A Dictionary of
Hinduism

FIRST EDITION

W. J. JOHNSON

OXFORD
UNIVERSITY PRESS

OXFORD
UNIVERSITY PRESS

Great Clarendon Street, Oxford, OX2 6DP,
United Kingdom

Oxford University Press is a department of the University of Oxford. It furthers the University's objective of excellence in research, scholarship, and education by publishing worldwide. Oxford is a registered trade mark of Oxford University Press in the UK and in certain other countries

First published 2009
First published as an Oxford University Press paperback 2010

Published in the United States of America by Oxford University Press
198 Madison Avenue, New York, NY 10016, United States of America

British Library Cataloguing in Publication Data
Data available

Library of Congress Cataloging in Publication Data
Data available

ISBN 978–0–19–861026–7

For Pat, Jonathan, and Patrick—who might otherwise have wondered precisely what it was that kept me at the top of the house for three years.

Contents

Preface

What is the subject of this dictionary? Under its own entry, I define the term 'Hinduism' as: 'A noun of convenience, or construction, encompassing, whether actively or retrospectively, the religious and cultural traditions (i.e. the various beliefs, values, social practices, and rituals) of those identified by themselves or others as "Hindus".' This is plainly and deliberately a tautology. It might also be considered an evasion, reflecting a notoriously evasive subject. However, the cross-reference involved directs the reader from the abstract ('Hinduism') to the concrete ('Hindu'), and so to the location of this religious and cultural complex in its original, geographical context of South Asia (essentially subcontinental India). This permits the understanding, if not precisely the definition, which, for workaday purposes, I adopted in the compilation of this dictionary. Broadly, it treats 'Hinduism' as a term used to designate a wide range of Indian religious traditions, which, in one way or another, have been, and continue to be, historically, ritually, theologically, ideologically, socially, and culturally linked. In line with the current consensus, the breadth of that range has not been understood as extending to traditions which, in the Common Era, have originated outside the subcontinent (e.g. Islam, Christianity, Zoroastrianism), or to those which have sooner or later come to identify themselves as autonomous (principally Buddhism, Jainism, and Sikhism). Nevertheless, for the sake of context, survey entries have been included on Buddhism, Jainism, Islam, and some other traditions which, for long periods of Indian history, have interacted, both positively and negatively, with what has come to be classified as Hinduism. Where groups or individuals have only subsequently (or sometimes never) been labelled 'Hindu', 'non-Hindu', 'Muslim', or 'Sikh'—some of the medieval bhaktas, for instance—each case has been treated on its own merits, but with a bias towards inclusion. In short—and in spite of the neuroses of those academics determined to prove that the rest of the world is made up not only of Orientalists, busy constructing politically loaded 'others', but also of essentialists and literalists, who are bound to misconstrue 'Hinduism' merely because such a coinage exists—I have treated the terms 'Hinduism' and 'Hindu' as necessary, if not always entirely reliable, signposts, rather than as elephant traps for the unwary.

The more capacious and inclusive the definition of 'Hinduism', the greater the gap between its reality—the reality of what 'Hindus' have done and, in many instances, continue to do—and the information that can be transmitted about it. Much has been knowingly omitted. Hindu traditions have produced thousands, perhaps hundreds of thousands of texts in a wide variety of languages, but most of them lie unstudied and effectively unknown. From this position of near ignorance, only those which have been prominent among prominent traditions, and for that reason have seemed important to scholarship, have been included. In the same spirit, only those elements of Vedic mythology which have been most significant for later Hinduism, will be found here; many minor gods have been neglected. Similarly, of the thousands of Purāṇic myths, I have only attempted to retell those that have had some further ritual, theological, or devotional significance. Gurus and ācāryas are ubiquitous, and their hagiographies immense, but they too have been filtered for historical or widespread influence. Some living gurus, but no living scholars, have been given their own entries. Not every temple complex has been described, nor has much iconography; again, the criterion for inclusion has been further cultic or historical importance. Maps have been provided showing the approximate locations of the major sites mentioned, but for practical reasons, some smaller sites are placed through reference to either a nearby city, or the part of the State in which they are situated. A different dictionary of Hinduism could have been written as a series of survey articles; those that have been included here, such as entries on 'caste' and 'food', are largely topics which have received extended theoretical explication in the secondary literature. But that list too could have been endless, and in most cases readers have been left to conduct their own surveys, should they wish to do so, by following the asterisks from the information provided in individual entries. In short, it would be absurd to claim for this dictionary, as the great Sanskrit Epic, the *Mahābhārata*, does for itself, that 'What is here may be found elsewhere, what is not here is nowhere at all'. Instead, I make the far more circumspect claim that, while much, if not all, of what is here may indeed be found elsewhere, usually in greater detail and at much greater length, the reader may also, in the first instance, find it convenient to have a concentrated version available in a single volume.

The cultural critic Raymond Williams once remarked that academic work is largely clerical. In that respect, this dictionary is exemplary: in terms of information and analysis, it is of necessity heavily dependent on the scholarship of others—scholarship which crosses numerous disciplines, from Anthropology to Zoology. To attribute sources in the normal way would, however, be perversely cumbersome in a work of this kind. I refer readers who would like to encounter this scholarship at first hand to the titles given under Principal Sources and Further Reading, and to their more specialized bibliographies. In this way, I hope that some of the academic debts I have incurred may be repaid through attracting the attention of a wider readership to areas that are sometimes neglected or overlooked. For that reason part of the bibliography is skewed towards sources I have found valuable above and beyond the common currency of Indological scholarship, including poetry and fiction. It is, in any case, supposed to be an indicative rather than a definitive list, and the majority of entries refer readers to the next level of detail, i.e. to longer introductory and survey articles.

The way in which this dictionary functions is intended to be self-explanatory, but readers may be interested in some of the underlying principles and hidden constraints which have informed both the choice of entries and the form they have taken.

The use of copious—some may think mechanical—cross-referencing to other headwords (indicated by an asterisk at the first occurrence of the word in a particular entry) is intended in itself to convey something about the interdependence of certain major themes, which persistent or regular readers will discover for themselves. (The only exceptions to this principle are those very common words, such as 'India', 'Hindu', and 'God', which almost any reader might expect to have separate entries in a dictionary of this kind.) Sometimes the connections may be unexpected, and, it is hoped, the more illuminating for that; at other times a particular individual may find them irrelevant. In so far as it can be sensibly limited at all, the range of possible meanings that the label 'Hinduism' has for me (and for the scholarship I have relied upon), will, in the end, be far more evident in this web, or nexus of cross-references, than in any single definition. Where connections seem especially pressing, or are not necessarily obvious, even among the asterisks, I have inserted directions at the end of particular entries to *See* X, or to *See also* Y. Most interesting, perhaps—and also probably most representative of recent academic study in this area—are the dozens, if not hundreds, of separate stories, which start, peter out, leave false trails, or take unpredictable turns on page after page of what follows.

It is worth noting that the length of any particular entry should not be taken as an invariable indicator of the importance of the term dealt with. Indeed, some of the more important terms may have relatively short specific entries, simply because they occur with such frequency in so many other contexts. Conversely, I have sometimes allowed less well known subjects (some modern religious movements, for instance) more space when basic information about them seems not to be easily available elsewhere, or they are not otherwise referred to in the dictionary. Nevertheless, since most information on this scale has to come from beyond any individual's more specialized interests, the author of a dictionary is largely at the mercy of scholarly fashions and clusters of research, so whereas the detail mined from some texts and practices has been thrown up in such quantities that it has had to be ruthlessly condensed to create readable entries, at the other extreme, entire traditions have, it seems, barely been noticed at all, and the compiler is left scrabbling for anything that looks like a reliable foothold. Linguistically, and to some extent culturally, there has been a subcontinental division, as well as a complex interplay, between the predominantly northern speakers of Indo-European languages (Sanskrit and its derivatives), and the speakers of the Dravidian languages of the South (notably Tamil). I have attempted to represent both of these major aspects of Hindu culture in this dictionary, although, in terms of available resources and coordinated information, it may be that a historical imbalance in the study of Hinduism in favour of the Sanskritic, at least in the Anglophone world, has been mirrored here as well.

Even when a particular text can, with good reason, be identified as the work of a single author, rather than the product of many hands and continuous accretion, it has frequently proved difficult to assign it an approximate date, even in terms of centuries. This is also true of the named authors of texts, and the origins of major movements or trends, such as bhakti and Tantra. Every set of dates, unless otherwise specified, should therefore be taken as a relative approximation. (This also applies to the dates in the Chronology.) Sometimes conflicting sets of dates are given, one assigned by the tradition itself, and one suggested (or more often contested) by modern scholarship. A common way of dividing up Indian religious history in the secondary literature, also sometimes employed in this dictionary, is to distinguish between four or more overlapping periods, typically the Vedic or Brahmanical (*c.*1700 BCE–*c.*200 CE), the Epic or Purāṇic (*c.*200 BCE–*c.*500/700 CE), the classical or mediaeval (*c.*500/700 CE–*c.*1500 CE), and the modern (*c.*1500 CE to the present). Some secondary sources (but not this one, which covers the period from *c.*1700 BCE to the present) attempt to distinguish 'Hinduism', conceived as a product of the post-Vedic period, from Vedic or Brahmanical religion. Given that there have been few pan-Indian empires (perhaps none at all in the strictest reading), and that most ruling dynasties have exercized only a local influence, no attempt has been made, except at the level of specific, individual entries, to link religious developments and dynastic periods. The most important dynasties have their own entries in the text, and are included in the Chronology.

Italics are used only for the names of texts in their original language. Unless otherwise indicated, the reader should assume that language, when not English, to be Sanskrit, or a Sanskrit derivative. Apart from the common names of countries, Union Territories, and Indian States, all Indic words, with the exception of some Anglicized modern names, have been spelt with diacritical marks to aid pronunciation (a Pronunciation Guide is provided). Where relevant, alternative spellings, and spellings without diacritical marks which significantly change the appearance of the word, have also been given. Roman alphabetical order is followed: for example, entries under 'S' (which includes three different Sanskrit sounds—ś, ṣ, and s) are treated as though they all begin with the same letter. Where the names of Indian cities have been subject to change, I have usually kept them in period—Bombay in the 19th century, Mumbai in the 21st—or printed both versions.

By way of seeking indulgence for the inadequacies and peculiarities of a dictionary that attempts to exemplify, although never to encompass, the vast complex of human concerns we have come to call 'Hinduism', I can do no better than quote my namesake, the great Dr Samuel Johnson, who in the Preface to his *A Dictionary of the English Language* (London, 1775: §93) expressed the hope that:

> there can never be wanting some... who will consider that no dictionary of a living language ever can be perfect... that a whole life cannot be spent upon syntax and etymology, and that even a whole life would not be sufficient; that he, whose design includes whatever language can express, must often speak of what he does not understand... that what is obvious is not always known, and what is known is not always present...

This seems especially apposite, insofar as 'Hinduism', like any great religious tradition, is itself a particular 'language'—a language that, even if it happens to be one's native tongue, often requires translation. And although, for some of the reasons Dr Johnson gives above, no good translation can ever be achieved through a dictionary alone, it may not always be the worst place to start.

Finally, I must thank my editors at OUP—Ruth Langley for suggesting the project in the first place, and for smoothing its early passage—Judith Wilson for seeing it through the press. I am also grateful to my colleagues in the School of Religious and Theological Studies at Cardiff University for allowing me to coordinate a period of research leave with the push to complete a task which at times seemed to require, but never knowingly received, divine intervention.

WILL JOHNSON
Cardiff 2008

Abbreviations

adj.	adjective	H.	Hindi
alt.	alternatively	lit.	literally
Ang.	Anglicized form	M.	Malayalam
B.	Bengali	masc.	masculine
b.	born	n.	noun
BCE	before the Common Era (= BC)	neut.	neuter
c.	circa	nom.	nominative
CE	in the Common Era (= AD)	P.	Prākrit
d.	died	pl.	plural
ed.	edition/editor	Punj.	Punjabi
esp.	especially	R.	Rajasthani
fem.	feminine	r.	ruled
fl.	flourished	sing.	singular
G.	Gujarati	Skt.	Sanskrit
Gītā	*Bhagavadgītā*	trad.	traditionally
Gk.	Greek	Tam.	Tamil

Note to the Reader

According to one convention, sometimes used in works that, unlike this dictionary, do not employ diacritical marks, the Sanskrit sounds 'ca', 'ci', etc. are romanized as 'cha', 'chi', etc., resulting in spellings such as 'Chaitanya' rather than 'Caitanya', 'chit' rather than 'cit'. Similarly, sounds such as 'śa', 'śi', etc. (and more rarely 'ṣa', etc.) are sometimes romanized as 'sha', 'shi', (and 'sha'), etc., resulting in spellings such as 'shakti', 'Shiva', and 'Vishnu', rather than 'śakti', 'Śiva', and 'Viṣṇu'.

A

abhaṅg(a) *See* BHAJAN(A).

Ābhāsvaras ('shining', 'bright') Name of a class of 64 deities, attendant on *Śiva, and associated with spiritual enlightenment.

abhāva **1.** ('non-apprehension', 'non-cognition') Recognized as a means of valid knowledge (*pramāṇa) by the *Mīmāṃsā and *Vedānta *darśanas. **2.** ('non-existence', 'absence') In the developed *Nyāya-Vaiśeṣika system, a fundamental category of reality.

Abhaya ('fearless', 'not dangerous', 'safe') Name of *Śiva.

abhaya ('freedom from fear') A formal vow taken by *saṃnyāsins never to kill or do violence to any living creature.

abhaya-hasta *See* ABHAYA-MUDRĀ.

abhaya-mudrā ('gesture of fearlessness') In iconography a hand gesture (*mudrā) in which the palm of a deity's or teacher's right hand is raised towards the devotee to inspire trust and dispel fear. Frequently represented on Hindu, *Buddhist, and *Jaina images.

abhicāra ('incantation', 'magic') The use of spells for harmful purposes.

Abhijñānaśākuntalam ('The Recognition of Śakuntalā', *c.*4th to 5th century CE) A *Sanskrit drama by *Kālidāsa, widely considered the most perfect example of the form. Based on an episode in the **Mahābhārata*, it tells the story of the love of King *Duṣyanta and *Śakuntalā, a hermitage girl, their separation by a curse, and their eventual reunion. Erotic in mood (*rasa), it deals, among other things, with the tension between love (*kāma) and duty (*dharma). Sir William *Jones's English translation of 1798 caused a sensation in the West, and was instrumental in drawing European attention to Sanskrit literature.

abhimantraṇa ('addressing with a mantra') Consecrating anything by means of a special verbal formula (*mantra).

Abhimanyu One of the *Pāṇḍava faction in the **Mahābhārata*; son of *Arjuna and *Subhadrā. At the age of sixteen, he is killed in a cowardly fashion on the thirteenth day of the war against the *Kauravas, leaving his widow, Uttarā, pregnant with the future *Parikṣit.

Abhinavagupta (*c.*975–1025) Greatest of the *Kashmiri Śaiva theologians. His works deal with the theoretical, *yogic, and ritual aspects of the *Tantric *Trika and *Krama traditions, the theology of the *Pratyabhijñā school, and aesthetics. He argued for a 'supreme *nondualism' (paramādvayavāda), which regarded both plurality and unity as ways in which the Absolute represented itself through the independent power of its *consciousness. In his writings on the nature of aesthetic experience (*rasa), he developed a subsequently famous theory which regarded rasa as a distinct mode of experience situated between ordinary awareness and enlightenment, although it differs from the latter only in degree. His principal works include a commentary on the root text of the Kashmiri Śaiva tradition—a **Tantra* he considered to be the highest revelation—the **Mālinīvijayottara Tantra* (the *Mālinīślokavārttika*), the immense **Tantrāloka* ('Light on Tantra'), its summary, the **Tantrasāra* ('Essence of Tantra'), and, in the field of aesthetics, his commentaries on *Bharata's **Nāṭyaśāstra* (*Abhinavabhāratī*) and *Ānandavardhana's *Dhvanyāloka*. His influence (filtered through the works of his pupil, *Kṣemarāja) was crucial to the history of *Śaivism, first in Kashmir, and then at *Cidambaram in Tamil Nadu.

abhiniveśa ('the will to live', 'fear of death') According to *Patañjali's **Yoga Sūtra* it is one of the five afflictions (*kleśas) that ensure the individual goes on suffering, and is classified as a form of ignorance (*avidyā).

Abhīras Non-*Āryan pastoral tribe of the Gangetic plain and northern Deccan. They hero-worshipped *Kṛṣṇa-Gopāla, and may have been responsible in part for the spread of his legend throughout India.

abhiṣeka ('sprinkling') **1.** Act of consecrating a *king or the image of a deity, involving bathing with water and/or other substances, such as milk and honey. **2.** A specific element in the *rājasūya and *aśvamedha rituals in which the king's divinity is (re)affirmed. It is normally administered by a *brahmin.

abhyāsa ('repetition', 'practice') In *Yoga philosophy, the positive mental effort required to retain purity of the mind.

ācamana ('sipping') Sipping water from the palm of the hand for *purification.

ācamanīya **1.** Water for rinsing the mouth; one of the basic requirements for the hospitable reception of a guest according to *Sanskrit literature. **2.** Water offered to the deity for this purpose—one of the sixteen offerings/services (*upacāras) which are component parts of *pūjā. **3.** The vessel used for purposes of *ācamana, and for carrying water to a deity during *worship so that it can rinse its mouth (worship being modelled on *hospitality).

ācāra ('conduct') An established rule of conduct, based on tradition, for a specific *caste or religious group. *See also* DHARMAŚĀSTRA(S).

ācārya ('teacher') **1.** Someone who knows or teaches the rules (*ācāras), especially a spiritual guide or teacher responsible for initiating and instructing individual pupils within a particular lineage (*paramparā). In the *Vedic tradition the ācārya performs the pupil's *upanayana, and is then responsible for teaching him all, or some, of the **Vedas*. **2.** A specific line of teachers, beginning with *Nāthamuni, and including *Rāmānuja, which is revered by the *Śrī Vaiṣṇavas.

Achchūtānanda, Swami (1879–1933) An initiated *ascetic and radical social reformer from Uttar Pradesh, who was one of the leaders of the *Ādi Hindu *Dalit reform movement in the 1920s and 1930s.

acintya ('inconceivable') Name of *Śiva.

acintya-bhedābheda ('inconceivable difference in identity') In *Gauḍīya Vaiṣṇavism the characterization of the relationship between the devotee and the Lord (*Kṛṣṇa), reflecting that between *Rādhā and Kṛṣṇa, a stance associated with the 18th century *Vedāntin teacher, *Baladeva.

action *See* KARMA.

Acyuta ('not fallen', 'imperishable') Name of *Viṣṇu (and *Kṛṣṇa). Epithet of *Yudhiṣṭhira.

adharma ('injustice', 'irreligion', 'unrighteousness', 'wickedness', 'disorder') The opposite, or absence, of *dharma, and like that word dependent for its precise meaning on the context in which it is applied. Meanings therefore range from the infraction of particular ritual rules, and of *caste or occupation-specific laws (requiring various reparations or *prāyaścittas), to breaches of general moral principles, especially that of *ahiṃsā (non-violence). In the *Mahābhārata*, adharma is conceptualized as a state of cosmic imbalance and disorder, which has to be rectified through the restoration of dharma. The process of the decay of dharma into adharma, dharma's restoration, and the continuing alternation of the two, characterizes the cyclical nature of *time. *Kṛṣṇa (God in this context) intervenes at the apposite moments in this temporal and cosmic cycle to ensure that balance is restored. In the **Bhagavadgītā* (4.7–8), Kṛṣṇa, in an embryonic statement of the *avatāra doctrine, explains this regulating and protective function: 'Whenever there is a falling away from the true law (dharma) and an upsuge of unlawfulness (adharma), then...I emit myself. I come into being age (*yuga) after age (yuga), to protect the virtuous and to destroy evil-doers, to establish a firm basis for the true law (dharma)'.

adhikāra ('qualification') The entitlement to perform a particular ritual, and, by extension, the necessary qualifications for undertaking a specific type of study, or for obtaining membership of a particular group.

adhikāraṇa ('the act of placing at the head') A subject or topic; a section of a text.

Adhiratha In the **Mahābhārata*, the name of *Karṇa's foster-father.

adhvara A *sacrifice, especially the *Soma sacrifice.

adhvaryu ('one who institutes an adhvara') Any officiating or overseeing *priest, but more specifically a class of *Vedic priests responsible for the construction of the altars (*vedis), the collection and preparation of sacrificial vessels and other requisites, the lighting of the fire, and the immolation of the sacrificial animal during the *yajña. Adhvaryus accompany these actions with the recitation of prescribed *yajus from the **Yajur Veda*, hence they are also known as Yajurveda priests.

adhyāsa ('imposing', 'superimposition') According to *Śaṅkara's *Advaita Vedānta, the mistaken belief that an object has certain attributes which in reality it does not have, classically illustrated by the man who, in the dark, mistakes a coiled rope for a snake. By analogy, this explains the way in which, according to Śaṅkara, reality or *brahman (neut.), which is actually beyond *nāmarūpa—names and forms—and devoid of all distinctions, comes to be experienced, under the superimposition of names and forms, as the world of appearances.

Adhyātma Rāmāyaṇa (the 'spiritual' Rāmāyaṇa, *c.*15th century CE) A *Sanskrit rendition of the story of *Rāma from an *Advaita perspective, which views the events and characters as a divine allegory, thus making Rāma himself a manifestation of the supreme *Viṣṇu from the outset. It played an important part in the development of the Rāma cult in North India, being one of the sources for *Tulsīdās's **Rāmcaritmānas*. It is the sacred text of the *Rāmānandī sect, and theoretically a part of the **Brahmāṇḍa Purāṇa*.

Ādi Brāhmo Samāj ('Original Brahman Association') Name given to one division, composed of Debendranāth *Tagore and his followers, of the 19th century Hindu reform movement, the *Brāhmo Samāj. In this way it distinguished itself from the other division, Keshab Chandra *Sen's '*Brāhmo Samāj of India'.

Adi Da *See* DA.

Adidam *See* DA.

Ādi Granth The sacred scripture of the *Sikhs, also known as the *Gurū Granth Sāhib*, it contains the teachings of *Gurū Nānak and the four Gurūs who immediately succeeded him. The *Ādi Granth* also includes a large number of verses attributed to (pre-Nānak) Hindu and *Muslim saints in the north Indian *bhakti tradition, among them *Kabīr and *Raidās. It was compiled by the fifth Sikh Gurū, Arjan, in 1603–4.

Ādi Hindu Movement A predominantly north Indian urban reform movement, made up of *Dalits (mostly *camārs). Active in the 1920s and 1930s, they identified themselves with the 'original' (ādi) pre-*Āryan inhabitants of India, who they saw as practising a form of *bhakti devoid of *caste discrimination, reflected in the works of such *sants as *Kabīr and *Raidās. Their leadership, such as Swami *Achchūtānanda, came largely from disillusioned members of the *Ārya Samāj.

ādikāvi ('original poet') *See* Vālmīki.

ādikāvya ('first epic poem') *See* Rāmāyaṇa.

Ādiparvan ('The Book of the Beginning') The first book of the *Sanskrit **Mahābhārata*, providing its framing stories, listing various genealogies, and recounting the birth, education, and alliances of the main protagonists.

Ādi Purāṇa *See* Brahmā Purāṇa.

Ādiśaiva(s) ('first followers of Śiva') A subcaste of hereditary and endogamous *Tamil *temple *priests, who are specialists in *Śaiva Siddhānta ritual. They are also known as Śaivabrāhmaṇa ('*Śaivite *brahmins').

Ādiśaṅkarācārya ('the first Śaṅkara in the line of teachers') The title given to *Śaṅkara (also called Ādiśaṅkara) to distinguish him from the teachers, known as *Śaṅkarācāryas, who succeeded him in the lineage he founded.

Ādi Sant *See* Kabīr.

Ādiśeṣa ('original serpent') The name of the serpent upon which *Viṣṇu reclines in his *Vaikuṇṭha heaven. There is a well-known image depicting this in the inner sanctum of the *Śrīraṅgam temple. *Śrīvaiṣṇavas regard Ādiśeṣa as a personification of eternal servitude to Viṣṇu. *See also* Ananta, Śeṣa.

Aditi ('boundless', 'freedom') *Vedic goddess of unbounded space. Viewed as the Great Mother (and father) of all gods and all creation, encompassing and comprising everything, both internal and external. As the goddess of nature, the energy infusing the cosmos, she is associated with the fertile earth and the *cow. The *Ādityas are her sons.

Āditya(s) In the singular, the sun. In the plural, the sons of *Aditi, and major figures amongst the *Vedic *devas. Linked to natural phenomena, they are also personifications of the most important social functions. They first appear in the **Ṛg Veda*, where they number between five and eight, chief among them *Mitra and *Varuṇa. In the **Śatapatha Brāhmaṇa* their number is increased to twelve to represent the months of the year.

ādivāsi(s) ('original inhabitants') Name sometimes given to the indigenous tribal peoples of India.

adri ('rock') In *Vedic ritual, the stone used for pressing or grinding *soma in order to extract its juice.

Adrijā ('mountain-born') Name of the goddess *Pārvatī.

adṛṣṭa ('unseen') According to *Vaiśeṣika *karma theory, the unseen power of actions, stored as a quality of the individual's *soul (*ātman). Depending on the nature of such actions, good or bad consequences follow for the person concerned. The term is also used by *Jaimini in his (*Pūrva-*) *Mīmāṃsā Sūtra*, where it is synonymous with *apūrva (an indefinable unseen force), which is either good or bad. Good adṛṣṭa/apūrva follows from the performance of actions enjoined in the **Veda*, bad from actions prohibited there. Good adṛṣṭa is itself of two kinds, either resulting in prosperity in this world or the next (i.e. it leads to heaven (*svarga)), or leading to liberation (*mokṣa). The latter is the result of ritual actions performed without any desire for particular results. *See also* APŪRVA; KARMA.

Advaita Vedānta ('Non-dualistic Vedānta', 'non-dualism') One of the major theological cum philosophical schools of the *Vedānta *darśana, now closely associated with the teachings of *Śaṅkara (Śaṅkarācārya). The earliest identifiable Advaita text, the **Gauḍapādīya Kārikā*, was said to have been composed by Śaṅkara's *paramaguru (his teacher's teacher), *Gauḍapāda. The *Kārikā* propounds the non-dual (advaita) nature of ultimate reality (*brahman (neut.)), and the complete identity of brahman and *ātman. It regards the world of apparent change and multiplicity as ultimately an illusion (*māyā), and teaches that nothing has ever really come into existence (*ajātivāda doctrine). Śaṅkara wrote a commentary on the *Kārikā*, and it was clearly a major influence on the development of his own thought, at the core of which is the perception that brahman alone is real, in the sense of being the one, indivisible existent. Much of his exegesis is therefore taken up with explaining the nature of the apparent (because ultimately unreal) relationship between brahman and the individual (ātman), and, by extension, the nature of conventional experience. At the core of this is superimposition (*adhyāsa), the mistaken belief that an object has certain attributes which in reality it does not have, classically illustrated by the man who, in the dark, mistakes a coiled rope for a snake. By analogy, this explains the way in which, according to Śaṅkara, reality or brahman (which is actually beyond *nāmarūpa—names and forms—and devoid of all distinctions) comes to be experienced, under the superimposition of names and forms, as the world of appearances. This persistent mistaking of appearance for reality is the source of ignorance (*avidyā); conversely, liberating knowledge (*vidyā) is the ability to distinguish between what is superimposed on the self and its true nature, which is brahman. With this discrimination (*viveka), it is not just avidyā that is dispelled, but also *māyā, the cosmic power of 'illusion' or artifice, which is coeval with ignorance, and its ultimate cause. For Śaṅkara, the logical problems caused by attributing reality or unreality to avidyā itself are irrelevant to the soteriological imperative of realizing its ultimate disconnection from brahman or the self. (Later Advaitins, however, continued to wrestle with the conundrum of avidyā's ontological status.) Discursive knowledge of the world of appearances, of names and forms, is characterized by Śaṅkara as *vyavahāra ('conventional' or 'relative'), as opposed to the *paramārtha ('supreme' or 'absolute') knowledge which is the direct realization of the non-dual brahman/ātman. Similarly, he distinguishes between *saguṇa brahman (brahman as experienced through conventional knowledge, i.e. as *Īśvara, a personal deity and object of devotion) and *nirguṇa brahman (brahman experienced as the non-dual reality, transcending all qualities and categories). (Although, following the **Upaniṣads*, the latter state is characterized by later Advaitins as the reality/state of being which is pure consciousness and bliss (*saccidānanda).)

According to Śaṅkara, liberating knowledge of brahman can only come from *Vedic revelation (essentially the *Upaniṣads*); it is therefore only accessible to those of the *twice-born *varṇa who have, at the very least, received *upanayana and undertaken Vedic studentship (*brahmacarya). He differs from the *Pūrva Mīmāṃsakas in so far as that, while he regards ritual (*karma) as necessary in order to remove the impurities which obstruct knowledge, he considers it to be incapable, in itself, of bringing the highest goal of liberation or immortality. That is to be achieved through reflection and meditation on the true nature of the self, knowledge of which can only be gained, in the first instance, through hearing the seemingly external voice of Vedic revelation

a

(i.e. through the teachings of the *jñānakāṇḍa—especially, according to the tradition, the *mahāvākya). The ritual life should therefore culminate in *renunciation, something which, according to Śaṅkara, can be done from any *āśrama.

Śaṅkara was succeeded in the Advaita tradition by his disciples *Sureśvara and *Padmapāda, the latter at the start of a commentarial tradition which led to the *Vivaraṇa subschool. Another subschool, the *Bhāmatī, began with the sub-commentary on Śaṅkara's *Brahmasūtrabhāṣya* by *Vācaspati Miśra, synthesizing Śaṅkara's views with those of his probable contemporary, *Maṇḍana Miśra. (Until this point at least, Maṇḍana seems to have been the better known teacher in the Advaita tradition.) From this time onwards, Advaita continued to attract commentators and to provide the theological underpinnings for various sectarian groupings, and monastic orders, such as the *Daśanāmis, said to have been founded by Śaṅkara himself. Other notable Advaitins, of whom there are many, include *Śrīharṣa, *Mādhava (1) (Vidyāraṇya), *Sadānanda (1), *Appaya Dīkṣita, *Madhusūdana Sarasvatī, and *Dharamarāja (2). Since the 19th century Advaita has become the best-known Hindu theology outside India, thanks to *Neo-Hindu reformers and teachers, such as *Vivekānanda and *Radhakrishnan, who presented it as the pure core of Hindu thought.

Advaitin A follower or proponent of the *Advaita Vedānta tradition.

aesthetics *See* RASA.

Āgama(s) ('come down') **1.** A general name for (non-*Vedic) canonical texts, sanctioned by tradition, and usually regarded as revelation (*śruti) by their adherents. Texts of this kind may also be known as **Tantras*. The term 'Āgama' is also used to describe particular collections of texts made by the *Buddhists and the *Jains. **2.** The 28 canonical texts of the *Śaiva Siddhānta tradition (composed of the ten *Śiva-Āgamas* (*Śaivāgamas*), and the eighteen *Rudra-Āgamas*), containing what is regarded as direct revelation from *Śiva himself.

Āgamaśāstra *See* GAUḌAPĀDĪYA KĀRIKĀ.

Agastya (Agasti) A legendary *Vedic seer, who is frequently mentioned in the **Ṛg Veda*, and subsequently appears in the **Purāṇas*, the **Mahābhārata*, and the **Rāmāyaṇa*. He is particularly associated with South India, and popularly credited with the introduction of *Sanskrit culture into this region. He is also supposed to have written a *Tamil grammar, the *Āgastyam*, which is no longer extant. Many Tamil Hindus consider that he is still living on Agastya Malai, a mountain named after him in Tamil Nadu. He is also identified with the brightest star in the southern Indian sky, Canopus.

Aghamarṣaṇa ('sin-effacing') Name given to hymn 10.190 of the **Ṛg Veda*, and to the seer said to have composed it.

Aghora ('non-terrifying', 'not terrible') A euphemistic epithet of *Śiva, applied to him in his awe-inspiring or terrible mode, whether mythologically or iconographically (Aghora-mūrti). Sometimes referred to as Aghora-*Bhairava. Iconographically, the term is also applied to Śiva's southern face, representing universal Law (*dharma).

Aghoraśiva 12th century *Śaiva Siddhānta theologian.

Aghorī A member of a *Śaiva *ascetic sect, related to the now defunct *Kāpālika tradition, that worships *Śiva in his *Aghora (terrible) form. Most prevalent in *Vārāṇasī (but now few in number), Aghorīs live and meditate in *cremation grounds, where they eat from skulls, and, in theory at least, perform a ritual which involves consuming the meat of human corpses. Their transgression of social and ritual taboos is regarded as a means of acquiring power (*siddhi).

Āgneya Purāṇa *See* AGNI PURĀṆA.

Agni ('fire') A term that can be used to designate fire in any of its manifestations, the most significant being the sacrificial fire. Agni is also the name given to the embodiment of fire, and as such he is one of the most significant *Vedic gods (*devas). As the essential prerequisite and instrument of *sacrifice (*yajña), he is, after *Indra, the deity most frequently invoked in the **Ṛg Veda*, where over two hundred hymns are addressed to Agni. Moreover, since it is fire that carries the oblation from the sacrificial altar (*vedi) upwards towards the gods, it is Agni who acts as the crucial mediator between the human and divine worlds, and it is he who is ultimately responsible for the benefits and wealth the sacrificer hopes to attain. Agni is therefore considered to be not only the *priest of the gods, but, by association, the god of human priests (*brahmins). In the orthodox *Brahmanical tradition, fire for both cooking and ritual is central to the life of the *householder, and it is the installation of domestic and ritual fires at *marriage that signifies a man's transition to full social status. Given the variety of uses to which fire can be put, and the range of possible sacrifices, it is not surprising that what is essentially a single element is thought to have multiple aspects (e.g. the purificatory fire of the *funeral) and a wide range of metaphorical associations, including, for example, the fire of digestion. Agni is therefore multifaceted, and like all manifestations of power, ambivalent, in so far as he can be both destructive and creative. *See also* ARAṆI.

agnicayana ('the piling of the fire [-altar]') The most complicated and atypical of the *śrauta sacrifices; nearly one third of the **Śatapatha Brāhmaṇa* (where it is associated with the *ṛṣi Śāṇḍilya) is devoted to its exposition. Agnicayana probably began as an independent rite, which was then incorporated into the system of *soma sacrifices; it is not obligatory at every soma sacrifice, but it is always combined with one. Its unique characteristic is that one of the offering altars (*vedi), the uttaravedi, is constructed by piling up (cayana) five layers of fired clay bricks in the form of a bird of prey (śyena) (this is the only form to have been archaeologically attested, although other forms are theoretically possible). Built into this construction are the 'heads' of a man, a horse, a bull, a ram, and a he-goat, all of which can optionally be made of gold or clay. After this cayana, which is done with various offerings, the procedure of the soma sacrifice is followed. The sacrificer (*yajamāna) who has performed agnicayana has to observe certain special *vows for a year, with variations if he performs it more than once. The duration of the ritual, and the distribution of the rites over particular days, is not clear from the classical manuals, although some rites may have been extended over a year. It obviously entailed enormous expenditure. The *Nambūdiri performance witnessed by the *Indologist Fritz Staal (b. 1930) in 1975 was a compressed version lasting for twelve days. Symbolically, it appears to represent a ritual recreation of the original sacrifice of the cosmic man (*Puruṣa/*Prajāpati), through which the universe was created and ordered, and his re-ordering to ensure the continuity of the seasons and the well-being of the sacrificer. *See also* AMṚTACITI.

agnihotra ('fire-offering', 'oblation to Agni') In the orthodox *Brahmanical tradition, the simplest of the *śrauta rituals, an obligatory twice-daily sacrifice (*yajña) to be performed at the junctions (*saṃdhyā) of dawn and dusk. The oblations consist of milk, oil, and sour gruel poured into the sacrificer's (*yajamāna's) fires. In each case the ritual, taking about fifteen minutes, involves about a hundred actions, accompanied by the individual wishing, through the recitation of *mantras, for various results, such as sons, cattle, rain, and a long life. To maintain this

a

on a daily basis, the *householder needs at least two cows, as well as thousands of cow-dung cakes and fuel-sticks. The wider purpose of the ritual is to ensure that the sun survives the night.

Agnihotri, Pandit Shiv Narayan (Satyānanda Agnihotri, Dev Bhagwan Ātma) (1850–1929) A leading member of the *Brāhmo Samāj from 1873, Agnihotri broke with them in 1886 and, the following year, founded the *Dev Samāj (Divine Society). Rejecting Brahmo rationalism, he taught that only he, as *guru and enlightened being, could show the way to eternal bliss, eventually making himself the sole object of worship for his followers. *See also* DEV SAMĀJ.

***Agni Purāṇa* (*Āgneya Purāṇa*)** (*c.*9th? century CE) Classified as one of the eighteen 'great **Purāṇas*' (*mahāpurāṇas*) in the *tāmasa group, i.e. those said (somewhat artificially) to relate to *Śiva. In fact, the text is mixed, in the sense that it deals partly with *Viṣṇu and his *avatāras, but predominantly with Śiva. The *Agni* is generally eclectic and encyclopaedic in character, and, in its surviving form infused with *Tantric material. *See also* PURĀṆAS.

agnisthāpana ('establishing the fire') The name given to the ritual in which the *Brahmanical sacrificer and his wife set up the *gṛhyāgni ('domestic fire') at the time of their *marriage.

agniṣṭoma A 'one day' *soma sacrifice that culminates in the offering of soma three times in a single day (although the entire ritual normally extends over five days). The ritual, involving a special consecration (*dīkṣā) of the *śrauta sacrificer (*yajamāna), is to be performed each Spring on the new or full moon day; it requires the services of sixteen or seventeen *priests, and involves lavish fees (*dakṣinās). The agniṣṭoma is a necessary component of, and provides the paradigm (*prakṛti (2)) for, all soma sacrifices which take less than twelve days.

agnyādhāna *See* AGNEYĀDHEYA.

agnyādheya ('installation of the fire') A two-day ritual performed by the sacrificer (*yajamāna) and his wife to establish the three (or five) fires necessary to become a *śrauta ritualist. Thereafter he is known as an *āhitāgni, and is obliged to perform the full range of śrauta rites until he dies, or renounces and becomes a *saṃnyāsin.

āgrayaṇa ('first seizing') The first *soma libation at the *agniṣṭoma sacrifice.

Ahalyā The wife of the *Vedic seer (*ṛṣi) *Gautama, who is at the centre of a number of stories in (e.g.) the **Śatapatha Brāhmaṇa*, the **Mahābhārata*, and the **Rāmāyaṇa* concerning her seduction by *Indra, disguised as her husband. This results in Gautama cursing her to invisibility (or, in some accounts, turning her into stone), although she is eventually restored—according to the *Rāmāyaṇa*, thanks to an act of *hospitality to *Rāma. Because of her loyalty to her husband, she has come to be regarded as one of five exemplary wives, who are supposed to be invoked every morning by Hindu women.

ahaṃkāra ('the making of self', 'I-maker') In *Sāṃkhya philosophy, the second evolute of *prakṛti (primal matter); it is the source of the sense of 'I' and 'mine' (so sometimes called the ego), and a major barrier to liberation for the spiritual self (*puruṣa), which, out of ignorance, identifies with it, even though it belongs to an entirely different ontological category.

āhavanīya ('to be offered as an oblation') Name of the eastern sacrificial fire, one of the three major fires of the *śrauta ritualist. Like the *dakṣiṇāgni, it is expanded from the *gārhapatya or 'householder's' fire; it is established on a square mound to the east of the sacrificial area and receives the cooked oblations to the gods (*devas).

Ahi ('snake') In the **Ṛg Veda* a demonic snake, also known as *Vṛtra, which is responsible for drought and darkness, but is ultimately defeated by *Indra.

ahiṃsā ('non-harming', 'non-violence', 'non-injury') As an ethical value, ahiṃsā first came to prominence in the renouncer (*śramaṇa) culture associated with the early **Upaniṣads* and the heterodox systems of the *Buddhists and, especially, the *Jains. Chief among the practices they were renouncing was the *sacrifice, and particularly the *animal sacrifice, which regulated and defined the life of the orthodox *Brahmanical *householder. As the *purity associated with renouncer practices was assimilated by Brahmanical orthodoxy, so many *brahmins distanced themselves from the violence (hiṃsā) of the *Vedic sacrifice, both by leaving such sacrifices to specialists, and through classifying sacrificial killing (which had always needed careful handling) as non-violent. This went hand in hand with the adoption of *vegetarianism and sexual restraint as activities deemed free of the *impurity associated with blood and *death. *Kings (and *kṣatriyas in general) were necessarily implicated in violence, which brought their specific duty (*dharma) to protect and punish into conflict with the doctrine of ahiṃsā. The anxiety caused by this is exemplified by the emperor *Aśoka's renunciation of warfare. Another solution to this problem was to redefine battle as a 'sacrifice', and therefore to remove it from the category of violence altogether, in the technical sense. (Some argue that this is the stance taken by the **Mahābhārata*.) A related strategy, advocated in the **Bhagavadgītā*, was to detach one's self from the fruits of one's actions, including violence, and to fight simply because it was one's duty (*svadharma) as a *kṣatriya to do so.

While ahiṃsā persisted as a prescribed practice for those following particular spiritual disciplines—it is, for instance, the first restraint (*yama) named in *Patañjali's **Yoga Sūtra*—the concept also acquired a more universal and positive resonance as the active pursuit of values such as compassion (*dayā). In the early twentieth century, it was his development of this wider understanding of the term—to make it a condition of truth, and ultimately to equate it with God—that led M. K. *Gāndhī to promote ahiṃsā as the quintessential religious and political value, and to employ it as a technique for actively resisting violence. *See also* SĀDHĀRAṆA DHARMA.

Ahirbudhnya Saṃhitā (*c.*600 CE) An important *Pāñcarātra text dealing with ritual and cosmological matters.

āhitāgni ('one who has laid [the śrauta] fires') The term designates a *śrauta ritualist—i. e. one who has established three (or five) *fires outside the home for the accomplishment of his ritual life. He is to be distinguished from the *ekāgni, who performs his rituals with a single domestic fire (*gṛhyāgni). *See also* AGNYĀDHEYA.

Aihole (6th–8th centuries CE) A major early architectural and sculptural site in Karnataka, containing the ruins of about seventy *temples.

Aikṣvāka dynasty Another name for the *Solar dynasty, derived from the name of its founder, *Ikṣvaku.

air One of the five material substances (*dravya) or elements (*bhūta) according to *Vaiśeṣika ontology.

Airāvaṇa *See* AIRĀVATA.

Airāvata (Airāvaṇa) ('produced from the ocean') The name of the four-tusked, white elephant that emerged from the *Churning of the Ocean, and which *Indra took as his mount or vehicle (*vāhana).

aiśvarya ('lordship', 'power') One of the six divine qualities (*guṇas) of *Viṣṇu according to *Pāñcarātra theology, an idea later developed by *Rāmānuja.

a

Aitareya Āraṇyaka One of two *Āraṇyakas* attached to the *Ṛg Veda*, and included in the *Aitareya Brāhmaṇa*. Divided into five sections, one of which concludes with the *Aitareya Upaniṣad*, it treats both the practice of ritual and the underlying nature of reality. *See also* KAUṢĪTAKI ĀRAṆYAKA.

Aitareya Brāhmaṇa One of two *Brāhmaṇas* attached to the *Ṛg Veda*, the *Aitareya* is principally concerned with the *soma *sacrifice. *See also* KAUṢĪTAKI BRĀHMAṆA.

Aitareya Upaniṣad Attached to the *Ṛg Veda*, the *Aitareya* is one of the oldest and shortest of the **Upaniṣads*. It deals with different aspects of the *ātman or self.

Aiyaṉār (Iyenar) (Tam.: 'lord', 'master') A village god in Tamil Nadu who is thought to act as a night-watchman, patrolling village boundaries and dispersing *evil spirits. He is a *pure, *vegetarian god with royal characteristics. His temples contain terracotta horses, and figures of elephants donated by devotees; they also usually house a shrine to *Karuppan, a little deity who acts as Aiyaṉār's servant. A cockerel is displayed on his banner. *See also* AIYAPPAṈ.

Aiyappaṉ (Ayyappaṉ) (Tam.) A popular god in Kerala and Tamil Nadu, also known as Hariharaputra—'Son of *Harihara (*Viṣṇu/*Śiva)'—and Śāstā ('ruler, teacher'). In mythology, he is the son of Śiva and *Mohinī, a female form of Viṣṇu. His function is essentially protective, whether at the regional or the village level; in this respect he plays a similar role to that of *Aiyaṉār, who is considered by some scholars to be his alternative form in Tamil Nadu, although their iconographies differ. At his principal *temple, and increasingly popular *pilgrimage site, at *Sabarimalai (on a mountain in Kerala), he is worshipped as an unmarried god and 'lord of *celibacy'.

Aiyars *Tamil-speaking *smārta *brahmins of Tamil Nadu.

Ajamila A dissolute *brahmin who, according to a popular *Vaiṣṇava story, was saved at the moment of *death by inadvertently calling out '*Nārāyaṇa!', one of the names of *Viṣṇu.

ajanani ('cessation of existence') A *Sanskrit curse: 'ajananir astu tasya' ('may he cease to exist!'), found, for instance, in the *Pañcatantra.

Ajaṇṭā Site of *Buddhist cave *temples in Maharashtra, containing famous murals.

Ajātaśatru *See* YUDHIṢṬHIRA.

ajātivāda ('doctrine of non-origination') Teaching, originating in the earliest *śāstra of the *Advaita Vedānta system, the **Gauḍapādīya Kārikā*, that nothing has ever really come into existence (i.e. that change is illusory).

Ajita Keśakambalin A heterodox teacher, apparently flourishing at the time of Gautama *Buddha, whose materialist doctrines (described in the *Buddhist Pāli Canon), seem to anticipate those of the later *Cārvāka or Lokāyata school of thought.

Ājīvika ('Follower of the Way of Life') Name given to members of a heterodox *ascetic order, apparently founded at the same time as the *Buddhist and *Jaina orders, and now extinct, although active in South India as late as the 13th century. No first-hand record survives of Ājīvika doctrines, so what is known about them is derived largely from the accounts of their rivals. According to Jaina sources, the Ājīvika's founder, Makkhali *Gosāla, was for six years a disciple and companion of the *Jina-to-be, *Mahāvīra, until they fell out. Although they seem to have shared some practices, such as nudity, with the *Digambara Jains, the Ājīvikas were a discrete ascetic corporation, supported by a distinct community of lay followers. The nature of Ājīvika doctrine is not clear; his rivals accused Gosāla of teaching that human effort was useless in the face of destiny (niyati), or *fate, but this is probably a distorted account. Early Jainism, particularly in its *cosmology and *karma theory, may have been influenced by Ājīvika teachings.

ājya Melted or clarified butter, used as a sacrificial oblation itself, or for anointing other oblations. The term may also refer to substitutes for clarified butter at the *sacrifice, such as oil and milk. *See also* GHĪ.

akam (Tam.: 'the interior world') A category of *Tamil literature which deals with the 'interior world', essentially the nuances of love between men and women, set against a variety of landscapes, as opposed to *puram literature which deals with the 'exterior world' of life outside the family (from the valour of *kings, to wars, to ethics, to *death and dying). Five of the eight *Caṅkam anthologies are dedicated to akam poetry.

ākāśa ('space', 'ether'). In the *Vedic texts and the **Upaniṣads*, ākāśa is used to convey the idea of world-space, i.e. the expanse in which everything lives and operates (that which allows space); in the **Chāndogya Upaniṣad* this space is equated, among other things, with *brahman (neut.). There was, however, a shift in meaning, so that by the *Epic period, ākāśa was taken to represent one of the five elements, namely, ether. In *Nyāya-Vaiśeṣika ontology, ākāśa, as ether, is characterized as one of the five material or atomic substances (*dravyas). As the unperceivable, infinite and all-pervading substratum of the quality of sound, it is clearly differentiated from the immaterial substance, space (*dik).

ākāśagaṅgā ('Ganges in the sky') The name of the celestial river *Gaṅgā (Ganges), which flows down from the sky.

Akbar (b. 1542, r. 1556–1605) *Mughal emperor, known as 'The Great'. He showed a constructive interest in Hindu and other non-*Muslim religious ideas, as well as encouraging a variety of religious practices, including Hindu *yoga. At the same time, he abolished the jizyaḥ, a discriminatory tax on non-Muslims. In the modern period, some Indian nationalists saw his behaviour as a model for the kind of religious and social toleration to which an independent and democratic India should aspire.

akhāḍā *See* ĀKHĀRĀ.

Akhaṇḍ Bhārat ('Undivided India') A term indicating the aim of some Hindu nationalists—to return India to a reunified, pre-*Partition state, an aspiration that was part of the election manifesto of the *Hindū Mahāsabhā party.

ākhāṛā (akhāḍā) (H.) Name denoting a 'regiment' or 'division' of naked warrior-*ascetics (*Nāgās). Such groups have been in existence since the medieval period, when they were first gathered together by local *kings to fight their enemies, to act as guardians of public order, and to protect trade routes in northern India. Originally organized on sectarian principles, ākhāṛās today are often simply associations devoted to physical exercise, meeting in a simple enclosure. *Hanumān, who wielded his club on behalf of *Rāma, is particularly honoured by contemporary ākhāṛās.

ākhyāna ('telling', 'communication') A general term for a narrative portion of a *Sanskrit text, or a tale; specifically, a name for the *Epic category of literature.

Akkā Mahādevī *See* MAHĀDĒVIYAKKĀ.

Akrūra ('not cruel') In the **Mahābhārata* the name of *Kṛṣṇa's paternal uncle, one of the *Vṛṣṇi generals who dies in the final battle.

akṣa A die for gambling; a nut used as a die. The archaeological record shows that gambling with dice or their equivalent has been popular in India since the period of the *Indus valley civilization. A hymn in the *Ṛg Veda* (10.34), known as 'The Gambler's Lament', vividly illustrates gambling's addictive power. The akṣa was originally a small hard nut called, variously, vibhīṣaka, vibhīdaka, or vibhītaka. Later, a die with four scoring sides, marked by spots, was used, although the exact rules are not known. The throws (or perhaps separate dice) were designated as *kṛta (four), tretā (three), dvāpara (two), and *kali (one). These terms were subsequently employed, metaphorically, to designate the sequence of world ages or *yuga. Perhaps the most celebrated, but least successful gambler in Indian literature is *Yudhiṣṭhira, who loses his kingdom (twice), his wealth, his brothers, himself, and, controversially, his wife, *Draupadī, in a rigged dicing match essential to the plot of the **Mahābhārata*. Yudhiṣṭhira's situation is mirrored in the *Mahābhārata* itself by the story of *Nala, another *king whose life turns on dicing. The association of gambling with kings is not fortuitous: a dicing match was probably the ritually required postscript to a royal consecration ceremony (*rājasūya), and in the later *Vedic period royal palaces were built with a gambling hall attached. The akṣāvāpa, 'the keeper of the gambling table', was regarded as an important royal official.

akṣamālā A generic term for a garland or rosary of 'beads', which may consist of any appropriate object (e.g. skulls for some forms of *Śiva). It is a frequent iconographic attribute of gods, as well as *ascetics. The number of beads may correspond to the sounds of the *Sanskrit alphabet (50), or conform to some *auspicious number (such as 108).

Akṣapāda Gotama *See* GAUTAMA.

Akṣarā ('word', 'speech') In the **Ṛg Veda*, a personification of *Vāc (Speech).

akṣara ('imperishable', 'unalterable') **1.** Grammatically, a syllable. More specifically, a term applied to the syllable and *mantra *oṃ (auṃ). According to the **Māṇḍūkya Upaniṣad* (1), 'The syllable (akṣara) is all this', and it is therefore equated with *brahman (neut.), *ātman, and everything that exists. **2.** The smallest time unit in South Indian classical music.

Akshar Puroshottam Sanstha *See* SVĀMĪNĀRYAṆA.

Akūpāra *See* KŪRMA.

Alagār A local hill deity in Tamil Nadu, said to be a form of *Viṣṇu. Once a year he is carried through the countryside on a *festival procession to *Madurai in order to attend the wedding of *Mīnākṣī and *Sundareśvara.

Aḻakiya Maṇavāḷa Perumāḷ Nāyaṉār (13th–14th century CE?) A theologian of the southern (*Teṉkalai) school of *Viśiṣṭādvaita *Śrī Vaiṣṇavism. The younger brother and pupil of *Piḷḷai Lokācārya, he was the author of a number of exegetical works, including a detailed commentary on the *Tiruppāvai* ('Sacred Lady') of *Āṇṭāḷ.

Alakṣmī (Jyeṣṭhā) ('misfortune') Personifed as the sister, and, in terms of her characteristics, opposite of the goddess of fortune, *Lakṣmī. *See also* JYEṢṬHĀ.

alaṃkāra An 'ornament' of the sense or sound of a word. In classical Indian literary theory alaṃkāra refers specifically to the skilful use of poetic figures of speech, based on image-building and suggestion, including metaphor, simile, and punning. *Sanskrit critics subjected this to an extensive and subtle analysis, producing a catalogue of around one hundred stock tropes, which both reflected and encouraged the creation of an exceptionally ornate and complicated poetry.

alaukika ('ultra-mundane', 'not relating to this world'). A term used in *aesthetics and *bhakti to describe the type of non-egotistic emotion felt by the spectator or devotee. It is opposed to *kāma, which is a worldy or *laukika emotion. More generally, it refers to something that is not part of the ordinary custom of the world (*loka (2)).

ālaya ('house', 'dwelling') By extension, a *temple—the house of the deity.

Alberuni *See* AL-BĪRŪNĪ.

al-Bīrūnī, Abū Raihān (Rayḥān) (973–1051) An Islamic scholar, scientist, and polymath from Persia who, in the first half of the 11th century CE, was forced to accompany the Turkic warrior Maḥmūd of Ghazna on his invasions of northern India. While there, al-Bīrūnī travelled widely and learnt *Sanskrit; this enabled him to converse with *paṇḍits, and to read Hindu religious texts and scientific treatises in the original. As a result, he provided in his Arabic al-Hind ('India', composed in 1030), the first extensive, disinterested account of Hindu beliefs and practices from a foreign perspective. For the outside world this remained the major source of information about India for a number of centuries, and its methods anticipate by hundreds of years the scientific and comparative study of religions.

alchemy The goal of Hindu alchemy is to achieve *immortality. What makes it distinctive, however, is the means it employs to attain this end: the transmutation and ultimate perfection of the body. The precise techniques for producing a perfected (*siddha) body vary. One broad channel (which includes both Hindu and *Buddhist methods) is referred to as 'the way of essences' (rasāyana), since it draws on *Sāṃkhya cosmological ideas about emission from, and reabsorption into an original essence. Another, specifically Hindu approach, is designated 'mercurial' (dhātuvāda) alchemy, since it uses mercury and drugs as its transformative agents.

A large number of alchemical texts, produced over a period of a thousand years (from the 2nd century CE) are attributed to a legendary figure, or series of figures, called Nāgārjuna. Indian alchemy draws on, and is intimately bound up with *Tantric thought and practice, and the two flourish alongside each other from the 6th to the 15th centuries CE. What counted as 'alchemy' for the *siddhas was a mixture of alchemy proper, *yoga, and Tantric practices. In short, any spiritual or physical technique that was thought to work could be employed. The goal was to make a body immutable as gold, hard as diamond, and capable of supernatural powers (*siddhis). Success resulted in *jīvanmukti, liberation while still embodied, a godlike state of immortality and power.

alcohol In *Tantric rituals alcohol, along with blood and *meat, is commonly offered to *Bhairava, and to goddesses such as *Kālī to placate their wrath. For the orthodox *brahmin of the *Vedic tradition, however, alcohol is considered a *polluting substance, associated with low *caste behaviour, and its consumption is forbidden in **Dharmaśāstra*.

Alexander of Macedonia (Alexander the Great) (356–323 BCE) Alexander made a military incursion into India between 327 and 325 BCE. Although this had little direct historical or political effect, the Greek settlements Alexander established in the region of what is now Afghanistan and Northwestern Pakistan, continued to exert a cultural influence on the area for centuries to come. The incursion also introduced the legend of Indian holy men—'naked gymnosophists'—to the West, since one such *ascetic (possibly a *Jain) attached himself to Alexander's army and subsequently caused a sensation by immolating himself.

Allahābād ('City Of Allah') The *Muslim name for the ancient city of *Prayāga.

a

Allama-Prabhu (Guhēśvara ('lord of caves', his characterization of *Śiva)**)** (12th century CE) A South Indian poet-saint at the beginning of the *Liṅgāyat(a) (Vīraśaiva) tradition. A contemporary of *Basava (Basavaṇṇa), *Mahādēviyakka, and other Vīraśaiva poets composing religious lyrics (*vacanas) in the *Dravidian language of *Kannada, Allama was considered to be their Master (prabhu) and *guru. His life, and the legends surrounding it, are told in various works, including the 13th-century *Śūnyasaṃpādane* ('Achievement of Nothingness'). A selection of his poetry in English translation can be found in A. K. *Ramanujan's *Speaking of Śiva* (Penguin Books, 1973).

almsgiving *See* DĀNA.

altar *See* VEDI.

Āḻvārs (Āḷvārs, Azhvars) (Tam.: 'saints', 'sages', 6th–9th centuries CE) The name given to twelve South Indian poet-saints, whose works, and the personal experience of God that they evoked, were highly influential in the development and practice of *Śrī Vaiṣṇava *bhakti, and devotional Hinduism in general. The Āḻvārs, who were disparate in class background, and included one woman, composed their poetry in the *Tamil vernacular (as opposed to *Sanskrit, the language of the *Brahmanical tradition), thus ensuring themselves a potentially wide and mixed audience. This constituency reflected their 'theology', which was predicated on absolute and ecstatic devotion to *Māyōn (*Viṣṇu/*Kṛṣṇa in one or more of his various forms) as the only qualification for the religious life, making questions of *caste or gender irrelevant. The Āḻvārs' uninhibited and highly emotional dependence on God (manifested in dancing and weeping, as well as singing) emphasized their own inadequacies and their total reliance for salvation on the *grace and forgiveness of the deity. Yet, in spite of this *possession-like strength of religious feeling, the poetry and songs in which the Āḻvārs expressed their devotion show a high degree of literary sophistication, accessing and manipulating the symbols of an older, secular tradition of Tamil love poetry. It was this literary tradition that provided both a model for the way in which passionate devotion can break all social conventions, and the emotional register of 'love in separation' which, in the religious context, becomes *viraha bhakti, the devotion of longing.

The Āḻvārs' poetry delineates the sacred geography of South Indian *Vaiṣṇavism between the 6th and 9th centuries: Viṣṇu's presence, in a variety of specific forms, is evoked and praised in 97 different *temples. This reflects a culture of *pilgrimage from site to site as a form of devotion in itself, a practice instrumental in encouraging conversions and establishing Vaiṣṇava centres, the most notable being the famous temple of *Śrīraṅgam. Two of the twelve Āḻvārs are said to have been *brahmin temple *priests, and temple worship, along with *meditation, is already an important element in the practice of the earlier poet-saints. In this way God is conceived as both immanent and transcendent, localized and universal. As the specific object of the Āḻvārs' devotion, Māyōn shows himself in three different ways: through his mythical actions (drawn from stories about *Kṛṣṇa and Viṣṇu's *avatāras), through his incarnation in South Indian temple statues, and through his residence in the hearts of his devotees. Part of the Āḻvārs' success in South India was achieved through the elevation of some of their number to divine status: they came to be seen as *avatāras of Viṣṇu himself, of his wife, *Śrī, or of various elements associated with the god's iconography (and so his temple *image), such as his conch and mace.

The most celebrated of the Āḻvārs is the low-caste *Nammāḻvār; but also well-known is the female saint *Āṇṭāḷ. Their compositions, along with the poetry of the other Āḻvārs, were codified in the 10th century in a collection variously known in Tamil as the *Nālāyirappirapantam*, the *Nālāyiram*, the (*Nālāyira*) *Tivviyappirapantam* or the *Tivyaprapantam*, and in Sanskrit as the *(Divya) Prabandham*, or the *Nālāyira Divyaprabandham*. In English this anthology, traditionally ascribed to the Śrī Vaiṣṇava theologian *Nāthmuni, and subdivided into four books, known as the 'First', 'Second', 'Third', and 'Fourth Thousands', is usually referred to as the 'Four Thousand Divine Compositions (Stanzas)'. (The longest and most significant section—the **Tiruvāymoḻi* ('the ten decads'), which belongs to the Fourth Thousand—contains Nammāḻvār's songs.) Thereafter, the *Divyaprabandham* was ritually recited, first in the temple at Śrīraṅgam, and then in Vaiṣṇava temples throughout South India, marking the transformation of the Āḻvārs personal soteriology into an organized and highly successful bhakti movement, one that, through the medium of other traditions and theologians, eventually spread into North India, and was instrumental in diminishing the influence of the heterodox systems of the *Buddhists and the *Jains. *See also* ARAIYARS; BHAGAVĀTA PURĀṆA; KULACĒKARA(N); MATURAKAVI.

āmalaka (fruit of the Emblic Myrobalan; a gourd) **1.** A tree and its fruit (Indian gooseberry) associated with *Viṣṇu, and used in *Āyurvedic medicine. **2.** An architectural term denoting a notched ring-stone, or 'sun-disc', at the very top of a *temple (North India), symbolizing the celestial world.

amaṅgala ('unhappiness', 'misery', 'something inauspicious') *See* AUSPICIOUS(NESS) AND INAUSPICIOUS(NESS).

Amaracandra (13th century CE) The author of a *kāvya epic, the *Bālabhārata* (based on the **Mahābhārata*), which was produced in Gujarat in the 13th century, and subsequently became popular in Rajasthan.

Amarakośa (***Nāmaliṅgānuśāsana*** ('teaching concerning names and types'), ***Trikāṇḍī*** ('composed of three sections')) ('Amara's dictionary') The earliest surviving *Sanskrit 'dictionary', compiled by the lexicographer *Amarasiṃha, containing lists of synonyms arranged in simple verse. It is divided into three sections, containing approximately 13 000 terms in total, and covering a wide range of subjects, from the sky, to the earth, to human beings, to language itself. This arrangement provided the model for nearly all subsequent lexicons, and it has been the subject of over forty commentaries.

Amarasiṃha (*c.*5th–6th centuries CE) The earliest known, and most famous Indian lexicographer, who compiled the **Amarakośa*. He was a *Buddhist, and possibly a contemporary of *Kālidāsa.

Amarāvatī ('the abode of the immortals') **1.** A name for the capital of *Indra's heaven (*Indraloka, *svarga) and the home of the gods. **2.** An early *Buddhist monastic site in Andhra Pradesh, notable for its great stūpa (intact until the 18th century CE) and sculptures.

Amarnāth A *tīrtha in Kashmir, where an ice formation, discovered in the 19th century, is worshipped as a *Śiva *liṅga. Although in an area currently liable to terrorist attacks, it remains a popular *pilgrimage destination during the summer months.

amāvāsyā **1.** The night of the new *moon; the first day of the first quarter on which the moon is invisible. **2.** A *sacrifice offered at that time.

Ambā ('mother') **1.** Another name for *Ambikā. *See also* AMMĀ(N). **2.** In the **Mahābhārata* the eldest daughter of the king of *Kāśi. With her sisters, she is carried

a

off by *Bhīṣma to marry his half-brother, Vicitravīrya. But she is already secretly betrothed to an *asura prince, who subsequently rejects her because she has spent time in Bhīṣma's house. To avenge herself on Bhīṣma, she eventually commits *satī, and is reborn as one of *Drupada's sons, Śikhaṇḍin. This enables her/him to kill the otherwise invulnerable Bhīṣma during the Mahābhārata war.

Ambālikā *Pāṇḍu's mother in the **Mahābhārata*. She turned pale during intercourse with *Vyāsa, hence her son was born sickly pale.

Ambedkar, Bhimrao Ramji (1891–1956) Born into the *Mahār '*untouchable' *caste, Dr. Ambedkar became a lawyer, and, as a member of *Nehru's cabinet, played a prominent role in drawing up India's post-independence constitution. He fell out with the *Congress Party and M. K. *Gāndhī over the question of caste, and the continued social exclusion of the 'untouchables'. In 1956 Ambedkar publicly renounced Hinduism, and converted to *Buddhism, an example followed by thousands of his 'untouchable' followers. The Maharashtran Mahārs still consider themselves Buddhists.

Ambikā (Ambā) ('little mother') **1.** Another name for the goddess *Durgā. Iconographically, the name may be reserved for Durgā when she is seated on, or attended by, a lion or tiger. The name is also applied to *Umā (*Parvatī), and to goddesses in general. **2.** A *Jain attendant goddess, perhaps originally of independent status, who is attached to the Nemi, the twenty-second Jain *tīrthaṅkara, and associated with childbirth and prosperity. Her mount is a lion. **3.** *Dhṛtarāṣṭra's mother in the **Mahābhārata*. She shut her eyes during intercourse with *Vyāsa, hence her son was born blind.

Ambudeśvara ('lord of clouds') An epithet of *Indra. The clouds are rain-giving.

American Oriental Society Founded in 1842 to encourage basic research in the languages and literatures of the whole of Asia from a humanistic perspective, its scope is now considerably wider. The society's journal (*Journal of the American Oriental Society*, or *JAOS*) and monograph series are the major organs for classical *Indology in the United States.

ammā(n) ('mother') In the *Dravidian languages of South India, a cognate of *ambā, widely used as an affix to the names of goddesses (particularly *village and clan goddesses), and to the names of women in general.

āmnāya ('stream', 'current') A word referring to a particular 'stream', 'current', or transmission of teachings and practices, which flows from *teacher to pupil through the generations. The term is used by both *Śaiva and *Vaiṣṇava traditions.

amṛta ('not dead', 'immortal') **1.** The name given to the nectar of *immortality (sometimes referred to as ambrosia), a liquid produced from the ocean when the *devas and *daityas churned it for that purpose at the beginning of time. As its name suggests, it bestows deathlessness. Various *yogic practices were developed to generate and imbibe it in the practitioner's body, in the form of transmuted semen. *See also* CHURNING OF THE OCEAN. **2.** In the **Ṛg Veda*, and subsequently, a synonym for *soma.

amṛtaciti ('piling up immortality') The piling up of sacrificial bricks in the *agnicayana ritual, which is thought to confer *immortality.

amṛtaghaṭa(ka) A pot containing the nectar of *immortality, which is depicted in the hands of various deities, such as *Brahmā. It can be synonymous with *amṛtakalaśa.

amṛtāharaṇa ('nectar stealer') An epithet of *Garuḍa.

Amṛtahṛdayāṣṭāṅgaguhyopadeśa-tantra ('The Book Teaching the Secrets of Medicine [called] the Essence of Immortality') A *Sanskrit medical treatise, now only preserved in an 8th-century Tibetan translation. It describes techniques unknown to ancient *Āyurvedic medicine, such as using the pulse for diagnosis, and was considered the most important work of its kind in Tibet before the modern era.

amṛtakalaśa **1.** A vessel containing *amṛta; it can be synonymous with *amṛtaghaṭa(ka). **2.** The finial of a temple, made in this shape, and placed on the *āmalaka (2) to symbolize the *immortality to which the worshipper aspires.

Amṛteśvara ('Lord of Immortality') A name of *Śiva.

aṃśa ('portion', 'share') **1.** As a proper name, one of the *Ādityas, who represents acquired wealth (booty), and luck in acquiring it. **2.** A sacrificial share. **3.** A partial *incarnation (aṃśāvataraṇa) of a deity, in so far as it embodies only a portion or aspect of its power. *Viṣṇu appears in this way at moments in the cosmogonic cycle when *dharma is in decline.

anādhāra ('without support') The idea that the world is without support. An heretical view, ascribed by *Vaiṣṇavas to *Viṣṇu's *Buddha *avatāra, and designed to delude his enemies, especially the *daityas, to lead them to self-destruction.

anādyanta ('without beginning and end') A name of Śiva.

anāhata cakra According to *Tantric physiology, the fourth *cakra of the body, a twelve-petalled, deep red *lotus in the region of the heart, and the seat of the element of air.

anāhata nāda (anāhata śabda) ('a sound produced other than by beating') An 'unstruck sound' heard by *sants and *yogins as the immediate prelude to enlightenment or *samādhi, sometimes equated with *oṃ. Its manipulation is a common element in *haṭha-yoga practice.

Ānakadundubhi *See* VĀSUDEVA.

ānanda ('bliss') A term used of *brahman (neut.), as ultimate reality, from the earliest **Upaniṣads* onwards. In *Advaita *Vedānta it is combined with *sat ('being'), and *cit ('awareness, sentience, consciousness') into *saccidānanda, a single term conveying the spiritual and unitary character of the absolute. Consequently, according to this school, salvation is a state of pure bliss (ānanda). In theistic systems, ānanda is frequently listed as a quality of God (e.g. of *Śiva).

Ānandamaṭh ('The Sacred Brotherhood', lit. 'The Monastery of the Ānandas', 1882). The best known fictional work of the Bengālī novelist Bankim Chandra *Chatterjee. It depicts the 1770 *Saṃnyāsī uprising in Bengal as a war of liberation against foreign rule, and was instrumental in promoting the cult of *Bhārat Mātā. See also BANDE MĀTARAM.

Ānandamāyī Mā ('Mother Steeped in Bliss', 1896–1982) Perhaps the best known 20th century female *guru, she is considered by many in India to have been a major religious teacher. Born into a devout and ecstatic *Vaiṣṇava *brahmin family in East Bengal (now Bangladesh), Nirmala (as she was known to begin with) had no formal education, but experienced trances from an early age. Much of her life thereafter appears to have been spent in a state of religious ecstasy. She married, but lived in a state of *celibacy with her husband, who later accepted her as his *guru. Ānandamāyī performed her own initiation (*dīkṣa), after which she kept a three year vow of silence. Her lifestyle was *ascetic (she gave up feeding herself and had to rely on an attendant), and she is said to have undergone various physical changes while in the grip of religious rapture. Her yogic powers (*siddhis) and healing ability attracted a large following. Like many modern gurus, Ānandamāyī's 'theology' was eclectic, and she cannot be identified as belonging to a specific sectarian tradition, although she sometimes ascribed her actions to a personal God. Nevertheless, her basic stance appears to have been non-dualistic: she considered individual identity to be a spiritual defect. Her followers established *āśramas across India, run in accordance with high-*caste *purity regulations. When present, Ānandamāyī taught through question and answer sessions. She travelled extensively, and impulsively, around North India, accompanied by her attendants and followers, and was held in high esteem by other religious teachers. By the time of her death, Ānandamāyī was a famous *saint with a substantial following in India and abroad (especially the USA). She was considered by many to be an incarnation of the *Goddess.

Ānandamūrti *See* Ānand Mārg.

ānandatāṇḍava (tāṇḍava) ('dance of bliss') From the 10th century CE, the standard sculptural representation in South Indian *temples of *Śiva *Naṭarāja, the best-known example being at *Cidambaram, where it represents Śiva wildly and ecstatically dancing one world age (*yuga) to destruction and ushering in the next. The figure is four-armed: the upper right hand holds a drum, the lower right makes the *abhaya-mudrā, the upper left holds a flame, the lower left points to the god's raised left foot, beneath which the devotee may take refuge. With his right foot, Śiva is standing on the dwarf, *Apasmāra, who symbolizes ignorance. The whole image is usually surrounded by a flaming aureole.

Ānandatīrtha *See* Madhva.

Ānandavardhana (9th century CE) A Kashmiri religious poet and *rasa

Ānandatāṇḍava

theoretician, author of, inter alia, a linguistically highly complex prayer to the *Goddess, the *Devīśatakam* ('Hundred stanzas on the Goddess'), and an influential treatise on poetics, the *Dhvanyāloka* ('The Mirror of Resonance'). Ānandavardhana applied *Bhartṛhari's vocabulary to poetics, and, in his turn, his works became the subject of commentaries by *Abhinavagupta. He developed, and was a master of, the *dhvani theory of aesthetics.

Ānand Mārg ('Path of Bliss') A Hindu movement founded in 1955 by Ānandamūrti (P. R. Sarkar, 1921–1990). The Ānand Mārg is *ascetic and *Tantric in orientation. Fully ordained monks and nuns lead celibate lives and wear Indian dress. Most followers, however, belong to the lay community. Ānandamūrti claimed to be an *incarnation of God, with the avowed aim of establishing God's 'dictatorship' over India. He, and his movement, have been linked to various acts of terrorism and violence, and the Ānand Mārg was banned in India during the 1970s emergency. Ānandamūrti himself spent five years in jail after his wife accused him of committing 35 murders, mostly of former sect members who had become disloyal. He was subsequently acquitted. The movement now promotes itself as a charitable organization promoting social development in the Third World. It also continues to teach *meditation and *yoga, as well as a version of its founder's socio-economic and political system, a compound of Marxism and capitalism. It has established centres around the world and claims to have up to a million members, many of them based in Europe, with a particular following in Germany.

Anaṅga ('bodiless') An epithet of the love god *Kāma, referring to his state after *Śiva had reduced him to ash for disturbing his *ascetic practice by causing him to desire *Pārvatī.

Anaṅgaraṅga *See* KĀMAŚĀSTRA.

Ananta ('endless', 'infinite', 'eternal') **1.** A name of the serpent *Śeṣa. Following the *pralaya, the dissolution of the universe, *Viṣṇu is depicted sleeping on Śeṣa in the interval that comes between two world periods (*kalpas). *See also* ĀDIŚEṢA. **2.** An epithet of various gods.

Anantaśayana ('reclining on Ananta') Iconographically, the depiction of *Viśṇu asleep on the serpent Ananta.

anārya ('not noble', 'ignoble') **1.** A noun used by the *Vedic *Āryans to designate others (i.e. non-Āryans), including tribal peoples. **2.** An epithet applied to behaviour considered unworthy, or atypical, of a person designated as belonging among the Āryans.

Anasūyā The wife of the *Vedic *ṛṣi *Atri, and mother of *Durvāsas.

anātman ('not-self', 'the absence of self') A key early *Buddhist doctrine which denies any permanent, unchanging essence or self (*ātman) either to persons or things. It was formulated to contradict the ātman-*brahman doctrine of the early **Upaniṣads*.

āṇavamala *See* MALA.

ancestor *See* PITṚ.

aṇḍa ('egg') *See* BRAHMĀṆḌA.

Āṇḍāḷ *See* ĀṆṬĀḶ.

Andhaka (Andhakāsura) ('blind') **1.** The name of an *asura, the son of *Kāśyapa and *Diti. He symbolizes spiritual blindness, a condition conveyed by his gait, which is that of a blind man, although he is many-eyed and many-limbed. **2.** A blind demon son of *Śiva and *Pārvatī, born from Śiva's sweat. According to some myths, after attempting to abduct Pārvatī, he was killed, and so liberated, by Śiva.

Āndhra Bhāratamu A Telugu version of the **Mahābhārata*, begun by Nannaya around 1025 CE, and completed by Tikkana Somayājī and Errana in the 13th–14th centuries.

aṅga ('a limb of the body') **1.** A common name for a 'limb', or subdivision, of a body of texts. **2.** A 'subsidiary rite', according to the **Kalpa Sūtras*.

Angalamman *See* AṄKĀḶAMMAṈ.

Aṅgāraka The planet Mars.

Aṅgavidyā ('science of limbs') Knowledge of lucky or unlucky marks on the body, and the art of prediction based on bodily movements.

Aṅgiras 1. The name of a famous *Vedic seer (*ṛṣi) and priest. Many of the hymns of the **Ṛg Veda* are attributed to Aṅgiras, or to the poets of the Aṅgirasa clans named after him. He is renowned as a great *teacher, ritualist, law-giver, and astronomer, and is identified with the planet Jupiter. In later mythology he is identified as one of the *Prajāpatis who create the universe. **2.** By extension, the name of Aṅgiras's priestly family, which is associated with the *Atharvans. **3.** With 'Atharvan', a name for the verses of the **Atharva Veda*.

Āṅgirasa(s) Priestly descendants of *Aṅgiras (or *Agni), and members of various clans to which many of the poets of the **Ṛg Veda* belonged. Also related mythological figures, personifying light and fire.

a

Angkor Wat *See* CAMBODIA.

aṇimā ('minuteness') The power to become minute—as small as an atom (*aṇu): one of the eight powers (*siddhis) listed in the **Yoga Sūtra*.

animal sacrifice *See* BALI; PAŚUBANDHA.

animiṣa ('unblinking') This refers to a characteristic of the gods: unlike humans, they are unblinking. Various stories (for example, the *Nala episode of the **Mahābhārata*) make use of this as a means of recognizing deities in disguise.

Aniruddha ('unobstructed') **1.** The son of *Pradyumna, and therefore *Kṛṣṇa's grandson. He is one of the five heroes of the *Vṛṣṇi clan. The story of how Uṣā fell in love with Aniruddha after seeing him in a dream, and how they eventually married, is told in the **Viṣṇu Purāṇa*. **2.** According to *Pāñcarātra cosmology, Aniruddha is one of the three *vyūha forms ('emanations') of *Viṣṇu (*Vāsudeva). He is emanated by the *Saṃkarṣaṇa form. Thirty-eight further forms or manifestations (*vibhavas) emanate from the Aniruddha vyūha; these include the *avatāras of later *Vaiṣṇavism. The vyūha forms are differentiated for purposes of creation, and for visualization in the different stages of worship (*pūjā). *Vaikhānasa theology regards Aniruddha as the irreducible form of Viṣṇu, one of a total of five forms in all.

añjali(mudrā) ('gesture of honouring/salutation') The typical gesture of the devotee before an image of a god, or a living *guru, and the gesture of respectful greeting in general. It involves placing the hands together, palms slightly hollowed, and holding them in front of one's chest. They may be raised to the forehead (a gesture known as añjalibandhana) as a mark of supplication.

Añjanā An *apsaras who, because of a curse, became a monkey. She could change her shape at will, and while in human form was overwhelmed by *Vāyu, the wind god; as a result she became pregnant with the monkey-hero *Hanumān.

Āñjaneya Name of *Hanumān.

Aṅkāḷamma<u>n</u> (Angalamman) (Tam.) The name of a village goddess (*grāmadevatā), well-known throughout Tamil Nadu for making her power available to devotees. She is usually represented without a male consort, although her marital state is deliberately ambiguous. Often identified with *Kālī, her cult has its centre at the Mēl Malaiya<u>n</u>ūr temple near Gingee (Ceñci).

aṅkuśa ('hook') An elephant driver's hook or goad. An emblem of royalty, and iconographically an attribute of many deities, notably of the elephant-headed god himself, *Gaṇeśa.

anna *See* FOOD.

Annamācārya (1408–1503) A South Indian poet-saint of the *Śrī Vaiṣṇava tradition. He is said to have composed more than 32 000 songs in Telugu in praise of *Veṅkaṭeśvara—*Viṣṇu as 'Lord of Veṅkaṭa Hill' (*Tirupati). Annamācārya was born into a *smārta *brahmin family in Tallapaka village in Andhra Pradesh. He became a member of the *Vaiṣṇava *sampradāya to which *Vedāntadeśika had belonged, and was subsequently put in charge of *saṃkīrtana singing at the famous Tirupati *temple. He is credited with originating the Telugu tradition of *bhakti in the saṃkīrtana form.

annaprāśana ('feeding food') Feeding a child solids (usually cooked rice) for the first time, five or six months after birth. The seventh of the *saṃskāras (transformative rituals) incumbent on the *three higher *varṇa, according to **Manusmṛti* and other sources of *dharma.

Annapūrṇā ('she who is full of food') A benevolent, household form of the

*Goddess (perhaps a reconstitution of *Iḍā), whose worship averts famine. Regarded as the goddess of plenty, she is worshipped either as a full-bellied pot, or as a female figure with a ladle across her lap. Annapūrṇā has a popular temple in *Vārāṇasi.

Anquetil du Perron, Abraham-Hyacinthe (1731–1805) A French scholar and traveller in India between 1754 and 1761. His Latin translation of the *Upaniṣads* (in fact a commentary based on a 17th-century Persian version of 52 *Upaniṣads* by *Dārā Shukōh, entitled *Oupnek'hat*, and published in 1802, was the source of Arthur *Schopenhauer's knowledge of these texts. From the same Persian source, Anquetil du Perron had published an earlier translation of just four *Upaniṣads* in 1786.

anṛta ('false', 'not true') A term used in *Vedic texts to denote the violation of cosmic and social law (*ṛta). It is conceptually similar to the later Hindu *adharma.

antaḥkaraṇa ('inner organ') According to the *Sāṃkhya and *Vedānta systems, a complex of 'intellect' (*mahat/*buddhi), 'the sense of I' (*ahaṃkāra), and 'mind' (*manas), and so the basis of all mental life.

antaka (lit. 'causing an end') Another name for, or epithet of, *Yama. *See also* DEATH.

Āṇṭāḷ (Āṇḍāḷ, Kōtai ('Flower-Garland')**)** (Tam.: 'the Lady', 9th century CE) Āṇṭāḷ is the one woman among the twelve South Indian poet-saints, the *Āḻvārs. She is said to have been the adopted daughter of *Periyāḻvār, a *brahmin *priest at the temple of Śrīvilliputtūr in Tamil Nadu, who was himself an Āḻvār. Her poetry turns on the unbearable tension created by the absence of the beloved (*Kṛṣṇa/*Viṣṇu), an absence that eventually engenders an ecstatic experience. According to legend, after marrying *Viṣṇu's statue at *Śrīraṅgam at the age of sixteen, she was absorbed into it, and thereafter worshipped as an incarnation of *Śrī. Two poems are attributed to her, both in the 'First Thousand' of the *Nālāyirap-pirapantam*: the *Tiruppāvai* ('Sacred Lady'), which has generated its own commentarial tradition in both *Sanskrit and *maṇipravāḷam, and the *Nā(y)acciyār-tirumoḻi*, containing the *Vāraṇamāyiram* ('A Thousand Elephants') hymn sung at *Vaiṣṇava *weddings.

antarīkṣa ('middle-air') In the *Veda the intermediate space between sky and earth.

antaryāmin ('inner ruler') A word designating *Viṣṇu's manifestation within the heart of all beings as their 'inner controller', an idea common to all *Vaiṣṇava traditions.

antyeṣṭi (śrāddha) ('the last sacrifice') The death ritual and funeral rites performed in the first thirteen days following *death, and marking the last *saṃskāra (transformative ritual) of a *twice-born person according to *Brahmanical legal texts (*Dharmaśāstra*). The ritual is designed gradually to remove death, and the *impurity associated with it, from the family of the dead person, so allowing them to re-enter normal social life. It is also designed to create a body for the deceased (*preta) in the next world, and unite him with his ancestors, thus preventing his spirit from wandering homelessly, and bothering the living.

In summary, the funeral rites (in their most compressed version) are conducted through the following stages (mostly performed by *priests or the eldest son): the dying or dead person is laid on the floor, head to the *south; the corpse is washed, anointed, and wrapped in a shroud; six of the first sixteen *piṇḍas ('rice balls' or 'dumplings') are sacrificed; on the day of death, if possible, the corpse is carried to the *cremation grounds in an all-male procession; there, its feet are placed in water, representing the liberating *Gaṅgā; the deceased's *domestic fire is relit at the cremation grounds; the grounds are purified, the pyre is stacked, and the corpse laid out on it, feet to the south; the fire is lit from the deceased's domestic fire by the head mourner; the skull of the corpse is smashed to allow the soul to leave through the opening (*brahmarandhra), marking the ritual time of death and beginning a ten- to thirteen-day period of impurity for the survivors (from this point, the śrāddha rites in a more specific sense begin); the wind is fanned and libations made; the head mourner bathes, circumambulates the corpse, smashes a clay pot, and returns home without looking round; from the first to the thirteenth day after the death a grass doll is worshipped on odd days, and it is during this period that the bones or ashes are gathered and scattered in the river and/or hung in a clay pot; on the tenth or eleventh day, the *sapiṇḍīkaraṇa, the ritual to make an after-death body for the deceased, begins with the sacrifice of the remaining ten of the first sixteen piṇḍas; the deceased's personal utensils, money, bedding, and clothing are given to the priests, along with a year's supply of grain; the chief mourner is shaved, bathes, and receives a new *sacred thread; the cow-giving (godāna) ritual is performed to help the deceased cross the river separating this world from *Yama's realm; from the eleventh to the thirteenth day, a second (and perhaps third) set of sixteen piṇḍas are presented, and invited *brahmins are fed; the sapiṇḍīkaraṇa (which, in the extended version of the rites, take place exactly a year after death—the deceased being cared for in the meantime through monthly, new moon śrāddha rites, called ekoddiṣṭas) culminates with the deceased being ritually bound to the forefathers (*pitṛs). *Ganeśa is worshipped; new clothes are presented to the head mourners; a meal is held with relatives and neighbours. Subsequently, periodic (e.g. monthly and annual) śrāddha rituals (ancestor worship) may also be performed. *See also* PIṆḌA; SAPIṆḌA; ŚRĀDDHA.

aṇu ('minute', 'an atom') **1.** The smallest, indivisible entity according to the *Vaiśeṣika system. All objects of the material world are produced by different combinations of triads of atoms, the triad being the smallest perceivable object whose magnitude is finite (for example, a mote in a sunbeam). Atoms in themselves are uncreatable and indestructible. **2.** *See* PAŚU.

Anugītā Part of the **Āśvamedhikaparvan* of the **Mahābhārata*, containing an address by *Kṛṣṇa to *Arjuna, supposedly based on their earlier discourse in the **Bhagavadgītā*, but, on the grounds of style and philosophical content, considered by many scholars to be a late insertion into the *parvan.

anugraha The *Śaiva Siddhānta term for *Sadāśiva's *grace, synonymous with *liberation.

anuloma ('with the hair') According to **Dharmaśāstra*, a name for a mixed *marriage between a man of a higher *varṇa, and a woman of a lower one. The term is also applied to any offspring of that marriage. Its name derives from the perception that, unlike a *pratiloma union, it is in line with the natural order.

anumāna ('inference') Considered a means of valid knowledge (*pramāṇa) by the six *darśanas (orthodox philosophical systems), a claim rejected by the *Cārvākas (materialists).

Anuśāsanaparvan ('The Book of the Teaching') Book 13 of the **Mahābhārata*, containing *Bhīṣma's teaching to *Yudhiṣṭhira, effectively constituting an anthology of Hindu thought and practice.

anuṣṭubh ('following in praise') A metrical form, consisting of four *pādas, or quarter-verses, of eight syllables each. It became popular in the later hymns of the *Ṛg Veda*, and later developed into the *śloka, the principal *epic metre. It is admirably accommodating to the requirements of narrative verse.

Aṇuvyākhyāna *Madhva's summary in 88 verses of his commentary on the *Brahma Sūtra*.

anvāhāryapacana *See* DAKṢIṆĀGNI.

ānvīkṣikī ('investigation through reasoning') **1.** A term identified by some earlier *Indologists as an equivalent to the western term 'philosophy', but it is more accurately seen as an investigative method, based on logical reasoning and critical inquiry, which can be applied to a number of cognitive disciplines. **2.** An older name for the *Nyāya system of thought.

Apabhraṃśa ('falling away', *c.*600–1000 CE) A medieval Middle *Indo-Āryan vernacular language of northern and western India, used by the *Jains and others for extensive literary and religious compositions.

āpad-dharma ('duty in a time of distress') Provisions or metarules made in *Dharmaśāstra* to cover instances when the normal rules of *dharma cannot be applied because of extenuating or unusual circumstances. For instance, 'The Laws of Manu' (*Manusmṛti*) 2.241 states that, in extremity, it is permissible to learn the *Veda* from a non-*brahmin. Conversely, a common use of āpad is to allow brahmins to engage in non-priestly professions, such as trade, which are not normally ascribed to their class.

Apāṃ-napāt ('son of the waters') A *Vedic deity; probably an aspect of *Agni.

apāna *See* PRĀṆA.

aparāvidyā ('lower knowledge') Knowledge produced through the senses and the intellect, and therefore limited to the impermanent and ever-changing world. Distinguished, in the *Upaniṣads*, from *parāvidyā ('higher knowledge').

Apasmāra Name of the demonic dwarf, symbolizing ignorance, who is crushed beneath *Śiva's right foot in the god's dance of bliss (*ānandatāṇḍava).

Āpastamba The founder of a ritual and scholastic tradition belonging to the *Taittirīya branch of the *Black Yajur Veda*. The *Āpastamba* *Kalpasūtra* takes his name, although it is not clear whether he is the author, or whether it simply belongs to the tradition named after him. The *Kalpasūtra* is composed of the *Āpastamba* *Śrautasūtra*, the *Āpastamba* *Mantrapāṭha*, the *Āpastamba* *Gṛhyasūtra*, the *Āpastamba Dharmasūtra*, and the *Āpastamba* *Śulvasūtra*.

Āpastamba Dharmasūtra (*c.*3rd century BCE) Probably the earliest *Dharmasūtra* text, belonging to the *Taittirīya branch of the *Black Yajur Veda*. Part of the voluminous *Āpastamba* *Kalpasūtra* ascribed to *Āpastamba, the *Āpastamba Dharmasūtra* deals with such topics as the rules governing the life of the *Vedic student, the life of the *householder, matters of criminal and civil law, the *āśramas, and the duties of the *king.

Āpastamba Kalpasūtra *See* ĀPASTAMBA.

apauruṣeya ('not coming from men') A term used by the *Pūrva Mīmāṃsā school to indicate that the *Veda* is not of human origin; rather, it is uncreated, authorless, and self-validating.

Apirāmī (Abhirāmī) ('Beautiful One') *See* APIRĀMĪ ANTĀTI.

Apirāmī Antāti ('One Hundred Verses in Honour of the Goddess Apirāmī') An 18th-century *Tamil devotional work praising the goddess Apirāmī, viewed as both *Pārvatī, the consort of *Śiva, and as a deity in her own right. (She is

a

still worshipped in the *temple at *Tirukkōṭṭiyūr.) It was composed by a *brahmin court poet called Cuppiramaṇiya Aiyar, also known as Apirāmapaṭṭar.

Appar (Tirunāvukkaracu ('Lord of Divine Speech')**)** (7th century CE) A *Tamil *Śaiva *saint and *bhakti poet, and among the most prominent of the 63 *Nāyaṉmār, Appar is regarded as one of the founders of the *Śaiva Siddhānta tradition in southern India. Born into a Śaiva family, he briefly converted to *Jainism, which was then strong in South India, before returning to Śaivism and playing a significant part in its revival. (He is subsequently said to have converted his *king, Mahendra, from Jainism to Śaivism.) By travelling about praising Śiva at his various *temple sites, Appar helped to establish a network of *pilgrimage sites across South India. His poetry is filled with a sense of his own sinfulness and inadequacy, and his utter dependence on Śiva for forgiveness. His songs appear in the **Tirumuṟai*, alongside the works of *Campantar and *Cuntarar, notably in what became known as the **Tēvāram* portion, compiled in the 12th century by *Nampi Āṇṭār Nampi. Iconographically, Appar is represented amongst the Nāyaṉmār with a hoe on his shoulder, since he is said to have vowed to keep the temple precincts clear of grass and weeds.

Appaya Dīkṣita (1554–1626) An *Advaitin commentator, probably of the *Bhāmati subschool, whose compendious *Siddhāntaleśasaṃgraha* nevertheless summarizes the views of other Advaita schools. He is also credited with expanding the teachings of the *Śivādvaita school.

apsaras (apsarās, apsarā) ('going in the waters', 'between the waters of the clouds') A class of female divinities or spirits, often translated as 'nymphs', who feature in Indian religious stories from the **Ṛg Veda* onwards. Born from the *Churning of the Ocean, they live in *Indra's *heaven, where, as the mistresses of the *Gandharvas, they dance for the gods. Apsarases are fond of the waters and often visit the earth, where they can assume any shape at will. According to some *Purāṇic texts, they are ubiquitous, especially in forested areas. They are frequently sent by the gods to seduce *ascetics and *ṛṣis, in order to drain them of the power they have acquired through *ascetic practice. *Śakuntalā, whose story occurs in the **Mahābhārata*, and who is the heroine of *Kālidāsa's play, **Abhijñānaśākuntalam*, is the abandoned offspring of one such seduction. Another of Kālidāsa's plays, *Vikramorvāsī*, tells the story of the love between the chief apsara, *Urvaśī, and King *Purūravas.

apūrva ('unpreceded') A concept developed by *Pūrva Mīmāṃsā to explain the interval between the *sacrifice and its result. According to *Kumārila (in his *Tantravārttika*), a sacrificial action immediately produces a storable 'potency' called an apūrva in the person who has performed it. This takes the form of a trace or disposition (*saṃskāra) which automatically works itself out as a fruit or consequence for the sacrificer at some later date. (According to *Śabara, it is the injunction prescribing an action, e.g. 'He who desires *heaven sacrifices', that brings the apūrva into being as its necessary corollary.) This consequence may occur in another life, since the apūrva is transmissible from *death to *rebirth as an element of the *subtle body. Although the specific connection is not made by the Mīmāṃsakas, the term apūrva is used by *Śaṅkara in relation to *karma. It is synonymous with the term *adṛṣṭa.

Araiyars The name given to the groups of men responsible for enacting, through chanting, gesture, and simple religious drama, the poetry of the *Āḻvārs contained in the **Nālāyirappirapantam* anthology. In the chronicle of the *Śrīraṅgam temple, the **Kōyil Oḻuku*, which describes the Araiyars' duties, they are also called Viṇṇapañ-ceyvār ('supplicants'). Araiyar hereditary lineages have been continuous since at least the 11th century CE, and male descendants perform today in the *Śrīraṅgam, Śrīvilliputtūr, and Āḻvārtirunagari temples in Tamil Nadu, as well as in the Melkote temple in Karnataka.

araṇi ('being fitted into', 'turning round') The fire-drill, used for kindling *fire by friction. It is composed of two sticks, upper (uttarāraṇi) and lower (adharāraṇi), the latter being 'drilled' into by the former to produce a fire. They are personified in the *Vedic texts as *Purūravas and *Urvaśī with considerable sexual symbolism.

araṇya ('wilderness', sometimes trans. 'forest') From approximately the time of the **Upaniṣads* the wilderness (araṇya) and the village (*grāma) are contrasted as the loci of two different world-views. Whereas the wilderness evokes the celibate *renouncer—the economically and ritually inactive seeker after *liberation, the village is the domain of the married *householder, who remains economically and ritually active, hoping for good things now and a better *rebirth later.

Araṇyakāṇḍa ('The Wilderness/Forest Book') The third book of the **Rāmāyaṇa*, narrating *Rāma's life with his companions in the *Daṇḍaka forest. It includes *Rāvaṇa's abduction of *Sītā.

Āraṇyakaparvan **(Vanaparvan** ('The Forest Book')**)** ('The Book of the Wilderness/Forest') The third book of the **Mahābharata*. This is one of the longest books in the epic, but it contains much non-narrative material, swelling out the *Pāṇḍavas' twelve years of exile in the forest with various supernatural adventures, stories, and teachings. Among others, it contains the famous story of *Nala and Damayantī, and the equally well-known account of the devoted wife *Sāvitrī, and her encounter with *Yama.

Āraṇyaka(s) ('wilderness [texts]') The third layer of *Vedic literature according to the traditional division. Much of the material the *Āraṇyakas* contain is linguistically and chronologically adjacent to the later **Brāhmaṇas* and **Upaniṣads*, to which they are closely related. They conclude a number of *Brāhmaṇas*, and are themselves usually terminated by *Upaniṣads*, or even have the latter embedded within them. For instance, the last book of the **Śatapatha Brāhmaṇa* is referred to as an *Āraṇyaka*, as is the *Upaniṣad* that completes it, the **Bṛhadāraṇyaka*. The *Āraṇyakas* in general remained open to the inclusion of a significant amount of later material, including post-Vedic *Upaniṣads*, such as the **Mahānārāyaṇa*, which was attached to the **Taittirīya Āraṇyaka*. They are referred to as 'wilderness texts' because, initially at least, they were concerned with secret and dangerous *śrauta rituals that had to be learned and recited outside the village (*grāma). They were not, therefore, the concern of *ascetics or *renouncers, but of *brahmin *householder ritualists.

āratī (ārtī) Honouring the deity with light (dīpa). Āratī is one of the sixteen offerings (*upacāras) made during worship (*pūjā). It typically involves the worshipper, or a *priest, taking an oil lamp with five wicks, or a single-flamed camphor lamp, and circling it in a clockwise direction in front of the image of the deity. Further actions, such as the sounding of handbells and other instruments, and hymn singing, may accompany āratī, but it is the circling of the flame that has come to be considered both the climax and the defining component of Hindu pūjā—so much so, that the terms (āratī and pūjā) are effectively synonymous, and āratī is commonly performed on its own as a standard ritual. In a *temple, a number of āratīs will take place each day. According to some commentators the camphor flame, in particular, symbolizes the identification of the worshipper and the deity, in so far as it provides a common focal point for the ideal *darśana. The deity's protective grace (*prasāda) is transferred to the worshippers as they cup or pass their hands through the flame, and then touch their eyes or heads with their fingertips. *See also* PŪJĀ.

arcā ('[image] to be worshipped') A term used to designate the properly consecrated image (*mūrti) of *Viṣṇu (or one of his *avatāras) in a *temple or shrine, with the understanding that the god is present in the image. *See also* ARCĀVATĀRA.

arcāvatāra ('the descent [into an image] to be worshipped') The incarnation (*avatāra) of *Viṣṇu in an image or a statue. The god is thought to be physically present in such images, and so permanently available for worship by devotees. According to the theology of the *Śrī Vaiṣṇavas (which draws on that of the *Pāñcarātrins), such an image—which should represent one of the *vyūha or *vibhava forms of Viṣṇu, and be installed in a *temple or a private *pūjā room—contains all six of the divine qualities (*guṇas) ascribed to the god. Nevertheless, the presence of Viṣṇu in, or as, the image does not compromise or localize in any way his supreme power.

arccakaṉ (Tam.) The name given to a type of hereditary *Śaiva Siddhānta *priest. In *temple ritual the arccakaṉs follow *Tantric rites derived from the *Āgamas*.

architecture *See* ŚILPAŚĀSTRA; ŚULVASŪTRA; TEMPLE.

Ardhalakṣmīhari ('part Lakṣmī, part Hari') A depiction of *Viṣṇu and *Lakṣmī combined as a single figure, one side male, the other female. It was probably developed in imitation of the better known *Ardhanarīśvara.

Ardhanārīśvara (Ardhanārī ('half female')**)** ('The lord who is half female') A depiction of *Śiva and *Pārvatī combined as a single figure, the right side male, the left side female, demonstrating the union of Śiva and his *śakti.

arghya ('respectful reception of a guest') **1.** Water offered as part of the respectful reception of a guest, and, by extension, before worship and meals. **2.** The welcoming of a deity through such an offering—one of the sixteen offerings/services (*upacāras) which are component parts of *pūjā. See also HOSPITALITY.

Arjuna ('white') In the **Mahābhārata*, Arjuna, the son of *Kuntī and *Indra, is the third of the five *Pāṇḍava brothers. Renowned for his skill as an archer, he takes a hero's leading role in most of the major episodes of the epic. Notably, it is Arjuna who wins the contest for *Draupadī's hand in *marriage, although he subsequently has to share her with his brothers. He becomes the friend of *Kṛṣṇa, whose sister, Subhadrā, he marries. (Their son, *Abhimanyu, is killed in the *Kurukṣetra war.) During the Pāṇḍavas' exile in the *forest, Arjuna journeys to Indra's *heaven to obtain weapons; he also spends a period practising *asceticism in the mountains and acquires more weaponry from *Śiva. Arjuna passes the thirteenth year of exile posing as a eunuch at the court of King Virāṭa, where the Pāṇḍavas are living in disguise. In the subsequent negotiations between the Pāṇḍavas and their hostile cousins, the *Kauravas, Arjuna secures Kṛṣṇa as a non-combatant charioteer and adviser. On the brink of war, stationed between the two armies in his chariot driven by Kṛṣṇa, Arjuna is suddenly overcome by disabling scruples at the prospect of killing his kinsmen and teachers. This marks the beginning of the famous **Bhagavadgītā* section of the *Mahābhārata*, which ends with Arjuna's renewed determination to fight. During the eighteen day battle that ensues, Arjuna kills a number of notable opponents, including *Karṇa who, unbeknown to him, is his half-brother. After the war, Arjuna follows the horse his eldest brother King *Yudhiṣṭhira has released as part of a horse sacrifice (*aśvamedha), and fights many great battles across the breadth of the earth during its wanderings. Much later, he performs his friend Kṛṣṇa's *funeral rites and, in the company of his brothers and Draupadī, renounces the world and journeys to Mount *Meru, intending to ascend to heaven. He dies in the attempt, but, like the others, is subsequently discovered in heaven, cleansed of his sins, dwelling with his father Indra.

Arjuna's importance in the *Mahābharata* is emphasized by the fact that the entire text is portrayed as being recited to his great-grandson, *Janamejaya. Beyond his renown as a great hero (compared by some to other *Indo-European heroes, such as Achilles, and Odysseus), he is above all the recipient of the *Bhagavadgītā* and, as such, a model for those in search of the correct way to act. *See also* BHAGAVADGĪTĀ; MAHĀBHĀRATA.

arka A plant (*Calotropis gigantea*) whose larger leaves are used in *Vedic rituals.

Arnold, Sir Edwin (1832–1904) British translator and playwright who produced a metrical translation of the **Bhagavadgītā*, called *The Song Celestial* (1885). This was the version through which M. K. *Gāndhī first became familiar with the text.

ārṣa marriage ('marriage of the sages') According to 'The Laws of Manu' (**Manusmṛti*) and other *Sanskrit legal texts (**Dharmaśāstras*), one of the eight possible types of *marriage, involving the bridegroom making a gift of one or two pairs of oxen to the bride's father.

artha ('object', 'that which one seeks') **1.** An ambiguous term, conveying both the sense of 'aim' or 'purpose', and the object aimed at or purposed. By extension, it can therefore convey the cause, motive, or reason for something. It also designates the object to which a word points, in terms of both its meaning and its particular use.

2. In a specific application of 'aim', artha appears as one of the four legitimate 'aims or goals of human life' (*puruṣārthas), namely, pursuing and acquiring material wealth and worldy success. Because this is something *kings are supposed to do on behalf of their subjects, 'artha' also comes to designate the means to this end, i.e. statecraft. *See also* ARTHAŚĀSTRA; DHARMA; KĀMA; MOKṢA.

arthāpatti ('presumption', 'postulation') Recognized as a means of valid knowledge (*pramāṇa) by the *Mīmāṃsā and *Vedānta *darśanas.

Arthaśāstra (***Kauṭilya Arthaśāstra***) ('Treatise on Statecraft') A *Sanskrit text of 5000 *sūtras, attributed to *Kauṭilya, a minister of *Candragupta Maurya. The extant version, discovered at the beginning of the 20th century, is probably a compilation dating from the 2nd century CE, but it remains the earliest surviving text of its kind, and clearly refers to still earlier sources. Its chief concern, and what constitutes *artha in this context, is with polity and statecraft. Under that umbrella, it treats widely and exhaustively of all matters to do with government, including the role of the *king, warfare, espionage, taxation, criminal law, and the civil service. The aim is to create and preserve a stable and ordered society, which is pictured as requiring persistent state intervention, and an elaborate bureaucracy. (It is worth noting, however, that the *Arthaśāstra* implies that political and religious authority operate in separate spheres.) As a unique source of information about all aspects of Indian life and society, including agriculture, medicine, and technology, it has proved invaluable to historians of the period, even if the precise extent of that period, and the question of whether the polity it evokes was actual, or merely ideal, remain matters of debate.

a

arthavāda ('eulogy', 'description') According to the *Pūrva *Mīmāṃsaka exegetes, arthavāda is the division of the **Veda* into which descriptive statements fall. Such statements complement injunctions (*vidhis) and prohibitions (*pratiṣedhas). Through their glorification of what is enjoined and their excoriation of what is forbidden, their function is simply to incite the ritualist to act or to abstain from action. Such statements as: 'The sun is the sacrificial post', '*Indra hurled the thunderbolt at *Vṛtra'—indeed, all statements about gods and *heaven—fall into this category of arthavāda. Their purpose is not to signify independently existent entities, but simply to shore up the sacrificer's performance. Their only form is as words in the *mantras when the offering is made.

ārtī *See* ĀRATĪ.

ārtīpūjā *See* ĀRATĪ.

arulśakti (Tam.: **arul̤catti**) ('energy that is grace')) A term used in *Śaiva Siddhānta theology to characterize *Śiva's *grace, which takes the form of his *śakti (i.e. the *Goddess), and which leads the devotee to direct experience of the god.

Āṟumuka Nāvalar (Arumuga Navalar) (1822–1879) An exponent of *Śaiva Siddhānta, based on the Jaffna peninsula of Sri Lanka, who wrote and published works in *Tamil on the correct performance of *temple worship. His purpose was to educate the *Śaiva population of Sri Lanka and southern India, and thereby to protect them against the criticisms and proselytizing of Protestant *Christian missionaries.

Aruṇa ('ruddy'). Dawn, and the god of dawn, personified as the sun god *Sūrya's charioteer.

Aruṇācaleśvara Temple ('The Temple of the Lord of the Red Mountain', mostly 16th–17th centuries CE) One of the great South Indian *Śaiva *temple complexes and *pilgrimage sites, situated at *Tiruvaṇṇāmalai.

Aruṇanti (Arul̤nanti) (13th century CE) A South Indian *brahmin *ascetic, the author of perhaps the best known *Śaiva Siddhānta **śāstra*, **Civañāṉacittiyār* (1253), which is partly a commentary on his *guru *Meykaṇṭār's *Civañāṉapōtam*, teaching the immanence of Śiva and his active non-difference from the individual *soul. Another composition of Aruṇanti's on the same theme was *Irupāvirupaḫtu* (1254), cast in the form of a dialogue with Meykaṇṭār.

Āruṇi *See* UDDĀLAKA ĀRUṆI.

arūpa *See* RŪPA.

āryā ('the lady') In *Sanskrit prosody the most common example of a metre scanned according to the number of syllabic instants (mātrās). Very different from, for example, the *anuṣṭubh or *śloka, it was probably adopted into Sanskrit from more popular sources.

Āryabhaṭa I (5th century CE) A mathematician and astronomer whose *Āryabhaṭīya* and *Āryabhaṭasiddhānta* (the latter no longer extant) were highly influential works in the development of both disciplines in India. Āryabhaṭa suggested that the earth rotated on its axis as well as around the sun. *See also* JYOTIṢA.

Ārya(n) ('hospitable', 'noble', 'honourable') **1.** The self-designation of the people whose language (*Sanskrit) and culture (*Vedic) dominated northern India from the middle of the 2nd millennium BCE, and who slowly spread their influence through the sub-continent, establishing a degree of cultural hegemony over South India by around the 6th century CE. Controversy, some of it fierce and politically tendentious, has come to surround the question of their pre-history and origins. Until recently, most scholarship has accepted the hypothesis propounded by western *Indology that the Āryans entered

India from the northwest sometime between 1750 and 1200 BCE. Initially, this incursion was claimed to be by conquest, given that the Āryans were clearly horsemen and charioteers; more recently there have been arguments in favour of a gradual migration into the area, conditioned by changing patterns in agriculture. Against these theories of outside origin, it has been maintained, mostly, but not exclusively, by Indian scholars, that the Āryans were indigenous to the subcontinent. This hypothesis depends largely upon the as yet unproven assertion that the *Indus Valley civilization spoke an *Indo-European language related to Vedic Sanskrit, which would indicate that Āryan or Vedic culture had subcontinental roots stretching back to the Neolithic period. Opponents of this view argue that the language of the Indus Valley seals probably belongs to the *Dravidian language group, and that the textual and archaeological records demonstrate both continuity and discontinuity between the Āryan and Indus Valley cultures. (In other words, the Āryans were originally unrelated to the earlier indigenous culture, and subsequently replaced it, displaced it, or integrated with it as the dominant partner.) The question is unlikely to be quickly or neatly resolved to the satisfaction of all parties, since ultimately it depends, as it has from the beginning, on a particular model of the geographical and temporal distribution of the Indo-European language family, one that will either be confirmed, or shown to be in need of redrawing, only if the Indus Valley script is conclusively deciphered.

Our knowledge of the Āryans comes almost exclusively from their body of texts, the **Veda*. It is there that they distinguish themselves from the *anāryans (non-Āryans), principally their adversaries the Dasyu or *Dāsas. In the developed social structure, reflected in the post-*Ṛg Vedic texts, 'Āryans' are those who belong to the three highest classes (*varṇas); they are also known as the '*twice-born' because they have been initiated into the *Veda*, and are therefore eligible to participate in the sacrificial ritual. This distinguishes them from those belonging to the fourth class, the *śūdras or serfs, who are considered to be non-Āryan. Some have taken this to indicate a division between the subjugated indigenous population and the subjugating Āryans, but the origins of this ideologically constructed hierarchy are clearly more complex than that simple division suggests. As Western readers will be aware, the term 'Āryan' was appropriated in the 20th century by the Nazi party in Germany as part of their racist agenda, but it would be both anachronistic and misleading in the extreme to read anything back from that into the original Sanskrit term.

2. A term of respect, used by the Buddhists in particular to indicate someone venerable. It was probably adopted by early *Buddhism as part of a deliberate strategy to redefine Vedic terminology for polemical purposes.

Āryanization *See* SANSKRITIZATION.

Ārya Samāj ('The Āryan [Noble] Society') A society founded in Bombay in 1875 by *Dayānanda Sarasvatī to promote his version of reformed Hinduism. Through it he advocated what he saw as a return to a pure, **Veda*-based, pre-**Mahābhārata* war form of the religion, shorn of its *Epic, *Purāṇic, and *devotional elements, and focused on an impersonal God. Dayānanda understood the *Veda* as containing the blueprint for all things, including apparently modern inventions. This combination of traditional authority and openness to technology appealed to members of the merchant *castes in the Punjab and Northwest India, and it was here that the Ārya Samāj attained a significant following. Encouraged by this, Dayānanda moved the society's headquarters to (pre-*Partition) Lahore.

From the outset Dayānanda's purpose was broadly political, in so far as he sought

a

to counter the attacks made on Hinduism by *Christian missionaries, to reconvert low-caste Indian *Muslims and Christians, and to promote a national identity based on the *Sanskritic tradition. His advocacy of radical social reforms, such as the availability of a traditional *Vedic education for women and the low *castes, an end to *child and arranged *marriages, and a reinterpretation of the caste system along meritocratic lines, was designed to further this reforming, neo-traditionalist agenda. Dayānanda's ultimate aim was Hindu unity in the face of the perceived threat of other religions, particularly *Islam and Christianity. Many members of the Ārya Samāj subsequently took prominent roles in the nationalist movement, and in more recent times others have been closely associated with the various militant organizations dedicated to the establishment of a Hindu state.

After its founder's death, the Ārya Samāj split into two branches, one conservative and Sanskritic, the other aiming to provide a 'progressive', English-medium education in its schools and colleges. There are now 'Dayānanda Anglo-Vedic' (DAV) colleges in many Indian cities, as well as Ārya Samāj centres across India and abroad. Current membership of the society is claimed to be over one million.

Āryāvarta (Madhyadeśa ('middle country')**)** ('homeland of the Āryans') Initially the region around the *Gaṅgā in northern India, which came to be dominated by the *Āryans in the 2nd millennium BCE, and so developed into the epicentre of *Vedic and *Brahmanical religion. Late in this period, **Manusmṛti* describes the Āryāvarta as lying between the *Himālayas and the Vindhya mountains (central India), and stretching from the eastern to the western sea (2.22).

āsana ('sitting', 'seat', 'posture') **1.** A name used to designate the postures assumed in *yogic practice. Posture (āsana) is one of the *aṣṭāṅgas, the eight limbs of (or aids to) *yoga according to the classical, or rājayoga system expounded in *Patañjali's **Yoga Sūtra* (2.29). Best known among the āsanas is the 'lotus position' (*padmāsana), but there are many such postures; the essential thing is to assume a stable and easy posture as a prerequisite for the practice of *prāṇāyāma, the control of the vital breath, and the eventual attainment of *samādhi. In the *haṭha-yoga tradition, āsanas become ever more elaborate and physically taxing, as a means of perfecting and purifying the body. **2.** Offering a seat to the deity—i.e. ritually installing it. One of the sixteen offerings/services (*upacāras) which are component parts of *pūjā.

asatkāryavāda ('doctrine that the effect does not (pre)-exist in its cause') A philosophical doctrine concerning origination or causation, according to which the material effect differs from, or does not pre-exist in the material cause. This position is held by the *Nyāya and *Vaiśeṣika schools, as well as by certain *Buddhist schools, and *Madhva's *Dvaita *Vedānta. For example, the Nyāya-Vaiśeṣikas maintain that a wooden table is a new object that is neither identical with nor pre-existent in the wood from which it was made. More significantly, it leads them to postulate an agent or efficient cause of the universe, namely God (*Īśvara). *See also* SATKĀRYAVĀDA.

aśauca ('impurity', 'pollution') *See* PURE AND IMPURE.

ascetic *See* ASCETICISM.

asceticism A term derived from the Greek word for a monk or hermit, denoting the practice of religious abstinence and austerity. It is used by *Indologists to designate a wide variety of practices, of varying intensity, in which the individual ascetic restrains or controls him-(or rarely her-)self in order to attain a particular spiritual, material, or supernatural goal.

Broadly speaking, practitioners aim either at *liberation from *karma and *rebirth, or the attainment of magical powers (*siddhis). Some of the major restraints involved include *celibacy, bodily mortification, homelessness, mendicancy, and fasting (*upavāsa). The origins of asceticism in India have been much debated by academics, some arguing for a source in certain elements of the *Vedic and *Brahmanical ritual, others for an extra-Vedic origin (sometimes conflated with the hypothetical religious practices of the non-*Āryan population). Others, again, have suggested multiple points of Vedic and extra-Vedic origin.

Whatever its beginnings, by the middle of the 1st millennium BCE asceticism was regarded as typifying, or synonymous with, the behaviour of many kinds of renouncers (*saṃnyāsins), and in the following centuries was slowly integrated (or domesticated) into the Brahmanical mainstream via the *āśrama system.

From the Vedic period to the present it has been widely believed that mortification of the body, combined with celibacy, results in an accumulation of internal power in the form of heat (tapas), which can then be used for obtaining gifts, or compelling the gods to act in the ascetic's favour. (The term 'tapas' is frequently used as a synonym for the process by which it is acquired, i.e. self-mortification; similarly, a tapasvin, a 'possessor of tapas', is an ascetic.) Many stories in the *Epic and *Purāṇic material tell of irascible ascetics, or *ṛṣis, and their weapon-like use of tapas for destructive purposes. They also recount the attempts of the gods to reduce this threat to their own power and the stability of the world through engineering situations in which the ascetic's tapas will be dispersed through seduction (the end of celibacy) or an outburst of anger.

The basic techniques of mortification and celibacy can be adapted to an individual's or group's specific theological needs, and further combined with, or modified by, *yogic and meditational practices. In this way the purpose of asceticism becomes spiritual transformation and the manipulation of the effects of karma. Nevertheless, to the extent that yoga and meditation can be seen as techniques to control the mind, so tapas and asceticism are aimed in the first instance at subduing and removing the passions. Among the more extreme practices, many of them still current, are imitating the foraging behaviour of animals, fasting for long periods, sleeping upright, gazing into the sun, tree-hanging, and lying on the proverbial bed of nails. A well-attested ancient exercise to increase inner heat involves the ascetic sitting between four fires, with the sun beating down as a fifth. (Known as the '*five fire sacrifice/mortification' (pañcāgni-tapas), in **Manusmṛti* (6.23) this is listed among the practices of those who have entered the *saṃnyāsa āśrama.)

Of the great Hindu gods, it is *Śiva who is regarded as the supreme ascetic. He is frequently depicted as a wandering mendicant with an emaciated body, matted hair, and wrapped in a tiger or elephant skin, his body smeared in *cremation ground *ash. In his appearance and behaviour he thus provides a model for *Śaiva ascetics, especially those, such as the skull-carrying *Kāpālikas, who worship his more ferocious forms.

From an early period, asceticism entered the repertoire of universal Indian religious practices, and it has been by no means confined to renouncers. It remains common for *householders to take temporary ascetic vows—to fast in particular ways, or to practise celibacy, for instance—in order to make spiritual progress and acquire karmic *merit. *See also* BRAHMACARYA; GOVRATA; SAṂNYĀSA; UPAVĀSA.

ashes *See* BHASMAN.

Asiatic Society of Bengal (Bengal Asiatic Society) A society founded in Calcutta

a

in 1784 by Sir William *Jones for 'enquiring into the History, Civil and Natural, the Antiquities, Arts, Sciences and Literature of Asia'. Under Jones's presidency, and through its journal, *Asiatik Researches*, the society became the first major channel to Europe of information about classical Indian culture.

asmitā ('I-am-ness') One of the five defilements (*kleśas) according to *Patañjali's **Yoga Sūtra*. It denotes the individual's erroneous association with their body, including the contents of their mind (a kind of egoistic self-consciousness), and is classified as a form of ignorance (*avidyā).

Aśoka (r. *c.*272–231 BCE) The third *Mauryan emperor, son of Bindusāra and grandson of *Candragupta. He claimed to have abandoned war and violence after his conquest of the Kaliṅga region of Northeast India (modern day Orissa), and thereafter promulgated 'Dhamma' ('*Dharma') through his rock and pillar edicts. He is said to have favoured *Buddhism, since his 'Dhamma' seems consonant with the ethical outlook of a lay Buddhist, but it has been argued that it represents more of a pragmatic code of conduct, encouraging social responsibility and religious harmony in a large and variegated empire, than an indication of any particular religious allegiance.

aśoka ('free from sorrow') An evergreen tree (*Saraca indica*) with a spectacular red flower. Sacred to *Śiva, it is associated with chastity, and is said to bloom if kicked by a *pure girl.

āśram(a) ('hermitage', Ang.: 'ashram') Probably originally a term for a hermitage in which *brahmin *householders practised their religious life beyond the *village, it came to be applied more widely to the residence of any *ascetic, or group of ascetics (*teachers and pupils), situated in the *forest. If the *Epics and **Purāṇas* are anything to go by, these were often self-contained communities of both sexes (*Śakuntalā was brought up in an āśrama), subject to frequent visits by royalty and others in an early form of religious tourism or *pilgrimage. In the modern period, āśramas are commonly situated in cities as well, where they attract *householders for temporary periods of religious exercise. M. K. *Gāndhī established an āśrama for his followers on the banks of the Sabarmatī in Ahmedabad, which now serves as a memorial to him.

āśrama An order of life. As part of the classical *varṇāśramadharma complex, the term designates an idealized trajectory for the life of a high-*caste male through four orders, from celibate studentship (*brahmacarya), through householder status (*gārhasthya), to the order of forest dweller (*vānaprasthya), and an eventual complete retirement from the domestic world in renunciation (*saṃnyāsa) and the life of a wandering *ascetic. It is clear from the **Dharmasūtras* that these orders were originally conceived (perhaps around the 5th century BCE, or somewhat later) as voluntary alternatives to the preferred norm (the life of a householder), any one of which, including 'studentship' or scholarship, could be chosen as a lifelong āśrama by an adult male, after a temporary period of *Vedic studentship under a *guru. By the time of the **Dharmaśāstras*, however, the āśramas had been arranged, for ideological purposes, into a single path through life marked by four successive stages, which each individual was supposed to pass through in turn. Some later texts (such as the *Jābāla* [**Saṃnyāsa*] *Upaniṣad*) allow for the option of renouncing from any of the first three āśramas. In practice, however, most adults have lived and died in the householder āśrama.

The original motive for constructing the āśrama theory seems to have been the need to redefine and defend the traditional *Brahmanical way of life—typified by the domestic ritualist or 'householder' (*gṛhastha)—at a time when various forms of celibate renunciation were being presented as legitimate and permanent alternative lifestyles. This may have been combined with a desire on the part of the renouncers themselves to align their particular orders with *Vedic orthodoxy. The āśrama system was thus an attempt to resolve this tension through assimilating the renouncer's ways of life into a wider pattern of behaviour, one which, in its best known, although by no means universal form, required men to pay their '*debts' (ṛṇas) to orthodox society, in the form of *studentship, *sacrifice, and the production of *sons, before they renounced for good.

Āśramavāsikaparvan ('The Stay in the Hermitage') Book 15 of the *Sanskrit *Mahābhārata*; it tells of *Dhṛtarāṣtra, *Gāndhārī, and *Kuntī retiring to the *forest, and eventually perishing in a forest fire.

Aṣṭādhyāyi ('Eight Chapters', *c.*4th century BCE) The name of *Pāṇini's grammar, in which he analysed the whole phonology and morphology of *Sanskrit in fewer than 4000 *sūtras (aphorisms), designed for memorization and *oral transmission. This description of the language used by the educated *brahmins of his time was quickly accepted as being so inclusive and accurate that it became the authoritative source for all questions of usage from that point onwards, and thus superseded all previous grammars, which disappeared as a result. What is now known as 'Classical Sanskrit' is the language codified in the rules and metarules of Pāṇini. A. L. *Basham justly describes the *Aṣṭādhyāyi* as 'one of the greatest intellectual achievements of any ancient civilization, and the most detailed and scientific grammar composed before the 19th century in any part of the world'.

aṣṭadikpālas ('the eight guardians of the directions') Sculpturally portrayed in the appropriate position in Hindu *temples, the eight guardians of the cardinal directions, namely: *Indra (E), *Agni (SE), *Yama (S), *Nirṛti (SW), *Varuṇa (W), *Vāyu (NW), *Kubera (N), and *Īśāna (NE), or variations on these. The guardians each have their own bull-elephant (also called dik- or loka-pāla), on which they are frequently shown mounted.

aṣṭākṣara ('eight syllables') A *mantra addressed to *Viṣṇu by his devotees thrice daily in order to gain *liberation: 'oṃ namo nārāyaṇāya'.

aṣṭamahālakṣmīs ('eight great Lakṣmīs') A group of deities representing different aspects of the goddess *Lakṣmī, thought to be an especially powerful representation of good fortune.

aṣṭamaṅgalas ('eight auspicious objects') A collection of eight lucky or *auspicious objects required for large public occasions, such as a coronation, or a *wedding by Hindus, *Buddhists and *Jains, and a fertile source for decorative art. Their exact combination varies, and may depend on the locality and the region, but the following are common: a lion, a bull, an elephant, a water-jar, a fly-whisk, a flag (*dhvaja), a trumpet, a lamp, a mirror, a goad, a drum, and a pair of fishes.

aṣṭamūrti ('eight-formed') A name of *Śiva indicating the totality of his manifestation through his presence in the five elements, *moon, *sun, and chanting *priest (i.e. people); or the elements, plus mind, *ahaṃkāra, and matter (*prakṛti), according to some lists.

aṣṭāṅga-yoga ('eight-limbed yoga') One of two types of *yoga outlined in *Patañjali's **Yoga Sūtra* (2.28–55; 3.1–8), and associated by some with Patañjali himself. The eight limbs are divided between 'outer' (bahir-aṅga) and 'inner' (antar-aṅga). The outer limbs are *yama (restraint, ethics), *niyama (self-discipline), *āsana (posture), *prāṇāyāma (control of the vital breath), and *pratyāhāra (withdrawal of the senses). These are considered prerequisites for the more advanced inner limbs: *dhāraṇā (concentration), *dhyāna (meditation), and *samādhi (absorbed concentration). *See also* KRIYĀ-YOGA.

āṣṭavināyakas *See* GĀṆAPATYAS.

Āstika ('he who makes it exist') The name of a *brahmin, born from a serpent mother, who intervenes to save the *snake that killed *Parikṣit from the latter's son, *Janamejaya, in one of the framing stories at the beginning of the **Mahābhārata* (recounted in a sub-section called the *Āstīkaparvan*).

āstika ('one who affirms "it exists"') Term used to designate those who acknowledge the absolute authority of the **Veda* as revelation, including those who subscribe to one of the six orthodox *darśanas and the *Brahmanical tradition in general. It can also be used less specifically to mean a believer, in God, etc. The term was probably coined as the positive of *nāstika.

astrology *See* JYOTIṢA.

astronomy *See* JYOTIṢA.

aśubha ('inauspicious', 'bad', 'not beautiful') *See* AUSPICIOUS(NESS) AND INAUSPICIOUS(NESS).

aśuddha ('impure') *See* PURE AND IMPURE.

aśuddhi ('impurity') *See* PURE AND IMPURE.

asura ('lord', 'anti-god', 'demon') In the **Ṛg Veda*, asura is a term applied as an honorific to the gods (*devas), and simply means 'lord'. (This accords with its use in Iranian religion, where Ahura (=asura) Mazdā is the 'Wise Lord'.) In the **Brāhmaṇas* and later literature, however, it is used to designate the opponents of the devas, with the sense of 'anti-god' or 'demon', although both groups are said to have been born from *Prajāpati. There has been considerable speculation about the reasons for this change in meaning. It may be that 'asura' was an *Indo-European term for the primordial gods, who were subsequently overthrown by the devas. The asuras may also represent the gods of the *Dāsas, ranged against the devas of the *Āryans. Whatever the case, the asuras come to be represented as the devas' cosmic opponents in the battle which is the central theme of *Epic and *Purāṇic mythology, although in terms of their actions the antagonists can often scarcely be distinguished. In ritual terms, the difference between them is that the asuras, unlike the devas, do not accept sacrificial offerings and consequently they provide no assistance to human beings. In *Vaiṣṇava mythology the descent of a particular asura, or of multiple asuras, into the world is concomitant with the rise of disorder (*adharma) which presages the end of a world-age (*yuga). It is the job of Viṣṇu's *avatāras to defeat such asuras and, by doing so, to restore *dharma. Well-known individual asuras include *Rāvaṇa and *Mahiṣāsura.

āsura marriage *See* MARRIAGE.

aśva ('horse') The horse seems to have been unknown to the *Indus Valley civilization, and it was probably introduced to, or popularized in India by the *Āryans, who were horsemen and charioteers. Naturally enough, the horse came to be associated with royalty, power, military might, conquest, fertility, and speed. Historically, the subcontinent has relied on central Asia and then Arabia to maintain its equine blood-stock. *See also* AŚVAMEDHA.

Āśvalāyana Reputed author of the *Āśvalāyana *Śrauta-* and **Gṛhya-Sūtras*, both belonging to the *ṚgVedic branch of the *Veda.

aśvamedha ('horse sacrifice') An elaborate *Vedic *śrauta ritual, culminating in the sacrifice of a horse. First mentioned in the *Ṛg Veda (but with parallels across *Indo-European cultures), it is discussed at length in the *Brāhamaṇas. Only a great *king could initiate this ritual, the purpose of which was to extend and substantiate his power. It involved the release of a stallion, which, escorted by the king's army, was allowed to roam freely for a year across neighbouring territories in an assertion of sovereignty. On the horse's return, the king underwent a three day consecration, at the climax of which the beast was killed. The chief queen then simulated copulation with the corpse of the horse, following which the animal was dismembered and portions offered to *Prajāpati and others. In this way the divine power and fertility of the horse were channelled, via the queen, to the king and his kingdom. In the opening of the *Bṛhadāraṇyaka Upaniṣad, the bodily parts and actions of the sacrificial horse are equated to cosmic and natural entities such as the sun and the seasons.

In Book 14 of the *Mahābhārata, the Aśvamedhikaparvan, *Yudhiṣṭhira performs a horse sacrifice at the end of the war to atone for the *Pāṇḍavas' destruction of their *Kaurava cousins. This provides the occasion for *Arjuna to fight many great battles as he escorts the horse in its wanderings across the entire earth. Historically attested performances of the aśvamedha after the Vedic period are rare.

Aśvamedhikaparvan *See* AŚVAMEDHA.

aśvattha (*Ficus religiosa*) A sacred fig or pipal tree (also known as the bodhi tree), the roots of which are thought to be 'above' or in *heaven (see, for example, the *Kaṭha Upaniṣad* 6.1, where it is identified with *brahman (neut.)). It is also connected in many *Vedic texts with *Kurukṣetra, since each is envisaged as being at the centre of the world. Its wood is sometimes used for making the fire drill (*araṇi).

Aśvatthāman A protagonist in several key episodes in the **Mahābhārata*. The son of *Droṇa, and so a *brahmin warrior, he fights for the *Kaurava faction in the battle against the *Pāṇḍavas. When his father dies as a result of being told by *Yudhiṣṭhira that 'Aśvatthāman is dead' (it is in fact an elephant of the same name), Aśvatthāman swears to destroy both the *Pāñcālas and the *Pāṇḍavas for this *adharmic act. As recounted in Book 10 of the *Mahābhārata*, the **Sauptikaparvan* ('The Massacre at Night'), his opportunity finally comes at the end of the battle when, as one of the four surviving Kauravas, he is inspired by the sight of an owl destroying a tree full of sleeping crows to attack his enemies' camp at night. Possessed by *Śiva at the entrance to the camp, he and his two companions massacre all the sleeping warriors, with the exception of the five Pāṇḍava brothers who have been removed by *Kṛṣṇa. *Draupadī demands revenge, and the Pāṇḍavas catch up with Aśvatthāman on the banks of the *Gaṅgā where he tries to use a magical weapon to bring about universal destruction. Instead, its power is diverted into the wombs of the Pāṇḍava women, making them barren. Kṛṣṇa, however, promises that he will later revivify the foetus in the womb of *Abhimanyu's widow, which is later born as *Parikṣit. The defeated Aśvatthāman is condemned to wander the earth in misery for 3 000 years, allowed to live only because he is a *brahmin and the son of the Pāṇḍavas' *teacher.

Āśvina (Āśvayuja) The month (September–October) during which the monsoon comes to an end.

Aśvins (Nāsatyas) ('possessed of horses', 'the charioteers') Twin gods who, according to *Vedic mythology, appear riding a three-wheeled chariot through the sky as the harbingers of dawn. They are the children of the sun (*Sūrya) by a nymph in the shape of a mare, and so are represented as horse-headed. Because of a connection with medicinal plants, healing powers were attributed to them, and they came to be regarded as the physicians of both warriors and the gods, as well as the guardians of *Amṛta. (Traditional physicians claimed a special relationship with them.) The Aśvins are identified with the constellation known in the West as Castor and Pollux (Greek: Dioscuri; Latin: Gemini). In the *Mahābhārata* they are said to be the fathers of the *Pāṇḍava twins, *Nakula and *Sahadeva, by *Mādrī.

Atharvan **1.** The reputed author of the *Atharva Veda*, a famous *Vedic seer (*ṛṣi) and *priest, who, as the son of *Brahmā, is said to have been the first to use *fire and to offer *soma. **2.** By extension, the name of Atharvan's priestly family, which is associated with the *Aṅgirases. **3.** With Aṅgiras, a name for the verses of the *Atharva Veda*.

Atharvāṇas Priestly descendants of *Arthavan, associated with those of *Aṅgiras and *Bhṛgu.

Atharvaśiras Upaniṣad A late *Upaniṣad* containing *Śaiva material.

Atharva Veda **(*Brahma Veda*)** ('The Knowledge/Veda of the Atharvans') The fourth of the *Vedic *Saṃhitās*, different in character to the *Triple *Veda*, and added to it at a later date. About a sixth of its 360 hymns are held in common with the *Ṛg Veda*, and some of its material may be even earlier. Its compilation dates from around 1100 BCE. Preserved in two recensions, those of Paippalāda and Śaunaka, the *Atharva Veda* is sometimes characterized as a collection of spells, since the main purpose of its hymns is to protect against demons and misfortune, and to procure wealth, health and *sons. Its aims, if not its methods, are therefore similar to those of the sacrificial ritual, and its final book attempts to link the *Atharva* with the preoccupations of the other *Vedas*. As part of this assimilation, it was eventually ascribed to the overseeing *brahman (masc.) priest at the *śrauta *sacrifice. From the sacrificial perspective, however, it remains less relevant and less authoritative than the Triple *Veda*. The *Atharva Veda's* contents reflect the diversity of its origins, veering from repetitive incantation to sophisticated verse. It also contains a greater proportion of hymns speculating on the nature of the universe and other cosmic matters than is to be found in the other three *Vedas*, material that to some extent anticipates the content of the early *Upaniṣads*.

atheism When used in a pejorative sense, the equivalent of *nāstika, but otherwise a factually descriptive adjective applied to the completely orthodox (*āstika) beliefs of, for example, the *Sāṃkhya and *Pūrva Mīmāṃsaka systems, which discount the significance of either a personal or impersonal God.

atimārga ('outer path') One of the two main branches of *Śaivism described in the Śaiva *Āgamas* or *Tantras* (the other being the *mantramārga, or 'path of *mantras'). The atimārga, which is entered on solely in order to attain *liberation, is open only to *ascetics. It has two divisions, the *Pāśupata, and the *Lākula, itself a development from within the Pāśupata tradition; both are concerned with *Śiva in his wild and terrible form of *Rudra.

atithi *See* HOSPITALITY.

ātithya ('hospitality rite') A component part of the *soma *sacrifice in which the sticks from the soma plant are ritually received as an honoured guest—i.e. as a *king or a *brahmin.

Ātmabodha ('Knowledge of the Self') A short work ascribed to *Śaṅkara, apparently aimed at popularizing the teachings of *Advaita Vedānta.

ātman ('self') A term that can be used either as a reflexive pronoun ('myself', 'yourself', 'itself', etc.), or as a noun meaning 'the self' (sometimes translated as 'soul'). In the early **Upaniṣads* 'ātman' is used in a wide variety of ways, perhaps most frequently to designate the living, breathing body; it is also sometimes equated with '*prāṇa' ('breath', 'life-force'). The understanding of ātman as the eternal, unchanging essence of the person developed out of an increasing concern in *Brahmanical literature to establish the nature of the 'real' (what is not subject to *death and change), and to distinguish it from the 'unreal' (what is impermanent and mutable), both in terms of the individual and of the universe at large. In a continuation and expansion of sacrificial thought, the *Upaniṣads* postulate an equation between the underlying power and essence of the universe (called *brahman (neut.)) and the essence of the individual (ātman), however understood. This correspondence was further developed and analysed by the *Vedāntins, since the precise nature of the relationship is crucial to an understanding of how the individual should behave in order to attain salvation or *liberation. (The ātman is regarded as being either actually, or apparently, trapped in a world of suffering and change from which it requires release.) For *Advaita Vedānta, which views the ātman and brahman as identical, the realization of that identity through knowledge (*jñāna) is liberating. For *Viśiṣṭādvaita Vedānta, however, the individual self is seen as a distinct mode of an all-powerful God, and so ultimately the self depends upon God for liberation. At the opposite pole to the Advaita view, *Dvaita Vedānta holds that God, or the absolute, and the individual self are completely and eternally distinct; liberation therefore depends on devotion (*bhakti) and God's *grace. In the *Nyāya-Vaiśeṣika system, ātman is designated as one of the four non-material substances (*dravya).

ātmanivedana ('self-surrender', 'offering oneself') Complete surrender to *Viṣṇu, the ninth stage or degree of devotion (*bhakti) according to the **Bhāgavata Purāṇa*.

atonement *See* PRĀYAŚCITTA.

Ātreyas *See* ATRIS.

Atri The name of a legendary *Vedic *ṛṣi. A number of Vedic hymns and a law code (the *Atrismṛti*) are attributed to him. He is said to have been the *purohita of the early *Āryans, and through his connection with the sacrificial *fire is credited with immense power. In later mythology, he is identified as one of the *Prajāpatis who create the universe. In the **Rāmāyaṇa*, he and his wife, *Anasūyā, are visited in their *forest hermitage by *Rāma and his companions.

Atris Descendants of *Atri who are credited with the composition of a number of *Ṛg Vedic hymns.

Aughara One of the *panths ('paths') of the *Nāth Siddha *sampradāya.

auṃ *See* OṂ.

Aurangzēb 'Ālamgīr (r. 1659–1707) *Mughal emperor who reversed many of the reforms made by his great-grandfather *Akbar, antagonizing many Hindus as a result. One of his main opponents was the *Marāṭhā chief *Śivājī.

Aurobindo Ghose (Śrī Aurobindo) (1872–1950) A thinker, teacher and *yogin, whose system of 'Integral Yoga' has acquired a dedicated following, mainly among English-speakers, in India and the West. Aurobindo was born in Bengal but educated in England. On his return to

India, he became a leading figure in the Independence movement, and it was during his imprisonment for seditious journalism that he underwent a spiritual transformation while practising *yoga. As a result, he abandoned politics in favour of the spiritual regeneration of India and, shortly after his acquittal, retreated to the French enclave of Pondicherry, where he established an *āśram, and spent the next forty years writing and meditating. His philosophical system has its roots in *Vedānta and the **Bhagavadgītā*, but as its name, 'Integral Yoga', suggests, it draws on a wide variety of practices and ideas, including different methods of yoga, *Tantric teachings, and science, especially the theory of evolution. The aim of Integral Yoga is to chart a path through progressively higher states of *consciousness, culminating in the divinization and perfection of both human beings and the material world. This philosophy is developed at length, but not always systematically, in Aurobindo's voluminous writings in English, the best known of which is probably *The Life Divine* (1st pub. 1914–19; rev. ed. 1939–40). 'Integral Yoga' was further disseminated through the teachings of Mirra Richard (Alfasa), a Frenchwoman of Egyptian descent, known as 'The Mother', who joined the āśram at Pondicherry in the 1920s, and became its co-leader. On Aurobindo's death, she took over its spiritual leadership, and, in 1968, with the support of UNESCO and the Indian government, founded Auroville, a township near Pondicherry dedicated to the promotion of international peace and unity. Centres promoting Aurobindo's teaching were also set up in the West, especially North America, throughout the 1950s, 60s, and 70s, but Auroville remains the focus of attention. In 2004 its community was made up of over 1 000 people from around 30 different countries, involved in environmental, artistic, and educational projects aimed at furthering the transformation of the world envisaged by Aurobindo.

Auroville *See* AUROBINDO GHOSE.

auspicious(ness) and inauspicious(ness) The conceptual opposition of the auspicious (śubha, maṅgala) and the inauspicious (aśubha, amaṅgala) conditions the management of day to day life in much of Indian society. It is a dichotomy that is thought to reflect a natural order or division in the universe. In the light of this, the general aim is to utilize the auspicious to obtain good fortune, while avoiding the inauspicious and protecting oneself and one's family from the misfortune thought to attend it. Almost any thing or event tends to be assessed as either more or less auspicious. In particular, times and dates, linked to their specific astronomical conjunctions, are governed by this division; events such as *weddings, and new undertakings in general, are therefore arranged in consultation with an astrologer in order that they may coincide with an auspicious moment in the *calendar. On the same principle, combinations of dates and movements (travel arrangements, etc.) have to be carefully considered and planned; harmful supernatural beings may make use of inauspicious moments in order to strike, and the influence of the malevolent planet Saturn has to be avoided.

Inauspiciousness is personified by certain people (*widows and *funeral *priests are prime examples); merely the sight of such a person is enough to bring about misfortune; conversely, the auspiciousness personified in a bride, for instance, symbolized by her 'thread of auspiciousness' (maṅgalasūtra or tali), will bring good fortune to those who see her. *Marriage in itself is thought to make a Hindu woman auspicious, especially among the higher *castes; in the same way, *widowhood makes her highly inauspicious. Traditionally, the overall auspiciousness of society was a matter for the *king, whose duty it was to create the right environment for good fortune and prosperity.

austerities *See* ASCETICISM; TAPAS.

āvāhana ('inviting', 'bidding', 'invocation') The 'calling' of the deity to be present in the image (*mūrti) at the beginning of worship—one of the sixteen offerings/services (*upacāras) which are component parts of *pūjā. With permanently consecrated images, in which the deity is thought to be ever-present, this is more of a framing device for the offering ritual, and a reminder of the unrestricted nature of God, than an actual calling. With images that are not permanently consecrated, āvāhana is an invitation to the deity to take up temporary, or even momentary residence for the purposes of immediate pūjā. *See also* VISARJANA.

Avalon, Arthur (1865–1936) Nom de plume of Sir John Woodroffe, a pioneering Western writer on Hindu *Tantra. His works, now mostly superseded, include *Introduction to Tantra Śāstra* (1913), *Śakti and Śākta: Essays and Addresses* (1918), and *The World as Power* (1921).

avarṇa Outside or beyond the *varṇa system (the 'class' system as validated by *Brahmanical ideology), and so effectively *outcaste or *untouchable.

avarṇadharmī bhakti A term sometimes applied to the kind of devotion (*bhakti) initiated in North India by various poets, *sants, and theologians, who rejected class (*varṇa), *caste, and, in some cases, gender distinctions (e.g. *Kabīr, *Mīrābāī, *Raidāsa). *See also* VARṆADHARMĪ BHAKTI.

avatāra ('descent'; Ang.:'avatar') A term applied principally to the 'descent-forms' or 'incarnations' of *Viṣṇu, but also more widely to any manifestation of a deity in a particular physical form, including living *gurus and famous teachers from the past. *Kṛṣṇa provides what is taken to be the earliest theological justification of the concept, and to some extent its template, in the **Bhagavadgītā* (4.7–8): 'Whenever there is a falling away from the true law (*dharma) and an upsurge of unlawfulness (*adharma), then... I emit myself. I come into being age (*yuga) after age, to protect the virtuous and to destroy evildoers, to establish a firm basis for the true law'. This prefigures the developed understanding of the concept in *Vaiṣṇava mythology, where the incarnation of Viṣṇu is always related to a particular cosmic period or age (*yuga), and generally to the rise of adharma in the form of an incarnated *asura or asuras.

What become the systematized lists of Viṣṇu's avatāras emerge only slowly in the *Epic literature. Lists vary as to numbers (from four to twenty-nine plus) and personnel, but by the 8th century CE the standard number in the Vaiṣṇava *Purāṇic texts is given as ten: *Matsya ('The Fish'), *Kūrma ('The Tortoise'), *Varāha ('The Boar'), *Narasiṃha ('The Man-Lion'), *Vāmana ('The Dwarf'), *Paraśurāma ('Rāma with the axe'), *Rāma (also known as Rāmacandra, and Rāma Dāśarathi), Kṛṣṇa, the *Buddha, and *Kalkī. (Where Kṛṣṇa is considered the supreme deity, he is substituted in the list by his brother, *Balarāma; Balarāma can also appear instead of the Buddha; others too make appearances.) Some or all of these figures were originally independent deities incorporated through the avatāra doctrine into the Vaiṣṇava tradition. Underlying this is the perception that Viṣṇu, as the supreme God, transcends all particular forms. *See also* AṂŚA (3); ARCĀVATĀRA.

āveśa *See* POSSESSION.

āveśāvatara ('possessed descent') Designation of a temporary (i.e. short of a life time) descent of a deity into a human being or other figure.

Avesta (*c.*1000 BCE) The sacred book of the Iranian religion of Zoroastrianism, attributed to Zarathustra. (The Zoroastrians who migrated to India in the medieval

a

period are known as the *Parsis). In terms of both its language and religious vocabulary, the *Avesta* has clear affinities with the **Ṛg Veda*, and thus provides important evidence for the common origins of the ancient Iranian and *Vedic religious cultures.

avibhāgādvaita ('indistinguishable non-dualism') *See* VIJÑĀNABHIKṢU.

avidyā ('ignorance') In general terms, the ignorance in question is that of one's real nature, and so of one's true relationship with the world; the result of such ignorance is suffering. What constitutes one's real nature, and therefore the precise meaning of avidyā, is variously interpreted by different Indian religious and philosophical systems. In the *Brahmanical literature, particularly the **Upaniṣads*, ignorance is seen as the inability to recognize the essential connection (*bandhu) between the self (*ātman) and the power underlying the universe (*brahman (neut.)). This insight is developed in the various schools of *Vedānta, but it is most significant for *Śaṅkara's *Advaita Vedānta, where ignorance is seen as the persistent tendency, through superimposition (*adhyāsa), to mistake appearance for reality. It is thought to be beginningless, and coeval with *māyā; it is, however, possible to end such avidyā through knowledge (i.e. realization) of brahman (neut.). According to *Patañjali's **Yoga Sūtra*, avidyā is one of the five defilements (*kleśas); as such, it is both its own cause and the cause of the other kleśas. More widely, ignorance is often simply the assumed negative of esoteric or spiritual knowledge; such knowledge or wisdom (*vidyā), which may well involve ritual action and/or devotion (*bhakti), is therefore its antidote.

Avimukta *See* VĀRĀṆASĪ.

avyakta ('unmanifest', 'non-distinct'). In *Purāṇic cosmogony and *Sāmkhya, avyakta is synonymous with *pradhāna and *prakṛti, 'original Nature' or undifferentiated matter. In the **Bhagavadgītā* (9.4), Kṛṣṇa characterizes the entire universe as being pervaded by his unmanifest form (avyakta-mūrti).

Ayodhyā One of the seven ancient holy cities of India, it is said to have been *Rāma's birthplace and capital; much of the action which opens and closes the **Rāmāyaṇa* takes place there. In December 1992 a small town in Uttar Pradesh bearing the same name became the epicentre of the worst Hindu-*Muslim communal violence since independence, when around 100 000 Hindu activists were incited for nationalist political purposes to demolish the town's Bābrī Masjid mosque. The intention was to (re) build a Hindu *temple on the razed site, since the mosque (built in 1528) was claimed to have been erected on the spot (Rāmajanmabhūmi) where Rāma had been born. The consequences of this violence were still being felt at the time of writing (2007), when the ultimate fate of the site remained unresolved. Since the 18th century the religious life of the town has been dominated by the *Rāmānandīs.

Ayodhyākāṇḍa The second book of *Vālmīki's **Rāmāyaṇa*, set in the city of *Ayodhyā.

āyudhapuruṣa ('persons that are weapons') In iconography, the anthropomorphic personification of a deity's weapons.

Āyurveda ('knowledge of life') Although it is traditionally an *Upaveda associated with the **Atharva Veda*, and mythologically derived from the gods, classical Indian medicine (āyurveda) has its historical roots in the lost precursors of the medical encyclopaedias that appeared around the beginning of the Common Era. (It has been suggested that this material evolved from the medicine practised in *Buddhist and other *ascetic communities.) The most important of these compendia were those of *Caraka (*Carakasaṃhitā*, 1st–2nd centuries CE) and Suśruta (*Suśrutasaṃhitā*, *c.*4th century CE), the latter particularly well-known for its sophisticated surgical techniques. Their attitude to the body is essentially empirical rather than metaphysical, and is based on balancing the three bodily humours (*doṣas): wind, bile, and phlegm. Therapeutic techniques include the use of herbal drugs, massage, diet, and exercise. Much of the literature is concerned with herbal medicine, its application and effects. Āyurveda has had a significant influence on other Indian traditions, including *Tantra, and on medical practice in both Asia and the Arabic-speaking world through translations of Caraka and Suśrata. In contemporary India, āyurveda plays a well-supported complementary role to modern medicine, and its status as an alternative therapy has generated considerable interest in the West.

āyus Life; duration of life.

Ayyappaṉ *See* AIYAPPAṈ.

B

Bābrī Masjid mosque *See* AYODHYĀ.

Bādāmi A site in the Deccan, once known as Vātāpi, famous for its Hindu and *Jain rock-cut *temples, and for the 7th-century Malegiṭṭi Śivālaya temple.

Bādarāyaṇa (early centuries CE) The author or redactor to whom the **Brahmasūtra* (*Vedāntasūtra*) is attributed.

Badrīnāth (Badarīnātha, Badrī) A major *pilgrimage site in the *Himālayas, close to the source of the *Gaṅgā in Uttaranchal (formerly in Uttar Pradesh), and sacred to *Viṣṇu as *Nara-Nārayaṇa. *Śaṅkara is said to have spent four years there as a student. It is regarded as one of the four *dhāmas (dwelling places of the gods). Four subsidiary sites are also known as 'Badrīs'; with Badrīnāth itself they make up the Pañcabadrī ('Five Badrīs'). *See also* DHĀMA; JYOTIRMAṬH.

Bahiṇābāī (*c.*1628–*c.*1700) A *Vaiṣṇava poet-*saint from Maharashtra. She left an autobiography (*Ātmanivedana*) in Marathi verse from which we learn that she was married at six or seven to a violent *brahmin widower with a dubious past. The family was forced to lead a wandering life during which Bahiṇābāī became familiar with the images in the Vaiṣṇava *temples of the region, and especially the songs sung there in praise of *Viṣṇu and *Kṛṣṇa. To her husband's fury she came to know the *Vārkarī poet-saint *Tukārām, and mixed with the low *caste group that surrounded him. It was at this point, under the influence of an intense religious experience, that she began to write her own vernacular devotional poetry (*abhaṅgas) in praise of *Viṭhobā (Viṣṇu), 473 hymns which remain popular today.

Bairāgīs *See* RĀMĀNANDĪS.

Bālabhārata A 10th-century CE *Sanskrit play by Rājaśekhara, based on the **Mahābhārata*.

Baladeva 1. *See* BALARĀMA. **2.** (18th century CE) The founder of a *Vedānta *sampradāya. His *Govindabhāṣya* belongs to the *Gauḍīya *Vaiṣṇava tradition; it characterizes the relationship between the devotee and *Kṛṣṇa as *acintyabhedābheda ('inconceivable difference in identity').

Balāhaka The name of one of *Kṛṣṇa's chariot horses.

Bālakāṇḍa ('The Childhood Book') The first book of the **Rāmāyaṇa*. Probably a later addition, it provides a framework for the main narrative by telling the story of *Rāma's life up to his *marriage.

Balarāma ('Rāma the strong') Kṛṣṇa's elder brother (also known as Rāma, Bala, Balabhadra, Baladeva, Saṃkarṣaṇa ('the ploughing'), et al.). An *avatāra of *Viṣṇu; also considered to be an avatāra of *Ananta or *Śeṣa, the cosmic serpent, hence his occasional depiction as a *nāga or snakeman. He may have been a folk hero who was later transmuted into an agricultural deity, associated with ploughing and irrigation. Balarāma is the subject of a considerable mythology, featuring, for instance, in the **Mahābhārata* (especially the **Harivaṃśa*), the **Bhāgavata Purāṇa*, and the **Viṣṇu Purāṇa*, but he has had a limited appeal as an independent object of worship. According to *Tamil mythology, he is Viṣṇu's elder brother, and is referred to as Vāliyōṉ.

Bālarāmāyaṇa A 10th-century CE *Sanskrit play (probably the longest ever written) by Rājaśekhara, based on the **Rāmāyaṇa*.

Baḷarāmdās (15th–16th century CE) Author of the **Jagamohana Rāmāyaṇa*, an Oriya version of the **Rāmāyaṇa*.

Bali **1.** The king of the *asuras, and grandson of *Prahlāda, who, in a well-known *Epic and *Purāṇic myth, secures rulership of the three worlds from *Indra and the gods. To retrieve the situation, *Viṣṇu incarnates himself as the dwarf, *Vāmana, and secures from Bali land equivalent to three strides. The god instantly becomes large enough to cover the universe in two steps, whereupon Bali presents his head to accommodate Viṣṇu's third stride (hence Viṣṇu's epithet, *Trivikrama). Because of this *devotion, Viṣṇu promises Bali that he will be reborn as Indra in a future world-age (*yuga). In the meantime he is sent to rule over *hell. In Kerala, where he is regarded as the *king of the the perfect age (*kṛtayuga), Bali's brief return to earth each year is the cause of celebration.

2. An Indonesian island where over 3 million of the 3.5 million population are Hindu. Hinduism (referred to as 'Āgama Hindu Dharma') came to Bali between the 7th and 16th centuries CE, partly as a result of immigration by *Javanese Hindus fleeing *Muslim rule. Culturally isolated for centuries from India, Balinese Hinduism developed its own forms and practices, some of which are synthesized with *Tantric *Buddhism and indigenous local traditions. A *caste hierarchy based on four *varṇas is maintained, although 90% of the *jātis fall into the *śūdra category. The major god is *Śiva, who manifests himself as *Sūrya, the sun god, represented by the *svastika. (*Brahmā and Viṣṇu are also worshipped.) Ritual (yadnya = *yajña) (separated into five different categories) has the dual, *dharma-like function of removing *karmic *impurities from the individual to prevent a bad *rebirth, and sustaining the order and well-being of the cosmos and society. A particular concern is the ritual *exorcism of *evil spirits, involving blood sacrifice. Among the rites of passage is the well-known tooth-filing ritual, in which the pubescent child's canine teeth are filed down to symbolize the transition from the animal emotions of childhood to the greater restraint of the adult world. *Death requires *cremation; the deceased joins the divinized ancestors (dewas = *devas) and is worshipped alongside them in the household shrine. Larger, public rituals, often tied to particular *festivals, are conducted in *temples by *priests (whose wives too are qualified to perform ritual). *Brahmin priests (pedanda) are considered to be the most pure, although priests are found across all classes. A major function of the priest is to consecrate the purifying water which plays a central role in Balinese ritual. A prominent vehicle of Hindu culture and religion in Bali remains the representation, retelling, and re-enactment, notably in shadow puppet theatre (wayang), of the stories of the **Rāmāyaṇa* and the **Mahābhārata*. In the 20th century, and particularly since Independence in 1945, anthropologists have noted increased Indianization, in the sense of attempts to configure the indigenous religion in terms of subcontinental models, perceived by some to have greater authenticity.

bali ('sacrifice') **1.** A common term for an animal *sacrifice; it can also refer to an offering made with vegetable substitutes. **2.** A daily propitiatory offering of grain, rice, or flowers made to the disembodied spirits (*bhūta) by the *householder as one of the 'five great sacrifices' (*mahāyajñas). *See also* BHŪTABALI.

Bāli(n) *See* VĀLIN.

b

Balmikis (Valmikis) (Punj.) A society formed in the late 19th century by Punjabi-speaking members of the sweeper *caste, which takes its name from *Vālmīki, the author of the *Sanskrit **Rāmāyaṇa*. In their worship the Balmikis attempt a synthesis of Hindu and *Sikh practice, giving equal weight to the **Gurū Granth Sāhib* and the *Rāmāyaṇa*. Their original impetus was an attempt to improve their status in society.

Bāṇa (7th century CE) A *Sanskrit poet active at the court of king *Harṣa of Kanauj. According to his own account, although he came from a *brahmin family, he led a wandering life as a young man, mixing with all levels of society. His works include the *Harṣacarita* ('The Deeds of Harṣa')—an account of Harṣa's early life, the prose-poem *Kādambarī*, and the **Caṇḍīśatakam*, which applies *kāvya techniques to a religious subject.

bāṇaliṅga A small, white ellipsoid stone found in the *Narmadā river and worshipped as a form of *Śiva *liṅga.

Banāras *See* VĀRĀṆASĪ.

***Bande Mātaram* (*Vande Mātaram*)** ('Homage to the Mother') The name of a hymn eulogizing an unnamed 'mother' by Bankim Chandra *Chatterjee. First published in his journal, *Bangadarshan* (1875) as part of the serialization of Chatterjee's novel, **Ānandamaṭh*, it subsequently became the anthem of the Indian National Congress in a setting by Rabindranath *Tagore, the 'mother' being identified with *Bhārat Mātā ('Mother India').

bandhu(s) ('connection[s]', 'bond[s]') A word used widely in the *Vedic ritual and ritual-related texts (**Saṃhitās* and **Brāhmaṇas*) to convey the idea of 'equivalences' or 'homologies' between elements of the sacrifice (*yajña) and the cosmos. This principle is extended in the **Āraṇyakas* and **Upaniṣads*, where it culminates in the equivalence of the essence of the individual (*ātman) and the power underlying the universe (*brahman (neut.)).

baniā The name of a merchant *caste of western India; often used as a synonym for 'merchants'.

banyan (*Ficus benghalensis/indica*) A tree with both aerial and grounded roots, the former sprouting from its branches and trailing to the ground like additional trunks hence its *Sanskrit names 'nyagrodha' ('growing downwards') and 'vaṭa' ('surrounded'). The banyan is sacred to a number of deities, including *Viṣṇu, *Śiva, and *Cāmuṇḍā, and is frequently taken to symbolize the universe. Some *Indologists have used it as a metaphor for Hinduism.

banyan

Ban-yātrā *See* BRAJ.

barhis ('that which is plucked up') Sacrificial grass; a layer of *kuśa grass spread across the sacrificial ground and the altar (*vedi) to serve as a surface for the oblations, and a seat for the sacrificers (as well as the gods).

Baroda Oriental Institute Formally instituted in 1927, and incorporated into the new University of Baroda in 1949, the Institute houses a famous collection of manuscripts. Among its well-known publications are the Gaekwad Oriental

Series, and a critical edition of *Vālmīki's **Rāmāyaṇa*. Critical editions of the **Viṣṇu* and **Mārkaṇḍeya Purāṇas* are currently in preparation.

Basava (Basavaṇṇa) (*c*.1106–1167) The founder of the *Liṅgāyats. Various accounts of his life have been given. According to a sympathetic biographer, Basava was brought up by foster parents as a *Śaiva *brahmin. At sixteen he rejected his ritual and *caste background and made his way to Kappaḍisaṅgama ('where three rivers meet') in northern Karnataka. *Śiva as 'Lord of the Meeting Rivers' became his chosen god, and is named in all Basava's religious lyrics (vacanas), composed in the *Dravidian language of *Kannada. After a period of study with a *guru in Kappaḍisaṅgama, Basava went to Kalyāṇa, married, and eventually succeeded his uncle as minister to the local ruler, King Bijjaḷa. It was here that he fostered the growth of a religious community devoted to Śiva (the Liṅgāyats), which ignored distinctions of caste, class and sex, and so rejected the authority of the **Veda* and its brahmin guardians. (Such anti-Vedism may have been agreeable to the large number of *Jains who were said to have been converted by Basava.) This heterodox and heteroprax egalitarianism gave rise to a political crisis. When the community conducted a *marriage between a brahmin woman and an *outcaste, Bijjaḷa had their respective fathers put to death. A Liṅgāyat rebellion ensued during which Bijjaḷa was assassinated, and the Liṅgāyats eventually dispersed. According to some accounts, Basava himself was opposed to the violence, and retired to Kappaḍisaṅgama, where he spent the rest of his life. The community he founded survives and flourishes as an influential religious force in some parts of Karnataka. A selection of Basava's vacanas have been translated into English by A. K. *Ramanujan (*Speaking of Śiva*, Penguin Books, 1973).

Basham, Arthur Llewellyn (1914–1986) A prominent Western *Indologist whose encyclopaedic survey, *The Wonder That Was India* (1954), continues to be instrumental in introducing students to the depth and variety of classical Hindu culture. Basham was the Professor of the History of South Asia at SOAS (University of London), before taking up a post as Professor of Asian Civilizations at the Australian National University, Canberra. He was awarded many honorary degrees, both in India and the rest of the world. Other publications include *The History and Doctrine of the Ājīvikas* (London, 1951), and *A Cultural History of India* (editor and contributor) (Oxford, 1975).

Basu, Mālādhar (15th–16th century CE) A Bengali poet, his *Śrīkṛṣṇavijaya* (1473–80) uses parts of the *Sanskrit **Bhāgavata Purāṇa*, and other sources, as the basis for a Bengali poem eulogizing *Kṛṣṇa, and his relationship with *Rādhā. *Caitanya is said to have been influenced by this work.

bath/bathing *See* SNĀNA.

Baudhāyana The founder of a ritual and scholastic tradition belonging to the *Taittirīya branch of the **Black Yajur Veda*. The *Baudhāyana *Kalpasūtra* takes his name, although it is not clear whether he is the author, or whether it simply belongs to the tradition named after him. The *Kalpasūtra* (which has many additions and interpolations) is composed of the *Baudhāyana *Śrautasūtra*, the *Baudhāyana *Śulvasūtra*, the *Baudhāyana *Gṛhyasūtra*, and the **Baudhāyana Dharmasūtra*.

Baudhāyana Dharmasūtra (*c*.mid 2nd century BCE) A **Dharmasūtra* text belonging to the *Taittirīya branch of the **Black Yajur Veda*. Part of the *Baudhāyana *Kalpasūtra* ascribed to *Baudhāyana, the *Baudhāyana Dharmasūtra* deals

b

with such topics as the rules governing the life of the *Vedic student, the life of the *householder, matters of criminal and civil law, the *āśramas, the duties of the *king, the procedure for *renunciation, and quite an extensive treatment of rituals.

Baudhāyana Kalpasūtra *See* BAUDHĀYANA.

Bāuls (B.: 'mad', *c.*15th–17th centuries CE) The name given to the followers of a *bhakti tradition originating in Bengal, whose characteristic activity is to renounce the *householder life and wander the countryside singing ecstatic devotional songs. While their behaviour seems 'mad' to the orthodox, in so far as they reject the *caste system and conventional religious practice, they regard themselves as 'mad with love for God'. Many of their songs evoke the pain of their continued separation from the divine.

Bāuls come from the margins of society, and their membership in the past has cut across the conventional Hindu–*Muslim divide. Since *Partition, however, a distinction is sometimes made between the 'Muslim Bāuls' of Bangladesh (usually known as 'fakirs') and the 'Hindu Bāuls' of West Bengal. Thanks to the patronage of Rabindranath *Tagore, the Bāuls' folk songs, composed and transmitted in colloquial Bengali, have come to be appreciated for their literary qualities. At the same time, their religious practices, which are closely related to these compositions, have been largely ignored by outsiders until relatively recently. Study of these show the Bāuls to be a *Tantric *yogic sect, drawing eclectically from Tantric *Sahajiyā practices (*Buddhist and Hindu), *Gauḍīya Vaiṣṇavism, *Śaivism, and *Sufism. Individual reliance on a *guru, as the intermediary between man and God, is central to their practice and spiritual progress, as is the use of sex for yogic purposes, and the ingestion of conventionally *impure substances. They reject the authority of texts such as the **Vedas* and **Purāṇas*, and the efficacy of external rituals; instead they seek to return to an original non-dual state, while still alive, through the bodily experience of divine love. This is to be achieved through practices such as breath control and semen retention during sexual intercourse.

Lālan Fakir (Lāln Shāh, ?1774–1890) is thought to be the greatest of the Bāul poets; like other Bāuls, he rejected sectarianism and caste distinctions, resisting any attempt to classify him as either a Hindu or a Muslim.

Beatles *See* MAHARISHI MAHESH YOGI.

beef eating *See* COW.

begging *See* BHIKṢĀ.

bel *See* BILVA.

Belūr The name of a site in Karnataka containing the first major *Hoysaḷa *temples.

Belūr Maṭha *See* RĀMAKṚṢṆA MAṬHA.

Benares *See* VĀRĀṆASĪ.

Benares Hindu University Founded in 1916 in *Vārāṇasī (Benares) by Pandit Madan Mohan *Malaviya, with the support of British officials, Indian princes, and Annie *Besant, the BHU is now the largest residential university in India. It was established to provide, inter alia, an education in 'Hinduism', derived from the classical *Sanskritic culture of the **Vedas* and the *Epics. Some of its teaching takes place in *Sanskrit. Sarvepalli *Radhakrishnan was Vice-Chancellor from 1939–48.

Bengal Asiatic Society *See* ASIATIC SOCIETY OF BENGAL.

Bengali Vaiṣṇavism *See* GAUḌĪYA VAIṢṆAVISM.

Bentinck, Lord William (1774–1839) Governor-General of the *East India

Company (1829–35). Influenced by Utilitarianism and an evangelical *Christian background, Bentinck supported *Macaulay's view that India should be modernized through Westernization, rather than through the updating of Hindu traditions. It was his administration that formally forbade the practice of widow-burning (sahamaraṇa/*satī (2)).

Besant, Annie (1847–1933) A British theosophist and writer who, after settling in India in 1893, became active in the cause of Indian nationalism and founded the Indian Home Rule League. She supported the foundation of *Benares Hindu University in 1916, allowing her own Hindu College to be incorporated at its centre. The following year, she was elected the president of the Indian National Congress. She had succeeded Colonel Olcott (1832–1907) as president of the *Theosophical Society in 1907, and was later responsible for the education and training of Jiddu *Krishnamurti.

Bhadrākālī ('auspicious Kālī') A form of *Durgā sprung from *Devī's wrath when her husband *Śiva had been insulted by *Dakṣa.

Bhaga ('share') One of the *Vedic *Ādityas; personified as 'Luck', and so the god of good luck.

Bhagats *See* GUGA.

Bhagavadgītā ('Song of the Lord') An episode of seven hundred verses embedded in book six (**Bhīṣmaparvan*) of the *Sanskrit **Mahābhārata*. As the *Kauravas and *Pāṇḍavas prepare to fight, the Pāṇḍava hero *Arjuna is stationed between the two armies in a chariot driven by his friend and ally, *Kṛṣṇa. At this juncture Arjuna is suddenly overcome by disabling scruples at the prospect of killing his kinsmen and *teachers. His dilemma is either to fight what appears to be a just but ethically disastrous war, or to renounce his inherent duty (*svadharma) as a *kṣatriya (a member of the warrior class), and withdraw from the battle altogether, with disastrous consequences for himself and his brothers. Kṛṣṇa intervenes and teaches him that it is his duty as a warrior to fight without further motivation, i.e. without desire for, or attachment to, the results of his actions (*karma). Indeed, such a desire would be deluded, for Kṛṣṇa himself, who in the *Bhagavadgītā* is presented as God omnipotent, is the only real actor. It is therefore to God alone that the results of actions accrue, and the ostensible actor (in this case Arjuna) is merely his instrument. It follows from this that the solution to the problem of karma and its results is to act in a spirit of devotion (*bhakti), offering the fruits of all one's actions to God, because they are his anyway. In a great theophany (Ch. 11), which is also an image of the end of a world age (*yuga), Kṛṣṇa allows Arjuna to see him in his overwhelming universal form, as Time (*Kāla), the destroyer of the universe, mangling the warriors on both sides between his jaws. The *Bhagavadgītā* ends with Kṛṣṇa's guarantee to Arjuna (and to devotees generally) that he will be released from all evils because he is dear to him. Arjuna takes up his bow ready to fight.

In addition to discussions of karma and bhakti as routes to *liberation, the text also deals with knowledge (*jñāna), and subsumes all three means under the discipline of *yoga (hence the common assertion that the *Bhagavadgītā* teaches three kinds of yoga). Much of its underlying ontology and *cosmology—what counts as 'knowledge'—is derived from versions of *Sāṃkhya theory. It also contains what is taken to be the earliest theological justification of the concept of the deity's *avatāras, or incarnations. In general, the text internalizes some of the radical ideas that came out of the *renouncer traditions, but argues for a socially conservative position, derived from orthodox *Brahmanical values.

In its present form, the *Bhagavadgītā* (or *Gītā* for short) may have been composed in the 1st century CE, although its date, and its precise relation to the rest of the *Mahābhārata*, are disputed by scholars. In spite of the *Epic's formal status as tradition (*smṛti) rather than revelation (*śruti), for many the *Gītā* is plainly the word of God, and from at least the 7th century CE it has been glorified as a religious text in its own right, notably in the **Purāṇas*. The *Gītā* has generated a large number of commentaries, starting with *Śaṅkara's 8th-century *Bhagavadgītābhāṣya*. Since then, the *Vedānta tradition has considered it one of the three essential texts (*prasthāna traya) requiring commentary by anyone wanting to found a new (sub-)school. Notable commentaries in this line, which were increasingly coloured by a more emotional bhakti than that adumbrated in the original epic context, include those by *Rāmānuja and *Madhva. Such was its popularity that *Śaivas too wrote commentaries on the *Gītā*, including one by *Abhinavagupta exploring its esoteric meaning. At the other extreme, simply to recite the *Gīta*, or to hear it recited, regardless of how well or badly one understands the Sanskrit, has often been considered 'meaning' enough and the vehicle of God's *grace.

Beyond the commentarial traditions, the *Bhagavadgītā*'s teachings have, in a generalized form, become cornerstones of belief for most *Vaiṣṇavas—the text is usually recited at Vaiṣṇava *funerals—and for most modern Hindus in general. Indeed, it has proved particularly popular in modern India, where its teaching has been interpreted, inter alia, as a call for the restoration of Hindu *dharma through violent political action, and an assertion of the non-violent struggle for truth. The former view was developed by the nationalist leader, B. G. *Tilak in his widely read and influential Marathi commentary, *Gītārahasya*, the latter in the writings of M. K. *Gāndhī. Other extensive modern commentaries include those by *Aurobindo and *Prabhūpada.The *Bhagavadgītā* has been subject to multiple translations, and as a result has become the best known Hindu text outside India. It was first translated into a modern European language (English) in 1785 by Charles *Wilkins, and it has been estimated that over 300 further translations into English alone had appeared by the end of the 20th century. (It is interesting to note that Gāndhī was introduced to it through Sir Edwin *Arnold's celebrated late Victorian version, *The Song Celestial*.) The *Bhagavadgītā*'s status as *the* emblematic Hindu text is as strong now as at any time in its 2 000 year history. *See also* BHAGAVĀN.

Bhagavān (1st person, masc. nom. sing. of Bhagavat: 'fortunate', 'having shares', 'adorable', 'Lord', 'God') **1.** The name applied by the *Vaiṣṇava *bhakti traditions to God, as the supreme being actively and intimately involved in his creation and with his devotees. It is from this word that the latter acquire their designation as *Bhāgavatas ('devoted to Bhagavān'). 'Bhagavān' is therefore a title appled to *Viṣṇu-*Nārāyaṇa/*Vāsudeva-*Kṛṣṇa; the 'Bhagavat' (= Bhagavad-) of the **Bhagavadgītā* is Kṛṣṇa. Used in this way, 'Bhagavān' is equivalent to the English 'God', i.e. it designates the object of monotheistic worship. **2.** A term of respect, applied to a deity or to any other figure worthy of honour, such as a *guru. *See also* BHAGAVATĪ.

Bhagavan Das (Ram Dass) (b. 1945) A California-born *bhakti-*yogin who lived in India and *Nepal as a renunciant in the 1960s. On his return to the USA he mixed with other popularizers of Indian culture, such as Alan Ginsberg and Alan Watts. He has published a number of books and recordings, the latter a mixture of devotional *kīrtana and pop rhythms, designed to appeal to a Western youth audience.

Bhagavat *See* BHAGAVĀN.

Bhāgavata Purāṇa ('the *Purāṇa* devoted to or related to God (Bhagavān)')

The best-known *Purāṇa, and one of the most popular and influential of all Hindu texts, the *Bhāgavata* is a *Vaiṣṇava work produced in South India in the 9th or early 10th century CE. It is probably the work of a single author, who recast the basic narrative of the **Viṣṇu Purāṇa* in a form of *Sanskrit that, despite the date of its composition, deliberately echoes the pre-classical language of the **Vedas*. The fact that it draws on much non-Vedic material, notably the devotional poetry of the *Āḻvārs, and is saturated with *bhakti, makes this attempt to legitimize itself as part of the older, orthodox tradition all the more necessary. The '*Bhagavān' of the title is *Kṛṣṇa; Book 10, a quarter of the *Purāṇa*, and its clear focal point, is taken up with the narratives of Kṛṣṇa's early life and his 'pastime' or 'divine play' (*līlā/ *rāsa līlā) among the *gopīs, the wives of the cowherds in *Vṛndāvana (*Braj/Vraj). Amongst the other cosmic and mythic concerns of a *Purāṇa*, the previous nine books deal, in a general bhakti context, with *Viṣṇu's *avatāras prior to Kṛṣṇa. In what becomes the foundational statement for the theology of the later Kṛṣṇa sects, however, these incarnations are said to be merely 'partial' (*aṃśa), whereas Kṛṣṇa is Bhagavān himself (1.3.28).

The *Bhāgavata*'s underlying theology is that of *Advaita Vedānta: the sole reality is *brahman (neut.), here viewed as identical to Kṛṣṇa. The general perspective, however, is that of ecstatic devotion to God through the medium of *viraha bhakti, 'love in separation'—a devotion evoked through the erotic yearning of the gopīs, during the famous *rāsa līlā ('dance pastime'), for the unaccountably absent Kṛṣṇa. The high poetry in which this is presented relies on a novel combination of *Tamil devotional idiom and content (translations or paraphrases of the poetry of the Āḻvārs), and the techniques of Sanskrit love poetry.

The *Bhāgavata Purāṇa*'s role in the development of medieval and subsequent Hinduism is difficult to exaggerate. Through its influence on such teachers as *Caitanya and *Vallabha, whose ecstatic bhakti it anticipates, the *Bhāgavata* was instrumental in transmitting the devotionalism of the Ālvārs to northern India, where it became an authoritative source for the *Gauḍīya Vaiṣṇava tradition. In tandem with its other roles, the *Bhāgavata Purāṇa* has also been a major resource for devotional art: subjects such as Kṛṣṇa's lifting of Mount *Govardhana, his stealing the gopīs' clothes, and the rāsa līla have all been drawn, directly or indirectly, from the *Bhāgavata*. In time, the text accrued over 80 extant commentaries in Sanskrit (including one by *Madhva), and was the source of multiple translations into all the other major Indian languages. Its influence (especially the theological pre-eminence of Book 10) is clearly evident in the teaching and related practices of more recent Vaiṣṇava movements such as the *Svāmināràyaṇas and *ISKCON, popularly known as the Hare Krishna movement. ISKCON's devotional translation of the *Bhāgavata Purāṇa* into English (known as the *Śrīmad Bhāgavatam*) has been the principal vehicle of its attempt to convey the Kṛṣṇa-bhakti of Caitanya to a Western audience. Perhaps because of misunderstandings about the erotic and 'adulterous' nature of Kṛṣṇa's relationship with the gopīs, in marked contrast to the **Bhagavadgītā* other translations into English have been few and far between. The first translation into a European language was made by the French Orientalist Eugéne *Burnouf in the mid 19th century.

Bhāgavata(s) ('related to or devoted to Bhagavān') **1.** A term widely applied to *Vaiṣṇavas (i.e. devotees of *Viṣṇu and *Kṛṣṇa) of all traditions. **2.** The name of those devoted to the worship of *Nārāyaṇa, *Vāsudeva (=Kṛṣṇa), and Saṃkarṣaṇa (=*Balarāma)—a tradition sometimes referred to as 'Bhāgavatism'—originating in western India around 150 BCE or earlier. The earliest known use of the term occurs on inscriptions from this period (often on *Garuḍa pillars) bearing witness to a Bhāgavata cult patronized by local rulers, and apparently combining *temple worship with *Vedic rituals. The association of aristocrats with Bhāgavatism seems to have persisted in some form until the 8th century CE, but the extent of the cult is unclear from the scanty evidence available. Some have attempted to connect the **Bhagavadgītā* with this tradition. The term 'Bhāgavata' also occurs in 5th and 6th century CE sources to designate the *priests responsible for the installation and worship of Viṣṇu images (*mūrti) in some Indian and Southeast Asian temples, and again in relation to a group of *smārta *brahmins, aligned to the **Bhāgavata Purāṇa*, and seemingly active in South India into the 20th century.

Bhagavatī ('fortunate', 'Goddess') Feminine form of *Bhagavān, referring to the supreme autonomous deity in a female form, sometimes known simply as 'the Goddess', but perhaps more frequently named (e.g. as *Durgā). *See also* DEVĪ.

Bhāgavatism *See* BHĀGAVATA.

Bhagīratha *See* BHAGĪRATHĪ.

Bhāgīrathī A name of one of the three main branches of the *Gaṅgā, derived from its legendary association with a *king of *Ayodhyā, Bhagīratha, who through his *tapas was instrumental in bringing the celestial river to earth.

Bhagwan Shree Rajneesh *See* RAJNEESH.

Bhairava ('the fearsome') A ferocious form of *Śiva; infused with a terrifying and ecstatic power, he is worshipped by *Kāpālikas and others. The myth associated with him tells how he was generated from Śiva's fury at the boasting of *Brahmā, cut off the latter's fifth head, and, as a great penance (*mahāvrata), was condemned to make a long *pilgrimage with the god's head stuck to his hand. Bhairava is therefore frequently depicted as a dishevelled, wandering mendicant *ascetic, skull in hand, accompanied by an *impure and *inauspicious dog, and haunting *cremation grounds—a perfect role model for the behaviour of his Kāpālika devotees. In *village Hinduism, Bhairava (also known as *Bhairon, or Bheru) frequently has a protective function, and is worshipped as the tutelary deity of a village (*grāmadevatā) or a clan (*kuladevatā). He can also be found as the guardian or watchman of Śiva *temples. *See also* SVACCHANDABHAIRAVA.

Bhairava Tantras With its subdivisions, a body of texts representing one major division of the *mantramārga branch of the *Śaiva **Āgamas* or **Tantras* (the other being the *Tantras* of the *Śaiva Siddhānta). They take their name from *Bhairava, a fearsome form of *Śiva, whose answers to the questions posed by the *Goddess (*Bhairavī) provide the content of the *Tantras*.

Bhairavī A name of a fearsome form of the *Goddess; *Bharaiva's consort.

Bhairon A synonym of *Bhairava, especially in North India and *Nepal.

bhajan(a) (abhaṅg(a)) A devotional hymn, or collection of hymns, usually sung collectively (in *satsaṅg). Singing bhajans is the principal mode of worship among *bhakti sects in many regions of India. The hymns are often the work of medieval bhakti poet-saints (*sants), such as *Mirābāī, and they are frequently accompanied by music. Entire texts, such as the **Gītagovinda*, may be sung in this fashion. In the latter case, devotees may imagine themselves as *Rādhā addressing her lover, *Kṛṣṇa. It is quite usual for men to assume female roles when worshipping Kṛṣṇa in this way. Similarly, divisions of *caste and social status, as well as of sex, may be overcome for the duration of the session, the shared intensity of the religious emotion aroused bonding the participants together. Weekly, monthly, and annual bhajana sessions of varying lengths may be organized by particular groups of devotees. These are perhaps more usually, but not exclusively, *Vaiṣṇava in orientation: bhajans addressed to Kṛṣṇa or to *Rāma being particularly popular. These frequently take the form of a continuous repetition of the deity's name or names. In the 20th century cassettes and CDs of bhajans have become popular with Hindu communities across the world, and the professionals who sing them attract a similar kind of attention to that enjoyed by pop or film stars. *See also* KĪRTAN(A).

bhakta ('devoted to', 'worshipper') Someone who practises *bhakti; i.e. a devotee of a particular deity.

bhakta (*Vaiṣṇava*)

bhakti ('participation', 'worship', 'devotion'; usually derived from Skt. 'bhaj' ('to share with or in', 'to partake of')). A generic (i.e. non-sectarian) term for a complex of religious attitudes and practices predicated on total devotion to a supreme deity with whom the devotee (*bhakta) has a personal relationship. Through that deity's *grace, such devotion is the principal or exclusive means to salvation, however defined. In this general sense, bhakti is now the dominant and most evident characteristic of Hinduism, if not of Indian religions in general, but the precise nature of the devotion involved, the underlying theology, and the related forms of worship all differ from tradition to tradition, and, to some extent, from individual to individual.

Historically, bhakti as a means to *liberation makes its first appearance in the *Brāhmaṇical tradition in a muted form in the **Śvetāśvatara Upaniṣad*, and more explicitly in the **Bhagavadgītā*. In comparison to later, more obviously emotional forms of devotion, the bhakti of the *Bhagavadgītā* is sometimes interpreted as being 'cool', or intellectual in tone: *Arjuna is enjoined by *Kṛṣṇa to offer the fruit of all his actions to God in a spirit of devotion (*bhakti-yoga). Ultimately, he is to devote himself entirely to Kṛṣṇa as the supreme God (*Bhagavān)—a God who, through his grace (*prasāda) returns that affection and frees the individual to come to him.

As a distinct religious movement of an incontestably ecstatic kind, bhakti has its roots in the poetry of the *Tamil saints—the *Śaiva *Nāyaṉmār and the *Vaiṣṇava *Āḻvārs who flourished in South India between the 6th and 9th centuries CE. Partly through the *Sanskrit **Bhāgavata Purāṇa*, which absorbed and transmuted the emotional bhakti of the Āḻvārs, and partly through the influence of itinerant singer-saints (*sants), using regional languages, bhakti spread northwards through the subcontinent in the following centuries, so that by the 16th century it had become the dominant form of religious expression in North India. Subsequently well-known Vaiṣṇava traditions established during this period include the *Vārkarī Panth, the *Vallabhasampradāya, the *Gauḍīyās of Bengal, including the *Gosvāmīs, and the *Rāmānandīs—traditions formed in the wake of influential poet-saints such as *Jñāneśvara and *Caitanya. Among the notable texts originating from this milieu are *Jayadeva's **Gītagovinda* and *Tulsīdās's *Rāmcaritmānas*. This period also saw the rise of *Muslim influenced bhakti sants, such as *Kabīr and *Nānak, the founder of *Sikhism.

In South India the growth of bhakti had coincided with the development of *temples and temple culture from the 6th century CE onwards. The poetry of the Tamil bhakti saints underscored temple ritual, echoing and reinforcing long-standing popular devotional attitudes to local deities—gods and goddesses that became increasingly assimilated to the great *Purāṇic deities, i.e. *Viṣṇu, *Śiva and the *Goddess. Bhakti of this kind was a key element in the development of both *Śrī Vaiṣṇavism and Tamil *Śaiva Siddhānta, each in their different ways stressing a direct and exclusive relationship between the devotee and God. Similarly, the markedly antinomian *Liṅgāyat culture of Karnataka was predicated on just such a direct devotion to the one God; all other considerations, whether of *caste, class, or sex, were considered at best irrelevant to salvation, which was entirely dependent upon Śiva's grace.

Although the basic attitude of the bhakta to the deity is one of devotion, this has been conceptualized in numerous ways. For instance, within Gauḍīya Vaiṣṇavism the devotee can assume a number of different *bhāva or 'attitudes' towards Kṛṣṇa, ranging from servitude to the kind of love experienced by the *gopīs. And the predominantly Vaiṣṇava **Bhakti Sūtra*, attributed to *Nārada (2), gives a list of eleven possible forms that devotion might take. Whatever the specific attitude, however, the underlying stance is one of complete surrender (*prapatti) to an immanent God in expectation of his saving grace. This can make all other action (including external ritual action), and theories of *karma in general, irrelevant. *Renunciation may likewise be pointless, since salvation can be achieved in the world (society), here and now, through God's saving grace, perhaps mediated through a *guru. With the devaluation of karma theory, such salvation tends to be seen less in terms of liberation from *saṃsāra, and more in terms of union (or some close relationship) with the deity, both in this world and the next.

While Vaiṣṇava devotionalism perhaps more obviously both defines and fits the bhakti typology, and Śaiva and *Śāktā worship is, in general, more deeply implicated in *Tantric ritualism, such distinctions are often blurred in practice. And just as few forms of Hinduism since the medieval period have been unaffected by *Tantra, so few have been untouched by bhakti. The popular, theistic Hinduism, dominated by the great sectarian deities of the *Epics and *Purāṇas* is, in the widest sense, a religion of bhakti.

bhakti-mārga ('path of devotion') *See* BHAKTI-YOGA.

bhakti-rasa ('the taste of devotion', 'religious ecstasy') According to the aesthetic theology constructed by *Caitanya's disciples, Rūpa *Gosvāmī, and his cousin, Jīva Gosvāmī, an experience of transcendent bliss triggered by the devotee's inner realization of the emotional bond between *Rādhā and *Kṛṣṇa. *See also* GAUḌĪYA VAIṢṆAVISM.

Bhaktisiddānta Sarasvatī (1874–1937) *See* KEDARNATH DATTA.

Bhakti Sūtra **1.** An 8th century CE *Sanskrit philosophical treatise on the nature of *bhakti, attributed to *Śāṇḍilya. **2.** A 12th-century(?) CE text, attributed to *Nārada (2), enumerating various degrees (eleven in all) of *Kṛṣna bhakti.

Bhaktivedānta Swāmi ('Prabhupāda'), A. C. (1896–1977) Founder in New York, in 1966, of the *International Society for Krishna Consciousness (ISKCON), popularly known as the Hare Krishna Movement. Born in Calcutta, Bhaktivedānta Swāmi was the disciple of a *Gauḍīya Vaiṣṇava *guru, Bhaktisiddhānta

Sarasvatī Gosvāmi (the son of *Kedarnath Datta). In the 1950s he lived and studied in *Vṛndāvana, and took *saṃnyāsa in 1959. On the instructions of his teacher, he travelled to the USA in 1965. After founding ISKCON, he established 'New Vrindaban', an 'experimental *Vedic community' in West Virginia. This was followed by a Vedic school in Texas (1972). With the success of ISKCON, he also undertook extensive worldwide lecture tours. Bhaktivedānta Swāmi was responsible for over 60 publications, issued through the Bhakti Vedanta Book Trust (est. 1972), including devotional versions of, and commentaries on, the **Bhagavadgītā* (*Bhagavad-Gita As It Is*), and the multivolume **Bhāgavata Purāṇa* (*Śrīmad Bhāgavatam*), the latter completed by his followers after his death.

Bhaktivinoda Ṭhākura *See* KEDARNATH DATTA.

bhakti-yoga ('the discipline of devotion') A socially- and gender-inclusive path to *liberation outlined in the **Bhagavadgītā*, involving complete surrender (*prapatti) to *Kṛṣṇa as supreme and omnipotent God. Usually contrasted with what are taken to be the other paths to liberation described in the *Gītā* (*karma-yoga and *jñāna-yoga), bhakti-yoga is said to supersede or incorporate them. Although the *Bhagavadgītā* itself does not present these three as systematic or exclusive paths (*mārgas), some modern commentators have adopted and adapted the division to chart three distinctive Hindu paths to liberation. *See also* BHAGAVADGĪTĀ; BHAKTI.

Bhāmatī A sub-commentary on *Śaṅkara's *Brahmasūtrabhāṣya* by *Vācaspati Miśra, synthesizing Śaṅkara's views with those of *Maṇḍana Miśra. Subsequently the *Bhāmatī* gave its name to a school of interpretation within the *Advaita Vedānta tradition, one which stressed the importance of *yoga and contemplation as means to liberating knowledge, and defined ignorance (*avidyā) as being peculiar to the individual.

Bhandarkar Oriental Research Institute (BORI) Founded in Pune in 1917 in honour of Sir Ramkrishna Gopal *Bhandarkar. Among its many outstanding scholarly achievements was the production of the critical edition of the **Mahābhārata* in 27 volumes (1933–72) under the direction of V. S. Sukthankar. In 2004 its collection, which included many invaluable *Sanskrit manuscripts, was badly damaged when a mob, whipped up by the *Marāṭhā nationalist Sambhaji Brigade, ransacked the library because some had taken exception to a book about *Śivajī written by a Western scholar who had acknowledged the help of some members of the Institute.

Bhandarkar, Sir Ramkrishna Gopal (1837–1925) An outstanding Hindu *paṇḍit and *Indologist who was knighted by the British in 1911. A member of the Hindu reform movement the *Prārthanā Samāj, he opposed *child marriage, and supported the remarriage of *widows, arguing from his detailed knowledge of Hindu tradition. Among other academic posts, he held the Chair in *Sanskrit at Elphinstone College, Bombay, and was later vice-chancellor of Bombay University. Bhandarkar produced many scholarly works, of which perhaps the best-known is *Vaiṣṇavism, Śaivism and Minor Religious Systems* (1913), which holds its academic currency into the 21st century. In 1917 the *Bhandarkar Oriental Research Institute in Pune was founded in his honour.

bhaṅgā (bhang, vijayā) A narcotic drug derived from the hemp plant, sometimes used for ritual purposes or to induce a state of trance.

Bharadvāja A legendary *Vedic seer (*ṛṣi) and priest, who subsequently appears in the *Epics and **Purāṇas*, where he is said to have been the son of *Bṛhaspati and the father of *Drona.

Bharata 1. A prototypical ruler, often perceived to be the forerunner of all Indian culture. In the **Mahābhārata* (and in *Kālidāsa's **Abhijñānaśākuntalam*), he is depicted as the son of King *Duṣyanta and *Śakuntalā. Destined to become a world-emperor (*cakravārtin), Bharata gives his name both to the country (*Bhāratavarṣa) and to his descendants (the *Bhāratas). **2.** The name of a tribe or family in the **Ṛg Veda*. **3.** In the **Rāmāyaṇa*, *Rāma's half-brother, the son of *Daśaratha and *Kaikeyī, who acts as regent of *Ayodhyā during Rāma's exile.

Bharata-(Muni) The name of the legendary sage and mythical first 'actor' to whom 'The Drama Manual' (**Nāṭya-śāstra*) is ascribed.

Bhārata-nāṭyam ('Bharata's dance-drama') The name given to the modern, South Indian classical dance form, which is descended from earlier solo dance-dramas, and seems to have originated as a *temple dance performed by women. The poses and movements involved can be found sculpted in the 10th- and 11th-century temples of *Gaṅgaikoṇḍa-coḻapuram (the Bṛhadīśvara temple) and *Cidambaram, although it was developed musically in the *Tañjavūr courts of the 18th and 19th centuries.

Bhāratanāṭyaśāstra *See* NĀṬYAŚĀSTRA.

Bhārata(s) ('descendant(s) of Bharata') **1.** In the **Mahābhārata* ('the great [story] of the descendants of Bharata'), the term is used to describe both the *Kurus and the *Pāṇḍavas. With the exception of the blind *king, *Dhṛtarāṣṭra, 'Bhārata' as a singular epithet is more frequently used of various Pāṇḍavas, e.g. *Yudhiṣṭhira, *Arjuna, and *Bhīma, than of particular Kurus. **2.** The name given to the modern Republic of India: '[the land of] the descendants of Bharata'.

Bhāratavarṣa ('land of the *Bhāratas') An ancient name for India, found principally in *Purāṇic *cosmology where, as the land south of the *Himālaya mountain range, it is one of the nine divisions of the continent of *Jambudvīpa, and, since it is a *karma-bhūmi, the only one from which *liberation can be attained. It is also associated with the area over which the dismembered body of the goddess *Satī falls.

Bhāratī A name of the goddess *Sarasvatī.

Bharati, Subramania (1882–1921) A *Tamil religious poet who drew eclectically on a wide range of traditional and modern poetic forms and languages. His late prose poems on *Vedic themes are said to be particularly striking.

Bhāratīya Janatā Party (BJP) ('Indian People's Party') The most significant Hindu nationalist political party, which was formed in 1980 out of the Janatā Party and its predecessor, the Jana Saṅgh, in order to promote what it considered to be Hindu values, in opposition to the secularism of the *Congress Party. Its leaders were implicated in the violence surrounding the destruction of the Bābrī Masjid mosque at *Ayodhyā in 1992. Briefly in coalition government in 1996, as the largest single party the BJP again formed coalition governments in 1998 and 1999, with Atal Behari Vajpayee as Prime Minister. Among its controversial policies was the rewriting of school textbooks in order to present Hindus as the victims of a series of invasions from outside, and to glorify ancient Hindu civilization. By 2003 the BJP had, in public, toned down its sectarian Hindu and anti-*Muslim rhetoric, campaigning on the strength of the economy rather than questions of religion. Having lost the support of millions of the rural poor, who had failed to benefit from India's economic boom, and having alienated some voters through their rejection of secularism, the BJP was defeated in the 2004 election by Sonia Gandhi's Congress Party.

Bhāratīya Vidyā Bhavan ('Indian Arts Association') The Bhavan was founded in India in 1938 by Dr. K. M. Munshi to revive and preserve Indian art, culture, and education from a perspective of secular, Gandhian universalism. It now has over a hundred branches in India as well as four abroad (in New York, Lisbon, Mexico City, and London—the oldest and largest), all running programmes of cultural and educational events, and issuing publications.

Bhārat Mātā ('Mother India') The name given to the geographical land of India conceived as a goddess. Apparently first appearing in this form in mid-19th century Bengal, by the early 20th century she had become a pan-Indian goddess, identified by her devotees with *Devī or *Durgā, and thus presented as an ancient Hindu deity. Inspiring patriotic poetry in many languages and attracting the allegiance of all types of Indian nationalists and religious revivalists, Bhārat Mātā has had *temples built in her honour (notably one in *Vārāṇasī housing a large relief map), has been widely depicted on posters and calendar art, and has more recently become a symbol of militant Hindu nationalism.

Bhārgava(s) 1. The name given to the descendants of the *Vedic sage *Bhṛgu. According to V. S. Sukthankar, the editor of its Critical Edition, the **Mahābhārata*, which was originally a *kṣatriya work, was reworked and expanded by this family of *brahmins, and thereby infused with *Brahmanical ideology and the values associated with orthodox *dharma. **2. (Bhārgava Rāma)** A name given to Rāma Jāmadagnya (*Paraśurāma), who in a well-known story annihilates all the kṣatriyas; he appears to have been included in the *Mahābhārata* as a Bhārgava hero.

Bhartṛhari 1. (*c.* 5th century CE) The most important thinker in the field of *vyākaraṇa (linguistic analysis/grammar), and largely responsible for its establishment as an independent *darśana (philosophical system). A grammarian of the school of *Pāṇini, in his major work, *Vākyapadīya* ('Of Sentences and Words'), Bhartṛhari developed a complex, unique, and highly influential theory of speech (*śabda) or language. Language for him is an activity that can be likened to the vibration (*spanda) of consciousness. It has two levels: underlying or inner speech (*sphoṭa), the bearer of meaning, which is an integral part of everyone's consciousness, and its derivative, or manifestation, articulate sound (*nāda, also known as *dhvani), through which meaning 'bursts forth'. The entire universe has evolved out of a single principle, the *śabda-brahman (the 'eternal verbum' or 'word-essence'), i.e. the ultimate reality. Language and the universe it refers to are therefore one, an indivisible whole. Underlying this essentially monistic and idealistic theory is a soteriology that promotes knowledge, acquired through precise linguistic analysis, as a means to *liberation. This results in realization of the absolute, unity with the śabda-brahman. Bhartṛhari's thought had an effect on the development of both *Advaita Vedānta and *Buddhist philosophy, but its most direct influence was on *Kashmiri Śaivism and the work of such figures as *Utpala and *Abhinavagupta. **2.** (date indeterminate) A great *Sanskrit poet (according to some the same person as the grammarian—see (1)), the author of the *Śatakatraya* ('Three Centuries'), a collection of verses divided into three sections, dealing with polity, *renunciation, and passionate love.

Bhāsa (*c.*4th century CE) A master *Sanskrit dramatist; he is the author of what are probably the earliest surviving complete plays in the *nāṭaka genre, as well as of various short dramas based on episodes from the *Epics. His masterpiece, 'The Vision of Vāsavadattā' (*Svapnavāsavadattā*), was rediscovered, along with twelve other plays, in 1912.

b

Bhāskara 1. (7th century CE) A *Vedānta teacher who was a near contemporary of *Śaṅkara, but disagreed with the latter's *Advaita, maintaining instead a *bhedābheda (identity in difference) stance: the world is one (*brahman (neut.)), but its diversity is real. **2. (Bhāskara I)** (5th–6th century CE) A Hindu astronomer and pupil of *Āryabhata I. **3. (Bhāskara II)** (12th century CE) A great mathematician, well-known for his discoveries in the field of the theory of numbers, several of which were well in advance of European knowledge. Among other proofs, he established mathematically that infinity remains infinite, however divided. Sections of his *Siddhānta Śiromani* were widely used, notably the *Līlavatī* and the *Bījaganita*, both receiving Persian translations in the 16th and 17th centuries respectively.

Bhāskararāya Makhin (18th century CE) A *brahmin polymath, *Tantric practitioner, and influential commentator associated with the *Śrī Vidyā tradition, notable in particular for his commentaries on the **Kaula Upaniṣad* and the **Lalitāsahasranāma*.

bhasman (vibhūti) Ash widely used as a purifying substance and, when mixed in a paste, for marking the body with sectarian insignia, particularly amongst *Śaivas. Indicating his great *ascetic and purificatory power, *Śiva himself is smeared in ashes, a practice followed by his *yogic devotees during initiation. (Mythologically, this is said to be a result of Śiva's incineration of *Kāma, the god of Love.) Although specifically associated with the *cremation ground culture of Śaiva ascetics, ashes also have a general symbolic and theological significance in Hinduism as a medium of *purification and an index of spiritual power. A characteristic activity of Sat(h)ya *Sai Baba has been the 'mental' production of sacred, miracle-working ash (*vibhūti).

bhāṣya A detailed explanatory work or commentary, especially on technical *sūtras.

bhaṭṭa An honorific title for a learned brahmin, either prefixed or suffixed to his name.

Bhāṭṭa (Mīmāṃsā) A *Pūrva *Mīmāṃsaka subschool named after its founder, *Kumārila Bhaṭṭa. *See also* MĪMĀṂSĀ.

Bhaṭṭa Jayanta *See* JAYANTA BHAṬṬA.

Bhaṭṭa Lakṣmīdhara *See* KṚTYAKALPATURA.

Bhaṭṭa Rāmakaṇṭha (*c.*950–1000 CE) *See* RĀMAKAṆṬHA.

Bhava ('existence', 'becoming') The name of a *Vedic deity, connected with *Rudra as *Śarva, and later one of the names of *Śiva.

Bhavabhūti (*c.*700 CE) An outstanding *Sanskrit poet and dramatist, three of whose works survive: *Mālatīmādhava*, *Mahāviracarita*, and *Uttararāmacarita*, the latter two based on parts of the **Rāmāyaṇa*. *Uttararāmacarita* ('Rāma's Last Act') is generally acknowledged as one of the greatest works of Sanskrit literature.

Bhavānī ('wife of Bhava') A name given to the *Goddess as the consort of *Śiva; *Kālī. *See also* BHAVA.

bhāva(s) ('state', 'emotion', 'attitude') **1.** In aesthetic theory the eight particular emotions, 'felt' by a character in a play, and evoked through the component parts of a drama to produce a corresponding mood (*rasa) in the audience. **2.** In *Gauḍīya Vaiṣṇavism the devotee can assume a number of different *bhāvas ('attitudes' or emotional states) with regard to *Kṛṣṇa. Five are commonly listed: awe and insignificance (śānta), servitude (dāsya), familial affection (vātsalya), friendly affection (sākhya), and intimate, erotic love (mādhurya), such as that experienced by the *gopīs and *Rādhā. It is the last, experienced through the associated *rasa of pure bliss, which is thought to be salvific.

Bhāve, Vinobā (1895–1982) A social and religious reformer who was a follower of M. K. *Gāndhī. In the immediate aftermath of Independence, he was the chief proponent of the Sarvodaya ('welfare of all') movement, designed to improve the lot of peasants through the 'voluntary gift of land' (H.: bhū-dān). His single-minded devotion to the welfare of others has resulted in a near saint-like status.

Bhaviṣya(t) Purāṇa ('the *Purāṇa* about the future') Classified as one of the 18 'great **Purāṇas*' (*mahāpurāṇas*) in the *rājasa group, i.e. those said (somewhat artificially) to relate to *Brahmā, it is principally *Śaiva in orientation. The *Bhaviṣya* purports to prophesy the future from the perspective of the 5th century CE, referring to a number of well-known late medieval figures such as *Akbar, and Gurū *Nānak, and even to British rule. It is thus the most open-ended of the *Purāṇas*. The majority of its contents are, however, more concerned with ritual than history.

bhedābheda(vāda) ('[the doctrine of] identity in difference') A doctrine, first systematically expounded in *Bādarāyaṇa's **Brahmasūtra(s)*, designed to explain the relationship of the individual or *ātman to the absolute or *brahman (neut.). Each self is regarded as non-different (abheda) from brahman, which is its cause. However, the individual self is essentially only part of brahman, and so lacks some of the absolute's qualities, such as creative power, and freedom from impurity. The two are therefore in some ways different (bheda). According to the *Advaitin *Śaṅkara's interpretation of this, however, such difference is ultimately illusory: ātman and brahman are really non-different (abheda). This reading is, in turn, rejected by the *Viśiṣṭādvaitin *Rāmānuja, who emphasizes that the individual self and brahman are not completely identical: rather, individual selves are both real and 'modes' (prakāra) of brahman, upon whom they depend as the body depends on the soul. This seems very close to the position of the *Brahmasūtra(s)*, and others have described Rāmānuja as subscribing to the bhedābheda doctrine. Rāmānuja himself, however, associates the bhedābheda doctrine with *Bhāskara, and specifically rejects it, along with both the abheda and bheda positions. This seems to be because he regards the absolute as possessing personal qualities, subject to real modifications, in contrast to the unqualified absolute of the bhedābhedavāda, the modification of which appears to be problematical. *Nimbārka's *Dvaitādvaita is also sometimes characterized as a bhedābheda teaching.

Bheru *See* BHAIRAVA.

bhikṣā ('begging') Asking, or making oneself available for alms (chiefly *food) as part of an *ascetic way of life. By extension, it may therefore be considered to be a spiritual practice in itself. *See also* DĀNA.

Bhikṣāṭana *Śiva depicted in the form of a naked beggar or mendicant (bhikṣu). See also BHAIRAVA.

Bhīma 1. (Bhīmasena, Vṛkodara ('Wolf's Belly')**)** ('fearful', 'formidable') In the **Mahābhārata*, Bhīma, the son of *Kuntī (Pṛthā) and *Vāyu (the Wind), is the second of the five *Pāṇḍava brothers (as the son of the Wind, he is also the half-brother of *Hanumān). Renowned for his great strength, size, coarseness, appetite, and wrath, he plays a major role in the epic conflict. Among his notable exploits are his rescue of his brothers from the fire trap that is the lacquer house; his survival of an attempt to poison him by *Duryodhana; the killing of the cannibal demon Hiḍimba in a wrestling match, followed by his marriage to his opponent's sister, Hiḍimbā; his disguise as a cook at the court of King Virāṭa, where he kills Kīcaka, who has attempted to seduce *Draupadī; and, in fulfilment of vows he made when Draupadī was humiliated after the dicing match, his killing of both *Duḥśāsana, whose blood he drinks, and

Duryodhana, his great enemy, whose thighs he breaks in contravention of the rules of war. Eventually, Bhīma ascends to *heaven with his brothers and their common wife, Draupadī. *See also* MAHĀBHĀRATA. **2.** ('the terrible') One of the eight names of *Rudra/*Śiva.

Bhīmasena *See* BHĪMA.

Bhimbhetka The central Indian site of a group of inhabited rock shelters, many with paintings, from the Paleolithic period.

Bhīṣma ('terrible') In the **Mahābhārata*, Bhīṣma is the forefather of the *Lunar (*Kuru) Dynasty. He was born on earth as an incarnation of the god *Dyaus ('sky'). The son of the celestial *Gaṅgā and King Śāṃtanu, Bhīṣma was the only one of the eight *Vasus to avoid being drowned at birth by their mother in order to return them to the sky. Later, Śāṃtanu wanted to marry Satyavatī; but her father would only consent if Bhīṣma renounced the succession to the Lunar Dynasty for himself and his descendants. This he was happy to do; moreover, he took a vow to become a celibate *ascetic, ensuring that he would remain sonless. As thanks, Śāṃtanu granted Bhīṣma the ability to die only when he willed it.

When the *Kaurava and *Pāṇḍava cousins are growing up, it is Bhīṣma who is their overall *teacher. Later, when the war breaks out, he is made the reluctant commander of the Kaurava troops by *Duryodhana. Bhīṣma refuses, however, to fight Śikhaṇḍin, one of the Pāṇḍava army, since in Śikhaṇḍin's previous life as a woman (called *Ambā), Bhīṣma had been responsible for her rejection by her chosen husband, and so he/she now pursues him with implacable hatred. Bhīṣma commands the Kauravas for the first nine days of the battle. On the eve of the tenth day the Pāṇḍavas visit Bhīṣma in his camp to ask him how they can kill him. He advises *Arjuna to fight him from behind the human shield of the man-woman Śikhaṇḍin, against whom he has sworn not to defend himself; he thereby wills his own death. On the tenth day of battle, the Pāṇḍavas, with Śikhaṇḍin at their head, consequently shoot down Bhīṣma in the presecribed fashion. Although mortally wounded, he postpones his death, and remains suspended above the earth, on a 'bed' made of the arrows that have pierced him, to witness the outcome of the battle. He lies there until the conclusion of the war, at which point *Kṛṣṇa asks him to instruct the victorious *Yudhiṣṭhira. This he does at extraordinary length (in the **Śāntiparvan* ('The Peace')), discoursing on kingly duties, social order, morality, and every kind of cosmological, religious, and soteriological matter. This continues in the following book, **Anuśāsanaparvan* ('The Teaching'), and only comes to an end when Bhīṣma, who has been lying on his bed of arrows for fifty-eight nights, finally dies. His *soul passes from his body through the crown of his head and he ascends to *heaven.

Bhīṣmaparvan ('The Book of *Bhīṣma') The sixth book of the **Mahābhārata*, covering the beginning of the epic battle, including the **Bhagavadgītā*, and Bhīṣma's period as the commander of the *Kaurava army.

bhogabhūmi ('enjoyment realm') In *Purāṇic cosmology, the three regions of the universe (*bhūrloka, *bhuvaḥloka, *svarloka) in which the effects of actions (*karma) performed in the *karmabhūmi of *Bharata are 'enjoyed' by the *souls reborn there.

Bhojadeva (Bhoja Paramāra) (11th century CE) King Bhoja of Dhārā, a *Śaiva Siddhānta theologian and commentator. Among his independent works is the *Tattvaprakāśa* ('Elucidation of the Fundamental Categories'). He takes a dualist position, arguing that the *self is distinct from *Śiva, although finally equal with him. He is also credited with a commentary on *Patañjali's **Yoga Sūtra*, the *Bhojavṛtti* or *Rājamārtaṇḍa* ('Royal Sun Bird'), and a version of the **Rāmāyaṇa*, the *Campū Rāmāyaṇa*.

bhojana *See* FOOD.

Bhṛgu A legendary *Vedic sage from whom the *Bhārgavas take their name. In the **Śatapatha Brāhmaṇa* and the **Taittirīya Upaniṣad* he is said to be the son of *Varuṇa, elsewhere the son of *Indra, *Prajāpati, *Brahmā, or the first *Manu. In later mythology he is identified as one of the *Prajāpatis who create the universe.

Bhṛgus *See* BHĀRGAVA(S).

Bhṛṅgi A *ṛṣi exclusively devoted to *Śiva. His neglect of *Pārvatī led her to weaken him to the point where he could no longer stand, whereupon Śiva strengthened him with a third leg, equipped with which he appears in *Śaiva iconography.

bhū *See* BHŪR(LOKA).

Bhubaneswar *See* BHUVANEŚVAR(A).

Bhū Devī (Bhūmi, Pṛthivī) ('Goddess Earth') The personification of the world, and a secondary consort of *Viṣṇu. In mythology, she frequently needs saving from the *asuras and other threats. For instance, when a *daitya throws her into the ocean, she is rescued on his tusks by *Varāha, Viṣṇu's boar *avatāra; and at the outset of the **Mahābhārata* the gods take human form specifically to relieve the burden of the goddess Earth, who is being afflicted by the asuras. She is not usually worshipped independently.

bhukti ('enjoyment') A word designating involvement in, and enjoyment of, the pleasures of the world. In the context of the specified outcomes of a *vow or ritual practice, bhukti is usually considered the opposite of, or alternative to *mukti ('liberation'). Those in pursuit of such ends are designated 'bubhukṣu' ('desirous of worldly enjoyment'), as opposed to 'mumukṣu' ('desirous of liberation'). In the *Tantric context, bubhukṣus are those seeking powers (*siddhis).

Bhūmi *See* BHŪ DEVĪ.

bhūr(loka) **1.** In *Vedic *cosmology, the earth or terrestial world. In *Purāṇic cosmology it is expanded to include the lower regions (*Pātāla) and *hells. **2. (bhū(ḥ))** 'Earth': one of the three exclamations (*vyāhṛtis) to be pronounced twice daily by orthodox *brahmins at the twilight (*saṃdhyā) ritual.

Bhuśuṇḍi Rāmāyaṇa (*c.*14th century CE) An esoteric *Sanskrit rewrite of the **Rāmāyaṇa*, which models its story of *Rāma's childhood on the *Kṛṣṇa *bhakti of the **Bhāgavata Purāṇa*, infused with *Advaitin theology. For a long time it may have been available only to *Rāmānandī rasik sects, although it also appears to have been one of the influences on *Tulsīdās(a)'s **Rāmcaritmānas*.

bhūtabali (bhūtayajña) ('offering to the beings/spirits') In the *Vedic tradition, one of the five 'great sacrifices' (*mahāyajñas), a daily minimal ritual offering by which a *householder acquits himself of his ritual obligations to the *bhūtas, or disembodied spirits. It usually takes the form of a *bali offering of portions of *food scattered on the ground.

Bhūtanātha *See* BHŪTEŚVARA.

bhūta(s) **1.** ('has beens', i.e. ghosts) Malevolent spirits, often referred to collectively as 'bhūta-preta' (Tam.: pēys). Belief in bhūtas is widespread in popular and *village Hinduism; they are thought to be the ghosts of the those who have died premature, and thus 'bad' deaths, whether by accident or design, or those whose *funerary rites have not been properly performed. As a result, they remain half in this world, deliberately causing misfortune for the living, especially in the forms of physical and mental illness, and childlessness. They achieve this through *possession, entering their victims and taking control of them, and so causing them to fall ill, etc. (This type of malevolent possession should be distinguished from the 'good' kind caused by a deity.) The 'treatment' is *exorcism by a diviner or a deity (i.e. through its *temple *image). The bhūta then has to be relocated, usually by enshrining it and worshipping it as a deity itself (this is particularly the case when the possessed person was a member of the spirit's family); many village deities began their careers in this fashion. Control is uncertain, however, and further possessions or outbreaks of malevolence may occur. **2.** According to *Nyāya-*Vaiśeṣika philosophy, the five fundamental material or atomic substances (*dravya): earth, water, fire, air, and ether (*ākāśa).

bhūtayajña See BHŪTABALI.

Bhūteśvara (Bhūtanātha) ('lord of spirits') An epithet of various gods, most commonly of *Śiva as the haunter of *cremation grounds.

bhuvaḥ(loka) (bhuvarloka, bhuvas) **1.** In *Vedic and *Purāṇic *cosmology, the atmosphere, which is the realm of the sun. **2. (bhuvaḥ)** ('atmosphere') one of the three exclamations (*vyāhṛtis) to be pronounced twice daily by orthodox *brahmins at the twilight (*saṃdhyā) ritual.

Bhuvaneśvar(a) (Bhubaneswar) An archeologically important *Śaiva *temple site in Odisha (Orissa).

Bhuvaneśvara ('lord of the world') An epithet of *Śiva.

Bhuvaneśvarī ('mistress of the world') An epithet of the *Goddess in various forms, including the tutelary deity of Odisha (Orissa).

bīja ('seed', 'seed syllable') A sound composed of a single syllable that is employed as part of a *mantra, or as an entire mantra in itself, the best known example of the latter being *oṃ. A seed syllable has no semantic content in itself, but in *Tantra it actualizes particular powers, and is the sonic form taken by a deity.

Bījak *See* KABĪR BĪJAK.

bilva (bel) The name of a tree (the wood apple tree *Aegle marmelos*), the leaves of which are sacred to *Śiva. The bilva is often found growing in the courtyards of older *Śaiva *temples.

Bilvamaṅgala (14th century CE?) A follower of *Viṣṇusvāmin's *Vaiṣṇava *bhakti sect, and author of the *Sanskrit text, *Kṛṣṇakārnāmṛta* ('Nectar of the Acts of Kṛṣṇa').

bindu ('drop', 'dot', 'spot') **1.** A name for the coloured spot worn between her eyebrows by a married woman, or for any large sectarian or decorative mark made on the forehead (H.: bindā). **2.** Semen, especially the seed of *Śiva. **3.** In *devanāgarī orthography, the dot over a letter, often cradled in an upturned crescent, representing the anusvāra (the nasalization of the preceding vowel). **4.** An important term in *Tantric theology, associated with (2), expressing the concentrated 'drop' of energy that bursts forth to manifest the cosmos. In this sense it is represented as the central point of the *śrīcakra diagram (*yantra).

birth rites The birth of a child, from conception to the actual birth and beyond, like all other stages in life, should be attended, according to **Dharmaśāstra*, by various rites of passage or transformative rituals (*saṃskāras). These are designed to control the *pollution of the birth (which affects both mother and baby), 'ensure' a male child, and generally secure an *auspicious birth and childhood for the infant. If the child *is* male, then the father has repaid one of his 'debts' (*ṛṇas) to orthodox society.

Members of the three higher classes (*varṇas), but particularly *brahmins, are considered to be 'twice-born' (*dvija) once they have been initiated into the *Veda (i.e. completed the saṃskāra of *upanayana). It should be noted, however, that these normative birth saṃskāras are seldom fully performed in the modern period, were never performed in this way for female children, and were, and are, often replaced by regional and local rites. Giving a name and establishing a horoscope for the child are probably considered the most important rites by many modern Hindus.

BJP *See* BHĀRATĪYA JANATĀ PARTY.

Black Yajur Veda **(*Kṛṣṇa Yajur Veda*)** One of the two major recensions of the *Yajur Veda*. The adjective 'Black' distinguishes it from the other recension, the **White* or *Pure Yajur Veda* (*Śukla Yajur Veda*), as does its mixing of *mantras or *yajus with explanatory prose formulae (*brāhmaṇas). The *Black Yajur Veda* is divided between four collections (**Saṃhitā*), each preserved by its own school (*śākhā): the **Taittirīya-Saṃhitā*, **Maitrāyaṇī-Saṃhitā*, **Kapiṣṭhala-(Kaṭha)-Saṃhitā*, and **Kāṭhaka-Saṃhitā*.

Blavatsky, Helena Petrovna ('Madame') (1831–1891) *See* THEOSOPHICAL SOCIETY.

bliss *See* ĀNANDA.

boar avatāra *See* VARĀHA.

Boden Professorship of Sanskrit The chair in *Sanskrit at Oxford University, the oldest, and now the only surviving chair of its kind in the United Kingdom. Established with a bequest from Colonel Joseph Boden of the East India Company in 1827, its first professor, Horace Hayman *Wilson, was elected in 1832. He was succeeded by Sir Monier *Monier-Williams. A number of distinguished scholars followed, including, recently, Thomas *Burrow and Richard Gombrich.

bodhi tree See AŚVATTHA.

Bodhgayā The site of the *Buddha's enlightenment in present day Bihar, now restored as a major Buddhist *pilgrimage site.

body *See* SŪKṢMA ŚARĪRA.

Böhtlingk, Otto (1815–1904) A German *Sanskrit scholar, lexicographer, and translator who, with Rudolf Roth and Albrecht Weber, was responsible for the compilation of the seven-volume St. Petersburg Sanskrit-German Dictionary (*St. Petersburg Wörterbuch* (also known as the *St Petersburg Lexicon*), 1852–1875), according to many the greatest achievement of 19th-century European *Indology, and the basis for Sir Monier *Monier-Williams' *Sanskrit-English Dictionary*.

Bopp, Franz (1791–1867) A Bavarian who, inspired by Charles *Wilkins' *Pāṇini-based *Sanskrit grammar, and the work of Sir William *Jones, attempted to reconstruct proto-*Indo-European, and so helped to found modern comparative philology and the science of lingusitics.

'bow songs' **(**Tam.: **vil pāṭṭu)** Stories about local deities or heroes, told to the accompaniment of percussive music at *village *temple *festivals in southern Tamil Nadu. The performances are closely linked to temple ritual, and involve some members of the audience becoming *possessed.

brahm *Hindi term for the malevolent ghost (*bhūta) of a dead *brahmin, likely to possess its victims; also known as a brahmarākṣasa.

Brahmā **(Pitāmaha** ('grandfather'), **Svayaṃbhū** ('self-born'), **Haṃsavāhana** ('he whose vehicle is a goose')**)** According to Hindu mythology the creator god, one of a trinity (*trimūrti) completed by *Viṣṇu (the preserver) and *Śiva (the

b

destroyer). The significance of this grouping is, however, almost entirely mythological and artistic, as opposed to theological or ritual, and the same could be said of Brahmā himself. He appears in numerous myths from the late *Vedic period onwards, but hardly ever seems to have been a serious object of worship (there are now only a handful of *temples in India dedicated to him). It has been suggested that a reason for this is his lack of soteriological power: he has the unique ability to confer the gift of *immortality (unending life), but not *liberation. His limited power is further exemplified in his specialized role as the demiurge or creator of the material world, which he does at the command of greater gods (such as Viṣṇu or Śiva), or as the instrument of impersonal cosmic cycles. This secondary role is perhaps best illustrated by the *Purāṇic account of how, at the end of an interval between world cycles, Brahmā sits in a *lotus that has sprouted from the sleeping Viṣṇu's navel, ready to (re)create the universe.

Brahmā's creative role is taken over from the *Vedic *Prajāpati, with whom he becomes synonymous in the *Purāṇic and *Epic periods; but his name (masculine singular in form) obviously links him to *brahman (neut.), the power underlying the universe, and *brahman (masc.), one of the priests at the Vedic sacrifice (*yajña). There is some evidence that, from around the 2nd to 1st centuries CE, Brahmā may have been worshipped as a combination of the personified and popularized brahman of the **Upaniṣads* and a Prajāpati-derived creator god. His association with *brahmins continues in the *Epics, as does his ability to create through thought. Iconographically, Brahmā is represented with four heads (Śiva cut off a fifth), and four arms. His consort is *Sarasvatī; their vehicle (*vāhana) is a goose (*haṃsa).

Brahmā Bābā *See* BRAHMĀ KUMĀRĪS.

brahmacārin ('one who walks the path of brahman') A high-caste male, especially a *brahmin, who is a celibate student of the **Veda*. According to the **Dharmasūtras*, this celibate way of life (*brahmacarya) could be chosen as a permanent *āśrama after an initial period of Vedic studentship under a *guru. Such a student would be known as a 'permanent' (naiṣṭhika) brahmacārin. By the time of the *Dharmaśāstras*, however, brahmacarya was considered to be synonymous with the period of Vedic studentship itself, and thus a temporary state that provided a doorway to the other three āśramas taken in sequence, and so effectively a preparation for the householder (*gṛhastha) way of life. Apart from strict self-control and memorizing the *Veda*, the chief characteristic of this āśrama is total subservience to and reverence for the *teacher and his family. The regulations for this pattern of life are laid out in great detail in the *Dharma texts.

brahmacarya The chaste and celibate state of a student of the **Veda* (*brahmacārin). It is therefore synonymous with study of the *Veda*, and, more generally, with any religious state of continence and chastity. Narrowly, brahmacarya is the first of the *āśramas, or 'stages of life', through which, according to the classical theory, all '*twice born' males are supposed to pass immediately following *upanayana, and prior to *marriage and the assumption of the role of the householder (*gṛhastha). This studentship can extend for anything up to 36 years, according to the **Manusmṛti*, but in practice lasts for as long as it lasts, although 12 years is sometimes suggested as the norm. More widely, brahmacarya can refer to the practice of any of the three celibate āśramas, i.e. those of the brahmacārin (student), the *vānaprastha (forest dweller), and the *saṃnyāsin (renouncer). The practice of chastity (semen retention) is thought to generate internal heat (*tapas) and, therefore, power, which can threaten even the gods. Many stories and myths therefore revolve around attempts to seduce *ascetics in order to break their vow of brahmacarya and thus drain them of their power.

Brahmagupta (7th century CE) A mathematician and astronomer who, amongst other discoveries, provided the most popular—and, by modern standards, accurate—estimate for the circumference of the (spherical) earth (5 000 *yojanas).

Brahmakaivarta Purāṇa *See* BRAHMAVAIVARTA PURĀṆA.

Brahmā Kumārīs ('daughters of Brahmā') A religious order run by celibate women. Its activities are mediated through its 'World Spiritual University', the headquarters of which are situated on Mount Abu in Rajasthan. The Brahmā Kumārīs were founded by Dada Lekhraj (1876–1969), later known as Brahmā Bābā ('Father Brahmā') a wealthy Hyderabad diamond merchant who was born into the *Vaiṣṇava *Vallabha *sampradāya. In 1936, at the age of 60, he experienced a series of spiritual visions of *Śiva and *Viṣṇu, as well as a message that he was an *avatāra of *Kṛṣṇa, whose job it would be to establish a golden age after the coming destruction of the cosmos. To propagate this message he formed what later became known as the Brahmā Kumārī World Spiritual University. After moving the 300-strong organization to Karachi in 1937, he formed a managing committee of eight women, and then handed over all his property and assets to a trust administered by them. The character of the movement, which was initially apocalyptic, inward-looking, and world-renouncing, changed after the move to Mount Abu in 1950. Lekhraj began to send out 'sisters' to establish *rājayoga and *meditation centres in the major Indian cities in the interests of 'world service'. The general objective was to hasten the end of the *kali yuga and institute a new golden age through bringing about the spiritual transformation of individuals. This movement into the world was so successful that, by 1996, the Brahmā Kumārīs World Spiritual University claimed to have established approximately 3 200 meditation centres in over 70 countries, with in excess of 450 000 'students'.

Since 1969, the movement has been run by two of the original managing committee, Dadi Prakashmani and Dadi Janki, and, perhaps uniquely in the Indian context, nearly all the administrators and teachers are women. *Celibacy, the renunciation of family ties, and *purity are stressed, and the practice becomes more demanding the further a devotee progresses. The messages received by Lekhraj were written down in a work known as the *Murli* (Skt.: muralī ('flute')), echoing the connection with the flute-playing Kṛṣṇa. These were intensively studied by more advanced students, since they were thought to be the words of God or the 'Highest Soul' (identified as Śiva). After Lekhraj's death, he continued to send further messages from an angelic realm via a medium, Sister Gulzar. Lekhraj himself is now a principal object of devotion. The *bhakti of the Brahmā Kumārīs is, however, muted and unemotional, and their practice revolves around attempting to connect with the Highest Soul and the highest in oneself through rājayoga and the power of 'positive thinking'. In line with its attempt to transform the world, the movement has become increasingly involved in social and humanitarian work, and has affiliated itself to organizations such as the United Nations and UNICEF. It appears to be particularly well funded, and has some impressive purpose-built centres around the world (notably in North London). In their public presentation, especially in the West, the Brahmā Kumārīs adopt a somewhat

b

occluded stance to their Hindu roots: ideas such as *karma and the *cosmology of *yugas, which underlie elements of their teaching, are mixed with New Age spirituality and the affirmation of the unity of religions to produce what some have called a 'new religion'.

Brahmaloka ('the world of Brahmā / brahman') The highest world or *heaven in the cosmology of the **Purāṇas*, also known as 'Satyaloka' ('the world of truth'). Whether this is the world of Brahmā, or of brahman (neut.), is ambiguous and is variously interpreted: is the Brahmaloka a place or a state? Whatever the case, it is clear that those attaining it have gone beyond the world of change and *rebirth. The term also appears in the early **Upaniṣads* where it refers to brahman, and appears to be synonymous with the *devaloka of the **Brāhmaṇas*.

brāhma marriage *See* MARRIAGE.

brahman (Brahman) (neuter: bráhman) The etymology of 'brahman' is unclear. It appears as an already established term in the **Ṛg Veda* with a wide variety of meanings. Perhaps its most frequent usage there is to designate both the 'hymns' or formulae, which are part of the ritual, and the ritual itself. Principally, it is something uttered or chanted by the inspired *priest, an utterance that manifests a sacred power. It is this power that causes the ritual to work, and, according to the ritual texts, justifies the performance of the sacrifice (*yajña) as the means to accessing it. By extension, 'brahman' comes to designate the entirety of ritual knowledge, i.e. the **Veda* itself (and its symbol, the syllable *oṃ). In the *Upaniṣadic literature, the power underlying and manifesting itself in the sacrifice (brahman), comes to be regarded as the power underlying and connecting all things, i.e. the universe in its entirety. This belief is derived from the idea that the sacrifice's cosmic cum social function, as the creator, regulator, and maintainer of the world, is only possible through the potency that is brahman. As a result of the progressive internalization of the sacrifice (it becomes something that the individual performs within himself), this eternal, underlying reality, which interconnects all things, is equated in the **Upaniṣads* with the real or essential nature of the individual, the *ātman. Ātman-brahman is shown to be the one, subtle, imperceptible first cause and essence of all things, as opposed to any particular (i.e. separate) thing or principle as normally encountered (see, for instance, **Chāndogya Upaniṣad* 6.13.1ff). Brahman can, however, be known (in the sense of experienced) as pure bliss (*ānanda). Such knowledge comes from the realization of the identity, or nonduality of one's self, brahman, and the universe; it is that which is liberating, and which frees one from *death.

In the more theistic *Upaniṣads*, such as the **Īśā* and the **Śvetāśvatara*, the ātman is identified less with an impersonal brahman, and more with a personal 'Lord' (*Īśvara/Īśa). This prefigures the attitude of sectarian Hinduism, where brahman's function and 'character' may be subsumed in the omnipotence of a great deity (*Viṣṇu, *Śiva, or the *Goddess), and *bhakti rather than *knowledge becomes the primary route to *liberation. Nevertheless, in the wake of its appearance in the *Upaniṣads*, the ātman-brahman equivalence has had a long and significant history in Indian religious thought, especially in the influential *Vedānta tradition, where the differences between the various schools are a direct result of differing understandings of the nature of brahman and its precise relation to the ātman. It is largely through an awareness of *Advaitin readings of brahman that some modern Hindus, perhaps wishing to play down sectarian differences, assert that all gods are really one. *See also* ĀTMAN; NIRGUṆA; SAGUṆA; VEDĀNTA.

brahman (masculine: brahmán) **1.** The name of one of the four main types of priest at the *Vedic *śrauta sacrifice. In the *Ṛg Veda* the brahman priest recited the *mantras to Indra in the *soma sacrifice. Subsequently, it became the brahman's job to oversee the rites in silence. He knows everything about the ritual and its complex interconnections, but does nothing unless called upon to heal some breach in the process through prescribed *prāyaścittas or 'reparations' (he is the 'physician of the sacrifice'). The *adhvaryu priest, however, has to ask his permission to perform most actions, and he responds with muttered *mantras and an affirmation. In so far as he understands the three-quarters of speech (i.e. the **Veda*) that is not articulated, the brahman is regarded as the 'mind' (*manas) of the sacrifice. That is to say, he understands *brahman (neut.), a power not expressed through speech, but, rather, that through which speech expresses itself. Although he is supposed to know the *Triple *Veda*, at a later period the brahman had the **Artharva Veda* nominally ascribed to him. **2.** *See* BRĀHMAṆA (MASC.).

brāhman *See* BRĀHMAṆA (MASC.).

brāhmaṇa (brāhman, brāhmaṇ, brahman, Brahman) (masculine) For the sake of clarity, when the referent is someone belonging to the first *varṇa (i.e. a member of the priestly class) this dictionary uses the Anglicized form, *brahmin, to encompass all these spellings (with the exception of common derivatives, such as *Brahmanism, where usage has been standardized).

Brahmānanda Sarasvatī (1870–1953) A *guru and *saṃnyāsin. Born into a *brahmin family in Uttar Pradesh, he began a life of wandering mendicancy at the age of nine. Initiated as a *Daśanāmi saṃnyāsin when he was 32, he led a reclusive life until, in 1941, he became the first *Śaṅkarācārya of the revived Daśanāmi *maṭha at *Jyotirmaṭh. *Maharishi Mahesh Yogi was among his pupils.

Brāhmaṇa(s) (neuter: 'relating to brahman') A general term for a prose explanation (brāhmaṇa) appended to a ritual text. More specifically, the second layer of *Vedic literature according to the traditional division. Composed in the period between about 1 000 and 500 BCE, the *Brāhmaṇas* are an extensive category of ritual texts containing prescriptions for the performance of the *śrauta sacrifice, alongside detailed explanations of the significance of particular ritual acts, tendentious etymologies, and much supporting mythological material. The exegetical tradition distinguishes between the rules of the ritual, including ritual injunctions (known as *vidhi), and explanatory cum philosophical passages (known as *arthavāda). The latter are concerned with establishing *bandhu, 'equivalences' or 'homologies' between the sacrificer, elements of the *sacrifice, society, and the cosmos. This method reaches its apogee in the *ātman-*brahman equivalence of the **Upaniṣads*, which, along with the **Āraṇyakas*, were originally counted as part of the *Brāhmaṇa* literature.

The division of the major extant *Brāhmaṇas* follows that of the four **Vedas*, with groups appended to each of the four **Saṃhitā* or *mantra collections. The oldest brāhmaṇa material, complemented and continued by that found in its *Brāhmaṇa* proper, the **Taittirīya*, is contained in the **Black Yajur Veda*, where it is intermixed with mantras. (The other *Brāhmaṇas* attached to the *Black Yajur Veda*—those of the **Kaṭha*, **Kapiṣṭhala*, and **Maitrāyaṇi* schools—have only survived in fragments.) The other three *Saṃhitā* collections, and the **White Yajur Veda*, separate their mantras from their brāhmaṇa material. Of these *Brāhmaṇas*, the **Aitareya* and the **Kauṣītaki* belong to the **Ṛg Veda*; the **Pañcaviṃśa* and **Jaiminīya* to the **Sāma Veda*, and, the best-known and most important of all the *Brāhmaṇas*, the **Śatapatha*, to the *White Yajur Veda* (the **Vājasaneyī Saṃhitā*). The **Atharva Veda* has one *Brāhmaṇa*, the **Gopatha*. The *Brāhmaṇas* are the key texts for the *Mīmāṃsā school of exegesis.

Brahmaṇaspati *See* Bṛhaspati.

Brahmāṇḍa ('Brahmā's egg') A name given to the universe in *Purāṇic *cosmogony because *Brahmā (equated here with *Puruṣa) is said to be born from the eternal, unmanifest first cause inside a golden egg. (This is perhaps connected with the idea that *brahmins, like birds, are *dvija, 'twice-born'.) According to **Manusmṛti* (1.12), after a year, Brahmā divides the egg (himself) in two through the power of thought, and thus creates the physical and psycho-physical worlds. The egg, however, remains unhatched, and so in the **Purāṇas* the universe is conceived as a closed, egg- or ball-shaped entity. It is divided into twenty-one zones, comprised (from top to bottom) of six *heavens, the earth, the seven lower regions of *Pātāla (inhabited by various mythical creatures, such as *nāgas), and seven hellish regions (*naraka).

Brahmāṇḍa Purāṇa ('The Brahmā's Egg *Purāṇa*') Classified as one of the 18 'great **Purāṇas*' in the *rājasa group, i.e. those said (somewhat artificially) to relate to **Brahmā*, it may have been derived from the **Vāyu Purāṇa*, and is essentially a collection of *bhakti hymns. The **Adhyātma Rāmāyaṇa* is, in theory, attached to it, as is the **Lalitāsahasranāma*.

Brahmāṇī *See* Brāhmī.

brāhmaṇī The wife of a *brahmin.

Brahmanic(al) *See* Brahmanism.

brahmanicide The killing of a *brahmin (brāhmaṇahatyā) is the worst sin (mahāpātaka) possible according to the (brahmin-derived) **Dharmasāstra* literature. Penance involves practices such as living as a mendicant for twelve years, with a skull as a banner or begging bowl. This great vow (*mahāvrata) was undertaken by the *Kāpālikas and *Lākulas in imitation of *Bhairava (*Śiva), whose brahmanicide consisted in cutting off *Brahmā's fifth head.

brahmanirvāṇa An ambiguous compound occuring in the **Bhagavadgītā* (1.72), which is interpreted variously as the *nirvāṇa that is *brahman (neuter), or the nirvāṇa of brahman. Its use there may be a deliberate attempt to reinterpret the *Buddhist nirvāṇa as the *Vedic and *Upaniṣadic absolute.

Brahmanism (Brahminism) (adj.: 'Brahmanic(al)') A term used by *Indologists to designate the **Veda*-derived religious culture of North India in the first millennium BCE, and its later developments. The term refers specifically to the dominant *brahmin ideology, manifested in such institutions as *varṇāśramadharma and a generally *Sanskrit-based culture. At its narrowest, the term is intended to distinguish 'Brahmanism' from both the 'Hinduism' of medieval India, and heterodox movements, such as *Buddhism and *Jainism. 'Vedism' (adj. 'Vedic') is sometimes used in much the same sense.

Brahmanization *See* Sanskritization.

Brahmā Purāṇa* (*Brahma Purāṇa, Ādi Purāṇa ('The First *Purāṇa*')**)** Classified as one of the eighteen 'great **Purāṇas*' (*mahāpurāṇas*) in the *rājasa group, i.e. those said to relate to *Brahmā, much of it actually seems to relate to the worship of *Kṛṣṇa (as *Jagannātha) in Odisha (Orissa); it also contains *Śaiva, *Vaiṣṇava, and *Saura oriented material. Despite one of its names, it is a relatively late text, which borrows heavily from other *Purāṇas* and the **Harivaṃśa*.

brahmarākṣasa *See* brahm.

brahmarandhra ('Brahmā's aperture') A suture or aperture in the crown of the head. At *death the *soul is supposed to leave the body by this route, which is why the skull of the corpse is smashed during the funeral ritual (*antyeṣṭi).

Brahmasampradaya The name by which the *Dvaita Vedānta tradition, founded by *Madhva, came to be known by the *Vaiṣṇavas of North India.

Brahma Shankar Misra (1861–1907) *See* RADHASOAMI SATSANG.

Brahmaśiras ('the [fifth] head of Brahmā') The name of a weapon of universal destruction, thought to contain all the destructive powers of the *brahmins, and by extension, of *brahman (neut.). One of a number of powerful magical weapons in the **Mahābhārata*, and sometimes thought to be identical with *Śiva's *pāśupata weapon.

brahmāstra ('Brahmā's missile') An infallible weapon that appears in the *Epics; perhaps synonymous with the *Brahmaśiras weapon.

Brahmasūtra(s) **(*Vedāntasūtra(s), Śārīrakasūtras, Uttaramīmāṃsāsūtra*)** (redacted early centuries CE) An aphoristic (*sūtra) text attributed to *Bādarāyaṇa, but drawing on earlier material, which attempts to synthesize the *Upaniṣadic teachings. The first sūtra reads: 'Now the enquiry into *brahman' (neut.), subsequently defined as the sole cause and source of everything. The text is divided into four parts (*pādas), dealing with brahman, the relationship between brahman and *ātman (refuting the *Sāṃkhya position, amongst others), the means to realizing brahman, and the way to liberation (*mokṣa). For the *Vedānta tradition, the *Brahmasūtra* is one of the three essential texts (*prasthāna traya) requiring commentary by anyone wanting to found a new school. The earliest surviving commentary of this nature is *Śaṅkara's *Brahmasūtrabhāṣya* (*c.*700 CE); this, along with the commentaries of other significant *Vedāntins, gave rise to further important (sub-)commentaries, the aphoristic nature of Bādarāyaṇa's text allowing for considerable freedom of interpretation within a basic Vedānta framework.

Brahmavaivarta Purāṇa ('The *Purāṇa* of Brahman's Transformations') Classified as one of the 18 'great **Purāṇas*' in the *rājasa group, i.e. those said to relate to *Brahmā, its material is essentially concerned with a relatively late form of *Kṛṣṇa *bhakti. *Gaṇeśa is also celebrated. It is known in South India as the *Brahmakaivarta.*

brahmāvarta ('the land where brahmins live' / 'the land of the *Veda*') The traditional heartland of *Brahmanism in northern India. **Manusmṛti* (2.23) designates it as the area between the divine *Sarasvatī and *Dṛṣadvatī rivers.

Brahma Veda *See* ATHARVA VEDA.

brahmayajña ('sacrifice to *brahman (neut.)') The daily recital of a portion of the **Veda*, which, according to the **Dharmaśāstra* literature, is obligatory for an orthodox *brahmin as one of the five 'great sacrifices' (*mahāyajñas). The recital can, however, be compressed into the syllable *oṃ.

Brāhmī 1. (Brahmāṇī) The name of *Brahmā's *śakti. According to some *Purāṇic accounts, she was also the god's daughter, and gave birth to the first *Manu as a result of their incestuous union. She is one of the seven or eight *mātṛkas. **2.** The name of an important early script, well-adapted to the phonetics of the *Indo-Āryan languages, and one of two used for *Aśoka's edicts. It formed the basis for numerous later scripts, including *devanāgarī. Brāhmī's origins are unclear and remain a matter of debate.

Brahminism *See* BRAHMANISM.

b

brahmin(s) 1. An Anglicized form of *brāhmaṇa, a masculine word referring to a member of the first *varṇa, the priestly class. Through their ownership of the *Veda* and through their monopoly on its associated sacrificial ritual, brahmins as a class exercised ideological dominance over *Vedic society. (In the **Puruṣasūkta*, the brahmin is represented as the mouth of the cosmic Man.) *Brahmanism thereafter remained a major influence on the development of Indian religious and social history. Exclusive access to Vedic education (i.e. to the *mantras of the orally transmitted *Veda*), and, through its manifestation in the sacrifice (*yajña), to *brahman (neut.), the power which underlies all things, enabled the brahmins to become the self-appointed guardians of *dharma. They saw it as their ritual responsibility to repair, re-order, and maintain the principle or 'law' (*dharma) that ensures the universe and society operate in a harmonious and hierarchically ordered way. This is one of the reasons **Manusmṛti*, part of the **Dharmaśāstra* literature the brahmins formulated, could refer to the brahmin as 'the lord of this entire creation' (1.93), and assert that, because of his control of the sacrifice, even the gods were dependent upon him (1.95). Brahmins thus claimed to be 'human gods' with special privileges and superior status, and the only worthy recipients of gifts (*dāna).

The brahmins' claim to superiority within the class or *caste *hierarchy is based not just on their monopoly on religious learning, but also on their inherently superior ritual *purity; this is the consequence of being born to brahmin parents, and thus unattainable by those of lesser birth. Such *purity, which enables them to be effective ritualists, can, however, easily be compromised or degraded, since the purest are the most vulnerable to *pollution. Brahmins as a class are therefore subject to a great number of restrictions in order to protect their purity. This is particularly evident in the need to marry within the brahmin caste and the rules governing the preparation and consumption of *food, which, when cooked, can only be accepted from someone of an equal or higher status. These and other restrictions have their corollary in the rules governing the way in which the other classes should interact with them, since the brahmins' purity can be maintained only if lower castes carry out polluting tasks on their behalf.

From the *Upaniṣadic period onwards, many brahmin *householders assimilated to themselves the purity-preserving values and practices associated with the renouncer or *saṃnyāsin. They distanced themselves from the violence of the Vedic sacrifice, both by leaving such sacrifices to specialists, and through classifying sacrificial killing (which had always needed careful handling) as non-violent. This stress on *ahiṃsā (non-violence) went hand in hand with the brahmins' adoption of *vegetarianism and *sexual restraint as activities deemed equally free of the *impurity associated with blood and *death. This behavioural shift led to the present situation, where those brahmins who pursue their traditional class occupation as priests are in a small minority. The latter's status is generally considered lower than that of 'purer', non-priestly brahmins—they are less pure because of their increased professional contact with others—and this frequently confines them to subcastes whose members are not permitted to intermarry with non-priestly brahmins. Because of the pollution of death, the lowest ranking brahmins of all are the death priests (*mahābrāhmaṇas).

Brahmin claims to pre-eminence are by no means unchallenged, especially by the politically and economically dominant castes and subcastes of a particular locality. Ambivalence in this respect mirrors the traditional relationship between brahmins and *kṣatriyas in general, and brahmins and the *king in particular. Although, from the brahmins' point of view, their purity makes them superior to the king, who is necessarily implicated in the operation of worldly power, they nevertheless depend upon the king's (or landholder's) patronage for their own welfare, and may be obliged to serve him to that end. From the perspective of the patron, and of the classes who are dependent upon and serve him, this therefore accords him the superior status. *See also* CASTE; JĀTI; VARṆA.

2. A term used to indicate those who are religiously superior, and so worthy of donations. In this sense 'brahmin' was used subversively by the *Buddhists and *Jains to redefine themselves as the 'true brahmins', i.e. the true religious aristocracy, whose status was due to their ethically pure actions, rather than their birth into a particular class (*varṇa). Hindus, particularly modernizers and reformers, have themselves used the term in this redefined sense to designate those who are superior by virtue of their ethical actions rather than their birth.

Brāhmo *See* BRĀHMO SAMĀJ.

brahmodya ('to be spoken about brahman') The name of a riddling contest, staged between the various sacrificial *priests, and between the priests and the sacrificer (*yajamāna) as a component part of a *Vedic ritual. The best known example occurs during the horse sacrifice (*aśvamedha), when the contestants ask questions such as: 'Who roams alone?' ('The sun'), and 'What is the furthest limit of the earth?' ('This *vedi (sacrificial altar)'). The purpose is to affirm an understanding of the hidden connections (*bandhu) between the sacrifice (*yajña) and the cosmos. The 'winner' is the silent *brahman (masc.) who holds all the connections together, and thereby demonstrates his knowledge of *brahman (neut.). This brahmodya format is also used in *Upaniṣadic debates, such as that beginning at *Bṛhadāraṇyaka* 3.1.

Brāhmo Sabhā ('The Theistic Association') The original name of the *Brāhmo Samāj.

Brāhmo Samāj ('The Theistic Society', 'Congregation of Brahman') The first modern Hindu reform movement, the Brāhmo Samāj (initially known as the 'Brāhmo Sabhā') was founded in Calcutta in 1828 by the Bengali intellectual Rāmmohun *Roy. Reorganized by Debendranāth *Tagore in 1843, it split in 1866 into Tagore's *Ādi Brāhmo Samāj ('Original Brahman Association') and Keshab Chandra *Sen's 'Brāhmo Samāj of India'. In 1878 the latter movement abandoned Keshab and reformed itself as the *Sādhāraṇ ('General') Brāhmo Samāj.

In response to *Christian missionary work and Western scientific rationalism, the general aims of the movement were to fashion a reformed and universalized 'real Hinduism', shorn of what Roy regarded as its superstitious and idolatrous practices (*pūjā and *temple ritual), and returned to its pure, monotheistic origins, as represented in his reading of the *Upaniṣads* and other *Vedānta aligned texts. Alongside this theological agenda, the Brāhmo Samāj aimed to reform those social practices that Roy saw as concomitant with 'idol worship' and polytheism. Widow burning (*satī), polygyny, *child marriage, infanticide, *caste discrimination, and the lack of female education were all subject to criticism and active campaigning. After Roy's death, the theological stance of the Society began to shift under the leadership of Tagore. In 1843 he instituted a 'Brāhmo Covenant' requiring members to worship one God. However, it became increasingly clear, in the light of criticism from Christians, rationalists within the movement, and Hindu traditionalists, that only a very selective reading of the *Vedas* (such as that employed by Roy) could provide textual support for such a deity, and Tagore reluctantly jettisoned reliance on the authority of *Sanskrit texts. This process was accelerated under the influence of Keshab Chandra *Sen, who joined the Brāhmos in 1858. The group that gathered itself around him was much more radical in its rejection of traditional Hindu practices and attitudes than Tagore's followers, and took an aggressively missionary stance, drawing on Western models while rejecting the Christianity of the missionaries. The tension between the two groups within the Samāj resulted in the split of 1866. Sen became ever more idiosyncratic in his religious practice, and increasingly indifferent to social reform. This led to his abandonment by many of his followers, who formed the Sādhāraṇ Brāhmo Samāj in 1878. Sen himself gathered the remnant into the 'Church of the New Dispensation' in 1881. In the meantime, Tagore's Ādi ('original') Brāhmo Samāj had dwindled into little more than an association of family and friends. Despite its disintegration as a Society, the Brāhmo Samāj's influence persisted. The questions it raised about the 'true' nature of Hinduism were taken up by other organizations, such as the *Ārya Samāj, and thereby helped to generate the movement for Indian independence. *See also* NEO-HINDUISM.

Braj (Braj-bhūmi, Braj-maṇḍal, Mathurā-maṇḍal, Vraj) The area surrounding the ancient city of *Mathurā (now the western part of the Mathurā district of Uttar Pradesh) on the banks of the *Yamunā river. Renowned as the district in which *Kṛṣṇa-*Gopāla grew up, played among the *gopīs, and accomplished many extraordinary feats, it includes his specific home of *Vṛndāvana ('the forest of Vṛndā'). From the early 16th century onwards it became the focus of attention for many Kṛṣṇa devotees (*bhaktas), especially the followers of *Caitanya, the *Gauḍīya Vaiṣṇavas, who viewed it as in some sense coterminous with the heavenly Braj where Kṛṣṇa plays eternally with *Rādhā and the gopīs. To be in the earthly Braj is thus to be drawn closer to God and *heaven; every grove and pond is connected with a particular 'pastime' (*līlā) of Kṛṣṇa. According to the hagiographical literature of the Caitanya and *Vallabha sects, their founders were instrumental in the rediscovery of these places, known as a *līlā-sthala, in the 16th century. It is not surprising therefore that Braj has become a great *Vaiṣṇava *pilgrimage centre, attracting millions each year, especially during the rainy season when the Ban-yātrā, the circumambulation (*parikrama) of the whole area and its various *tīṛthas, takes place.

Braj bhāṣā A dialect of *Hindi spoken in the *Braj region: it is the language of much medieval *Vaiṣṇava *bhakti literature, such as the chronicles of the *Vallabha sect and the poetry of *Sūrdās, as well as being the vehicle of classical Hindustānī music.

breath *See* PRĀṆA.

Bṛhadāraṇyaka Upaniṣad ('The Great *Āraṇyaka Upaniṣad*') The concluding section of the **Śatapatha Brāhamaṇa* of the **White Yajur Veda*, the *Bṛhadāraṇyaka*, is regarded as both an **Āraṇyaka* and an **Upaniṣad*. As a whole, it is thought to be the oldest of the *Upaniṣads*, although the **Chāndogya*, with which it shares some specific teachings, may contain pockets of older material. The *Bṛhadāraṇyaka*, as we have it, is an edited text, probably compiled in the 7th or 6th century BCE, which survives in two recensions, the Mādhyandina and the Kāṇva. (Although according to the *Brahmanical tradition, the *Bṛhadāraṇyaka*, like the rest of the **Veda*, is unauthored revelation (*śruti).) The longest, and one of the most important *Upaniṣads*, much of it is set in *Videha, and takes the form of dialogues and debates about the underlying nature of the sacrifice (*yajña), the cosmos and human beings—debates that involve the learned King Janaka, his famous teacher, *Yājñavalkya, and various other *brahmins and *kṣatriyas, including a number of women. After a characteristic *Āraṇyaka* passage, in which the sacrificial horse is identified with the universe, the *Bṛhadāraṇyaka* enters on its main themes, the identity and nature of *brahman, brahman's relation to the self (*ātman), and how to avoid redeath (*punarmṛtyu) through *knowledge. It includes the earliest teachings about *karma, *rebirth and *saṃsāra in various forms, including the famous '*five fires' doctrine, and the account of the two paths of the dead, the *devayāna and the *pitṛyāna. The *Bṛhadāraṇyaka Upaniṣad* has inevitably attracted many commentaries, including one by *Śaṅkara.

Bṛhaddevatā ('The Index of Deities') A hymn by hymn 'index' of the deities addressed in the **Ṛg Veda*, relating through various stories and myths how each hymn was first spoken to the god. It is traditionally attributed to a sage called *Śaunaka, but recent philological research has redated it to the time of the early **Purāṇas*, the pattern of which it seems to anticipate.

Bṛhaddharma Purāṇa ('The Great *Purāṇa* Concerning Duty') In spite of its name, it is classified as one of the minor or **upapurāṇas*. Based on the **Mahābhārata* and the **Dharmaśāstra* literature, it shows considerable *Tantric influence, eulogizing the *Goddess as the highest deity.

Bṛhadīśvara temple *See* Tañjāvūr.

Bṛhannārada Purāṇa A composite *Vaiṣṇava *bhakti text, sometimes confused with the **Nārada Purāṇa*. Its earlier sections may date from around the 10th century CE, the rest appear to be from the 16th or 17th centuries.

Bṛhannāradīya Purāṇa *See* Nārada Purāṇa.

Bṛhaspati ('Lord of the Ritual Formula') **1.** In later hymns of the **Ṛg Veda*, Bṛhaspati is the *priest of the *Vedic gods (it is possible that his name derives from an epithet of *Indra). In this role, his counterpart on earth is the overseeing *brahman (masc.) at the *śrauta sacrifice. As a god, Bṛhaspati's role diminishes in later texts, but he frequently appears as a great seer (*ṛṣi), and is traditionally associated with the priestly *Aṅgiras family. **2.** Perhaps the same as (1), but alleged to be the founder of an ancient school of materialism. *See also* Cārvāka.

Bṛhatkathā ('The Great Story') The assumed source (apparently lost, although ascribed to an author called Guṇāḍhya writing in *Paiśācī) of a huge amount of Indian story material, for which it is also the collective name. From the end of the 1st millennium CE, this material found its way, in a variety of languages, into numerous collections, dramas, and reconstructions, including *Somadeva's **Kathāsaritsāgara*.

Bṛhatsaṃhitā ('The Great Compendium') The greatest work of the 6th century CE astronomer and astrologer, *Varāhamihira. It treats of *jyotiḥśāstra under three main headings: mathematics, horoscopic astrology, and divination.

Brindaban *See* Vṛndāvan(a).

Brindāvan(a) *See* Vṛndāvan(a).

British East India Company *See* East India Company.

Brook, Peter (b. 1925) British born theatre director whose English language theatrical version of the **Mahābhārata* (1985), performed by a multi-national cast, toured the world. Rapturously received in the West, its relative compression, and deviation from traditional modes of presentation, drew criticism from India, although it was never performed there. Brook subsequently filmed the production, and it has had an afterlife on video and DVD.

bubhukṣu *See* BHUKTI.

Buddha ('the awakened/enlightened one', *c.*485–405 BCE) The title given to Siddhārtha Gautama, the historical Buddha, and, from an outsider's perspective, the founder of *Buddhism. He was born just inside what is now *Nepal, but spent his pedagogic and monastic life in the *Brahmanical heartland of Northeast India. Traditional accounts of his career prior to his enlightenment show him renouncing his married life as a prince to undertake a period of religious experimentation amongst the unorthodox *śramaṇas and *ascetics active at this time. Eventually adopting a 'Middle Way' between asceticism and worldly indulgence, he achieved enlightenment after a period of intense *meditation. His career as a Buddha began when he formed his group of followers into an order of monks and nuns under his tutelage. While accepting the general renouncer view that human existence was governed by the laws of *karma and *rebirth, and the soteriological need to free oneself from *saṃsāra, much of the Buddha's teaching was formulated as a deliberate response to orthodox Brahmanical values and to the kinds of doctrines about the nature of reality and human beings found in the early **Upaniṣads*. Using the same technical vocabulary as his opponents, but radically redefining it, he rejected the authority of the **Veda*, and so the *brahmins' claims to religious and ritual superiority through birth. For the Buddha, the 'true brahmin' is the Buddhist monk, and it is he, rather than the priestly brahmin, who is worthy of receiving donations. Similarly, the effects claimed for the *Vedic *sacrifice are delusions: the significant, saving action (karma) is ethical not ritual. Just as there is no equation between the sacrificer and the cosmos, so there is no equation between a permanent, unchanging self (*ātman) and an absolute universal power (*brahman): both self and brahman (or God) are illusory. Liberation (*nirvāṇa) is the extinction of the fires of greed, hatred, and delusion that fuel this false sense of self.

In the wake of centuries of religious and cultural rivalry, but also of co-existence, the later sectarian Hinduism of the **Purāṇas* integrated the Buddha into some of the lists of *Viṣṇu's *avatāras. It is perhaps significant that this occurred (*c.*10th–12th centuries CE) at the time when Buddhist influence was starting to wane in India, and, according to some, losing its identity in pan-Indian *Tantric forms of religion. From one perspective, therefore, the Buddha's 'descent' as an avatāra of Viṣṇu was perhaps simply an attempt to bring an increasingly theistic looking Buddhism under the *Vaiṣṇava umbrella; from another, the Buddha avatāra was viewed not as a saviour, but as a destroyer, whose appearance was necessary to encourage latent atheists (*nāstikas), such as the Buddhists to declare themselves openly and so accelerate their own destruction.

buddhi ('intellect', 'intelligence') In *Sāṃkhya philosophy, the first evolute of *prakṛti (primal matter); the faculty of discrimination and judgement, it is the basis of all intellectual and psychological activity in the individual. It is through the buddhi that the *puruṣa will eventually be recognized as different from all that is prakṛti. At the cosmic, or universal level, it is known as mahat ('the great one'); the buddhi of the individual is a part or 'spark' of this.

buddhīndriya ('sense') According to *Sāṃkhya ontology, the five senses or sense capacities (hearing, feeling, seeing, tasting, smelling) evolve from *prakṛti.

Buddhism A Western term coined in the 19th century to refer to the teachings, or *dharma, of the *Buddha, and to the religion practised by his followers in South and Southeast Asia. Buddhism in a variety of forms was a major and, in some places, dominant tradition in India from the 4th century BCE until around the 12th century CE, after which it ceased to have any significant following there. It was only in the 19th century that Western *Indologists realized that the Buddha had been an historical figure, and that the forms of Buddhism so prevalent throughout the rest of Asia had evolved from Indian originals. Since the 20th century there has been a limited revival of Buddhism in India, aided by the conversion of B. R. *Ambedkar and his '*untouchable' followers. Many of the Indian and Nepalese sites associated with the Buddha are now major international *pilgrimage centres.

Indian Buddhism's relationship to *Brahmanism and later sectarian Hinduism is a highly complex history of interaction, co-existence, mutual influence, and rivalry for patronage and political dominance. Through their refusal to acknowledge the authority of the **Veda* and its custodians, Buddhists eventually became the paradigmatic heretics or *nāstikas for orthodox *brahmins. Much Hindu philosophical and polemical writing is therefore concerned to refute or differentiate itself from various Buddhist doctrines, and can hardly be understood without some knowledge of the particular forms of Buddhism concerned. Rivalry (but often creative and influential debate) at the philosophical level, was complemented at the popular level by a broadly similar ritual culture, in so far as both Buddhist and Hindu practices were subsumed in *bhakti and *Tantra as pan-Indian religious movements. The interplay between Tantric *Śaivism and Vajrayāna Buddhism is particularly apparent, as are the parallels between the multiple Buddhas and Bodhisattvas of the Mahāyāna in general, and the pantheons of Hindu devotionalism. Through a combination of the attenuation and destruction of its monastic base, by both *Muslims and Hindus, and a convergence at the popular level with Tantric Hinduism, Buddhism all but disappeared as an Indian religious tradition. Its cultural influence, however, especially on literature, architecture, and philosophical thought, was extensive, and its significance for any proper understanding of the religious history of India cannot be overestimated.

Buffalo demon *See* MAHIṢĀSURA.

Bühler, Georg (1837–1898) An outstanding and influental Austrian scholar of *Sanskrit and *Prākrit, Bühler held a chair at Elphinstone College, Bombay, and was keeper of the oriental manuscripts in the Bombay Presidency. He returned to Europe to the Sanskrit chair at Vienna, where he helped to found the Oriental Institute. Perhaps his best known work in the English-speaking world is his translation of 'The Laws of Manu' (**Manusmṛti*) (1886) for the **Sacred Books of the East* series.

burial For Hindus the normal means of corpse disposal is *cremation; however, the bodies of children (who have not yet entered on the ritual life) and of *saṃnyāsins and other *ascetics (who are considered to have already 'died' and been cremated through the internalization of their ritual fires) are buried. In the case of the latter, this is often in a sitting posture, as though still in *meditation. Others likely to be buried include those who have been victims of smallpox or snakebites, and lepers. The *Liṅgāyats (*Vīraśaivas) also practise burial rather than cremation. *See also* ANTYEṢṬI; JĪVANSAMĀDHI.

burning of widows *See* SAHAMARAṆA; SATĪ.

Burnouf, Eugéne (1801–1852) Pioneering French Orientalist who worked on *Zoroastrian and *Buddhist material, and produced a three volume edition of the *Bhāgavata Purāṇa in *Sanskrit and French (1840–47), the first translation of this work into a European language. He held the chair in Sanskrit at the Collége de France, where he numbered Rudolph Roth and Max *Müller among his students.

Burrow, Thomas (1909–1986) *Boden Professor of *Sanskrit in the University of Oxford (1944–76). Mainly a philologist, his publications included *The Sanskrit Language* (1955) and joint authorship of *A Dravidian Etymological Dictionary* (1961).

C

Caitanya (Kṛṣṇacaitanya) (*c.*1486–1533) The initiator and figurehead of the *bhakti movement that developed into *Gauḍīya (Bengal) Vaiṣṇavism. According to the hagiographic accounts, Caitanya (whose given name was Viśvambharamiśra) grew up as an orthodox *Vaiṣṇava *brahmin in the town of Navadvīpa (Nadiā) in Bengal. At the age of 22, while in Gayā (in Bihar) to perform *śrāddha for his father, he had a sudden and overwhelming religious experience, triggered by a South Indian *ascetic, who then initiated him into *Kṛṣṇa bhakti. Abandoning his life as a married *householder, Caitanya thereafter devoted himself to praising God. This took the form of organizing and participating in the collective singing of *kīrtana about Kṛṣṇa's life with the *gopīs in *Vṛndāvana, and the erotic love between *Rādhā and Kṛṣṇa, a practice that induced ecstatic trances in Caitanya, during which he was effectively possessed by the deity. In 1510 he was initiated as a *saṃnyāsin (with the name Śrīkṛṣṇacaitanya) and, after years of ecstatic wandering, settled in Purī in Orissa, although he continued to make *pilgrimages to South India, and to Vṛndāvana. In Purī, his devotion was focused on the famous *Jagannātha image of Kṛṣṇa in the main *temple.

The only work ascribed directly to Caitanya is an eight verse poem called *Śikṣāṣṭaka* ('The Eight Verse Teaching'), evoking the bliss experienced through his devotion to Kṛṣṇa. Drawing on sources favoured by their *teacher, such as the **Bhāgavata Purāṇa* and *Jayadeva's **Gītagovinda*, it was Caitanya's immediate followers, the six *Gosvāmīs, who composed the works of aesthetic theology and ritual that became the scriptural basis for the Gauḍīya tradition. The popular view, expressed in the Gauḍīya Bengali sources, as opposed to the more *Advaitin stance of some of his *Sanskritic followers, is that Caitanya was himself either an *avatāra of Kṛṣṇa or identical with the god. Caitanya's influence is evident in a number of other Vaiṣṇava traditions, including the *Rādhāvallabhīs and the *Tantric *Sahajiyās, who regarded him as their teacher, the joint incarnation, in one body, of Rādhā and Kṛṣṇa.

caitanya *See* CONSCIOUSNESS.

Caitanyabhāgavata The first Bengali biography of *Caitanya, written in the mid 16th century by Vṛndāvana Dāsa, a few years after its subject's death.

Caitanyacaritāmṛta ('The Immortal Deeds of Caitanya') A 16th-century Bengali hagiographical work by *Kṛṣṇadāsa Kāvirāja, describing the life of *Caitanya.

caitya A sacred spot or memorial, often on the outskirts of a *village, usually identified by a tree, a grove, or a tumulus (sometimes containing the ashes of a local chief), and thought to be the haunt of various supernatural beings, such as *yakṣas and *nāgas. *Buddhist stūpas are, in part, a development and expansion of the caitya cult.

cakra ('wheel', 'discus', 'circle') **1.** A symbol, probably derived from the *sun, of the Universal Ruler's (*cakravartin's) dominion over the entire earth. As displayed on the palms of his hands (where it may be associated with *Viṣṇu's cakra), it is one of the infallible physical signifiers of a cakravartin.

2. As a steel discus, one of the weapons of Viṣṇu, and a symbol of his protective power, placed, iconographically, in his upper right hand. Viṣṇu's cakra is sometimes represented in a personified form (as an *āyudhapuruṣa or cakrapuruṣa), and worshipped independently as the god *Sudarśana.

3. In *Tantra and *yoga one a series of 'wheels' or centres of spiritual energy spaced along the vertical axis of the *subtle body, i.e. along the central channel of the spinal column, known as the *suṣumna *nāḍī. It is through this, and its related web of veins (*nāḍīs), that the *prāṇa, the energy or life-force which animates the body, flows. This conception of cakras originated in an unsystematized form in Tantric texts of the 10th and 11th centuries CE, such as the *Kubjikāma Tantra* (dedicated to the goddess *Kubjikā) and the **Mālinīvijayottara Tantra*, and then spread to most yoga schools, in what became a more or less standardized form of six (plus one) cakras (ṣaṭcakra). According to a formulation used in *haṭha-yoga, the cakras are located at the levels of the perineum (the 'root' or mūlādhāra cakra), the genital region (the 'self-based' or svādhiṣṭhāna cakra), the solar plexus (the 'gem' or maṇipūra cakra), the heart (the 'new' or anāhata cakra), the throat (the 'pure' or viśuddha cakra), between the eyebrows (the 'understanding' or ājñā cakra), and at the top of the head (the 'thousand-petalled lotus' or sahasrāra cakra). The aim of haṭha-yogic practice is to force the individual's *śakti (the serpent power or *kuṇḍalinī, which is dormant in the 'root' cakra) up the suṣumna, from cakra to cakra, until it merges with the unlimited power of the sahasrāra padma ('the thousand-petalled lotus' at the crown of the head) in blissful *liberation (envisaged as permanent union with *Śiva). The ascension generates ever-increasing spiritual power in the practising *yogin. Each cakra is described as a lotus with petals (numbering 4, 6, 10, 12, 16, 2, and 1 000, respectively), and colours, and is assimilated to particular sounds and deities. Quite recently cakras have been integrated into some forms of medical practice.

4. The cakra at the centre of the Indian national flag is based on those found on the lion capital of the *Aśokan pillar from Sārnāth. At independence this symbol of an Indian empire replaced the Gandhian spinning wheel that, since 1931, had been at the centre of the flag adopted by the Indian National Congress.

5. In *Buddhism, a symbol of the *Buddha's *dharma or teaching, and especially of his first sermon, hence 'Dharma Cakra', the 'Wheel of the Law'. The *Jains also use the wheel to indicate that *tīrthaṅkaras teach as well as meditate.

6. The term may also be used of any circular formation or construction, such as a ritual enclosure, and of ritual diagrams, when it is synonymous with the terms *maṇḍala or *yantra.

Cakradhar(a) (Cakradhāra Svāmī) (13th century CE) The founder, or organizer, of the Maharashtrian anti-*Vedic and antinomian *Mahānubhāva movement. He was later deified by the tradition as one of the 'five *Kṛṣṇas'. He is the subject of an extensive hagiographical literature (e.g. the *Sūtrapāṭha* and the *Līḷācaritra*) in Marathi.

cakravartin ('universal ruler') The ideal *king, who is divinely ordained to restore temporal *dharma by ruling over the entire earth (cakravartikṣetra). The concept seems to have originated in *Mauryan times, and is related in the **Purāṇas* to developing cosmological ideas: the cakravartin appears at certain necessary moments in the cosmic cycle. *Bharata, the prototypical Indian king, is certainly regarded as a cakravartin, but rulers within historical times have also aspired to, or claimed the title. A future cakravartin is said to be born with a long list of auspicious and infallible signs, such as webbed fingers and *cakras (1) on the palms of his hands, all of which are supposed to denote physical and spiritual perfection. For the *Buddhists and *Jains, the cakravartin is the temporal equivalent of a *Buddha or a *tīrthaṅkara.

Cakreśvara ('lord of the discus') An epithet of *Viṣṇu as wielder of the *cakra (2).

calendar Although the western, Gregorian calendar, or its equivalent, the Indian National Calendar (based on the *Śaka *era, beginning 78 CE), is now used for secular purposes in India, all religious and astrological activities are governed by various traditional calendars. In *Nepal and much of India the basis for the latter is the lunar day (tithi), although solar calendars, based on the sun's passage through the houses of the zodiac, are also used, particularly in eastern India and in Tamil Nadu and Kerala. The lunar month lasts for thirty days, and is divided equally between the *auspicious 'bright fortnight' (śuklapakṣa), which ends on the full-moon (pūrṇimāvāsyā), and the *inauspicious 'dark fortnight' (kṛṣṇapakṣa), which ends on the new moon (amāvāsyā/bahulāvāsyā). The twelve lunar months (with their Western equivalents) are as follows, starting with the New Year: Caitra (March–April), Vaiśākha (April–May), Jyaiṣṭha (May–June), Āṣāḍha (June–July), Śrāvaṇa (July–August), Bhādrapada/Prauṣṭhapada (August–September), Āśvina/Āśvayuja (September–October), Kārttika (October–November), Mārgaśīrṣa/Āgrahāyaṇa (November–December), Pauṣa/Taiṣa (December–January), Māgha (January–February), and Phālguna (February–March). (It should be noted that the first of Vaiśākha, rather than Caitra, may be celebrated as the first day of the lunar year.) Every thirty months an inauspicious leap-month (malamāsa) is added after Āṣāḍha or Śravaṇa in order to bring the lunar and solar calendars back into alignment. There are traditionally six seasons of two months each, divided approximately as follows: vasanta (spring, March–May), grīṣma (summer, May–July), varṣā (rainy season, July–September), śarad (autumn, September–November), hemanta (winter, November–January), and śiśira (cool season, January–March). The dates of pan-Indian *festivals are fixed on lunar days in particular lunar months. This is also true of most regional and *temple festivals, except in the far south, where they are determined by the solar calendar. Because of the importance of precisely determining the dates for religious and ritual occasions, and the mismatch between the secular and religious calendars, astrologers and other specialists are frequently consulted, especially about the auspiciousness of particular dates. Printed almanacs (pañcāṅgas), containing astrological tables, are widely available to aid such calculations. Days of the week, and particular lunar days, are considered sacred to particular deities, or inauspicious because governed by malevolent planets. *See also* ERAS.

camār (H. = Skt. carmakāra) The name of a *caste of leather-workers, who, because of their association with the *pollution of *death, have traditionally been regarded as *untouchables by *Brahmanical orthodoxy. The *bhakti poet *Raidās was a camār, and has subsequently been regarded as their patron *saint.

Cambodia Introduced by traders, Hinduism flourished in Cambodia from the early centuries CE until the preferment of Theravāda *Buddhism (*c.*13th century CE onwards). During this period, the Khmer *kings (late 8th–15th century), who, on the model of Jayavarman II (consecrated 802 CE) were regarded as both *cakravartins and devarājas ('god kings')—*avatāras of the great Hindu gods—provided notable material patronage in the shape of the great *temple complexes

C

constructed near their capital of Angkor (*c.*200 miles northwest of modern Phnom Penh). These included the celebrated Angkor Wat (built in the first half of the 12th century by Suryavarman II), and Angkor Thom (built *c.*1200 by Jayavarman VII). Although the early Khmer kings had been associated first with *Śiva worship (their consecration involved *Tantric rituals), and then with the composite *Harihara, Angkor Wat was dedicated to *Viṣṇu, with its groundplan modelled on the *Vaiṣṇava *Purāṇic cosmos, and an elaborate set of towers erected at its centre representing the peaks of Mount *Meru. The important part played in Cambodian Hinduism by both Purāṇic myths and the *Epics, particularly the **Rāmāyaṇa*, is evident in the world's longest bas-relief, found on the first level at Angkor Wat. The site, which became a Buddhist monastery in the 15th century CE, was effectively rediscovered as a Hindu monument in the early 20th century CE by scholars of the École Française d'Extréme Orient, and it is still being investigated and restored.

Campantar, Tiruñāṉa (Jñānasaṃbandar/Gnanasambandar, Tiruñāṉa Sambandhar) (*c.*7th century CE) A *Tamil *Śaiva saint and *bhakti poet, and among the most prominent of the 63 *Nāyaṉmār, Campantar is regarded as one of the founders of the *Śaiva Siddhānta tradition in southern India. His songs appear in the **Tēvāram* ('Garland of God') section of the **Tirumuṟai*, alongside the works of *Cuntarar, and those of his close friend, *Appar. Campantar is said to have reconverted the king of *Madurai from *Jainism; and, along with Appar, he was largely responsible for the disappearance of both *Buddhism and Jainism from the region. In his ecstatic songs he variously addresses *Śiva as master and lord, friend, lover, spouse, and bridegroom. He advocates worship of Śiva through a *bhakti that is not only emotional but also intellectual, in so far as it requires inner contemplation of and *meditation on the deity as the means to *liberation. Ultimately, complete self-surrender is required, which will result in a state of loving union with the god. Iconographically, Campantar is represented amongst the Nāyaṉmār holding a cup, since, as a three year old, he is said to have been given an inspirational cup of divine milk by Śiva's consort, *Pārvatī.

camphor An organic compound, crystallized from an oil distilled from the camphor laurel tree (*Cinnamomum camphora*), which is widely used to fuel the lamps used in Hindu worship (*pūjā), especially *āratī. The camphor flame symbolizes the identification of the worshipper and the deity, in so far as it provides a common focal point for the ideal *darśana ('viewing'). The deity's protective grace (*prasāda) is transferred to the worshippers as they cup or pass their hands through the flame, and then touch their eyes or heads with their fingertips.

Campū Rāmāyaṇa 11th-century version of the **Rāmāyaṇa* by the scholar *king, *Bhojadeva.

Cāmuṇḍā (Cāmuṇḍī) One of the *saptamātṛkās, a popular and terrible manifestation of the Goddess (*Devī), who, according to the **Mārkaṇḍeya Purāṇa*, sprang as *Kālī from the forehead of the goddess *Ambikā (*Durgā) in order to destroy the *asuras Caṇḍa and Muṇḍa. Iconographically, she is similar to, or indistinguishable from Kālī, appearing as a skeletal hag, garlanded with skulls, and brandishing various lethal weapons.

Cāṇakya *See* KAUṬILYA.

caṇḍāla The name given to the *caste of 'fierce' '*untouchables', said by **Manusmṛti* to originate from the union of *brahmin women and *śūdra men, and thought to be the lowest and most *impure group in society. In theory at least, it was their responsibility to undertake the highly *polluting task of laying out corpses and carrying them to the *cremation ground. The term is often used as a generic term for a member of any untouchable caste, i.e. a person or group lying outside the *varṇa system altogether, and considered by those above them in the hierarchy to be maximally polluting.

candana A fragrant paste made from ground sandalwood dust, commonly used to decorate the human body and the images of deities for ritual purposes (i.e. during *pūjā). It is thought to have cooling properties.

Caṇḍī (Caṇḍā, Caṇḍikā) ('fierce') A name given to the form that the *Goddess (*Devī/*Durgā) takes to destroy *Mahiṣāsura the buffalo demon. See also DURGĀ.

Caṇḍīdās(a) ('Caṇḍī's slave', *c.*14th–16th century CE) A composer of *Vaiṣṇava devotional songs in Bengali (in a collection known as *Śrīkṛṣṇakīrtana*). According to legend he was a *brahmin who fell in love with a low- *caste washerwoman, Rāmī, and then made their relationship public in an attempt to have it recognized by other brahmins. In his songs he identified Rāmī with *Rādhā and himself with *Kṛṣṇa, in the belief that love of God (*bhakti) could only be based on love of a particular human being. According to some, his songs influenced *Caitanya, and he is considered an important figure in the development of Bengali literature.

Caṇḍīśatakam ('The Hundred Stanza Poem about the Goddess') A *Sanskrit poem by *Bāṇa, applying *kāvya techniques to the story of how the *Goddess (*Caṇḍī) defeats the buffalo demon, *Mahiṣāsura. It focuses on the moment she kills him by stepping on his head, an action which, paradoxically, is also the cause of his salvation.

candra (candramas) The moon and its personification as a god. The moon is associated with both *amṛta and *soma (personified as King Soma, the founder of the *candravaṃśa or 'Lunar Dynasty'). According to the **Bṛhadāraṇyaka Upaniṣad*, it is the receptacle of those who have taken the *pitṛyāna, the way of the ancestors, after death. There they will become *food that is consumed by the gods, and, entering the natural cycle again, be subject to *rebirth.

Candragupta Maurya (r. *c.*317–297 BCE) The emperor who founded the *Mauryan dynasty, establishing his capital at *Pāṭaliputra (modern Patnā), and eventually conquering and ruling over much of northern India and Afghanistan. He was the grandfather of *Aśoka; his chief minister is said to have been *Kauṭilya.

candravaṃśa (Somavaṃśa) ('The Lunar Dynasty') According to myth, one of the two great dynasties of ancient India, the counterpart to the *Sūryavaṃśa or 'Solar Dynasty'. Traditionally founded by the moon (King *Soma), it was divided into *Yādava and *Paurava branches, derived from *Yayāti's two sons, *Yadu and *Puru. In the **Mahābhārata*, the **Ādiparvan* of which recounts the Lunar Dynasty's early history, *Kṛṣṇa and *Balarāma belong to the former branch, the warring *Pāṇḍava and *Kaurava cousins to the latter.

Caṅkam literature (Saṅgam) (Tam.: 'academy literature') Over 2 300 poems in classical *Tamil collected into eight 'caṅkam' anthologies, dating from the early centuries CE onwards. Two of the later anthologies (both *c.*5th century CE) have religious themes: the **Paripāṭal* contains poems celebrating the gods, *Cevvēḷ and *Tirumāl, and the **Pattuppāṭṭu* begins with a long poem in praise of *Murukaṉ, the **Tirumurukāṟṟuppaṭai*. In the 11th century CE, the latter was incorporated into the eleventh book of the *Śaiva Siddhānta **Tirumuṟai* collection. In general, the literary conventions of caṅkam literature of both genres ('*akam' or love poetry of the 'interior world', and '*puṟam' or praise poetry of the 'exterior world') provided models for many of the *bhakti poems of the Tamil tradition, whether *Vaiṣṇava or *Śaiva in orientation.

Caraka (1st–2nd centuries CE) A renowned physician and medical theorist who is said to have been the *Kuṣāṇa *king Kaniṣka's court physician. The medical treatise *Cārakasaṃhitā* is credited to him.

Caramaśloka *See* RAHASYA.

caraṇa *See* ŚĀKHĀ.

cār dhām *See* DHĀMA.

Carey, William (1761–1834) The first Baptist *Christian missionary to arrive in India (1793). He set up a mission with two others in the Danish colony of Serampore, outside Calcutta, in 1799. He was influential in persuading *Bentinck to legislate against the practice of widow-burning (*sahamaraṇa/*satī).

Cārvāka (Lokāyata ('worldly')**)** A name given to what was claimed to be a heterodox 'school' (*darśana) of materialist philosophers. No texts belonging to such a school survive, and its doctrines and arguments can only be inferred from the assertions of its opponents. The latter accuse it of denying the existence of any kind of supernatural authority or reality, including an afterlife or *rebirth, and promoting hedonism, or at least the avoidance of suffering, as the only sensible way of life. Sense perception is the only valid means of knowledge (*pramāṇa); the material body and the *self are identical; ritual and religious practices are meaningless activities promoted by self-serving charlatans. Since such beliefs would, from their opponent's point of view, seem to make an ideal preliminary position (*pūrvapakṣa) from which to launch a counter argument, it seems likely that they are intended to represent a generally materialistic or empirical attitude to the world, rather than the doctrines of a formally constituted school. This is not to deny that a materialist stream of thought, sometimes associated with the *ṛṣi *Bṛhaspati, has been evident in India from at least the period of the **Upaniṣads* onwards, but its codification by a 'school' or darśana must be open to doubt.

caste A term claimed to be derived from the Portuguese 'casta' ('pure'), and widely adopted to designate the principle on which traditional Indian society is perceived to be organized ('the caste system'). The *Sanskrit equivalents are *varṇa ('class' (lit. 'colour')) and, more accurately, *jāti ('[position assigned by] birth'), the former indicating a *Brahmanically established, idealized hierarchy based on social function, the latter a complex social reality composed of 'castes', 'subcastes', and 'sub-subcastes'.

From the point of view of *brahmin ideology (as represented in the varṇa system), Indian society is ranked in a complementary hierarchy, the levels of which are differentiated by particular social functions assigned by birth. The earliest textual authority for this is found in the **Puruṣa Sūkta* (*Ṛg Veda* 10.90), where society (conceived as a cosmic man) is portrayed as divided into four 'classes' (varṇa), with the *brahmins, the least *polluted, at the top, and the servants (*śūdras), the most polluted, at the bottom. In between come, first, the ruling or warrior class, the *kṣatriyas, and then the people or 'commoners', the *vaiśyas. According to the Brahmanical *dharma texts, each of these classes has an ascribed duty or function that helps to sustain the body (i.e. society) as a whole. Deviation from this norm, particularly the unregulated mixing of classes through intermarriage, is portrayed as bringing disaster both for the individuals involved and society as a whole. As Louis *Dumont has shown, the ordering principle underlying this hierarchy is the religious or ritual opposition of the *pure and the *impure. It is designed to safeguard the inherent ritual purity, and therefore, in their eyes, superior status of the brahmins, by assigning what are thought to be polluting tasks, such as barbering, laundering, and the disposal of corpses, to specific low-ranking castes. The members of the very lowest castes, often referred to as '*untouchables', are thought to be avarna (or pañcama, the 'fifth' group)—outside the class system altogether—but nevertheless entirely necessary as the complementary opposite of the brahmins. The system is thus mutually reinforcing: lower castes take on the major pollutions of *death, excretion, and other bodily functions for the castes above them. They are prevented from doing anything else because, by virtue of their birth, they are inherently impure. That is to say, nothing can be altered or purified by change of occupation: an individual is born into a caste and only death ends their membership of it; moreover, if that caste is thought of as impure, then its members, regardless of their actual occupations, are thought of as polluting to those above them in the hierarchy. On this principle, even the various 'untouchable' castes are considered more or less impure than each other, and ranked accordingly.

The reality of social segmentation, as opposed to the brahmins' attempt to interpret and shape it through the ideology of the varṇa system, is highly complex, and despite **Manusmṛti's* claim that the various jātis are the result of the disastrous intermarriage of members of the separate varṇas, an evolutionary relationship between varṇa and jāti has never been established. Rather, anthropologists have shown that in any particular Indian *village, the population is composed of people belonging to a number of different jātis ('castes'), whose most immediate identification may be with a subcaste or a division of a subcaste (themselves often simply referred to as 'castes') rather than with the more inclusive jāti, let alone with one of the four varṇa. There may therefore be twenty or more such 'castes' within a single village, each differentiated from the others in terms of their use of public and living space, their social ranking at village events, and to some extent their occupations. (Although each caste may have a traditional occupation, it is not necessarily followed by all, or even many, of its members: occupations such as working on the land are not caste-specific, neither are those connected with the modern, city-based economy and the rise of technology.) Castes differentiated like this within the village may combine for various purposes at a regional level, and may therefore be regarded from outside as a single caste group. Boundaries between various jātis are to some extent controlled by rules regarding commensality and *marriages: the latter, which are usually arranged between the families, should be either endogamous (between a man and a woman of the same jāti) or, in some cases, hypergamous (the woman marrying into a higher jāti). But the precise balance of the relationship between members of different castes and subcastes depends on the context, and the nature of the particular interraction—whether it be ritual, economic, or political. Castes, and various caste groupings therefore identify each other through their relationships, rather than through self-definition. This is why the system is often described as both fluid and segmentary. It is also explains why 'caste' is not just a Hindu phenomenon: other groups, such as *Jains, *Christians, and *Muslims are involved in the same network of relations and have to be ranked accordingly.

Caṭakōpaṉ *See* NAMMĀḺVĀR.

cāturmāsya ('four monthly [sacrifice]') A sacrifice (*yajña) requiring five *priests; it may be performed three times a year on the full moon days at the beginning of spring, the rainy season, and autumn/winter as part of the duties of the *Vedic *śrauta sacrificer. Individually these sacrifices are known as Vaiśvadeva, Varuṇapraghāsa, and Sākamedha, each comprising a *parvan or 'part' of the sequence as a whole. A fourth sacrifice, Śunāsīrīya, for which there is no fixed time, may also be performed at will. The cāturmāsyas may either be performed throughout the sacrificer's (*yajamāna's) life or for one year only. *Heaven is said to be the reward.

caturmukha ('four-faced') A term usually employed in an iconographic context to describe an *image with four faces or aspects. Perhaps mostly commonly used of *Brahmā, it can also be applied to images of *Viṣṇu, and *Śiva.

caturvarga ('collection of four') *See* PURUṢĀRTHA.

caturvarṇāśramadharma *See* VARṆĀŚRAMADHARMA.

cauḍa *See* CŪḌĀ.

causation *See* ASATKĀRYAVĀDA; SATKĀRYAVĀDA.

Cēkkiḻār (12th century CE) The author, or compiler, of the most important *Tamil *Śaiva hagiographical work, the *Periya Purāṇam* ('Great *Purāṇa*') (also known as the *Tiruttoṇṭarpurāṇam*), which deals with the lives of the *Nāyaṉmār. Using the life story of *Cuntarar, the sixty-third *Nāyaṉār, to tell the stories of the other sixty-two, it was added to the **Tirumuṟai* as its twelfth and last book. Cēkkiḻār is said to have been a *Cōḻa minister, who composed his *Purāṇa* in *Cidambaram.

celibacy *See* BRAHMACARYA.

Cellattāmmaṉ (Celliyammaṉ) A *village goddess of Tamil Nadu; usually the guardian of the north of the village, she is said to defend the northern gate of *Madurai and owe her power to *Sundareśvara.

Celliyammaṉ *See* CELLATTĀMMAṈ.

Cennabasava (12th century CE) A *Liṅgāyat theologian; the nephew of *Basava.

Cevvēḷ *See* MURUKAṈ.

Cēyōṉ *See* MURUKAṈ.

chandas ('metre') The study of metre and prosody. One of the six *Vedāṅgas, or subsidiary fields of study, considered necessary for a proper understanding of the **Veda*, and so the correct performance of sacrificial ritual—in this case, the use of the correct metre (chandas) in the chants.

chandoga ('singer in metre') A name for the *Udgātṛ *priest who chants the **Sāma Veda*.

Chāndogya Upaniṣad ('The *Upaniṣad* of the Singers [of the *Sāma Veda*]') A section of the *Chāndogya Brāhmaṇa* belonging to the Tāṇḍya school of the **Sāma Veda*, the *Chāndogya Upaniṣad* is one of the two earliest **Upaniṣads*. Like the **Bṛhadāraṇyaka Upaniṣad*, with which it shares some material, the *Chāndogya* is an edited prose text that was probably compiled in the 7th or 6th century BCE, although it clearly contains earlier material. It appears to have been composed in the western part of the North Indian *Brahmanical homelands (*Kuru-Pañcāla), since Pravāhaṇa, the king of the Pañcāla region, and the teacher and debater *Uddālaka Āruṇi, who has been independently identified with the region, both make significant appearances in it, as does Uddālaka's son, Śvetaketu. The **Upaniṣad* begins with a series of speculations about the cosmic and ritual correspondences of the udgītha, the central element of the *sāman chant used in the *soma sacrifice. It goes on to consider the nature of *brahman (neut.) and *ātman, teaching that the ātman lies deep in the heart, that it is identical to brahman, and that after *death one becomes brahman (ideas attributed to *Śāṇḍilya). Like the *Bṛhadāraṇyaka*, the *Chāndogya* also gives accounts of the two paths of the dead (the *devayāna and the *pitṛyāna), the '*five fires' doctrine, and what, to some *brahmins at least, was the new doctrine of *karma. Among many passages that have attracted the attention of later commentators, there is the famous instruction given by Uddālaka to Śvetaketu, in which he uses a number of images from the natural world (rivers in oceans, salt in water, seed in a fruit) to show how the world is in essence the ātman, concluding with the refrain: 'tat tvam asi' ('You are that' or 'That's how you are').

Chatterjee, Bankim Chandra (1838–1894) An influential Bengali novelist and nationalist, whose best known work, **Ānandamaṭh* ('The Sacred Brotherhood'; lit. 'The Monastery of the Ānandas', 1882), includes the hymn, **Bande Mātaram* ('Homage to the Mother').

chattra ('parasol', 'umbrella') A symbol of royal power, and the emblem of a number of deities, including *Varuṇa.

Chaudhuri, N. C. (1897–1999) A long-lived writer of elegant English and classical Bengali. A persistent critic of the direction taken by Indian nationalism, he was condemned in India for his apparent admiration of the British Raj and European culture. After 1970 he lived in England. He is best known for his memoir, *The Autobiography of an Unknown Indian* (1951), and its sequel, *Thy Hand, Great Anarch!* (1987). Among his other works is *Hinduism* (1979).

chāyā ('shadow') **1.** A substitute for herself created by Saṃjñā, the wife of *Sūrya, the sun god, when she could no longer bear the intensity of her husband's light. **2.** A translation of, or an aid to understanding, a text, or part of a text, especially the translation of a *Prākrit passage into *Sanskrit.

Chetananda, Swami *See* NITYĀNANDA INSTITUTE.

child marriage Still quite widely practised in some rural parts of India, despite the fact that, since 1978, following the initial legislation of 'The Child Marriage Restraint Act' of 1929, the minimum legal age of *marriage has been fixed at 21 for males, 18 for females.

Chinmaya Mission *See* CHINMAYĀNANDA, SWAMI.

Chinmayānanda, Swami (1916–1993) A teacher in the *Neo-Vedānta tradition and a pupil of *Swami Śivānanda. Chinmayānanda was instrumental in the founding of the Hindu nationalist *Viśva Hindū Pariṣad in 1964. He worked outside India under the auspices of the international Chinmaya Mission, which was designed specifically to further his agenda, and is now an organization devoted to spreading his teachings. His death prevented him from being the official president of the Hindu representatives at the Centennial Conference of the Parliament of World Religions in Chicago in 1993.

Chinmoy (Śrī Chinmoy) (b. 1931) A *yoga teacher and writer. Born Chinmoy Kumar Ghose, as a 12 year old, Chinmoy entered the *Aurobindo *āśram near Pondicherry. In 1964 he left India for the USA, where he established *meditation centres based on *guru *bhakti, including one at the United Nations.

Chinnamastā ('decapitated') A *Tantric form of the *Goddess, conventionally listed as one of the ten *Mahāvidyas, and

Chinnamastā

depicted as carrying her decapitated head, either under her arm or in her hand.

Chittirai festival *See* MĪṈĀKṢĪ.

C

choṭī *See* ŚIKHĀ.

Christianity A minority religion in India since at least the 6th century CE, and probably earlier. The Thomas Christians of Kerala, whose tradition may have been introduced by traders from Syria, were subject to Hindu influence in terms of integration into the *caste system, and the bureaucratic organization of their Church. Concerted missionary activity began in the 16th century in Goa with the Portuguese Catholics, and in time Indians began to be ordained as priests. In the 17th century the Italian Jesuit, Roberto Nobili, established the pattern for a different strategy, living as a *brahmin at *Madurai in an attempt to influence the priestly caste. Tension between higher and lower caste congregations, and the fluctuating attitudes of the Church authorities with regard to caste continued to generate problems for the small Christian communities. Protestant missionaries became active from the beginning of the 19th century, but because of their reluctance to compromise with Hindu culture they made little tangible headway. By the beginning of the 20th century various accommodations were being made—such as the setting up of Christian *āśrams—in the attempt to give Christianity a less Western appearance. According to the 2001 census, Christians comprised 2.3% of the population of India, in absolute terms about 24 million people. The most prominent Christian working in India in recent times has been Mother Teresa (1910–1997), whose work among the poor of Calcutta has received widespread publicity in the West. In spite of its long history in India, Christianity is still subject to attacks from Hindu nationalists as a 'foreign' religion, intent on conversion.

Churning of the Ocean **(samudramathana/samudramanthana)** An *Epic and *Purāṇic myth telling how the *devas (gods) and *daityas (demons) churned the primeval ocean at the beginning of time to obtain *amṛta, the nectar of immortality, and, through the chaos caused, brought about the secondary creation and ordering of the world. In the earliest extant version, given in the **Ādi Parvan* of the **Mahābhārata*, the gods and demons initially co-operate, using Mount Mandara as a churning stick, with its tip placed on the back of the tortoise (*Viṣṇu as *Kūrma according to some accounts), and the serpent king *Vāsuki as a cord. The ocean becomes milk, from which *Soma, the *sun, and other personified deities appear, as well as the elephant, *Airāvata. The ocean then gives up the *kālakūṭa (halāhala) poison, which *Śiva nullifies by holding it in his throat before swallowing it, thus earning the epithet 'Blue-throated' (*Nīlakaṇṭha). After further creation, *Dhanvantari, the physician of the gods, appears holding the amṛta in a pot. To prevent the demons acquiring it, *Nārāyaṇa (Viṣṇu) takes the form of the enchantress *Mohinī, and seduces the demons who hand over the amṛta. Mohinī then gives it to the gods to drink. This sets off a cataclysmic battle, which the gods eventually win. The nectar of immortality is given into the care of Viṣṇu. The myth has proved very popular with artists.

Cidambaram **(Citamparam/Ciṭamparam)** (Tam.) A South Indian *temple complex in Tamil Nadu dedicated to *Śiva. Dating mostly from the 12th and 13th centuries CE, it became an important religious and political centre under the patronage of the *Cōḻa dynasty. Cidambaram contains the best-known image of Śiva's *ānandatāṇḍava ('dance of bliss'), and is supposed to be the place where it was first performed. *See also* DĪKṢITAS.

Cidānanda, Swami (b. 1916) The pupil and successor of Swami *Śivānanda, Cidānanda took over the presidency of the *Divine Life Society on the death of his mentor in 1963, and thereafter widened the activities of the Śivānanda Āśram (of which he had been a member since 1943) both in India and abroad.

Cidvilāsānanda, Swami(nī) (Gurumayi Chidvilasananda) (b. 1955) Born Malti Shetty, Cidvilāsānanda has been the head of the *Siddha Yoga organization since 1982, when, after years as his follower and translator, she was chosen by Swami *Muktānanda to be his successor. Her younger brother, Swami Nityānanda (Subhash Shetty), who was appointed with her, subsequently stood down to leave her as the sole living 'master' in the tradition.

Cilappatikāram ('The Story of the Anklet', *c.*5th century CE) 'The *Tamil Epic', traditionally attributed to the *Jain renouncer Iḷaṅkōvaṭikaḷ, is a poem telling the 'tragic' story of Kōvalaṉ (a merchant who squanders his wealth on a prostitute), and his faithful wife Kaṇṇaki, who eventually becomes a goddess.

circumambulation *See* PRADAKṢIṆĀ.

cit *See* CONSCIOUSNESS.

Citamparam *See* CIDAMBARAM.

Citragupta In *Purāṇic mythology, Citragupta is born from *Brahmā to be the scribe of the gods; later he becomes *Yama's attendant, recording humans' good and bad deeds.

Citrāṅgadā In the **Mahābhārata* the princess of Maṇipūra, and sole heir to the throne (*putrikā). She marries *Arjuna during his period of exile, and he obtains a son for her who will inherit the throne from his maternal grandfather.

Citraratha In the **Mahābhārata* a *gandharva who is friendly to *Arjuna. As the king of the gandharvas and *apsarases, he constructs a celestial grove, called Caitaratha, for *Indra.

citta ('mind-field') A technical term used in *Patañjali's **Yoga Sūtra* to designate the complex of *buddhi, *ahaṃkāra, and *manas. *Yoga is defined (*Yoga Sūtra* 1.2) as 'the control of the fluctuations of the mind-field' ('cittavṛttinirodha').

Cittar (Tam. = Skt. siddha) A name given collectively to various *Tantric, *yogic, and antinomian *Tamil religious poets, such as *Civavākkiyar; it is also applied to the numerous authors of alchemical and medical treatises who were active in South India between the 10th and 15th centuries CE.

Civañāṉacittiyār See ARUṆANTI.

Civañāṉa Muṉivar (d. 1785) *Tamil author of the *Tirāviṭamāpāṭiyam*, the most important commentary on the *Civañāṉapōtam* of *Meykaṇṭār.

Civañāṉapōtam See MEYKAṆṬĀR.

Civavākkiyar (*c.*14th or 15th century CE) An antinomian *Tamil poet, classified as a *Cittar (*siddha), who opposed the authority of the **Vedas* and the *Brahmanical religion associated with it, as well as Hindu sectarianism and *temple worship. His name is derived from his collection of poems *Civavākkiyam* ('*Śiva's Utterance').

Cokāmeḷā (1293–1338) A low-*caste (*Mahār) Maharashtrian *sant and *bhakti poet belonging to the Marāṭhā *Vārkarī tradition, and associated with *Nāmdev. He was a devotee of *Viṭṭhala at Paṇḍharpur, but was unable to enter the *temple because of his *untouchable status. He is said to have been crushed by a wall that fell on him while he was working as a forced labourer. Until their mass conversion to *Buddhism by B. R. *Ambedkar in 1956, the Mahārs regarded Cokāmeḷā's memorial, which lay outside the temple precincts, and marked the closest point at which he or they could approach the shrine, as a focal point for their worship. His hymns (*abhaṅgs) remain popular with Vārkarīs.

C

Cōḻa One of the great *Tamil dynasties, at its height in South India (and briefly Sri Lanka) between the 9th and 13th centuries CE.

Colebrooke, Henry Thomas (1765–1837) The most accomplished of the early British *Sanskrit scholars and an enthusiastic champion of Indian civilization. Colebrooke, who was a civil servant with the *East India Company, took up the mantle of Sir William *Jones in developing the *Asiatic Society of Bengal into a major scholarly institution. After his retirement, he founded the *Royal Asiatic Society in London (1823). As well as translating from the Sanskrit, Colebrooke wrote extensively on the **Vedas*, Sanskrit grammar, Hindu law, and Indian mathematics, science, and geography.

Congress Party The Congress Party developed out of the Indian National Congress (founded 1885) and has been the dominant force in Indian politics for most of the period since Independence (1947). The family of the first Prime Minister of India, Jawaharlal *Nehru, has in turn dominated the Party, providing further Prime Ministers in Nehru's daughter, Indira Gandhi, and her son Rajiv, both assassinated. After a politically disastrous period in the 1990s, Rajiv's widow, Sonia Gandhi (b. 1946), led Congress back to power in the 2004 elections, although she declined to become Prime Minister herself. In contrast to the Hindu nationalist stance of its recent major rival, the *Bhāratīya Janatā Party (BJP), Congress has always campaigned on a non-sectarian and secular platform. However, it was comprehensively defeated by the BJP, under Narendra Modi, in the 2014 elections.

consciousness 'Caitanya', 'cetanā', 'cit', and 'vijñāna' are among the *Sanskrit terms used to designate 'consciousness', which is identified in a number of important Hindu traditions—from the **Upaniṣads*, through *Sāṃkhya (where it is equated with *puruṣa), *Advaita Vedānta, and various forms of *Tantra—as either a defining characteristic of the individual, and what differentiates it from insentient matter, or the essence of both the person and the universe. Pure (often contentless) consciousness is thus equated with *liberation, and the occlusion or limitation of consciousness with *karmic bondage. In Advaita, for instance, *brahman (neut.) is considered to be *saccidānanda, 'being, consciousness, and bliss'; in Tantric traditions, such as that of the Kashmirian *Śaiva theologian *Abhinavagupta, *Śiva, and thus reality itself, is envisioned as a unitary or non-dual consciousness, the nature of which is, nevertheless, dynamically to transform itself; for a modern teacher such as *Aurobindo Ghose, the divinization and perfection of both human beings and the material world is achieved through a *yogic ascent through progressively higher states of consciousness.

consecration *See* ABHIṢEKA.

Coomaraswamy, Ananda Kentish (1877–1947) Sri Lankan born writer on classical Indian art and culture, who became the first keeper of Indian and Islamic arts at the Boston Museum of Fine Arts. In his major publications, including *The Dance of Śiva* (1918), he stressed the spiritual and *yogic origins of Indian art.

cosmogony Early *Vedic ideas about the creation of the universe are speculative. The **Ṛg Veda* uses a variety of metaphors to convey the act of creation, including building, shaping, weaving, and sacrificing. The gods (*devas) are said to produce and order the material universe, including themselves. Alternatively, fire generates heat in the primaeval waters to produce sun and rain, and then the various worlds. The relatively late, tenth book of the *Ṛg Veda* contains a number of well-known cosmogonic hymns; one, *Ṛg Veda* 10.129 (*Nāsadīyasūkta*), contains a series of paradoxical statements and provocative questions about the origins of everything, ending with what seems like radical uncertainty; another, the famous **Puruṣasūkta* (*Ṛg Veda* 10.90), envisages creation and the ordering of society as a self-creating *sacrifice in which the cosmic man (*puruṣa), representing the totality of things, is both the subject and the object of the sacrifice made by the gods; yet another hymn (*Ṛg Veda* 10.121) introduces the idea of the *hiraṇyagarbha, the 'golden embryo', who arose in the beginning as the one lord of creation. Ideas such as these are developed and reconstituted in later literature. In the **Brāhmaṇas*, Puruṣa, who is both immanent and transcendent, is identified with the creator or demiurge *Prajāpati ('Lord of Creatures'), the vital force in, and of, creation. Prajāpati, in turn, becomes identified with *Brahmā, the creator of the **Purāṇas*, and the 'golden embryo' mutates into Brahmā's egg (*Brahmāṇḍa), establishing the basic, closed shape of the *Purāṇic universe.

The cyclical and unending nature of time, first suggested in the **Upaniṣads* in relation to the doctrine of *karma and rebirth, is linked in the *Purāṇas* to cosmogonic ideas. The question of the absolute beginning of things is therefore no longer a consideration. Furthermore, in the eyes of the devotee (*bhakta), time, like the material universe, is simply another aspect of God. Cosmogonic thought is therefore concerned with the beginning and ending of particular cycles—with 'creation' (*sarga) and dissolution (*pralaya) at the beginning and end of each *mahākalpa (or 'life of Brahmā'), and, within that longer period, the secondary 'creation' (*pratisarga) and dissolution at the beginning and end of each 'day of Brahmā', also known as a *kalpa (or, according to some, 1 000 kalpas). (A kalpa is further subdivided into *mahāyugas, the cycles of ages (*yugas) which regulate the appearance of *avatāras.) At the end of a day of Brahmā, the universe enters a period of quiescence or night, during which, according to a well-known Purāṇic myth, *Viṣṇu (*Nārāyaṇa) sleeps on the cosmic ocean (sometimes identified with the serpent *Śeṣa) before becoming, or giving rise to, the demiurge, Brahmā, who inaugurates the new cycle. A less theistic reading of this is that the universe emerges from and dissolves back into the unitary absolute that is *brahman (neut.). Partially integrated with this scheme is the *Sāṃkhya *yogic and evolutionary model, through which, at the beginning of each cycle of primary creation, the supreme Puruṣa (also known as the supreme brahman) causes undifferentiated matter (*avyakta or *prakṛti) to evolve into the various constituents which comprise both the individual and the universe (equated, when fully evolved, with 'Brahmā's egg'). These constituents will eventually be reabsorbed into the Puruṣa at the end of the cycle, i.e. at the end of a life of Brahmā, or, at the microcosmic level, as part of an individual's yogic practice. *See also* COSMOLOGY.

cosmology Hindu cosmological ideas are various, complex, frequently incompatible, and only imperfectly integrated with soteriological and *yogic thought. The following presents a summary of some of the principal, mostly cosmographic concepts, but details vary considerably from tradition to tradition, and from text to text. In the early *Vedic period the cosmos is divided either between the sky (the masculine *Dyaus) and the earth (the feminine *Pṛthivī), or between earth (*bhūr), atmosphere (*bhuvaḥ), and sky (*svar). It is only in the **Atharva Veda* and the **Brāhmaṇas* that human behaviour and its consequences start to be matched to regions of the universe, resulting in a vaguely delineated concept of a *hell located in an underworld. The *Upaniṣads offer a wide variety of cosmographic images: inter alia, the universe is compared to a tortoise, and to an egg (the prototype of *Brahmāṇḍa). The introduction of the doctrine of *karma and *rebirth is linked to the *pitṛyāna and the *devayāna—paths that the transmigrating individual takes across the universe, the latter leading out of (or abolishing) the cosmos altogether. The tripartite Vedic universe is vertically extended to seven levels, with the addition of the mahas-, janas-, tapas-, and satyam-lokas, which are partly the spatialization of meditational states. Later, the three upper levels are seen as providing refuge from the *pralaya, the destruction of the world at the end of a day of *Brahmā; and the highest world, the satyam, is equated to the *Brahmaloka.

In the *Purāṇas, the physical universe is assumed to be contained within 'Brahmā's egg' (Brahmāṇḍa), divided into 21 zones, comprised (from top to bottom) of six upper regions or heavens, the earth, the seven lower regions of *Pātāla (inhabited by various mythical creatures, such as *nāgas and *asuras), and seven (or more) hellish regions (*naraka). The horizontal arrangement of the universe contained within this egg is extensively elaborated. The earth is conceived as a flat disc made up of seven concentric islands (dvīpa), separated from each other by a series of oceans. At the centre of the innermost island, Jambudvīpa ('the rose-apple island'), stands the conical, golden, Mount *Meru, the *axis mundi*, extending into both heaven and hell. In the more intricate accounts, Jambudvīpa itself is divided, by a series of mountains, into nine regions, the southernmost of which is *Bharatavarṣa, the only *karmabhūmi among the regions. The sun, moon, and planets are said to move above the earth in chariots. The dimensions of this universe are vast: its diameter is said to measure 500 000 000 *yojanas. From one perspective it provides the cosmic theatre in which the drama of karma and rebirth is acted out—the *saṃsāra from which the *yogin seeks *liberation; from another, it is the body, or material nature of God, who can determine the fate of his devotees, both within and beyond such a universe. *See also* COSMOGONY.

cow The cow (Skt.: 'go') has been venerated in India from an early period. In *Vedic times cattle, and their products, were an index of wealth, and so of good fortune and prosperity. They were also among the offerings made in the Vedic sacrifice (*yajña). Cow-killing and beef-eating were therefore accepted, and even required in the contexts of ritual and *hospitality until around the beginning of the Common Era. Over the following millennium a situation slowly developed in which the worship of the cow as a sacred animal came to prominence, and its inviolability was established—ultimately in pointed contrast to the *Muslim practice of beef-eating. Since then the cow has remained a popular symbol of Hindu values, and a complete ban on its slaughter remains a vote-catching policy for Hindu nationalist politicians. The cow's importance as a draught animal, and as the provider of the 'five products of the cow' (pañcagavya)—milk, curds, butter, urine and dung (a source of fuel)—simply reinforces the animal's sanctity for most Hindus. Such products, whether singly or mixed, are regarded as both purifying and medicinal. In this context, *Kṛṣṇa's early life as a cowherd, and his role as 'protector of cows' (*gopāla) both reflect and further endorse the animal's status.

cremation The normal means of corpse disposal for Hindus. The general principle is that the fire conveys the deceased to another world. According to the **Bṛhadāraṇyaka Upaniṣad* (6.2.13–16), the cremated person proceeds either via the flame to *liberation, or via the smoke to eventual *rebirth. From another perspective, after a lifetime of making ersatz sacrificial offerings, the *āhitāgni finally becomes the oblation himself, and in a complex transformation is both offered and reconstituted. *Death and cremation in *Vārāṇasī (known as mahāśmaśāna, 'the great cremation ground'), where one's ashes will be scattered in the *Gaṅgā, is thought by many to guarantee liberation. *See also* ANTYEṢṬI; BURIAL; DEVAYĀNA; PITṚYĀNA.

cremation ground (śmaśāna) A space set outside normally inhabited areas, since, because of the presence of corpses, it is considered by most Hindus to be exceptionally ritually *polluting and *inauspicious. For this very reason, since the *Upaniṣadic period or earlier, cremation grounds have been sought out by various *ascetics and *Tantric practitioners, such as the *Kāpālikas. Emulating and worshipping terrible forms of *Śiva or the *Goddess, among other impurities they embrace that of *death, in an attempt to transcend orthodox dichotomies and gain access to various powers (*siddhis).

crore Ten million.

cūḍā (cūḍākaraṇa) ('tonsure', 'ceremonial haircut') The eighth of the *saṃskāras (transformative rituals) incumbent on the *three higher *varṇa, to be performed in a male child's first or third year, according to **Manusmṛti* and other sources of *dharma.

Cuntarar (Sundarar, Suntarar) (7th–8th century CE) A *Tamil *Śaiva *saint and *bhakti poet, and among the most prominent of the 63 *Nāyaṉmār. Cuntarar is regarded as one of the founders of the *Śaiva Siddhānta tradition in southern India. His songs appear in the **Tirumuṟai*, notably in the **Tēvāram* ('Garland of God') portion, alongside the works of *Appar and *Campantar. From the fact that he records the names of the 62 other Nāyaṉmār in his poetry, he appears to have been at the end of this line, and the 12th century hagiographer, *Cekkiḻār, uses Cuntarar's life story as a framework to tell the stories of the other 62 Nāyaṉmār in the twelfth and final book of the *Tirumuṟai*, the **Periya Purāṇam*. According to the traditional account, Cuntarar was born into a *brahmin family at Tirunāvalūr, although he was later married to two low *caste women. He was close to Cēramāṉ Perumāḷ, a *king who is also numbered among the Nāyaṉmār. Cuntarar's 1 026 poems express a single-minded devotion to *Śiva, mixed with a sense of his own deep inadequacy, and the hope of eventual union with the object of his bhakti.

Cyavāna (Cyavana) The name of a legendary *Vedic *ṛṣi, said to be a *Bhārgava. Married as an old man to the youthful Sukanyā, he is the subject of various *Epic and *Purāṇic myths, notably one in which he is rejuvenated by the *Aśvins, an event that eventually leads to the latter's inclusion in the *soma sacrifice.

D

Da (Da Free John, Da Avabhāsa Kalki, Avatar Adi Da Samraj, Bubba Free John) (b. Franklin Albert Jones, 1930) The New York-born founder of a Hindu-derived movement currently known as Adidam, or 'The Way of the Heart', but, like Da himself, known previously by at least ten different names. Da was a disciple, first of Swami *Rudrānanda, and then, in India in the late 1960s, of Rudrānanda's teacher, Swami *Muktānanda, under whom he experienced some form of '*yogic liberation'. He returned to America to form his own movement, initially known as The Dawn House Communion (1970). Da considers himself to be God in human form, and is worshipped as such by his followers. The beliefs and practices of the 'Daists' are eclectic, but draw heavily on Hindu and *Buddhist *Tantric models, infused with 'crazy wisdom'. Since the mid 1980s, lawsuits by former members, and accusations of physical and sexual abuse have dogged the movement and its founder, who now lives in retreat in Fiji. Da is responsible for over twenty books, all published by his own house, The Dawn Horse Press.

Dada Lekhraj *See* Brahmā Kumārīs.

Dadhīca *See* Dadhyac.

Dadhikrā (Dadhikrās, Dadhikrāvan) A celestial, divine horse mentioned in a number of hymns in the **Ṛg Veda*.

Dadhyac (Dadhyañc, Dadhīca) ('Sprinkled Curds') The name of a *Vedic *ṛṣi, the son of *Atharvan, and the subject of a number of myths, including one in which the *Aśvins protect him from *Indra's wrath by giving him a horse's head.

Dādū (Dādū Dayāla) (1544–1604) A Rajasthani poet-saint (*sant) who, after his death, became the devotional focus of the *Dādūpantha. What is known of his life is derived from the hagiography (*Dādū janam līla*, *c.*1620) of his disciple, Janagopāla. Dādū was born in Gujarat, probably into a low-*caste *Muslim family. As a young man, he had a series of religious experiences, and thereafter—with the exception of ten years as a married householder—led the life of an itinerant *ascetic and preacher. His wandering encompassed much of Rajasthan, and it was there that he eventually died, in a small town (Naraiṇā, near Jaipur) that subsequently became the centre of one branch of the Dādūpantha tradition. His teachings and devotional songs, composed in *Braj bhāṣā, were collected by one of his disciples, Rajjab. In their non-sectarianism (Dādū was followed by both Hindus and Muslims), their critical attitude to formal religion, and their style, his songs are comparable to those of *Kabīr, many of whose poems were preserved in the manuscripts of the Dādupantha tradition. Dādū is thus frequently identified as a follower of Kabīr.

Dādūpantha A North Indian *bhakti tradition, drawing on the songs and practices of 'five saints'—chief among whom are their founder, the 16th century *sant, *Dādū, and *Kabīr (The other three are *Nāmdev, *Haridāsa, and *Raidāsa.) Devotees (Dādūpanthīs) attempt to induce a state of non-dual dependence on God by chanting his name. The movement has two main branches: the Khālsā, based at Nairaiṇā in Rajasthan, and the Uttarādhā.

Membership is now restricted to the higher *castes, and has both lay and *ascetic (virakta) divisions. A Dādūpanthī *Nāgā regiment was formed in the 17th century, but has since been domesticated.

daityas ('descendants of Diti', 'demons', 'giants', 'titans') In *Purāṇic mythology, a class of beings represented as opponents of the gods (*devas). The daityas are frequently assimilated to the *Vedic *asuras, and play a prominent role in the story of the *Churning of the Ocean.

daiva 1. ('what comes from the gods (devas)', 'fate') A significant term in the **Mahābhārata*, where, as a constraint beyond human control, it is often opposed to free will and human effort (pauruṣa). *Dhṛtarāṣṭra and *Duryodhana, in particular, blame it for their predicament. While its operation is, at best, opaque to human beings, fate is, nevertheless, not random, since it refers to a real and active power that shapes and blocks the results of human actions, and does so in order to work out a universal plan. It is not that humans are constrained in all their actions, simply that fate demands certain outcomes. Some actions therefore accord with fate while others do not. As the narrative core of the *Mahābhārata* reaches its conclusion, *Kṛṣṇa's will (God's will) and fate become virtually indistinguishable, since Kṛṣṇa has not only taken over the collective cosmic powers of the *Vedic gods, but he also intervenes in human affairs in a personal way to guarantee cosmic outcomes. **2.** According to **Manusmṛti* and other *Sanskrit legal texts (**Dharmaśāstra*), one of the eight possible types of *marriage, in which a daughter is given to an officiating priest at a sacrificial ritual as part of his fee (*dakṣinā).

ḍākinī(s) Flesh-eating demonesses, who appear naked and act as if *possessed. They attend on *Kālī, and play a subsidiary or intermediary role in *Buddhist and Hindu *Tantra, sometimes assimilated to a single figure ('Ḍākinī').

Dakṣa ('skilled') In the **Ṛg Veda*, Dakṣa appears as the male principle of creation or creative energy. This role is modified and personified in *Epic and *Purāṇic mythology, where Dakṣa is said to be (a) *Prajāpati, produced by *Brahmā; he is regarded as a secondary creator (or son of the secondary creator) and seer (*ṛṣi), present in each cycle of creation (*manvantara), and particularly associated with the power of the sacrifice (*yajña). The best-known myth concerning Dakṣa tells how his sacrifice was destroyed by *Śiva (in his ferocious *Vīrabhadra form) after the god had been deliberately excluded from it. Dakṣa was then decapitated by Śiva, but restored to life (in some accounts with a goat's head) once Śiva had been promised his proper share of the sacrifice by the other gods. Some versions of the myth tie Śiva's anger to the suicide of his wife, Dakṣa's own daughter, *Satī, caused by the insult her father offered the god.

dakṣinā 1. ('right','southern') Right is *auspicious, left (*vāma) generally *inauspicious. The right hand is therefore used for interaction with all things auspicious, including making offerings to the gods; the left for contact with the inauspicious, such as in making offerings to the spirits (*bhūtabali). On the same principle, circumambulation (*pradakṣinā) of an image, place, or revered person takes place in a clockwise direction, with the object of attention to the walker's right. By extension, the term 'dakṣinā' also means 'south', because a person facing east has the south to his or her right. The south is the direction generally associated with the dead. **2.** The 'sacrificial fee' or 'gift' offered to the officiating *priests at a *śrauta sacrifice by the sacrificer (*yajamāna), and, by extension, at other rituals. The prototypical dakṣinā is a *cow (the original referent of the term in this context), but fees are various, ranging from cows, gold, and garments, to fruits and edible roots, depending on the scale of the sacrifice and the number of priests involved. According to the **Śatapatha Brāhmaṇa* (4.3.4), the minimum fee for a *soma sacrifice is 100 cows per priest. A sacrifice without dakṣinā is considered neither complete nor effective, and is effectively prohibited. Those who can provide only meagre fees are advised by **Dharmaśāstra* not to sacrifice at all. *See also* DĀNA.

dakṣiṇācāra ('right-handed practice/path') A form of *Tantric *pūjā in which *Devī is worshipped in a 'pure' or *Vedic way, without material recourse to the 'five Ms' (*pañca-makāra) associated with 'left-handed' (*vāmācāra) worship, which are either substituted or visualized instead.

dakṣiṇāgni (anvāhāryapacana) ('southern fire') One of the three main fires used in *śrauta ritual. Like the *āhavanīya, the dakṣiṇāgni is expanded from the *gārhapatya or 'householder's' fire; it is established on a semi-circular mound to the south of the sacrificial area and is used for the *piṇḍapitṛyajña, the monthly offerings to the ancestors (*pitṛs), since they live in that direction. It also protects against maleficent powers and spirits, such as *rākṣasas.

dakṣiṇāmūrti ('southern image') An auspicious form of *Śiva, particularly popular in South Indian iconography, in which the god is represented as the supreme *ascetic *teacher. Commonly, he is shown addressing his *yogin followers from a seat beneath a tree, one foot trampling the demon of ignorance. 'South' may be a reference to the direction in which he faces to deliver his teachings.

Dakṣineśvara temple (Dakshineshwar temple) A 19th-century *temple near Kolkata (Calcutta), dedicated to *Kālī. In their youth, *Rāmakṛṣṇa and his elder brother were *priests there.

Dalit ('oppressed') The self-designation of members of a 20th-century social and political movement, comprised of those known by others as '*untouchables', 'outcastes', 'scheduled castes', or, in the case of M. K. *Gāndhī, *harijans. The general purpose of the movement has been to raise the status and awareness of such noncaste groups (which may include *Buddhists, *Christians, and *Muslims) and to organize them as a political and cultural force.

ḍamaru The name of a small hour glass-shaped drum, carried by various deities, most notably by *Śiva in his *Naṭarāja form. Śiva's ḍamaru is fashioned from two half-skulls, and is said to represent the primeval sound (*śabda) from which the universe emerges, and into which it is reabsorbed. A similar instrument is carried by sectarian followers of Śiva, particularly in North India and *Nepal.

Damayantī *See* NALA.

Dāmodara ('having a rope around the belly') An epithet of *Kṛṣṇa, referring to his foster-mother's attempt to tie him to a pillar as a young child.

dāna ('the act of giving', 'a donation', 'a gift') According to **Dharmaśāstra*, religious 'giving' (dāna) is the characteristic activity of the *householder, and there is extensive discussion of it in *Epic and *Purāṇic texts, as well as in the *dharma literature, where elaborate rules are laid down governing donees, donors, suitable times, and the right kind of gift. Although almost anyone can give and receive gifts (deya), the most suitable recipient is a learned and *ascetic *brahmin (it is he who is considered a pātra—one worthy to receive a gift), and it is only brahmins who can practise pratigraha ('acceptance of gifts') as a means of livelihood. Whether the donee is a brahmin or not, the underlying principle is that the merit (*puṇya) obtained, or 'returned', to the donor is proportionate both to his own worth and mental attitude, and to the worth and *caste of the original recipient of the gift. In this way, goods—typically *food, a *cow, other *auspicious animals, or land—are reciprocated through immaterial religious *merit. It is this model that underlies both the *dakṣiṇā, or sacrificial fee, presented to the *priests at the *śrauta ritual, and the offering made to the deity at *pujā, which is returned in the form of *prasāda ('favour' or 'blessing'). According to many anthropologists and textual scholars, this kind of ritual giving is a vehicle for the shedding or transmission of *impurity and *inauspicious qualities from donor to donee. Brahmins and gods are suitable recipients precisely because they are capable of absorbing such impurity. While this confirms their superiority to the donor (they have the capacity to deal with impurity), in the case of the brahmin, it also compromises his purity. For this reason, brahmins who accept gifts as a living (including dakṣiṇā) are considered inferior to those who do not.

Dānavas The descendants of Danu (one of the daughters of *Dakṣa) and *Kaśyapa. In *Purāṇic and *Epic mythology, they are frequently identified with the *daityas and *asuras as opponents of the gods (*devas).

dance *See* ĀNANDATĀṆḌAVA; BHĀRATANĀṬYAM; KATHAK; KATHĀKALĪ; LĀSYA; MANIPURĪ; NAṬARĀJA; NĀṬYAŚĀSTRA; RĀS(A) LĪLĀ.

daṇḍa ('rod', 'staff') **1.** As wielded by the *king, a symbol of judicial authority, and so synonymous with the administration of justice and punishment. According to **Dharmaśāstra*, it is the king's duty, through the ceaseless application of daṇḍa, to maintain *dharma (social order) and manage the state. At the mythological level, *Yama, the god of death, also wields the daṇḍa (and so is known as 'Daṇḍadhara ('rod-bearer')), with a similar function. **2.** The name of the staff given to a twice-born man (*dvija) at initiation (*upanayana), or to a *saṃnyāsin as part of his insignia.

Daṇḍaka forest (Daṇḍakāraṇya) The vast forest in which, according to the **Rāmāyaṇa*, many of *Rāma and *Sītā's adventures take place. Its location and extent are variously described: according to some it reaches as far north as the *Gaṅgā, others locate it more specifically in the Deccan.

daṇḍi(n) ('staff-bearer') A title or epithet of a *Daśanāmi *saṃnyāsin, who carries a staff as part of his insignia.

Daṇḍin (7th century CE) A *Sanskrit author, best-known for his prose collection, *Daśakumāracarita* ('Tales of the Ten Princes'/'What Ten Young Men Did'), which attains a degree of realism in its depiction of ordinary life.

Danu *See* DĀNAVAS.

Dārā Shukōh (Dara Shikoh) (1613–1659) Son of the *Mughal emperor *Shāh Jahān (1592–1666). He regarded classical Hindu *Sanskritic teachings and the Qur'ān as mystically compatible, and, in collaboration with Hindu *paṇḍits, made a Persian translation of 52 of the **Upaniṣads*. This was subsequently 'translated' into Latin by *Anquetil du Perron, and so conveyed to Europe.

darbār (Persian; Ang.: 'durbar') A royal court or assembly.

darbha A type of grass used in *Vedic sacrificial rituals. Spread across the altar (*vedi) and the whole sacrificial enclosure, it is burnt at the end of the ritual. Considered both sacred and powerful, darbha also has less specific ritual and symbolic uses. Sprouting darbha is referred to as *kuśa, but the two terms are often used synonymously.

darśan(a) **1.** ('looking at', 'viewing') Derived from the *Sanskrit root 'dṛś' ('to see', 'to look at'), darśana, in the form of the meeting of the devotee's and the (iconic) deity's eyes, is both an act of worship in itself and central to any extended form of *pūjā. The principle is expanded to cover the *auspicious sight of any sacred place (especially *tīrthas—pilgrimage sites—and their associated deities), or person (i.e. particular holy men or *sādhus). This is not passive gazing, but an active exchange through which the devotee receives the deity's or sādhu's blessing. For this reason, people go to the *temple 'for darśan'; there, the deity presents itself to be seen, 'giving' darśan, while the devotees 'take' or 'receive' it. **2.** ('point of view', 'perspective') A term used to designate a 'school of philosophy'. In modern works, there are said to be six such, purportedly complementary, Hindu, or 'orthodox' (*āstika) systems, grouped into pairs: *Nyāya and *Vaiśeṣika, *Sāṃkhya and *Yoga, *Mīmāṃsā and *Vedānta. This distinguishes them from the 'heterodox' (*nāstika) systems of the *Cārvākas, *Jainas, and *Buddhists. The term 'darśana' is used for the first time in a Buddhist context in the 5th century CE, and many premodern lists contain both Buddhist and *Śaiva schools, as well as Jaina 'philosophy', at the same time omitting Yoga and Vedānta.

darśapūrṇamāsa ('[the sacrifice offered on] the days of the new and full moon') A twice-monthly *Vedic *śrauta sacrifice, to be performed on each full and new moon day, requiring four *priests. It is regarded as the model (*prakṛti (2)) for all other offerings (*iṣṭis), and so receives extensive treatment in the **Śrauta Sūtras*.

Daśa ('ten') A common prefix denoting a group of ten (deities, etc.).

Daśabodha A Marathi anthology of his own writings made by the Maharashtrian *saint and religious leader, *Rāmadāsa.

Daśaharā (H.: **Daśahrā**) *See* DASARA.

Dāsakūṭa *See* HARIDĀSAKŪṬA.

Daśanāmis (daṇḍa-svāmis, daṇḍi(n)s) ('those who follow the [order with] ten names') An *ascetic and monastic order said to have been founded by *Śaṅkara in the 8th century CE, but according to some scholars up to six hundred years later than that. It derives its name from a division along *caste lines into ten sections (four of them specific to *brahmins): Āraṇya ('wilderness'), and Vana ('forest'), based at *Purī (the seat of the head of the order, the *jagadguru); Giri ('mountain'), Parvata ('mountain'), and Sāgara ('ocean'), at *Jyotirmaṭh (near *Badrināth); Tīrtha ('ford'), and Āśrama ('hermitage'), at *Dvārakā; Purī ('city'), Bhārati ('learning'), and Sarasvatī ('speech'), at *Śṛṅgeri. Daśanāmis, distinguished by their ochre robes and the *Śaiva sectarian *lakṣaṇa of four horizontal white lines on the forehead, are generally renowned for their learning. They adhere to an *Advaitin form of *Vedāntic orthodoxy, with a markedly Śaiva affiliation. Initiated members (who add their '*caste' name as a suffix to their monastic name) are normally resident in monasteries (*maṭhas) under the direction of their *guru or *Śaṅkarācārya. It is claimed that Śaṅkara founded a fifth maṭha at *Kāñcī(puram), and so it too has become the seat of one of the Śaṅkarācāryas. Because they were recruited as protectors of the order, some sources consider the naked warrior-ascetics, the *Nāgas, to be part of the Daśanāmi tradition.

Dasara (Dassera, Dussera, Dussehra, Dashami, H.: **Daśahrā,** Skt.: **Daśaharā)** ('the tenth day [festival]') The tenth day, and culmination, of the 'nine night' (*Navarātri) *Durgā-pūjā festival in Bengal, celebrating the *Goddess's defeat of the buffalo-demon *Mahiṣāsura. The term is also used synonymously for the Navarātri festival in its entirety. In North India, Dasara coincides with the climax of the *Rāma Līlā festival, on the tenth day of which (known as vijayā-daśamī ('victory tenth')) *Rāma's victory over *Rāvaṇa is celebrated—the victory of a deity over a demonic power providing the point of convergence between the two festivals. Studies have been made of the particularly complex and martial Dasaras celebrated in both Mewar and Mysore (for at least five hundred years in the latter case) under the patronage of local rulers, where the festival has served not just to reinforce the universal victory of *dharma, but also to ensure victory in the military campaigns that follow on the end of the rainy season.

Daśaratha ('ten chariots') In the **Rāmāyaṇa*, the king of *Ayodhyā, who is forced by his second wife, *Kaikeyī, to exile his son *Rāma to the forest, providing the catalyst for the *Epic narrative.

Dāsa(s) ('slave(s)') **1.** An epithet, applied in the **Ṛg Veda* to the enemies of the *Āryans, also known as 'Dasyus'. **2.** A pejorative term used to designate someone of low *caste, such as a fisherman. **3.** The self-description and assumed name of a *bhakta, often suffixed to the deity's name (e.g. *Kālidāsa ('servant of *Kālī'), *Rāmdās ('servant of *Rāma')).

daśāvatāra *See* AVATĀRA.

Dasgupta, Surendra Nath (1885–1952) A Hindu philosopher, whose five-volume *History of Indian Philosophy* (1922–55) became the standard academic work on the subject. Educated in both the Indian *Sanskritic tradition and European philosophy, Dasgupta spent most of his professional career in Kolkata (Calcutta). His own philosophy was derived from a synthesis of various Indian and Western traditions, combined with evolutionary science.

Dāsimayya, Dēvara (Jēḍara Dāsimayya ('Dāsimayya of the weavers')) ('God's Dāsimayya', 10th century CE) A South Indian poet-*saint, who was probably the earliest major author of the *Liṅgāyat(a) tradition. His religious lyrics (*vacanas), composed in the *Dravidian language of *Kannada, are addressed to Rāmanātha ('Rāma's lord'), i.e. *Śiva as worshipped by *Rāma. Legends tell of his missionary and miracle-working activities, and he is said to have converted the Cālukya king, Jayasiṃha, from *Jainism. A selection of his poetry in English translation can be found in A. K. *Ramanujan's *Speaking of Śiva* (Penguin Books, 1973).

Dassera *See* DASARA.

Dasyu *See* DĀSA(s) (1).

Dattātreya 1. In western India, and especially Maharashtra (where he is known as Dattobā), Dattātreya is considered a composite deity, incorporating *Brahmā, *Viṣṇu, and *Śiva. He is portrayed either as a three-headed god (accompanied by four dogs, representing the **Vedas*), or as the three gods together, usually with Viṣṇu as the dominant partner. **2. (Datta)** The son of the *Vedic *ṛṣi *Atri, and *Anasūyā. He is thought to be an *avatāra of Viṣṇu. **3.** (12th–13th century CE) The reputed founder of the Avadhūta subsect (*panth) of the *Nāth Siddhas, and author of a number of works on *yoga and *Tantra, including the *Dattātreya Tantra*; sometimes conflated with (1).

Dattobā *See* DATTĀTREYA.

dayā ('compassion') An ethical stance sometimes represented as the positive or active pursuit of non-violence (*ahiṃsā), and a component part of the practice of *dharma. Dayā personified is therefore (personified) Dharma's wife.

Dayānand(a) Sarasvatī (1824–1883) A prominent Hindu reformer who founded the *Ārya Samāj. Born into a family of orthodox *Śaivite Gujarati *brahmins, as Mūl Śaṅkar, he changed his name after being initiated into the Sarasvatī *Daśanāmi order as a *saṃnyāsin (1848), partly to avoid his relative's attempts to see him married. This was the culmination of a ten year period of disillusionment with his family's devotional religious practices, which had been triggered, at the age of fourteen, by the sight of mice running over the image of *Śiva during the *Śivarātri vigil. After twelve years as a wandering mendicant, he became the pupil of the blind *Vedic scholar, Svāmī Virajānanda, under whose influence he further rejected *Purāṇic and devotional Hinduism in favour of a 'pure', *Veda-based form of the religion, focused on an impersonal God. At the beginning of his public career (1868), he matched these convictions with a traditional style of oral teaching through the medium of *Sanskrit, but, after contact with the *Brāhmo Samāj, switched to the more accessible *Hindi. His most influential written work, the *Satyārth Prakāś* ('Light of Truth'), in which he virulently rejected the claims of other religions (including what he saw as the corruption of the Vedic tradition), was published in 1874, just prior to his founding of the Ārya Samāj. He died in 1883, apparently poisoned by one of his many enemies, but his reforming influence persisted to become a shaping force in the development of 20th-century Hindu nationalism. *See also* Ārya Samāj.

death/Death (antaka, kāla, mṛtyu, Yama, etc.**)** In Hinduism, as in other religions, the fact, nature, and meaning of death have been integral to almost every kind of ritual and *yogic practice, and to every variety of metaphysical speculation throughout its history. With the possible exception of the *Cārvākas, no Hindu tradition has claimed that death marks the end of existence. Although in the earlier hymns of the **Ṛg Veda*, the notion of an afterlife seems vague, and '*immortality' frequently equated to a 100-year lifespan, the later hymns are aware of an after-death realm, ruled over by Yama, the first man to die and so the *king, or god, of the dead. In the developed ritual system, reflected in the **Brāhmaṇas* and *Mīmāṃsaka analysis, the sacrificer's goal is to defeat death by creating first a temporary, then a permanent, place in a heavenly world (*svarga-loka). The possibility of dying again—of suffering redeath (*punar-mṛtyu) in the next life and/or world, if not properly sustained or conditioned, either by surviving *ancestors, or one's own efforts while still alive—leads in the **Upaniṣads* to the concept of a potentially endless cycle of *rebirths. The goal then becomes a state of immutable deathlessness that transcends both time (*kāla—itself synonymous with death), and location—perhaps a reconstitution of the *Vedic idea of *amṛta, itself synonymous with the ingestion of *soma. Such deathlessness can be achieved, according to some *Upaniṣads*, and *Advaita Vedānta, by realization of the essential identity of the individual soul (*ātman) and *brahman (neut.). The conceptualization of this state as lying outside and beyond the power of death is prefigured in the status of those *renouncers pursuing such a goal: both socially and ritually they are considered to be already dead. Progress towards liberation (*mokṣa) of this kind is conditioned by *karma, the bonds of which accompany the individual from life to life, from death to death, unless otherwise dissolved (through, for example, *yogic and *meditational practices). Even the gods (*devas) in heaven are ultimately subject to this law. In *Purāṇic *cosmogony the death and *rebirth of the individual is mapped onto the cyclical 'death and rebirth' (dissolution and creation) of the universe and time, a process governed by the great sectarian gods of monotheistic Hinduism.

With increasing soteriological reliance on unconditional devotion (*bhakti) and direct access to the power of particular sectarian deities by *Tantric means, the problems of repeated death and rebirth (and so the consequences of karma) become less pressing. Death for the devotee or initiate will lead to eternal bliss in heaven, and/or to some degree of liberating identity, or permanently close relationship, with God, or the *Goddess.

A gap exists between such metaphysical and mystical beliefs, concerning the nature of death, and liberation from it, and the rationale for performing the various rituals associated with the death of a close male relative, as prescribed in the *Brahmanical legal texts (*Dharmaśāstra*). This 'last sacrifice' (*antyeṣṭi) and the subsequent *śrāddha rites appear to be more closely aligned with earlier, persistent ideas about the afterlife, since they predicate a situation in which the ancestors (*pitṛs) require feeding after death. Death in general is considered to be both extremely *inauspicious and *polluting. Funerary rituals are therefore a way of circumscribing and controlling the pollution involved.

In parallel with both metaphysical speculations about the fate of the dead, and the rationale for elaborate death rituals, there remains a widespread belief in popular and *village Hinduism in the continued survival of the dead in close proximity to, and interpenetration with the world of the living. This is particularly the case with those who have died 'bad' or accidental deaths; such spirits, known as *bhūta (-preta) are usually malevolent, and the cause of misfortune, illness, and *possession among the living. The ancient *Vedic tradition of a daily ritual offering of *food to the spirits (*bhūtabali) is one way of attempting to appease their hunger and avert their malevolence. Conversely, those who have achieved 'good' or heroic deaths—for example in *meditation, in an act of (sometimes suicidal) devotion, as a *satī, or in battle, if they are a *kṣatriya—are thought to attain heaven, or liberation, immediately, and are thereupon frequently deified. *See also* KARMA; REBIRTH.

Deb, Rādhākānta *See* DHARMA SABHĀ.

debt(s) (Skt.: **ṛṇa(s)**) According to *Brahmanical theology, a *brahmin (in this context, any *twice-born man) owes three 'debts': of studentship (*Vedic study) to the seers (*ṛṣis), of *sacrifice to the gods (*devas), and of offspring to the fathers (*pitṛs). (Some texts—e.g. the *Śatapatha Brāhmaṇa*—add a further debt: of *hospitality to men.) Their characterization as 'debts' (ṛṇas) indicates that these are both obligations, and in some sense 'faults' that have to be remitted; they are said to be automatically and universally (for the twice-born) incurred at birth, although they cannot start to be paid until the individual has undergone *upanayana (initiation into the **Veda*, thus paying his debt to the seers). Furthermore, payment to the gods in the form of sacrifice requires *marriage (since only then can one set up the requisite fires), as does the birth of a *son, the payment to the fathers. Since it is the first-born son who is qualified to perform his father's funeral rites (*antyeṣṭi), thus ensuring the dead man's transformation into a pitṛ himself, his birth marks the point at which the father's debt is paid and, in a sense, passes to the next generation. The implication of this obligatory 'theology' of debt (made explicit in, for instance, **Manusmṛti* 6.35–7) is that *renunciation can only take place, if at all, once the debts have been paid. In historical terms, it may therefore be seen as a conscious attempt to legitimize, or shore up, the Brahmanical institutions of sacrifice and marriage in the light of a perceived threat from the *ascetic and renouncer values of internalized sacrifice and celibacy (*brahmacarya). *See also* ĀŚRAMA.

Deussen, Paul (1845–1919) A German philosopher and *Sanskrit scholar who held posts in Berlin and Kiel. Deussen was the editor of *Schopenhauer, and a friend of Friedrich Nietzsche (1844–1900); a great admirer of *Vedāntic culture, he travelled widely in India, where he was known by his preferred Sanskrit name, 'Devasena'. His numerous publications include *The Philosophy of the Upaniṣads* (1899; English trans. 1906), and extensive translations into German of the **Upaniṣads*, parts of the **Mahābhārata*, and *Śaṅkara's *Brahmasūtrabhāṣya*, among others.

devadāsī ('servants of the god') A term used to refer to a woman who was ritually 'married' to the *temple god, or treated as one of his courtesans. Either presented to the temple by her parents in childhood, or born of a devadāsī herself, the girl (considered to be beyond *caste restrictions) was trained to attend on the god, and to entertain him by singing and dancing. She also acted as a prostitute to the male devotees. In the medieval period, some temple complexes, especially in South India, had hundreds of devadāsīs under the control of the temple *priests. The attitude towards devadāsīs was ambivalent: although regarded by many as *auspicious, since they were married to the god, and highly respected for their education and training, particularly in the arts, they were also thought to be unchaste and not fit to enter the inner sanctum of the temple. Some made considerable fortunes, part of which might be returned to the temple in the form of endowments. The practice of presenting female children to the temple was made illegal in 1947, but the devadāsīs' artistic accomplishments have been increasingly appreciated.

Devakī As recounted in texts such as the **Harivaṃśa*, the seventh wife of *Vasudeva, and the mother of *Balarāma and *Kṛṣṇa.

devaloka ('heavenly world') *See* SVARGA.

devanāgarī (nāgarī) ('divine city writing', 'the city script of the gods (devas)') The central Indian script (derived from *brāhmī) which was widely adopted for printed *Sanskrit texts, as well as for publications in the modern languages of *Hindi and Marathi.

deva(s) ('heavenly' 'divine', 'deity', 'god', fem.: devī(s)) Used generically to designate the supernatural and celestial beings, or 'gods', praised and invoked in the **Ṛg Veda* as a component part of the sacrificial ritual. Conventionally 33 in number, like their brothers the *asuras (their opponents in the ritual and, subsequently, the cosmic context), they were born from *Prajāpati. The devas are both the personifications of natural forces, and the embodiment of particular powers or concepts, and are accordingly distributed between the three worlds (*loka) of heaven (*svar), the atmosphere (*bhuvaḥ), and earth (*bhūr). They are frequently described in unequivocally concrete and anthropomorphic terms. In particular, they require the '*food' offered to them in the *sacrifice by human beings. *Agni (the ritual fire) and *Soma (a plant, and the drink made from it)—the devas who act as intermediaries between humans and heaven—are therefore among the more important gods. Most frequently invoked in the *Ṛg Veda* is the warrior *king, *Indra (in post-*Vedic mythology invariably identified as the king of the gods), the leader of the storm gods, the *Maruts. Other significant devas include the *Ādityas (the sons of *Aditi), chief among them *Mitra and *Varuṇa, who, as well as being linked to natural phenomena, are regarded as personifications of the important social functions. Natural phenomena themselves, such as the sun (*Sūrya), the sky (*Dyaus), the earth (*Pṛthivī), and the wind (*Vāyu), are also conceived of as deities. Some goddesses (*devīs), including *Uṣas (the dawn), and *Vāc (speech), are invoked, but the majority of divine beings are thought to be male. *Viṣṇu and *Rudra (later a name of *Śiva), although appearing amongst the devas, play only minor and circumscribed roles in *Vedic religion.

In the **Brāhmaṇas*, and later ritual texts, the power and significance of the devas is substantially transferred to the performers of the sacrifice (*yajña), the *brahmin priests, referred to as the 'human gods' (Skt.: mānuṣya devāḥ). This is reflected in the theology of the *Pūrva Mīmāṃsaka exegetes, where statements about the devas are said to be *arthavāda, their purpose being not to signify independently existent entities, but simply to shore up the sacrificer's performance. In *Epic and *Purāṇic mythology, the Vedic devas exist alongside, and interact with the great gods of devotional Hinduism—Viṣṇu, Śiva, and the *Goddess, although ultimate power, and religious significance, now rests with those sectarian deities. *See also* ASURA.

devatā ('deity') A generic term for a village (*grāma), clan, or little deity, which may, formerly, have been a malevolent spirit (*bhūta). The term can encompass the full range of minor deities and vaguely defined spirits worshipped at small shrines, where they may be represented by stones, or other natural objects.

devayajña ('sacrifice to the gods') The daily offering into the fire for the gods, which, according to **Dharmaśāstra*, is obligatory for an orthodox *brahmin as one of the five 'great sacrifices' (*mahāyajñas).

devayāna ('the way of the gods') Also referred to as the 'northern path', one of three paths taken by the self, or its subtle body, after *death, according to the **Upaniṣads* and *Vedāntic theology. (The others are the *pitṛyāna, 'the way of the fathers', or the 'southern path', and the path to *Yama's world—known as *saṃyamana.) According to the **Bṛhadāraṇyaka Upaniṣad* (6.2.15), those on the devayāna (those with knowledge of the meaning of the *sacrifice, or knowledge of *brahman (neut.), according to *Śaṅkara) follow the route through the *funeral fire into the day, from the day into the fortnight of the waxing moon, from there into the six months when the sun moves north, from those into the world of the gods (*devaloka); from there through the sun into the region of lightning, and thence to the 'worlds of *brahman', from which they are not reborn in this world. This destination has been variously interpreted either as the state of *liberation, or as some intermediate state prior to realization of *nirguṇa brahman.

Dēvayāṉai *Murukaṉ/*Skanda's first wife.

Dev Bhagwan Ātma *See* AGNIHOTRI, PANDIT SHIV NARAYAN.

Devī (Goddess) 1. A general term, synonymous with *Śakti, for the Great Goddess (Mahādevī) as the principal or supreme deity. She is also known under a wide variety of specific names or representations, each typically categorized as either benevolent (e.g. *Lakṣmī, *Pārvatī, *Śrī) or fierce (e.g. *Durgā, *Kālī). Devī is further identified in the form of innumerable village goddesses (*grāmadevatās). Depending on the context, such specific or localized goddesses are thought either to manifest aspects of her power, or to be identical to the Goddess herself. Beyond this, Hindus share the familiar generalized perceptions of the Goddess as a mother, and most widely as 'mother earth' (*Bhū Devī).

Worship of the Goddess as the supreme creative power and/or theological absolute is usually referred to as '*Śāktism', and her worshippers as '*Śāktas'. In this respect Śāktism has been identified as one of the three great sectarian streams in medieval and later Hinduism, alongside *Vaiṣṇavism and *Śaivism. Like them, it is evoked through a rich *Purāṇic mythology, notably in texts such as the **Devīmāhātmya*, **Kālikā Purāṇa*, the **Mahābhāgavata Purāṇa*, and the

d

Devībhāgavata Purāṇa. The phenomenon of Goddess worship is, however, a complex one, in so far as veneration of the female principle is not only evident in early *Vedic material but was also clearly a prominent feature of pre- and extra-Vedic practices as well, although it was only gradually assimilated into *Sanskritic religion. Moreover, since both *Viṣṇu and *Śiva have wives or consorts personifying their *śakti (energy or power), the degree to which a localized tradition can be labelled Śākta, rather than, for instance, Śaiva, will vary, depending on how much emphasis it gives to the female aspect of the supreme. In Bengal, for instance, there has been a long and close historical connection between Śāktism and various forms of Śaivism. One way in which Śāktism distinguishes itself theologically is by characterizing the dynamic and active female principle, manifested in the material world, as identical with the absolute. Female power thus encompasses and contains the passive male, or 'spiritual' principle (represented by the male deity) in an all-embracing, energized union which is ultimate reality.

Unsurprisingly, given *Tantra's preoccupation with the attainment and manipulation of power (śakti), much worship of the Goddess (whether in her ferocious or benevolent forms, whether as an unmarried goddess or as a male deity's consort) is imbued with *Tantric elements, although the two religious types are by no means identical. Within Śākta Tantrism, schools are broadly aligned with either fierce or benevolent forms of the goddess, and categorized, on a similar division of their Tantras, as either *Kālīkula, 'belonging to the family of the Black Goddess' (originating in north-eastern and northern India) or *Śrīkula, 'belonging to the family of the Auspicious Goddess' (originating in Kashmir and the South, notably in the *Śrī Vidyā tradition).

In ritual, blood *sacrifice is a distinguishing component of the worship of the Goddess (and goddesses), particularly at the village level. For *brahmins, this potential *impurity may be removed to a symbolic or mythological realm, but there is a common perception that the Goddess's bounty demands to be repaid through the blood of sacrificial victims (especially buffaloes), mirroring Durgā's violent destruction of the buffalo demon, *Mahiṣāsura. It is only in this way that fertility and fecundity can be renewed, and *evil defeated. More widely, this reflects the perception that, as the supreme and all-encompassing power, the Goddess has violently destructive, as well as motherly, preservative, and creative aspects.

Both the material immanence and the universally sustaining nature of the Goddess are reflected for Śāktas in the idea that the subcontinent is plotted with *tīrthas or pilgrimage places, known as *śaktipīṭhas ('places of power'), where, according to a well-known myth, the dismembered body of the goddess *Satī, manifests itself in local topography. A similar perception of an ancient and underlying unity appeared in a politicized form in the 19th and 20th centuries with the idea of *Bhārat Mātā ('Mother India'), the subcontinent conceived as a goddess. Such conceptions continue to be derived from, and reinforce, the claim that Devī is *the* pan-Indian deity. *See also* TANTRA. **2.** Feminine form of *deva in the **Ṛg Veda*, and a generic term for any female deity.

Devībhāgavata Purāṇa Traditionally classified as one of the **upapurāṇas* (Minor **Purāṇas*), it celebrates *Devī as the highest independent principle in the universe (*nirguṇa brahman), and recounts various myths associated with her. Composed by a *brahmin, possibly in *Vārāṇasī in the 13th or 14th century CE, it reinterprets much earlier Purāṇic material for the glorification of the Goddess, and appears, in part, to be an imitation of the **Bhāgavata Purāṇa*, with Devī replacing *Kṛṣṇa as the object of *bhakti. From its own perspective, however, it is the 'real' *Bhāgavata Purāṇa*, and so replaces the latter as a **Mahāpurāṇa*.

Devī Mahātmya **(*Durgāsaptaśatī*, *Durgāpāṭha*, *Caṇḍīpāṭha*)** ('The Glorification of the Goddess') The earliest and best-known *Sanskrit text consistently glorifying *Devī as the supreme and autonomous creator, preserver, and destroyer of the universe. Probably composed in the 6th century CE, the *Devī Mahātmya* was a thirteen-chapter addition (Chs. 81–93) to the (*c.*4th-century CE) **Mārkaṇḍeya Purāṇa*, although its significance as a source for the mythology, theology, and ritual culture associated with the Goddess has resulted in it being treated, like the **Bhagavadgītā* in the **Mahābhārata*, as a textual authority in its own right.

Within a framing story, the *Devī Mahātmya* treats of three episodes displaying the Goddess's saving power in relation to other deities and the universe at large, and therefore, by extension, her power to save her devotees. In the first, she is depicted as the force underlying the universe, which enables *Viṣṇu to defeat Madhu and Kaiṭabha, threatening demons who have emerged from the dirt or wax in his ear. The Goddess is characterized as *Yoganidrā ('sleep of yoga'); only when she agrees, at *Brahmā's request, to leave Viṣṇu's body can he awake from his absorption, prior to creation. The story is therefore also related to cosmogonic power. In the second episode, the Goddess, in the founding version of what comes to be her best known myth, is brought into being by the fused lustre (*tejas) of all the gods, including *Śiva and *Viṣṇu, in order to rid them of the demon Mahiṣa (*Mahiṣāsura), who has appropriated their powers. Kitted out by the gods with weapons, ornaments, and a lion mount, the beautiful Goddess lays waste Mahiṣa's armies, and then confronts Mahiṣa himself, who has now taken the form of a buffalo. In an incident that subsequently became a favourite subject for sculptors and painters, the Goddess, riding her lion, fells the buffalo, plants her foot on its neck, and decapitates the demon as he emerges from its body. So the gods and the world are saved, and the Goddess duly praised by the gods for accomplishing something they could not. In the third episode, the Goddess is again called upon to save the world from the demon brothers, Śumbha and Niśumbha. A variety of different goddesses appear, including *Pārvatī, *Ambikā, *Kālī, and *Cāmuṇḍā; these are shown to be essentially one with each other and identical with Devī. In a similar fashion, the 'seven mothers' (*saptamātṛkās) emerge as *śaktis from the bodies of seven gods during the battle, and are eventually absorbed into the body of the victorious Goddess. The episode ends with the gods addressing a *bhakti infused hymn of praise, the *Nārāyaṇī Stuti*, to the Goddess, in which, in spite of her many names, she is represented as being the singular and all-powerful creator, preserver, and destroyer of the universe, and the liberator of her devotees.

The *Devī Mahātmya*'s popularity is largely attributable to its recitation, as a vehicle of bhakti and a means of wish fulfilment, in a wide variety of ritual contexts, especially those involving an *animal sacrifice. The most notable occasion of this kind is the autumn *Navarātrī or *Durgā-pūjā (in Bengal), when the text is recited on each of the nine days of the *festival for the benefit of both listeners and reciters.

Devīśatakam *See* ĀNANDAVARDHANA.

devotion *See* BHAKTI.

Dev Samāj (Divine Society) An organization formed in 1887 by Pandit Shiv Narayan *Agnihotri after his split from the *Brāhmo Samāj. Rejecting Brahmo rationalism, he taught that only he, as

d

*guru and enlightened being, could show the way to eternal bliss, and by 1895 he had made himself the sole object of worship for the educated, high-*caste Punjabis who made up his following. Worship of Agnihotri was combined with a strict ethical code (which required, inter alia, *vegetarianism) and a radical social programme, including the lifting of all *caste restrictions, a ban on *child marriage, and the promotion of women's education and rights, including *widow remarriage. In the 1920s the Samāj had over 3 500 members, but, although remaining active in educational work, the organization has declined since Agnihotri's death in 1929.

dhāma ('dwelling place') A specific location thought to be infused with the light of divine power. There are four of these (H.: cār dhām—'four dwelling places') in the subcontinent, located at the cardinal points of the compass: *Badrīnāth in the North, sacred to *Viṣṇu as *Nara-Nārayaṇa, *Purī in the East, sacred to *Kṛṣṇa as *Jagannātha, *Rāmeśvaram in the South, sacred to *Rāma, and *Dvārakā in the West, Kṛṣṇa's capital city. Individually and collectively, as well as microcosmically in *Vārāṇasī, they are major *pilgrimage sites. A smaller network, also referred to as cār dhām, is the *Himālayan grouping of Badrīnāth, *Kedārnāth, *Gaṅgotrī, and *Yamunotrī.

Dhanaṃjaya ('wealth winner') A name of *Arjuna.

Dhaṇṇā (*c.*15th century CE) A medieval *bhakti saint from Rajasthan who belonged to the Jāṭ (peasant-farmer) *caste. Three of his hymns are included in the *Sikh sacred book, the **Ādi Granth*.

Dhanurveda ('science of archery') A treatise on warfare and archery, traditionally regarded as an **Upaveda* attached to the **Yajur Veda*, and attributed either to *Bhṛgu or *Viśvāmitra. More widely, the knowledge of martial arts.

Dhanvantari The *Vedic gods' physician and the bearer of *amṛta at the *Churning of the Ocean. According to the **Purāṇas*, he was the originator of *Āyurveda (classical Indian medicine).

dhāraṇā ('concentration') The sixth limb of *Patañjali's *aṣṭāṅga-yoga ('eight-limbed yoga'), as outlined in his **Yoga Sūtra* (2.28–55; 3.1–8). There, and elsewhere, the term designates the discipline of concentrating the mind on a single object and continuously returning to it in the attempt to achieve one-pointedness (*ekāgratā). The object of attention may be material, verbal, or a mental. For *bhaktas it usually takes the form of a visualized deity.

Dharma The personification of *dharma as a god. In the **Mahābhārata*, he is the father of *Yudhiṣṭhira.

dharma A polysemic term, the more precise meanings of which depend upon the context in which it is used. Less precise meanings range from 'truth' and 'order' (both cosmic and social), to 'law' (both universal and particular), 'teaching', 'duty', 'virtuous behaviour', and 'religion'. The term first appears in the **Ṛg Veda*, referring to those (predominantly ritual) actions and laws (dharmas) that maintain *ṛta, the inherent active power, or truth, which informs and orders the universe and human society. (The *Mīmāṃsaka ritualists systematized this view: for them *dharma and **Veda* are synonymous; moreover, the sole means of knowing dharma is through the ritual injunctions—the prescribed ritual actions or *vidhis.) Subsuming ṛta, dharma subsequently becomes synonymous with the underlying order itself, as well as with the activities—prototypically, sacrifice (*yajña)—which express and maintain it. The concept has therefore been characterized as being both descriptive—it designates the way things are (ideally), and prescriptive—it specifies the way things should be. It is dharma in the latter sense—the maintenance of what, at one and the same time, is both the cosmic and the social order—which becomes the prime concern of the *Brahmanical dharma literature. In other words, if the responsibility of the *brahmins is to (re)-create universal order in the sacrifice, then what that order should look like in terms of both the individual, and an increasingly complex society, also needs to be delineated. Taking their cue from the sacrificial ordering of society into a hierarchy of classes (*varṇa) (evoked, for example, in the **Puruṣasūkta*), the **Dharmasūtras* were concerned to explicate the ritual, moral, and social question of how people should conduct themselves in relation to varṇa and *āśrama ('stage of life') in the light of *Vedic injunction and customary practice. These and other concerns were taken up in an expanded form in the **Dharmaśāstra* literature, which addressed such topics as *ācāras ('rules of conduct')—the orthodox, and therefore 'correct', performance of social and ritual duties (including *saṃskāras) in the light of *varṇāśramadharma; *prāyascittas—reparations for infringements of dharma; and *vyavahāra—the civil and criminal law through which *kings should administer their justice, the king being dharma's instrument on earth. At its widest, dharma in this context therefore refers to the rules governing any traditional occupation or social role (e.g. *strīdharma ('women's dharma')) in the light of Brahmanical precept.

Another way of expressing this Brahmanical obligation to conform to certain predefined patterns of behaviour (dharma) was to cast it in terms of an individual's 'inherent duty' or *svadharma. In the *Bhagavadgītā*, it is the negative consequences of failing to comply with one's svadharma that are stressed, even when following it is perceived as bringing one into conflict with other values (such as *ahiṃsā). In an explicit rejection of the institution of *renunciation, *Kṛṣṇa tells *Arjuna: 'It is better to practise your own inherent duty (svadharma) deficiently than another's duty well. It is better to die conforming to your own duty; the duty of others invites danger' (3.35). In other words, contravening svadharma—in this case, the *kṣatriya's obligation to fight, or more widely the king's obligation to maintain the dharma of his kingdom through force—engenders the imbalance and disorder which characterize dharma's opposite, *adharma. And yet, at the same time, Kṛṣṇa shows the warrior how, through an internalization of renouncer mores, he can achieve the soteriological goal of the renouncer even while conforming to his prescribed svadharma.

Universal ethical principles (such as ahiṃsā, truthfulness, control of the senses), as opposed to the particularized *ethics of varṇāśramadharma, begin as alternatives to the latter in the shared codes of conduct common to members of particular renouncer groups. Such principles are, however, incorporated into *Dharmaśāstra* as adjuncts to the dharma of 'class' and 'stage of life', and themselves classified as 'common' or *sādhāraṇa dharma, i.e. dharma common to all people regardless of varṇa, āśrama, or gender. It is precisely this juxtaposition (particularly of sacrificial and martial violence with ahiṃsā) which creates the internal tension in a tradition striving to reconcile itself to dharma in both these senses.

Although the *Bhagavadgītā* developed its own, 'best of both worlds' compromise, in the **Mahābhārata* in general, dharma is represented as being in perpetual crisis at all levels—individual, social, and cosmic. This is evoked through dramatizations of the tension which exists between those newly or partially assimilated values and practices, such as ahiṃsā and *yoga, with their goal of *mokṣa, and the older, svadharmic values, rooted in a ritually ordered society and cosmos, designed to secure good things in both this life and the next. Nowhere is this tension more evident than in the perpetual agonizing which afflicts the person responsible for maintaining the dharma of the realm, *Yudhiṣṭhira, the 'King of Dharma', himself. The developed āśrama and *puruṣārtha schemes—the latter including both dharma and mokṣa among the four legitimate 'aims of human life'—were further attempts from within Brahmanical orthodoxy to resolve this ambiguity or paradox in a system striving to incorporate both svadharmic and renouncer values.

At the same time, the *Epics, in so far as they reflect and embody the rise of devotional religion (*bhakti), foreshadow a different solution, since, in a monotheistic context, dharma and the will of the omniscient, omnipotent deity are necessarily conflated. (Although received understandings of dharma and God's will may by no means coincide.) For bhaktas, therefore, the theoretical problem of apparently antithetical dharmic values is to some extent resolved, or perhaps simply subsumed in the actions of the great gods, and their *avatāras, such as Kṛṣṇa and *Rāma. Similarly, *Purāṇic cosmology envisions dharma as subject to cyclical fluctuations of decay and renaissance, synchronized to the appearance of *avatāras, and the creative and destructive powers of the great monotheistic deities. At an individual level, devotion to God, therefore cuts across dharmic considerations, nowhere more clearly than in the antinomian poetry of many of the medieval *sants.

Dharma has, however, remained a potent and multivalent concept, not just for Brahmanical orthodoxy, but also, in the modern period, as a badge of the eternal and universal truth (*sanātana dharma) which, for *Neo-Hindu reformers, underwrites the Hindu tradition. *See also* ETHICS; KINGSHIP.

Dharmakṣetra ('field of dharma') Referred to in the opening *Sanskrit words of the **Bhagavadgītā*, where it is used synonymously with *Kurukṣetra, the '*Kuru field' on which the **Mahābhārata* war is to be fought.

Dharmanibandhas Medieval compendia of Hindu *dharma, dealing, inter alia, with ritual 'law' and *saṃskāras (life-cycle rituals).

Dharmarāja ('King of Dharma', 'Just King') **1.** An epithet of *kings, especially of *Yama, the king of the *dead, and *Yudhiṣṭhira, the son of *Dharma. More generally, it may be applied to any embodiment of kingly perfection. **2.** (17th century CE). A much studied *Advaitin commentator whose *Vedāntaparibhāṣā* includes a summary of Advaita approaches to ontology and epistemology, including the *pramāṇas.

Dharma Sabhā An orthodox association formed in 1830 by Rādhākānta *Deb and others to oppose legislation against *satī (*sahamaraṇa), and generally to counter the changes to Hindu ritual practice proposed by reformers such as Rām Mohan *Roy.

dharmaśālā A rest house for travellers and *pilgrims, often distributing alms in the form of *food and shelter, and endowed by the well-off as an act of *merit.

Dharmaśāstra ('treatise on the Law', 'Law code', 'science of dharma') In the widest sense, the term designates not just the literature treated below, but also the **Dharmasūtras*, and the later commentaries and digests. However, it is most usually applied as the collective name given to a voluminous category of verse literature dealing with *Brahmanical dharma. Classified as *smṛti, *Dharmaśāstra* addresses such topics as *ācāras ('rules of conduct')—the orthodox, and therefore 'correct', performance of social and ritual duties (including *saṃskāras—life-cycle rituals) in the light of *varṇāśramadharma, especially as it applies to the behaviour of *brahmins; *prāyascittas—reparations for infringements of dharma; and *vyavahāra—the civil and criminal law through which *kings should administer their justice. The foundation text of this genre, and the direct source of much of the later *Dharmaśāstra* literature, is the **Manusmṛti* or *Mānava Dharmaśāstra* ('The Law Code of Manu'), whose authority had been established by around the 4th century CE. Another prominent, and more systematic dharma text from this period is the **Yājñavalkyasmṛti*. From about the 9th century CE onwards, the influence of *Dharmaśāstra* literature was expanded through commentaries (particularly on *Manu* and *Yājñavalkya*), and increasingly through the compilation of systematic **Nibandhas* or 'digests' of dharma from a wide variety of sources. The latter were the main source of the Indian legal system devised by the British in the 18th century; but whether *Dharmaśāstra* is supposed to be prescriptive in a literal sense, or the expression of an ideal, remains a matter of debate. A valuable modern digest for scholars is P. V. *Kane's five volume *History of Dharmaśāstra* (1930–62). *See also* DHARMASŪTRAS.

Dharmasūtras ('aphorisms on the Law') The collective name for the four extant works of this type: the **Āpastamba*, **Gautama*, **Baudhāyana*, and **Vasiṣṭha Dharmasūtras*, probably composed between the 3rd and 1st centuries BCE. Classified as belonging to the **Kalpasūtra* literature of the **Vedāṅga* (and therefore as *smṛti), these are the sole survivors of what was once a much larger body of largely prose work from this period dealing with *dharma—in this context, less the question of civil law (although this is touched on) than the ritual, moral, and social questions of how people should conduct themselves in relation to *varṇa and *āśrama in the light of *Vedic injunction and customary practice. These and other concerns were taken up in an expanded form in the **Dharmaśāstra* literature, to which, in the widest sense, the *Dharmasūtras* belong.

dharmic Anglicized adjective: in accordance with or derived from *dharma.

dhātuvāda *See* ALCHEMY.

dhenu A milch *cow; or its substitute, offered as part of the fee (*dakṣinā) to *brahmin *śrauta ritualists.

Dhenuka A demon in the form of an ass, killed by *Kṛṣṇa's elder brother, *Balarāma, after a dispute in a palm grove, according to *Purāṇic mythology.

Dhṛṣṭadyumna In the **Mahābhārata* the brother of *Draupadī, who after the death of his father *Drupada at the hands of *Droṇa, becomes the king of the *Pāñcālas, and their commander in the war against the *Kauravas. He revenges himself on Droṇa and is, in his turn, trampled to death in a demeaning way by Droṇa's son, *Aśvatthāman. *See also* MAHĀBHĀRATA.

Dhṛṣṭaketu Son of *Śiśupāla, and an ally of the *Pāṇḍavas during the *Mahābhārata* war.

Dhṛtarāṣṭra ('who holds the kingdom firmly') In the **Mahābhārata* the name of the blind *Kuru *king who, although disqualified by his infirmity, has to take the throne after the death of his brother, *Pāṇḍu. Husband of *Gāndhārī, and father of the *Kauravas, Dhṛtarāṣṭra reluctantly presides over the events leading to the war with his brother's sons, the *Pāṇḍavas. In a passage that includes the **Bhagavadgītā*, his driver, *Saṃjaya, relates the course of the battle to him. Dhṛtarāṣṭra was born blind as a result of his mother, *Ambikā, closing her eyes during intercourse with his father,

Kṛṣṇa Dvaipāyana *Vyāsa. *See also* MAHĀBHĀRATA.

Dhruva ('fixed', 'constant') The pole star, which, according to *Vaiṣṇava mythology, was raised there by *Viṣṇu as a reward for the *ṛṣi Dhruva's great austerities.

dhvaja ('flag', 'banner') The banner on which the emblem of a hero, or the mount of a deity, is represented. (*Arjuna is described in the **Mahābhārata* as kapidhvaja, 'ape-bannered'.) It is counted as one of the 'eight auspicious objects' (*aṣṭamaṅgalas). In *temples—especially *Śaiva temples—the banner may be mounted on a flag pole, or dhvaja-sthambha, opposite the entrance to the main shrine.

dhvani ('articulate', 'audible', 'material sound') According to *Bhartṛhari (who also refers to it as *nāda), dhvani is the articulate sound that is a derivative or manifestation of inner speech (*sphoṭa). This distinction between sound, or reverberation, and essential meaning is taken up in *Sanskrit poetic (*rasa) theory, which analyses and champions the poet's use of dhvani ('resonance' or 'suggestion') as the means by which emotions are evoked in the listener.

Dhvanyāloka *See* ĀNANDAVARDHANA.

dhyāna ('meditation') A general term for *meditation across a variety of Hindu traditions. More specifically, one of the *aṣṭāṅgas, the eight limbs of (or aids to) *yoga, according to the classical, or *Rāja Yoga system expounded in *Patañjali's **Yoga Sūtra* (2.29). Along with *dhāraṇā (concentration) and *samādhi (absorbed concentration), dhyāna is considered one of the more advanced, inner limbs. It represents a state of mind characterized by total and immersive concentration on, and insight into, the nature of the object of meditation, to the exclusion of all other objects or ideas (*Yoga Sūtra* 3.2).

diaspora (Gk. for 'dispersion') A term sometimes used in Western works to refer to Hindu populations outside the traditional homelands of India and *Nepal, numbering between 20 and perhaps 30 million (approximately 2.3–3.5% of the total Hindu population). The largest concentrations (in very approximate figures) are in Bangladesh (15 000 000; 12% of the total population), Indonesia (7 250 000; 3.4%), Sri Lanka (2 000 000; 15%), Pakistan (2 000 000; 1.3%), Malaysia (1 630 000; 9%), USA (1 032 000; 0.3%), South Africa (800 000; 1.5%), Myanmar (890 000; 0.5%). In 2001, the UK had a Hindu population of 559 000 (0.9%).

Digambara ('sky-clad') The name given to one of the two major *Jaina sects, so-called because their *ascetics go naked. *See also* ŚVETĀMBARA.

digvijaya ('the conquest of the quarters/regions') A term for the conquest of the whole earth—the heroic and idealized aspiration of ancient Indian *kings. By extension, the defeat of all opponents in, for example, religious debate.

Digvijayaparvan A subsection of the **Sabhāparvan* of the *Sanskrit **Mahābhārata*.

dik (space) One of the four non-material substances (*dravyas) according to the *Nyāya-*Vaiśeṣika systems of philosophy.

dikpāla *See* AṢṬADIKPĀLA.

dīkṣā ('consecration', 'initiation') A consecration undergone by an individual that both marks and facilitates the passage from one state of being, or stage of life, to another. Underlying this is the understanding that the 'one who has been ordained' (the dīkṣita) has been reborn through the generation of a new body. The paradigmatic dīkṣa is that of the *yajamāna (the *śrauta sacrificer) in the *Vedic *agniṣṭoma ritual—an initiation that enables the dīkṣita to be transported, for the duration of the rite, to the world of the gods. From an early date in *Vedic history the most crucial dīkṣa was that of *upanayana, a *saṃskāra ('rite of passage' or 'transformative ritual') through which a young male, born into one of the upper three *varṇas, was initiated, and thus 'reborn', into both the *Veda* and *Āryan society. In this way a permanent change was effected in both his ritual and social status. In a wider sense, formal entry into any religious order or *sampradāya usually requires dīkṣā by a *guru. This may take a wide variety of forms, but typically involves the transmission of *mantras from teacher to pupil. In a similar fashion to Vedic dīkṣā, this kind of initiation acts as a saṃskāra on the initiate, equipping and qualifying them for their new life. As is the case in some forms of *Śaivism, the act of initiation itself may be thought to engender or guarantee *liberation.

Dīkṣitas (Tam.: **Tīṭcitars/Tīkṣitars)** The name given to the two hundred hereditary priests who own and operate the *Śaiva temple complex at *Cidambaram in Tamil Nadu. Said to be descended from *brahmin migrants from North India, they conduct the elaborate daily *pūjās and an extensive calendar of *festivals according to *Vedic rather than, for Śaivas, the more usual *Tantric rites. They are assisted in this by five families of *Aiyar *smārta brahmins.

Dīpāvalī *See* DIVĀLĪ.

Dīrghatapas *See* GAUTAMA.

Diti ('bounded') *Vedic goddess of the earth. The sister and antithesis of *Aditi. In *Purāṇic mythology, the wife of *Kāśyapa and mother of the *daityas (the Vedic *asuras); she is also—inadvertently—the mother of the *Maruts.

Divālī (Dīpāvalī) ('row of lamps') A major pan-Indian *festival celebrated around the day of the new moon in October–November (bridging the months of *Āśvina and *Kārttika), lasting from two to five days. Its name is derived from the characteristic lighting of rows of small oil lamps, placed in houses, *temples, and on *rivers to dispel the darkness on the night preceding the new moon. Various rationales are given for this practice, and there are numerous regional variations, but the general theme is one of renewal, and it may have begun as a fertility festival at the end of the rainy season. The festival, especially the lighting of the lamps itself, is now most widely connected with the return of *Rāma and *Sītā to *Ayodhyā at the end of their exile, and thus the restoration of divine order and light over demonic disorder and darkness. It is also closely associated with *Lakṣmī, the *auspicious goddess of wealth, good fortune, and household prosperity, especially amongst the traders and business people of western India, for whom the festival marks the beginning of the new financial year. In modern India, Divālī is a major commercial festival as well, accompanied by the exchange of gifts and ubiquitous firework displays.

Divine Life Society Established in 1936 to propagate the teachings of it founder, Swami *Śivānanda, the Divine Life Society has its headquarters at the Śivānanda Āśram in Rishikesh (*Hṛṣīkeśa), which now oversees a good number of other branches both in India and abroad (notably in Canada). The current president is Swami *Cidānanda, who took over on the death of his mentor in 1963.

Divine Light Mission (Elan Vital) A new religious movement, founded in the 1960s by Shri Hans Ji Maharaj, and derived in part from the syncretic Hindu-Sikh *sant tradition. The spiritual leadership of the movement passed to Ji Maharaj's youngest son, Guru Maharaj Ji in 1966, when he was eight years old. In the early 1970s he moved to the US, where he attracted a substantial following, propagating the 'Knowledge', a form of primordial energy, which was to be obtained through four types of *meditation designed to realize the inner divinity of the individual. His followers, known as 'premies', established a network of *āśrams, both in the US and around the world, but the movement went into decline and lost most of its Indian religious dimension after Maharaj married one of the premies. This caused his mother to return to India with many of the Indian teachers of the 'Knowledge'. In 1983 Maharaj Ji reconstituted the movement as 'Elan Vital', and subsequently changed his name to Maharaji.

Divya Prabandham *See* ĀḺVĀRS; NĀTHMUNI.

domestic fire *See* GṚHYĀGNI.

domestic rites/sacrifices *See* GṚHYA-YAJÑA(S).

doṣa ('fault', 'taint', 'sin') **1.** A word applied to the source of misfortune or *inauspiciousness (often an impersonal force), as well as to the effect it produces in terms of physical, mental, ritual, and moral defects. *See also* AUSPICIOUS(NESS) AND INAUSPICIOUS(NESS). **2.** The humours (wind, bile, phlegm) according to *Āyurveda.

Draupadeyas *See* DRAUPADĪ.

Draupadī (Kṛṣṇā) A major figure in the **Mahābhārata*; an incarnation of the goddess *Śrī, the daughter of the *Pāñcāla king, *Drupada, sister of *Dhṛṣṭadyumna, and wife of the five *Pāṇḍava brothers. A contest (*svayaṃvara) is held to determine whom she will marry. All the Pāṇḍavas fall in her love with her, but it is *Arjuna who wins the contest. Returning to the forest with his bride, Arjuna calls out to his mother: 'see what we have found!' Thinking he is simply referring to alms, she replies without looking: 'share it together!' As a result of this, and of the need for *Yudhiṣṭhira as the eldest to marry first, Draupadī (in a rare instance of polyandry in the *Sanskritic tradition) becomes the wife of all five brothers. She has a son by each of them (known collectively as the Draupadeyas). In the rigged dicing match with Śakuni, *Yudhiṣṭhira eventually stakes, and loses, Draupadī. In the ensuing dispute, she is humiliated by the *Kauravas—the general inspiration for Pāṇḍava acts of vengeance in the war to come—but manages to secure her husbands' release. Subsequently, she follows them into their twelve-year exile in the forest where, among other adventures, she is abducted by *Jayadratha, the king of Sindh, and then rescued by *Bhīma and Arjuna. In the Pāṇḍavas' thirteenth year of exile in disguise, Draupadī is again the subject of unwelcome attentions, this time from Kīcaka, one of Virāṭa's generals, who, for his pains, is killed by Bhīma. Later, in the preparations for the war, Draupadī reminds *Kṛṣṇa, who is acting as a potential peacemaker, of her humiliation at the hands of the Kauravas, and demands war. At the conclusion of the ensuing battle, Draupadī's sons, the Draupadeyas are killed by *Aśvatthāman. Draupadī begins a fast to the *death, which she will end only if Aśvatthāman is found and killed. After his defeat, she accepts the jewel he wears on his head in lieu of his death. Much later, at the conclusion of the *Epic, Draupadī accompanies her husbands in their renunciation of the world, and dies in the attempt to ascend Mount *Meru. She is subsequently reunited with them in *heaven. Symbolizing, at one level, the Earth, Draupadī has been depicted as both the cause of the war and its greatest victim.

Draupadī is worshipped both as a pan-Indian goddess and, in a transposition of the *Mahābhārata* into a localized idiom, in the Draupadī *temple cult, which is concentrated in the *village traditions of Northeastern Tamil Nadu.

Drāviḍa *Sanskritic name, possibly derived from the word '*Tamil', for the speakers of the non-*Indo-European languages of South India, and by extension for their culture, including their architectural style.

Dravidian Adjective, derived from *Drāviḍa, applied to the languages and cultural forms associated with the peoples of South India, principally the inhabitants of Tamil Nadu (dominant language: *Tamil), Andhra Pradesh (Telugu), Karnataka (Kannada), and Kerala (Malayalam). It is deduced by linguists that classical (and so modern) Dravidian languages originated from an ancient, less differentiated tongue, no longer extant, referred to as Proto-Dravidian. Some scholars have argued that the undeciphered *Indus valley seals are in a Dravidian language. If true, this would lend force to the suggestion that the earlier inhabitants of the Indian subcontinent were driven south, or absorbed into the newly arrived *Vedic *Sanskrit- (and therefore *Indo-European-) speaking *Āryan population. Whatever the original position, what is now designated 'Hinduism' is, at its most inclusive, the result of a complex amalgam of, and interplay between, Dravidian- and Āryan-derived cultures.

dravya ('substance') Used technically in the *Nyāya-*Vaiśeṣika systems of philosophy to designate the underlying substances in which qualities (*guṇas), characteristics, and actions (*karma) inhere, and which are a prerequisite for any change to occur. They are divided between the five material or atomic substances (*bhūtas)—earth, water, fire, air, and ether (*ākāśa)—and the four non-material substances—time (*kāla), space (*dik), soul (*ātman), and mind (*manas).

Droṇa A protagonist in several key episodes in the first half of the *Mahābhārata*. A great *brahmin warrior (the son of the *ṛṣi *Bharadvāja), Droṇa is the teacher of both the *Kauravas and the *Pāṇḍavas, including his great favourite, *Arjuna. In the war, Droṇa fights on the Kaurava side, and succeeds *Bhīṣma as the commander of their army. By his own account he can only be defeated if tricked. This comes about when he is told by *Yudhiṣṭhira that 'Aśvatthāman', his son, is dead, although this 'Aśvatthāman' is in fact an elephant. Believing Yudhiṣṭhira, a renowned man of truth, Droṇa allows himself to die in a *yogic pose, and is subsequently beheaded by *Drupada's son, *Dhṛṣṭadyumna, in revenge for Droṇa's killing of his father. The real *Aśvatthāman swears to destroy both the *Pāñcālas and the Pāṇḍavas for these *adharmic acts.

Droṇaparvan ('The Book of Droṇa') The seventh book of the *Sanskrit **Mahābhārata*, recounting the events leading to the death of *Droṇa after his succession to the command of the *Kaurava army. It also includes descriptions of the deaths of *Abhimanyu and *Jayadratha, and the killing of Ghaṭotkaca—a gigantic *rākṣasa son of *Bhīma—by *Karṇa.

Dṛṣadvatī A North Indian river, of uncertain identity, apparently flowing into the *Sarasvatī. According to **Manusmṛti* (2.23), the area between the two rivers is the *brahmāvarta ('the land of the **Veda*').

Drupada **(Yājñasena)** In the **Mahābhārata* the king of the *Pāñcālas; father of *Draupadi, *Dhṛṣtadyumna, *Śikhaṇḍin, and others; the sworn enemy of *Droṇa, who kills him during the battle.

Dubois, Abbé J. A. (1770–1848) Author of a celebrated early *Orientalist work on India, based on personal observation: *Hindu Manners, Customs and Ceremonies* (1st pub. East India Company, 1816; and multiple reprints).

duḥkha ('suffering', 'the unsatisfactory nature of life', 'the corollary of impermanence') An existential given for *Sāṃkhya-Yoga and other systems intent on providing the individual with a path to freedom from duḥkha and its effects. Analysis of the nature of duḥkha is a major element in *Buddhist discourse.

Duḥṣanta *See* DUṢYANTA.

Duḥśāsana In the *Sanskrit **Mahābhārata*, a brother of *Duryodhana. Because of his role in the humiliation of *Draupadī after the rigged dicing match, *Bhīma vows to drink his blood—a vow fulfilled towards the end of the war.

Dumézil, Georges (1898–1986) An influential French scholar of comparative philology and mythology, who developed the theory of a tripartite division underlying *Indo-European thought and social structures, in which the functions of particular deities correspond to the three major divisions of society—i) priests and rulers, ii) warriors, and iii) producers. His work was comparative and thematic in method, and much of his analysis was derived from Indian materials, particularly the **Mahābhārata*. His writings continue to be influential, if controversial, in some areas of Western *Indology, especially in *Epic and mythological studies, and in discussions of the origins of the *varṇa system.

Dumont, Louis (1911–1998) A French anthropologist, the appearance of whose essay, 'World Renunciation in Indian Religions' (1959; English trans. 1960), followed by his monumental study of the Indian *caste system, *Homo hierarchicus: essai sur le système des castes* (1966; English trans. 1970), provided two landmarks in modern *Indology. The claims of the latter, in particular, continue to be fiercely debated. Based on extensive fieldwork, *Homo hierarchicus* demonstrates that the ordering principle, or ideology, underlying caste hierarchy is the religious or ritual opposition of the *pure and the *impure, giving rise to a nexus of interlocking and complementary group relations. Controversially, he sees this holistic, socially coherent, and inegalitarian caste society as being a necessary complement to Western individualism and the ideology of equality.

durbar *See* DARBĀR.

Durgā (Ambikā, Ghaṇṭī) ('difficult of access', 'unattainable') A name given to the most prominent, fierce form of *Devī, especially in her role as the warrior goddess who destroys the buffalo demon, *Mahiṣāsura (hence the epithet Mahiṣāsuramardiṇī, 'crusher of the buffalo demon [Mahiṣa]'), although the two names—Durgā and Devī—are often used interchangeably. Durgā's defeat of the buffalo demon has its textual origin in the **Devī Mahātmya*, and its most notable ritual celebration in the annual Bengali *Durgā Pūjā *festival. In her most violent form, Durgā is often thought to be identical with *Kālī. See also AMBIKĀ; BHĀRAT MĀTA; CĀMUṆḌĀ; CAṆḌĪ; DEVĪ; DEVĪ MAHĀTMYA; KĀLĪ.

Durgā

Durgā Pūjā ('worship of Durgā', 'Durgā's festival') The name by which the pan-Indian autumnal *festival of *Navarātri (*Dasara) is known in Bengal, culminating in the blood sacrifices made to the goddess Durgā in her guise as the destroyer of the buffalo demon, *Mahiṣāsura. Central to the goddess's worship, in

Kolkata (Calcutta) and beyond, is the fashioning of her image in unbaked clay, and the creation of many thousands of individual and community tableaux, celebrating both her return to her parental home and her defeat of *evil and chaos. Worshipped for nine days, on the tenth day (*Dasara or Dashami), such images or tableaux are then immersed in the *river or the sea. This is followed (at least in the major temples) by various animal sacrifices, principally of goats, sheep, fowl, and, in rare instances these days (following a government attempt to proscribe the practice), actual buffalo. The specific purpose is to satisfy the fierce Goddess with the blood she requires; more widely the intention is to replicate the decapitation of the demon in a creative act of destruction, and where a local ruler is involved to reinforce his power and authority by association with the Goddess.

Durgā Saptaśati ('Seven Hundred Verses about Durgā') *See* DEVĪ MAHĀTMYA.

Durvāsas ('the badly dressed') A legendary brahmin *ṛṣi, the son of *Atri and Anasūyā, notorious in *Purāṇic and *Epic myth for his short temper. The best known episodes involving him include his cursing of *Indra, which leads indirectly to the *Churning of the Ocean; in the **Mahabhārata*, his angry prediction of *Kṛṣṇa's death, and his gift of a god-summoning *mantra to *Kuntī; and in *Kālidāsa's **Abhijñānaśakuntalam* his cursing of *Śakuntalā, who has inadvertently kept him waiting. He is thought to be an incarnation of *Śiva.

Duryodhana ('difficult to conquer') In the **Mahābhārata*, the eldest son of *Dhṛtarāṣṭra and *Gāndhārī, and the leader of the *Kaurava faction in the struggle against the *Pāṇḍavas. He is also said to be born from a portion of the *asura *Kali (Discord), living up to this parentage in his persistent attempts to prevent his Pāṇḍava cousin, *Yudhiṣṭhira, coming to the throne. It is Duryodhana who is instrumental in the rigged dicing match that brings about the Pāṇḍavas' twelve years of exile in the forest. At the end of the subsequent war, he has his thighs broken by *Bhīma, yet lives long enough to rejoice in *Aśvatthāman's massacre of the sleeping *Pāñcālas and Pāṇḍavas, and ascends to *heaven declaring his adherence to *kṣatriya *dharma. At the end of the *Epic, Duryodhana, enthroned and radiating splendour, is the first person Yudhiṣṭhira sees on entering *heaven. *See also* MAHĀBHĀRATA.

Dusse(h)ra *See* DASARA.

Duṣyanta (Duḥṣanta) The husband of *Śakuntalā and father of *Bharata according to the **Mahābhārata* and *Kālidasa's **Abhijñānaśākuntalam*.

Dvaitādvaita ('dualistic non-dualism', 'dualism and non-dualism') One of the four major *Vaiṣṇava *sampradāyas, a theistic school of *Vedānta, founded by *Nimbārka in the 11th or 12th century CE. Its teaching is also sometimes characterized as propounding *bhedābheda ('identity in difference') and is similar in some respects to *Rāmānuja's *Viśiṣṭādvaita. Like Rāmānuja, Nimbārka recognizes three principles: the sentient or spiritual (cit; also known as bhoktṛ—the enjoyer), the non-sentient or non-spiritual (acit; also known as bhogya—the object of enjoyment), and *Īśvara or *Brahman. These three are related neither though their difference (bheda) from each other nor their identity (abheda); instead, they are conceived of as real entities naturally existing in a state of equilibrium between the opposing poles of difference and identity. Nevertheless, for Nimbārka, the other two principles are not, as they are for Rāmānuja, attributes of Īśvara, although they are inseparable from him. Since, for the

Nimbārka tradition, Īśvara or Brahman is indistinguishable from the personal God, *Kṛṣṇa, *liberation can only be achieved by following the path of total surrender (*prapatti) to the latter, or, according to some texts, his representative (i.e. the devotee's *guru). *See also* NIMBĀRKA.

Dvaita Vedānta ('Brahmasampradāya' (N. India)) ('Dualistic Vedānta') One of the four major *Vaiṣṇava *sampradāyas, a theistic school of *Vedānta founded by *Madhva. It is dualistic in so far as it maintains, in contrast to *Śaṅkara's *Advaita Vedānta and *Rāmānuja's *Viśiṣṭādvaita, an absolute and irreducible distinction between the world and *Brahman, its creator and Lord (equated with *Viṣṇu by Madhva). Madhva develops this further by positing a fundamental distinction—five differences, or pañcabheda—between Brahman and individual selves (*cit or *jīvas), Brahman and matter, matter and individual selves, individuals and other individuals, and one material object and another. Only Brahman can be regarded as independent (svatantra): all other entities, whether selves or material objects, are dependent upon omniscient, omnipresent, and omnipotent Brahman for their existence. Selves are entrapped in matter because of their actions (*karma); *liberation can only be attained by total devotion (*bhakti) to God. *See also* MADHVA.

dvāpara yuga *See* YUGA.

Dvārakā (Dvarka, Dwarka) ('the gated') A major *pilgrimage site on the Saurāṣṭra peninsula of Gujarat, on the coast of the Arabian Sea. The *temple there is said to be the only surviving remnant of *Kṛṣṇa's capital city (and that of his people, the *Vṛṣṇis, according to the *Mahābhārata*), which was otherwise submerged at his death. The site is regarded as both one of the seven holy *tīrthas and the western representative of the four *dhāmas (dwelling places of the gods). It is also the site of one of the four *Daśanāmi *maṭhas (monasteries) founded, according to tradition, by *Śaṅkara in the 8th century CE.

dvārapāla ('doorkeeper', 'doorguardian') Sculptural representations of powerful and *auspicious figures placed at the entrance to *temples. They often take the form of armed and ferocious warriors, bearing the emblems of the main deity enshrined in the temple.

dvija ('twice-born') **1.** An *Āryan male belonging to one of the three higher *varnas who has been 'born again' through taking *upanayana—initiation into the *Veda* and *Vedic ritual. **2.** A synonym for a *brahmin.

dvīpa ('island', 'continent') *See* COSMOLOGY.

Dwarf *See* VĀMANA.

Dwarka *See* DVĀRAKĀ.

Dyaus ('sky', 'heaven') In the *Vedic hymns, the sky, and so the 'father of light' (i.e. *Sūrya, the sun). He is frequently paired with the earth (*Pṛthivī), as Dyāvāpṛthivī, the parents of the gods. *See* also COSMOLOGY.

Dnyandeo *See* JÑĀNEŚVAR(A).

E

earth (as a goddess) See Pṛthivī.

East India Company Until the British Crown took control in 1858, a trading company with its headquarters in Calcutta (Kolkata), which, from the 17th to the mid 19th century, was the embodiment of British power in India. Its official, but not necessarily its actual policy (one obvious exception being the Governor-General, Lord William *Bentinck) was one of non-interference in Indian social and religious concerns. In reality, the often conflicting views of its employees had a shaping effect on the way in which Hinduism was (re)defined by various 19th-century reformers, such as Rāmmohun *Roy (at one time a Company employee himself), and the members of the *Brāhmo Samāj.

eclipses *See* Rāhu.

Edgerton, Franklin (1885–1963) Salisbury Professor of *Sanskrit and Comparative Philology at Yale University (1926); visiting professor at *Benares Hindu University (1953–4). Edgerton was a linguistic scholar who produced over two hundred works on Indian textual traditions, including a Buddhist Hybrid Sanskrit Grammar and Dictionary. His exceptionally literal translation of the **Bhagavadgītā* is still widely used by Western students of Sanskrit.

egg, cosmic *See* Brahmāṇḍa.

Eggeling, Hans Julius (1842–1918) Prominent 19th-century *Indologist and secretary of the *Royal Asiatic Society, London. He made the first English translation of the **Śatapatha Brāhmana*, published in the **Sacred Books of the East* series (1882–1900), although, like many of his contemporaries, he failed fully to understand or appreciate its contents.

ekadaṇḍi ('bearing one staff') The suborder of *saṃnyāsins within the *Vaiṣṇava *Ekānti tradition to which *Madhva belonged, distinguished by their members carrying one staff rather than the more usual three.

ekāgni ('having one fire') In the *Brahmanical context, the domestic ritualist who performs his sacrifices (*gṛhya-yajñas) on a single fire (*gṛhyāgni) within his own house. *See also* Āhitāgni.

ekāgratā ('one-pointedness') A state of mind, aimed at by those practising *yoga, and achieved through concentration on a single object. *See also* dhāraṇā.

Ekalavya In the **Mahābhārata*, the king of the *Niṣādas. He complies with the request of *Droṇa, his archery teacher, to cut off one of his thumbs, ensuring that he is therafter not as skilful an archer as Droṇa's other favourite pupil, *Arjuna. Later, Ekalavya attacks *Dvārakā, but is eventually killed by his opponent, *Kṛṣṇa.

Ekanātha (Eknāth) (*c.*1548–*c.*1608) A Brahmin *bhakti poet and saint (*sant) in the *Marāṭhā *Vārkarī tradition, who, in a deliberate and locally controversial divergence from the Sanskritic norm, translated the *Sanskrit **Bhāgavata Purāṇa* into Marathi and wrote a commentary on its 11th chapter. In addition, he composed numerous devotional and moralistic verses, as well as longer narrative poems and commentaries, including the first Marathi version of the *Rāmāyaṇa. He was also the first to produce a scholarly edition of *Jñāneśvar's *Jñāneśvarī. There is a *temple dedicated to him in his home town of Paithan, near Aurangabad (Aparānta).

e

Ekānti Vaiṣṇavas A South Indian *Vaiṣṇava monastic *renouncer tradition. *Madhva belonged to its *ekadaṇḍi sub-order.

Ekaśṛṅga ('one-horned') Epithet of *Viṣṇu, probably derived from the single horn attributed to *Matsya, his fish *avatāra. In the *Ahirbudhnya Saṃhitā*, Ekaśṛṅgatanu is listed as number 28 in a list of 39 avatāras of Viṣṇu.

Ekliṅga The name given to *Śiva, as the tutelary divinity of the Rajasthani state of Mewār. He is worshipped in this form at the Ekliṅgji temple near Udaipur.

ekoddiṣṭa *See* ANTYEṢṬI.

Elephanta An island in Mumbai (Bombay) harbour which is the site of a celebrated 6th-century cave *temple dedicated to *Śiva. The temple contains some of the great large-scale works of Hindu sculpture, depicting the god in various forms (such as *Naṭarāja, *Mahādeva, *Ardhanārīśvara, and *Lakulīśa), as well as with his consort, *Pārvatī.

Eliade, Mircea (1907–1986) Romanian born historian of religions whose early research was into religious experience in Hindu traditions, especially *yoga. From 1928–31 he was a student of *Sanskrit and Indian philosophy at the University of Calcutta, following which he spent six months in an *āśram at *Rishikesh. Returning to Bucharest, he completed his PhD thesis, which was subsequently translated into English (1954) as *Yoga: Immortality and Freedom*. He continued his academic career in Romania, Paris, and Chicago, publishing widely and influentially on myth, comparative religion, and the history of religious ideas. The *Encyclopedia of Religion* (1987) was produced under his general editorship.

Ellorā (Ellūrā) A site containing 35 rock-cut *temples near Aurangabad in Maharashtra, constructed between the 6th and 9th centuries CE. The Hindu group contains the famous Kailāsa temple, carved directly from the mountainside and dedicated to *Śiva (as a 'replica' of the god's Himālayan home) by the *Rāṣṭrakūṭan *king, Kṛṣṇa I (757–783).

embryo, golden *See* HIRAṆYAGARBHA.

Emerson, Ralph Waldo (1803–1882) An American poet and man of letters. As one of the New England Transcendentalists he was instrumental in popularizing certain Hindu and *Vedāntic ideas in the West. His once well-known poem 'Brahma' draws on the *Bhagavadgītā*.

emotions *See* BHĀVA(S).

Epics A common collective designation of the *Mahābhārata* and the *Rāmāyaṇa*, corresponding roughly to the *Sanskrit term *itihāsa.

eras The designation of a calendar year as belonging to a particular era, and so its assignation to a particular date, has varied widely on the subcontinent, depending upon geographical region and local history. Among the better known conventions are the *Śaka era (1=77/78 CE), used for the Indian National Calendar, and the *vikrama era (1=57/58 BCE). 'Saṃvat' indicates 'in the year... of the vikrama era'. CE (Christian or Common Era) is widely used for secular purposes. For the mythological conceptions of eras, *see* COSMOGONY; YUGA.

eroticism *See* KĀMA.

ethics While there is no ready equivalent in Hindu discourse to the Western theological and philosophical discipline of 'moral philosophy', ethics in the more general sense—how individuals and societies as a whole should behave in relation to each other, and in relation to the power or powers that are thought to govern life, time, and the universe—are, of course, as essential to Hindu traditions as they are to all other cultures. In the Hindu context, the formal discussion of principles and rules governing correct behaviour is most obvious in the *dharma literature. The separate but related question of whether, or to what extent, dharma represents a system of universal as opposed to particular, or context-bound values (*sādhāraṇa-dharma vs *varṇāśrama-dharma) has exercised various *Neo-Hindu thinkers in the 19th and 20th centuries, especially in the face of challenges from Protestant *Christian missionaries who claimed to have access to the uniquely saving truth. In contrast, the ritual, devotional, and *Tantric emphases of many Hindu traditions operate with a different set of assumptions, one that requires particular kinds of conduct by particularly qualified people in particular circumstances. A corollary of this is that while the state of liberation or salvation (*mokṣa) may in itself be portrayed as transcending ethics, the means to attaining it is usually tied to context-specific behaviour, such as devotion to a personal deity (*bhakti), or various forms of *purificatory or transgressive ritual—behaviour which at some level may be governed by ethical principles. *See also* DHARMA; EVIL.

Europe *See* ORIENTALISM.

evil The English word 'evil' does not translate any specific term in Indian languages, but is used to evoke, more and less imprecisely, a whole range of context-dependent meanings and connotations. In general, evil is not thought to exist as some absolute metaphysical principle in Hindu traditions; rather it is seen as a concomitant of life in the world, and so relative to both the human condition and cosmic cycles of time (*yugas). In *Vedic and *Purāṇic mythology, the experience of human suffering and cosmic disorder (*adharma) is mirrored in the conflict of the *devas and *asuras. In monotheistic contexts, this becomes the contest between the all-powerful and effortlessly triumphant deity and a succession of threatening 'demons' (asuras). The ability to overcome threats to the natural order (*dharma) is thus an index of the deity's power as manifested in the world. This is particularly evident in the *Vaiṣṇava notion of the deity's 'descents' (*avatāras), which are linked to cosmic increments in adharma. Such relative distinctions of 'good' and 'bad', dharma and adharma, are, however, ultimately transcended in the oneness of the absolute, whether evoked as *brahman (neut.), or as a personal deity's higher nature.

The problem of 'evil' at the individual level is frequently resolved in terms of *karma doctrine, derived from *renouncer ideology. Evil and misfortune, like all other experiences, are envisaged as concomitants of an individual's previous actions (karma), whether in this life or in those preceding it. The root cause of such actions may be identified as ignorance (*avidyā)—often itself used as a synonym for 'evil'—in the sense of an epistemological mistake, a misreading of the way things really are in terms of the nature of the self, its relation to others and to God. Such ignorance inevitably leads to wrong actions (karma), frequently characterized as *pāpa ('wicked', 'evil', or 'bad'), an adjective applied to both ethical and ritual deficiencies. In daily life, anything *inauspicious (aśubha, amaṅgala)—particular dates, astrological combinations, *widowhood, etc.—may be regarded as 'evil'. *See also* ADHARMA; ASURA; AUSPICIOUS(NESS) AND INAUSPICIOUS(NESS); AVIDYĀ; PĀPA.

evil eye (dṛṣṭi-doṣa, H.: **kudṛṣṭi, nazar/najar,** Tam.: **tiṣṭi,** etc.**)** Associated with the conscious or unconscious gaze of the envious, and perceived to be a universal danger. Young children are thought to be particularly vulnerable, and considerable energy is expended on ritual and magical protections.

exorcism/exorcist *See* BHŪTA(S); POSSESSION.

expiation *See* PRĀYAŚCITTA.

F

faith *See* ŚRADDHĀ.

family *See* KULA.

fast/fasting *See* UPAVĀSA.

fate Popularly conflated with *karma as an impersonal force, generated in past lives, which accounts for current personal circumstances. *See* DAIVA.

fathers *See* PITṚ(S).

fee, sacrificial *See* DAKṢINĀ.

festival (utsava, mahotsava, melā) A generic term for a wide range of seasonal or cyclical celebratory occasions, ranging from *village festivities, focused on local *temples, to great pan-Indian festivals. The dates of the latter are fixed on lunar days in particular lunar months. This is also true of most regional and temple festivals, except in the far south, where they are determined by the solar *calendar. Village festivals are highly variegated, but in general they are performed collectively, with the intention of benefitting the whole village and reinforcing a sense of unity and solidarity among the local population. In North India the main annual village festival usually coincides with *Dasara or *Holī; in the south it is more likely to be the village tutelary goddess whose *image is processed through the streets on a decorated chariot (*ratha) in celebration. The occurrence of a temple festival may draw large numbers of local and national pilgrims to a specific site, with music, dancing, and drama, all contributing to the carnivalesque and fair (*mela)-like proceedings.

Filliozat, Jean (1906–1982) A French *Indologist and brilliant linguist with wide-ranging scholarly interests. He was director of the École Française d'Extrême-Orient from 1956 to 1977, as well as the founder director of L'Institut Français d'Indologie in Pondicherry (1955), where he established a collection of *Śaivite manuscripts. He published on a wide variety of subjects, giving equal weight to both *Sanskrit and *Tamil sources. Among his better known publications are his collaboration with Louis *Renou (1896–1966) on *L'Inde Classique* (vol. 1, 1947; vol. 2, 1953), his works on classical Indian medicine, and his studies of the influence of the Sanskritic tradition on Southeast Asia.

fire *See* AGNI.

fire sticks *See* ARAṆI.

five fire sacrifice (pañcāgni-tapas, pañca-sādhana, pañca-tapas) A practice in which an *ascetic 'cooks' himself by sitting between four fires (one for each quarter) under the midday sun (the fifth fire).

'five fires' doctrine A teaching given in the **Bṛhadāraṇyaka* (6.2.8ff.) and **Chāndogya* (5.4ff.) *Upaniṣads* in which the natural and human life-cycles are depicted in sacrificial terms.

'five great sacrifices' *See* MAHĀ-YAJÑAS.

'five Ms' *See* PAÑCA-MAKĀRA.

food From the *Vedic period onwards the preparation, offering, consumption, and transformation of food has been central not just to the daily life of Hindus, but also to their ritual, social, and soteriological activities. Its conceptual significance is first established in the Vedic sacrificial ritual (*yajña), which involves human participants offering food (anna) to the gods. The raw offering is cooked in the sacrificial fire, and thus transported by *Agni to the heavenly gods for their consumption; in return, they provide food and other benefits for the human world, symbolized by the remnants, or leavings, of the sacrifice. In an extension of this idea of reciprocal exchange, any substance offered, and the benefit received in return, may be seen in the widest sense as 'food' (anna). In the **Taittirīya Upaniṣad* (2.2) (cf. *Bhagavadgītā* 3.11–16) food itself is characterized as the foremost of beings, since all creatures are born out of it, live by it, and pass in to it; in this way it is equated with *brahman (neut.). It is food which constructs the body, both here and in other worlds; hence the necessity to create a new body for the deceased through the offering of *piṇḍa in the death ritual (*antyeṣṭi), and thereafter to go on feeding the *ancestors in the next world. It is this concern about starvation after death which leads in the **Brāhmaṇas* and early **Upaniṣads* to speculation about the prospect of 're-death' (*punar-mṛtyu) and the means to avoid it, a process which culminates in the internalization of the sacrifice and its effects in the person of the *renouncer, whose daily meals become a sacrifice both to and within the *ātman or self.

Food is thought to be particularly susceptible to ritual *pollution—a pollution which may then be transferred to those who consume it. Bhojana, or the taking of food, is therefore extensively treated in the *Brahmanical **Dharmasāstra* literature: frequency of consumption, the kinds of foods permitted or forbidden, the ways in which food may be polluted, who may take food from whom, and at which times, are among the subjects considered in exhaustive detail. The underlying assumption is that made in the early *Upaniṣads*—that the ingestion of pure food is an essential precondition of mental purity and consequently *liberation. This is combined with a heightened awareness that the ingestion of improper foods—those not consonant with one's *caste status, stage of life (*āśrama), or ritual state—or of proper foods in improper, i.e. *inauspicious or polluting circumstances, will be both physically and spiritually damaging. As with the *caste system in general, those considering themselves the most ritually pure (the *brahmins) have the most to lose; consequently, they are the most strictly regulated in terms of their permissible foods and eating patterns: cooked food, for instance, requires a non-polluting brahmin cook, and in North India especially, boiled (kaccā) food is considered less resistant to pollution than food fried in *ghī (pakkā food).

Given the hierarchical nature of traditional Indian society, one of the chief ways in which all groups differentiate between themselves at all levels of caste society is through their cooking and eating practices. Who can give food to whom, and what food they can receive, is of crucial importance. From this perspective, you are, indeed, what you eat. It is hardly surprising, therefore, that foodstuffs are classified in multiple ways—raw and cooked, 'hot' and 'cold', as well as according to various qualities (*guṇas) and flavours (*rasas) (see, for example, *Bhagavadgītā* 17.7–10). In relation to the guṇas, foods are popularly designated as sattvic, rajasic, or tamasic, corresponding to the effects they are supposed to have on the bodies and temperaments of those who consume them. Sattvic foods, such as fruits and grains, are thought to be energizing; rajasic foods, which are oily and spicy, engender negative emotions and sensuality; cold, stale, overcooked, and leftover foods are regarded as tamasic, leading to ignorance and laziness. Many foods change their quality as a result of being cooked with other ingredients, or if left out for a period of time (e.g. milk turns from sattvic to rajasic).

Vegetarianism, in particular, comes to be viewed as an index of purity (by the brahmins), and therefore of higher caste status. At the ritual level *Vaiṣṇavas are most often vegetarian, whereas some *Śaivas and, in particular, *Śāktas (worshippers of the *Goddess), may consume meat as part of their *Tantric practices. Worship (*pūjā), whether conducted in the home or the *temple, mirrors this, in so far as vegetarian food is offered to vegetarian deities, such as *Viṣṇu, *Rāma, and *Kṛṣṇa, and returned to the worshipper in the form of *prasāda (leftovers which have been blessed by the deity), an act which in itself establishes a hierarchical relationship of superior to inferior. Similarly, goddesses may receive offerings of meat and, the equally impure, *alcohol, which may or may not be returned to the devotee as prasāda. *See also* AHIṂSĀ.

ford *See* TĪRTHA.

forest *See* ARAṆYA.

Frauwallner, Erich (1898–1974) An Austrian *Indologist and Buddhologist who held the chair of Indian and Iranian studies at the University of Vienna. His *History of Indian Philosophy* (*Geschichte der Indischen Philosophie*, 2 vols. 1953), although never completed, contains valuable analyses of early *Upaniṣadic material, and the *Sāṃkhya, *Yoga, and *Vaiśeṣika systems.

funeral rites Members of the lower *castes, children, and holy men are usually buried. Ascetics (*saṃnyāsins) 'die' to the social and ritual world when they renounce; their ritual of *renunciation is therefore synonymous with their funeral (*antyeṣṭi). An orthodox *Brahmanical *renouncer, who has internalized his sacrificial fires, and so made a perpetual *sacrifice of himself, is therefore also buried, or placed in a *river, rather than cremated after his physical *death. For Brahmanical rites for the *twice born, *see* ANTYEṢṬI.

funerary rites *See* FUNERAL RITES.

G

gada ('mace', 'club') A weapon, constructed from wood or iron, and a proverbial index of strength, since it can be wielded only by the most powerful warriors, such as *Bhīma and *Duryodhana, who engage in a famous single combat with maces in the **Śalyaparvan* of the **Mahābhārata*. The mace is one of the attributes of *Viṣṇu, complementing his other weapon, the *cakra. This gada, symbolizing the god's universal power, is sometimes represented in a personified form (as an *āyudhapuruṣa), and worshipped independently for its protective qualities, notably in the form of the goddess Kaumodakī. In an attempt to account for the name, a story in the **Agni Purāṇa* tells how *Viśvakarman made a mace from the bones of Gada, a demon defeated by Viṣṇu, and presented it to the god.

Gadādhara (17th century CE) Author in the Bengali *Navya Nyāya (new logic) tradition who wrote a commentary on *Raghunātha Śiromaṇi's *Anumānadīdhiti*.

Gāgābhaṭṭa (17th century CE) A well-known *Sanskrit *paṇḍit from *Vārāṇasī, who performed the coronation of *Śivājī in 1674. He appears to have been a rival of Śivājī's teacher, *Rāmadāsa.

Gajalakṣmī ('elephant-Lakṣmī') The name by which the goddess of good fortune and wealth, *Lakṣmī, is known when depicted as seated on a *lotus and being showered with water from pots wielded by a pair of elephants (gajas). The earliest images of the goddess, dating from the 1st century BCE, show her in this form, demonstrating her connections with fertility, rain, and royal power (associated with elephants). Depictions of this type are often found carved on the lintels of *Vaiṣṇava *temples.

Gajendramokṣa ('deliverance of the elephant king') A favourite subject of paintings—the depiction of *Viṣṇu saving an elephant from a crocodile. In a previous life the elephant had been a royal devotee of the god, but had been cursed by a sage to be reborn as an elephant. His devotion (*bhakti) to Viṣṇu saves him and ensures his return to human form.

gaṇa ('troop') *Śiva's retinue of anarchic demigods, made up of troops of minor *Vedic deities, and often portrayed as pot-bellied dwarves. They are led by *Gaṇeśa, the 'lord of the gaṇa'.

Gaṇapati *See* GAṆEŚA.

Gāṇapatyas ('Gaṇapati worshippers') The collective name given to members of *bhakti sects who worship *Gaṇeśa as the accessible embodiment of *brahman (neut.), and so view him alone as the supreme deity. By the 10th century CE a number of such groups were sufficiently distinct from their *Śaiva parentage to have established their own (Śaiva-derived) ritual practices and iconographies. Evidence of the sects' continued development can be found in the **Gaṇeśa* and **Mudgala Purāṇas* (12th and 14th centuries respectively), which, with the **Vedas*, became the canonical texts of the later tradition. The modern Gāṇapatya cult has its origins in 17th-century Maharashtra, thanks to the influence of the South Indian teacher, Morayā Gosāvi. As the result of a series of visions of Gaṇeśa at Morogoan near Pune, he came to believe that he himself, and those following in his lineage, would become vehicles for the incarnation of the god. Subsequently, Morayā underwent *jīvansamādhi—'living entombment'—in the village of Cincvad (also near Pune), which thereafter became the headquarters for the sect. Under the patronage of the local rulers, the *Marāṭhās, the Gāṇapatya sect (which now also worshipped Morayā Gosāvi and his successors) continued to flourish among the higher *caste Hindus of Maharashtra and South India into the 19th century. After a period of quiescence under British rule, its activities have revived. This is particularly evident in the numbers of devotees undertaking the *pilgrimage to the āṣṭavināyakas, the 'eight Gaṇeśas'—forms of the deity established in eight *temples in the Pune area. These include Gaṇeśa as Mayureśvara ('lord of peacocks') at the Morogoan shrine, which is also the twice-yearly destination of the Cicvad Gaṇeśa image, carried there in a processional pilgrimage by its *priests and devotees.

Gāndhārī In the *Mahābhārata* the wife of the blind *Dhṛtarāṣṭra and the mother of the *Kauravas, who wears a blindfold out of sympathy for her husband. Mourning the death of her children at the end of the war, she curses *Kṛṣṇa for having failed to prevent the slaughter, predicting the end of the *Vṛṣṇis and his own death. Kṛṣṇa, for his part, blames Gāndhārī, who, as *Duryodhana's mother, can be considered responsible for the conflict. Fifteen years later, she retires with Dhṛtarāṣṭra and *Kuntī to practise *asceticism in the forest, where they subsequently die in a fire. Later, her curse on the Vṛṣṇis and Kṛṣṇa is seen to take effect. *See also* MAHĀBHĀRATA.

gāndharva marriage A *marriage rite (vivāha), so-called because it is witnessed only by *Gandharvas, which, according to *Manusmṛti* (3.32), takes the form of a mutually desired union between the bride and bridegroom expressed through sexual intercourse. In the *Śakuntalā episode of the *Mahābhārata* (1.67.25ff.), it is described as 'done in secret between two lovers, unaccompanied by mantras'. The arrangement is unconventional but, according to *Dharmaśāstra*, it has legal force as a form of marriage for couples from the *kṣatriya *varṇa.

Gandharva(s) 1. (sing.) In the *Ṛg Veda* a name given to an atmospheric deity, also called Viśvāvasu, associated with rain. He is the guardian of the heavenly *soma, and the physician of the gods. **2.** (pl.) A class of male (and sometimes female) divinities or spirits, often characterized as 'heavenly musicians', who feature in Indian religious stories from the *Ṛg* and *Atharva Vedas* onwards, initially as attendants on *Indra and the other gods. In *Purāṇic and *Epic texts they are often paired with the *Apsarases. Like many supernatural beings, despite their seductive beauty, they are considered both powerful and dangerous, and can be a threat to humans, especially in remote parts of the forest, or wilderness (*araṇya). In the *Mahābhārata*, *Citraratha is designated *king of both Gandharvas and Apsarases.

Gandharvaveda (Gandharvavidyā) ('knowledge of music') An *Upaveda*, sometimes classified as a subsidiary branch of the *Sāmaveda*, dealing with music and performance.

Gāndhī, Mohandas Karamchand (Gandhi, Mahātma ('great soul')**, bāpū** (G.: 'father')**)** (1869–1948) A moral, political, and religious leader, who played a key role in the struggle for independence from British rule; he is probably still the best-known Indian outside the subcontinent. Born in Gujarat into a *vaiśya family, he was brought up in an eclectic religious environment. His parents were both *Vaiṣṇavas, although his mother belonged to the *Praṇāmī sect, which includes among its authoritative texts the *Muslim Qur'an, and his father mixed in Gujarati *Jain circles. Gāndhī trained as a barrister in England, where he came across the *Bhagavadgītā* for the first time in Sir Edwin *Arnold's translation. From 1893 to 1915 he practised law in South Africa. It was there, in the face of racial discrimination, that he developed many of the strategies he was to employ after his return to India in 1915. Chief among these was satyāgraha—a tenacious adherence to the truth which, in the public sphere, expressed itself through active but non-violent resistance to oppression. At the heart of this was a commitment to universal justice, combined with the ancient Indian ethical principle of *ahiṃsā ('non-violence'). The latter is regarded as a condition of truth (satya), and since, for Gāndhī, truth is equated with God, ahiṃsā becomes the quintessential religious and political value. Starting with the assumption that such truth is universal, Gāndhī's hope was that ahiṃsā would be expressed both through religious tolerance, particularly between Hindus and Muslims, and—flying in the face of traditional *varṇāśramadharma—through the pursuit of equality between Hindus. The touchstone of the latter was the treatment of those considered by the rest of society to be the most ritually *impure, the so-called '*untouchables'—renamed *harijans ('children of God') by Gāndhī, although they themselves later preferred the epithet *Dalit ('oppressed').

After 1916 Gāndhī became a leading figure in the Indian National Congress, striving to promote, through numerous publications and direct action, these essentially religious and ethical values in the wider context of the struggle for independence. This, combined with his vision of an indigenous economy which rejected modern industrialism and technology in favour of a self-supporting rural means of production (such as hand-loom produced cloth), brought him into conflict with the British, and like other members of Congress he was often imprisoned. Part of his response was to exert moral pressure on his opponents by fasting (*upavāsa), an increasingly effective measure given his growing fame. His organized campaigns of mass civil disobedience culminated in an event which received worldwide publicity, the 1930 march to the coastal village of Dandi to protest against the imposition of a salt tax by the colonial government. This act of satyāgraha led in the following year to the London talks which, in turn, paved the way to eventual post-war independence. The form that independence took, with the formation of Pakistan as a separate state, and the intercommunal violence that attended *Partition, represented a defeat for Gāndhī, whose hope had been for an Indian state based on tolerance between all religious traditions (which he viewed as essentially pursuing the same truth), and especially between Muslims and Hindus. It was his even-handed treatment of the Muslim cause, and his desperate attempts, including a final fast, to bring the violence to an end, that, six months after independence, provoked his assassination by Nathuram Godse (1912–49), a member of the militant Hindu nationalist organization, the *Rāṣṭrīya Svayamsevak Saṅgh (RSS). Although still revered as a great political and religious figure in India and throughout the world, Gāndhī's teachings—including his universal ethic of non-violence, and its corollary, his ahistorical approach to Hinduism and other religious traditions—have only had a marginal effect on the development of post-Independence India. But his personal religious practices, based on a concern for self-purification and the spiritual rewards of leading a simple, not to say *ascetic life, align him with a long tradition of Indian religious 'strivers' or *śramaṇas.

Gaṇeśa (Gaṇapati) ('lord of the *gaṇa') The popular god of 'obstacles' (Vigneśvara): he removes them—hence the name, Vināyaka, 'remover'—but, if not properly propitiated, he can also impose them. He is therefore invoked at the beginning of almost any undertaking, whether ritual, literary, or simply setting out on a journey. This means he plays an essential, although limited role in the daily life of many, if not most Hindus. A related function is Gaṇeśa's guardianship of doorways and entrances. Images of the god in this role are ubiquitous on lintels throughout India. There, as elsewhere, he is portrayed as elephant-headed and human-bodied, with a snake-entwined pot belly and the limbs of a chubby child. Of his various attributes, an elephant goad, a noose, and a bowl of sweetmeats (laḍḍus) are among those most frequently depicted. His *vāhana ('vehicle') is a rat.

Historically, Gaṇeśa may have been a tribal totem, or a separate elephant god, who was subsequently absorbed into the group of deities associated with *Śiva, as the leader of his gaṇa ('troop'). He does not appear in iconographic form until after the 5th century CE, but his close association with Śiva and *Pārvatī thereafter is reflected in numerous *Purāṇic myths. One popular mythological account of how Gaṇeśa acquired his head, which also mirrors his absorption into *Śaivism as a subordinate deity, tells of how Pārvatī, when washing herself, created a child (Gaṇeśa) from the dirt scraped from her legs. When Śiva returned, he found an unknown youth, guarding the entrance, and so blocking his way to Pārvatī. In the ensuing row, Śiva decapitated him. On learning his true identity, Śiva ordered one of his followers to bring him the head of the first creature he came across—which happened to be an elephant. And so Gaṇeśa was resurrected with an elephant's head. Images of him with a broken tusk reflect another popular story, that he broke it in order to act as *Vyāsa's scribe as he recited the *Mahābhārata* for the first time.

Although Gaṇeśa is embedded in Śaiva mythology, his appeal crosses sectarian and, indeed, religious boundaries; there are *Buddhist and *Jain equivalents. A small number of *bhakti sects, known as the *Gāṇapatyas, have worshipped him in various forms as the supreme deity, and he has been particularly popular in Maharashtra, where the yearly *Ganeśa Catūrthi festival takes place. (Since the 19th century, this has taken on a particularly nationalist flavour.) He is one of the five gods worshipped by *smārta *brahmins.

Gaṇeśa

Ganeśa Catūrthi A popular *festival celebrating *Gāṇeśa's birthday. In Maharashtra it is held on the fourth day (catūrthi) of the bright lunar fortnight in Bhādrapada/Prauṣṭhapada (August–September); but in *Vārāṇasī, for instance, during Māgha (January–February). The festival, which may last for up to ten days, involves the domestic worship of temporary, painted clay images of Gaṇeśa, as well as the setting up of more elaborate, sponsored tableaux, all of which are subsequently ritually immersed in *tanks, *rivers, or the sea, to mark the conclusion of the celebrations. This also marks the time when business people and students present their written accounts and books to the god (as the scribe of the **Mahābhārata*) to ensure good fortune. *See also* TILAK, BALA GANGADHARA.

Gāṇeśa Purāṇa One of the canonical texts of the *Gāṇapatya sects, bringing together various mythological stories about *Gaṇeśa, whom they regard as the supreme deity. It was probably composed in the 12th century CE, and is traditionally classified amongst the **Upāpurāṇas*.

g

Gaṅgā (Ang.: **Ganges**) ('swift-goer', 'fast-flower') A North Indian *river, flowing from *Gaṅgotrī in the *Himālaya(s) to the Bay of Bengāl, which is considered the most sacred and *pure water on earth. As the phenomenal form of the goddess Gaṅgā (the eldest daughter of *Himavat and *Menā), the river is frequently referred to as 'Mother Gaṅgā' ('Gaṅgā Mātā'). All other rivers are thought to be concentrated in the Gaṅgā, just as she is in them, and they therefore share her purifying powers. The actual river and its waters are, however, believed to be the most efficacious, guaranteeing the complete destruction of sin (*pāpa), and so *mokṣa or liberation from *rebirth for those whose ashes or bones are immersed in it. This ritual and symbolic power to purify, heal, and liberate is thought to be particularly concentrated where the Gaṅgā flows through the sacred *tīrtha of *Vārāṇasī, hence the desire of many Hindus to make a *pilgrimage there to bathe in its waters, and, ultimately, to be cremated on its banks.

According to mythological accounts, there is a celestial Gaṅgā (*ākāśagaṅgā), who issues from *Viṣṇu's left foot and flows across the sky as the Milky Way. She was persuaded by the *ṛṣi *Bhagīratha to fall to earth to purify the ashes of his ancestors, enabling them to attain *heaven. Earning the epithet Gaṅgādhara ('bearer of the Gaṅgā'), *Śiva broke the torrent with his *ascetic's locks, allowing it to flow across the plains of Northeast India to the sea. In the **Mahābhārata*, *Bhīṣma, the forefather of the *Lunar (*Kuru) dynasty, is the eighth, and only surviving son of the celestial Gaṅgā and King Śāṃtanu. There is also said to be a Gaṅgā beneath the earth. *See also* GHĀṬ(S).

Gaṅgādhara ('bearer of the Gaṅgā') An epithet of *Śiva. *See* GAṄGĀ.

Gaṅgaikoṇḍacōḻapuram ('city of the Cōḻa, conqueror of the Ganges') Site close to the great Bṛhadīśvara *Śaiva *temple at modern day *Tañjāvūr in Tamil Nadu, constructed by the *Cōḻa dynasty *king, Rājendra I (r. 1012–44 CE), to celebrate his conquests in the north. The city itself has not survived.

Gaṅgāputra ('son of Gaṅgā') Epithet of *Bhīṣma. *See also* GAṄGĀ.

Gaṅgāsāgar *See* SĀGAR ISLAND.

Ganges *See* GAṄGĀ.

Gaṅgeśa (*c.*14th century CE) One of the major philosopical teachers in medieval India, whose *Tattvacintāmaṇi* ('Thought-Jewel of Reality'), with its emphasis on the *pramāṇas ('valid means of knowledge'), was instrumental in firmly establishing the *Navya Nyāya (new logic) school.

Gaṅgotrī A popular *tīrtha in Uttarakhand (formerly in Uttar Pradesh) in the high *Himālaya(s), marking the point where the celestial *Gaṅgā is thought to have come to earth, and close to the glacier from which the actual *river emerges. In the accessible summer months, the goddess Gaṅgā is worshipped there in a shrine built in the 18th century on the banks of the *Bhāgīrathī (the name of the river at this point in its course). *See also* DHĀMA.

gaṇita *See* JYOTIṢA.

garbhādhāna ('impregnation of the womb') **1.** According to **Dharmaśāstra*, the *saṃskāra to be performed after menstruation, and before and after sexual intercourse, to ensure the conception and proper embryonic development of a child. Its origins appear to be ancient, the equivalent rite appearing in the **Atharva Veda*. **Manusmṛti* and some other *dharma texts refer to niṣeka, a synonym of garbhādhāna.

2. (garbhadhāna) A rite performed during the building of a *temple in which the *priest 'implants' the'seed' of the temple in the *garbhagṛha, in the form of a small box. Symbolically, this seed grows through the *śikhara, directly above it, to the heavens above, on a line representing the axis mundi.

garbhagṛha ('womb-house') The inner sanctuary of a *temple, housing the principal image of the deity. It is usually, a small, dark, and cave-like room, placed at the centre of a passageway designed for the *pradakṣiṇā (circumambulation) of devotees. Traditionally, access to the garbhagṛha itself was restricted to the *priest in charge of the temple, and devotees would take *darśan of the deity through an aperture or doorway.

Gārgī Vācaknavī Female teacher in the **Bṛhadāraṅyaka Upaniṣad* (3.6; 3.8) who challenges *Yājñavalkya twice in a debate concerning the ultimate nature of reality.

gārhapatya fire (gārhapatyāgni) ('the householder's fire') The sacrificial fire expanded from, and superseding the *gṛhyāgni ('domestic fire'). One of the three major fires of the *śrauta ritualist, it is produced during the *agnyādheya ritual, and thereafter must be continually maintained. Considered five times more powerful than the gṛhyāgni, it is set up on the west side of the sacrificial area, and is expanded to make the *āhavanīya and dakṣiṇa (*dakṣiṇāgni) fires.

gārhasthya *See* GṚHASTHA.

Garīb Dās (1717–1778) A North Indian poet-saint (*sant) born into a *Vaiṣṇava family in the village of Chhudani in Haryana, which remains the devotional centre for his followers, the Garībdāsīs. His collection of hymns, the *Granth Sāhib,* was influenced by previous sants, such as *Dādū, *Nānak, and especially *Kabīr.

Garībdāsīs *See* GARĪB DĀS.

Garuḍa (Tārkṣya) A mythical creature, hatched from an egg, with a man's body and the beak and talons of a bird of prey. He is associated with the sun's rays, and is famous for his serpent-destroying power. Various stories are told to account for this antipathy to the *nāgas, including his defeat of the two giant snakes guarding *Indra's heavenly *amṛta. Garuḍa needs to steal the amṛta in order to free his mother, *Vinatā, who has been imprisoned by the mother of the nāgas, her sister *Kadrū. Various stories also connect Garuḍa with emeralds, the touch of which is popularly supposed to act as an antidote to snakebites. Garuḍa pillars (garuḍastambhas) erected in front of a number of *temples in the early centuries BCE provide evidence of Garuḍa's role in the first detectable *Bhāgavata cults, a connection with *Viṣṇu which is confirmed in numerous *Purāṇic myths, where he acts as the god's *vāhana ('vehicle'). In this role he has been a popular subject for sculptures connected with *Vaiṣṇava worship of all kinds.

Garuḍa Purāṇa ('*Purāṇa* taught by Garuḍa') Classified as one of the 18 'great **Purāṇas*' (*mahāpurāṇas*) in the *sāttvika group, i.e. those said to relate to *Viṣṇu, it is a long work, which exists in many versions, and much of its material may be relatively late. It has been variously dated between the 6th and 11th centuries. Among its disparate contents are *Saura and *Gāṇapatya sections, and the *Pretakalpa* (possibly a late addition to the rest of the text), which deals with *funeral rites, what happens to the deceased (*preta) after death, questions of *karma and *rebirth, and evocations of numerous *hells.

Gauḍapāda (*c.*6th century CE) Reputed author of the earliest identifiable *Advaita text, the **Gauḍapādīya Kārikā*, he is considered by the tradition to be the teacher of *Govindapāda, and so *Śaṅkara's *paramaguru (his teacher's teacher). A commentary on the **Sāṃkhya Kārikā*, the **Gauḍapāda Bhāṣya*, is also attributed to him. Some modern commentators have suggested that he may have been a *Buddhist, but, at most, he seems to have reconstituted certain Yogācāra ideas.

Gauḍapāda Bhāṣya (*c.*6th century CE?) An influential commentary on the **Sāṃkhya Kārikā*, attributed with no great certainty to the early *Advaitin teacher, *Gauḍapāda.

***Gauḍapādīya Kārikā* (*Āgamaśāstra*, *Māṇḍūkya Kārikā*)** (*c.*6th century CE) Attributed to *Gauḍapāda, the *Kārikā* is the earliest identifiable *Advaita text; it takes the form of a 215-verse commentary on the **Māṇḍūkya Upaniṣad*, hence its alternative title, the *Māṇḍūkya Kārikā*. *Śaṅkara wrote a commentary on it, and it was clearly a major influence on the development of his own thought. The *Kārikā* itself propounds the non-dual (advaita) nature of ultimate reality (*brahman (neut.)), and the complete identity of brahman and *ātman. The world of apparent change and multiplicity is ultimately an illusion (*māyā), and nothing has ever really come into existence. In its conflation of *consciousness and the objects of consciousness, it seems to have been influenced by the 'mind only' teachings of Yogācāra *Buddhism. *See also* AJĀTIVĀDA.

Gauḍīya Vaiṣṇavism (Bengal/Gauḍīa Vaiṣṇavism) (referring to the Gauḍa region of southern Bengal) A major *bhakti movement, instigated in the 16th century by the immediate followers of *Caitanya, at his behest, in order to promulgate and systematize his teachings and devotional practices. It was these followers—the six *Gosvāmīs—who composed the works of aesthetic theology and ritual which became the scriptural basis for the Gauḍīya tradition, and who helped to establish *Vṛndāvana and *Mathurā as major *pilgrimage sites. Central to Gauḍīya bhakti, and following a pattern established by Caitanya himself, is an intense devotion to *Kṛṣṇa. This is expressed through various repetitive ritual practices, including the collective singing of *kīrtanas, *temple *pūjā, and a theology predicated in general on Kṛṣṇa's life with the *gopīs in *Vṛndāvana (as narrated in the **Bhāgavata Purāṇa*), and in particular on the mutual erotic love between the god and his beloved *Rādhā, portrayed in texts such as *Jayadeva's **Gītagovinda*. This love is conceptualized as an expression of the spiritual relationship which exists between Kṛṣṇa, as the supreme Lord, and his human devotee (the individual soul or *jīva)—a relationship ultimately characterized as *acintyabhedābheda ('inconceivable difference in identity'). The only way to achieve the permanent realization of this connection—which is an experience of divine love (*preman) concomitant with *liberation (either in this body or at death)—is through a persistent and all-encompassing, yet fundamentally desireless, devotion to Kṛṣṇa.

Both the theology and practice of Gauḍīya Vaiṣṇavism have a wide variety of registers, ranging from the repetition of Kṛṣṇa's names (*nāmajapa), and *temple worship, to the internalized and aestheticized devotion developed by Rūpa *Gosvāmī. For many Gauḍīyas, who conceived of him as either an *avatāra of Kṛṣṇa or identical with the deity, Caitanya himself remained central to their practice, and was worshipped accordingly. His influence is therefore evident in a number of more and less mainstream traditions, including the *Rādhāvallabhīs and the *Tantric *Sahajiyās, who regarded him as the joint incarnation, in one body, of Rādhā and Kṛṣṇa. For those drawing on the *Sanskritic and aestheticized tradition of the Gosvāmīs, the emphasis for the devotee was more typically on assuming and enacting one of a number of different *bhāvas ('attitudes' or 'emotions') towards Kṛṣṇa, ranging from servitude and subservience to the intense erotic love experienced by Rādhā and the *gopīs. In practice, it was the latter bhāva which was soteriologically significant, since it could be refined and savoured as its corresponding *rasa, the salvific and divine love of (and for) Kṛṣṇa.

Various *guru-lineages developed in the wake of the Gosvāmīs, many of them promoting sophisticated *yogic techniques based on the internalization of *Braj's sacred topography and inner participation in Kṛṣṇa's *līlā. For a period in the 17th and 18th centuries more physical practices, involving ritualized sexual intercourse, also seem to have been employed. Nineteenth-century urban reformers of the tradition, such as *Kedarnath Datta, succeeded in establishing a more conservative theological and ritual agenda for mainstream Gauḍīya Vaiṣṇavism. This was the form in which the tradition was carried to the West by *Bhaktivedānta Swāmi, founder of the *International Society for Krishna Consciousness.

Gaurī ('golden', 'brilliant', 'fair') A benign form of *Pārvatī, depicted with a fair complexion.

Gaurī Mā (1857–1938) A female teacher within the *Rāmakṛṣṇa tradition. At the age of eighteen she had become an itinerant devotee of *Kṛṣṇa, but after encountering Rāmakṛṣṇa in 1880, she worked, at his behest, for the education of women, and in 1884 founded the Śrī Śrī Śāradeśwarī Āśrama for women next to the *Gaṅgā in Barrackpore, north of Calcutta.

Gautama 1. (Akṣapāda Gotama, Dīrghatapas) (*c.*250 CE or earlier?) Traditionally credited with the authorship of the **Nyāyasūtra*, and therefore the founder of the *Nyāya *darśana (2). **2.** The name of a *Vedic *ṛṣi, traditionally associated with the **Sāma Veda*. The **Gautama Dharmasūtra* takes his name.

Gautama Dharmasūtra (*c.*3rd century BCE) One of the four extant **Dharmasūtra* texts; while it has no formal connection with any *Vedic school, there is some internal evidence of a link with the **Sāma Veda*, with which *Gautama, to whom it is ascribed, has a traditional association. It deals with such topics as the rules governing the life of the Vedic student, the life of the householder (*gṛhastha), the occupations of the four *varṇa, matters of criminal and civil law, the *āśramas, and the duties of the *king.

Gayā The name of a town in Bihar regarded as one of the seven ancient holy cities of India. It is a major *pilgrimage site, sacred to both Hindus (as one of the three major *tīrthas on the Gaṅgā) and *Buddhists (as Bodhgayā, the site of the *Buddha's enlightenment). A myth of origin, found in the **Māhātmya* sections of the **Agni* and **Vāyu Purāṇas*, tells how the gods persuaded the *asura Gaya to sacrifice himself there to maintain the world order, and created a site where it would be particularly efficacious to make offerings (*piṇḍas) to the ancestors (*pitṛs).

Gāyatrī The personification of the *Gāyatrī *mantra as a goddess, said to be the wife of *Brahmā and the mother of the four *Vedas.

Gāyatrī mantra (Sāvitrī mantra) The most sacred and powerful *Sanskrit *mantra (named in this case after the *Vedic metre in which it was composed), addressed to the Sun (*Savitṛ—hence 'sāvitrī'). Taken from **Ṛg Veda* 3.62.10 (tat savitur vareṇyam bhargo devasya dhīmahi dhiyo yo naḥ pracodayāt—'we meditate on that excellent radiance of the Sun god. May he inspire our thoughts'), it is supposed to be recited by every 'twice-born' (*dvija) male at his morning and evening rites, and is a component part of the *agnihotra ritual. Knowledge of the verse is often considered to be synonymous with initiation into the *Veda* (*upanayana), the *saṃskāra in which it is first transmitted to the initiate. Like all mantras its potency is in its sound and repetition, and it can be considered as a concentration of the power of the entire *Veda*. Although theoretically accessible to the top three *varṇas, *brahmins have traditionally considered the mantra to be exclusively theirs.

ghaṇṭā ('bell') One of the instruments commonly used in *pūjā, and an attribute or weapon of various deities.

Ghaṇṭākarṇa ('bell-eared') A local deity associated with *Śiva. Particularly popular in Gujarat, he is thought to give protection from skin diseases, such as smallpox.

Ghaṇṭī A name given to *Durgā, derived from her use of a bell (*ghaṇṭā) as one of her weapons.

Ghaṭotkaca *See* HIḌIMBA.

ghāṭ(s) (ghats) ('step(s)') **1.** A flight of steps, leading to a *river or *tank, which as well as servicing a landing place, allows access for ritual purposes, such as a bathing (*snāna). The ghāṭs leading into the *Gaṅgā at *Vārāṇasī are thought to be particularly sacred, each being its own *tīrtha. These include the two cremation grounds, or 'burning ghāṭs', Hariścandra and Maṇikarṇikā. **2.** Chains of mountains and hills (western and eastern) stretching across peninsula India.

Gheraṇḍa Saṃhitā (*c.*1700 CE) A relatively late but encyclopaedic, *haṭha-yoga manual, composed in *Sanskrit and teaching a unique sevenfold path to perfection. The text, which shows *Vedāntin influence, is said to have been revealed by a teacher called Gheraṇḍa (seemingly a *Vaiṣṇava) to a disciple with a *Śaiva name, Caṇḍakāpāli ('furious skull-bearer').

ghī (H.: 'clarified butter', Skt.: ghṛta, Ang.: ghee) Butter clarified through boiling and skimming. Widely used for cooking, and as the basic oblation (*homa) offered into the sacrificial fire. *See also* ĀJYA.

Ghose, Aurobindo *See* AUROBINDO GHOSE.

ghosts *See* BHŪTA(S).

gift *See* DĀNA.

Gītābhāṣya (contraction of *Bhagavadgītābhāṣya*) The generic term for a commentary on the **Bhagavadgītā*, such as those by *Śaṅkara and *Rāmānuja.

Gītagovinda ('Govinda in Song') A courtly *Sanskrit poem about the love-play (*līlā) of *Kṛṣṇa (*Govinda), *Rādhā, and the *gopīs, composed in Bengal by *Jayadeva towards the end of the 12th century CE. The poem—a series of erotic lyrics in the *kāvya style, linked by a narrative, and intended to be sung—plays on the ideas of 'love in separation' (*viraha) and reunion. Whether or not Jayadeva intended his poem to have some super-literary religious function, it became a key source for the *Gauḍīya Vaiṣṇava *bhakti tradition, which, through *Caitanya and the *Gosvāmīs, interpreted the relation between Kṛṣṇa and his lovers as a template for that between God (*Bhagavān) and his devotees (*bhaktas).

Gītā-mandira ('Gītā-temple') The name given to a type of modern Indian *temple dedicated to the worship of the **Bhagavadgītā* as both goddess and textual object. The walls are usually inscribed with the full text of the *Gītā* in *Sanskrit.

Gītārahasya B. G. *Tilak's widely read and influential Marathi commentary on the **Bhagavadgītā* (1915; English trans. 1936).

Gnanasambandar *See* JÑĀNASAṂBANDAR.

go *See* COW.

Gobila Reputed author of the *Gobila* **Gṛhya-Sūtra*, which belongs to the texts attached to the **Sāma Veda*.

God/god An English word used to translate a variety of Indian-language terms. Its precise denotation depends on the context: each of the all-powerful deities of sectarian Hinduism (i.e. *Śiva, and various forms of *Viṣṇu—especially *Kṛṣṇa and *Rāma) is likely to be referred to as 'God' by his devotees. The term may also be used to refer to the monistic absolute, *brahman (neut.), either viewed as an impersonal principle, or as synonymous with one of the great sectarian gods. *See also* BHAGAVĀN; BHAGAVATĪ; GODS (VEDIC); ĪŚVARA.

Godāvarī One of India's seven sacred rivers, and a *tīrtha in its own right; it flows through the Deccan plateau, from Maharashtra to the Bay of Bengal.

goddess/Goddess A generic English term for any female deity. Capitalized as 'Goddess', it refers to *Devī, or one of her manifestations. *See also* DEVA(S); GRĀMADEVATĀ(S).

'god-men' English-language term for a variety of modern Hindu religious teachers, whose authority and claims to divinity are largely self-validated, and based on charismatic practices such as miracle-working.

'god posters' A term applied by some to Hindu calendar art, a popular means of representing a wide variety of deities, executed in primary or luminescent colours.

gods (Vedic) *See* DEVA(S).

Godse, Nathuram (1912–1949) *See* GĀNDHĪ, MOHANDAS KARAMCHAND.

Gokarṇa ('cow-eared') A Śaiva *tīrtha on the coast in northern Karnataka.

Gokhale, Gopal Krishna (1866–1915) An influential Maharashtrian reformer and Indian nationalist who, in 1905, founded the *Servants of India Society, dedicated to educational, economic, and social uplift, particularly for women and the poorer classes, and to communal harmony.

Gokula ('cow station') A place near *Vṛndāvana, frequented by *Kṛṣṇa (*Gopāla) in his youth, according to the **Bhāgavata Purāṇa* and *Gauḍīya Vaiṣṇavism.

Gokulāṣṭamī *See* KṚṢṆA JAYANTĪ.

golden age *See* KṚTAYUGA.

goloka ('world of the cows') In *Gauḍīya Vaiṣṇavism the name given to *Kṛṣṇa's *heaven, variously conceived as a place on Mount *Meru, where the *bhakta can hope to live after *death in an intimate relationship with the deity, and as a realm within *brahman (neut.), which Kṛṣṇa has to himself beyond his devotees.

Golwalkar, Madhav Sadashiv (1906–1973) Leader of the militant, right-wing Hindu nationalist organization, the *Rāṣṭrīya Svayamsevak Saṅgh (RSS), who succeeded its founder, K. B. *Hedgewar, in 1940, and thereafter developed its cultural ideology, based on an idea of Hindu nationhood.

Gonda, Jan (1905–1991) A Dutch *Indologist and *Sanskritist, who held the chair at the University of Utrecht, and published extensively on many aspects of Hinduism. His books included *Aspects of Early Viṣṇuism* (1954), *Die Religionen Indiens* (1960–64), *Change and Continuity in Indian Religion* (1965), *Loka: World and Heaven in the Veda* (1965), *Viṣṇuism and Śivaism: A Comparison* (1970), and *Vedic Ritual: The Non-Solemn Rites* (1980).

good *See* DHARMA; ETHICS; EVIL; PUṆYA.

gopa A male cowherd.

Gopāla Bhaṭṭa *See* GOSVĀMĪS.

Gopāla(ka) ('Cowherd') An epithet of *Kṛṣṇa (sometimes compounded as Kṛṣṇa-Gopāla), referring to his childhood and youth among the *gopas and *gopīs of *Vṛndāvana and *Braj.

Gopāṣṭamī A *festival celebrating *Kṛṣṇa's transition to an adult cowherd, held on the eighth day of the bright fortnight of Kārttika (October–November).

Gopatha Brāhmaṇa A relatively late **Brāhmaṇa*, perhaps belonging to the *Paippalāda school, and the only one attached to the **Atharva Veda*. It appears to have been mostly compiled from other *Brāhmaṇa* texts.

gopī A female cowherd. Much of the **Bhāgavata Purāṇa* is taken up with the narratives of *Kṛṣṇa's early life and his 'pastime' or 'divine play' (*līlā) among the gopīs, the wives of the cowherds in *Vṛndāvana (*Braj/Vraj). For the *Vaiṣṇava devotee (*bhakta), the gopīs' erotic yearning for their unaccountably absent lover, Kṛṣṇa, evoked, along with union and reunion, during the famous *rāsa līlā ('dance pastime'), is the paradigmatic instance of *viraha bhakti, 'love in separation/devotion of longing'. (In general, the devotee identifies him- or herself with the gopīs in their ecstatic devotion to Kṛṣṇa.) For *Jayadeva's **Gītagovinda*, and much of *Gauḍīya Vaiṣṇava theology and practice, one gopī in particular, *Rādhā, is singled out as Kṛṣṇa's lover and consort. As well as the rāsa līla, popular stories, such as Kṛṣṇa stealing the gopīs' clothes, have become a major resource for devotional art and poetry.

gopura(m)s The towered gateways found at the entrances to South Indian *temples. They are often richly decorated with *Purāṇic and other mythological scenes, and may be substantially larger than the temple itself.

Gorakhnāth(a) (Gorakṣanātha) (*c.*9th–13th centuries CE) Little is known for certain about Gorakhnāth; according to tradition he is the third *Nāth and an incarnation of *Śiva. Some scholars now believe that the name signifies an amalgam of an earlier, legendary 'Gorakh', and a 12th–13th-century 'Gorakhnātha', who was a western Indian systematizer and reformer of a number of loosely constituted *Tantric and *yogic traditions. Whatever the historical case, the Gorakhnāth to whom a number of important texts were attributed, and who became the subject of various miracle-saturated hagiographies and legends, was a highly influential figure in the development of medieval Hinduism. He and his equally elusive teacher, *Matsyendranāth, are credited with systematizing *haṭha yoga within the *Śaiva *Nāth Siddha tradition (one which includes the *Kānphaṭa yogīs and the *Gorakhnāthīs)—a *sampradāya (institutionalized order) effectively created by them. Gorakhnāth is said to have composed two works in *Sanskrit, the *Siddha Siddhānta Paddhati*, and the *Gorakṣaśataka*, as well as a number of didactic works in old *Hindi verse, teaching, inter alia, *yogic techniques for perfecting the body as a means to *liberation.

Gorakhnāthīs One of the names applied to members of the *Śaiva *Nāth Siddha tradition, indicating those who trace their lineage back to *Gorakhnāth, the reformer of the order.

Gorakhpur A town in Uttar Pradesh, named after *Gorakhnātha, which is the site of an important *Nāth Siddha monastery and publications' centre.

Gorā-kumbhār ('Gorā the potter', c.13th–14th centuries CE) A low-*caste Maharashtrian poet and *sant belonging to the *Vārkarī Panth. According to a well-known story, he was so intent on chanting the name of God (*Viṭhobā/Viṣṇu) that he crushed his own baby as he worked his potter's clay; but the child was miraculously restored to life as a reward for Gorā's devotion.

Gosāla, Makkhali (P.; Skt.: Gośāla, 5th century BCE) Founder of the heterodox ascetic order, the *Ājīvikas. His name indicates that he was born in a cowshed.

Gosvāmi, Jīva *See* GOSVĀMĪS.

Gosvāmī, Rūpa (*c.*1489–1564) A poet, dramatist, and theologian who, as one of the six *Gosvāmīs, helped to establish the *Gāuḍīya Vaiṣṇava tradition at the behest of *Caitanya. Originally from a *brahmin family, he and his brother, Sanātana Gosvāmī, had been employed by the *Muslim ruler of southern Bengal before they devoted themselves to Caitanya. Rūpa was the author of two major works in *Sanskrit, *Ujjvalanīlamaṇi* ('The Beautiful Sapphire') and *Bhaktirasāmṛtasindhu* ('The Ocean of the Immortal Nectar of Devotion'), which applied the classical *rasa theory of Sanskrit poetics to the practice of *Kṛṣṇa devotionalism (*bhakti). According to these, the means to realizing one's loving relationship with God starts in repetition of his name (*nāmajapa), and proceeds through various emotional states (*bhāvas), which are engendered in a meditational engagement with Kṛṣṇa's *līlā. This process culminates in an identification with Kṛṣṇa's lover, *Rādhā, and it is this experience (or rasa) of a comprehensive divine love (*preman) which is concomitant with salvation.

Gosvāmīs ('lords of cows') (16th century CE) The six immediate followers of *Caitanya: the brothers Sanātana and Rūpa *Gosvāmī, their cousin Jīva Gosvāmī, the south Indians Gopāla Bhaṭṭa and Raghunātha Bhaṭṭa, and Raghunātha Dāsa. In over two hundred written works, they established the scriptural and ritual basis of the *Gauḍīya Vaiṣṇava tradition, as well as delineating the sacred geography of *Braj as the focal point for *Kṛṣṇa *bhakti. Unlike Caitanya himself, their medium of communication was *Sanskrit, deliberately adopted to align the nascent tradition with *Vedic orthodoxy (five out of the six came from *brahmin families). Their conception of the **Veda*, however, stretched to include the **Purāṇas*, and especially the **Bhāgavata Purāṇa*. While Raghunātha Dāsa produced a collection of ecstatic devotional hymns, it was Sanātana and, especially, Rūpa and Jīva Gosvāmī who were primarily responsible for the metaphysical thought and aestheticized theology which came to characterize the tradition. Gopāla and Raghunātha Bhaṭṭa are generally considered to have established the rituals to be used in *temple worship. No works by Raghunātha survive, but Gopāla's **Haribhaktivilāsa* has been highly influential.

gosvāmīs ('lords of cows') The name given to men who belonged to a lineage of hereditary *householder initiates in the *Nimbarkī tradition. It is also a title given to the members of the (similarly householder) lineage of teachers in the *Vallabhasampradāya (or *Puṣṭimārga). The latter are also addressed as 'mahārājas' ('great kings').

gotra ('cowshed') One of a number of (originally *brahmin) groups (49 according to some accounts), defined by their line of descent from various legendary *Vedic seers (*ṛṣis). According to **Dharmaśāstra*, there should be no intermarriage between members of the same gotra, even though they belonged to the same *caste. The other two *twice-born *varṇa also adopted the gotra system, aligning themselves in theory to the gotra of the brahmins who performed their domestic rituals, but in practice, paying more attention to their own, equally legendary ancestors. *See also* PRAVARA.

Govardhana ('increasing cattle') **1.** The name of a hill in the *Braj region near *Mathurā. In a story told in the **Bhāgavata Purāṇa* and elsewhere, *Kṛṣṇa hoists the hill up like a giant umbrella, and supports it on just one of his fingers for seven days. In this way he protects the cowherds and their cattle from a storm which has been summoned by the *Vedic deity *Indra in angry response to the cowherds transferring their devotion to Kṛṣṇa. Thanks to the latter's intervention, Indra is eventually forced to concede. It has proved a popular subject with artists. **2.** (late 12th century) A prolific East Indian poet, whose *Sanskrit love poetry was mixed with theistic devotion.

Govardhanadhara ('upholder of Govardhana') An epithet of *Kṛṣṇa.

Govinda ('tender of cattle') An epithet of *Kṛṣṇa.

Govindadās(a) (16th–17th century) A Bengali Vaiṣṇava *sant and *bhakti poet who used the conventions of secular Indian love poetry for his own devotional ends.

Govindalīlāmṛta ('The Nectar of Govinda's Divine Play', 16th century CE) A *Sanskrit poem attributed to *Kṛṣṇadāsa Kavirāja, about the love play of *Rādhā and *Kṛṣṇa. It is used in *Gauḍīya Vaiṣṇavism as part of a meditational practice involving the visualization (*līlā-smaraṇa) of the devotee as one of Kṛṣṇa's favourite companions.

Govindapāda (7th century CE?) According to the *Advaita Vedānta tradition, the name of *Śaṅkara's *guru, about whom nothing is otherwise known.

Govindaprabhu (Guṇḍam Rāül) (13th century CE) A Maharashtrian *saṃnyāsin, renowned for his unconventional or 'mad' behaviour. He was worshipped by the antinomian *Mahānubhāvas as an incarnation of God (*parameśvara); he was believed to be the guru of their founder, *Cakradhar.

govrata ('cow-vow') A practice followed by some *ascetics and *saṃnyāsins involving the imitation of a *cow, in so far as they sleep anywhere, and feed and cover themselves with whatever happens to be at hand.

grace A key supposition of theistic *bhakti movements is that a devotee's *liberation is ultimately dependent on the grace of the all-powerful deity. *See also* ANUGRAHA; PRAPATTI; PRASĀDA; PUṢṬIMĀRGA.

grāma ('village') In spite of increasing migration to the cities, over two-thirds of India's population still lives in villages, which remain the principal locus of *caste society. In so far as each village functions as a well-defined community, tied to a specific area of land, with its own particular guardian deities or *grāmadevatās (usually goddesses), and its own set of cyclical and seasonal *festivals, the inhabitants remain economically and ritually dependent on each other. In *Brahmanical and *renouncer discourse, the village (as opposed to the 'wilderness' or *araṇya) is conceived as the domain of the economically and ritually active, married male *householder. However, the dominant role of women in village ritual cycles has been increasingly recognized in contemporary studies, as has the part played by low-caste *priests and *exorcists in the day to day religious life of the community. *See also* ARAṆYA; CASTE; FESTIVALS.

grāma-devatā(s) (amma(n), mātās) ('village deities') A collective term for the numerous local deities, usually goddesses, worshipped in villages (*grāma) across India, where they are closely associated with fertility and the annual agricultural cycle. They are represented in various ways, from the aniconic (rocks, pots of water, etc.) to a lone, consortless image, placed in a dedicated shrine or *temple. Their functions are equally various, although many are considered to be the guardian deities of specific localities, especially in South India. Unmarried goddesses, such as the smallpox (and now AIDS) goddess, *Śītalā (who is thought to control the disease by possessing the afflicted), are invariably perceived to be both fierce and jealous: they demand blood (animal) *sacrifice in order to be placated. This is aligned to a general perception that such goddesses are 'hot', in the sense of being charged with unreleased sexual energy and violence. This makes them simultaneously powerful and dangerous; it also associates them with the impurities of blood and sex, and so aligns them with lower *caste behaviour. Nevertheless, they may also be conceptualized as multiple forms of *Devī, so that, depending on the context, they are thought either to manifest aspects of her power, or to be identical to the Great Goddess herself.

grammar/grammarians *See* VYĀKARAṆA.

gṛhastha ('householder', 'man-in-the-world') According to the *āśrama theory, a high *caste male who is a member of the householder stage or order (gārhasthya). In the *Dharmasūtras* this represents the preferred norm of life, although by the time of the *Dharmaśāstras* the āśramas had been arranged, for ideological purposes, into a single path through life marked by four successive stages, which each individual was supposed to pass through in turn. In practice, however, most adults have lived and died in the householder āśrama, reflecting **Manusmṛti*'s view (3.77–78) that the householder represents the best of all the āśramas, since it supports the other three. In this context, the 'householder' is therefore the married domestic ritualist, whose duty it is to perform *sacrifices (either as a *gṛhya or a *śrauta ritualist), and to produce *sons in partial fulfilment of his *debts to orthodox society. Ideologically, he functions as the complementary opposite to the world-renouncing *saṃnyāsin. The *king may be considered to represent the ideal or archetypal householder.

gṛhya ('domestic', 'household') Usually applied as an adjective to distinguish the limited, single fire (*ekāgni) ritualism of the domestic sacrificer from the expanded and extended ritualism of the *śrauta sacrificer, but applied more generally to the domestic rules, rituals, and rites of passage laid out in the **Gṛhyasūtras*. *See also* GṚHYĀGNI; GṚHYASŪTRA; GṚHYA-YAJÑA(S).

g

gṛhyāgni ('domestic fire') A ritual fire set up by the *Brahmanical sacrificer and his wife at the time of their marriage in a ritual known as *agnisthāpana ('establishing the fire'), and on which they perform their domestic rites (*gṛhya-yajñas). It is conceptually separate from the ordinary cooking fire (pacanāgni), although the latter may be physically collapsed into it.

Gṛhyasūtra ('Domestic *Sūtra*', *c.*800–300 BCE) A category of late *Vedic texts, classified as belonging to the **Kalpasūtra* literature of the **Vedāṅga* (and therefore as *smṛti), which deals with the proper performance of the domestic rituals (*gṛhya-yajñas), as well as containing details of various rites of passage (*saṃskāras)—such as Vedic initiation (*upanayana), *marriage, and *death—and descriptions of day-to-day religious concerns from the perspective of the householder (*gṛhastha). The *Gṛhyasūtras*' content overlaps to some extent with that of the **Dharmasūtras*.

gṛhya-yajña(s) (pāka-yajñas ('feeble' sacrifices)**)** ('domestic rites/sacrifices') The *sacrifices performed by the *Brahmanical sacrificer and his wife on the *gṛhyāgni. These rituals are a simplified form of the *śrauta sacrifices: a twice daily *agnihotra with grains (not milk), and fortnightly new and full moon sacrifices, for instance. They function to protect the family and the home, and to secure domestic prosperity. By the time of *Manusmṛti*, domestic ritualism has been further reduced or concentrated into the five 'great sacrifices' (*mahā-yajñas).

Guḍimallam *See* LIṄGA.

Guénon, René (Sheikh 'Abd Al Wahid Yahya) (1886–1951) A French writer on esoteric religious traditions, who was initiated into a North African *Sufi order. He wrote a number of influential works on Hinduism, including *Introduction générale à l'étude des doctrines hindoues* (1921) and *l'Homme et son devenir selon le Vêdânta* (1925).

Guga A legendary *Rājpūt prince and hero (R.: bīr; Skt.: vīra). Throughout Rajasthan, parts of the Panjab, Haryana, and north-western Uttar Pradesh, he is worshipped at local shrines as a deity with power over *snakes and the ability to cure those bitten by them; he is therefore particularly popular during the snake-infested rainy season. He is thought to derive his powers from *Gorakhnātha, and, according to some, he is also an incarnation of *Janamejaya, the auditor of the **Mahābhārata*. Guga's story is the subject of a sung epic, usually told over one night by Bhagats, the ritual specialists associated with his cult. Iconographically, he is represented with his horse and accompanied by blue and yellow standards. Some believe that he converted to *Islam before his death, and in places he is worshipped by both Hindus and *Muslims as a Muslim saint or pīr.

Guhēśvara *See* ALLAMA-PRABHU.

Guhyakālī A terrible goddess who, since the 10th century CE, has been at the centre of the northern transmission of the *Kaula *Kālī cult of *Tantric *Śaivism.

guhyaka(s) ('the hidden ones') A class of demigods, attendant on *Kubera (the god of wealth), and guardians of his treasures. Half horse, half bird in appearance, they are thought to live in caves in the mountains.

Guhyeśvarī ('goddess of the secret') Popular Nepalese form of the goddess *Guhyakālī, a major local deity since *c.*800 CE, and subsequently the tutelary goddess of *Nepal.

guṇa ('strand', 'quality', 'attribute', 'constituent of matter') **1.** At its most general, a quality or even a virtue. This sense is perhaps related to the more specific *Nyāya-Vaiśeṣika view of guṇas as the perceivable attributes which indicate the existence of a substance (*dravya). Lists of such qualities most commonly include those available to the senses (taste, touch, colour, etc.), and the mind (cognition, volition, attraction, etc.).

2. According to *Sāṃkhya-Yoga ontology, the (tri)guṇas are the three inextricably intertwined strands, or constituents, of material nature (*prakṛti), the dynamic interaction of which constitutes the physical universe—i.e. everything except the non-material 'persons' or *puruṣas. For purposes of analysis, the guṇas are separated into pure (*sattva), passionate (*rajas), and dark (*tamas) strands—the sattva guṇa representing the principle of pure thought, the rajas guṇa that of kinesis, and the tamas guṇa that of inertia. Prior to the evolution of the universe, these three guṇas exist in a state of perfect equilibrium or unmanifest potentiality (*pradhāna); but once their balance is upset by the influence of puruṣa, they manifest themselves in the evolutes, which make up the variegated world. Thereafter, it is the predominance, or otherwise, of particular guṇas in material nature (including the mind) which constrains beings to act in particular ways.

Versions of this understanding of the guṇas can be found across a significant number of Indian religious and philosophical systems, often tailored to particular ends. So the **Bhagavadgītā*, for instance, which is more concerned with the transformation of already embodied individuals than with the evolution of the universe per se, associates the sattva guṇa with knowledge and freedom from *pollution, the rajas guṇa with activity, energy, and greed, and the tamas guṇa with inertia and *ignorance; but ultimately it subsumes all three within God's (*Kṛṣṇa's) lower nature.

Guṇāḍhya *See* BṚHATKATHĀ.

Guṇātītānanda (Gunatitanand) *See* SVĀMĪNĀRĀYAṆA.

Guṇḍam Rāūl *See* GOVINDAPRABHU.

Gupta (*c*.320 CE–*c*.6th century CE) The ruling dynasty of an empire which extended across northern and central India. Their governance was marked by a period of cultural and religious creativity during which many of the religious and artistic forms that subsequently came to dominate medieval Hinduism were established and developed.

guru ('weighty', 'venerable') Used loosely as a term for any spiritual teacher or, indeed, for anyone due veneration (such as an older relative), guru is more specifically a term for a teacher within a particular tradition or lineage (*sampradāya), who is responsible for transmitting the religious knowledge validated by that tradition to individual pupils (śiṣyas). This oral, and often secret, transmission is particularly crucial in *Tantric traditions. There, and elsewhere, the process begins with the *dīkṣā, or formal initiation of the pupil into the order by the guru, typically involving the transmission of *mantras. Thereafter, the pupil becomes a 'son' in the guru's family until the end of his period of studentship, or until he takes pupils himself. In this way the (guru)paramparā, the unbroken line of direct transmission from teacher to pupil which authenticates the tradition, is maintained.

Normatively, the pattern of the relationship is prescribed in the context of the *brahmacarya *āśrama, the chief observable characteristic of which is total subservience to and reverence for the guru and his family. The regulations for this pattern of life are laid out in great detail in *Dharmaśāstra*. In *bhakti traditions, the guru is often treated as an incarnation of the deity, and, in some cases, gurūpasatti ('worship of the guru') may be regarded as the only means to *liberation. Conversely, the deity himself may be considered the only true guru.

Gurū Granth Sāhib *See* ĀDI GRANTH.

gurukula ('guru's house') The name given to a religious establishment or school following the *Brahmanical tradition of celibate studentship in a teacher's (*guru's) household. The *Ārya Samāj attempted to revive this tradition in schools (which it called 'gurukulas') for children and students of both sexes, between the ages of four and twenty.

guruparamparā *See* GURU.

gurūpasatti *See* GURU.

Guruvāyūr The location of a well-known *temple and *pilgrimage site on the Keralan coast, dedicated to Guruvāyūrappan ('The Lord of Guruvāyūr'), a form of *Kṛṣṇa.

Gvāy Dvoraḥbī A Laotian variation on the **Rāmāyaṇa*.

gyān *See* JÑĀNA.

H

hala ('plough') An attribute of *Balarāma, who is therefore also known as Haladhara or Halabhṛt ('plough-holder') and Halāyudha ('plough-weaponed', i.e. carrying a weapon shaped like a ploughshare).

halāhala See KĀLAKŪṬA.

Haḷebiḍ ('old capital') The modern day name for a hamlet in Karnataka marking the site of the *Hoysaḷa capital, Dvārasamudra; its *temple complex includes the elaborately sculpted Hoysaḷeśvara temple (built 1141–82).

Hampī *See* VIJAYANAGARA.

haṃsa ('goose') A term sometimes translated in older western works as 'swan', although it is generally taken to refer to the bar-headed goose, a bird that migrates to India in the winter. Since the time of the **Ṛg Veda*, it has been widely revered across Indian religious traditions, and is frequently represented in poetry and art. Notable for its white plumage and its grace in flight, the haṃsa was initially regarded as a symbol of masculine fertility and associated with the *sun, but, thanks to its migratory existence, it was increasingly evoked as a symbol of the transmigrating soul, or *ātman, which nevertheless has the aspiration and capability to transcend the elements (water, earth, and sky in the case of the haṃsa) in which it lives. It also comes to represent knowledge, since geese have the proverbial power to filter water from milk with their beaks (i.e. falsehood from truth). In mythology, the haṃsa is the vehicle (*vāhana) of *Brahmā and his consort *Sarasvatī, although it can be taken to symbolize a number of deities, and is included in some lists as an *avatāra of *Viṣṇu. The term is also applied to a class of *ascetics.

Hanumān (Hanumat, Hanūmān, Hanūmat) ('large-jawed') The monkey-hero of the **Rāmāyaṇa*, famous for his devotion to *Rāma; since the medieval period, he has been widely worshipped as a powerful deity in his own right. Usually portrayed with a monkey's head, a human body, and wielding a club, he is the son of *Añjanā and *Vāyu, the wind god, and exhibits his father's immense physical strength. In the *Rāmāyaṇa* he is a minister of Rāma's ally, the *Vānara (monkey-) king, *Sugrīva. Searching for *Sītā, Hanumān is able to leap the ocean to Laṅkā, where he eventually discovers and, by presenting her with Rāma's ring, reveals himself to the abducted princess. She gives him a jewel to present to Rāma, but, instead of returning with it immediately, he lays waste to Laṅkā. In this he is unwittingly assisted by the demon *Rāvaṇa, who, in setting fire to his tail, provides him with a brand to complete the destruction. After returning to *Kiṣkindhā to report his discovery, Hanumān helps Rāma in the final battle to free Sītā, at one point flying to the *Himālayas and returning with an entire, medicinal-herb-covered mountain, to revive the host. Eventually, he returns with the victors to *Ayodhyā.

Because of his relationship with Rāma, Hanumān comes to be regarded by the *Vaiṣṇava tradition as the exemplary devotee (*bhakta), a role reinforced in subsequent retellings of the *Rāmāyaṇa*, such as *Tulsīdās's **Rāmcaritmānas*. In addition to his role as Rāma's greatest devotee, he is widely worshipped across India, sometimes as a form of *Śiva, or Śiva's attendant, but frequently as an object of devotion (*bhakti) in his own right. Although invoked for numerous purposes, his physical strength is perhaps the most usual reason for seeking his aid and protection, whether for personal or political ends; he is particularly popular across northern and central India as a protective *village deity. Contemporary *Ākhāṛās, amongst others, consider him their patron deity. Other associations include fertility, his power to cure spirit *possession, and his skill as a *grammarian. Many *temples are dedicated to Hanumān, and images of him are seemingly ubiquitous.

Hanumān

Hanumān Kherapati A popular North Indian tutelary deity ('lord of the village').

Hanumat *See* HANUMĀN.

haoma Iranian and *Zoroastrian equivalent of *soma.

Hara ('carrying off', 'destroying') An epithet of *Śiva, evoking his destructive aspect.

Harappā The name given to the archaeological remains of one of the major cities of the *Indus Valley civilization, situated on the southern bank of the Rāvī river (a tributary of the Indus) in the Punjab, in what is now Pakistan. Employing the modern name of the site, archaeologists frequently refer to the entire culture as 'Harappan'.

Harappan. *See* HARAPPĀ.

Hardās *See* HARIDĀSA, SVĀMĪ.

Hardwār (Hardvār, Haridvār(a) ('Hari's gate'), less freq. **Haradvār(a)** ('Hara's gate')**)** One of the seven ancient holy cities of India; a major *pilgrimage site, situated in the foothills of the *Himālayas where the *Gaṅgā meets the North Indian plain in Uttar Pradesh (Uttaranchal), hence another name for the town, 'Gaṅgadvāra' ('Gaṅga's gate'). Every twelve years the *Kumbh(a) Melā is held there, with an Ardha Kumbha, or 'half-Kumbha', every six years. The town is the gateway to the *Himālayan shrines at *Kedārnāth (to *Śiva) and *Badrīnāth (to *Viṣṇu), and a close neighbour to *Hṛṣīkeś.

Before its destruction at the end of the 14th century, the town was known as *Kapila after the *Vedic *ṛṣi who was said to have lived there, and it continues to be a centre for religious teachers and institutions. A number of well-known mythological or legendary events are associated with Hardwār, including episodes from the **Mahābhārata*, *Dakṣa's sacrifice, and Gaṅgā's descent to earth. Viṣṇu's footprint, imprinted in a stone at Hari-ka-pairi ghāṭ, draws many devotees.

Hardy, Friedhelm (Fred Hardy) (1943–2004) Born and educated in Germany, Hardy completed his doctorate at the University of Oxford. He joined the staff at King's College London in 1973, where he subsequently held the chair in Indian Religions from 1996 until his premature death. A scholar with an exceptionally wide knowledge of Indian religions and languages, and a particular expertise in

South Indian religious history and literature, he published two important monographs: *Viraha-Bhakti: The Early History of Kṛṣṇa Devotion in South India* (1983), and *The Religious Culture of India: Power, Love and Wisdom* (1994).

Hare Kṛṣṇa mantra A *Gauḍīya Vaiṣṇava devotional *mantra in praise of *Kṛṣṇa/*Viṣṇu, designed for repetitive chanting, and popularized in the West by the Hare Kṛṣṇa movement (*ISKCON): hare kṛṣṇa, hare kṛṣṇa, kṛṣṇa kṛṣṇa, hare hare, hare rāma, hare rāma, rāma rāma, hare hare.

h

Hare Kṛṣṇa Movement *See* ISKCON.

Hari ('yellow, reddish brown, or green') An epithet of *Viṣṇu (and so of *Kṛṣṇa), derived by some from the *Sanskrit root hṛ, 'to take away evil'.

Haribhaktivilāsa A popular *Gauḍīya Vaiṣṇava ritual text ascribed to the *Gosvāmī, Gopāla Bhaṭṭa (16th century CE). It includes some *Tantric elements.

Haridāsa, Svāmī (Hardās, Haridās) ('servant of Hari', 16th century CE) A North Indian *Vaiṣṇaiva *bhakti poet who was a devotee of *Rādhā and *Kṛṣṇa. He is associated with a number of sites in *Vṛndāvana, which has remained the base for his followers, the Haridāsīs, until the present day. Their alternative name, the Sakhī *sampradāya (or *Sakhibhāvas), reflects the way in which Haridāsa assumed the role of a female attendant or close girl-friend (*sakhī) of Rādhā in his *Braj bhāṣā devotional poetry, notably in the *Kelimāl* ('Garland of Divine Love Play'). Beyond the sampradāya (which is composed of *ascetic and *householder branches, following a 17th-century split), Haridāsa is renowned in North India as a singer and musician, and one of the founding figures of Hindustānī devotional music. He is linked with *Hitaharivaṃśa and Harirāma *Vyāsa as one of the 'triad of Hari', also known as the 'triad of connoisseurs' (rasika-trayī) because of their concern to evoke a sense of aesthetic delight or *rasa in their audience.

Haridāsakūṭa (Dāsakūṭa) A Kannada *bhakti tradition of wandering poet *saints, which derived its theology from *Madhva's *Dvaita Vedānta. Their devotional practices focused on the image of *Viṭṭhala in the *temple at *Paṇḍharpur in Maharashtra. Well-known followers included *Kanakadāsa and *Purandaradāsa.

Haridāsasampradāya *See* HARIDĀSA, SVĀMĪ.

Haridāsīs *See* HARIDĀSA, SVĀMĪ.

haridra (H.: **haldi**) Turmeric. In addition to its medicinal properties, because of its yellow colour haridra is regarded as *auspicious when used as a powder or dye. It is notably employed in *marriage rites and in rituals associated with pregnancy.

Haridvār(a) *See* HARDWĀR.

Harihara 1. The name given to a composite or synthetic deity, half *Viṣṇu (*Hari), half *Śiva (*Hara). *Images show a figure divided from head to foot, the right half (from the viewer's perspective) Hara, the left Hari. Worship of the god appears to have developed in the medieval period, when a number of *temples were dedicated to him, especially in the Deccan under the patronage of the *Vijayanagara dynasty (14th–16th centuries CE). It is notable that one of the co-founders of that dynasty was himself called 'Harihara'. **2.** A 15th-century CE Kannada poet and verse biographer of the *Vīraśaiva *saints.

harijans ('children of God') A term coined by *Gāndhī (1869–1948) to designate the so-called '*untouchables' (those at the foot of the *caste hierarchy) in an attempt to raise their status, although they themselves later preferred the epithet *Dalit ('oppressed').

Harivaṃśa ('Chronicle of Hari') A *Purāṇa-like appendix (khila) to the *Sanskrit *Mahābhārata*, much of which was probably compiled over several centuries at the beginning of the Common Era. It was subsequently divided into three books, the *Harivaṃśaparvan*, the *Viṣṇuparvan*, and the *Bhaviṣyaparvan*. The first of these contains material on *cosmogony, secondary creation, genealogies (including that of the *Vṛṣṇis, as requested by *Janamejaya in the frame story), and other material conforming to the *pañcalakṣaṇa. The last, the *Bhaviṣyaparvan*, contains Janamejaya's genealogy, a description of his performance of an *aśvamedha, and an evocation of the *kaliyuga. But it is the middle book, the *Viṣṇuparvan*, which has been most influential in the subsequent history of Hinduism, since it contains the first extended and complete account of *Kṛṣṇa's childhood, later life and death, including his and Saṃkarṣaṇa's (*Balarāma's) sport among the cowherds (and, briefly, the *gopīs) at *Vṛndāvana. The *Harivaṃśa* (undoubtedly drawing on previous folk-religious stories) thus provides the model for later accounts of Kṛṣṇa's life and deeds, such as those in the **Viṣṇu Purāṇa* and the **Bhāgavata Purāṇa*—a model that presents a very different Kṛṣṇa from the warrior god of the *Mahābhārata*.

Harivaṃśa *See* HITAHARIVAṂŚA.

Harṣacarita *See* BĀṆA.

Harṣa (-Vardhana) (*c.*590–647 CE, r. *c.*606–647 CE) North Indian emperor. Thanks to *Bāṇa's account of his patron's early life, the *Harṣacarita* ('The Deeds of Harṣa'), and the description of his court given by the Chinese pilgrim, Hsüan Tsang, Harṣa's reign is better documented than that of other early Indian *kings. He appears increasingly to have favoured the *Buddhist monastic community; one of the three *Sanskrit plays attributed to him, the *Nāgānanda*, has a Buddhist theme.

hasta *See* MUDRĀ(s).

Hastināpura (Hāstinapura) An ancient city (destroyed by floods, and now an archaeological site) on a tributary of the *Gaṅgā, northeast of Delhi, identified in the **Mahābhārata* as the capital of the *Kauravas.

Hastings, Warren (1732–1818) The first British Governor-General of Bengal (1773–85).

haṭha-yoga ('yoga of force') A form of *yogic practice designed to bring about *liberation and immortality in this life (*jīvanmukti), through the purification and manipulation of the practitioner's body. In addition to conditioning practices, such as ingesting and expelling water through various bodily orifices, this is to be achieved through the superimposition of a complex esoteric anatomy (or '*subtle body'), composed of channels (*nāḍīs) and 'wheels' (*cakras) onto the physical body, which is subsequently controlled through a variety of demanding postures (*āsanas), visualizations, the regulation of inner sound (*anāhata nāda), and breathing techniques (*prāṇāyāma) to concentrate the life-force (*prāṇa). More specifically, haṭha-yogic practice aims to force the individual's *śakti (the serpent power or *kuṇḍalinī, which is dormant in the 'root' cakra) up the central channel of the spinal column (the *suṣumna nāḍī), from cakra to cakra, until it merges with the unlimited power of the sahasrāra padma ('the thousand-petalled lotus' at the crown of the head) in blissful liberation (frequently envisaged as permanent union and identification with the absolute, however defined). The ascension generates ever-increasing spiritual powers (*siddhis) in the practising *yogin.

Although probably practised in some form from at least the 6th century CE, haṭha-yoga was developed as a systematized discipline by the *Nāth Siddhas from about the 9th century onwards. A sophisticated, internalized understanding of its practice informs such later literature as the **Siddhasiddhānta Paddhati* and the **Gheraṇḍa Saṃhitā*, and, in particular, its textual locus classicus, Svātmarāma's **Haṭhayoga-pradīpikā*. Of all the forms of Indian yoga, haṭha has probably been the most influential on modern Western understandings of the discipline.

Haṭhayoga-pradīpikā ('Light on the Yoga of Force') The best known *hatha-yoga text, probably composed in the 15th century CE by Svātmarāma.

h

havelī (H.) A western Indian 'mansion', and the name used by the *Vallabhasampradāya (*Puṣṭimārga) for their *temples—i.e. a place of hospitality where *Kṛṣṇa (who is thought to be literally embodied in his *image) is properly entertained.

haviryajña *See* HAVIS.

havis A simple oblation, such as *ghī, milk, *soma, or grain, or an animal, offered into the fire as the essential component of a *Vedic sacrifice in a process known as haviryajña ('the offering of havis').

Hayagrīva (Hayaśiras ('horse-headed'), **Hayāsya** ('horse-mouthed')**)** ('horse-necked') As suggested by his name, a horse-headed figure who first appears in the **Mahābhārata* and the **Purāṇas*. One group of stories recounts how, as a *daitya, he steals the **Vedas* from *Brahmā, dives to the bottom of the ocean, and is killed by *Viṣṇu in his *Matsya *avatāra; another group identifies him as the saviour of the *Vedas*, and assimilates him to *Vaiṣṇavism as the eighteenth avatāra of Viṣṇu himself.

heaven *See* SVARGA.

Hedgewar, Keshav Baliram (1889–1940) A Maharashtrian *brahmin, he had been a member of the Indian National Congress, but tired of *Gāndhī's non-violent methods, and in 1925 founded the militant, right-wing Hindu nationalist organization, the *Rāṣṭrīya Svayamsevak Saṅgh (RSS).

hell *See* NARAKA.

henotheism A term coined by the *Indologist Max *Müller in an attempt to convey his idea that each deity in the apparently polytheistic *Vedic pantheon was actually experienced as supreme when focused on by a particular individual.

Hiḍimba (Hiḍimbā) A cannibal *rākṣasa in the **Mahābhārata*, who threatens the *Pāṇḍavas while they are in the *forest, disguised as *brahmin *ascetics. *Bhīma kills him in a wrestling match, then marries his sister Hiḍimbā. Their son Ghaṭotkaca appears during the final war to fight for the Pāṇḍavas.

Hiḍimbā *See* HIḌIMBA.

hierarchy The ranking principle which underlies the ordering of traditional Indian society ('the *caste system'), the cosmos, *ritual systems, deities, and other groupings.

Himālaya(s) ('house of snow') The name given to the mountain range bordering northern India. Personified as *Himavat, it has traditionally been identified as the dwelling place of the gods—in particular *Śiva, who dwells on Mount *Kailāsa—and is therefore thought to be especially sacred. The Himālayan range contains many famous *tīrthas and *pilgrimage sites, such as *Kedārnāth, *Badrīnāth, and (in its foothills, on the *Gaṅgā) *Hardwār and *Hṛṣīkeś(a). In *Purāṇic *cosmology the Himālaya is situated in *Jambudvīpa ('the rose-apple island') at the point where mythology and topography intersect—the northern boundary of *Bhāratavarṣa ('land of the *Bhāratas'), i.e. India. Its place in the cultural and religious imagination of northern India, in particular, is only rivalled by that of its personified daughter, the Gaṅgā.

Himavat (Parvata) ('snow-clad') The personification of the *Himālaya. In *Purāṇic mythology he is said to be married to *Menā. Their eldest child is *Gaṅgā; another daughter is *Śiva's consort *Umā (also known as *Pārvatī, 'the daughter of the mountain').

hiṃsā ('violence') *See* AHIṂSĀ.

Hindi (Hindī) A North Indian *Indo-Āryan vernacular which, in its medieval dialects, was the medium of much *bhakti literature, such as the works of *Kabīr, *Mīrābāī, and *Tulsīdās(a). In the 20th century, Hindi—a *Sanskritized version of *Hindustānī written in the *devanāgarī script—was controversially promoted as the 'national' or 'official' language of India to distinguish it from the similarly Hindustānī-based, but Persianized, *Urdū, which became the national language of Pakistan. In the face of vigorous opposition, mainly from speakers of the *Dravidian languages, it has been recognized that, although designated India's 'official' language, Hindi is in practice only one among a number of languages used for 'official' purposes (eighteen are named in the Constitution). Hindi remains, however, in its various dialects, the most widely used modern Indian language, spoken by over 420 million people (41% of the population) according to the 2001 census. *See also* BRAJ BHĀṢĀ.

Hindu A word derived from Persian, Greek, and *Muslim renderings of the *Sanskrit term for the river *Sindhu* (subsequently known as the *Indus), designating the population to the east of that river. There is debate about whether this remained simply an ethnic and geographical marker until the British took it up to designate what they perceived as the majority 'religion' practised by the inhabitants of South Asia (so inventing '*Hinduism'), or whether the term was already being used indigenously to signify a developing sense of a core set of (non-Muslim) beliefs, values, social practices, and rituals found across a wide variety of traditions. Whatever the case, the term is now used universally to differentiate 'Hindus' from adherents of what are perceived to be other South Asian religious traditions, whether identified as subcontinental in origin (*Buddhism, *Jainism, *Sikhism), or not (*Islam, *Christianity, *Judaism, *Zoroastrianism). As a noun in current usage, it is therefore loosely applied to a follower of, or practitioner within, any of the traditions belonging to the family of culturally related religions collectively labelled 'Hinduism'. As an adjective, it is applied (for example) to the rituals, texts, and beliefs, as well as the cultural and social practices associated with any of the branches of that family tree. At the time of the 2001 census, there were 827 million Hindus in India (80% of the total population), 18.5 million in *Nepal (80%), and at least a further 20 million to 30 million throughout the rest of the world, making Hinduism, in this collective sense, the world's third largest 'religion' after *Christianity and *Islam. *See also* DIASPORA.

Hinduism A noun of convenience, or construction, encompassing, whether actively or retrospectively, the religious and cultural traditions (i.e. the various beliefs, values, social practices, and rituals) of those identified by themselves or others as '*Hindus'. Many present-day scholars attempt to make a distinction between the '*Vedic' or '*Brahmanical' religion of northern India in the first millennium BCE, which can be defined in relation to the ultimate authority of the **Veda*, and the less easily definable, all-encompassing 'Hinduism' whose emergence is mirrored in the *Epics and **Purāṇas*. From the medieval period onwards, it is this 'Hinduism' which demonstrates such a huge variety of social, devotional and ritual practices, along with their associated theologies and ideologies, while retaining and reconfiguring older elements such as notions of *purity and *pollution. *For a further indication of how the term is used in this dictionary, see the Preface. See also* HINDU.

Hinduization A term employed by some scholars to evoke the process by which non- or pre-Hindu religious elements—such as local gods—are assimilated into Hinduism by identifying them with specifically Hindu elements, such as the great gods and goddesses of medieval devotionalism.

Hindū Mahāsabhā ('Great Hindu Assembly') A right-wing Hindu political party, formed in 1909 by Pandit Madan Mohan *Malaviya (subsequently the first vice-chancellor of *Benares Hindu University) as an off-shoot of the *Ārya Samāj, advocating 'Hindu' rule under 'Hindu' law. Under Vinayak Damodar *Savarkar (president of the party, 1937–1942) it espoused the ideology of *Hindutva.

'Hindu Renaissance' A term used by Western scholars and others to characterize 19th-century Hindu reform movements, such as that instigated by Rām Mohan *Roy.

Hindustānī A term used by the British to designate Khaṛī bolī (H.), a dialect of the Delhi region, which became India's lingua franca for purposes of trade. In the 19th century its usage was divided on religious grounds into what became, at *Partition, the 'separate' 'national' languages of *Hindi (India) and *Urdū (Pakistan).

Hindusthān ('land of the Hindus') The name given by some to *Bhārata.

'Hindu Trinity' A misleading term, derived from a *Christian model and applied by some earlier Western commentators to *Brahmā, *Viṣṇu, and *Śiva because of their perceived complementary functions (creator, preserver, and destroyer) in *Purāṇic *cosmology. *See also* TRIMŪRTI.

Hindutva ('Hindu-ness') A term that first surfaces in literary form in the mid 1870s in Bankim Chandra *Chatterjee's serialization of his novel **Ānandamaṭh* in the journal, *Bangadarshan*. It was subsequently employed by Vinayak Damodar *Savarkar in his book *Hindutva: Who is a Hindu* (1923) to convey the idea of a universal and essential Hindu identity. As used by its author, and other right-wing nationalist ideologues, it is predicated on an assumed consensus about what constitutes Hindu identity and distinguishes it from the ways of life and values of other (implicitly 'foreign') people and traditions, especially Indian *Muslims. Savarkar attempted to distinguish between Hindu *dharma—the religious traditions conventionally grouped together as '*Hinduism'—and 'Hinduness', a cultural and political force underpinned by a racially and geographically defined, *Āryan history.

Hiraṇyagarbha ('golden embryo') A cosmogonic principle introduced in **Ṛg Veda* 10.121 where it appears as the one lord of creation who arose in the beginning. In later texts, hiraṇyagarbha mutates into 'Brahmā's egg' (*Brahmāṇḍa), establishing the basic, closed shape of the *Purāṇic universe.

Hiraṇyakaśipu ('golden-garments') According to *Purāṇic myth, an ignorant and powerful *daitya king, renowned for his expensive clothing. Much to his father's displeasure, his son, Prahlāda, was an ardent devotee of *Viṣṇu; and it was the latter, in a demonstration of his omnipresence, who killed Hiraṇyakaśipu after bursting out of a pillar in his *Narasiṃha ('Man-Lion') *avatāra.

Hiraṇyakeśi Kalpasūtra *See* HIRAṆYAKEŚIN.

Hiraṇyakeśin The founder of a ritual and scholastic tradition belonging to the *Taittirīya branch of the **Black Yajur Veda*. The *Hiraṇyakeśi* **Kalpasūtra* takes his name, although it is not clear whether he is the author, or whether it simply belongs to the tradition named after him. The *Kalpasūtra* is composed of the *Hiraṇyakeśi* **Śrauta-*, **Gṛhya-*, and **Dharmasūtras*, although the latter is effectively a copy of the **Āpastamba Dharmasūtra*.

Hiraṇyākṣa (Hiraṇyanetra, Hiraṇyalocana) ('golden-eye') According to *Purāṇic myth, an ignorant and powerful *daitya, the brother of *Hiraṇyakaśipu, who threw the Earth (*Bhū Devī) into the ocean. She was rescued by *Viṣṇu in his *Varāha ('Boar') *avatāra, who killed Hiraṇyākṣa for his pains.

Hitaharivaṃśa (Hit Harivaṃś, Harivaṃśa ('Flute of Kṛṣṇa')**)** (1502–1553) A North Indian *Vaiṣṇaiva *bhakti poet who was the founder of the *Rādhavallabhī *sampradāya. Born into a *brahmin family near *Mathurā, he moved in his thirties to *Vṛndāvana where, in 1535, he consecrated an image of Kṛṣṇa called Rādhavallabha ('Lover of Rādhā'). Hitaharivaṃśa himself was devoted to *Rādhā, assuming the role of a female attendant or close girl-friend (*sakhī), the better to contemplate the eternal union of her and her husband *Kṛṣṇa, in the hope of engendering a liberating emotion or aesthetic experience (*rasa) of joy (hita). Given this exclusive devotion, his attitude to orthodox *Brahmanical practices seems to have been antinomian; indeed, according to the hagiographies, he was initiated directly and miraculously by Rādhā herself into the *sampradāya which he effectively founded. (There is, however, a *Gauḍīya tradition that, before a falling out, he was originally a disciple of *Gopāla Bhaṭṭa.) Three works of devotional poetry can be reliably attributed to him, the *Sanskrit *Rādhā-sudhānidhi*, and two *Braj bhāṣā anthologies, *Caurāsīpada* (*Hitacaurāsī*) and *Spuṭavāṇī*, each the subject of numerous commentaries. Hitaharivaṃśa is linked with Svāmī *Haridāsa and Harirāma *Vyāsa as one of the 'triad of Hari', also known as the 'triad of connoisseurs' (rasika-trayī) because of their concern to evoke a sense of aesthetic delight or *rasa in their audience.

Hitopadeśa ('Beneficial Instruction') A *Sanskrit collection of fables and folk wisdom, compiled by Nārāyaṇa in 12th century Bengal, and well-known in India and beyond as a Sanskrit 'reader'. The first English translation was made by Charles *Wilkins in 1787, but many of the stories had found their way to Europe in Arabic and Persian versions well before that. It is a radically altered version of the **Pañcatantra*.

Holākā *See* HOLĪ.

Holī (Holākā) The name of a spring *festival (*vasantotsava), particularly popular in North and Central India, which is held on the last two days of the lunar month of Phālguna—February–March. Holī is characterized by a degree of social reversal and chaos before the start of the New Year. Its more obvious manifestations include the throwing of coloured powder and water, the shouting of risqué jokes and obscenities, consumption of bhang (*bhaṅgā), and the lighting of bonfires. The festival's name is usually derived from its association with a demoness called Holikā. Various stories are told about her, all culminating in her eventual destruction, marking the end of *evil, and/or the symbolic destruction of the old year. Holikā's *cremation, for instance, is re-enacted in the lighting of the bonfires. It has been suggested that Holī, or its precursors, may, as fertility rituals, have contained more explicitly erotic elements. Some of this may be reflected in the North Indian association of the festival with *Kṛṣṇa and his love-sport with the *gopīs.

Holikā *See* Holī.

homa Specifically, the act of making an oblation to the gods (*devas) by pouring *ghī into the sacrificial fire. Generally, any oblation of cooked *food; more generally still, any oblation or *sacrifice.

horse *See* Aśva.

h

horse sacrifice *See* Aśvamedha.

hospitality Traditionally considered a duty and an act of ritual worship. According to **Manusmṛti* (3.70), the honouring of guests (atithis) is the 'sacrifice to humans' (manuṣya-yajña), i.e. the fifth of the 'five great sacrifices' (*mahāyajña) incumbent upon the householder (*gṛhastha). The technical definition of a 'guest' in this literature (written from the *brahmins' point of view) is a brahmin who spends a single night with his host; the term does not imply that the person has been specifically invited. Others too may be treated as 'guests' as long as they fulfill certain conditions, such as having used up their own provisions, and arriving from another *village at a mealtime. The generosity of hosts should not, however, be abused. Basic hospitality consists of offering a seat, water (for washing the feet and rinsing the mouth), *food, and, if necessary, somewhere to sleep. The more important the guest—a *saṃnyāsin, for example, would be considered important—the greater the hospitality required. Just as the guest is regarded as doing the host a favour by giving him the opportunity to fulfill his obligations, as well as to earn *merit, so neglect of a guest is thought to have disastrous consequences. Notable examples of the latter are *Śakuntalā's neglect of the brahmin *ṛṣi *Durvāsas in *Kālidāsa's play, rewarded with a curse, and Death's keeping the brahmin Naciketas waiting in the frame story of the **Kaṭha Upaniṣad*, which requires three gifts as compensation. The general idea that hospitality is an obligation is, however, widespread, throughout South Asian cultures, and by no means confined to *Brahmanical circles. Since hospitality itself is a kind of ritual worship, then it is not surprising that in many forms of *pūjā the deity is treated as an honoured guest whose particular needs must be supplied by the worshipper.

hotṛ (Hotar) The name of the chief *priest at the *Vedic *śrauta sacrifice; his main responsibility is to recite the appropriate verses (*mantras) from the **Ṛg Veda*. The term is also used generically to refer to any officiating priest who offers an oblation (*homa).

householder *See* gṛhastha.

Hoysaḷa Dynasty (Hoyśala) (*c.*1050–1350) A South Indian Hindu dynasty, responsible for the building of elaborately sculpted *temple complexes at their capital city Dvārasamudra (*Haḷebiḍ), *Belūr, *Somnāthpuram, and other sites in the Deccan.

Hṛṣīkeś(a) (Hrishikesh, Rishikesh) A wooded valley on the *Gaṅgā, fifteen miles upstream from *Hardwār in Uttaranchal (formerly in Uttar Pradesh). It marks the beginning of the route to the *Himālayan *pilgrimage sites, such as *Kedārnāth and *Badrīnāth. It has become a popular site for religious teachers and their associated *āśrams.

human sacrifice (puruṣamedha) Conceptually the highest form of *Vedic sacrifice (*yajña), modelled on the primeval dismembering of the cosmic *puruṣa in the **Puruṣasūkta* of the **Ṛg Veda*. In principle, all sacrifices require the immolation of the patron (*yajamāna); in ritualized practice, however, the human victim is replaced by a substitute. It is not possible to judge the extent to which suggestions of the necessity of human sacrifice in, for instance, the *agnicayana ritual, or in the construction of buildings and bridges, were at one time intended to be taken literally. From the accounts in some **Purāṇas* (e.g. the *Kālikā*), it is clear that some *Tantric worship of the Goddess (*Devī) was thought to require regular human sacrifice, and its practice in some *temples is reported into the 19th century. Stories of individually motivated human sacrifice in remote areas of northern India still appear from time to time in the national press.

humours *See* DOṢA (2).

I

icon *See* MŪRTI.

Iḍā The goddess of nourishment. In the **Śatapatha Brāhmaṇa*, she is said to be the daughter of the first man, *Manu, who, after surviving a great flood, created her from the offerings made in the *iḍā ritual.

iḍā **1.** A *Vedic rite in which various oblatory milk products (*ghī, etc.), also known as iḍā, are distributed among the officiating *priests and the *yajamāna, prior to their consumption. The oblation is held in a vessel called the iḍā-pātra.

2. One of the three principal channels, or *nāḍī, of *yogic and *Tantric physiologies, associated with the *moon and the river *Gaṅgā. It runs up the body to the right of the central channel (*suṣumṇā) to the right nostril.

ignorance *See* AVIDYĀ.

Ikṣvāku Said to be the son (or grandson, through *Iḷa) of *Manu Vaivasvata, and the first king of *Ayodhyā. He was the founder of the dynasty named after him (also known as the *Solar dynasty); since *Rāma was one of his descendants, his genealogy is given, inter alia, in the **Ayodhyākāṇḍa* of the **Rāmāyaṇa*.

Iḷa/Iḷā Said to be the son (Iḷa) and/or daughter (Iḷā) of *Manu Vaivasvata, he/she is subject to various changes of sex in a number of *Purāṇic stories. As Iḷā, she gave birth to a son, *Purūravas, and so founded the *Lunar dynasty.

illusion *See* MĀYĀ.

image *See* MŪRTI.

image worship *See* MŪRTI; PŪJĀ.

immortality (amṛta) The state of being 'not dead', as variously defined. In the **Ṛg Vedic* hymns, for humans it is either a long life (of a hundred years or more), or a ritually created, but not necessarily permanent, existence in another, post-death world (*loka). For the gods (*devas), it is 'deathlessness' bestowed by the nectar of immortality (*amṛta). With the development of the doctrines of *karma and *rebirth, immortality comes to be seen as a permanently blissful state altogether removed from the cycle of *saṃsāra, and from which, after bodily *death, one is never again reborn. In the early **Upaniṣads* this state is attained through realization of the identity, or non-duality of one's self (*ātman), *brahman (neut.), and the universe; it is that 'knowledge' which is liberating, and which in itself frees one from *death.

Among prominent conceptions of immortality in sectarian Hinduism are ideas of an eternal life in *heaven (in some cases in a perfected body, as in *Viṣṇu's *Vaikuṇṭha heaven), or as identity with God. Such deathlessness may be bestowed by the *grace of the all-powerful deity, as a result, or concomitant, of an individual's personal devotion (*bhakti); it may also be attained through various *yogic practices (some of which aim at physical immortality), or through *Tantric ritual.

impure *See* PURE AND IMPURE.

impurity *See* PURE AND IMPURE.

inauspicious(ness) *See* AUSPICIOUS(NESS) AND INAUSPICIOUS(NESS).

incarnation *See* AVATĀRA.

India(n) A word derived from Persian, Greek, and *Muslim renderings of the *Sanskrit term for the Sindhu (subsequently known as the *Indus), designating the land surrounding, and to the east of that river. It is now used as a name for the modern Republic of India, although the official name for the latter is *Bhārata, '[the land of] the descendants of *Bharata'. As both noun and adjective (e.g. 'Indian religions') the term is frequently used by historians and others to encompass the 'Indian subcontinent' before *Partition (1947)—i.e. to include modern Pakistan, Bangladesh, and sometimes the *Himālayan states, such as *Nepal.

Indian National Congress A political organization founded in 1885, which, under the leadership of *Gāndhī and others, became the major vehicle of the Indian independence movement in the first half of the 20th century. Its successor, the *Congress Party, has been the dominant force in Indian politics for most of the period since Independence (1947) and the declaration of the Indian Republic(1950).

Indo-Āryan A term coined by philologists to distinguish the Indian, or Indic, branch of the Indo-Iranian language group from its Iranian counterpart. This model is predicated on the assumption that there was at one time an undivided population speaking a common *Indo-European language ('Indo-Iranian'), which separated over time into Iranian (Persian) and Indian subgroups while migrating, and/or invading, in a broadly West to East direction. When applied specifically to languages and their development, the term is subdivided into 'Old' (*Vedic and classical *Sanskrit), 'Middle' (the *Prākrits), and 'Modern' (*Hindi, Gujarati, etc.) Indo-Āryan. On some counts there are more than five hundred Indo-Āryan languages now spoken in central and northern parts of the Indian subcontinent. *See also* INDO-EUROPEAN; ĀRYAN.

Indo-European A term coined by Western philologists to designate a family of languages with an inferred common ancestor (Proto-Indo-European), whose membership includes, on the Indian side, the *Indo-Āryan languages, and, on the Western, such language groups as Germanic (including English), Italic (including Latin, French, Spanish), Greek, Slavic, and Celtic. Some scholars, notably Georges *Dumézil, have used comparative philology and the study of mythology in the attempt to uncover common Indo-European thought-patterns and social structures. *See also* JONES, SIR WILLIAM.

Indo-Iranian *See* INDO-ĀRYAN.

Indology The academic study of the languages, cultures, histories, and religions of the Indian subcontinent.

Indra The most frequently invoked god (*deva) in the **Ṛg Veda*, where he is characterized as the thunderbolt (*vraja)-wielding, *Āryan warrior-king, the leader of the storm gods (*Maruts), and the heroic conqueror of the *anāryans. Through the *sacrifice, he is the chief recipient of offerings prepared from the *soma plant, which he himself has brought from *heaven to earth for the benefit of humans. (In a similar fashion, he liberates the *cows from heaven to allow them to wander the earth.) Imbibing soma in this way, Indra acquires its power—power he can use to ensure life-giving rain and human fertility. A well-known hymn (*Ṛg Veda* 1.32) tells how, fortified by soma, he defeats the drought- and chaos-causing demon, *Vṛtra, frees the waters, and creates order and prosperity in the world, in the process earning the epithet, Vṛtrahan ('Slayer of Vṛtra').

In post-*Vedic mythology, Indra is invariably identified as the *king of the gods (devas), and the chief opponent of the *asuras. But with the rise of the great saving deities of sectarian Hinduism (*Śiva, *Viṣṇu, and *Devī), whose assistance Indra persistently requires to re-establish *dharmic order, and to whom, according to the *Purāṇic and *Epic accounts, he is therefore subservient, his status, along with that of the devas in general, declines. In the process, many of his previous functions (including his creative and ordering powers) are transferred to greater gods, notably Śiva. He remains, however, the epitome of warrior (*kṣatriya) values, and, at the level of mythology, a pan-South Asian deity, playing a part not only in popular stories and dramas, but also in *Buddhist and *Jain mythologies.

Indrāgni (Indra-Agni) A dual deity composed of *Indra and *Agni in the form of twin brothers.

Indrajit ('conqueror of Indra') A epithet of Meghanāda, the elder son of *Rāvaṇa, earned because he captured *Indra and refused to release him from *Laṅkā until the other gods had given him the gift of *immortality. He is responsible for *Hanumān's willing capture in the *Rāmāyaṇa*, and, in spite of his gift, dies in the battle for Laṅkā.

Indraloka (Svarloka, Svarga) ('Indra's world/heaven') A sensual paradise ruled over by *Indra from his capital, *Amarāvatī. It is said to be north of Mount *Meru.

Indrāṇī *Indra's beautiful wife; also known as *Śacī, and Paulomī (the daughter of the demon Puloman). She is one of the seven *mātṛkās.

Indraprastha ('Indra's place') In the *Mahābhārata*, the capital of the *Pāṇḍavas. It is said to have been situated in what is now old Delhi.

indriya ('sense', 'sense organ') In an elaboration of the usual five senses (indriyas), *Sāṃkhya ontology posits five sense capacities, or 'organs of knowledge' (*buddhīndriyas), and five motor organs or 'organs of action' (*karmendriyas), which it regards, along with *manas, as evolutes of *ahaṃkāra.

Indus Traditionally, one of the seven sacred rivers of the Indian subcontinent. Known in *Sanskrit as the Sindhu, the term 'India' was derived from it. *Partition (1947) allocated it to Pakistan, through which it flows to the Arabian sea.

Indus Valley civilization (Harappan culture) (fl. *c.*2500–1800 BCE) A term coined to denote the urban civilization whose archaeological remains have been unearthed over an increasingly large number of sites in the north of the Indian subcontinent, some close to the river *Indus, but others further south and east. Apart from evidence of meticulously planned and constructed cities (at, for example, *Mohenjo-Daro and *Harappā), suggesting a centralized administration, there are the remains of a distinctive pottery, and various steatite seals and copper plates bearing a script ('the Indus Valley script') which is yet to be deciphered. The remains of what appear to be *temples and *tanks, the numerous seals depicting what are apparently goddesses, possible *liṅgas, and the speculation that one seal at least (the '*Paśupati seal') depicts a 'proto-*Śiva' figure, suggest to some scholars a continuity between this civilization's religious and ritual practices, and those of later, *Dravidian forms of Hinduism. The extent to which these constitute real continuities, rather than simply reflections of general human concerns, such as fertility, is yet to be established. Similarly, the precise nature of the relationship between the Indus Valley culture and its presumed successor (according to some, destroyer), the *Āryan and *Vedic culture of North India, remains a matter of considerable controversy, hingeing, as it does, on presumptions about the language family (Dravidian or

*Indo-European) to which the Indus Valley language belonged. See also ĀRYAN.

Indus Valley civilization (seal showing a horned god with animals)

inference *See* ANUMĀNA.

initiation *See* DĪKṢĀ; UPANAYANA.

installation *See* PRATIṢṬHĀ(PANA).

Integral Yoga *See* AUROBINDO GHOSE.

intention *See* SAṂKALPA.

intermixing (of varṇas) *See* VARṆA-SAṂKARA.

International Society for Krishna Consciousness (ISKCON, Hare Krishna Movement) Initially a proselytizing and fundraising organization, founded in New York in 1966 by *Bhaktivedānta Swāmi, ISKCON is the principal form in which the *Gauḍīya Vaiṣṇava tradition has been carried to the West. With its headquarters at 'New Vrindaban' in West Virginia, USA, it has devotees (including *diaspora Hindus) across the world, and has established itself in this Westernized form in India as well, notably at *Vṛndāvana. Although conservative and orthodox in most of its practices, ISKCON is radical in its acceptance of those born outside the Hindu *caste system. Once initiated, either as celibate students or married *householders, members are given Hindu names and adopt traditional dress. In public, they are instantly recognisable in the West through their saffron robes and their continuous chanting (*japa) of the sixteen names of *Viṣṇu in the *Hare Kṛṣṇa mantra, although this is now not so central to their activities as it was in the 60s and 70s. ISKCON's principal scripture is a multi-volume English devotional version of the **Bhāgavata Purāṇa*, known as the *Śrīmad Bhāgavatam*. Since the death of Bhaktivedānta Swāmi, there have been a number of theological and organizational disputes, resulting in the establishment of splinter groups, such as the ISKCON Revival Movement.

International Transcendental Meditation Society *See* TRANSCENDENTAL MEDITATION.

invocation *See* ĀVĀHANA.

Irāmāvatāram ('The Incarnation of Rāma', *c.*12th century CE) An influential *Tamil retelling of the **Rāmāyaṇa* composed by the poet *Kampaṉ under the *Cōḻa dynasty. The founding classic of Tamil literature, it follows the structure of *Vālmīki's *Rāmāyaṇa*, but uses multiple verse forms (some derived from *caṅkam literature), and extended episodes, to recast the story as a *Vaiṣṇava epic, infused with *Āḻvār devotionalism. Its *bhakti is directed towards *Rāma, imagined as an omnipotent, saving deity—an *avatāra, who through his destruction of *evil, brings about the restoration of *dharma.

Īśāna ('Lord') In the *Vedic period a name of *Agni; later an epithet of *Śiva. In the feminine (Īśānā), an epithet of *Durgā.

Īśānaśivagurudevapaddhati (*c.*12th century CE) A text named after its supposed author, Īśānaśivagurudeva, which is used in Keralan *temple ritual as part of the *Tantric *Śaiva Siddhānta tradition.

Īśa Upaniṣad ('The *Upaniṣad* of the Lord'); also known as the Īśāvasya ('Dwelt in by the Lord') *Upaniṣad*, and the *Saṃhitā Upaniṣad*. At eighteen verses, the shortest of the principal **Upaniṣads*, but the one placed first in all Indian collections. Deriving its name from its first word (īśā—'by the Lord'), it belongs to the **Vajasaneyi Saṃhitā* of the **White* (*Śukla*) *Yajur Veda*, and quotes signficantly from the **Bṛhadāraṅyaka Upaniṣad*. Its content suggests that it was composed, like other theistic **Upaniṣads*, in the final centuries BCE. Its last four verses have been incorporated into the Hindu *funeral rites.

ISKCON *See* INTERNATIONAL SOCIETY FOR KRISHNA CONSCIOUSNESS.

Islam The religion of Indian Muslims, introduced to South India through trading links in the 8th century CE. Sustained Islamic military incursions into North India date from the 11th century CE, when raids were made from Afghanistan to plunder the riches of various palaces, *temples, and monasteries. A series of Muslim dynasties was subsequently established in North India, known collectively as the Delhi Sultanate (1211–1526). This paved the way for the *Mughals (of Turko-Mongolian descent) to establish their empire across most of the subcontinent during the 16th and 17th centuries. Many of the Muslim rulers of this period, such as the Mughal emperor *Akbar, were protective of the *dharma of their Hindu subjects, and patrons of *Sanskritic culture. Other notable Mughal emperors include *Shāh Jahān, and the less accommodating *Aurangzēb 'Ālamgīr.

As is increasingly stressed by contemporary scholarship, Muslims, Hindus, and others have interacted in a wide variety of complementary ways throughout their history together on the subcontinent, and attempts to present this situation in terms of ideologically motivated conflicts and divisions produces a distorted, not to say distorting, picture, especially when applied to pre-modern India. In relation to patterns of both theology and worship, there was a complex interplay between various Islamic (especially mystical or Sufi) traditions, and forms of Hindu *bhakti, notably among the *sants. *Kabīr, for instance, is famously claimed by both Hindus and Muslims.

Some have described this inclusive culture, which was clearly the norm in many Indian *villages throughout the Mughal period, as 'composite'. The British, who replaced the Mughals as the dominant political power, helped to foster more rigid divisions between Muslims and Hindus—a pattern which continued through the upheavals of the 20th century, chief among them the rise of the *Hindutva movement, *Partition (1947), and periodic outbreaks of communal violence, such as those triggered by the razing of the Bābrī Masjid mosque in *Ayodhyā (1992), and the Gujarat riots of 2002.

Before Independence, Muslims composed about a quarter of the subcontinent's population, and in spite of the mass migrations to the newly created state of Pakistan, engendered by Partition, India still has one of the largest Muslim populations in the world (138 million in 2001: 13.4% of the population).

iṣṭa-devatā ('chosen deity') A deity chosen by an individual for his or her private, but not necessarily exclusive, *pūjā.

iṣṭi In *Vedic *śrauta ritual, an oblation composed of vegetables or fruits, nested within a more extensive *sacrifice; the complex version usually requires four *priests. More generally, a term for any sacrifice or offering.

Īśvara ('lord', 'God') **1.** An honorific or title given to the supreme deity in the context of *bhakti, and theistic Hinduism in general. The term is perhaps most frequently applied to *Śiva.

2. In *Patañjali's **Yoga-Sūtra* (1.24), and so in the *Sāṃkhya-Yoga tradition, Īśvara is described as a 'special *puruṣa', an omniscient being, eternally untouched by defilements (*kleśas), such as ignorance (*avidyā), or by the workings of *karma. He is viewed as an object of meditation, expressed by the syllable *oṃ, but not as an active creator. For *Śaṅkara, Īśvara is *saguṇa brahman.

Īśvaragītā ('Song of the Lord [Śiva]') A *Pāśupata insertion into the *Kūrma Purāṇa*, providing a *Śaiva response to the *Vaiṣṇava *Bhagavadgītā*.

Īśvarakṛṣṇa (4th–5th century CE) Author or compiler of the *Sāṃkhya Kārikā*, the foundational text of philosophical *Sāṃkhya.

Īśvara-praṇidhāna ('contemplation of the lord') A form of intense concentration on the deity (*Īśvara), which forms part of the *kriyā-yoga ('*yoga of action') outlined in *Patañjali's *Yoga-Sūtra* (Ch. 2), with the ultimate aim of attaining *samādhi.

Itihāsa ('so indeed it was') A term for narrative texts widely regarded within the tradition as true and, therefore, in the widest sense, historical stories, although Western sources usually classify them as 'mythical'. The term is specifically applied to the two *Epics, the *Mahābhārata* and the *Rāmāyaṇa*. It is often combined with *Purāṇa* (itihāsa-purāṇa) to designate a huge body of authoritative narrative material embodying the tradition (*smṛti) which informs theistic Hinduism.

Iyenar *See* AIYANĀR.

i

J

Jābāla Upaniṣad (*c.*1st–3rd centuries CE) One of the **Sāṃnyāsa Upaniṣads*. Inter alia, it teaches that, with sufficient detachment, it is possible to renounce from outside the traditional *āśramas.

Jābāli A *brahmin who, in one of the rare didactic passages in the **Rāmāyaṇa*, attempts to persuade *Rāma to return and claim his throne by employing materialist (*Cārvāka) arguments.

Jacobi, Herman (1850–1937) The leading German *Indologist of his generation. He held the Chair of Indology and Comparative Linguistics at Bonn University from 1889–1921. His early work was mostly in *Jainism, but he later turned his attention to the *Epics and to *Sanskrit poetics. Many of the leading scholars of the next generation were his students.

Jagaddhara Bhaṭṭa (Jagadar, Mahākavi) (14th–15th century CE) A Kashmiri *Śaiva *Tantric poet.

Jagad Gaurī *See* MANASĀ.

jagadguru ('world teacher') The title given to the head of the *Daśanāmi order, the *Śaṅkarācārya based at *Purī.

jagamohana (mukhaśālā) The front hall of a *temple, where worshippers assemble.

***Jagamohana Rāmāyaṇa* (*Dāṇḍi Rāmāyaṇa*)** (early 16th century CE) A version of the **Rāmāyaṇa*, composed by *Baḷarāmdās in the Oriya language of East India.

Jagannāth(a) ('Lord of the World') A form of *Kṛṣṇa worshipped in West Bengal and Orissa, notably at the Jagannātha *temple complex in *Purī, which also contains *images of the god's brother, Balabhadra (*Balarāma), and his sister, *Subhadrā. All three wooden images share a peculiar, tribal-looking, and perhaps tribal-derived, iconography, with flattened faces and widened mouths; they are ritually renewed every twelve years. The major attraction for the large numbers of *pilgrims who make their way to Purī is the yearly *ratha-yātrā, or 'chariot *festival', held in āṣāḍha (June–July). Accompanied by his siblings in their slightly smaller vehicles, Jagannātha, on a 16-wheeled, 14-metre high, temple-shaped vehicle, is pulled through the streets to a garden retreat by thousands of devotees in a carnival atmosphere. After seven days, the images are returned the two miles to the temple, and the chariot dismantled, only for an exact replica to be built the following year.

The temple was begun in the 12th century CE under the Eastern Gaṇga *king, Anantavarman Coḍa (1076–1148), in what seems to have been an attempt to colonize the area by combining local tribal deities with *Viṣṇu in a royal commemorative cult. Initially the temple was dedicated to the *Puruṣottama form of Viṣṇu, but the name was changed to Jagannātha in the 15th century. The accidental and, occasionally, devotionally suicidal crushing of some devotees beneath the chariot's wheels, was a conspicuous feature of early reports by Westerners, and led to the coining of the English term, 'juggernaut'.

Jagannātha Dās ('Servant of Jagannātha', 16th century CE). A *Vaiṣṇava *bhakti poet and disciple of *Caitanya, who, apart from works in *Sanskrit, composed an Oriya version of the **Bhāgavata Purāṇa*, which remains popular in Odisha (Orissa).

Jaimal Singh (1838–1903) *See* RADHASOAMI SATSANG.

Jaimini **1.** A legendary *Vedic sage and pupil of *Vyāsa, from whom he is said to have received the **Sāma Veda*. **2.** The name of the teacher to whom the foundational *Mīmāṃsā text, the (*Pūrva*-) *Mīmāṃsā Sūtra* is ascribed, perhaps with the intention of linking its authorship to Jaimini (1). *See also* MĪMĀṂSĀ.

Jaiminībhārata **(*Jaiminīyāśvamedha*)** (12th century CE) A *Sanskrit retelling of the **Āśvamedhikaparvan* of the *Mahābhārata*, ascribed to *Jaimini (1).

Jaiminīya A recension of the **Sāma Veda*, named after *Jaimini (1), and composed of the *Jaiminīya Brāhmaṇa*, an *Upaniṣad* (the *Jaiminīya Upaniṣad Brāhmaṇa*, which includes the **Kena Upaniṣad*), and **Śrauta* and **Gṛhya Sūtras*.

Jainism A Western term coined to refer to the teachings of the *Jinas (or Tīrthaṅkaras), and to the religion practised by their followers (the Jains or Jainas) on the Indian subcontinent. The most recent Jina, and according to Western scholarship the effective founder of Jainism in its current form, was *Mahāvīra (5th century BCE). Regarded by some as a Hindu sect, Jainism has had a sufficiently distinctive religious and cultural history, analogous in some respects to that of *Buddhism, to justify its classification as a separate tradition. Indeed, many Western Jains now promote it as a 'world religion'. Its major internal division is between the *Śvetāmbaras, followers of male and female white-robed *ascetics, and the *Digambaras, followers of naked, male ascetics.

Although there are only approximately 3.35 million Jains in India today, with a further 100 000 in the diaspora, Jainism has been a major cultural influence in many parts of the subcontinent since at least the 4th century BCE. Well known for its premium on non-violence (*ahiṃsā), and the punctilious care its ascetics take to avoid harming the living creatures (*jīvas) which, according to Jains, inhabit all parts of the material world, Jainism is also highly visible through the lay activity of *temple building. Historically, its interaction with Hindu traditions has been complex, and varied according to region and political patronage. However, unlike the other great non-*Vedic renouncer religion, Buddhism, Jainism never developed a *Tantric soteriology, which may have contributed to its survival as a distinctive tradition through the medieval period and beyond. From the outset, Jain ascetics were opposed to *Brahmanical sacrificial practices and rejected the authority of the **Veda* in favour of the universal truth taught by the Jinas. They also opposed the idea of an all-powerful or creator God, the universe being subject to perpetual temporal cycles in which creatures are governed by the law of *karma. Nevertheless, in their stories and worship, Jains utilized many of the deities (particularly the goddesses) of pan-Indian mythology as mundanely powerful but ultimately limited beings. At the same time, they satirized the supposed creative and soteriological abilities of the great monotheistic deities, producing their own, ethically reconstituted versions of the *Epics. Unlike its interaction with *Śaiva traditions, which has often been antagonistic, Jainism's relationship with *Vaiṣṇavism, particularly in northern India, has been more complex and amicable. For instance, *Kṛṣṇa, although berated for his violence, is incorporated into Jain mythology as a relative of Nemi, the twenty-second Tīrthaṅkara. Moreover, similar dietary practices (especially *vegetarianism), as well as membership of the same subcastes, has made intermarriage between members of the two communities relatively easy.

Jajmānī system The system by which the dominant *caste (the jajmān or 'patron') in a locality receives goods and services from other castes, usually of a ritual nature, and reciprocates with other goods, cash, or the use of land. The term is derived from the *Sanskrit word for the patron of the *Vedic ritual, the *yajamāna.

Jālandhara **1.** Situated in the Punjab, one of the four great *pīṭhas ('seats') at which parts of *Satī's dismembered body are said to have fallen to earth. **2.** (Jālandhari, Hāḍi-pā) The name of one of the nine 'historical', lineage-founding *Nāth *Siddhas.

Jalaram **(Jalaram Bapa)** (1800–1881) Born into a merchant family in the village of Virpur in Gujarat, Jalaram became well known in the locality for his acts of charity, particularly towards mendicants and *sādhus. A devotee of *Rāma, he was credited with intercessory and miraculous powers, and subsequently became an object of devotion himself, especially among Gujaratis. His birthplace is a popular *pilgrimage centre, and *temples have been dedicated to him throughout India and beyond.

Jamadagni A legendary *Vedic *ṛṣi who appears in the *Purāṇas* and the *Mahābhārata*. According to the *Viṣṇu Purāṇa*, he is one of the seven great sages of the current *manvantara, and is married to *Reṇukā; one of their sons is *Paraśurāma.

Jāmba Purāṇa A Telugu folk narrative recounting the origins of the '*untouchable' Mādiga leatherworkers of Andhra Pradesh. Dating to at least the 16th century CE, it is a 'live' text, subject to improvements and up-dating in performance.

Jāmbavat In the *Rāmāyaṇa* the king of the bears, and one of *Sugrīva's counsellors. He assists in the attack on Laṅkā.

Jambūdvīpa ('the rose-apple island') *See* COSMOLOGY.

Janābāī (*c.*1263–1350). A Maharashtrian *bhakti poet. Born into a *śūdra family, she was taken as a child to *Paṇḍharpur to work for the family of the *Vārkarī poet-saint *Nāmdev, to whom she became completely devoted. Over 340 of her Marathi devotional songs (*abhaṅgas) were preserved alongside her master's. They are mostly addressed to *Viṭhobā, whom she sometimes conceptualizes as female (Viṭhabāī). Her songs are still sung in Maharashtrian *temples.

Janaka The king of *Videha, he first appears in the *Bṛhadāraṇyaka Upaniṣad* (3.1.1) in a debate with *Yājñavalkya. He is subsequently cited as an exemplar by *Kṛṣṇa in the *Bhagavadgītā* (3.20), and appears elsewhere in the *Mahābhārata*. In the *Rāmāyaṇa*, he plays an important role as the father of *Sītā, whom he brought to existence from a ritually ploughed furrow. His capital city is *Mithilā.

Jānakajānanda A 17th-century work by Kalyalakṣmīnṛsiṃha, based on the *Rāmāyaṇa*.

Jānakī *See* SĪTĀ.

Jānakīharaṇa (*c.*6th century CE) A *Sanskrit retelling of the *Rāma story, attributed to the Sri Lankan *king, Kumāradāsa.

Janakpūr A city in *Nepal, just inside the border with India, said to be the site of the ancient city of *Mithilā. Identified as the birthplace of *Sītā, and the city in which she was married to *Rāma, it was effectively founded by the *Rāmānandīs in the

18th century, since when it has been a major *tīrtha for *Vaiṣṇava devotees of the divine couple. A large *Jānakī *temple was built there at the beginning of the 20th century, and there is an annual *festival (known as Vivāha Pañcāmī) in Mārgaśīrṣa (November–December), during which the *wedding of the deities is re-enacted.

Janamejaya In the outer framing story of the **Mahābhārata*, King Janamejaya is the great grandson of *Arjuna and *Subhadrā; he is therefore a direct descendant of the *Pāṇḍavas, and the son of *Parikṣit, whose death by snakebite he avenges in a great *snake *sacrifice. The first recitation of the *Mahābhārata* itself is made to him by *Vaiśaṃpāyana.

Janārdana ('agitating men') An epithet and, according to some lists, *avatāra of *Viṣṇu.

Janārdana Swāmi (1504–1575) A devotee of *Dattātreya, and the *guru of *Ekanātha. A number of other teachers have also taken this name.

Jana Saṅgh (Bhāratīya Jana Saṅgh) A Hindu nationalist party founded in 1951 by S. P. Mookerjee in an attempt to provide an anti-*Muslim alternative to the *Congress Party, especially in the north of India. In 1977 it merged with other Hindu parties to form the *Janatā Party, which briefly took power after the defeat of Indira Gandhi (1917–1984) in the post-'emergency' election.

Janatā Party A coalition of anti-*Congress, Hindu and secular parties, including the *Jana Saṅgh, which briefly took power after defeating Indira Gandhi (1917–1984) in the post-'emergency' election of 1977. It was succeeded in 1980 by the *Bhāratīya Janatā Party.

janëu *See* SACRED THREAD.

jaṅgamas Members of an hereditary priestly subcaste among the *Liṅgāyatas, so-called because they are seen as 'moving' (jaṅgama) *liṅgas. There are *householder and *ascetic divisions.

Janmāṣṭamī *See* KṚṢṆA JAYANTĪ.

japa ('muttering') The constant repetition of a *mantra, or of the name of God, often performed sotto voce, or internally. It may be accompanied by the telling of a rosary (*mālā), and is variously considered as a form of *purification, a variety of *tapas, a means of controlling the breath (*prāṇāyāma), and salvific in its own right.

jāpaka Someone who practises *japa as a soteriological discipline in its own right.

Jāpakopākhyāna A sub-section (Critical Edition: 12.189–93) of the **Śāntiparvan* of the **Mahābhārata* in which *Bhīṣma eulogizes *japa as an independent spiritual discipline.

jaṭā ('matted locks') Matted hair, worn as a sign of mourning, and also as a distinguishing mark by *ascetics. *Śiva, as the archetypal ascetic, is invariably portrayed as wearing his hair in this fashion, often formalized or elaborately extended for artistic effect—hence his epithets jaṭādhara ('wearing the jaṭā') and jaṭāmukuṭa ('crown of jaṭā').

Jātavedas ('all-possessor', 'knowing all beings') An epithet of *Agni.

Jaṭāyu(s) In the **Rāmāyaṇa*, a king of the vultures, and a friend of *Daśaratha. In attempting to foil *Rāvaṇa's abduction of *Sītā, he is fatally wounded, but survives long enough to point *Rāma and *Lakṣmaṇa in the right direction. They conduct his *funeral rites and see him ascend to *heaven in a chariot of fire.

jāti ('[position assigned by] birth', 'birth group') The word commonly translated as '*caste', 'subcaste', or 'sub-subcaste'.

jātismara ('remembrance of previous births') The recollection of previous lives, enabled by the right *karmic conditions. The ability to do this at will is considered an indicator of high spiritual accomplishment.

Javanese Hinduism Until the collapse of the Majapahit empire and the rise of *Islam in the 16th century CE, the Indonesian country of Java was ruled for over a thousand years by a series of Hindu and *Buddhist kingdoms. Hinduism, and particularly *Śaivism, had been introduced from India through trade in the first centuries CE, but achieved popular dissemination in the medieval period through the creation of Old Javanese versions of the **Rāmāyaṇa* and **Mahābhārata*, and an extensive *temple-building programme. Since the 1960s there has been a Hindu revival, drawing on the historical predisposition of many Javanese to follow Hindu practices while maintaining a nominal *Muslim identity.

Jayadeva (12th century CE) A *Sanskrit poet renowned for his authorship of the **Gītagovinda*. Little or nothing is known about his life, although he is traditionally associated with the *Jagannātha *temple complex in *Purī.

Jayadeva Pakṣadhara (15th century CE) The founder of a *Navya Nyāya *sampradāya in the tradition of *Gaṅgeśa.

Jayadratha (Saindhava) In the **Mahābhārata*, the king of Sindh(u), and the brother-in-law of *Duryodhana. An ally of the *Kauravas, he was responsible for the abduction of *Draupadī during the *Pāṇḍavas' exile in the *forest. Spared by the latter, he fought against them in the war, but was killed by *Arjuna.

***Jayadrathayāmala Tantra* (*Tantrarājabhaṭṭāraka* ('King of Tantras'))** A northern transmission *Tantric text of the *Kāpālika cults, through which *Kālī is to be worshipped, and realized, as the transcendent absolute.

Jaya Jagadīśa Hare ('Victory to the Lord of the Universe') A popular North Indian devotional hymn, sung during *āratī.

Jayākhya Saṃhitā (*c.*7th/8th century CE) One of the *Pāñcarātra *Saṃhitās, dealing, inter alia, with esoteric *cosmology, ritual, and *temple construction. It is one of the 'three jewels' which continues to provide the pattern for South Indian temple worship.

Jayanta Bhaṭṭa (9th–10th century CE) A *brahmin logician who was the author of the well-known work, *Nyāyamañjarī* ('Blooms of Nyāya'), dealing with *Nyāya vis à vis *Buddhism and the *Mīmāṃsaka *darśana. He also wrote a witty and satirical, but ultimately tolerant play (*Āgamaḍambara*—'Much Ado About Religion') about religious life in Kashmir during the reign of Śaṅkaravarman (883–902).

Jayarāśī Bhaṭṭa (*c.*650 CE) Author of the *Tattvopaplavasiṃha* ('Lion of Destruction of Philosophical Theories'), a work highly sceptical of all philosophies and epistemologies, and considered by some as a candidate for a surviving *Cārvāka text.

Jayaratha (*c.*13th century CE) Author of a major commentary (the *Tantrālokaviveka*) on *Abhinavagupta's **Tantrāloka*.

Jejurī *See* KHAṆḌOBĀ.

Jha, Sir Ganganatha (1871–1941) An eminent Indologist and teacher, whose work on *Nyāya, *Vedānta, and especially *Mīmāṃsā, fruitfully combined traditional *Sanskrit learning with modern scholarship. He was educated at the University of Allahabad, which he was later to serve as Vice-Chancellor from 1923–32. Among other posts, he was the first Indian to be appointed Principal of the Sanskrit College in *Vārāṇasī. He was honoured with both the traditional title

'Mahāmahopadhyāya' ('Great Teacher') and a knighthood from the colonial Government. His publications include *The Prabhākara School of Pūrva Mīmāṃsā* (1909), and *Pūrva Mīmāṃsā in Its Sources* (1942), as well as numerous translations of Sanskrit texts into English—the **Śābarabhāṣya*, **Ślokavārttika*, and **Tantravārttika* amongst them.

Jīmūtavāhana (12th century CE) Author of a Bengali treatise on Hindu inheritance law, the *Dāyabhāga*.

Jina ('conqueror') An epithet and alternative name for the *Jain Tīrthaṅkaras ('ford-makers' or omniscient teachers), indicating conquest of wordly passions and values. The Jain(a)s are therefore 'followers of the Jinas'. The term is also used in early *Buddhist literature to indicate the *Buddha.

jīva ('living', 'life principle', 'embodied soul') A term which is variously defined across a wide number of schools of thought and religious traditions. Essentially, it denotes the living individual, emphasizing its status as either an embodied sentient being, or as the essential *self, or soul. For *Rāmānuja, for instance, jīva is the eternal individual self, which is distinguished from God but dependent upon him. In some contexts it is synonymous with *ātman.

Jīva Gosvāmī *See* GOSVĀMĪS.

jīvanmukta ('liberated while alive and embodied') A person who has achieved *jīvanmukti.

jīvanmukti ('liberation while alive and embodied') The state of being liberated or saved (however defined) while still alive and in a physical, although possibly transformed, body. This may (as in *haṭha-yoga), or may not (as in *Advaita Vedānta), be concomitant with *immortality in the material sense of eternal life in one's current bodily condition. Some schools (e.g. *Viśiṣṭādvaita) reject the possibility of pre-death *liberation altogether.

jīvansamādhi ('living memorial') A practice in which an advanced *yogin or *saṃnyāsin brings his life to an end by being voluntarily entombed or buried alive while in a state of deep meditation (*samādhi). The tomb subsequently becomes his memorial (also known as jīvansamādhi).

jñāna (gyān) ('knowledge', 'knowing') Frequently employed in the sense of gnosis or 'realization' (i.e. of ultimate reality, or one's true nature), as opposed to conventional or discursive knowledge. Such 'knowledge' is considered free of the karmic consequences of action (*karma); it is therefore thought to be concomitant with the *renunciation of instrumental and passion-induced activity in general, regardless of whether it has been undertaken for ritual or worldly purposes. It is the quest for this liberating knowledge, identified as realization of the relationship between *brahman (neut.) and *ātman, which informs much of the teaching of the **Upaniṣads*, and which subsequently becomes the characteristic means to liberation (*mokṣa) advocated by the *Vedāntic tradition.

jñānakāṇḍa ('the knowledge section') The traditional designation of that part of the **Veda* (the **Āraṇyakas* and **Upaniṣads*) which deals with liberating knowledge (*jñāna), as opposed to the *karmakāṇḍa (the **Saṃhitās* and **Brāhmaṇas*), which deals with ritual.

jñāna-mārga ('path of knowledge') *See* JÑĀNA-YOGA.

Jñānasaṃbandar (Gnanasambandar) (*c.*7th century CE) *See* CAMPANTAR, TIRUÑĀṈA.

jñāna-yoga ('the discipline of knowledge') A path to *liberation outlined in the **Bhagavadgītā*. In its widest sense, what counts as 'knowledge' in the *Gītā* is a particular ontology and *cosmology derived from versions of *Sāmkhya theory. More specifically, jñāna-yoga is a discipline requiring realization of the *Upaniṣadic *brahman (neut.) as the absolute power underlying all things, including the individual, and associated with *renunciation of *householder life. It is usually contrasted with what are taken to be the other paths to liberation described in the text (*bhakti-yoga and *karma-yoga), although the *Gītā* itself does not present these as systematic or exclusive paths (*mārgas). Subsequent commentators have, however, adapted the division to chart three distinctive Hindu paths to liberation. So *Śaṅkara, for instance, in his commentary on the *Bhagavadgītā*, elevates jñāna-yoga above the other two yogas, as the ultimate means to *liberation. *See also* BHAGAVADGĪTĀ; JÑĀNA.

j

jñānendriya ('organs of knowing', 'sense organs') According to *Sāṃkhya ontology, the five cognitive senses (hearing, touch, sight, taste, and smell) which evolve from *prakṛti.

Jñāneśvar(a) (Jñānadeva, Dnyaneshwar, Dnyandeo) (1275–1296) A Marathi poet *saint, considered to be the founder of the *Vārkarī Panth. According to the hagiographies, he came from a high *caste, *brahmin background, but his father had been cast out of the local community for returning to the *householder life after previously becoming a *saṃnyāsin. Jñāneśvara was apparently initiated into the *Nāth tradition by his elder brother, Nivṛtti(nāth), who was therefore also his *guru. Together with their other brother, Sopān, and their sister *Muktabāī, they asked to be officially readmitted to their caste status after their parents had died. It was after being rebuffed in this attempt that Jñāneśvara began to acquire a reputation as a miracle worker, and, along with his siblings, devoted himself to *Viṣṇu as *Viṭhobā, thus initiating the Vārkarī tradition in Maharashtra. He is also said to have associated at this time with the poet saint *Nāmdev. His life ended when he practised *jīvansamādhi at the age of 22 at Ālaṇḍī, near Pune, where a shrine is dedicated to him. Subsequently, he has become an object of devotion in his own right, and his pālkhī (a decorated chariot carrying his pādukās, the imprint of his feet) plays a major role in the biannual Vārkarī *pilgrimage to the image of Viṭhobā at *Paṇḍharpur in South Maharashtra.

Jñāneśvara's major influence on both the history of Indian religions and the development of the Marathi language was achieved through the composition of the *Jñāneśvarī* (also known as *Bhāvārtha Dīpikā*) (1290)—a version of the **Bhagavadgītā* embedded in his own extensive verse commentary. This was not only the first vernacular commentary on the *Gītā*, but would also come to be seen as the most influential work of any kind in Marathi. In addition to stressing its *Vaiṣṇava *bhakti elements, Jñāneśvara's reading of the text also draws on *Advaita Vedānta and the *Śaiva *Nāth tradition, providing a rich mixture of material for subsequent commentary. A large number of poems and Marathi devotional songs (*abhaṅgas) are also attributed to him.

Jñāneśvarī *See* JÑĀNEŚVAR(A).

jogī *See* YOGI(N).

jogtī/jogtīṇ Male (jogtī) and female (jogtīṇ) religious mendicants, especially devoted to the goddess *Yellammā in Maharashtra and Karnataka.

Jones, Sir William (1746–1794) A British *Orientalist of Welsh origin, popularly known as 'Oriental' Jones. He was the first to recognize that *Sanskrit, Greek, and Latin had a common source (i.e. they all belonged to what was later called the *Indo-European language family), so paving the way for the science of comparative linguistics. He was also the first

European to begin the systematic study of *Sanskrit texts, thereby also initiating *Indology as an academic discipline.

Jones was a polymath and a prodigious linguist. Part of his early interest was in translating from the Persian; but, having trained as a jurist, he was sent to Calcutta in 1783 to join the Supreme Court of Bengal, and it was there that he began to learn Sanskrit in order to gain access to Hindu law books. This resulted in his translation of **Manusmṛti* as the *Institutes of Hindu Law, or, the Ordinances of Menu* (1794). In 1784 he founded the *Asiatic Society of Bengal, which, under Jones's presidency, and through its journal *Asiatik Researches*, became the first major channel to Europe of information about classical Indian culture. Among pioneering publications investigating everything from Indian classical music to subcontinental botany, Jones introduced Western audiences to the previously unsuspected riches of Sanskrit poetry and drama through his translations of (inter alia) Jayadeva's **Gītāgovinda* (*Gítagóvinda; or, The Songs of Jayadéva*) (1789), and *Kālidāsa's **Abhijñānaśākuntalam* (*Sacontalá, or, The Fatal Ring*) (1789)—works which were to have a profound effect on the development of European Romanticism.

Judaism A minority religion with a long history in India, probably originally initiated by trading links. There is reliable evidence of a Jewish presence on the West coast from the 11th century CE, although the Jews themselves assert a much older connection. The Jews of Kochi (Cochin), for instance, claim to have settled in Kerala after the fall of Jerusalem in 70 CE. Whatever their early history, they successfully integrated with the Hindu population, speaking the local language (Malayalam), and being assimilated for all practical purposes into the *caste hierarchy. Nevertheless, three separate, endogamous communities established themselves, each with their own synagogues. Another community, the Bene Israel, had settled largely in the western coastal regions and the Bombay (Mumbai) area. Further groups, known collectively as the 'Baghdadi Jews', arrived from the Middle East in the 18th century, settling in Calcutta and Bombay; there were also migrations into northern India from Iran, Afghanistan, and central Asia. More anomalous are the Bnei Menashe community, part of a tribal group living close to the Myanmar border in Mizoram, who claim to be descended from one of the 'lost tribes' of Israel. Since the Second World War the number of Indian Jews has decreased rapidly through emigration to Israel, North America, and elsewhere—from 30 000 in 1951 to probably no more than 5 000 in 2006, mainly in Maharashtra and Mizoram.

Jumnā *See* YAMUNĀ.

Jvālāmukhī ('she of the flaming mouth') The name of the *śaktipīṭha in Himachal Pradesh where *Satī's tongue is supposed to have fallen.

Jyeṣṭhā (Alakṣmī ('misfortune')**)** ('eldest', 'greatest') A South Indian goddess, who, in her pan-Indian form, is identified with *Śītalā, the smallpox deity. She is often portrayed as grotesquely old and ugly, and is associated with *Yama, the god of death.

Jyotiḥśāstra ('science of the skies', 'science of astrology') A category of **Vedāṅga* texts, also known as the *Jyotiṣavedāṅga*, partially dating from the 5th century BCE and preserved in two recensions (those of the **Ṛg* and **Yajur Vedas*), which deals with the movement of heavenly bodies (*jyotiṣa), and the divisions of time dependent on them, in order to fix a calendar of *auspicious dates and times for the performance of *Vedic *sacrifices. The term is also more generally applied to texts which follow in and expand upon this *Jyotiṣavedāṅga* tradition.

j

jyotirliṅga ('liṅga of light') The image or form of supreme *Śiva, which is said to have manifested itself in a gigantic and brilliant column (*liṅga) of light at twelve different *tīrthas across India—*Somanātha, Nāgeśvara, Bhīmaśaṅkara, Ghṛṇeśvara, Trimbakeśvara (Tryambakeśvara), Mahākāleśvara, Oṃkareśvara, *Rāmeśvaram, *Śrīśailam (*Mallikārjuna), *Kedārnātha, *Viśvanātha (in *Vārāṇasī), and Vaidyanātha—thus creating a network of *Śaiva *pilgrimage sites.

Jyotirmaṭh A town close to *Badrināth in Uttaranchal, it is the site of one of the four *Daśanāmi *maṭhas (monasteries) founded, according to tradition, by *Śaṅkara in the 8th century CE. The monastery fell into disuse in the late 18th century, but with the aid of other maṭhas was revived in 1941. There is however a continuing dispute about who has the best claim to be its head, or *Śaṅkarācārya.

jyotiṣa (gaṇita) ('science of the movement of heavenly bodies', 'astrology', 'astronomy') A combination of astronomy, astrology, and mathematics, explicated in a category of **Vedāṅga* texts known as *jyotiḥśāstra. It was initially developed as a key adjunct to the correct performance of ritual, since it was only through calculations made in the light of such knowledge, based on the *nakṣatra system of grouped stars or lunar mansions, that the *auspicious dates and times for *Vedic *sacrifices could be fixed in a *calendar. With the introduction of Greek planetary astronomy in the first centuries CE, jyotiṣa expanded to affect all significant areas of mundane life, so that any important time and date was invariably linked to its specific astronomical conjunction. This practice has persisted: events such as *weddings, *pilgrimages, the installation of *images, and new undertakings in general (including major public events), continue to be arranged in consultation with an astrologer (jyotiṣī) in order that they may coincide with an *auspicious moment in the calendar. On the same principle, combinations of dates and movements (travelling arrangements, etc.) have to be carefully considered and planned; harmful supernatural beings may make use of *inauspicious moments in order to strike, and the influence of the malevolent planet Śani (Saturn) has to be avoided. At an interpersonal level, events such as potential marriages, and *saṃskāras in general, continue to be governed by the casting and interpretation of birth horoscopes.

Jyotiṣavedāṅga *See* JYOTIḤŚĀSTRA

jyotiṣī An astrologer, responsible for the casting and interpretation of horoscopes. *See also* JYOTIṢA.

jyotiṣṭoma The name of a class of *soma rituals.

K

Ka ('who?') The *Sanskrit interrogative pronoun, used in the **Ṛg Veda* as a signifier of the unnamed and undefined universal power. In some hymns, notably in Book 10, Ka is identified with *Hiraṇyagarbha or *Prajāpati (i.e. the creative source of everything).

Kabīr (*c.*1398–*c.*1448) A North Indian poet and mystic. A substantial hagiographical literature and numerous legends have developed around his life story, but little is known for certain. He was born, either in *Vārāṇasī or in the nearby *Muslim enclave of Magahar, into a family of low-*caste Muslim weavers, or Julāhās (P.). (Once classified as Hindu *śūdras, the Julāhās had subsequently been Islamicized.) Kabīr was married and had several children, but seems to have been as critical of the *householder's life as he was of that of *renunciants or religious 'professionals'. A famous legend relates how, after Kabīr's death, his body was claimed by both Hindus and Muslims; but when it was revealed that his only mortal remains consisted of a spray of flowers, he received a double *funeral—a Hindu *cremation and a Muslim *burial. This reflects what was perceived to be his ambiguous position in relation to conventional religious identity, but perhaps it is his vanishing which is most significant, since Kabīr's poetry is notable for its insistent criticism of the external forms of all religions. Given the certainty of *death, he considers the only adequate response is simply to direct one's loving devotion (*bhakti) to the undifferentiated and unqualified (*nirguṇa) absolute, referred to as *Rām; this is identical with the realized *self and everything else, and it alone can save the devotee. Conventional worldly or religious behaviour of any kind, including *caste differentiation, is all equally misguided.

Kabīr was probably illiterate; his sayings (vāṇīs/bāṇīs), composed in his native dialect of old *Hindi, were orally transmitted for at least a century before they were first written down. Of the three early collections of verses attributed to him, modern scholarship is most confident about the authenticity of those contained in the *Sikh **Ādi Granth*. Others appear in the *Dādū-panthī *Kabīr Granthāvalī*, and the influential *Kabīr-panthī **Kabīr Bījak*. Many commentators remark on the uniquely direct, vigorous, ironic, and even rough style of his couplets, and their characteristic of being simultaneously resonant and obscure. In spite, or perhaps because of this, he is regarded by many as the greatest poet in the Hindi tradition, and is probably the most frequently quoted.

Modern scholarship has detected a gradual Hinduization, or even *Brahmanization, of Kabīr in terms of his biography and sectarian affiliation, with a concomitant attempt to remove his Muslim affiliations. He has come to be regarded by most Hindus as a *Vaiṣṇava nirguṇa *bhakta—the Ādi Sant who effectively initiated the *sant tradition of poet-saints in North India. He is also supposed (erroneously) to have been a disciple of the *Vaiṣṇava reformer, *Rāmānanda. His biography in particular has been expanded by the Kabīr-panthīs, who regard him not just as their founder, but as divine in his own right—an *avatāra of the supreme Being (Sat Purush) for the *kaliyuga. In general, 'readings' of Kabīr have been (and will no doubt continue to be) shaped by political and ideological preference. In the 19th century, *Christian missionaries were keen to claim a Christian influence. In the early 20th century he was admired by reformers and intellectuals, such as *Gāndhī and Rabindranāth *Tagore, as an exemplar of religious toleration, and even as the forerunner of a universal or synthetic (Hindu-Muslim) religion. His songs, or those attributed to him, are widely known across North India; he remains particularly popular in Bengal.

Kabīr Bījak A collection of verses (literally 'seed') attributed to *Kabīr, comprising the last book in the *Kabīr-panthīs' collection, the *Khās Granth*. The original manuscript is said to be housed in the Kabīr Chaurā Maṭh in *Vārāṇasī, where a copy is worshipped as part of the daily ritual. According to modern scholarship, the *Bījak* is an eastern Indian recension of Kabīr's sayings; it exists in two recensions, but in both cases the text is partly corrupt.

Kabīr Granthāvalī A collection of *Kabīr's verses preserved by the *Dādūpantha tradition of Rajasthan, whose founder *Dādū has been identified as a follower of Kabīr.

Kabīr-panthīs ('followers of the way of Kabīr') Members of a low *caste panth (spiritual path), who claim that it was founded by *Kabīr himself, although it probably originated in the 17th century. They regard Kabīr as an *avatāra of the supreme Being (Sat Purush) for the *kaliyuga, and worship him in a number of maṭhs (*temples) across northern and central India. Their chief temple is the Kabīr Chaurā Maṭh in *Vārāṇasī, which houses the manuscript of their most significant text, the **Kabīr Bījak*. Like their purported founder, the Kabīr-panthīs are monotheistic in their beliefs, and opposed to both *image worship and the institution of *caste; they do, however, consider themselves to be Hindus, and have developed a distinctive ritual culture.

kaḍamba A fruit-bearing tree with yellow flowers, sacred to *Śiva.

Kadrū According to *Purāṇic legend, one of the two wives of the *ṛṣi *Kaśyapa. She imprisons her co-wife, *Vinatā, but the latter is freed by her son, *Garuḍa, who then destroys Kadrū's thousand *nāga children.

Kaikeyī In the **Rāmāyana*, the princess of Kaikeya, and the second wife of *Daśaratha, king of *Ayodhyā. Granted two wishes by her husband, at the instigation of her servant, Mantharā, she forces him to exile *Rāma (his son by his first wife, *Kausalyā, and the heir-apparent) to the *forest, in the hope of installing her own son, *Bharata (3) in his place—actions which provide the catalyst for the *Epic narrative.

Kailāsa (Kailash) ('icy', 'crystalline') **1.** A 22000 ft mountain peak in the *Himālayas, situated in Tibet, close to the sacred lake Manāsa. (Ancient Indian *cosmology places it south of Mount *Meru). It has a long history as a *pilgrimage site, although it is now only intermittently open to Indian pilgrims. Its attraction derives from its identification as where *Śiva meditates in the mountains, his dwelling place and paradise. *Kubera is also supposed to reside there. **2.** See ELLORĀ.

kaivalya ('isolation') According to *Sāṃkhya philosophy and *Patañjali's *Yoga system, the state of blissful *liberation; the term indicates the individual *puruṣa's (or *soul's) realization (i.e. experience) of its complete differentiation from everything else—i.e. *prakṛti (material existence) and other puruṣas.

kāla ('time', 'black') **1.** A common term for 'time', derived from the *Sanskrit root kal, 'to calculate' or 'enumerate', and used in a wide variety of contexts. Inevitably, it is synonymous with *death: in the *Bhagavadgītā*, for example, *Kṛṣṇa describes himself as 'time (kāla) run on, destroyer of the universe, risen here to annihilate worlds' (11.32). **2.** A name or epithet of *Yama, the *king of the dead. **3.** In compounds (e.g. Mahākāla), a frequent epithet of *Śiva, either in his role as the destroyer of the universe at the end of a *cosmogonical cycle, and therefore lord of death (e.g. Kālabhairava, Kālanātha), or in his soteriological role as the conqueror of both time and death (e.g. Kālaharamūrti). In *Śaiva metaphysics, the two roles are often elided.

kālāgni ('fire of time') The fire which brings about the dissolution (*pralaya) of the universe at the end of a *yuga, or a *kalpa ('day of *Brahmā').

Kālahasti (Tam.: **Kāḷahatti/Kāḷatti**) A major *Śaiva *pilgrimage centre and *temple site in Andhra Pradesh, incorporating the 16th/17th century CE Kālahastīśvara temple, which contains one of the five *Śiva *liṅgas embodying the elements, in this case *Vāyu, the wind or air. There is also a shrine to the *Nāyaṉār *bhakta *saint, *Kaṇṇapar, who is said to have been liberated by Śiva because of his devotion to the liṅga.

Kālakūṭa ('dark-blue plant[?]') A deadly, world-threatening poison (also known as halāhala) produced during the *Churning of the Ocean, which *Śiva nullifies by holding it in his throat before swallowing it, thus earning the epithet, 'Blue-throated' (*Nīlakaṇṭha).

Kālāmukha ('black-faced', fl. *c.*9th–13th centuries, Karnataka) A South Indian order of celibate *ascetics belonging to the *Lākula division of the *Śaiva *atimārga. They worshipped *Rudra through various heterodox practices such as bathing in the ash (*bhasman) from *cremation-grounds. It is likely that by the 14th or 15th century they had been absorbed into the *Liṅgāyats.

Kālarātrī ('black night') A form of the Goddess (*Devī) personifying the power which brings about the dissolution (*pralaya) of the universe at the end of a *yuga, and who rules over the subsequent night.

kalā(s) A sixteenth part; a digit as one-sixteenth of the moon's diameter. *Tantra uses the term in a variety of contexts; notably, in *Śaiva Siddhānta ritual, kalās refer to parts of the deity's body, superimposed by the recitation of *mantras (kalā-*nyāsa), either on an *image, or on the ritualist's own body.

Kālasaṃkarṣiṇī An unmarried form of the goddess *Kālī, identified by the *Krama tradition of *Kashmiri *Śaivism, and manipulated in their ritual, as undifferentiated *consciousness.

Kāḷatti *See* KĀLAHASTI.

Kalhaṇa (12th century CE) Author of a verse chronicle history of Kashmir, the 'River of Kings' (*Rājataraṅgiṇī*).

Kālī (**Mahākālī** ('the great black one')) ('the black one' (fem.)) The name of a fierce and terrible (raudra/ghora) form of *Devī (the Great Goddess), often conflated with *Cāmuṇḍā. Perhaps originating in a variety of forms in a tribal milieu, Kālī was assimilated into the *Purāṇic and *Sanskritic tradition (notably in the *Devī Mahātmya* and the *Mārkaṇḍeya Purāṇa*) as the anger-generated and demon-destroying *śakti of Devī (*Durgā). By the 8th century CE, she was also the focus of a number of *Śākta *Tantric or *Kāpālika cults in northern and eastern India (such as the *Kālīkula school), which viewed her as the transcendent, but materially engaged absolute. In the Tantric context, her fierceness is at one with both her independence and her trangression of social and ritual norms; her *impurity, signified by her associations with *death (her haunting of the *cremation grounds) and blood (her demands for *animal, and, at times, *human sacrifice), is precisely the source of her power. Iconographically, she is usually depicted as either a young woman with black, dishevelled hair, or as an emaciated hag with shrivelled breasts; in either case, she wears a necklace of skulls, and a skirt of severed arms; her distended tongue protrudes from her mouth, covered in the blood of sacrificial victims; in her four hands she usually holds various lethal weapons, and a severed human head; in some depictions she offers protection through the *abhaya-mudrā. A well-known image of her absolute supremacy depicts her trampling on *Śiva's recumbent and passive body.

In a variety of forms, Kālī's worship spread throughout India, although she continued to be, and remains, most popular in Bengal, where, since the mid 18th century the ways in which she is worshipped have been recast by a succession of *bhakti poets, such as *Rāmprasād Sen. In the genre known as *śākta padāvalī, Kālī has also come to be viewed, through a complex variety of classical and local influences, as a motherly and compassionate, not to say beautiful deity. In the 19th century, *Rāmakṛṣṇa's devotion to Kālī as the 'Holy' or 'Divine Mother' also helped to maternalize the terrible Goddess. *See* Devī; *also* Cāmuṇḍā; Durgā.

kali A die (*akṣa), or side of a die, marked with a single spot, representing the lowest scoring throw. The term is used metaphorically to designate the last in sequence, and most degenerate, of the four *world ages or *yugas (the 'kaliyuga'), commonly, and anciently, supposed to be the age through which human beings are currently living. It is characterized by a shorter lifespan and a general moral and spiritual incapacity: what was possible in other ages is not possible now; there is an extreme imbalance between *dharma and *adharma in favour of the latter. The length of the kaliyuga has been variously calculated. It is generally supposed to have started either with the **Mahābhārata* war or, slightly later, with the death of *Kṛṣṇa. The imminence of its end (and so the cataclysmic conclusion of the current world age) was, however, increasingly postponed as the *Purāṇic literature struggled to synchronize differing chronologies.

Kālibangan A site on the banks of the dried-up river Ghaggar in Rajasthan, containing archaeological remains from the *Indus Valley civilization.

Kālidāsa (*c.*4th–5th century CE) Widely considered the greatest *Sanskrit dramatist and poet. He almost certainly lived in northern India, perhaps under the patronage of the *Gupta dynasty. Kālidāsa may well have been a *brahmin; the benedictions to his plays reveal that he was a devotee of *Śiva, and his name ('servant of *Kālī') suggests that he probably worshipped the *Goddess as well. His surviving works consist of three or four long poems (*mahākāvyas)—*Raghuvaṃśa* ('The Dynasty of Raghu'), *Kumārasambhava* ('The Birth of the War God'), *Meghadūta* ('The Cloud Messenger'), and, less certainly, *Ṛtusaṃhāra* ('The Gathering of the Seasons')—and three plays based on traditional themes—*Mālavikāgnimitra* ('Mālavikā and Agnimitra'), *Vikramorvaśīya* ('Urvaśī Won by Valour'), and the famous **Abhijñānaśākuntalam* ('The Recognition of Śakuntalā').

Kālīghāṭ (Kālīpīṭha) The name of a popular *temple site dedicated to *Kālī, close to the banks of the *Bhāgīrathī river in a suburb of Kolkata (Calcutta). The present temple is about two hundred years old, although the site itself is older. It is considered one of the *śāktipīṭhas—in this case marking the site were the toes of *Satī's right foot fell to earth. Animals—usually black goats—are slaughtered daily in the precincts of the temple in an attempt to propitiate Kālī with a blood *sacrifice.

Kālikā Purāṇa (*c.*10th century CE) A medieval *Śākta *Purāṇa*. Classified as one of the **upapurāṇas*, it focuses on the story of *Satī's dismemberment, and, in particular, the worship of the goddess as *Kāmākhyā at *Kāmarūpa in Assam.

Kālīkula ('belonging to the family of the Black Goddess') Within *Śākta *Tantrism, a designation of those schools, originating in northeastern and northern India, whose *Tantras are used to worship the Goddess (*Devī) in her fierce forms, such as *Kālī.

Kālīpīṭha *See* KĀLĪGHĀṬ.

Kālī Pūjā A one day Bengali *festival dedicated to *Kālī, falling approximately three weeks after *Durgā Pūjā.

Kāliya A *nāga king, prominent in the mythology of *Kṛṣṇa's childhood, where he appears as a five-headed serpent, living in the *Yamunā river near *Vṛndāvana. The child-god overcomes him by dancing on his middle head, and subsequently banishes him. A version of the story is related in the **Bhāgavata Purāṇa* (10.1.16). It is also celebrated in the South Indian *festival of *Nāga Pañcamī.

kaliyuga *See* KALI.

Kalkī (Kalkin) ('[having] a white horse') The tenth and future *avatāra of *Viṣṇu, whose appearance, according to the **Viṣṇu* and other *Purāṇas*, will end the current *kaliyuga and usher in the next 'golden age' or *kṛtayuga. Iconographically, he is portrayed as either a white horse, a sword-wielding warrior mounted on a white horse, or, perhaps most frequently, a warrior with a horse's head and a man's body. His function is to save the good and to restore *dharma. Consequently, he has been the focus of various millenarian fears and expectations, including the end of perceived foreign dominance.

Kaḷḷaḻakar (Tam.: 'Lord of the Kaḷḷar') A *Tamil form of *Viṣṇu. The *temple of Aḻakar, near *Madurai, is dedicated to him. He is said to be the brother of the goddess *Mīnākṣī.

kalpa A division or interval of time. In texts dealing with *cosmogony, it is known as a 'day of *Brahmā', marking a complete cycle of time from creation to destruction. A cosmic kalpa is variously measured, but a commonly accepted figure, given in the **Purāṇas*, is 4 320 000 000 years. It is also sometimes known as a *manvantara, i.e. a world age instigated by a *Manu. This kalpa may be subdivided into 1 000 *mahāyugas, the cycles of ages (*yugas) which regulate the appearance of *avatāras. *See also* MAHĀKALPA.

Kalpa Sūtras A category of *smṛti texts, belonging to the **Vedāṅga*, which prescribes the correct performance of ritual, and treats of *dharma in the social and civil senses of the term. It is normally thought to be composed of up to four types of text (although it is also used synonymously with the first of these): **Śrauta Sūtras*, which deal with the correct performance of the extended and public *Vedic rituals, classified as following *śruti; **Gṛhya Sūtras* which deal with the proper performance of the domestic rituals (*gṛhya-yajñas) and various rites of passage (*saṃskāras); **Dharma Sūtras*, which deal with the ritual, moral, and social question of how people should conduct themselves in relation to *varṇa and *āśrama; and *Śulvasūtras* (essentially a supplement to the *Śrauta Sūtras*), which deal with the geometry of Vedic altars (*vedis). A *Kalpa Sūtra* is attributed to each branch (*śākhā) of the four **Vedas*, but not all of those named are composed of a complete set of texts, or, in some cases, still extant in any form.

kāma ('desire', 'love', 'pleasure') **1.** One of the four legitimate 'aims or goals of human life' (*puruṣārtha), namely, pursuing pleasure in all its forms, including, paradigmatically, sexual pleasure. In **Dharmaśāstra* literature, kāma is sometimes considered of equal importance to the other puruṣārthas (*dharma and *artha)—an essential component of the triad (*trivarga), since, as a motivating impulse, desire underlies all activity—and sometimes as subordinate to, or in conflict with them.

2. A multivalent term, the precise significance of which depends on its context. At its most general, kāma signifies desire as an active and creative force: in some *Vedic accounts, desire for procreation and multiplicity is the impulse that leads to the creation of the universe. Linked to this creative and cosmological function, kāma is a key component in the sacrificial ritual (*yajñā), which at the same time sustains and recreates the universe (reproducing that primeval desire), and satisfies the individual desires of human sacrificers for results (phalas), such as *sons, wealth, cattle, and *heaven. With the *Upaniṣadic realization that such desire-impelled results were finite, particularly those which created a body for the individual in the next life, kāma began to be seen negatively: in conjunction with action (*karma), it was the major cause of human embodiment and *rebirth, and so of continued suffering. Desire in general, and sexual desire in particular—both indices of the householder's (*gṛhastha's) life—were therefore identified as prime targets for the *saṃnyāsin's *renunciation. In the **Bhagavadgītā*'s reformulation of renunciation as *karma yoga (action without attachment to, or desire for its results), desire is drained of its potency; and in the *Gītā*'s concomitant *bhakti yoga, God (*Kṛṣṇa) is shown to be not just the only real actor, but at the same time the completely disinterested (i.e. desireless) spectator of his own actions.

In the medieval *bhakti traditions, kāma, in the focused sense of desire for the all-powerful personal deity, is redefined, not as an obstacle, but as the actual means to *liberation or salvation. This kind of relationship between deity and devotee, using models such as the *gopīs' longing for Kṛṣṇa, is conceptualized with greater and lesser degrees of sexualization, particularly in the poetry of the *sants and other *bhaktas. At the same time, various *Tantric traditions, in a deliberate inversion of the negative view of desire held by *Brahmanical orthodoxy and those renouncer traditions aligned to it, allowed the sexual dimension of kāma to take precedence in their ritual practices as a manifestation of the active and material relationship between *Śiva and his *śakti, and a means to either powers (*siddhis) or liberation.

Kāma(deva) (Kandarpa) The god of love—i.e. the personification of sexual desire. He first appears in this form in the **Ṛg* and the **Atharva Vedas*, but his mythology and iconography are largely products of the *Epic and *Purāṇic periods. Kāṃa is portrayed as a youth wielding a bow strung with bees, and riding on a parrot, a *makara for his banner. He is married to the *apsaras Rati ('sexual pleasure'), and with his floral arrows he shoots desire into the hearts of his victims. Paradoxically, he is also characterized as bodiless (*Anaṅga), perhaps because, as an emotion, he lacks embodiment except in particular lovers. Mythologically, this is explained as the result of *Śiva reducing him to ash for causing the great god to desire *Pārvatī, and so disturbing his ascetic practice. Kāma plays a role in both *Vaiṣṇava and *Śaiva mythologies, particularly the latter.

Kāmadhenu (the 'wish[-fulfilling] cow', Surabhi) A mythical beast, generated from the *Churning of the Ocean, which can grant all desires. It symbolizes abundance and plenty—qualities which can be predicated of the *cow in general.

Kāmākhyā *See* KĀMARŪPA.

Kāmākṣī ('desire-eyed') A supreme but benign form of the *Goddess worshipped in the *temple of the same name at *Kāñcīpuram. She is connected with the *Śrīdevī of the *Śrīvidyā cult, and worshipped with the śrīvidyā *mantra.

Kamalākānta Bhaṭṭācārya (*c.*1769–1820) A Bengali *bhakti poet in the *śākta padāvalī tradition which had been initiated by his immediate predecessor, *Rāmprasād Sen. A *brahmin by birth, he became a local court *paṇḍit and poet. The majority of his poems are devoted to the goddess *Kālī. A *Tantric manual, *Sādhaka Rañjana* ('What Delights the Religious Aspirant'), is also ascribed to him.

kamaṇḍalu A water-jar or gourd used by *ascetics and *brahmins, and part of the iconography of a number of deities, especially *Śiva.

Kāmarūpa (Kāmākhyā) The site, near Guwahati/Gauhati in Assam, of the most significant *Tantric *Śākta complex in India. Considered the original *śaktipīṭha, *Satī's dismembered *yoni, represented by a spring-moistened cleft in the rock of Kāmagiri hill, is worshipped there in the form of the goddess Kāmākhyā, from whom the place takes its name. (The goddess is also identified with the *Mahāvidyā *Ṣodaśī.) The current *temple was built in the mid 16th century. As reported in texts such as the *Kālikā Purāṇa*, ritual at Kāmākhyā is said to have included voluntary *human sacrifice. After 1832 this was replaced by *animal (goat) sacrifice.

Kāmaśāstra ('Treatise on Pleasure') A *Sanskrit literary genre providing the sensual equivalent to **Artha*- and **Dharmaśāstra*, insofar as it gives instruction and guidance for the urban sophisticate in cultural and, specifically, sexual pleasures. The earliest extant, and best-known text of this kind is the **Kāma Sūtra*. This provided the model for later works, such as Kokkaka's *Kokaśāstra* (*Ratirahasya*, *c.*12th century) and Kalyāṇamalla's *Anaṅgaraṅga* (15th century).

Kāma Sūtra ('A Textbook of Pleasure', *c.*3rd–4th century CE) Attributed to Vātsyāyana (about whom nothing is known), and probably of North Indian origin, the *Kāma Sūtra* is the earliest surviving, best-known, and most influential *Sanskrit **Kāmaśāstra* text. It belongs to what is clearly an already established tradition of texts giving instruction not only in erotic love but also in the ideal life of pleasure and culture led by the sophisticate or 'urban man' (nāgarika); in the process it provides an invaluable insight into the social life of the period.

Kambaṉ *See* KAMPAṈ.

Kāmeśvarī *See* TRIPURASUNDARĪ.

Kampaṉ (Kambaṉ) (*c.*12th century CE) The author of the *Tamil retelling of the **Rāmāyaṇa*, the **Irāmāvatāram* ('The Incarnation of Rāma'). Nothing of significance is known about the poet's life.

kāmya ('optional') A class of rituals performed by an individual in order to obtain some desired object (such as *heaven or *sons), as opposed to obligatory (*nitya), or occasional (*naimittika) rites.

Kaṇāda (trad. 5th–4th century BCE) Through his authorship of the *Vaiśeṣikasūtra*, Kaṇāda is considered to be the founder of the *Vaiśeṣika *darśana. He is also called Kaṇabhakṣa/Kaṇabhuj, 'grain-eater' (in reference to the Vaiśeṣikas' atomic theory), and 'the owl' (ulūka), but nothing is known about his life. The extant *Vaiśeṣikasūtra* is probably a composite text, put together around the turn of the Common Era.

Kanakadāsa (16th century CE) A *Kannada *bhakti poet and devotee of *Viṭṭhala/*Kṛṣṇa. Born into a low *caste Karnataka family, like his contemporary, *Purandaradāsa, he was a follower of the *Haridāsakūṭa. Little is known of his life, but a well-known legend tells how the strength of his devotion caused the *image of Kṛṣṇa in the *temple at Udipi (Karnataka) to turn on its axis from East to West to allow Kanakadāsa to take *darśana through a chink in the wall. (He had been excluded from entry because of his low caste.) He composed numerous songs, as well as longer poetic works, including a popular Kannada version of the story of *Nala.

k

Kāñcī(puram) (Conjeeveram) A city in Tamil Nadu, southwest of Chennai (Madras), regarded as one of the seven holy *tīrthas of ancient India (and the only one situated in the South). It has been a major focus for southern Indian architectural, political, and religious developments (Hindu, *Buddhist, and *Jain) since its period (from the 6th to the 8th century CE) as the capital of the *Pal̲l̲ava dynasty. The city contains a large number of stone-built *temples, dedicated to both *Śiva (including the Kailāsanātha (8th century) and Ekāmbareśvara (16th–17th century) temples) and *Viṣṇu (including the Vardhamāna temple (12th century and later)). It is claimed that *Śaṅkara founded a fifth *maṭha here, and so it has become the seat of one of the *Śaṅkarācāryas. It is also the principal city for the *Vaṭakalai *Śrī Vaiṣṇavas. As a centre for traditional Hindu practice and learning, Kāñcīpuram is sometimes compared to *Vārāṇasī.

Kandarpa *See* KĀMA.

Kane, Pandurang Vaman (1880–1971) An expert on Hindu *law, and 'National Professor of Indology', he was the author of the seminal *History of Dharmaśāstra (Ancient and Mediaeval Religious and Civil Law)* (1930–62, 5 vols.).

Kannada A language belonging to the *Dravidian family; mostly spoken in Karnataka.

Kaṇṇaki. *See* CILAPPATIKĀRAM.

Kaṇṇappanāyaṉār One of the 63 *Nāyaṉmār *bhakta *saints. According to legend, he was a hunter so devoted to *Śiva that, when he saw blood dripping from the eye of a *liṅga, he plucked out his own eye to replace it, and would have done the same with his other eye if the god himself had not intervened. Gratified by such devotion, Śiva healed the hunter and caused him to be liberated, at the same time naming him Kaṇṇapar, 'Eye-giver'. There is a shrine to the saint close to the liṅga in the Kālahastīśvara *temple (*Kālahasti) in Andhra Pradesh, the supposed site of these events.

Kānphaṭa yogīs ('split-eared' yogīs) A name applied to some monastic members of the *Nāth Siddha order, distinguished by their large earrings (kuṇḍalas), and hence the piercing of their ear lobes which takes place at *initiation.

Kaṇva A legendary *Vedic *ṛṣi; his family, or descendants, the Kāṇvas, make up one of the clans to which a number of the poets who composed the **Ṛg Veda* are said to belong.

Kanyakā Purāṇa An oral (i.e. sung) epic peculiar to the Komaṭi caste of Andhra Pradesh, telling the story of their origins, and how their *caste rules were imposed by the goddess Kanyakā. Today the text is performed from a written *Sanskrit version associated with the **Skanda Purāṇa*.

Kanyā Kumārī ('virgin goddess') A form of the *Goddess, whose temple at Cape Comorin (now itself known as Kanyākumārī), on the southernmost tip of India, is a major *tīrtha or pilgrimage site.

kapāla An alms bowl made from a human skull, favoured by *Kāpālikas and other *Tantric *Śaiva *ascetics.

Kāpālika ('skull carrier') A devotee of *Bhairava (a ferocious form of *Śiva) and member of an early medieval *Tantric tradition which drew on the revelatory authority of the **Bhairava Tantras* to follow practices opposed, and inimical, to *Brahmanical orthodoxy. Chief among these was the ritual use of conventionally *impure substances such as meat, wine, and sexual fluids. Their name is derived from their characteristic possession of a human skull (*kapāla), for use as a cup cum begging-bowl, and a *khaṭvāṅga (a trident incorporating a human skull). Both are carried in imitation of Bhairava, who also provides the model for the Kāpālikas' covering themselves in ashes (*bhasman) and living in *cremation grounds. The Kāpālika tradition is now defunct, but many of the practices associated with it are consciously sustained by groups such as the *Aghorīs.

Kapila The name of a legendary seer, said to have founded the *Sāṃkhya system.

Kapiṣṭhala-(Kaṭha)-Saṃhitā The foundational texts of the Kapiṣṭhala branch (*śākhā) of the **Veda*, and one of the four collections originally constituting the **Black Yajur Veda*; only fragments survive.

Kāraikkāl Ammai(yār) (Kāraikkāl Ammāḷ) (Tam.: 'the lady of Kāraikkāl', *c.*6th century CE?) One of the 63 *Nāyaṉmār *bhakta *saints. According to the hagiographies, she was born into a *vaiśya family in the South Indian town of Kāraikkāl (south of Pondicherry). Her *Tamil poems in praise of *Śiva (the *Arputat tiruvantāti*, the *Tiruviraṭṭai maṇimālai*, and the *Tiruvālaṅkāṭṭu mūtta tiruppatikaṅkaḷ*), which are regarded as the oldest in the **Tirumuṟai* collection, are signed 'the demoness (*pēy) of Kāraikkāl'. This epithet seems to have inspired the story that she asked Śiva to change her from a beautiful woman into a frightening and skeletal figure, like the demons in his retinue (and/or to terrify her husband), which is how she is portrayed in the iconography. In her *bhakti poems she positions herself as *Śiva's slave or servant. Some commentators see this stance as being more intellectual and restrained than the full-blown emotionalism of some later bhaktas.

Kāraikkāl Ammai(yār)

karma (karman) ('act', 'action', 'activity', 'rite', 'motion') In its developed form, the lynchpin of a theory, or doctrine ('the law of karma'), which attempts to account for the origins and nature of an individual's mortal existence and suffering in the light of his or her actions (karma), past and present. At its heart lies the perception that any action normally has an unavoidable, but usually post-mortem, effect on its agent, and that, depending on the ritual or ethical quality of that action, such an effect is either 'good' (*puṇya) or 'bad' (*pāpa). Combined with the idea of *rebirth, this constitutes a theory of cosmic justice which accounts for the individual's current state and, at the same time, predicts their future condition, or 'birth', on the basis of their current actions. In this way it provides the incentive to moderate one's behaviour in order to avoid rebirth as, for example, a lower life form, or in one of the hells (*narakas) so vividly evoked in the *Purāṇic literature. Karma may therefore provide the means to achieve a better—perhaps a heavenly—rebirth; negatively, through its diminution or cessation, it may lead to escape from the cycle of rebirth altogether (i.e. the attainment of *mokṣa).

This general concept of karma has been pervasive in South Asian thought for over two thousand years, although its origins are unclear and widely debated. Some suggest that the 'doctrine' was formed by the coincidence of non-*Vedic ideas about rebirth, rooted in agricultural cycles, with the Vedic understanding of sacrifice (*yajña). At its simplest, the word 'karma(n)' signifies an action, and in the *Brahmanical period, the most conceptually significant action was that performed by the sacrificer (*yajamāna). As long as the ritual (karman) was performed correctly, the desired result (such as a heavenly afterlife) would be attained automatically through the operation of an unseen mechanism. Like all other actions, however, ritual was thought to have finite results, and was therefore in need of constant renewal. Consequently, a ritually created afterlife was thought to result, eventually, in redeath (*punar-mṛtyu). The way in which this problem was addressed led, inter alia, to the formulation of a 'doctrine' of karma, which finds its first expression in the **Bṛhadāraṇyaka* and **Chāndogya Upaniṣads*. In these, and in subsequent **Upaniṣads*, the ritual understanding of action and its effects is extended to include all of an individual's actions; in other words, everything the agent does is now considered significant for his future. What counts as a 'good' or a 'bad' action therefore becomes crucial. At one level, this is a function of the individual's *caste-prescribed role, or *sva-dharma; at another, it may depend on 'universal' moral principles (*sādhāraṇa dharma), such as not stealing, or not lying.

With the rise of renunciatory ideologies (including *Buddhism and *Jainism), which were intent on securing permanent release from rebirth and its concomitant suffering, the fact that all actions entailed finite effects became a stumbling block, and it was necessary to examine again what counted as a significant, i.e. consequence-causing, action. One solution was that proposed in the **Bhagavadgītā*'s path of *karma-yoga—that it was attachment to their results or fruits (phalas) which entailed consequences, not the actions themselves. With such an attitude, one could adhere to one's sva-dharma and still hope to achieve salvation. In its advocacy of another path (*bhakti-yoga), predicated on the assertion that God (*Kṛṣṇa) was the only true actor or agent, the *Gītā* also opened a way for the prevalent attitude of medieval and later *bhakti traditions that karma, rather than being an impersonal 'law', was subordinate to an all-powerful deity. The only appropriate reaction to God's total agency was to give oneself over to him, in total devotion, and thereafter to rely on his grace (*prasāda) to wipe out the consequences of one's other actions. In this context, karma comes close to converging with 'fate' or *daiva—a general means of accounting for one's current condition, and for events which are otherwise inexplicable, but ultimately not crucial to one's *liberation or salvation.

Of the classical *darśanas, the *Yoga system is the most rigorous in its treatment of karma, describing the process of bondage (and potential liberation from it) in broadly psychological terms. According to *Patañjali's *Yoga Sūtra*, an act performed with *ignorance and desire creates a karmic residue (karmāśaya). This in turn produces dispositions (*saṃskāras), which once activated engender afflictions (*kleśas); these lead to further purposive, ignorance- and desire-motivated actions. At death, afflictions which have not been activated, and thereby exhausted, gather in the mind (*citta), where they determine the length of life, the kind of experiences, and the body to which the individual, in the form of the citta, will then pass. The antidote to this, and the way to liberation, is to weaken the afflictions by pursuing various ethical restraints, combined with the practice of *dhyāna-yoga, the yoga of meditation.

Since its inception, the precise nature of the 'law of karma'—what counts as significant action, and its binding or, indeed, liberating effects—has been differently conceptualized by different Hindu traditions. This variety of frequently conflicting attitudes is evident in the *Epics, the **Purāṇas*, and in **Dharmaśāstra*. It is also apparent in popular stories, which emphasize the immediate and often luridly violent effects of actions, rather than their longer-term consequences, and in anthropological studies which show that, for many Hindus, karma is only one link in a wider nexus of causal explanations. Nevertheless, karma doctrine, in the broadest sense, is common to most Hindu traditions, as well as to their rivals, including Buddhism, and Jainism.

karmabhūmi ('realm of action') According to *Purāṇic *cosmology, a part of the cosmos where action (*karma)—and particularly ritual action—has results. *Rebirth in a karmabhūmi is therefore required in order to achieve *liberation. *Bhāratavarṣa (India) is thought to be the only such place in the continent of *Jambudvīpa.

karmakāṇḍa ('the rites section') The traditional designation of that part of the **Veda* (the **Saṃhitās* and **Brāhmaṇas*) which deals with ritual (*yajña), as opposed to the *jñānakāṇḍa (the **Āraṇyakas* and **Upaniṣads*), which deals with liberating knowledge (*jñāna).

karma-mārga ('path of action') *See* KARMA-YOGA.

karma-yoga ('the discipline of action') A path to *liberation outlined in the **Bhagavadgītā*, requiring an inner attitude of desireless detachment from the results or fruits (phalas) of one's actions (*karma), both ritual and social. In this way one can (indeed, should) conform to one's *sva-dharma, continue to live in the world, and at the same time achieve liberation from the results of action without needing to renounce in a social or material sense. The agent has renounced his agency and with it the karmic repercussions of his inescapable activity. Karma-yoga is usually contrasted with what are taken to be the other paths to *liberation described in the text (*jñāna-yoga and *bhakti-yoga), yet, since *Kṛṣṇa is perceived to be the only real actor, karma-yoga itself is ultimately subsumed in *bhakti—total devotion to God. Although the *Gītā* itself does not present these yogas as systematic or exclusive paths (*mārgas), subsequent commentators have, nevertheless, adapted the division to chart three distinctive Hindu paths to liberation. *See also* BHAGAVADGĪTĀ; KARMA.

karmendriya ('organ of action') According to *Sāṃkhya ontology, the five active senses (tongues/speaking, hands/grasping, feet/walking, excretory organs/excreting, and sexual organs/procreating) evolved from *prakṛti.

karmic The Anglicized, adjectival form of '*karma'.

Karṇa (Sūtaja, Rādheya, Vasuṣeṇa) ('ear') A major figure in the **Mahābhārata*, and perhaps the character most obviously resembling a Western 'tragic hero'. An ally of *Duryodhana, he is actually the *Pāṇḍavas' older half-brother, although this in unknown to himself and everyone else, with the exceptions of his mother, *Kuntī, and his father, the sun god *Sūrya. Born in full armour, and with the earrings from which he takes his name, Karṇa was secretly abandoned as a baby, and adopted by *Dhṛtarāṣṭra's charioteer, in whose employer's court he was brought up. After being excluded from Draupadī's *svayaṃvara because of his apparently low-*caste origins, he joined the *Kaurava cause and was rewarded with the *kingship of Aṅga by Duryodhana. As a warrior, he became *Arjuna's great rival, but towards the end of the war he was killed by the latter, in a contravention of *kṣatriya *dharma, when his chariot became stuck in the earth. His energy left his body and he entered his father, the sun. At the end of the battle, Kuntī discloses Karṇa's true parentage to her surviving Pāṇḍava sons, who then grieve for their elder brother. They are eventually reconciled in *heaven.

k

Karṇaparvan ('The Book of Karṇa') The eighth book of the *Sanskrit **Mahābhārata*, recounting the period in the war during which *Karṇa commands the *Kaurava forces. It includes *Bhīma's killing of *Duḥśāsana, and Karṇa's death at the hands of *Arjuna.

Karpātrījī Mahārāj (1898–1973) A *Vaiṣṇava *sādhu who, in the 1940s, founded the *Rāma Rājya Pariṣad, a right-wing Hindu political party, advocating that India should become an exclusively Hindu state. The party won a number of seats in the 1950s and early 1960s, but disappeared on merger with the Bhāratīya Jana Saṅgh, the precursor of the *Bhāratīya Janatā Party.

Kartābābā *See* KARTĀBHĀJĀS.

Kartābhājās Members of a *Caitanya-derived tradition who worshipped Kartābābā (d. 1783) and his son, Dulalchand, of Navadvīpa (Bengal). They also appear to have been influenced by the *Bāuls.

Kārttika (Kārtik) In the lunar *calendar, October–November—a particularly *auspicious month in the Hindu year, of particular significance to *Vaiṣṇavas.

Kārttika Pūrṇimā ('[the festival of] the full moon day of Kārttika') *See* TRIPURĪ PŪRṆIMĀ.

Kārttikeya (Skanda, Murukaṉ, Tam.: **Murugan, Kumāra, Subrahmaṇya, (Siddha)sena, (Mahā)sena,** etc.**)** According to the **Purāṇas*, the youthful god of war, and a son of *Śiva and *Pārvatī. His name is associated with a myth that he was brought up by the Kṛttikās, the six stars making up the Pleiades constellation. It is also connected with Kārttika, the month of October–November, which is supposedly the best time for making war. Kārtikkeya is frequently, but not invariably, represented with six heads, carrying a spear and other weapons, and riding on his peacock *vāhana, Paravāṇi. His wife, Senā (Kaumarī) is a personification of the divine army. In South India, where he is usually known by his *Tamil name, Murukaṉ, he is a major independent deity. *See also* MURUKAṈ.

Karuppan (Tam.) A popular *village god in Tamil Nadu. He is regarded as the servant of the god *Aiyaṉār, and the guardian of his *temples. Karuppan is said to have once been a *pēy (an evil spirit); he demands *animal sacrifices, and is served by non- *brahmin *priests.

Kashmir(i) Śaivism A *Tantric *Śaiva tradition which flourished in Kashmir between the 9th and 11th century CE, but which also influenced South Indian *Śaivism. The *Trika, its ritual system, developed out of the eastern *Kaula transmission, and represents a domestication for married *householders of more extreme Kaula practices. Worship is directed at *Śiva and his consort, placed, in the forms of Kuleśvara and Kuleśvarī, at the centre of a triangular *maṇḍala formed by three goddesses (Parā, Parāparā, and Aparā)—power manifestations of the universe conceived as a single *consciousness. The Trika initiate at this level could, optionally, take a further, secret *initiation, requiring the ritual use of *impure substances and a sexual partner, in the attempt to realize this state of pure consciousness. Supporting the Trika was a monistic (non-dualistic) theology which argued for the identity of the individual (as consciousness) with Śiva (as total consciousness). Theologians of the *Pratyabhijñā school, such as *Somānanda, *Utpala, and, most notably *Abhinavagupta and his pupil, *Kṣemarāja, worked this out with considerable sophistication.

Kāśī *See* VĀRĀṆASĪ.

Kāśīkhaṇḍa ('The Chapter on Kāśī') A hymn of praise (*māhātmya) to Kāśī (*Vārāṇasī) included in the **Skanda Purāṇa*.

Kāśīrahasya ('The Secret of Kāśī') A hymn of praise (*māhātmya) to Kāśī (*Vārāṇasī) included in the **Brahmavaivarta Purāṇa*.

Kaśyapa ('tortoise') A legendary *Vedic *ṛṣi and, according to some lists, one of the *Prajāpatis—a forefather and fashioner of the cosmos and its occupants. He is also conflated with *Prajāpati (sing.) as demiurge.

kathā (recitation) The specifically commissioned recitation of a text, conducted by a *brahmin, for the benefit (in terms of *merit, or wordly goods) both of the sponsor and of those who hear it.

Kathak A classical North Indian dance form, used for narrative and *bhakti purposes. It has a number of hereditary lineages and schools (gharānās) (notably those of Jaipur, Lucknow, and *Vārāṇasī) derived from both *temple and courtly dance traditions. Historically, its content has moved from temple-based religious narrative, through court entertainments, to a more modern emphasis on abstract elements, such as rhythm.

Kathākalī ('story drama') A highly stylized dance-theatre tradition, established in Kerala in the 17th century. Using the local language of Malayalam rather than *Sanskrit, it combines elements of folk and classical theatre to retell *Epic and *Purāṇic episodes, through elaborate movements accompanied by song. Its popularity in India, and especially beyond, has increased in the 20th century.

Kāṭhaka Saṃhitā The foundational texts of the Kāṭhaka branch (school) of the **Veda*, and one of the four collections constituting the **Black Yajur Veda*. Its **Brāhmaṇa* and **Āraṇyaka* have been almost completely lost, but an **Upaniṣad*, the **Kaṭha*, survives, although its connection with the *Vedic school has been attenuated. The Kāthakas, who appear to have been specialists in the construction of ritual fire-altars (*agnicayana), were probably based in the northwest of India.

Kaṭhāsaritsāgara ('The Ocean of Streams of Story') Somadeva's celebrated version of the **Bṛhatkathā* collection of popular stories, composed in verse in the 11th century CE.

Kaṭha Upaniṣad **(Kāṭhaka)** (*c.*3rd–1st century BCE) An important **Upaniṣad* belonging to the **Kāṭhaka Saṃhitā* of the **Black Yajur Veda*. It may have been part of a longer *Upaniṣad* which has since been lost. In its present form, it is divided into two parts, the second of which is, seemingly, a later addition. The *Upaniṣad* is initiated by a prose passage, taken from the **Taittirīya Brāhmaṇa* (but perhaps originally part of the lost *Kāṭhaka Brāhmaṇa*), relating how a *brahmin boy, Naciketas, wins three wishes from *Death. The bulk of the text, which is in verse, is taken up with Death's response to the boy's third wish—to be told what happens to an individual after death. The answer is not cohesive, but some of the major themes treated are the relation of the soul (here called the *puruṣa) to the body, the progressive restraint of the senses, the role of *knowledge in *liberation, and the *yogic means for separating the puruṣa from the body at death, and so achieving *immortality.

Kātyāyana (*c.*250 BCE) A *Sanskrit *grammarian and, in his *Vārttikas*, commentator on *Pāṇini's **Aṣṭādhyāyi*. He was a proponent of Sanskrit as the exclusive language of ritual and religious *merit.

Kaula (Kula) ('Family') The name applied to a complex of *Kāpālika-derived, early medieval *Tantric traditions (also known as 'Kaulism'), involving the worship of families of ferocious goddesses (*yoginīs). Of its four lines of transmission (*āmnāya), the 'northern' worshipped *Guhyakālī, from which the *Krama system evolved; the 'western', *Kubjikā; the 'southern', *Tripurasundarī, the source of the *Śrī Vidyā tradition; and the 'eastern', Kuleśvara (*Śiva) and Kuleśvarī (*Śakti), whose worship was central to the development of the *Trika ritual system of *Kashmir(i) Śaivism.

Kaulajñānanirnaya ('The Demonstration of Kaula Knowledge') An influential medieval *Tantric text, attributed to *Matsyendranāth, and containing his major teachings.

Kaula Upaniṣad ('The *Upaniṣad* of the Preceptors', *c.*9th–12th century CE) A short text epitomizing the philosophical essentials of *Tantric *Goddess worship. In his commentary on the text, *Bhāskararāya associates it with both *Kaula and *Śrī Vidyā teachings.

Kaumodakī *See* GADĀ.

Kauravas ('descendants of Kuru') The usual designation of the sons of *Dhṛtarāṣṭra and their followers in the **Mahābhārata* (although the *Pāṇḍavas are also descendants of Kuru). Under the leadership of *Duryodhana, they challenge their cousins, the Pāṇḍavas, in the epic war for the kingdom, but are ultimately defeated.

Kausalyā ('princess of Kosala') In the **Rāmāyaṇa*, the first wife of *Daśaratha, and mother of *Rāma.

Kauṣītaki Āraṇyaka **(*Śāṅkhāyana Āraṇyaka*)** One of two **Āraṇyakas* (the other being the **Aitareya*) attached to the **Ṛg Veda*, and included in the **Kauṣītaki Brāhmaṇa*. The *Āraṇyaka* internalizes the external *sacrifices, treated in its *Brāhmaṇa*, to inner ritual, such as the practice of *prāṇāgnihotra.

Kauṣītaki Brāhmaṇa One of two **Brāhmaṇas* (the other being the **Aitareya*) attached to the **Ṛg Veda*, the *Kauṣītaka* is principally concerned with the major *śrauta sacrifices.

Kauṣītaki Upaniṣad (*c.*6th–5th century BCE) Attached to the **Ṛg Veda*, and embedded in the **Kauṣītaki Āraṇyaka*, this prose **Upaniṣad* deals with various topics, including *death and *rebirth, the nature and realization of *brahman (neut.), and the significance of vital breath (*prāṇa). It shares material with several other *Upaniṣads*.

Kauṭilya (Cāṇakya, Viṣṇugupta) (*c.*4th–3rd century BCE) The person to whom the **Arthaśāstra* ('Treatise on Statecraft'; also known as *Kauṭilya Arthaśāstra*) is attributed. He was said to have been a *brahmin minister or *purohita of *Candragupta Maurya.

Kauṭilya Arthaśāstra *See* ARTHAŚĀSTRA.

Kāverī (Kāviri) South India's most sacred *river. Rising in Karnataka, and flowing through Tamil Nadu to the Bay of Bengal, its symbolic resonance for *Tamil culture is similar to the *Gaṅgā's for northern India. A place of *pilgrimage in itself, a number of famous *tīrthas are situated on the Kāverī's course, chief among them the *Śrīraṅgam island *temple complex at *Tiruchirāppaḷḷi.

kavi ('seer', 'singer', 'poet') A term for an inspired poet, and for the author of a *Sanskrit *kāvya. The legendary author of the *Rāmāyaṇa*, *Vālmīki, is sometimes said to be the 'first kavi'.

Kavi Karṇapūra (b. 1526 CE) A leading theologian and poet in the *Caitanya tradition, responsible for a number of important *Gauḍīya *Vaiṣṇava works in *Sanskrit, including the *Gauragaṇoddeśadīpikā* and the *Caitanyacaritamahākāvya*.

Kāviri *See* KĀVERĪ.

Kāvya ('literature', 'produced by a kavi') A general term for non-vernacular, chiefly *Sanskrit literature. More specifically, a poem, or piece of poetical prose produced by a single author, as opposed to, e.g., *itihāsa. Frequently composed in a courtly environment, poetry of this kind is often characterized by the ingenious use of a variety of elaborate metres. In modern languages, the term is reserved solely for verse. *See also* MAHĀKĀVYA.

Kedārnāth(a) (Kedāranātha) Situated in the high *Himālayas (in Uttaranchal, formerly in Uttar Pradesh), one of the twelve *Śaiva *jyotirliṅga *tīrthas, and the site of a modern Kedārneśvara *temple. The *svayambhū liṅga worshipped there is formed of ice. Four other local shrines, all similarly associated with parts of *Śiva's body, are grouped with Kedārnāth to make up the Pañcakedār ('Five Kedār') tīrthas. *Śaṅkara is said to have died at Kedārnāth. *See also* DHĀMA.

Kedarnath Datta (Bhaktivinoda Ṭhākura) (1838–1914) A *Vaiṣṇava theologian and activist who succeeded in establishing a reformed theological and ritual agenda for the *Gauḍīya Vaiṣṇava tradition in the second half of the 19th century. A career civil servant under the British, he had received a Western style education, and was friendly with many of the leading Bengal intellectuals of the time. In his late twenties he became a follower of *Caitanya's form of Vaiṣṇavaism, and thereafter devoted himself to systematizing the textual and ritual bases of the tradition to produce a kind of practice, predicated on a relatively conservative theology, which proved attractive to the growing urban middle classes. His work was continued by his son Bhaktisiddānta Sarasvatī (1874–1937), whose disciple *Bhaktivedānta Swāmi founded the *International Society for Krishna Consciousness, and so brought Kedarnath's reformed Gauḍīya tradition to the West.

Keith, Arthur Berriedale (1879–1944) A Scottish *Indologist and constitutional theorist. After an early career in Colonial administration, he was appointed Regius Professor of Language at Edinburgh in 1914. He published copiously on many subjects. Among his most significant Indological publications are *A History of Sanskrit Literature* (1920), and *The Religion and Philosophy of the Veda and Upanishads* (1925).

Kelimāl *See* HARIDĀSA, SVĀMĪ.

***Kena Upaniṣad* (*Talavakāra*)** (*c.*4th century CE) A short, half-verse, half-prose *Upaniṣad*, known after its first word in *Sanskrit, kena—'by whom'. It belongs to *Jaiminīya* branch of the *Sāmaveda Saṃhitā*, and forms part of the *Jaiminīya Upaniṣad Brāhmaṇa*. Its first half is a meditation on the overwhelming, irreducible, and inexpressible nature of *brahman (neut.); the second part tells a story of how the *Vedic gods fail to recognize brahman, who is then revealed as the source of their power and of the potency underlying everything.

Keśava ('long-haired') An epithet of *Kṛṣṇa.

Keśin 1. A 'long-haired one', referred to in *Ṛg Veda* 10.136, who, according to some, is a precursor of the *yogins and *ascetics of a later period. **2.** According to the *Viṣṇu Purāṇa*, a *daitya who attacks *Kṛṣṇa and is bisected for his pains.

Ketu *See* RĀHU.

Khajurāho A complex of 25 (originally 85) outstanding medieval *temples, constructed under the patronage of the Candella dynasty (9th–12th centuries) on the Central Indian site of their capital city in modern day Madhya Pradesh. Perhaps the most celebrated is the Kaṇḍarīya Mahādeo temple, dedicated (*c.*1000 CE) to *Śiva, but the site includes temples peculiar to many other traditions as well, including those of the *Vaiṣṇavas and the *Jains. Externally, many of the temples are covered in sensual and erotic sculptures, the original significance of which remains a matter of debate.

Khaṇḍobā (Khanderao, Mallari, Malhari, Mailar, etc.**)** A Maharashtrian form, or *avatāra, of *Śiva/*Bhairava, combining the functions of a regional and a pan-Indian deity. The folk origins of the god are prominently reflected in a localized mythology in which he is portrayed as a chieftain, or hunter, and in a distinct iconography—he is, for instance, attended by dogs, and rides a blue horse. Of his five wives, a merchant's daughter and a shepherdess play the most significant roles in stories about his life. His best known *temple is in the town of Jejurī, near Pune. It is served by non-*brahmin *priests, and is open to all *castes. It was a visit to the Jejurī temple which inspired a classic sequence of poems in English by the Maharashtrian poet, Arun Kolatkar (*Jejuri*, 1976). *See also* MURAḶĪ; VĀGHYĀ; YESHWANT RAO.

khaṭvāṅga An attribute of fierce deities (such as *Śiva) and their *ascetic followers, consisting of a staff or bone topped by a human skull.

khecarī mudrā A *haṭha-yogic practice, involving the bending of the tongue backwards into the space above the throat, in order to retain, through drinking, the accumulated nectar of immortality (*amṛta).

Kherapati *See* KṢETRAPĀLA; *also* HANUMĀN KHERAPATI.

Khmer *See* CAMBODIA.

king *See* KINGSHIP.

kingship (rāja-dharma) As a construct, a topic extensively treated in a number of Hindu texts, especially in relation to *dharma. According to *Dharmaśāstra*, the king, as the conduit for divine power, should be regarded as divinely ordained, or partially divine himself (he is addressed as *deva), by virtue of his consecration (*abhiṣeka) in the *rājasūya ritual. The ideal king (prototypically *Bharata) is, moreover, the *cakravartin or 'universal ruler'—the embodiment of physical and spiritual perfection who ritually unites the kingdom in his person. Mirroring this identification of the temporal and the spiritual, gods and other divine beings are often depicted with the insignia of kingship, and *pūjā is modelled on the entertainment due to a royal guest. The practical corollary of this understanding of kingship is that it is the king's duty (rāja-dharma) to maintain social order (i.e. *caste hierarchy—*varṇāśramadharma), and to protect the kingdom in its entirety. This is to be financed by taxes, and accomplished by administering justice and punishment through the ceaseless application of *daṇḍa. At least from the *Brahmanical perspective, the king is also the ideal *kṣatriya, the model householder, (*gṛhastha) and patron of the sacrifice (*yajamāna), who, through his power and wealth, supports the *brahmin class and its ideology. A seemingly more pragmatic, if highly interventionist, prescription for running a stable kingdom can be found in *Kauṭilya's *Arthaśāstra*.

In the medieval period (8th–13th centuries), the idea of divine kingship was expressed unambiguously, in a *Tantric milieu, as the king's identity with the deity. As a warrior god, his power was thought to be derived from his retinue of consort goddesses—a power conferred at abhiṣeka and through Tantric *initiation. Although actual kings disappeared with the end of colonialism, the idea of kingship, projected onto, or assumed by, the dominant local *caste, continues to configure social and ritual relations for much of Indian society.

kinnara (fem. kinnari, Skt.: kiṃnara—'what kind of man') One of a centaur-like class of semi-divine beings with human heads and horses' bodies (or vice-versa). Like the *Gandharvas, they are characterized as 'heavenly musicians'.

kīrtan(a) **(saṃkīrtana)** ('repeating', 'praising') Songs sung collectively in praise of *Kṛṣṇa. This practice is particularly popular in the *bhakti culture of *Gauḍīya (Bengal) Vaiṣṇavism; the model was provided by *Caitanya who organized and participated in the collective singing of *kīrtanas about Kṛṣṇa's life with the *gopīs in *Vṛndāvana, and the erotic love between *Rādhā and Kṛṣṇa. Such singing induced ecstatic trances in Caitanya himself, during which he was effectively *possessed by the god. *See also* BHAJAN(A); LĪLĀKĪRTAN(A).

kīrtimukha/kirttimukha ('face of fame/glory') Sculpturally, the face, or mask, of a lion-like animal found above arches and *temple doorways, where it has both a decorative and a protective function.

Kiṣkindhā In the **Rāmāyaṇa*, the capital of the monkey king, *Sugrīva.

Kiṣkindhākāṇḍa The fourth book of *Vālmīki's **Rāmāyaṇa*, in which *Rāma forms his alliance with the monkey king, Sugrīva, while staying at his capital, *Kiṣkindhā.

kleśa ('affliction', 'impurity', 'defilement') According to *Patañjali's **Yoga Sūtra*, five defilements or impurities (*avidyā—ignorance, *asmitā—'I-am-ness', rāga—attachment, dveṣa—aversion, abhiniveṣa—fear of extinction), which both give rise to and are formed by *impure or painful states of mind (vṛttis), and so perpetuate an individual's suffering and *karmic bondage. Avidyā is thought to engender the other four.

knowledge *See* JÑĀNA; VIDYĀ.

Kokaśāstra *See* KĀMAŚĀSTRA.

Konarak/Koṇāraka The site, in Odisha (Orissa), of an immense 13th-century *temple to the Sun god *Sūrya (the Sūrya Deul, also known as the 'Black Pagoda'), built by King Narasiṃhadeva I (1238–64). Although the temple is now ruined, its design, as the god's chariot, drawn by seven horses, is still evident, as are many of its sculptures, some of them erotic in theme, although the original significance of this remains a matter of debate.

Koṟṟavai (Tam.) According to the *Tamil *Caṅkam literature, the goddess of war, of the mountains, and of arid land. She demanded *animal sacrifice, including buffaloes, and the *sacrifice of men in battle; or even, in the case of the warrior *Marvars, ritual suicide. The goddess *Durgā may be to some extent modelled on Koṟṟavai.

Kosala-Videha **(Kośala-)** The name given to the eastern area of the Gangetic plain of northern India, which was part of the heartland of ancient *Brahmanism, and thought to be the home of the *Śukla school of the **Yajur Veda*.

Kōtai *See* ĀṆṬĀḶ.

Koṭikkavi (Tam.: 'flag of verse') An early 14th-century CE collection of *Tamil *Śaiva poems, composed by Umāpati

Civāriyar (*Umāpati Śivācārya), and dedicated to *Śiva *Naṭarāja at *Cidambaram. It was supposed to have been first performed at a flag-raising ceremony in honour of the god.

kōyil (Tam.) *See* TEMPLE.

Krama ('sequence', 'gradation') An esoteric *Tantric *Śaiva system, developed in Kashmir, and closely related to the *Trika and *Kaula traditions. (It appears to have evolved from the latter's 'northern' line of transmission.) The focus of Krama worship is the unmarried goddess *Kālasaṃkarṣiṇī, regarded, like everything else, as a manifestation of pure, or undifferentiated *consciousness. Its ritual requires the offering of what, from the *Brahmanical perspective, are *impure substances. The theoretical, *yogic, and ritual aspects of the Krama receive their most sophisticated treatment in the works of *Abhinavagupta.

kramapāṭha ('the step-by-step reading', 'syllabic separation') A traditional method of memorizing and repeating the *Vedic texts, in which the first and last syllables of any particular word are, in turn, combined with the last and first syllables of each of the preceding and succeeding words, the repetition accompanied by bodily movements.

Krishna *See* KṚṢṆA.

Krishnamacharya, Tirumalai (1888–1989) *See* VINIYOGA.

Krishnamurti, Jiddu (1895–1986) A South Indian of *brahmin parentage, who, as a 14-year-old, was taken up by the leading lights of the *Theosophical Society, including Annie *Besant, and trained to be a saviour figure, or contemporary *avatāra, at the head of a new world spiritual organization, the Order of the Star in the East (founded 1911). In 1929 he severed himself from the Theosophical Society, and, disavowing his saviour status, spent the rest of his life travelling and teaching independently. His published dialogues on a wide variety of spiritual and global issues, some of them conducted with prominent Western intellectuals, helped to increase his popularity, although he persistently rejected all religious authority, including his own, in favour of self-examination. His teaching, nevertheless, drew on a number of Indian traditions, including *Advaita Vedānta and *Buddhism; in essence it concerned the necessity for individuals to cultivate self-knowledge, and, through re- or deconditioning their mental processes, to create a pure, undifferentiated awareness. His work is now disseminated through numerous schools and foundations which he established in Europe, the US, and India.

kriyā An action, particularly of a ritual or sacrificial kind.

kriyā-yoga ('yoga of action') **1.** One of two types of *yoga outlined in *Patañjali's **Yoga Sūtra*, where it is described as consisting of *tapas (penance), study (svādhyāya), and devotion to *Īśvara (2.1–2). Its purpose is to produce *samādhi and minimize the effect of the *kleśas. *See also* AṢṬĀṄGA-YOGA.

2. A form of yoga (apparently unrelated to Patañjali's kriyā-yoga), said to be derived from the yoga taught by *Kṛṣṇa in the **Bhagavadgītā*. It is claimed that this ancient tradition was revived in the 19th century by a mysterious *guru known as Mahāvatar Babaji. It was disseminated to the West by Paramahaṃsa *Yogānanda through his establishment of the California-based *Self-Realization Fellowship.

Kriyāyogasāra (9th/10th century CE?) A *Bhāgavata text, included in the **Padma Purāṇa* but sometimes regarded as a separate **upapurāṇa*.

Kṛṣṇa ('black') One of the major Hindu gods, regarded by his devotees as the supreme deity. As worshipped since the medieval period, Kṛṣṇa has been characterized by some scholars as a 'composite' god, insofar as his character and story appear to be derived from the amalgamation of what were, originally, at least two different figures. Apart from some ambiguous appearances in the *Vedic literature, the earliest references to *Vāsudeva, a god identified as a precursor of the *Epic and *Purāṇic Kṛṣṇa, occur in *Sanskrit sources of the 5th and 6th centuries BCE, and in the works of Greek historians. This Vāsudeva may have originated as the deified hero or *king of the *Vṛṣṇi tribe. He was subsequently amalgamated with Kṛṣṇa, the similarly deified chief of the *Yādavas of *Dvāraka, so that, by the time of the Sanskrit **Mahābhārata*, Vāsudeva-Kṛṣṇa appears as a single deity, thought to be synonymous with, or an *avatāra of, the Vedic god, *Viṣṇu.

As *Bhagavān, the god of the *Bhāgavatas and the personal omnipotent deity of the **Bhagavadgītā*, Vāsudeva-Kṛṣṇa was, by the 4th century CE, further fused with another Kṛṣṇa, *Gopāla, the cowherd god of the semi-nomadic tribes inhabiting the banks of the *Yamunā. This Kṛṣṇa first comes to light in the appendix to the *Mahābhārata*, the **Harivaṃśa* (early centuries CE), which contains in its middle book, the *Viṣṇuparvan*, the first extended and complete account of *Kṛṣṇa's childhood, later life, and death, including his and Saṃkarṣaṇa's (*Balarāma's) play among the cowherds (and, briefly, the *gopīs) at *Vṛndāvana. Undoubtedly drawing on previous folk-religious stories, the *Harivaṃśa* thus provides the model for later accounts of Kṛṣṇa's life and deeds, such as those in the **Viṣṇu Purāṇa* and the **Bhāgavata Purāṇa* (9th–10th centuries), which in turn provide the narrative and theological basis for the medieval *bhakti movements.

In the *Bhāgavata Purāṇa*, in particular, Kṛṣṇa is regarded as not simply a partial avatāra of *Viṣṇu, but as *Bhagavān himself, i.e. God, the supreme being, actively and intimately involved in his creation and with his devotees. It is this God who is subsequently worshipped as Kṛṣṇa-*Gopāla by the *Gauḍīya Vaiṣṇavas (16th century onwards). Their intense devotionalism, expressed through various repetitive ritual practices, is supported by a theology predicated on Kṛṣṇa's life with the gopīs in Vṛndāvana (as narrated in the *Bhāgavata Purāṇa*), and, in particular, on the mutual erotic love between the god and his beloved *Rādhā, which had been portrayed in texts such as *Jayadeva's **Gītagovinda*, and by numerous bhakti poets. A more recent and conservative form of this kind of Kṛṣṇa devotionalism has been propagated in the West by the *International Society for Krishna Consciousness. Another important Kṛṣṇa bhakti tradition is the largely western Indian *Puṣṭimārga; based on the teachings of *Vallabha, it requires disinterested service (*sevā) of, and complete surrender to, the youthful or infant deity, and a blanket reliance on his *grace for spiritual progress and salvation.

As his name suggests, Kṛṣṇa is most usually depicted as a blue or dark-skinned young man. He has an extended and rich pan-Indian mythology, ranging from his exploits as a child and flute-playing youth in Vṛndāvana, to his identification with Viṣṇu, and his pivotal role in the *Mahābhārata*. In all such guises, he has been, and remains (with a wide variety of local and regional variations) an immensely popular subject for paintings, textile hangings, sculpture, and poetry, as well as the inspiration for dramatic performances, and musical compositions.

Kṛṣṇā *See* DRAUPADĪ.

Kṛṣṇacaitanya *See* CAITANYA.

Kṛṣṇadāsa Kavirāja (b. 1531?) A North Indian *Vaiṣṇaiva *bhakti poet who succeeded his father, *Hitaharivaṃśa, as head of the *Rādhavallabhī *sampradāya after the latter's death. His main work is *Karṇānanda* ('Delight of the Ears'), an accomplished *Sanskrit devotional poem evoking the divine *līlā of *Rādhā and *Kṛṣṇa, accompanied by his own commentary. He produced twelve other works in Sanskrit, including one praising his father, one in *Braj bhāṣā, and the **Caitanyacaritāmṛta* ('The Immortal Deeds of Caitanya'). The **Govindalīlāmṛta* ('The Nectar of Govinda's Divine Play') is also attributed to him.

Kṛṣṇa Dvaipāyana *See* VYĀSA.

Kṛṣṇa-Gopāla *See* GOPĀLA(KA); KṚṢṆA.

Kṛṣṇaism A term sometimes applied to the practice of those *Vaiṣṇava devotional traditions (such as *Gauḍīya Vaiṣṇavism) which worship *Kṛṣṇa as the supreme deity, as opposed to merely an incarnation of *Viṣṇu.

k

Kṛṣṇa Jayantī (Gokulāṣṭamī, Janmāṣṭamī) The *festival held in July–August (Śrāvaṇa) to mark *Kṛṣṇa's birthday, particularly celebrated by the great *Vaiṣṇava *temples of North India.

Kṛṣṇānanda (16th century CE) The Bengali compiler of the *Tantrasāra* ('Essence of *Tantra'), a compendium of earlier Tantric texts giving descriptions of various deities for purposes of visualization, and, to a lesser extent, iconography.

Kṛṣṇa-Vāsudeva. *See* KṚṢṆA; VĀSUDEVA-KṚṢṆA.

Kṛṣṇa Yajur Veda *See* BLACK YAJUR VEDA.

kṛta A die (*akṣa), or side of a die, marked with four spots, representing the highest scoring throw. The term is used metaphorically to designate the first in sequence of the four *world ages or *yugas (the kṛtayuga), the perfect, or golden age (also known as the satyayuga, the age of truth). It is characterized by an exceptionally long lifespan and the perfection of moral and spiritual achievement, the acme of *dharma.

kṛtayuga *See* KṚTA.

Kṛttivās(a) *See* OJHA, KṚTTIVĀS.

***Kṛtyakalpataru* (*Tīrthakalpataru*)** An important 12th-century *nibandha (anthology of *dharma sources), compiled by Bhaṭṭa Lakṣmīdhara, which includes an extensive list of *tīrthas.

kṣatriya A member of the second *varṇa, the warrior, governing, or princely class. Initially referred to as the rājanya ('kingly') class, the ideal member of the kṣatriya varṇa is the *king, who, from the *Brahmanical perspective, is the model householder (*gṛhastha) and patron of the sacrifice (*yajamāna). Through his power and wealth, he supports the *brahmin class and its ideology, but is classified by the latter as less *pure, and so of a ritually lower status. In reality, the kṣatriyas usually exercised political or economic supremacy; this has been mirrored at the local or *village level, where the dominant *caste of landowners (such as the *Rājpūts), often aspire to, or claim, kṣatriya status.

Kṣemarāja (*c*.1000–1050) A theologian of the *Pratyabhijñā school of *Kashmir(i) Śaivism, and pupil of *Abhinavagupta. He was the author of a number of works of non-dualistic theology, including the *Pratyabhijñāhṛdaya* and an authoritative commentary on the *Svacchanda Tantra*.

Kṣetrapāla ('protector of the fields') A generic term for a tutelary deity, who is regarded as the specialist protector of the *village and its fields, especially in southern India. The name is also applied to *temple guardians.

Kubera The pan-Indian god of wealth, and, as one of the *aṣṭadikpālas, the guardian of the North. In the **Purāṇas* and *Epics, he is said to be the leader of the *yakṣas and *rākṣasas, and the half-brother of *Rāvaṇa. He is normally included in the *Śaiva pantheon.

Kubjikā ('the crooked one') A Tantric form of the *Goddess, so-called because one of the forms she takes is that of a hunchback crone. Kubjikā was worshipped in the 'western' *Kaula tradition, active in *Nepal from the 11th century CE, and thereafter throughout India. The *Kubjikāmata Tantra,* which is the key *Tantra of the school, is the first text to outline the system of six *cakras, or centres of spiritual energy spaced along the vertical axis of the *subtle body. It also associates the goddess with *Kuṇḍalinī ('the coiled one'), of whom she may be a predecessor.

Kubjikāmata Tantra *See* KUBJIKĀ.

kula A term designating the family or clan. *See also* KAULA.

Kulacēkara(ṉ) (Kulacēkara Perumāḷ, Kulaśekhara Āḻvār) (*c.*8th–9th century CE) A Keralan chieftain, and one of the twelve *Āḻvār *bhakti poets. He was the author of the *Perumāḷtirumoḻi* ('Emotional Songs by the Perumāḷ King'), ten ecstatic songs devoted to *Kṛṣṇa and *Rāma. In the hagiographies, he is presented as a *king who eventually abdicated in order to spend his time in devotional activities.

kula-deva(tā) A male or female family (kula) or clan deity; although sometimes referred to as a 'chosen deity' (*iṣṭa-devatā), such deities are more tied to the family house or home (kula) than to the specific members of the family. They may be pan-Indian gods, such as *Bhairava or *Gaṇeśa, or more local in origin.

Kulaśekhara Āḻvār *See* KULACĒKARA(Ṉ).

Kuleśvara A form of *Śiva worshipped in the eastern transmission of *Kaula *Tantrism.

Kuleśvarī A form of the *Goddess (*Śakti) worshipped in the eastern transmission of *Kaula *Tantrism.

Kullūka (*c.*13th century CE) Author of an important commentary on **Manusmṛti.*

Kumāra *See* KĀRTTIKEYA.

Kumārasambhava ('The Birth of the War God') *See* KĀLIDĀSA.

Kumāra Tantra (pre-11th century CE) An early *Tantric text said to have been composed by the demon *Rāvaṇa. It deals with *possession, *exorcism, and the treatment of childhood illnesses.

Kumārila Bhaṭṭa (7th century CE) A *Pūrva *Mīmāṃsaka exegete. His major work (consisting of the *Ślokavārttika,* the *Tantravārttika,* and the *Ṭupṭikā*) is a free subcommentary on *Śabara's *Bhāṣya,* itself a commentary on *Jaimini's **Pūrvamīmāṃsā Sūtra.* Differences between Kumārila and *Prabhākara (1) in the interpretation of Śabara's text led to the creation of two *Mīmāṃsā subschools, the *Bhāṭṭa and the *Prabhākara (2). Kumārila was also an implacable opponent of the *Buddhists.

kumārī-pūjā ('worship of the young woman') A form of *Goddess worship (*pūjā), practised in northeastern India and *Nepal, in which a premenstrual virgin (kumārī) has the Goddess installed in her—i.e. becomes the Goddess for the duration of the ritual, or *festival—and is worshipped accordingly. She is sometimes referred to as a 'living goddess'.

Kumbakonam (Kumpakoṇam) (Tam.) An important religious, commercial, and agricultural centre in the *Tañjavūr district of Tamil Nadu since before the time of the *Cōḻas. A popular *tīrtha, it contains both *Śaiva and *Vāiṣṇava *temples, and the Mahāmaham (Tam.: Makamakam) *tank—the site every eleven to twelve years (most recently, 2004) of the great nine-day *festival of Kumbheśvara (*Śiva) (also known as the Mahāmaham festival). Held at the February–March full moon, the festival is marked by thousands of devotees ridding themselves of their

k

sins by bathing in the tank, which is believed to mark the confluence of all the holy *rivers of India, an event sometimes characterized as the South Indian *Kumbh(a) Melā.

Kumbh(a) Melā ('festival of the water-pot') An ancient *festival (dating from at least the 7th century CE) held every three years on the banks of the sacred *river flowing through one of four *pilgrimage sites (*tīrthas)—*Hardwār (on the *Gaṅgā), *Ujjain (Siprā), *Nasik (*Godāvarī), and *Prayāga (now called *Allahābād) at the confluence of the Gaṅgā, *Yamunā (Jumnā), and *Sarasvatī rivers. The festival's name is derived from its taking place in January–February when, astrologically, Bṛhaspati (Jupiter) enters Kumbha, the Water-Pot (Aquarius). Its celebration is also linked to a *Purāṇic myth about the gods resting at these towns after they had procured the pot of *aṃrtā, or drops of the liquid which had fallen there. A large number of *ascetics, and holy men and women of all kinds, converge on the site for ritual, debating, and organizational purposes; it is they who take precedence in the ritual *bathing, which is believed to wash away the results of *karma and ensure *immortality. This culminates, both in spiritual intensity and volume of bathers, on the new moon day (maunī amāvasyā (H.)).

A system of rotation means that each town hosts the full melā once every twelve years, while an ardha Kumbha, or 'half-Kumbha', is held every six years. The most important celebration takes place at the confluence of the rivers in Allahābād, which in 2001 hosted the Mahā ('Great') Kumbha Melā, the final festival in a cycle of twelve (i.e. the conclusion of a 144 year cycle). This resulted in what has been called the largest human gathering in history, with a crowd of over 30 million (according to some, 70 million, over 44 days)—so large that it was visible from space.

kuṃkum (kuṅkumā) A red powder, or saffron, used as an offering in *pūjā, particularly the pūjā of goddesses.

Kumpakoṇam *See* KUMBAKONAM.

kuṇḍalinī ('the coiled one') An individual's power or *śakti, visualized as a dormant serpent coiled at the base of the spine. The *yogic manipulation of kuṇḍalinī was developed in *haṭha-yoga and, from about the 8th century CE, as a pan-Indian *Tantric technique. The aim of haṭha-yogic practice is to force the individual's kuṇḍalinī, which is dormant in the 'root' *cakra, up the central channel of the spinal column (the *suṣumṇā *nāḍī), from cakra to cakra, until it merges with the unlimited power of the *sahasrāra padma ('the thousand-petalled lotus' at the crown of the head) in blissful liberation (frequently envisaged as permanent union and identification with the absolute, however defined). The ascension generates ever-increasing spiritual powers (*siddhis) in the practising *yogin. In Tantric traditions, such as the *Śrī Vidyā, kuṇḍalinī is conceptualized as the *Goddess (also called Kuṇḍalinī), and so as *Śiva's Śakti (a cosmic power), the aim being to unite the male and female principles in the practitioner's body. *Abhinavagupta developed a complex theological understanding of kuṇḍalinī, and the term in general is used with divergent meanings in different yogic and Tantric traditions.

kuṅkumā. *See* KUṂKUM.

Kuntī (Pṛthā) In the **Mahābhārata*, the daughter of the *Yādava king, Śūra; married first to Kuntibhoja (hence 'Kuntī'), she subsequently became the senior wife of *Pāṇḍu, and the mother of the three eldest *Pāṇḍava brothers—*Yudhiṣṭhira, *Bhīma, and *Arjuna. She was also, secretly, the mother of *Karṇa, the result of an earlier union with the Sun god, *Sūrya. Towards the end of the *Epic, she retires to the *forest with *Dhṛtarāṣṭra and

*Gandhārī, where she dies with them in a fire. *See also* MAHĀBHĀRATA.

Kuppuswami, Sethurama Sastri (1880–1943) A prominent *Sanskrit scholar and editor. The first principal of Madras Sanskrit College (1906), he was appointed in 1911 to the Chair of Sanskrit at Presidency College; he was also Curator of Manuscripts at the Oriental Library of Madras University. A research Institute bearing his name was founded in 1944.

Kūrattāḻvāṉ (Kureśa) (11th century CE) A *Śrī Vaiṣṇava theologian and disciple of *Rāmānuja. Five theological poems, collectively known as the *Pañcastavam*, are attributed to him.

Kūrma (Akūpāra) ('The Tortoise') According to the **Śatapatha Brāhmaṇa*, part of the cosmogonic process, in so far as it represents earth, atmosphere, and sky. In general, its stability makes it a representative of the earth, and, in particular, it symbolizes the subcontinent of India. According to the *Vaiṣṇava *Purāṇic texts, Kūrma is the second *avatāra of *Viṣṇu, which manifests itself at the time of the *Churning of the Ocean as a support for the 'churning stick', Mount *Mandara.

Kūrma Purāṇa (*c.*6th–11th century CE) Classified as one of the eighteen 'great **Purāṇas*' in the *tāmasa group, i.e. those said (somewhat artificially) to relate to *Śiva. It was probably initially a *Vaiṣṇava *Pāñcarātra manual, reformulated by the *Śaivite *Lākula sect. Its theology is close to that of the **Vāyu* and **Liṅga Purāṇas*, and reflects the general teaching of the *Śaiva **Āgamas*. It also contains the **Īśvaragītā*.

Kuru A descendant of *Bharata. Kuru's descendants (in the **Mahābhārata*, chiefly the sons of *Dhṛtarāṣṭra, but also the *Pāṇḍavas) are referred to as the *Kauravas or Kurus.

Kurukṣetra ('The Field of the Kurus/ Kuru') The name given to a vast region northeast of modern Delhi, said to have been ruled over by *Kuru, and subsequently the site of the *Kaurava capital, *Hastināpura. Said to have been an ancient sacrificial area, those dying there were thought to go immediately to *heaven. In the **Mahābhārata*, it is the location of the final battle between the *Kauravas and *Pāṇḍavas (see **Bhagavadgītā* 1.1).

Kuru-Pañcāla The name given to the region of northwestern India, around the upper to mid reaches of the *Gaṅgā and *Yamunā rivers, which in the later *Vedic period was part of the heartland of *Brahmanism. The term refers to the peoples who were thought to have lived there, the *Kurus and the *Pañcālas.

Kurus *See* KAURAVAS.

Kuśa One of the twin sons of *Rāma and *Sītā. He and his brother, *Lava, were taught the text of the **Rāmāyaṇa* by *Vālmīki, which in the frame story of the *Epic, they recite to Rāma himself.

kuśa *See* DARBHA.

Kuṣāṇa(s) (*c.*mid 1st–3rd century CE) A northern Indian dynasty of central Asian origin. They established their capital at the important religious and artistic centre of *Mathurā. Their most effective ruler was Kaniṣka (*c.*78–144 CE).

L

Lajjā Gaurī ('modesty Gaurī') One of the names given to a fertility goddess (others include 'shy woman', and 'shameless woman'), possibly of tribal origin, but incorporated into Hindu worship through a pan-Indian iconography (notable examples occurring in Odisha (Orissa) and the Deccan). She is most frequently represented naked, with her legs drawn up, as though she were giving birth, or sexually receptive. Her hands hold *lotus buds, touching the open lotus which replaces her head.

lakṣana ('sign', 'characteristic') An identifying mark, sectarian symbol, or characteristic attribute.

Lakṣmaṇa (Saumitri) ('endowed with auspicious signs') A major character in the *Rāmāyaṇa*; the son of King *Daśaratha and *Sumitrā, the twin of *Śatrughna, and the half-brother of *Rāma, whom he accompanies into his *forest exile. Epitomizing the devoted and loyal younger brother, he is also renowned for his devotion to *Sītā. Some lists of *avatāras give him as partial incarnation (aṃśāvataraṇa) of *Viṣṇu. *See also* RĀMĀYAṆA.

Lakṣmī (Śrī, Padmā) ('good fortune') The pan-Indian goddess (strictly speaking, personification) of good fortune, prosperity, wealth, and beauty; she is the consort of *Viṣṇu, and, according to *Vaiṣṇava mythology, the mother of *Kāma(deva). First appearing in late *Vedic texts, the goddess Śrī ('light', 'radiance') is specifically associated with prosperity and the fertility of the land. (A telling epithet is karīṣin, 'abounding in cow-dung'.) In *Epic and *Purāṇic accounts, Śrī/Lakṣmī is said to have appeared fully formed from the waters at the *Churning of the Ocean. She is depicted as a beautiful young woman, holding, and sometimes seated on, a lotus (*padma)—hence her epithet Padmā, or Kamala (the red of the lotus also being her colour). Sometimes she is shown with four arms, but more often with just two. Regarded as an entirely benevolent and *auspicious form of the *Goddess, because of her ability to grant wealth, Lakṣmī/Śrī is widely revered across India; among other *festivals, she is closely associated with *Divālī, which marks the beginning of the new financial year. Other auspicious images, such as burning oil lamps, and the *cow, are assimilated to her as the essence of auspiciousness. As Viṣṇu's consort she plays a pivotal part in a number of Vaiṣṇava theologies, especially that of the *Śrī Vaiṣṇavas. *See also* GAJALAKṢMĪ.

Lakṣmīdhara, Bhaṭṭa *See* KṚTYAKALPATARU.

Lakṣmī-Nārāyaṇa Iconographically, *Viṣṇu (*Nārāyaṇa) with the goddess *Lakṣmī seated in his lap, or, in some cases, the two deities combined in a single image.

Lakṣmī Tantra (*c.*7th/8th century CE) An important **Tantra* of over 3600 verses belonging to the *Vaiṣṇava *Pāñcarātra school. In a reconstitution of *Sāṃkhya ontology, it identifies the goddess *Mahā Lakṣmī (subdivided into three related goddesses) as the *śakti of *Puruṣa/*Viṣṇu, and therefore both the instrumental and material cause of the universe. In addition to its philosophy and metaphysics, the *Tantra* has sections devoted to the composition and use of *mantras, and the practice of ritual, enjoining the worship of Lakṣmī as the means to *liberation.

Lākula (fl. 1st millennium CE) One of two subdivisions of the *Śaiva *atimārga tradition, the other being the *Pāśupata, of which the Lākula was a more radical development. Composed entirely of *ascetics who identified themselves with *Rudra as *brahmin-killer and outsider, the Lākula distinguished itself by its adherence to *cremation ground culture and the bearing of skull bowls (*kapāla) and skull-topped staffs (*khaṭvāṅgas). It accepted the basic teachings of the **Pāśupata Sūtra*, but its own canonical texts have not survived. *See also* KĀLĀMUKHA.

Lākulīśa ('Lord of the Staff', 2nd century CE?) Regarded as an incarnation of *Rudra, and said to be the founder of the *Śaiva *Pāśupata tradition; the latter's only surviving text, the **Pāśupata Sūtra*, is attributed to him, although in its extant form it is significantly later (*c.*8th or 9th century CE?). Iconographic evidence from North India (*c.*7th–11th centuries CE) suggests that Lākulīśa was worshipped as a staff (lakuṭa/laguḍa)-bearing, ithyphallic *yogin.

Lālan Fakir *See* BĀULS.

Lalitā ('lovely') A benign form of the goddess *Parvatī, depicted with a mirror in her hand. *See also* TRIPURASUNDARĪ.

Lalitāsahasranāma ('The Thousand Names of Lalitā', 7th century CE?) A *Śrī Vidyā text, composed of 320 devotional verses; it takes the form of a dialogue between *Agastya and *Hayagrīva, praising the all-powerful, but benign goddess, *Tripurasundarī. Traditionally ascribed to *Śaṅkara, the text, like the cult associated with it, seems to have originated amongst *Kaula Śaivas, before moving south and assimilating elements of *brahmin *Vedānta culture. Now forming the second part of the **Brahmāṇḍa Purāṇa*, it has become an exceptionally popular work, claimed by some to be the most widely used *Śākta *Tantra in India. The best-known commentary appeared in 1728, composed by *Bhāskararāya Makhin.

Lalitā Tripurasundarī *See* TRIPURASUNDARĪ.

Lallā *See* LAL(LA) DED.

Lal(la) Ded (Lallā, Lalleśvarī) ('Granny Lal', 14th century CE) A Kashmiri *Śaiva poet and *saint, notable for her antinomian behaviour (she is, for instance, said to have given up wearing clothes), but most renowned for the literary and religious quality of her sayings. Collected in the *Lallā-vākyāni*, these 109 verses came to have classic status across all Kashmiri religious traditions and *castes, reflecting the poet's own anti-sectarianism.

Lallā-vākyāni *See* LAL(LA) DED.

language *See* BHARTṚHARI (1); MANTRA(S); PĀṆINI; SANSKRIT; VĀC; VYĀKARAṆA.

Laṅkā The name given in the **Rāmāyaṇa* to *Rāvaṇa's island stronghold where he holds *Sītā, and from which she is eventually rescued by *Rāma and his monkey army. It is not clear what relation the epic Laṅkā bears to what is now Sri Lanka (Śrī Laṅkā), formerly Ceylon.

Lāsya A prototypical, gentle but dramatic, dance form for women, said to have been invented by *Pārvatī as the counterpart to the vigorous male *tāṇḍava, attributed to *Śiva.

laukika ('mundane', 'relating to this world', 'usual custom', 'not sacred') Something characterized by, or related to, the ordinary custom of the world (*loka). This distinguishes it from the ultramundane or *alaukika, whether generally, or in the more specialized contexts of *aesthetics and *bhakti.

Lava One of the twin sons of *Rāma and *Sītā. He and his brother, *Kuśa, were taught the text of the **Rāmāyaṇa* by *Vālmīki, which, in the frame story of the *Epic, they recite to Rāma himself.

Lavaṇa According to *Purāṇic *cosmology, the name of the salt-water ocean surrounding *Jambūdvīpa, the innermost island constituting the flat disc which is the earth.

lāvṇī A Maharashtrian poetic genre, originating in the 16th century CE, combining the erotic and the religious in, for example, songs evoking *Kṛṣṇa's adventures with the *gopīs. These were originally delivered by dancing girls in order to reinvigorate *Marāṭhā soldiers.

law *See* DHARMA.

Laws of Manu *See* MANUSMṚTI.

Laya Yoga ('yoga of absorption/dissolution') A method of *yoga, which appears in various lists from at least the time of the the *Yogatattva Upaniṣad* (early centuries CE) onwards. Its practice typically involves the dissolution of the conscious mind, and/or (symbolically) the universe, as means of raising *kuṇḍalinī and attaining *samādhi. There appear to be numerous modern variations.

'left-handed path/practice' *See* VĀMĀCĀRA.

liberation *See* MOKṢA.

life-cycle rituals *See* SAṂSKĀRA.

līlā ('play', 'amusement', 'pastime', 'sport') The precise historical origins of this pan-Indian concept are unclear, but it may be understood from two interrelated perspectives, the theological and the anthropological. From the former perspective, līlā appears in the 1st centuries CE, with the rise of the great monotheistic systems, as an expression of God's spontaneous, joyful, and gratuitous creative power; in this respect, it is the corollary of his omnipotence and freedom, particularly from those constraints which are so characteristic of the limited human condition, i.e. desire (*kāma) and *karma. The first extant theological justification of this idea appears in the **Brahmasūtra(s)* (2.1.33) (redacted early centuries CE), the locus classicus for later, often divergent, commentaries within the *Vedānta tradition. The idea continued to inspire creative theology, and was later taken up by the sophisticated *rasa theoreticians of *Kashmir(i) Śaivism. Nevertheless, the most consistent development of the concept occurs in the context of *Kṛṣṇa *bhakti: in *Gauḍīya Vaiṣṇavism, for instance, it is thought to be the defining characteristic of Kṛṣṇa's childhood and youth (as narrated in the **Bhāgavata Purāṇa*), so that, in the earthly *Braj, every grove and pond is connected with a particular 'pastime' (līlā) of Kṛṣṇa, reflecting his eternal play with *Rādhā and the *gopīs in *heaven. Furthermore, through the enactment of various devotional practices, which narrate, visualize (in līlā-smaraṇa), or otherwise evoke these līlās, the devotee can hope to achieve a permanent, blissful, and liberating participation in this heavenly play, either while still alive, or after *death.

From the anthropological perspective, līlā is a descriptive label applied to numerous popular performance traditions—i.e. dramatized forms of ritual worship (*pūjā)—originating in specific localities. Characterized by a mixture of the staged—recitation of texts, song, ritual processions, and drama—and the spontaneous, examples include the *Līlākīrtan(a) of Bengal, the *Pāṇḍavalīlā of Garhwal, the *Rās(a)līlā of Braj, and the *Rām(a)līlā of *Vārāṇasī (the last two now having a pan-Indian significance).

Līlākīrtan(a) A Bengali performance form, originating in the 16th century CE and still very popular, involving a troupe of singers and drummers in the retelling, through song, dance, and dramatic movement, of stories about the *līlā of *Kṛṣṇa and *Rādhā, as well as episodes from the life of *Caitanya. The performance consists essentially of settings of 15th–18th century *Vaiṣṇava *bhakti lyrics, mainly in Bengali, designed to induce a state of aesthetic delight (*rasa) in the audience. The popularity of līlākīrtana across religious traditions, and the suspension of the usual *caste and gender distinctions during its performance, have been seen as major factors in the social integration and democratization of Bengali society. *See also* KĪRTAN(A).

līlā-sthala ('play places') The groves and ponds of the earthly *Braj, each connected with a particular 'pastime' (*līlā) of *Kṛṣṇa. According to the hagiographical literature of the *Caitanya and *Vallabha sects, their founders were instrumental in the rediscovery of these places in the 16th century.

liṅga ('sign', 'characteristic mark', 'emblem', 'phallus') An abstract or aniconic representation of *Śiva, which is the form in which the god is most usually worshipped, whether in *temples, smaller shrines, or as self-manifesting (*svayaṃbhū) in natural objects. The liṅga is a phallus-shaped, vertical shaft, usually set into a pedestal (pīṭha) in the shape of a *yoni (vulva), representing Śiva's *śakti, or female power. (The yoni may be shaped as a spout, enabling water, and other substances used in the *abhiṣeka of the liṅga, to drain away.) The liṅga and yoni together are taken to represent the undifferentiated unity of spirit (male) and matter (female), which is the god's unlimited, and continuously dynamic potency—his simultaneously creative and destructive energy. Despite its appearance (and perhaps its origins), the liṅga is therefore not regarded as a 'phallic symbol' in the Western sense; rather, it is viewed, and treated in *pūjā, in ways similar to any other representation of a supreme deity, including elaborate garlanding and dressing. Indeed, like many later images, the earliest surviving liṅga (2nd or 1st century BCE), still worshipped at Guḍimallam in Andhra Pradesh, combines the aniconic with an anthropomorphic or iconic rendering of Śiva. Such sculptures often include him as part of the shaft (usually just his face), or emerging from it. In fact, liṅgas are ubiquitous, and are represented in a wide variety of ways, depending on geographical and historical context, and the aspect of Śiva emphasized. *See also* JYOTIRLIṄGA; LIṄGĀYAT(A)S; LIṄGODBHAVAMŪRTI.

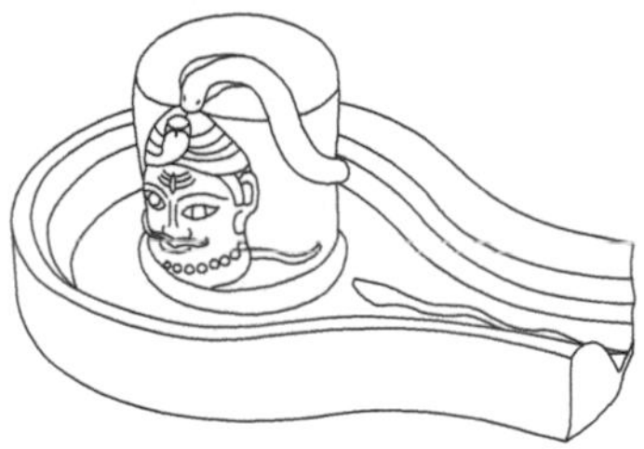

liṅga

Liṅga Purāṇa **(*Lainga Purāṇa*)** (*c.*500 CE?) Classified as one of the eighteen 'great *Purāṇas' in the *tāmasa group, i.e. those said to relate to *Śiva. In addition to the usual contents, this important *Śaiva *Purāṇa* contains material on various Śaivite sects, descriptions of Śiva, information on *asceticism and *yoga, and instructions about the installation of *liṅgas.

Liṅgarāja (originally Tribhuvaneś-vara—'Lord of the Three Worlds', c.1100 CE) An elaborate and archaeologically important *Śaiva *temple complex at *Bhuvaneśvar(a).

liṅga śarīra *See* SŪKṢMA ŚARĪRA.

Liṅgāyat(a)s (Vīraśaivas) ('wearers of the liṅga') A South Indian *Śaiva *bhakti tradition, founded by *Basava, with possible *Kālāmukha antecedents. It ignores distinctions of *caste (although it is treated as one itself), class, and, to a considerable degree, gender, and so rejects the authority of the *Veda* and its *brahmin guardians. Worship consists of daily devotion to a small *Śiva liṅga, worn by men, after initiation, in a silver box strung over the left shoulder. The aim of the devotee is to realize his or her essential identity with *Śiva, with whom they hope to be unified at *death. A priestly subcaste, known as *jaṅgamas, are responsible for performing the Liṅgāyatas' life-cycle rituals (*saṃskāras) (including *burial, rather than *cremation), and act as *gurus to the community. The most important texts of the tradition are the songs (vacanas) of Basava and other poets, notably, *Allama-Prabhu, Dēvara *Dāsimayya, and the female *saint, *Mahādēviyakka. The Liṅgāyat community, currently about eight million strong, is *Kannada-speaking, and strictly *vegetarian. It remains an influential religious force in Karnataka.

liṅgodbhavamūrti ('image springing from the liṅga') An image (*mūrti) of a four-armed *Śiva emerging from a blazing liṅga which represents an infinite column of light. A particularly popular image in South Indian *temples, it is derived from a *Purāṇic myth in which Śiva, by means of the infinite liṅga, demonstrates to *Brahmā and *Viṣṇu that he is greater than both of them.

little deities A term sometimes used by anthropologists, and others, to refer to *village or local deities.

logicians *See* NAIYĀYIKAS.

loka ('world') **1.** The name given to a particular realm or space, whether i) cosmological, such as the *Vedic three worlds of heaven (*svar), the atmosphere (*bhuvaḥ), and earth (*bhūr) (or heaven, earth, and the underworld), ii) a 'heaven' (*svarga), governed by a deity, or iii) a ritually and individually created ontological realm. **2.** The 'world' of conventional social transactions. *See also* LAUKIKA.

Lokācārya Piḷḷai *See* PIḶḶAI LOKĀCĀRYA.

loka-pāla *See* AṢṬADIKPĀLA.

Lokāyata *See* CĀRVĀKA.

Lothal The site of an *Indus Valley city, close to the Indian Ocean in Gujarat, revealing evidence of a large dock area and maritime activity.

lotus *See* PADMA.

love *See* KĀMA.

Lunar Dynasty The name given to the descendants of *Iḷā, and so of her son, *Purūravas, including the *Kauravas and *Pāṇḍavas of the *Mahābhārata*. *See also* CANDRAVAṂŚA.

M

Mā, Ānandamāyī *See* ĀNANDAMĀYĪ MĀ.

Macaulay, Thomas Babington (First Baron Macaulay) (1800–1859) An English poet, politician, and historian, who served on the Supreme Council of the *East India Company from 1834–38. During this time he instigated the policy of an exclusively English and Western education for a selected Indian elite, designed to create an administrative class to act as a bridge between the colonial power and the mass of those they governed. He was also responsible, as the Chair of the commission, for the drafting of the Indian Penal Code, which came into force in 1862.

Macdonell, Arthur A. (1854–1930) A British *Indologist; he spent most of his working life at Oxford University, where he held the *Boden Chair in *Sanskrit. His publications include *Vedic Mythology* (1897), *A History of Sanskrit Literature* (1900), *A Sanskrit Grammar for Students* (1901), and *A Practical Sanskrit Dictionary* (1929).

Mādhava 1. (Mādhavācarya, Vidyāraṇya) (14th century CE) Author of the *Sarvadarśanasaṃgraha* ('Compendium of All Philosophical Schools'), a summary of sixteen philosophical systems (*darśanas) from an *Advaita perspective. He is said to be identical with Vidyāraṇa, and therefore also the author of the Advaita manual, *Pañcadaśī*. Reputed to have been chief minister at the *Vijayanagara court of King Bukka, before renouncing to become head of the *Śṛṅgeri *maṭha, he collaborated on various works with his younger brother, *Sāyaṇa, the commentator on the **Ṛg Veda*. He is sometimes confused with *Madhva. **2.** ('descendant of Madhu') An epithet of *Kṛṣṇa.

Madhu A *Dānava killed by *Viṣṇu/*Kṛṣṇa, earning him the epithet Madhusūdana ('destroyer of Madhu').

Madhurakavi *See* MATURAKAVI.

Madhusūdana ('Destroyer of Madhu') An epithet of *Viṣṇu/*Kṛṣṇa. *See also* MADHU.

Madhusūdana Sarasvatī (*c.*mid 16th century CE) An influential Bengali *Advaitin teacher and *Vaiṣṇava *bhakti poet, who, while remaining a strict nondualist, argued for the efficacy of bhakti as a means to the realization of *ātman/*brahman (neut.). His best known philosophical work is the *Advaitasiddhi*; he also wrote a number of commentaries, including one on the **Bhagavadgītā* (the *Gūḍhārthadīpikā*).

Madhva (Ānandatīrtha, Madhvācārya) (1197/9?–1276, alt. 1238–1317) The founder of the *Vaiṣṇava, *Dvaita Vedānta *sampradāya. Hagiographies claim that he was born in Udipi (Udupi) in Karnataka, but later travelled around India, teaching and disputing with other traditions, before returning to establish a *maṭha in his home town. Initiated as an *Advaitin, he came forcibly to reject *Śaṅkara's teachings (in the process acknowledging the mythical *Vyāsa as his only *guru), and developed a dualistic, *Kṛṣṇa- *bhakti-oriented form of *Vedānta, partially derived from his exegesis of texts such as the **Mahābhārata* and the **Bhāgavata Purāṇa*, on both of which he wrote commentaries. Credited with 37 works in all, his principal philosophical treatises are his commentaries (*Bhāṣya* and *Anuvyākhyāna*) on the **Brahmasūtra(s)*. He also regarded *Pāñcarātra texts as authoritative, particularly in matters of *temple ritual.

Madhyadeśa *See* ĀRYĀVARTA.

Mādrī In the **Mahābhārata*, *Pāṇḍu's second wife, and mother (by the *Aśvins) of the twins *Nakula and *Sahadeva.

Madurai (Maturai) An ancient *temple city in Tamil Nadu, on a site which is at least 1 500 years old. Capital of the *Pāṇḍya dynasty, and subsequently part of the *Vijayanagara empire, Madurai flourished under the patronage of the *Nayaka ruler Tirumala (1623–60). It was he who was responsible for the construction of most of the city's best-known temple, the spectacular *Mīṇākṣī-Sundareśvara complex, named after Madurai's tutelary goddess, *Mīṇākṣī, and her consort *Sundareśvara (a form of *Śiva). (Madurai's main annual *festival—the twelve day *Chittirai festival—celebrates their wedding and the goddess's coronation.) The city remains at the heart of *Dravidian culture, and a major *pilgrimage site.

madya (wine) One of the 'five Ms' (*pañca-makāra) used in *Tantric ritual, and viewed as *impure by *Brahmanical religion.

Magadha An ancient northern Indian kingdom, situated east and south of the *Gaṅgā, including much of modern Bihar. Under its first *king, Bimbisāra (*c*.465–413 BCE), it was the breeding ground for various *renouncer movements, including *Jainism and, particularly, early *Buddhism. Bimbisāra's son, Ajātaśatru (*c*.413–381 BCE) expanded the kingdom into what is sometimes referred to as the first Indian empire. The *Mauryans subsequently ran their empire from Magadha, as did the *Guptas and the *Pālas, and it remained the heartland of Indian Buddhism until the middle of the 1st millennium CE. Initially at Rājgṛha, the capital subsequently moved to Pāṭaliputra.

Mahābalipuram *See* MĀMMALAPURAM.

Mahābhāgavatamu A 15th-century CE Telugu retelling of the **Bhāgavata Purāṇa*.

Mahābhāgavata Purāṇa (*c*.10th century CE or later) A medieval *Śākta **Purāṇa*. Classified as one of the **upapurāṇas*, it deals with the theology and mythology of *Devī in her various forms, including *Kālī. Narrated by *Śiva, it seems to be partly derived from the **Śiva Purāṇa*.

Mahābhārata ('The Great Story of the Descendants of Bharata') One of two great *Sanskrit *Epics (the other being the **Rāmāyaṇa*), its central narrative deals with the conflict between two sets of cousins, the *Kauravas and the *Pāṇḍavas (the descendants of *Bharata) for the lordship of *Kurukṣetra in northern India. The extant text, which exists in two major recensions (northern and southern), numbers approximately 100 000 verses, divided into eighteen 'books' (*parvan). Apparently gathered together, edited, and re-edited, over a period of perhaps 900 years (*c*.500 BCE–400 CE), some of its material (which was originally transmitted orally) may be very much earlier, perhaps even of *Indo-European origin. The *Mahābhārata* itself attributes its composition to the legendary *ṛṣi *Vyāsa, who instructs his pupil *Vaiśaṃpāyana to recite it for the first time at *Janamejaya's *snake *sacrifice. What he recites is a vast encyclopaedia of narrative and didactic material (the text refers to itself as the 'fifth **Veda*', and claims to contain everything), which continues to be interpreted, both from within the tradition and by academic scholarship, in multiple ways. The central concept is clearly the complex one of *dharma, which is represented as being in perpetual crisis at all levels—individual, social, and cosmic. Variously analysed and questioned, the resolution of this dharmic crisis becomes a key conundrum both for the protagonists and the audience.

The *Mahābhārata* contains some of the best-loved stories in Indian literature, many of them, like the central narrative itself, continuously recast in vernacular languages, and told again in countless dramatic performances, visual representations, and music. Particularly productive in this respect are the stories of *Śakuntalā, *Sāvitrī, and *Nala—not to mention the *Mahābhārata*'s own version of the *Rāma story (*Rāmopākhyāna*). Among the more didactic portions, the **Bhagavadgītā* (part of the **Bhīṣmaparvan*), is notable for being treated by many as an autonomous sacred text, effectively 'authored' by *Kṛṣṇa.

A highly condensed version of the principal narrative is as follows:

Book 1: **Ādiparvan* ('The Beginning'). The Epic begins with various genealogies and a number of narrative framing stories. It then deals with the origins of the *Lunar Dynasty and the seeds of the conflict, including the miraculous birth of the Pāṇḍavas (*Yudhiṣṭhira, *Bhīma, *Arjuna, *Nakula, and *Sahadeva) and their cousins, the Kauravas (*Duryodhana, his 99 brothers and one sister—the children of the blind king, *Dhṛtarāṣṭra). The cousins' education, and the creation of various alliances is recounted, including those of Duryodhana and the Pāṇḍavas' older half-brother *Karṇa, and the Pāṇḍavas themselves with Kṛṣṇa's people, the *Vṛṣṇis. The Pāṇḍavas' collectively marry *Draupadī.

Book 2: **Sabhāparvan* ('The Assembly Hall'). Yudhiṣṭhira performs a *rājasūya. He subsequently loses everything, including his brothers and himself in a rigged dicing match, organized by Duryodhana. Draupadī is humiliated by the Kauravas, but obtains the Pāṇḍavas' freedom. They are exiled to the *forest for twelve years, with a thirteenth year to be spent incognito if they are to regain their kingdom.

Book 3: **Āraṇyakaparvan* ('The Book of the Wilderness/Forest'). This tells of the Pāṇḍavas' twelve-year forest exile, including sections on Arjuna's journey to *Indra's heaven, his meeting with *Śiva, and Draupadī's abduction and rescue. Much of the material is incidental to the main narrative, such as the story of *Nala, and the **Rāmopākhyāna*.

Book 4: **Virāṭaparvan* ('King Virāṭa'). The Pāṇḍavas spend their thirteenth year of exile in disguise at the court of King Virāṭa of the *Matsyas, to whom they become allied.

Book 5: **Udyogaparvan* ('Preparations'). Both sides prepare for war, and eventually face each other at *Kurukṣetra.

Book 6: **Bhīṣmaparvan* ('Bhīṣma'). The book begins with the *Bhagavadgītā*, in which Kṛṣṇa dispels Arjuna's scruples about fighting his relatives and teachers. The battle starts and the Kaurava commander *Bhīṣma is fatally wounded.

Book 7: **Droṇaparvan* ('Droṇa'). *Droṇa now assumes command, but he eventually lays down his arms and is killed.

Book 8: **Karnaparvan* ('Karṇa'). Karṇa is now the Kaurava commander, but, at Kṛṣṇa's urging, he is killed, illegitimately, by Arjuna.

Book 9: **Śalyaparvan* ('Śalya'). Śalya too is killed. Of the Kauravas, only *Aśvatthāman, Kṛpa, Kṛtavarman, and Duryodhana survive. At Kṛṣṇa's instigation, Duryodhana is mortally wounded by Bhīma in contravention of the laws of battle.

Book 10: **Sauptikaparvan* ('The Massacre at Night'). With Śiva's help, Aśvatthāman, Kṛpa, and Kṛtavarman massacre the sleeping Pāṇḍava army; only the five brothers escape.

Book 11: **Strīparvan* ('The Women'). The surviving women grieve for those killed in the battle.

Book 12: **Śāntiparvan* ('The Peace'). Yudhiṣṭhira is crowned. From his death bed, Bhīṣma gives a wide-ranging and extensive discourse on religion, ethics, dharma, and *cosmology.

Book 13: **Anuśāsanaparvan* ('The Teaching'). Bhīṣma's instructions to Yudhiṣṭhira continue. Eventually he dies and ascends to *heaven.

Book 14: **Aśvamedhikaparvan* ('The Horse Sacrifice'). Yudhiṣṭhira performs a horse sacrifice (*aśvamedha) at the end of the war to atone for the Pāṇḍavas' destruction of their Kaurava cousins. This provides the occasion for Arjuna to fight many great battles as he escorts the horse in its wanderings across the entire earth.

Book 15: **Āśramavāsikaparvan* ('The Stay in the Hermitage'). Dhṛtarāṣṭra, and the Kaurava women retire to the forest, and eventually perish in a forest fire.

Book 16: **Mausalaparvan* ('The Battle with Clubs'). Thirty-six years after the war, Kṛṣṇa's people beat each other to death in a drunken brawl. Kṛṣṇa's brother, *Balarāma dies, and Kṛṣṇa allows himself to be killed in a hunting accident.

Book 17: **Mahāprasthānikaparvan* ('The Great Departure'). The five Pāṇḍava brothers renounce the world and set out for Mount *Meru. All die en route except Yudhiṣṭhira; after a final encounter with his father, *Dharma, he enters heaven.

Book 18: **Svargārohaṇaparvan* ('The Ascent to Heaven'). Yudhiṣṭhira enters heaven and sees his enemies enthroned, his brothers and wife in *hell. The gods reveal this to be an illusion: both Kauravas and Pāṇḍavas now reside in a heavenly region, free of enmity and suffering. The text closes its narrative framing stories. *See also the entries for the main characters listed above.*

Mahābhāṣya ('The Great Commentary', 2nd century BCE) *Patañjali's commentary on *Kātyāyana's *Vārttikas* to *Pāṇini's grammar (**Aṣṭādhyāyī*).

mahābhūta ('great element') According to *Sāṃkhya ontology, the five mahābhūtas, or 'gross material elements', are the final evolutes of *prakṛti. They consist of ether (space), air (wind), fire, water, and earth.

mahābrāhmaṇa (mahābrāhman) ('great Brahmin') The name given to the *priests (*brahmins) who conduct *funeral rites at *Vārāṇasī.

Mahādeva ('The Great God') An epithet of *Śiva (and, less often, *Viṣṇu).

Mahādevī *See* DEVĪ.

Mahādēviyakkā (Akkā Mahādevī, Mahādēvyakka, Mahādeviakka) (12th century) A South Indian female poet-*saint at the beginning of the *Liṅgāyat(a) tradition. A younger contemporary of *Allama-Prabhu, *Basava, and other Vīraśaiva poets composing religious lyrics (*vacanas) in the *Dravidian language of *Kannada, she signed herself 'Cennamallikārjuna' ('Lovely Lord White as Jasmine'), an epithet of that form of *Śiva to which she had become exclusively devoted. Although apparently married to a local lord, she abandoned him to wander naked, covered only by her long hair. Eventually, she was initiated into the Liṅgāyat(a) tradition by Allama-Prabhu, but continued to roam in her ecstatic quest for union with Śiva, the only bridegroom she recognized. She died in her early twenties. A selection of her poetry in English translation can be found in A. K. *Ramanujan's *Speaking of Śiva* (Penguin Books, 1973).

Mahākāla *See* KĀLA (3).

Mahākālī *See* KĀLĪ.

mahākalpa According to *Purāṇic *cosmogony, the cycle of time (known as a 'life of *Brahmā') which begins with 'creation' (*sarga) and ends with dissolution (*pralaya). At the end of a day of Brahmā, the universe enters a period of quiescence or night, during which, according to a well-known Purāṇic myth, *Viṣṇu (*Nārāyaṇa) sleeps on the cosmic ocean (sometimes identified with the serpent *Śeṣa) before becoming, or giving rise to, the demiurge, Brahmā, who inaugurates the new cycle. *See also* KALPA.

Mahākāvya ('great kāvya') A term applied to the *Sanskrit 'courtly epic' poems of *Kālidāsa (*c.*4th–5th century CE), and a few others, which combine poetic description with narrative. *See also* KĀVYA.

Mahā Lakṣmī ('Great Lakṣmī') An epithet of *Lakṣmī, especially as that cosmic form of *Devī who, in the **Devī Mahātmya*, for instance, embodies the *guṇa of *rajas.

Mahāmaham festival *See* KUMBAKONAM.

mahāmantra *See* HARE KṚṢṆA MANTRA.

Mahāmāyā ('The Great Illusion') An epithet of *Devī, expressing (in texts such as the **Devī Māhātmya*) her creative and overwhelming power, including her manifestation as the world of appearances (*māyā).

Mahānārāyaṇa Upaniṣad (*c.*3rd century BCE) A verse **Upaniṣad*, which, as the tenth book of the **Taittirīya Āraṇyaka*, belongs to the **Taittirīya* school of the **Black Yajur Veda*. It is named after *Nārāyaṇa (*Viṣṇu), whom it identifies as the absolute deity, both cosmically and within the individual; he is therefore synonymous with *brahman (neut.). The *Mahānārāyaṇa* is one of the first *Upaniṣads* to demonstrate theistic/monotheistic beliefs.

Mahānayaprakāśa ('Illumination of the Great Way', 10th–13th century CE) The name of three separate texts belonging to the Kashmiri *Krama tradition, one ascribed to Śatikaṇṭha, one to Arṇasiṃha, and one anonymous.

Mahānubhāva Saṃpradāya (Mānbhāvs, Manbhaus) ('those who have a great experience') An anti-*Vedic and antinomian *Kṛṣṇa-*bhakti tradition, founded by *Cakradhar in 13th-century Maharashtra. By the end of the following century, the tradition had separated into thirteen 'currents' (*āmnāyas), and isolated itself from the surrounding Hindu culture of *caste and *svadharma, partially by preserving its extensive Marathi literature—much of it hagiographical material about Cakradhar and his successors—in a secret code until the 20th century. Mahānubhāvas worship *Parameśvara, the one, absolute God, who manifests himself in the form of five *avatāras, the 'five Kṛṣṇas': i) Cakradhar, ii) his *guru, *Govindaprabhu, iii) Govindaprabhu's guru, iv) the composite deity, *Dattātreya, and v) Kṛṣṇa. Worship is largely internal and meditational. The āmnāyas, now reduced to two, are composed of lay followers and initiated male *saṃnyāsīns, although, in line with the early tradition's antinomianism, women were originally initiated as well.

mahāpralaya *See* PRALAYA.

Mahāprasthānikaparvan ('The Great Departure') Book 17 of the *Sanskrit **Mahābhārata*; it tells of how the five Pāṇḍava brothers *renounce the world and set out for Mount *Meru. All die en route except *Yudhiṣṭhira; after a final encounter with his father, *Dharma, in the shape of a dog, he enters *heaven.

mahāpurāṇa *See* PURĀṆA(S).

mahāpuruṣa ('great man', 'great soul') **1.** Honorific used of a great *ṛṣi or *ascetic. **2.** Epithet of *Viṣṇu. **3.** According to **Śilpaśāstra*, the foundational deity on whose dimensions a *temple is constructed. *See also* PURUṢA.

Mahār A Maharashtrian *untouchable *caste with a pronounced warrior tradition, expressed through their recruitment into various armies, such as those of *Śivaji, and the British Rāj, as well as the current Indian army. Most Mahārs converted to *Buddhism in the 1950s under the influence of their fellow caste member, Dr. *Ambedkar.

Maharishi Mahesh Yogi (1917–2008) Founder and *guru of the *Transcendental Meditation Movement. Thanks to successful marketing, and his espousal by the Beatles and other celebrities since the 1960s, the Maharishi is probably the best known Indian *yogī in the West. Born Mahesh Prasad Varma, his *guru was the *Śaṅkarācārya, *Brahmānanda Sarasvatī; in the mid 1950s, under the title Maharishi (*mahāṛṣi), he began to teach a traditional form of *meditation, later called Transcendental Meditation. Initially intended to bring about a Hindu spiritual reformation, it was later expanded into a global and technologically sophisticated enterprise with thousands of teachers and millions of practitioners. Throughout his career, a number of controversial allegations were made about the Maharishi's personal life. In his latter years, he lived in the Netherlands.

maharṣi(s) ('great sage(s)/seer(s)') An honorific, collectively used to designate 'the seven great sages (*ṛṣis)' in the **Veda*, and various similar groupings in the *Epics and **Purāṇas*.

Mahāsena ('having a great army') Epithet of *Skanda.

Mahāśivarātri *See* ŚIVARĀTRI.

mahat ('the great one') *See* BUDDHI.

mahātma ('great self/soul') An honorific (e.g. Mahātma *Gāndhī).

māhātmya ('glorification') A text praising a sacred place, person, or object (including the text itself), e.g. the **Devī Mahātmya* ('The Glorification of the Goddess').

mahāvākya ('great sayings') Short *Sanskrit sentences, or *mantras, from the **Upaniṣads* believed by many *Vedāntins to embody the essence of *Vedānta. They include tat tvam asi ('that is you'), ahaṃ brahmāsmi ('I am *brahman'), ayam ātmā brahma ('*ātman is brahman'), prajñānaṃ brahma ('wisdom is brahman'), and sarvaṃ khalu idaṃ brahma ('all this [everything] is brahman'). The first four are imparted by the *guru to his pupil as the latter undertakes the orthodox ritual of renunciation (*saṃnyāsa).

mahāvedi *See* VEDI.

Mahāvidyā(s) A name given to a group of ten transformations, or personifications, of *Devī in the *Śākta *Tantric literature, consisting, typically, of: *Kālī, *Tārā, *Ṣoḍaśī, *Bhuvaneśvarī, *Bhairavī, *Chinnamastā, Dhūmāvatī, Bagalā, Mātaṅgī, and Kamalā.

Mahāvīra ('great hero') **1.** An honorific applied to a spiritual 'hero'. **2.** (Vardhamāna) (5th century BCE) The name by which the twenty-fourth *Jaina teacher, or *Jina, is best known.

mahāvrata ('great vow') **1.** A fertility *festival, performed by the *Vrātyas at the winter solstice, and seemingly incorporated into the *aśvamedha rite. **2.** According to **Dharmaśāstra*, the penance to be undertaken for killing a *brahmin, involving carrying the skull of the victim as a banner, while living the life of a forest (*aranya) *ascetic—a practice followed by the *Śaiva *Pāśupatas in imitation of the brahminicidal Śiva/*Rudra, who, according to *Purāṇic myth, had cut off *Brahmā's fifth head.

mahā-yajña(s) ('great sacrifice(s)') A highly simplified or concentrated form of *Vedic ritual through which the householder (*gṛhastha) is thought to fulfill his daily ritual obligations to i) the gods (*devas), ii) the ancestors (*pitṛs), iii) the spirits (*bhūtas), iv) other human beings (typically *brahmins), and v) *brahman (neut.). These *yajñas, usually referred to as the 'five great sacrifices' (pañca-mahāyajñas)—consist, respectively, of i) *devayajña—a minimal oblation (such as a stick of wood) offered into the fire, ii) *pitṛyajña—the offering of food and water (the *tarpaṇa), iii) *bhūtayajña—the offering of a rice ball or flowers, iv) *narayajña— *hospitality (the offering of food) to *brahmins or the twice-born (*dvija), and v) *brahmāyajña—recitation of the **Veda* (i.e. of a Vedic *mantra). Seen originally, in the **Brāhmaṇas* and **Āraṇyakas*, as a way for the householder to pay off his *debts, they are regarded by **Manusmṛti* as expiations for the necessary violence (*hiṃsā) involved in householder life.

mahāyuga In *cosmology, a cycle of four *yugas. One thousand mahāyugas constitute one 'day of *Brahmā', also known as a *kalpa. *See also* COSMOGONY.

Maheśvara ('The Great Lord') An epithet of *Śiva.

Maheśvaras A name applied (e.g. by *Śaṅkara) to *smārta, or *Purāṇic, devotees of *Śiva.

Maheśvarī ('Maheśvara's Consort') A name of *Śiva's *Śakti; one of the'seven Mothers' (*Saptamātṛkās).

Mahīpati (1715–1790) The poet-author of collections of Marathi stories (of which the best known is the *Bhaktavijaya*) about the *Vārkarī *saints. *Tukārāma (*c.*1607–49) is said to have been his *guru.

Mahiṣāsura ('Buffalo Demon') According to the **Devī Mahātmya*, Mahiṣa was a demon (*asura) who ousted the gods from *heaven. Eventually, *Viṣṇu and *Śiva combined their powers to summon the *Goddess in the terrible form of *Durgā, who killed the shape-shifting demon when he assumed the form of a buffalo (mahiṣa), by decapitating the animal, and crushing the demon as he emerged from the carcass. This earned her the epithet *Mahiṣāsuramardiṇī ('crusher of the buffalo demon').

Mahiṣāsuramardiṇī ('crusher of the buffalo demon') Epithet of *Durgā.

maithuna ('sexual union') An element of some forms of *Tantric ritual (e.g. in the *Kaula tradition), involving the consumption of the fluids produced in ritual intercourse. It is one of the 'five Ms' (*pañca-makāra) of *Śākta Tantrism. In the plural (maithunas, also mithunas), it refers to the iconographic depiction of couples in sexual union on the exterior of medieval *temples, such as those at *Khajurāho.

***Maitrāyaṇī Saṃhitā* (*Maitrāyaṇi/Maitrāyaṇīya/Maitrāyaṇa Saṃhitā*)** The foundational texts of the *Maitrāyaṇī* branch (school) of the *Veda, and one of the four collections constituting the **Black Yajur Veda*. Its **Brāhmaṇa* and **Āraṇyaka* exist only as fragments, but an **Upaniṣad*, the **Maitrāyaṇī* survives.

***Maitrāyaṇī Upaniṣad* (*Maitrāyaṇīya/Maitrāyaṇa/Maitrī Upaniṣad*)** Considered to be the most recent of the 'major' **Upaniṣads*, the *Maitrāyaṇī* (named after its principal *teacher, Maitri) belongs to the **Maitrāyaṇī Saṃhitā* of the **Black Yajur Veda*. There is no general agreement about its date, but many detect evidence of *Buddhist influence and a well-developed *Vaiṣṇava theism in the *Maitrāyaṇī*, as well as references to a relatively late form of *Sāṃkhya-Yoga. This suggests a composite text, assembled over a lengthy period, possibly between the 4th century BCE and the early centuries CE.

Maitreya **1.** A *Vedic *ṛṣi who appears in the frame stories of the **Bhāgavata* and **Viṣṇu Purāṇas*. **2.** The name of the future *Buddha.

Maitreyī Wife and astute theological questioner of *Yājñavalkya in the **Bṛhadāraṅyaka Upaniṣad* (2.4ff.; 4.5ff.).

***Maitrī Upaniṣad* (*Maitri Upaniṣad*)** *See* MAITRĀYAṆĪ UPANIṢAD.

m

makara A large, mythical, aquatic animal, sometimes connected with the crocodile. It has long been popular as a decorative device on *temples, sculptures, and manuscripts.

Māl *See* MĀYŌṈ.

mala (āṇavamala) ('impurity', 'dirt', 'fine dust') According to *Śaiva Siddhānta theology, an essential and beginningless *impurity which is tied to the soul (*ātman); along with *karma and *māyā, it occludes the soul's true nature, and causes further *rebirth. Through successive lives, mala is said to 'ripen', and so gets worn away. In the Kashmiri form of Śaiva Siddhānta, it is thought to be destroyed by the act of initiation (*dīkṣā).

mālā ('garland', 'necklace', 'wreath', 'rosary') Variously made—typically from beads, berries, or flowers—mālās are regarded as *auspicious and protective. Flower mālās are used to honour deities (by garlanding their *images), as well as notable guests, particularly at *weddings and *festivals. Bead and berry mālās may be used as aids in the recitation of *mantras; in the case of *Vaiṣṇavas, the berries are usually those of the *tulasī plant, while *Śaivas favour *rudrākṣa berries. *Śiva himself is also often depicted wearing a garland of skulls.

Mālādhar Basu *See* BASU MĀLĀDHAR.

Malaviya, Pandit Madan Mohan (1861–1946) *See* HINDŪ MAHĀSABHĀ.

***Mālinīvijayottara Tantra* (*Mālinīvijaya Tantra*)** (9th–10th century CE) The root text of the *Kashmiri Śaiva tradition. It clearly had widespread appeal, and became central to the output of *Abhinavagupta, who not only wrote a commentary on the text (the *Mālinīślokavārttika*), but also two works expounding and summarizing it—the **Tantrāloka* and the **Tantrasāra*—recasting the *Mālinīvijayottara*'s dualistic *Śaivism in terms of his supreme non-dualism.

Mallikārjuna The name by which *Śiva is known at the 14th–16th century *temple (of the same name) at the *jyotirliṅga of *Śrīśailam.

Māmmalapuram (Mahābalipuram) A coastal site, in Tamil Nadu, 30 miles south of Chennai (Madras). It was the main port of the *Pal̲l̲ava dynasty (*c.*4th–8th centuries CE), which was responsible for constructing its seventeen rock-cut and monolithic *temples (7th–8th century) (including the well-known 'shore temple'), the earliest of their kind in southern India. It is celebrated for the quality of its sculptures.

māṃsa ('meat', 'flesh') One of the 'five Ms' (*pañca-makāra) used in *Tantric ritual, and viewed as *impure by *Brahmanical religion.

manana ('thinking', 'meditation') Understood by the *Vedānta tradition in the sense of discursive understanding or reasoning, the bridge between hearing (*śravaṇa), revelation (*śruti), and meditation (*nididhyāsana) upon it.

manas ('mind') Regarded by many Indian systems as a sixth sense organ—i.e. a material entity, itself processing subtle material entities, such as thoughts and physical impressions, to the essential *self. So, according to *Sāṃkhya ontology, for instance, manas is an evolute of *prakṛti, which is simply 'owned' by the spiritual *puruṣa, and in no way to be identified with it.

Manasā A *snake goddess, popular in northern and eastern India. Probably of tribal origin, and visibly worshipped in Bengal and Bihar from at least the 8th century CE, by the 14th or 15th century CE she had been absorbed into the mythology of great deities, such as *Śiva, through vernacular narrative texts, such as the Bengali *Manasā Maṅgal*. Invariably portrayed in human form, but usually with a canopy of cobras, like other goddesses of the type, she both rules over snakes and offers devotees protection from their venom. In eastern India her *festival is known as *Nāga Pañcamī.

Mānavadharmaśāstra *See* MANUSMṚTI.

Maṇavāḷamāmuṉi (1370–1443) *Śrī Vaiṣṇava teacher, and author of the *Tirumantrārtham*, a commentary on Lokācārya *Piḷḷai's *Mumukṣuppaṭi*, itself a commentary on the secret *mantras (*rahasyas) of the Śrī Vaiṣṇavas. Maṇavāḷamāmuṉi effectively formulated the theological basis for what later became the *Teṉkalai school.

Mānbhāvs *See* MAHĀNUBHĀVA SAMPRADĀYA.

maṇḍala ('circle', 'disc', 'ring') **1.** A type of sacred, and often complex, symbolic diagram, used, especially in *Tantric ritual, as an aid to visualization and a way of manifesting the deity, or group of deities, represented at its centre. The maṇḍala itself is thought to be a two-dimensional representation of the cosmos, and as such can contain potentially anything. On the same principle, a *temple is conceptualized as a three-dimensional maṇḍala, again representing the cosmos, with the deity at its heart. Maṇḍalas are usually circular at the periphery, and enclose various interlocking geometrical shapes, such as triangles. Their precise interpretation and ritual use is tradition- or practitioner-specific. *See also* YANTRA. **2.** The generic name given to each of the ten 'books', or sections, of the **Ṛg Veda*.

Maṇḍana Miśra (7th–8th century) An exponent of *Advaita Vedānta, and, after *Bhartṛhari, one of the most important thinkers in the field of *vyākaraṇa (linguistic analysis or grammar). According to the hagiographies, Maṇḍana was originally a *Pūrva *Mīmāṃsaka exegete and a pupil of *Kumārila Bhaṭṭa, but there must be considerable doubt about this, given that one of Maṇḍana's major works, the *Sphoṭasiddhi* ('The Establishment of the Essence of Meaning'), sets out to assert the *sphoṭa theory as the underlying metaphysical and epistemological principle of Vedānta precisely by disproving Kumārila's arguments and denying many *Mīmāṃsā assumptions. Similarly, a well-known story about Maṇḍana's 'conversion' to *Śaṅkara's form of Advaita after being defeated by the latter in a long debate, looks like sectarian propaganda, given that, initially, Maṇḍana seems to have been the better known teacher in the Advaita tradition through influential works such as the *Brahmasiddhi* ('The Establishment of Brahman'), although some claim that this was composed under Śaṅkara's influence. The conflation of Maṇḍana with Śaṅkara's pupil, Sureśvara, should also be rejected.

Mandara *See* CHURNING OF THE OCEAN.

mandir(a) ('dwelling', 'temple') *See* TEMPLE.

Māṇḍūkya Kārikā *See* GAUḌAPĀDĪYA KĀRIKĀ.

Māṇḍūkya Upaniṣad (early centuries CE) A short prose **Upaniṣad* assigned to the **Atharva Veda*. It deals with the sacred syllable *oṃ, which it equates with the cosmos, with *brahman (neut.), and with *ātman. It also considers the waking, dreaming, and deep-sleeping ātman, a theme expanded in the earliest identifiable *Advaita text, the **Gauḍapādīya Kārikā*, *Gauḍapāda's influential commentary on the *Māṇḍūkya*.

maṅgal A type of Bengali narrative verse drama recounting the myths of local deities (such as *Manasā), performed by professional singers known as (maṅgal) gāyaks.

maṅgal(a) *See* AUSPICIOUS(NESS) AND INAUSPICIOUS(NESS).

Māṇikkavācakar (Māṇikkavāsagar) ('whose words are like rubies', 8th/9th century CE?) The best-known and most revered *Tamil *Śaiva saint and *bhakti poet; although not officially listed among the 63 *Nāyaṉmār (he probably post-dates the original list), Māṇikkavācakar, along with *Appar, *Campantar, and *Cuntarar, has come to be regarded as one of the founders of the *Śaiva Siddhānta tradition in southern India. His chief works are the *Tiruvācakam* ('Sacred Verses'), a very popular collection of Tamil hymns devoted to *Śiva, which is still sung daily in *temples and homes in the Tamil region, and the *Tirukkōvaiyār*, a love poem addressed to the image of Śiva at *Cidambaram, in which the author adopts the persona of a young girl. Together these works constitute Book 8 of the **Tirumuṟai* collection. Māṇikkavācakar's hagiography seems to have developed between the 14th and 16th centuries: before renouncing and devoting himself entirely to *Śiva, he is said to have been the *brahmin chief minister of the Pāṇḍiya *king of *Madurai. There is an annual ten-day *festival (the 'Tiruvempāvai') in December–January, focused on the worship of his movable image in the *Mīnākṣī temple at Madurai, which involves the repeated singing of the *Tiruvempāvai* ('Our Sacred Lady'), a twenty-verse devotional hymn included in the *Tiruvācakam*.

Māṇikkavācakar

maṇipravāḷa(m) ('jewels and coral') A hybrid form of discourse in which *Sanskrit words were incorporated into *Tamil syntax. It was used by those attempting to 'sanskritize' or, from their point of view, elevate the status of Tamil literature.

Maṇipurī A classical dance form originating in the *temples of the Maṇipur region in northeastern India, evoking *Kṛṣṇa's 'divine play' (*līlā) among the *gopīs in *Vṛndāvana (*Braj/Vraj), and especially his relationship with *Rādhā. It thus acts as a component part of the *Rās Līlā performance tradition, which was initiated in the 18th century. Rabindranath *Tagore's enthusiasm for the Maṇipurī style led both to its wider dissemination, and the creation of a new style, based on its synthesis with *Kathākalī.

mantra(s) **1.** A synonym for the *Vedic **Saṃhitā* texts (*ṛc, *yajus, and *sāman), recited as an essential component of *Brahmanical ritual (*yajña); this portion of the **Veda* is distinguished from the prose explanations, or ritual exegesis, contained in the **Brāhmaṇa(s)*, as well as from the **Āraṅyakas* and the **Upaniṣads*. The term may therefore be used to refer to any Vedic hymn. **2.** A combination, or string of syllables (paradigmatically in *Sanskrit, and often a word or verse excerpted from a particular text), which, when known or recited, is believed to actualize an instrumental, performative, and/or transformative power. Mantras, or sequences of mantras, are therefore typically employed in activities such as ritual, *meditation, *bhakti, and *yoga. *Tantric ritual, in particular, manipulates the latent power of mantras for supernatural and/or soteriological purposes, and they are the major topic in nearly all Tantric texts. Mantras need to be formally acquired, and initiation (*dīkṣā) into a *sampradāya usually requires the transmission of a 'secret' *mantra from *guru to pupil. In other contexts, *namajapa alone—the chanting of a mantra consisting of the deity's name, such as the *Hare Kṛṣṇa mantra—is thought to guarantee *liberation. Like all power, that of the mantra is ambivalent, and can be used for a wide variety of purposes; for instance, in the **Mahābhārata*, magical weapons are activated or empowered through mantras. According to some, the most powerful mantra of all is the sacred syllable *oṃ.

mantramārga ('path of mantras') One of the two main branches of *Śaivism described in the Śaiva **Āgamas* or **Tantras* (the other being the *atimārga, or 'outer path'). The mantramārga is open to both *householders and *ascetics; some of the latter are concerned not just with salvation but also with the cultivation of *siddhis ('supernatural powers'). Its large body of texts is divided between the *Śiva-* and *Rudra-*Āgamas* which are authoritative for the *Śaiva Siddhānta tradition, and the voluminous **Bhairava Tantras* of *Kāpālika *Tantrism.

mantraśāstra ('the doctrine of mantras') A synonym for tantraśāstra, i.e. *Tantra, since knowledge of *mantras, and how to use them, is considered the most important part of Tantric teaching.

mantravāda ('magic') In Kerala, the specific manipulation of *mantras by a 'magician' or 'sorcerer' (mantravādin) for magical or supernatural purposes, such as averting misfortune, effecting cures through exorcism, and controlled '*possession'.

Manu 1. According to *Purāṇic myth, the first human being, and therefore the ancestor of the human race. (According to some, he is also the first *king.) His name first appears in the **Ṛg Veda*; in the **Brāhmaṇas*, he is the survivor of the great deluge; he is also said to have given birth to the race by removing one of his ribs. In the more developed Purāṇic *cosmologies, 'Manu' is the generic name given to the first man and instigator of the race at the beginning of each of fourteen successive world ages, known as manvantaras. Collectively, these progenitors are referred to in the plural as the 'Manus'. **2.** The mythical author of the **Manusmṛti*, also known as Svāyambhuva ('The Son of the Self-Existent'), the first manvantara-*avatāra in the cycle of fourteen manvantaras.

Manusmṛti **(*Mānava Dharmaśāstra, Manu Saṃhitā, Manu*)** ('The Laws of Manu', 'The Law Code of Manu', 'The Institutes of Manu', 1st century BCE–2nd century CE) The foundational text of the **Dharmaśāstra* literature, of which it remains the best-known and most influential example. As its name indicates, it is regarded as one of the most important *smṛti texts. Its composition is traditionally ascribed to the first *Manu (2), but its main historical author was clearly a North Indian *brahmin, perhaps working during the 2nd century CE (although there may well have been later additions); certainly, its authority had been established by the 4th or 5th century CE. A narrative framework depicts Manu being approached by some great *ṛṣis to explain the ordinance of the Creator (*Svayambhū = *Brahmā) with regard to the laws (*dharma) for all social classes (*varṇas) (i.e. the work is supposed to be normative and all-inclusive). Manu obliges over twelve chapters—topics covered include: *cosmogony and *cosmology; *svadharma and varṇa; the pre-eminence of the brahmin class; the nature and scope of dharma; the *saṃskāras; the rules for the *Vedic student (*brahmacārin); rules and rituals for the householder (*gṛhastha) *āśrama; forbidden *foods, *pollutions, and *purifications; qualifications and rules for the forest dweller (*vānaprastha), *ascetics, and *saṃnyāsins; the duties and responsibilities of *kings; civil and criminal law; domestic law, and the roles of wives and *sons; duties of *vaiśyas and *śūdras; rules for times of adversity or distress (*āpad-dharma); reparations or penances for infringements of dharma (*prāyascittas); *karma and *rebirth; the equation of *ātman with *brahman (neut.), and *liberation through the realization of brahman.

The earliest extant commentary on *Manu* is that of *Medhātithi; at least six others still exist, including Kullūka's, the one most commonly cited.

manvantara ('the reigns of the Manus') In *Purāṇic *cosmology, the collective name for the fourteen successive world ages, each instigated by a *Manu, and one of the classical 'five distinguishing marks' (*pañcalakṣaṇa) of a **Purāṇa*. *See also* Manu.

Māraṉ *See* Nammāḻvār.

Marāṭhā The name of a dominant *caste in western India (Maharashtra), which was united into an independent Marāṭhā kingdom (or empire) by *Śivajī in 1674. His successors, who eventually splintered into a confederacy, resisted first the *Mughals and then the British. After a prolonged series of wars, they were finally defeated in 1818.

mārga ('path') A prescribed religious discipline or route, leading to a particular goal, such as liberation (*mokṣa).

Marīci A legendary *ṛṣi, and one of the *Prajāpatis; the son of *Brahmā and father of *Kaśyapa.

Māriyammaṉ (Mariamman) A very popular South Indian tutelary goddess or *grāmadevatā, particularly associated with *smallpox. She appears in a similar, or identical form in most of the *villages across the region; because of her fearsome nature, she is considered to be a manifestation of *Durgā (a fierce form of the great Goddess, *Devī). Her annual *festivals, such as that at Samayapuram in Tamil Nadu, attract tens of thousands of devotees.

Mārkaṇḍeya A legendary *ṛṣi, renowned for his great age and *asceticism. He is the narrator of the **Mārkaṇḍeya Purāṇa*.

Mārkaṇḍeya Purāṇa (*c.*4th century CE) Classified as one of the eighteen 'great **Purāṇas*' (*mahāpurāṇas*) in the *rājasa group, i.e. those said to relate to *Brahmā, it is said to have been narrated by the *ṛṣi *Mārkaṇḍeya. Among passages on ritual and *yoga, it contains much *Vedic mythological material; its best-known section (Chs. 81–93) is the celebrated **Devī Mahātmya*, a later (*c.*6th or 7th century) addition to the main *Purāṇa*.

marriage (vivāha ('leading away of the bride [from her father's house]')**)** The most important rite of passage (*saṃskāra) for most Hindus. For women, it marks the transition to maturity, and is therefore classified by **Dharmaśāstra* (e.g. **Manusmṛti* 2.67) as the *upanayana (initiation rite) for women; it turns them into personifications of *auspiciousness (*sumaṅgalīs). For men, marriage represents entry into the *gārhasthya *āśrama, the 'householder' stage or order of life. Since this āśrama represents the best, or preferred norm of life for the authors of *Dharmaśāstra*, marriage is therefore considered the highest duty or *dharma. For the *Brahmanical sacrificer, whether performing the *gṛhya (domestic) or the extended *śrauta rites, marriage is likewise a sine qua non, since not only does the ritual require a married couple acting together, but the *gṛhyāgni, the 'domestic fire' from which all the other ritual fires can be expanded, is only set up at the time of marriage. From a similarly Brahmanical perspective, marriage is also a prerequisite for starting to pay off two of the three *debts (ṛṇas) that the *twice-born man incurs at birth, namely, those of *sacrifice to the gods (*devas), and of offspring to the fathers (*pitṛs). The production of offspring is often identified as the particular duty of the married couple and the raison d'être of their union.

Manusmṛti (3.30ff.) lists eight possible types of marriage: i) Brāhma—a father's free gift of his daughter to a Vedically educated groom of good character; ii) Daiva (Divine)—a father's gift of his daughter to an officiating *priest while he is performing the *sacrifice (i.e. as part of priest's *dakṣiṇā); iii) *Ārṣa (Seer's Marriage)—involving the bridegroom making a gift of one or two pairs of oxen to the bride's father; iv) *Prājāpatya—the bride is given after the couple have been exhorted to practise *dharma together; v) Āsura (Demonic)—marriage after the free payment of money (i.e. a 'bride-price') to the girl's relatives and the girl herself; vi) *Gāndharva—a mutually desired union between the bride and bridegroom expressed through sexual intercourse; vii) Rākṣasa (Fiendish)—marriage by the violent and forcible abduction of the bride; viii) Paiśāca (Ghoulish)—a form of marriage involving the secret rape of a sleeping, intoxicated, or deranged woman. Of these, the final two are considered illegal by *Manu*, although they are theoretically, perhaps pragmatically, assigned to *kṣatriyas in particular. The Gāndharva marriage is likewise thought to be the prerogative of kṣatriyas, especially of *kings in stories. Marriages i)–iv) are supposed to be reserved for *brahmins, although it is a version of the first of these, the Brāhma marriage, which has effectively become the norm for marriages involving all classes. Shorn of the necessity of *Vedic learning, a typical North Indian marriage (for instance) involves an arrangement made between two families, based on the compatibility of the bride and groom with regard to their *caste (it should normally be the same) and *gotra (it should normally be different), their horoscopes, their education, and their wealth. A dowry may also be negotiated (although, officially, this is illegal), a proverbial and sometimes ruinous expense for families with daughters. (However, among the middle classes, in particular, a dowry is not always required.) *Child marriage was common throughout the medieval period and into the 19th century, when it became a target for reformers. Under civil legislation, such marriages are now illegal, although still practised in some parts of the country (e.g. Rajasthan). Under civil law, the legal age for marriage is 18 for women and 21 for men.

Parts of the Hindu wedding ceremony are undoubtedly very ancient, although details vary according to time and place. The general pattern is as follows: the groom is accepted by the bride's family, and the couple are bethrothed. The wedding proper begins with the father giving his daughter away to the groom, who is now responsible for her. While the groom recites a *mantra, the couple circumambulate the sacred fire three times. The bride offers grain and *ghī for fortune and fertility; accompanied by the groom, and reciting a mantra, she then takes seven steps (the saptapadī ritual), at each one placing her right foot on a different pile of rice. Following this, in the āśmārohaṇa ritual, she puts her right foot on a millstone, as a sign of her steadfast commitment to the union. The couple may then look at that symbol of constancy, the Pole star. Towards the end of the ceremony, the groom gives his bride the 'gift of the thread of auspiciousness' (maṅgalasūtra-dāna), by tying a thread (also known as a tali) symbolizing her newly auspicious and fortunate status about her neck. The wedding feast is followed by the bride's ritual journey to her new home, and her welcome by the other women of the family. According to the law codes, it would be at this point that the couple would set up their domestic fire and begin their ritual life together. It is now their duty to consummate the marriage in the hope of producing a male child.

Maruts (Rudras) The *Vedic storm gods; companions and, according to some post *Ṛg Vedic texts, brothers of *Indra, they form his entourage. Their numbers (from

7 to 180) and parentage vary from text to text, but they are often identified as the sons of *Rudra. They are also closely connected with *Agni and *Vāyu.

Maṟvars An ancient *Tamil social group, portrayed in the *Caṅkam literature as *forest warriors or bandits, and said to be devotees of the goddess of war, *Koṟṟavai, for whom they committed ritual suicide. It is not clear whether the *caste of the same name is related to them.

Maskarin Gosāla *See* GOSĀLA; MAKKHALI.

mātā (mātājī) (nom. sing. of mātṛ—'mother') An honorific given to a goddess, particularly a *village goddess, and by extension to any holy woman or female religious teacher.

Mātājī Nirmala Devī (b. 1923) Founder and propagator of the Sahaja Yoga ('Innate/Spontaneous Yoga') movement (also known as 'Sahaja Yoga International' or 'Vishwa Nirmala Dharma'). Her *Christian parents were associates of *Gāndhī, and as a child she visited his *āśram; in the 1940s she was active as a youth leader in the independence movement. Married to the civil servant, Sir C. P. Srivastava, she had a religious experience in 1970 which convinced her that she had discovered a method (subsequently called Sahaja Yoga) through which people could realize their inner, spiritual selves by awakening their *kuṇḍalinī. This awakening, or Self Realization, brought about directly by Nirmala Devī herself, and then passed on from self-realized individual to individual, is claimed to bring about a total (physical, mental, and spiritual) transformation, one which is ultimately capable of solving all the world's problems. Sahaja Yoga centres have been established throughout India and around the world, teaching the meditational technique to lay people. The movement claims to have 20000 members, half of them in India. Clinics and 'hospitals' have also been founded, since it is claimed that the technique can help to cure otherwise incurable physical diseases. Nirmala is revered by her followers as the compassionate Divine Mother.

materialists *See* CĀRVĀKA.

maṭh(a)s The name given to teaching institutions, or 'monasteries', particularly those said to have been founded by *Śaṅkara. The latter, which are the monastic centres for the *Daśanāmi order, were established at *Purī, *Jyotirmaṭh, *Dvārakā, *Śṛṅgeri, and—on some accounts— *Kāñcī(puram). Each is under the headship of a *Śaṅkarācārya.

Mathurā An ancient city on the *Yamunā *river in what is now Uttar Pradesh (a modern city of the same name lies a few miles away), and one of the seven ancient holy cities of India. Mathurā lay at the meeting point of three major trade routes, which accounts, historically, for its immense commercial and cultural importance. Said to have been ruled over initially by the *Yādavas, it became the capital city of the *Kuṣāṇas, under whom some of the very earliest figurative *Jaina and *Buddhist art was produced. From the same period, Mathurā provides the first archaeological evidence of Hindu *temples in India. Its flowering as an artistic and religious centre continued under the *Gupta dynasty. Recognized by *Gauḍīya Vaiṣṇavism as the birthplace of *Kṛṣṇa, and lying at the heart of the *Braj region, close to the *Vṛndāvana forest, Mathurā was re-established as a major *pilgrimage site in the 16th century.

Matilal, Bimal Krishna (1935–1991) An important Indian philosopher and *Indologist who introduced many Western thinkers to Indian philosophical thought by demonstrating the common concerns of the two traditions. A brilliant *Sanskrit scholar, he was educated, and subsequently taught (1957–1962) at the Sanskrit College in Kolkata (Calcutta). His PhD on

*Navya Nyāya was obtained at Harvard (1965). After a period as Professor of Sanskrit at Toronto University, he was elected in 1977 to the *Spalding Chair of Eastern Religions and Ethics at Oxford University, which he occupied until his early death. His work was wide-ranging, covering not just *Nyāya-Vaiśeṣika, but *Mīmāṃsā, *Buddhist and *Jain philosophy, Ethics, and the philosophy of *language. He founded and edited the *Journal of Indian Philosophy*; his many publications include: *Navya Nyāya Doctrine of Negation* (1968), *Epistemology, Logic and Grammar in Indian Philosophical Analysis* (1971), *Logic, Language and Reality* (1985), and *The Word and the World: India's Contribution to the Study of Language* (1990).

Mātṛkā(s) (Mātṛ(s)) ('mother(s)') A 'divine mother', i.e. a goddess. In the plural, a class of goddesses of *Vedic origin, connected with fertility, but by *c.*500 CE typically depicted as a group of seven or eight. At one level they are presented as the *śaktis of male deities, as the names of the seven—the saptamātṛkās—suggest: *Brāhmī (*Brahmā), Maheśvarī (*Śiva), Kaumarī (*Kumara), Vaiṣṇavī (*Viṣṇu), *Varāhī (*Varāha), *Indrāṇī (*Indra), and *Cāmuṇḍā. (*Mahā Lakṣmī, the cosmic form of *Devī, is the eighth.) At another level, the 'mothers' are feared as ferocious and independent goddesses, thought to be particularly dangerous to young children; it is in this fierce form that they are associated with the *yoginī cults of *Tantric *Śaivism.

Matsya ('fish') **1.** According to the the *Vaiṣṇava *Purāṇic texts, the first *avatāra of *Viṣṇu. It takes the form of a fish which helps *Manu (and thus humankind) to survive the great deluge, and so ensures the repopulation of the world, as well as saving the *Vedas*. Matsya is often portrayed with a single horn, hence Visṇu's epithet, *Ekaśṛṅga ('one-horned'). **2.** One of the 'five Ms' (*pañca-makāra) used in *Tantric ritual, and viewed as *impure by *Brahmanical religion. **3.** In the *Mahābhārata*, the name of a people/ kingdom, ruled over by Virāṭa. It is among the Matsyas that the *Pāṇḍavas spend the thirteenth year of their exile.

Matsya Purāṇa (*c.*1st–6th century CE?) Classified as one of the eighteen 'great *Purāṇas' (*mahāpurāṇas*) in the *tāmasa group, i.e. those said (somewhat artificially) to relate to *Śiva, the *Matsya* is related to *Manu by *Matsya (*Viṣṇu), whose *avatāra myth it includes. Generally considered to be among the earlier *Purāṇas*, and composed of more than 14 000 verses (*ślokas), its contents are disparate, sharing material with the *Mahābhārata* and perhaps also the *Vāyu Purāṇa*. Among *Śaiva themes, it tells of the birth of *Kārttikeya, and the destruction of *Tripura, but the text also includes extensive *Vaiṣṇava and nonsectarian material.

m

Matsyendranāth(a) (Matsyendra) ('He Whose Lord is the Lord of Fishes', *c.*9th–13th centuries CE) The legendary second *Nāth (second only to *Śiva), said to be the founder of the *Yoginī *Kaula sect. Although an elusive figure historically (according to a text attributed to him, he was from a *caste of fishermen), a considerable hagiography has grown up around Matsyendranāth, which treats him as a semi-divine being who had been taught by Śiva himself. He is said to have been the *guru of *Gorakhnāth, and together, they are credited with systematizing *haṭha yoga within the *Śaiva Nāth *Siddha tradition (one which includes the *Kānphaṭa yogīs and the *Gorakhnāthīs)—a *sampradāya (institutionalized order) effectively created by them. According to legend, Matsyendranāth was continually having to be rescued from worldly and erotic entanglements by his more disciplined pupil. Eight works, exercizing a considerable influence on later *Tantric authors, are attributed to him: chief among them is the *Kaulajñānanirṇaya*, a synthesis of the Siddha and Yoginī Kaula traditions, which derives its authority from the claim that Matsyendranāth had recovered Śiva's original Tantric teachings. He is the tutelary deity of *Nepal.

Maturai *See* MADURAI.

Maturakavi (Maturākavi, Madhurakavi) (*c.*9th–10th century CE) One of the twelve South Indian poet-saints, the *Āḻvārs. A *brahmin, he was a contemporary of *Nammāḻvār, and, according to legend, after being led to him by a bright star, he became the younger man's disciple, and thereafter the popularizer of his works. A number of his own hymns, including those in praise of Nammāḻvār, have been anthologized.

Mauryan dynasty (*c.*317–185/187 BCE) The rulers over a major early northern Indian empire, radiating from the *Magadha region, with its capital at *Pāṭaliputra. Among the dynasty's ten rulers, the most celebrated are its founder, *Candragupta Maurya, and his grandson, *Aśoka.

Mausalaparvan ('The Battle with Clubs') Book 16 of the *Sanskrit **Mahābhārata*. It tells of the self-destruction of the *Yādavas, and the deaths of *Balarāma and *Kṛṣṇa.

māyā A *Sanskrit term, perhaps derived from the verbal root mā, which, in its earliest usages in the **Ṛg Veda*, refers to a god's supernatural power to manifest the world, or his own appearance, in a creative but sometimes bewildering sense. In the **Bhagavadgītā* (7.14), *Kṛṣṇa refers to the three *guṇas making up material nature (his own lower nature) as his divine māyā, in the sense of an 'appearance' generated by him. From their monistic or non-dual perspective, *Advaita Vedānta theologians used the term in a different way, giving it the sense of the cosmic power of 'illusion' or artifice, which causes beings to view as multiple and differentiated what is in reality one, i.e. *brahman (neut.). In other words, it accounts for the way in which the world is experienced by the unliberated, and is coeval with ignorance (*avidyā). For *Viśiṣṭādvaita, on the other hand, māyā represents the way in which God manifests the reality of *prakṛti. And for *Śaiva Siddhānta, it is the eternal material cause and unconscious substratum of the manifest universe, which remains ontologically distinct from *Śiva. At its simplest, māyā is the term used to evoke a magic trick or illusion, but, by an extension of this, it becomes for many *bhaktas a *līlā-like expression of God's mesmerizing, and often baffling, creative activity. In the **Purāṇas*, māyā is sometimes personified as a goddess, Māyādevī. *See also* YOGAMĀYĀ.

Māyōṉ (Māl ('the Great One'), **Tirumāl)** ('the Dark One') As the word suggests, a *Tamil name for *Kṛṣṇa, especially, at the popular level, the Kṛṣṇa of *bhakti and devotional poetry. He may have been introduced to the South in the 1st centuries CE through the **Mahābhārata* (**Bhagavadgītā*), but he also has pronounced elements of the *Purāṇic *Viṣṇu and *Nārāyaṇa. Thanks to the influence of the *Āḻvār poets, Māyōṉ became an object of devotion in a number of related contexts: through his mythical actions (drawn from stories about *Kṛṣṇa and Viṣṇu's *avatāras), through his incarnation in South Indian *temple statues (where his more Viṣṇu-like characteristics are emphasized, especially by the *Śrī Vaiṣṇavas), and through his residence in the hearts of his devotees.

meat *See* AHIṂSĀ; COW; FOOD; PAÑCAMAKĀRA.

medha According to *Vedic *ritual theory, the quality that makes an animal worthy of *sacrifice, and so, by extension, a name for both the sacrificial victim and the sacrifice itself, as, for example, in the name, *aśvamedha.

Medhātithi (9th century CE) Author of the earliest extant commentary on **Manusmṛti*.

medicine *See* ĀYURVEDA.

meditation A generic term in English for various practices involving mental concentration, or the auto-manipulation of the mind, in order to obtain specific effects, such as inner transformation. Frequently used as a translation of the *Sanskrit term, *dhyāna.

Megasthenes (*c.*350–*c.*290 BCE) An Ionian ambassador, sent by the Greek general Seleucus Nicator to the court of *Candragupta Maurya at *Pāṭaliputra. He wrote a four volume account (*Indikē*) of his eight year stay (306–298 BCE), which is no longer extant, although valuable fragments appear in the writings of later classical authors. Even in this condition, Megasthenes' description remains the earliest significant eye-witness report of India by a foreigner.

Meghadūta *See* KĀLIDĀSA.

Mehta, Narsī *See* NARSĪ MEHTA.

melā ('assembly', 'gathering') A term for a popular *festival—for instance, the *Kumbh(a) Melā ('festival of the water-pot')—usually with both religious and commercial elements.

Menā (Menakā) 1. According to *Purāṇic mythology, the wife of *Himavat, and the mother of, inter alia, the goddesses *Gaṅgā and *Umā (*Pārvatī). **2.** An *apsaras who gives birth to *Śakuntalā after seducing the *ṛṣi *Viśvāmitra; she subsequently abandons her daughter.

merit *See* PUṆYA.

Meru (Sumeru) According to *Purāṇic (and pan-Indian) *cosmology, the conical, golden mountain at the centre of Jambudvīpa, the innermost island of the earth, conceived as a flat disc. Meru is therefore the axis mundi, or 'navel' (nābhi), a mountain of extraordinary proportions (said by some sources to be 84 000 *yojanas (756 000 miles) high), extending into both *heaven and *hell. It is said to be the abode of various gods and their heavens.

Mewār A Hindu (*Rājpūt) principality in Rajasthan (from *c.*14th century CE), centred on Chitor (Cittauḍ) and then Udaipur. It gave its name to a important school of miniature painting, which flourished in the 18th and 19th centuries CE.

Meykaṇṭār (Meykaṇḍa) (given name: Maykaṇṭatēvar (Śvetabana), 12th–13th century CE) The first systematic *Śaiva Siddhānta theologian; author of the influential *Civañāṉapōtam* (*Śivajñānabodham*) ('Treatise on Śiva Knowledge') (*c.*1223 CE), a twelve-verse *sūtra text with autocommentary, treating of the relationship between *Śiva, the individual *self, and the world (and therefore also of the means to and nature of *liberation)—a relationship variously interpreted as either pluralistic or monistic by numerous later *Tamil commentators, including those of the *sampradāya named after Meykaṇṭār (pluralists). *See also* ARUṆANTI; CIVAÑĀṈAMUṈIVAR.

Mīmāṃsā (Pūrva Mīmāṃsā—'Prior Exegesis', as opposed to Uttara Mīmāṃsā—'Later Exegesis' = Vedānta) 'The School of *Vedic Exegesis', listed in modern works as one of the six *darśana or 'schools of philosophy'. The foundational *Mīmāṃsā text is *Jaimini's (*Pūrva-*) *Mīmāṃsā Sūtra* (*c.*200 BCE–200 CE), followed in importance by *Śabara Svāmin's commentary on Jaimini, the *Śābarabhāṣya* or *Bhāṣya* (*c.*3rd–6th centuries CE; trad. 1st century CE), and the subcommentaries by *Kumārila Bhaṭṭa and *Prabhākara (both 7th century CE). The two main Mīmāṃsaka schools are known, respectively, as 'the *Bhāṭṭa (Kumārila)' and 'the Prābhākara', after the latter pair of commentators. They differ principally on the nature of the unseen force (*apūrva) which ties a ritual action to its outcome, and on questions of epistemology.

The essential Mīmāṃsaka presupposition is that the **Veda* is self-existent—an uncreated and unauthored (*apauruṣeya) revelation (*śruti), the truth and authority of which is incontrovertible and infallible; it is therefore synonymous with *dharma. (Jaimini's *Mīmāṃsā Sūtra* begins: 'Now the investigation of dharma'.) Further, the *Veda*'s sole function as śruti is to ensure, or actualize, the correct performance of Vedic *śrauta ritual. The Mīmāṃsakas therefore classify the *Veda* as consisting of injunction (*vidhi—the sole means of knowing or practising dharma), prohibition (pratiṣedha), and eulogy (*arthavāda), the last of these having no conventionally descriptive or discursive function, but simply acting as a repository of *mantras which contribute to the efficacy of the sacrifice (*yajña).

m

In order to support their claims for the absolute authority of the *Veda*, the Mīmāṃsakas developed an epistemological realism, according to which perception is a direct way of knowing real objects external to consciousness, an inference which guarantees both the validity of śruti and its direct, unmediated transmission. The *sacrifice itself, the enjoined action (vidhi)—more specifically the injunctive verb—produces an unseen force (apūrva/*adṛṣṭa) which ultimately guarantees its success. 'Success' in this context, according to Jaimini, is the attainment of heaven (*svarga) after *death. According to *Kumārila, however, the ultimate aim of the Mīmāṃsaka ritualist is to attain *mokṣa (defined as a state of eternal, separate, and omnipresent bliss) through the performance of nothing other than prescribed and necessary actions, through which no further *karma accrues to the individual. More generally, the goal of Mīmāṃsā is to maintain the *Brahmanically-defined social order (dharma) through the monopolistic practice of sacrificial ritual, a sufficient end in itself. As part of their concern to establish the correct meaning of injunction (vidhi), the Mīmāṃsakas also developed an influential theory of language.

Mīmāṃsakas *See* MĪMĀṂSĀ.

Mīmāṃsā Sūtra *See* JAIMINI; MĪMĀṂSĀ.

Mīṇākṣī ('fish-eyed') A form of *Devī or *Pārvatī (she is also said to be the sister of *Viṣṇu), Mīṇākṣī is the tutelary goddess of *Madurai, a city which she rules over with her consort *Sundareśvara (a form of *Śiva). According to local legend, she was a queen of the *Pāṇḍya dynasty whose *digvijaya (conquest of the world) ended in defeat at the hands of Śiva in the *Himālayas. Later he joined her in Madurai, where they were married and took up residence in the Mīṇākṣī-Sundareśvara *temple. Their wedding, and Mīṇākṣī's coronation, is celebrated in the annual twelve day Chittirai *festival. Other festivals celebrate Mīṇākṣī in her unmarried state, as a single goddess.

Mīrā(bāī) (*c.*16th century CE) The most celebrated and popular North Indian poet-saint (*sant). The earliest extended hagiographical account of her life is that of Priyādās (1712 CE). According to this narrative (the basis of numerous variants and expansions in later hagiographies), Mīrā was a *Rājput princess who, although married to a prince of *Mewār, was so exclusively devoted to *Kṛṣṇa, whom she considered to be her real husband (in his guise as 'Lifter of Mount *Govardhana'), that she deliberately contravened all the usual class (*varṇa) and social expectations, preferring to keep the company of fellow devotees of all *castes, and to express her *saguṇa *bhakti through ecstatic singing and dancing. Miraculously surviving her husband's family's attempts to incarcerate and then poison her, she left home to lead the life of a mendicant poet and singer. First she travelled to *Vṛndāvana, where she acquired a considerable following; later, she settled in *Dvārakā, and it was at the *temple there that she vanished—drawn by the god into his own *image.

Mīrā's *Hindi songs (i.e. those attributed to her), many of them seemingly autobiographical, have maintained a wide and undiminishing appeal, and have been set to all kinds of music across the subcontinent. Inevitably, they are particularly popular in Hindi-speaking regions, and especially with lower-*caste women, who identify with their antinomian stance in relation to caste and gender differences, and their evocations of ordinary, daily life. In style too, her songs are redolent of the simple and repetitive idiom employed by women's folk songs. In this poetry, Mīrā frequently identifies herself as one of the *gopīs, and, because of her sex, she is perceived by her devotees to have a closer and more direct relationship with Kṛṣṇa than that enjoyed by male *bhaktas, who have to assume the woman's role. Going even further, some poems present her as married to the god, in the paradoxical union of two world-renouncing *yogīs—the union for which she so avidly aspires. Mīrā's 'biography', or legend, has been equally popular, inspiring, in the 20th century, comic strips, novels, dramas, and multiple cinematic renditions.

Mitākṣarā ('Comprehensive and Concise') Vijñāneśvara's celebrated 11th-century CE commentary on the **Yajñavalkyasmṛti*, a **Dharmasāstra* text.

Mithilā The capital city of *Videha, a Northeast Indian region ruled over by *Janaka (*Sītā's father in the **Rāmāyaṇa*). The site is said to be marked by the modern city of *Janakpūr in *Nepal.

mithuna *See* MAITHUNA.

Mitra ('agreement', 'contract') In the **Ṛg Veda*, and later, one of the *Ādityas, a *deva personifying, and so responsible for, tribal and social order. He is inevitably paired with *Varuṇa, the deva ruling over the wider cosmic and ethical order (*ṛta)—so much so that they are most usually invoked as the composite or single deity, Mitra-Varuṇa. Their roots were *Indo-European (cf. the Iranian Mithra), and their significance was already in decline in the early *Vedic period.

Mitramiśra (*c.*1610–*c.*1640) *Brahmin author of the *Vīramitrodaya*, a voluminous and widely distributed digest of **Dharmaśāstra* literature. He was also responsible for the *Pūjāprakāśa* ('The Elucidation of Worship'), a detailed *pūjā manual.

Mitra-Varuṇa *See* MITRA; VARUṆA.

mleccha(s) ('barbarian(s)') A noun used by the *Vedic *Āryans, and in subsequent *Brahmanical discourse, to designate foreigners (i.e. *anāryans). By definition, they speak languages other than *Sanskrit, but, more widely, they are beyond the pale insofar as they have no access to Vedic *dharma, and originate outside the Āryan homelands. *Muslims, *Christians, and other perceived outsiders, may find themselves placed in this category. They are also considered ritually *impure.

Mohenjo-daro The name given to the archaeological remains of what was perhaps the major city of the *Indus Valley civilization, situated on the northern bank of the *Indus river in what is now Pakistan. It was the excavation of this site in 1921 by R. D. Banerjee (1885–1930) and Sir John Marshall (1876–1958), which led to the modern discovery of this ancient culture.

Mohinī ('enchantress') An *avatāra of *Viṣṇu, in which he takes the shape of a beautiful and seductive woman. According to the *Churning of the Ocean myth,

Viṣṇu (*Nārāyaṇa) appears in this form to seduce the demons (*daityas) into handing over the *amṛta, which Mohinī then gives to the *devas to drink. According to another myth, the *Tamil god *Aiyappaṉ is the result of *Śiva's love affair with Mohinī. In South Indian *temples, especially preceding the annual *Vaikuṇṭha Ekadaśi festival, male images of Viṣṇu are ritually dressed as the female Mohinī.

mokṣa ('liberation', 'release') A term, synonymous with mukti, which was widely used from the *Upaniṣadic period onwards to designate the ultimate soteriological goal of an individual's ritual, ethical, or devotional striving. It is classically regarded as one of the four legitimate 'aims or goals of human life' (*puruṣārthas). As a concept, mokṣa is concomitant with the development of the doctrines of *karma and *rebirth, since it is predicated on a belief that in the unaltered, worldly course of events, beings will inevitably continue to suffer, die, and be reborn as a result of their actions (karma). It is precisely liberation *from* this suffering and cycle of rebirth (*saṃsāra) which constitutes mokṣa. Those in pursuit of such an end are designated 'mumukṣu' ('desirous of liberation'), as opposed to 'bubhukṣu' ('desirous of worldly enjoyment (*bhukti)').

The specific content or experience of mokṣa is variously evoked from tradition to tradition, since it depends upon factors peculiar to each, such as belief, or non-belief, in a supreme deity, the nature of the deity, and the conditioning features of karmic bondage—action, ignorance (*avidyā), passion, etc. In that it expresses escape from a condition of suffering, the term may be characterized in terms of the absence of negative experiences, such as ignorance, suffering, delusion, impermanence and change, unreality, separation, implication in matter, *death, etc. Conversely, it may also be described in terms of the positive corollaries of such states: knowledge (*jñāna), bliss, omniscience, love, permanence, reality, (re)union, isolation (*kaivalya), *immortality, etc. For theistic and *bhakti-driven systems, *mokṣa, as the highest goal, may be synonymous with a permanently blissful, personal relationship with God, coincident with the attainment of his heaven (*svarga); for monistic systems, such as *Śaṅkara's *Advaita *Vedānta, mokṣa may be the knowledge (i.e. realization) of the identity of the individual self (*ātman) with the absolute (*brahman (neut.)). According to some, it is possible to attain liberation while still alive and embodied (*jīvanmukti), although again the precise meaning of this is variously interpreted.

Mokṣadharma *See* ŚĀNTIPARVAN.

Monier-Williams, Sir Monier (1819–1899) Born in Bombay (Mumbai), Monier-Williams was educated in Oxford University, where he remained to be elected the second *Boden Professor of *Sanskrit, and, in 1883, to found the Indian Institute. As well as writing on the history of Indian religions and literatures, he made a number of translations from the Sanskrit, including a version of *Kālidāsa's **Abhijñānaśākuntalam* (1853). His lasting contribution to *Indology has been the still widely used, and frequently reprinted, *A Sanskrit-English Dictionary* (Oxford University Press: 1st ed., 1899).

moon *See* CALENDAR; CANDRA.

Morayā Gosāvi *See* GAṆAPĀTYAS.

morning ritual *See* SAṂDHYĀ.

Mother, The *See* AUROBINDO GHOSE.

mother(s) *See* MĀTṚKĀ(S)

Mṛgendra-Āgama (*c.*900 CE) A relatively short, but important **Āgama*, acknowledged by a number of *Śaiva traditions, north and south, although it is not included in the standard *Śaiva Siddhānta list of 28. Its sections on knowledge (*vidyā) and *yoga are sometimes treated separately as the *Mṛgendra-Tantra*. The *Mṛgendra* ('Lord of Animals'), which attempts to align Śaiva doctrine and ritual with *Vedic practice, is one of three texts which underwrite contemporary South Indian Śaiva *temple practice.

Mṛgendra Tantra *See* MṚGENDRA-ĀGAMA.

mṛtyu *See* DEATH.

Mudgala Purāṇa One of the canonical texts of the *Gāṇapatya sects, bringing together stories about nine different manifestations of *Gaṇeśa, whom they regard as the supreme deity. It was probably composed sometime after the 12th century CE, and is traditionally classified amongst the **Upāpurāṇa*.

mudrā(s) ('seal', 'signet ring', 'image', 'sign', 'mark') **1.** Hand gestures, usually accompanied by *mantras. Considered to be the deity, or aspects of the deity, in the form of physical movement, mudrās are part of the means by which a new, or purified body is created in *Tantric ritual. Various extended meanings are also commonly employed in Tantric texts and practices. **2.** A gesture which protects or 'seals' the body; a protective sign: the palm of the hand, or its imprint (synonymous with hasta—'hand'). **3.** Hand gestures used in iconography, dance, and drama to indicate a particular characteristic or attitude assumed by a deity or character (e.g. the *abhaya-mudrā). **4.** Parched grain; one of the 'five Ms' (*pañca-makāra) used in *Tantric ritual, and viewed as in some sense *impure by *Brahmanical religion, perhaps because of supposed aphrodisiac properties, or because it was typically offered by lower *castes.

Mughal (Mogul) The Persian-derived name for the *Muslim dynasty that ruled most of the subcontinent of India during the 16th and 17th centuries CE.

muhūrta In general, a moment of time; more specifically, a period of 48 minutes (i.e. a thirtieth part of the day).

mukta ('liberated') The individual who has attained *mokṣa; his or her state.

Muktābāī (1279–1297) A Marathi poet *saint. According to the hagiographies, she was the sister of *Jñāneśvara; like him and her two other brothers, she was devoted to *Viṣṇu as *Viṭhobā, and thus helped to initiate the *Vārkarī tradition in Maharashtra. Only eighteen when she died, and unmarried, Muktābāī has subsequently been revered as a *bhakti saint and the composer of some popular abhaṅgs (*bhajans). Perhaps the best-known is 'The Song of the Door', addressed, coaxingly, to Jñāneśvara who had locked himself away out of disgust for the world.

Muktānanda, Swami (1908–1982) A *guru drawing on the *Kashmiri Śaiva tradition and *kuṇḍalinī-based *yoga techniques, who founded the *Siddha Yoga organization. He was a pupil of Swami *Nityānanda, under whose instruction he built the Gurudev Siddha Peeth at Ganeśpuri, near Mumbai, and subsequently brought Siddha Yoga to a western audience in the 1970s. He set up further *āśrams and administrative centres in India and the USA, and wrote over a dozen books, including a 'spiritual autobiography', *Play of Consciousness* (1970). His designated successors were his American translator, *Cidvilāsānanda and her younger brother, although it was the former who subsequently became the sole living 'master' in the tradition.

mukti *See* MOKṢA.

Mukundarāja (12th century CE) The *brahmin author of two texts, *Paramāmṛta* and *Vivekasindhu*, which aimed, for the first time, to disseminate *Advaita Vedānta teachings in Marathi for the benefit of those who knew no *Sanskrit.

mūla The *Sanskrit word for 'root', variously compounded to convey the essential, primary, or fundamental form of something (e.g. mūla-*mantra, mūla-*prakṛti).

Müller, Max (Friedrich Müller) (1823–1900) A German-born *Indologist and *Sanskritist, who, after being educated in Leipzig, Berlin, and Paris, spent the rest of his academic life at Oxford University in England, where he was appointed to the Chair of Comparative Philology in 1868. It was in Oxford that he completed his edition of the *Ṛg Veda Saṃhitā* (6 vols., 1849–1873), and began his editorship of the translation series, *Sacred Books of the East* (1879–1894), to which he also contributed. Other publications include *Lectures on the Origin and Growth of Religion, as Illustrated by the Religions of India* (1878), *India, What Can It Teach Us?* (1898), *Rāmakrishna, His Life and Sayings* (1898), and *The Six Systems of Indian Philosophy* (1899). He was also influential in the attempt to establish the comparative study, or 'science' of religion (*Religionswissenschaft*) as an academic discipline. See also HENOTHEISM.

mumukṣu *See* MOKṢA.

Muṇḍaka Upaniṣad (*c.*3rd–1st century BCE) A short, predominantly verse **Upaniṣad* traditionally assigned to the **Atharva Veda*. According to its own frame story, it is received by Śaunaka, a householder, from the *Vedic *ṛṣi, *Aṅgiras. Some have interpreted its name as indicating an association with 'shaven-headed' (muṇḍaka) *ascetics. Certainly, it relegates the **Veda*, and the ritual complex derived from it, to the secondary position of lower knowledge, in contrast to the higher knowledge of *brahman (neut.) (contained in the *Vedānta), which is only fully attainable by those who have disciplined themselves through renunciation (*saṃnyāsa) (3.2.6).

muni A name given in the **Ṛg Veda* to inspired, but silent *ascetics, it comes to be used as a general term for a holy man, ascetic, or *renunciant.

muñja A species of rush-like grass, considered to be purifying, and employed in parts of the *Vedic ritual. In the form of a twisted girdle, it constitutes part of the insignia of a *brahmin, according to the **Dharmaśāstra* literature.

muraḷī (murli) A class of *devadāsī, attendant upon *Khaṇḍobā in Maharashtra, especially in his *temple at Jejurī.

mūrti The image, icon, or concrete form of a deity; i.e. its manifestation, or incarnation, whether temporary or permanent, in a particular shape or form—for example, in an anthropomorphic statue, a *liṅga, a natural object, or a revered person, such as a *guru. (In the right ritual circumstances—in some *Tantric rituals, for instance—it can also take the form of an individual's self or body.) It is precisely such a mūrti which is thought to be a suitable object for *pūjā and *darśana. *Temple mūrtis are produced according to the prescriptions of **Śilpaśāstra*, and need to be ritually installed (in a *pratiṣṭhā) to 'activate' the presence of the deity. Although normally housed in the temple, some mūrtis (known as *utsavamūrtis), such as those of *Jagannātha and his siblings at *Purī, or the portable bronzes of South Indian temples, are paraded through the streets as the focus of particular *festivals, or *utsavas.

Textually, the term 'mūrti' first occurs in the sense discussed here in the later **Upaniṣads*, and there are material remains of such images from the late centuries BCE, notably at *Mathurā. However, the great multiplication of Hindu mūrtis takes place only with the rise of the *bhakti movements and their associated temple culture, from around the 4th century CE onwards. See also ARCĀ.

Murukaṉ (Murugan) ('He Who Possesses Youth/Beauty') The *Tamil name for the god otherwise known as Cēyōṉ

('The Red One'), Cevvēḷ ('The Beautiful Hero'), and Neṭuvēḷ ('The Great Hero'); and in *Sanskrit as *Kārtikkeya, Kumāra, Skanda, Subrahmaṇya, (Siddha)sena, (Mahā)sena, etc. Easily the most popular of the South Indian gods, Murukaṉ's origins are thought by many to be very ancient. Certainly, he was worshipped as an independent folk or tribal deity in the late centuries BCE, long before his incorporation into the *Śaiva pantheon. In the *Caṅkam literature of the early centuries CE, Murukaṉ is evoked variously—as a hunter, as a forest-, tree-, or hill-deity, and as the god who causes mediums (known as vēlans), and, in particular, young girls, to become possessed, usually by means of a frenzied dance (the veṟiyāṭu/verī ayartal). As the exemplar of both worldly and divine love, and the acme of demon-destroying warrior heroism, he became an obvious focus for the northern-influenced *bhakti traditions, which began to develop in the early medieval period. This culminated in the fusion of the *Tamil Murukaṉ with the Sanskritic and *Purāṇic Kārtikkeya/Skanda, the god of war, who is the second son of *Śiva and *Pārvatī.

As worshipped today, Murukaṉ is normally depicted as a red or golden youth or boy, holding a spear, with a peacock for his vehicle (*vāhana); the cock and the fighting elephant are also associated with him. Reflecting his diverse origins, he is said to have two consorts: the Tamil huntress, Vaḷḷi, and the *Brahmanical Dēvayāṉai (Devasenā—'army of the gods'). Six *temple *pilgrimage centres (*tīrtha) in Tamil Nadu are traditionally associated with the god: *Paḻani, Tiruccēntūr, Tiruttaṇi, Tirupparaṅkuṉṟam, Cuvāmimalai, and Kunrāṭal, a name popularly interpreted as implying the totality of Murukaṉ shrines. Of these, the most important is Paḻani, which attracts millions of pilgrims a year. Perhaps the most significant Tamil literary treatment of his mythology, and of the places associated with his worship, is the Caṅkam **Tirumurukāṟṟuppaṭai*. *See also* KĀRTTIKEYA.

Murukaṉ

Muslims Followers of *Islam.

Mūvāḷakuḻicāmuṇḍī A local Keralan form of the goddess *Cāmuṇḍā.

N

Naciketas *See* KAṬHA UPANIṢAD.

nāda ('sound') A term, applied particularly by *yogic and *Tantric traditions, to designate the absolute—the power underlying creation—manifested as audible sound. *See also* ANĀHATA NĀDA; BHARTṚHARI (1); DHVANI.

nāda-brahman *See* ŚABDA-BRAHMAN.

nāḍī ('channel', 'vein') In the plural, the name given in *yogic and *Tantric physiologies to the hidden 'channels' (conventionally 35 million of them), which are thought to pervade the *subtle body and link the *cakras. They provide a conduit for the energy or life-force (*prāṇa) that animates the human body. The three most significant are the *piṅgalā, the *iḍā, and the central channel of the spinal cord, the *suṣumṇā nāḍī. *See also* KUṆḌALINĪ.

Nāga (Nāgā) 1. A generic term for a naked (from Skt. nagna) warrior-ascetic. Originally formed into *ākhāṛās or 'regiments' in order to act as guardians of public order, and to protect trade routes in northern India, from at least the 17th century, Nāgas were being used by local *kings in order to fight their enemies (including *Muslims and the British). Originally organized on sectarian principles, and further subdivided into various smaller groups, the Nāgas and their military power have gradually been attenuated into something resembling athletic associations. They remain, however, prominent participants in various *festivals, notably the *Kumbh(a) Melā, during which they are the first to enter the waters of the sacred *river. Said to have been recruited by *Śaṅkara himself for the protection of his monastic order, the best-known Nāgas are probably those affiliated to the *Śaiva *Daśanāmis. **2.** The inhabitants of the predominantly *Christian state of Nāgaland (in north-eastern India).

Nāga Pañcamī A pan-Indian snake (*nāga) *festival usually held on the fifth day (pañcamī) of the 'bright fortnight' (śuklapakṣa) of Śrāvaṇa (July–August). Apart from in eastern India, where it is the name given to *Manasā's festival, Nāga Pañcamī celebrates *Kṛṣṇa's defeat of the snake king *Kāliya. Characterized by *fasting, bathing, the sketching of snakes, and the *pūjā of nāga images, such as those of *Śeṣa (*Ananta), the festival is also notable for the way in which *food and drink are offered to both iconic and real snakes, usually in the form of milk, left near or poured into their holes.

Nāgara A name applied to the North Indian style of *temple architecture, in comparison to the southern, or *Drāviḍa style.

nāga(s) 1. ('snake', 'serpent') Widely worshipped in various ways across the subcontinent, snakes—especially cobras—are thought to be sacred animals, which need propitiation but which can also offer protection. Actual snakes may be considered indistinguishable from their mythological counterparts (2), since the former may be considered the guise in which the latter show themselves to humans. **2.** A class of male and female serpent deities, usually portrayed with human torsos and heads (often framed by a hood of cobras), and the lower bodies of snakes. Associated with water, and therefore with fertility, they keep watch over the subterranean worlds (*Pātāla) and their mineral wealth. Ancient in origin, the nāgas and their cult were a component part of classical Indian (Hindu, *Buddhist, *Jain) mythologies from their visible beginnings. Notable nāgas in developed Hindu mythology include *Kāliya, *Śeṣa (*Ananta), *Vāsuki, and the enemies of *Garuḍa. *See also* MANASĀ.

nāga stone ('snake stone') A stone, or slab, carved in the image of a snake (*nāga), usually placed beneath a tree, or by water, and worshipped by women for its supposed fertility-granting powers.

Nāgeśa Bhaṭṭa (*c.*late 17th–early 18th century CE) A *Śrī Vaiṣṇava philosopher, *grammarian, and author of commentarial works, including one on the *Vālmīki **Rāmāyaṇa*.

nāginī A female snake deity (*nāga).

Nahuṣa A legendary *king, who, because he insulted the *brahmins, was reborn as a snake (*nāga). In the **Mahābhārata*, *Yudhiṣṭhira releases him from this curse by answering his questions about what it means to be a brahmin. He is the father of *Yayāti.

Naigameṣa A ram-headed supernatural being, said to be inimical to children, unless propitiated. Connected with procreation, he also appears in *Śvetāmbara *Jaina mythology as Hiraṅyagameṣin, an antelope-headed deity who transports *Mahāvīra's embryo.

Naimiṣa In the outer framing story of the **Mahābhārata*, the name of the *forest where the *sūta *Ugraśravas first recites the text to the assembled *ṛṣis.

naimittika ('occasional') A class of rituals to be performed when a particular occasion arises (such as the birth of a child), as opposed to those classified as obligatory (*nitya), or optional (*kāmya) rites.

Nainā Devī The name of a *temple site, 700 miles northwest of Chandigarh in Himachal Pradesh, dedicated to the goddess *Satī. Regarded as a *sakti pīṭha, it is said to be the place where Satī's eyes fell to earth.

Nairuktas Etymologists. *See also* NIRUKTA.

naiṣṭhika brahmacārin *See* BRAHMACĀRIN.

Naiyāyikas ('logicians') Proponents of the *Nyāya (-*Vaiśeṣika) tradition.

Nakkīrar (Nakkiratēvar) A name shared by a number of *Tamil *bhakti poets. The tradition, however, has come to regard them as a single author, around whom a considerable hagiography has been constructed. Historically, the most important Nakkīrar is the *Caṅkam poet credited with the earliest and best-known devotional poem to *Murukaṉ, the **Tirumurukāṟṟuppaṭai*, 'Guide to Lord Murukaṉ', included in the **Pattuppāṭṭu* anthology (*c.*5th century CE). In the 12th century, along with eight other compositions attributed to Nakkīrar, this poem was included in the eleventh book of the **Tirumuṟai* collection.

nakṣatra ('constellation', 'lunar mansion') The ancient Indian system of constellations or lunar mansions (nakṣatras) was known from *Vedic times. By dividing the sky on the basis of the moon's relation to the fixed stars, a lunar month of initially 27 and then (through correction) 28 days was established by astronomers, the moon passing through a different nakṣatra on each day of its cycle. This information was then used to fix the *auspicious dates and times for *Vedic *sacrifices and to cast horoscopes. *See also* JYOTIṢA.

Nakula In the **Mahābhārata*, Nakula, the son of *Mādrī and the *Aśvins, is the fourth of the five *Pāṇḍava brothers, and the twin brother of *Sahadeva.

Nala Although it is incidental to the main narrative, the story of the Nala, the *king of Niṣada, his love for his wife, Damayantī, and the trouble he brings upon them both through his addiction to gambling, is one of the best-known and best-loved sections of the **Mahābhārata* (**Āraṇyakaparvan* 50–78).

Nālāyira Divyaprabandham *See* ĀḺVĀRS; NĀTHMUNI.

Nālāyiram *See* ĀḺVĀRS; NĀTHMUNI.

Nālāyirappirapantam ('The Four Thousand Divine Compositions', *c.*10th century CE) See ĀḺVĀRS; NĀTHMUNI.

Nālāyira Tivviyappirapantam *See* ĀḺVĀRS; NĀTHMUNI.

nāma ('name') A term used, particularly among the *sants, to evoke the Absolute, 'nameless', *nirguṇa Godhead. Sometimes synonymous with *Rām(a).

Nāmadeva *See* NĀMDEV.

nāmajapa (nāma(saṃ)kīrtana) The continual repetition of the deity's name. A common devotional practice in *bhakti traditions (e.g. the chanting of *Kṛṣṇa's names in *Gauḍīya Vaiṣṇavism), it is thought to be empowering or liberating in its own right. *See also* MANTRA.

nāmakīrtana *See* NĀMAJAPA.

nāmarūpa ('name and form') For many Indian philosophical systems, the twin designation given to the individual entities that constitute the 'external' world, whether real or apparent.

nāmasaṃkīrtana *See* NĀMAJAPA.

Nambūdiri Brahmin (Nampūtiri) A member of a group of *brahmins from the southwestern Indian state of Kerala. Some Nambūdiris still practise *śrauta rituals; they are also part of a distinctive, *temple-based, *Tantric ritual tradition, adapted to their high-*caste status and so shorne of *impurities, a context in which they are referred to as 'Tantris'. *Śaṅkara is said to have been a Nambūdiri.

Nāmdev (Nāmadeva) (trad. 1270–1350) A *Vārkarī poet-saint (*sant), said to have been a low-*caste Maharashtrian tailor. A devotee of *Viṣṇu as *Viṭhobā, but also of the undifferentiated and unqualified (*nirguṇa) absolute, referred to as *Rām, Nāmdev's hagiography is intertwined with the lives of a number of other *bhakti poets, including his maidservant, *Janābāī, *Cokāmeḷā, and, in particular, *Jñāneśvara. Vārkarīs consider him to be the latter's successor and a number of the abhaṅgas (*bhajan(a)) attributed to Nāmdev record their association; others are included in the **Ādi Granth*, reflecting a legend that Nāmdev lived for many years in the Punjab and visited other parts of northern India, where he is supposed to have initiated the tradition of devotional poetry. Nevertheless, he remains most closely linked to the *temple at *Paṇḍharpur in South Maharashtra, where he is said to have been buried.

A large number of the Marathi and *Hindi songs credited to Nāmdev are thought by modern scholars to be the work of later poets. Unsurprisingly, therefore, his highly influential work covers a wide spectrum of devotional attitudes, invoking both *saguṇa and *nirguṇa forms of the deity. However, he is most usually grouped with the *avarṇadharmī bhakti poets who rejected the idea that class (*varṇa) and *caste had any significance for devotional practice or soteriology.

Nammāḻvār (Caṭakōpaṉ, Māraṉ) (Tam.: 'Our Saint', *c.*880–930 CE) Nammāḻvār was the most celebrated of the South Indian poet-saints, the *Āḻvārs. A *śūdra, he was said to have spent his life in *fasting and *meditation, relying on a *brahmin disciple, Maturakavi (*c.*9th–10th century CE), to popularize his works. The majority of

Nammāḻvār's songs are preserved in the *Tiruvāymoli* ('Sacred Speech'), possibly the most significant section of the Āḻvār anthology, the **Nālāyirappirapantam*. In these songs he addresses *Viṣṇu/*Kṛṣṇa (by his *Tamil name, *Māyōṉ—'The Dark One') as both his *king and—using the poetic convention of the passionate love of a girl for her beloved—his lover. All other gods and religious practices are considered useless, since salvation is entirely dependent upon Māyōṉ's *grace. *Śrī Vaiṣṇavas refer to the *Tiruvāymoli* as the 'Tamil *Veda*', regarding it as the equal of the *Sanskrit **Veda*, with the added advantage of being accessible to all. *See also* TIRUVIRUTTAM.

Nampi Āṇṭār Nampi (12th century CE) A *Tamil *Saiva *bhakti poet who, under royal patronage, compiled the first eleven books of what became known as the **Tirumuṟai* collection. His own poetry, plus a description of his own and the other poets' activities, is included in Book 11.

Nampūtiri *See* NAMBŪDIRI BRAHMIN.

Namuci The name of an *asura, eventually overcome by *Indra.

Nānak, Gurū (1469–1539) The first *Sikh gurū. Born a Hindu in the Punjab, he taught an essentially monotheistic route to liberation from *karma, to be achieved through meditation on the divine Name (nām) of the transcendent deity, characterized as the Sat Gurū ('True Gurū'). Like other *bhakti *sants, such as *Kabīr and *Mīrabāī, Nānak preached non-sectarianism and the openness of this path to both Hindus and *Muslims; his status as the founder of a distinctive tradition (*Sikhism) becomes evident only with hindsight, and is partly the result of both his and his followers' rejection of Hindu ritualism and the ideology of *caste (although not of caste itself as a means of social organization). Nānak's hymns and teachings are among those collected in the **Ādi Granth*. A large number of hagiographies (janam-sākhīs) were subsequently composed, detailing his travels and supernatural attainments.

Nañcīyar (Nañjīyar) ('Our Ascetic', 1182–1287) A *Śrī Vaiṣṇava teacher who was the author of seven *Tamil commentaries, including the first on **Tiruvāymoḻi*.

Nanda 1. According to *Vaiṣṇava texts such as the **Bhāgavata Purāṇa*, *Kṛṣṇa's cowherd foster-father, married to *Yaśodā. **2.** A proverbially wealthy northern Indian dynasty of the 4th century BCE, overthrown by *Candragupta Maurya.

Nandā Devī The second highest mountain in the Indian *Himālayas in present day Uttaranchal. The peak is identified with the *Goddess, and thought to be both *Devī herself and her home. The mountain and surrounding sites are important *pilgrimage destinations.

Nandi(n) (Nandikeśvara, Adhikāranandin) ('the happy one') The name of *Śiva's vehicle (*vāhana) or mount. Said to be the son of *Kaśyapa and *Kāmadhenu, he is depicted at the entrance to Śiva *temples (often in his own pavilion) as a humped bull with his legs tucked beneath his body, gazing at the *liṅga. In southern India, he may also be shown as an anthropomorphic devotee of Śiva, barely distinguishable from the god himself.

Nandi(n)

Nañjīyar *See* NAÑCĪYAR.

Nara ('Man') The first or primeval man, linked, in the **Mahābhārata* and elsewhere, with *Nārāyaṇa, either as a single deity (Nara-Nārāyaṇa = *Viṣṇu) or as one of a pair of warrior gods (father and son, or brothers), who undertake *asceticism at the *Himālayan site of *Badrīnāth. *Arjuna (Nara) and *Kṛṣṇa (Nārāyaṇa) are said to be their *incarnations.

Nārada 1. The name of a legendary *Vedic *ṛṣi. Mentioned in the **Atharva Veda*, and said to be the composer of some **Ṛg Vedic* hymns, Nārada appears subsequently as an archetypal divine seer, involved either in the framing dialogues, or as the 'author' of a number of texts from the **Chāndogya Upaniṣad* onwards (such as the **Dharmaśāstra* text, the **Nāradasmṛti* (*c.*400 CE), and the **Nārada Purāṇa*). In the **Mahābhārata* and the **Purāṇas*, Nārada is seen as *Brahmā's son, and is therefore one of the *Prajāpatis. He is also supposed to be the inventor of the classical musical instrument, the *vīṇā, and to rule over the heavenly musicians, the *Gandharvas. **2.** The name given to, or assumed by, the author of the **Bhakti Sūtra*, a 12th century (?) CE *Kṛṣna *bhakti text.

***Nārada Purāṇa* (*Bṛhannāradīya Purāṇa*)** A **Purāṇa* ascribed to the *ṛṣi *Nārada, and included in most **mahāpurāṇa* lists (although sometimes given as an **upapurāṇa*). Some scholars consider it to be no older than the 16th century CE. *See also* BṚHANNĀRADA PURĀṆA.

***Nāradasmṛti* (*Nāradīyamanusaṃhitā*)** (*c.*400 CE) The name of a **Dharmaśāstra* text attributed to *Nārada. It deals with 'law' (*dharma) in the delimited sense of jurisprudence, including an extensive treatment of the use of ordeals (divyas) as evidence submissible in court.

Nāradīyamanusaṃhitā *See* NĀRADASMṚTI.

Narahari Sarkār(a) (d. 1568) A *Vaiṣṇava *bhakti poet and associate of *Caitanya, who worshipped the latter as a deity in his own right.

naraka(s) ('hell(s)') According to *Purāṇic *cosmology, the lowest zones contained within the physical universe are the hellish regions (narakas), ruled over by *Yama, the god of *death. Accounts differ as to the exact number of hells, ranging from six or seven to 28. In tune with the law of *karma, narakas are places of torment and punishment where those who have acted badly in their previous lives are reborn, and where they will remain until the effects of such actions have been exhausted or recompensed through tortures which are thought to fit their crimes. Birth in a hell is, nevertheless, no more permanent than any other condition, and eventually those suffering there will be reborn elsewhere. The gruesome accounts of hells in the *Purāṇas* and other literature are clearly intended to act as warnings about behaving ethically (e.g. non-violently) in this life, as well as allowing for some vicarious revenge on one's opponents.

Nara-Nārāyaṇa *See* NARA.

Narasiṃha (Nṛsiṃha) ('The Man-Lion') According to *Vaiṣṇava *Purāṇic texts, the fourth *avatāra of *Viṣṇu, so-called because of his human torso and lion's head. In his best-known legend, Narasiṃha bursts from a pillar to disembowel King *Hiraṇyakaśipu who had tried to prevent his son, *Prahlāda, from worshipping Viṣṇu. (An earlier version of the story sees Hiraṇyakaśipu as an overpowerful and over-confident *asura). Perhaps partly tribal in origin, Narasiṃha is worshipped as an independent deity in Orissa and Andhra Pradesh, and, in some instances, requires blood *sacrifice. *See also* PĀÑCARĀTRA.

***Narasiṃha Purāṇa* (*Nṛsiṃha Purāṇa*)** Generally classified as an **upapurāṇa*, the *Narasiṃha* takes its name from its glorification (inter alia) of *Viṣṇu's 'Man-Lion' (*Narasiṃha) *avatāra. It may have been composed between the 9th and13th centuries CE, but there is no agreement about its date.

narayajña ('sacrifice to humans') The daily offering of hospitality to guests, typically through the offering of food to *brahmins or the twice-born (*dvija), which, according to the **Dharmaśāstra* literature, is obligatory for an orthodox brahmin as one of the five 'great sacrifices' (*mahāyajñas).

Nārāyaṇa ('resting on the waters [narā]', 'resting place of men [nara]') **1.** A great deity, synonymous with *Viṣṇu/*Kṛṣṇa from approximately the 4th century CE onwards, Nārāyaṇa may have begun as an independent tribal god from the north-west. In the **Śatapatha Brāhmaṇa*, as the result of a *puruṣamedha, Nārāyaṇa is identified with the cosmic *puruṣa. This text may also be the source of his later role as the supreme god (also referred to as *Vāsudeva) worshipped by the *Pāñcarātrins. In the **Mahānārāyaṇa Upaniṣad*, he is recognized as the absolute deity, both cosmically and within the individual, and is therefore synonymous with *brahman (neut.). From around 150 BCE, the *Bhāgavatas worshipped him alongside Vāsudeva (= Kṛṣṇa), and Saṃkarṣaṇa (= *Balarāma). In both the **Mahābhārata* (notably the **Nārāyaṇīya* section) and the **Purāṇas*, his identity begins to fuse with that of *Viṣṇu, so that the two become indistinguishable. Perhaps the cosmic myth in which he is most often referred to as 'Nārāyaṇa' is that which portrays him asleep on the serpent *Ananta (*Śeṣa) in the interval that comes between two world periods (*kalpas). **2.** (12th century CE) The Bengali compiler of the **Hitopadeśa*. For Nara-Nārāyaṇa, *see* NARA.

Nārāyaṇa Guru (1854–1928) A widely revered Keralan reformer who fought to raise the status of his *caste, the *untouchable Izhavas, through a programme of school- and *temple-building. His general strategy was one of *Sanskritization, based on a reading of *Śaṅkara's non-dualistic *Advaita Vedānta which opposed it to caste and religious discrimination. He produced works in Malayalam, *Sanskrit, and *Tamil.

Nārāyaṇī Stuti *See* DEVĪ MAHĀTMYA.

Nārāyaṇīya The final section of the **Śāntiparvan* of the **Mahābhārata* (Critical Edition 12.321–39); dealing with the worship of *Nārāyaṇa, it contains what are probably the earliest references to *Pāñcarātra doctrine. Some scholars consider it a relatively late addition (*c*.3rd/4th centuries CE) to the *Epic text.

Nareśvaraparīkṣa *See* SADYOJYOTI.

Narmadā One of India's seven sacred *rivers, and a *tīrtha in its own right (some pilgrims trace it from the sea to its mountain source, before returning by the opposite bank). Flowing across northern central India to the Arabian Sea, it is renowned for the natural occurrence of *bāṇaliṅgas in its current, and is therefore particularly sacred to *Śiva.

Narsī Mehtā (Narsiṃh Mehta, Narasiṃha Mahetā) (1414–1480, or later) The most widely revered of the *Vaiṣṇava *bhakti poet-saints of Gujarat, little is known of Narsī's life, although there is an extensive hagiography, much of it depicting direct interventions by *Kṛṣṇa (as the lord of the *temple at *Dvārakā) on behalf of his devotee. Such stories appear to have been drawn from the content of the songs attributed to Narsī; other compositions are erotic in nature, playing on the relationship between *Rādhā (with whom the poet identifies) and Kṛṣṇa, and probably drawing on *Jayadeva's **Gītagovinda*. It has also been suggested that he belonged to the *Vallabha sect. A number of the non-erotic poems attributed to

n

Narsī (albeit in a modernized form of the language) are still widely used in the daily devotions of Gujarati speakers. Among them is *Vaiṣṇava jana*, a characterization of the ideal Vaiṣṇava devotee, which is said to have been one of *Gāndhī's favourite songs.

Nasik A celebrated *tīrtha in the northern Deccan. Considered one of the principal holy cities of Hinduism, it lies on the banks of the *Godāvarī river (18 miles downstream from its source at Trimbak). Every twelve years the *Kumbh(a) Melā is held at Nasik, but the city and a number of its *temples also have a particular association with the exile of *Rāma, *Lakṣmaṇa, and *Sītā, as portrayed in the **Rāmāyaṇa*. *See also* PAṆḌĀ (1).

nāstika ('denier', 'naysayer', 'disbeliever', 'non-affirmer', 'atheist') Literally 'one who says it is not/it does not exist', nāstika is a term which comes to be applied pejoratively to *darśanas or individuals with supposed heterodox views, especially those, such as the *Cārvākas, *Jains, and *Buddists, who deny the absolute authority of the **Veda* (and so of the *brahmins). More generally it denotes those who disbelieve in the existence of God, however conceived (hence the modern sense of the term—'atheist'), the law of *karma, or anything which contradicts the speaker's or writer's own position. *See also* ĀSTIKA.

nāṭaka ('drama') The most important and popular genre of *Sanskrit theatre, drawing its material from the *Epics, **Purāṇas*, and history. A nāṭaka's hero was usually a god or a *king, and its main *rasa either the erotic (śṛṅgāra) or the heroic (vīra). Examples include many of the best known plays in Sanskrit drama, such as *Kālidāsa's **Abhijñānaśākuntalam* ('The Recognition of Śakuntalā') and *Bhavabhūti's *Uttararāmacarita* ('Rāma's Last Act').

Nātamuṉi *See* NĀTHAMUNI.

Naṭarāja ('king/lord of the dance') An epithet of *Śiva, current from at least the early centuries CE, indicating his ecstatic, omnipresent, and unlimited power as the creator, sustainer, and destroyer of the universe, as expressed through his *ānandatāṇḍava, or cosmic 'dance of bliss'. From the 10th century CE, this became the standard sculptural representation of the god in South Indian *temples; of these, the best-known is the image installed at *Cidambaram, which is where the dance is said to have been first performed, and where Naṭarāja became, effectively, the tutelary deity of the *Cōḻa dynasty.

nāth(a) ('protector', 'lord') An honorific, used as a name for *Śiva; it also commonly appears as a suffix in compounds such as *Jagannāth(a) ('Lord of the World'), and *Matsyendranāth(a) ('He Whose Lord is the Lord of Fishes'). *See also* NĀTH SIDDHAS.

Nāthamuni (Nāthmuni, Tam.: **Nātamuni)** (*c.*10th century CE) The first *ācārya of the South Indian *Śrī Vaiṣṇava tradition and so, nominally, the first *Viśiṣṭādvaita teacher. Little is known for certain about his life, although there are a number of hagiographies dealing with how he came to codify the *Tamil poetry of the *Āḻvārs in the 'Four Thousand Divine Compositions (Stanzas)' collection (variously known in *Tamil as the *Nālāyirappirapantam*, the *Nālāyiram*, the *(Nālāyira) Tivviyappirapantam*, or the *Tivyaprapantam*, and in *Sanskrit as the *(Divya) Prabandham*, or the *Nālāyira Divyaprabandham*). He is said to have been a *brahmin who began as an officiant at the Rājagopāla *temple at Vīranārāyaṇapuram, near *Cidambaram, but subsequently became a temple *priest at the *Viṣṇu temple at *Śrīraṅgam. It was there that he initiated the recitation of the *Nālāyirappirapantam*/*Divya Prabandham* as part of the daily ritual, thus establishing its claim to be the equivalent of *Vedic *śruti, and the essential component of a redefined (Tamil) *Brahmanical orthodoxy. It is also claimed that he was influenced by the *Pāñcarātra ritual tradition. None of his doctrinal works survive, although extracts from a supposed Viśiṣṭādvaita treatise, the *Nyāyatattva*, are quoted by later Śrī Vaiṣṇava teachers, such as *Yāmuna, who is said to have been his grandson.

Nāthdvāra ('Door of the Lord') A town in southern Rajasthan which is the major *tīrtha and ritual centre for the *Vaiṣṇava *Vallabha *Puṣṭimārga *sampradāya. The focus of attention is the image of *Kṛṣṇa as *Śrī Nāthjī (in the *havelī of the same name), which was transferred from *Braj in 1671. The town is also a flourishing artistic centre, producing paintings and cotton wall hangings (pichavaī) for devotees.

Nāthmuni *See* NĀTHAMUNI.

Nāth Siddhas Followers of a North Indian *Śaiva *Siddha tradition made up of groups of largely itinerant *Tantric practitioners, including the *Kānphaṭa yogīs and the *Gorakhnāthīs. They are popularly referred to as '*Yogis' or 'Jogis'. Their legendary founders are *Matsyendra(nāth) and his pupil *Gorakhnāth, second and third of the Nine Nāths—the *yogic masters who are conventionally identified as the originators of the tradition's lineages. The Nāth *sampradāya probably emerged in the late 12th or early 13th century CE, and was subsequently divided into twelve *panths ('paths'). It has had considerable popular appeal, and the Siddhas themselves have usually been from the lower *castes. They are renowned as masters of *haṭha yoga and *alchemy, and as the possessors of this-worldly supernatural powers (*siddhis). In all these instances their principal aim is to achieve *immortality within, and through, a perfected (*siddha) physical body.

***Nāṭyaśāstra* (*Bhāratanāṭyaśāstra*)** (*c.*200 CE, or later) The 'Drama Manual', the earliest surviving treatise (a composite text) on the origins, nature, and performance of the *Sanskrit dramatic arts (theatre, dance, and music), ascribed to the legendary sage and mythical first 'actor', *Bharata-(Muni). Characterizing itself as a fifth **Veda*, it contains, inter alia, an influential, although ambiguous discussion of the evocation of emotional states (*bhāvas) and *rasa aesthetics. It has been the subject of multiple commentaries, including the celebrated *Abhinavabhāratī* of *Abhinavagupta.

Navadurgās ('nine Durgās') *Durgā multiplied by nine (nava), each manifestation representing a different aspect of the *Goddess.

navagrahas ('nine planets') According to traditional astrology (*jyotiṣa), the nine 'planets' consist of: Sūrya (Sun), Soma (Moon), Budha (Mercury), Śukra (Venus), Maṅgala (Mars), Bṛhaspati/Guru (Jupiter), Śani (Saturn), and the ascending (northern) and descending (southern) nodes, *Rāhu and Ketu. Their potential influence over the lives of individuals is thought by many to require continuous monitoring through consultations with astrologers and the reading of horoscopes. Appropriate propitiation (particularly of Śani, Rāhu, and Ketu, which are thought to be *inauspicious and dangerous) takes the form of *food offerings made to their personifications in local shrines and *temples. Some temples, particularly in southern India, have separate shrines dedicated to the navagrahas; alternatively, they may appear in sculpted relief above the door lintel, offering protection to the building and its worshippers.

Navarātra *See* NAVARĀTRĪ.

Navarātrī (Navarātra) ('nine night [festival]') Any 'nine night' *festival, but the term most frequently refers to a major pan-Indian autumnal festival, or complex of festivals, held over the first ten days of the bright fortnight of Āśvina/Āśvayuja (September–October). In general, Navarātrī celebrates the victory of a deity over a demonic power at what is otherwise an *inauspicious time of year, typically the *Goddess's defeat of the buffalo-demon *Mahiṣāsura, or *Rāma's victory over *Rāvaṇa. A well-known northern Indian example is the *Durgā-pūjā festival in Bengal. *See also* DASARA.

Navya-Nyāya ('New Nyāya') *See* NYĀYA.

Nayakas The name given to the rulers of a number of independent states in southern India in the 16th and 17th centuries, and to the artistic styles associated with this period.

Nāyaṉmār (Tam.: 'lords', 'leaders'; sing. Nāyaṉar) The collective title given to the 63 *saints of *Tamil *Śaivism, active between the 6th and 9th centuries CE. Many came from non-*brahmin backgrounds, and the movement in general advocated the unrestricted worship of *Śiva for all, irrespective of *caste. Their hagiographies are recounted in *Cekkiḻār's *Periya Purāṇam*, which became the twelfth and last book of the **Tirumuṟai*. The *Tirumuṟai* also contains the *bhakti poetry of a number of prominent Nāyaṉmār (including *Campantar, *Appar, and *Cuntarar)—works given canonical status, and incorporated liturgically into *Śaiva Siddhānta *temple ritual. Effectively the Nāyaṉmār established a sacred *Śaiva geography across the Tamil homeland, focused on the particular shrines and *temples to which they had made physical cum literary *pilgrimages.

Nehru, Jawaharlal ('Pandit Nehru') (1889–1964) The first Prime Minister (1947–64) of independent India, Nehru, who had been active alongside *Gāndhī in the struggle for independence, was a modernizer and reformer, intent on maintaining the unity of the country as a social democracy, and instrumental in constructing a secular constitution for the newly formed state. He and his family—the so-called 'Nehru dynasty'—have dominated Indian, and *Congress Party politics since the 1940s.

Neo-Hinduism A term applied by Western scholars to the forms in which some Hindu thinkers and reformers (such as *Vivekānanda, *Gāndhī, and *Aurobindo Ghose), and institutional movements (such as the *Brahmo Samāj) responded to the influence and challenges of *Christianity and Western thought in a period stretching from the early 19th century until Independence (1947). The main 'Neo-Hindu' stance was derived from the redefinition of Hindu *dharma as an essentially universal, ethical 'religion' (*sādhāraṇa dharma), based on principles of non-violence (*ahiṃsā) and compassion, as opposed to the traditional, particularistic or *sva-dharmic stance of *varṇāśrama dharma. This in turn led to the advocacy of various social reforms, especially in relation to the *caste system.

Neo-Vedānta A term used to designate the *Advaita Vedānta-derived teachings of *Vivekānanda. These provided the material for the *Vedānta Society and the *Rāmakrishna Mission to promote 'Hinduism' (essentially Advaita Vedānta) as a (in some sense *the*) world religion—one based on what were perceived to be universally valid, and scientifically consonant, ethical principles. *See also* NEO-HINDUISM.

Nepal A *Himālayan republic (until May 2008 a kingdom and the only official Hindu state in the world), where just over 80% of the population of 28 million (2006) identify themselves as Hindus. Beyond the Kathmandu valley (which had an ancient tradition of local *kingships), Nepal was effectively established as a unified kingdom in 1769 by Pṛthvī Nāryān Shah (Śāhā), an ancestor of the monarch (King

Gyanendra) who was deposed in May 2008. The Hindu population is composed of two groups, each with its own *caste system: the Newars, Newari speakers who are descended from the ancient inhabitants of the Kathmandu valley, and who practise forms of religion (both Hindu and *Buddhist) which may have been largely unchanged since the 14th century, and the Parbatiyas, Nepali speakers, whose practice is similar to that found among Hindus in northern India. Across the population, religion in Nepal is most obviously expressed through *pūjā to a wide range of deities, and the performance of numerous obligatory and optional rituals. Access to *Tantric deities, through the performance of rituals requiring the manipulation of *impure substances, is restricted to those of the higher castes who have received the appropriate *initiation. There have been a number of large scale public *festivals in which, until 2008, the king (conceived of as divine) played a key part, either personally or symbolically. Perhaps the best known example is Dasaiṃ (the equivalent of *Navarātrī / *Durgā Pūjā), during which thousands of animals, including buffaloes, are sacrificed to Taleju (= Durgā), represented by a *kumārī or 'living goddess'. In this way the power of the king (here identified as *Śiva), and the power of *kṣatriyas in general, was thought to have been maintained. In a similar way, the king's support of the *Śaiva Paśupatinātha *temple and *pilgrimage site in Kathmandu was also considered highly significant as a means of garnering and reinforcing the religious legitimacy of his reign. Nepal's newly elected assembly, led by former Maoist guerillas, abolished the monarchy and declared the country a secular republic on 28 May 2008.

neti neti ('not [this], not [this]' = sandhi form of Skt. na iti, na iti) A formula used a number of times in the **Bṛhadāraṇyaka Upaniṣad* (4.2.4, 4.4.22, etc.) to indicate the ungraspable and inexpressible nature of the *ātman (= *brahman (neut.)).

Netra Tantra* (*Mṛtyujit ('Conquering Death')**)** (*c.*9th century CE) A *Kashmiri Śaiva text, which takes its name from *Śiva as Netranātha ('Lord of the Eye'). Perhaps composed in court circles, it nevertheless contains significant popular material on *possession and exorcism rituals. There is an extant commentary (*Netratantroddyota*) by the *Pratyabhijñā theologian *Kṣemarāja (*c.*1000–1050).

Nibandhas The name given to a class of systematic 'digests' of *dharma, compiled from a wide variety of **Dharmaśāstra* literature from about the 9th century CE onwards. They were the main source of the Indian legal system devised by the British in the 18th century.

nididhyāsana ('repeated meditation') The repeated *meditation which, according to the *Vedānta tradition, should follow on from hearing (*śravaṇa), revelation (*śruti), and then thinking (*manana) about it.

nigama A term for the **Veda*, a *Vedic text, or a text auxiliary to the *Veda*.

Nighaṇṭu *See* NIRUKTA (2).

Nijānand Sampradāya *See* PRAṆĀMĪ.

Nīlakaṇṭha ('Blue-throated') **1.** An epithet of *Śiva, derived from the way in which, at the *Churning of the Ocean, he nullifies the *kālakūṭa (halāhala) poison by holding it in his throat before swallowing it. **2.** (fl. in second half of the 17th century) A Marathi-speaking *brahmin, active in *Vārāṇasī. Among over a dozen other commentaries, he composed the *Bhāratabhāvadīpa* on the **Mahābhārata*, an influential commentary which purports to uncover the *Epic's 'inner', *Vedāntic meaning. Nīlakaṇṭha's text provides the basis for the 'Bombay' edition of the *Mahābhārata* (1862–63).

Nimāvat *See* NIMBĀRKĪ.

Nimbārka (Nimbāditya) (*c.*12th–13th century) The founder of one of the four major *Vaiṣṇava *sampradāyas, the Nimbārka or Sanakādi tradition, known from a philosophical perspective as the *Dvaitādvaita ('dualistic non-dualism') school of *Vedānta. Nimbārka is said to have been a *brahmin from Andhra Pradesh. Later tradition claims that he lived in the *Braj region, the terrestrial 'homeland' of his personal God, *Kṛṣṇa. Among various suggested works, only a commentary on the **Brahmasūtras*, the *Vedāntapārijātasaurabha*, can be attributed to him with any confidence. *See also* DVAITĀDVAITA; NIMBĀRKĪ.

Nimbārkī (Nimāvat) A member of the Nimbārka or Sanakādi *sampradāya, a *Vaiṣṇava *bhakti tradition claiming the *Dvaitādvaitin, *Nimbārka as its founder. The early history of the sampradāya is not clear, but it appears to have been revived by the twenty-ninth *ācārya, Keśava Kāśmirī Bhaṭṭa (b. 1479), who established *Braj as an important centre for the Nimbarkīs. Succeeding ācāryas developed a theology focused on devotion to *Kṛṣṇa and *Rādhā as the male and female aspects of the supreme reality (*brahman (neut.)), the devotee taking the part of a devoted friend (*sakhī) of the couple. The thirty-first ācārya, Harivyāsadeva, created an hereditary lineage of male *householder initiates (*gosvāmīs), although women too are prominent in the tradition. There are also *ascetic branches. The sampradāya has divided over the centuries, but still has centres across northern India—in Rajasthan, *Vārāṇasī, and Bengal, as well as in *Vṛndāvana.

nirguṇa ('without qualities') An adjectival compound, indicating the transcendence of all qualities (*guṇa), properties, or predicates by the absolute (*brahman (neut.)), or by God, conceived as the absolute. *Śaṅkara distinguishes between the incomplete and limited apprehension (*vyavahāra) of brahman as a personal deity and object of devotion (*saguṇa brahman—brahman with qualities), and the higher knowledge (*paramārtha-satya), which apprehends—i.e. experiences—the non-dual reality of nirguṇa brahman. Somewhat paradoxically from a Śaṅkaran, *Advaitin perspective, some North Indian *bhakti movements, which worship *Viṣṇu as a deity beyond attributes, have been characterized as nirguṇa bhakti traditions, in an attempt to distinguish them (or themselves) from those saguṇa traditions which worship him as an embodied or anthropomorphic deity (e.g. as the *Kṛṣṇa of *Vṛndāvana). Some commentators therefore distinguish between nirguṇī and saguṇī bhakti poets and *sants.

Nirṛti ('destruction') A *Vedic goddess personifying *death, destruction, decay, and misfortune. She is evoked as a close relative of *adharma and *hiṃsā, and as the mother of Death (Mṛtyu), whose direction (the South/Southwest) she rules over. Sometimes a male equivalent (Nirṛta/Nairṛta) is found with the same characteristics.

nirukta ('explained', 'defined') **1.** The etymological explanation of a word. **2.** (*Nirukta*) A commentary on the *Nighaṇṭu* (a list of *Vedic words), attributed to *Yāska, and classified as one of the **Vedāṅgas*. The earliest extant work of its kind, the *Nirukta* attempts, through etymological analysis, to recover the meaning of, by that time, obscure Vedic passages in order to shore up ritual performance. Yāska argues that all nouns are derived from, and so traceable to, particular verbal roots or 'bases' (dhātus).

nirvāṇa ('blown out', 'extinguished', 'quieted') Perhaps better known as a key term in *Buddhist discourse—where it signifies the state that obtains when desire and its corollary, ignorance, have ceased to fuel the psychophysical entity that constitutes the 'person' and drive it on to further rebirth—nirvāṇa also appears in Hindu texts as a synonym of *mokṣa (liberation), or the realization of *brahman (neut.). In what looks like a deliberate attempt to reclaim the term from the Buddhists, the **Bhagavadgītā* (2.72; 5.24–6) refers to the state of freedom from all desires and possessiveness as the 'nirvāṇa of Brahman'.

nirvāṇa-dīkṣā An initiation (*dīkṣā) in some forms of *Tantric *Śaivism which guarantees liberation (*nirvāṇa) at *death.

Niṣāda A member of a tribal group inhabiting forest and mountain regions. Niṣādas, who are identified with the Bhīls of Gujarat, are thought by some to be descendants of the ancient aboriginal inhabitants of the subcontinent. Certainly, they are mentioned in parts of the **Veda*, the **Mahābhārata*, and the **Purāṇas*, where they are generally regarded as employed in un *Āryan and *polluting activities, such as hunting, fishing, and robbing.

Nisargadatta Mahārāj (1897–1981) A teacher from a humble background, who earned his living as a cigarette (bīdī) seller in Mumbai. Initiated into a *Nāth Siddha *sampradāya, he achieved wider fame with the publication of a collection of his tape-recorded sayings in English translation, *I Am That* (1973). His essentially *Advaitin teachings have since been championed by a number of Western, and Western-educated, disciples, such as the ex-banker, Ramesh Balsekar (b. 1919).

nīti ('conduct', 'policy') A class of stories teaching proper social, political, and moral behaviour, including collections of animal fables such as the **Hitopadeśa* and the **Pāñcatantra*.

nitya ('obligatory') Rituals performed as part of a regular, fixed, and obligatory cycle (such as the *agnihotra), as opposed to optional (*kāmya), or occasional (*naimittika) rites. The neglect, or omission, of rituals of this type is thought to result in demerit for the ritualist concerned.

Nityānanda, Swami (*c.*1896–1961) An influential and much-revered South Indian 'saint'. Abandoned and then adopted as a young child, Nityānanda ('Endless Bliss') was said to have become a wandering *ascetic and *yogin at the age of ten. Many stories are told of his power as a miracle-working healer, and of the supernatural events associated with his life. He wandered extensively in the 1920s, during which time he initiated a number of charitable construction projects. But in 1936 Nityānanda settled at Ganeśpuri, near Mumbai, where he had an *āśram built in which he spent the rest of his life. He attracted a large number of devotees, among them Swami *Muktānanda, whom he inspired to found the *Siddha Yoga organization. Nityānanda is worshipped in the Siddha Yoga *temples attached to the āśrams at Ganeśpuri and New York State. He also gives his name to the *Nityānanda Institute, an American *Kashmiri *Śaiva-based organization, which considers him the creator of its *guru lineage, since he initiated the teacher of its founder. Nityānanda's own teachings seem to have been non-sectarian, advocating the realization of the individual consciousness in its universal reality.

Nityānanda Institute An American organization teaching a form of *Kashmiri *Trika *Yoga. It was founded in 1971 in Portland, Oregon by the American-born Swami *Chetananda, and has *meditation centres in a number of North American cities, Oslo, and Kathmandu. It traces its *guru lineage to Swami *Nityānanda, whose pupil, Swami *Muktānanda, initiated both Chetananda (in 1978) and his immediate teacher, the former New York art dealer, Swami *Rudrananda (in 1966). Various allegations have been made about the propriety of the organization and its leader.

Niveditā, Sister (Margaret Noble, 1867–1911) An Irish-born supporter of Indian nationalism, initiated into the *Ramakrishna order by *Vivekānanda in 1898. She was involved in educational, cultural, and charitable activities, as well as the political struggle for independence.

nivṛtti ('withdrawal', 'disengagement') According to *Dharmaśāstra*, and orthodox *Vedic commentators such as *Śaṅkara, the attitude of withdrawal from engagement (pravṛtti) or involvement with the world, cultivated by the *renouncer who is intent upon *liberation. Nivṛtti and pravṛtti are regarded as complementary aspects of Vedic *dharma, the former defining the stance of the celibate *renouncer, who has abandoned ritual and economic activity to cultivate knowledge, the latter that of the married ritualist whose actions are motivated by specific desires, and who is still repaying his *debts.

niyama ('self-discipline') The second of the 'outer limbs' (bahir-aṅga) of the *aṣṭāṅga-yoga ('eight-limbed yoga') outlined in *Patañjali's *Yoga Sūtra* (2.28–55, 3.1–8). Niyama has five aspects: moral and psycho-physical *purity (śauca), contentment (saṃtoṣa), asceticism (*tapas), self-analysis (*svādhyāya), and devotion to/contemplation of the lord (īśvara-praṇidhāna).

Nobili, Roberto de (1577–1656) An early Italian *Christian (Jesuit) missionary, based in *Madurai. He was nicknamed the 'White Brahmin' because of his strategy of trying to present Christianity in terms recognisable to Hindus, not least through his personal adoption of *brahmin dietary and other customs, his acceptance of *caste, and his living the life of a *saṃnyāsin. He learnt both classical *Tamil and Telugu, and was probably the first Westerner to study *Sanskrit.

non-dualism *See* ADVAITA VEDĀNTA.

non-violence *See* AHIṂSĀ.

Nṛsiṃha *See* NARASIṂHA.

Nṛsiṃha Purāṇa *See* NARASIṂHA PURĀṆA.

nyagrodha *See* BANYAN.

nyāsa ('putting down', 'fixing') As a component part of *Tantric ritual, the empowering, or divinization of the body, through touching various of its parts while reciting the requisite *mantra. In this way the ritualist identifies him- or herself with the deity.

Nyāya ('reasoning', 'logic', 'method') 'The School of Reasoning' (also known as Ānvīkṣikī, and Tarkaśāstra), listed in modern works as one of the six *darśanas or 'schools of philosophy', where it is paired with the *Vaiśeṣika school. Drawing on *Vedic concerns with formal debate, and valid means of proof, the foundational Nyāya text is *Gautama's *Nyāyasūtra* (probably a composite text, redacted between 250–450 CE). As important for the subsequent tradition are two other texts: the first extant commentary on Gautama, Vātsyāyana's *Nyāyabhāṣya* (second half of 5th century CE), and *Uddyotakara Bhāradvāja's *Nyāyavārtikka* ('Elucidation of Nyāya') (6th century), a defence of the system in response to *Buddhist logic. Other major Nyāya works include *Vācaspati Miśra's commentary on Uddyotakara, *Nyāyavārtikka* ('Gloss on the True Intention of the Elucidation of Nyāya') (*c.*960 CE), and *Jayanta Bhaṭṭa's non-commentarial *Nyāyamañjarī* ('Blooms of Nyāya') (9th–10th century), dealing with *Nyāya vis à vis *Buddhism and the *Mīmāṃsaka *darśana.

A convergence of the Nyāya and Vaiśeṣika traditions is evident from the 12th century onwards, initially in the commentaries of Udayana (12th century), who continues the debate with the Buddhists in works such as *Ātmatattvaviveka* ('The Discernment of the Reality of Self'), and

Nyāyakusumāñjali ('A Handful of Blooms of Nyāya'), defending the existence of both a permanent *self and a God (*Īśvara). By the 14th century, a distinction was being drawn between Old Nyāya (prācīna-nyāya), and Navya-Nyāya ('New Nyāya'), the analytical side of the reformulated and synthesized tradition. Navya-Nyāya, with its increased emphasis on the *pramāṇas (valid means of knowledge), was firmly established in the *Tattvacintāmaṇi* ('Thought-Jewel of Reality') of *Gaṅgeśa. Gaṅgeśa's son, Vardhamāna, was also a notable commentator, as was the former's disciple, *Jayadeva Pakṣadhara, who established a Navya-Nyāya subschool based on his master's works. Further diversification followed with the creation of a Bengali *sampradāya, carried forward by such authors as Raghunātha and his commentator, Gadādhara.

The principal concern of the classical Naiyāyikas was to develop and defend an epistemology and method of reasoning capable of providing certain knowledge about the nature of the world (including the reality of both a permanent self and God—often identified as *Śiva), since it was precisely such knowledge which was thought to result in release (apavarga) from suffering. This approach was systematized into a list of sixteen topics, or categories of debate (*padārthas), of which the first two, *pramāṇa (the means of valid knowledge or cognition), and prameya (the objects of valid knowledge, i.e. what is known, a category subsuming the seven padārthas of the Vaiśeṣika system), were the most crucial. Nyāya recognized four pramāṇas: perception (*pratyakṣa), inference (*anumāna), analogy/comparison (*upamāna), and verbal testimony (*śabda). Much attention was paid to the manner in which the Naiyāyikas attempted a formal proof of inference through an elaborate five-part syllogism. The acquisition of knowledge through the pramāṇas, logic, and debate was supported and reinforced by various *yogic practices and ethical restraints (*yama). *See also* VAIŚEṢIKA.

Nyāyabhāṣya *See* NYĀYA.

Nyāyamañjarī *See* NYĀYA.

Nyāyasūtra *See* NYĀYA.

Nyāya-Vaiśeṣika *See* NYĀYA; VAIŚEṢIKA.

Nyāyavārtikka *See* NYĀYA.

O

Ojha, Kṛttivās(a) (Kṛttibāsa) (15th century CE) Author of a highly popular and influential Bengali narrative version of the **Rāmāyaṇa*. Its circulation was further increased after it was issued in five volumes from the Serampore Mission Press in 1802–3.

Olcott, Colonel Henry S. (1832–1907) *See* THEOSOPHICAL SOCIETY.

Oldenberg, Hermann (1854–1920) A pioneering German *Indologist, Oldenberg held chairs at the universities of Kiel and then Göttingen. His early work was on Pāli *Buddhism; later he turned his attention to the **Gṛhya Sūtras* and the **Vedic Hymns*, publishing English translations in the **Sacred Books of the East* series (vols. 29 (1886), 30 (1892), and 46 (1897)). His *Die Religion des Veda* (*The Religion of the Veda*) (1894) remains a classic account.

oṃ (auṃ, oṃkāra, praṇava, akṣara, ekākṣara) The best-known *Sanskrit seed syllable (*bīja). Placed at the beginning of texts, and muttered to start and conclude recitations, it is usually considered the most powerful *mantra of all. Its strength lies in its compression—the **Veda*, the *trimūrti, the entire universe, is thought to be contained in, or equivalent to, its three phonemes (a, u, m). According to the **Māṇḍūkya Upaniṣad* (early centuries CE), 'The syllable (akṣara) is all this', and it is therefore equated with *brahman, *ātman, and everything that exists. **Manusmṛti* (2.76–84) makes similar claims. For the **Yoga Sūtra* (1.27–8), it represents *Īśvara, and its repetition (*japa) leads to the first stages of *samādhi.

Oṃ

oral transmission The traditional means by which texts were passed from generation to generation. The paradigmatic instance is the oral transmission of the **Veda* through *brahmin lineages or 'schools' (*śākhas), trained to memorize the text exactly for ritual purposes (hence the epithet *śruti—'heard'). Underlying this is the conviction that the text's power as *mantra, and its efficacy as the agent of ritual action, lies in its sound. For this reason, there continues to be resistance among some brahmins to the writing down or printing of the *Veda*. (The first written versions probably date from around the 5th century CE.) The pupil-teacher (*guru-śiṣya) relationship of *Tantric and other traditions is predicated on the oral, and often secret, transmission of mantras and religious knowledge. More generally, popular stories, derived from the *Epics and elsewhere, continue to be orally transmitted by bards and singers, as well as through dramatic performances.

Orientalism A term originally designating the West's interest in, and sometimes imitation of, Eastern (Oriental) languages, cultures, and arts during the 18th, 19th and 20th centuries. Those engaged in the scholarly, particularly the linguistic, study of the Orient, were therefore known as 'Orientalists'. The term was recoined by Edward Said (1935–2003) in his influential 1978 book *Orientalism: Western Conceptions of the Orient*, to designate a European attitude to non-Western peoples and their cultures, based on a colonial need to categorize, subordinate, and control the Orient by representing it as irreducibly 'other'. While aimed initially at Western attitudes to *Islam and the Middle-East, the critique was rapidly expanded to include colonial and post-colonial relations with India, and in particular the ways in which (according to this argument) what was called 'Hinduism' had been constructed by classical *Indologists, and others, in order (consciously or unconsciously) to entrench the West's political advantage and perceived superiority.

Orientalist *See* ORIENTALISM.

Osho *See* RAJNEESH, BHAGWAN SHREE.

ōtuvār A non-*brahmin *temple functionary, employed to chant *Tamil hymns during *Śaiva rituals and *festivals connected to the *Cidambaram temple complex in Tamil Nadu.

outcastes *See* CASTE; DALIT; UNTOUCHABLES.

P

***Pābūjī* (Pāpūjī)** A Rajasthani oral epic telling the story of Pābūjī, a deified 14th-century *Rājpūt chieftan. It is performed (usually overnight) by low *caste professional singers (bhopos) in front of a scroll of cloth (paṛ) on which episodes from Pābūjī's life have been painted—a performance which constitutes a form of *pūjā before the cloth which is Pābūjī's *temple.

pacanāgni *See* GṚHYĀGNI.

pāda ('foot') A term commonly used to designate a quarter of something—e.g. a quarter line of verse, or one of the four sections of a text.

padapāṭha ('word for word') A means of memorizing and repeating the **Veda*, word by separate word (pada), without the application of the euphonic changes (sandhi) which occur when *Sanskrit words are recited continuously (*saṃhitāpāṭha). Traditionally, both these means of recitation are employed (along with *kramapāṭha) to ensure the accurate *oral transmission of the text.

padārtha ('category') **1.** The key term of *Vaiśeṣika ontology, indicating a fundamental category of existence, of which there are seven according to the developed tradition. *See also* VAIŚEṢIKA. **2.** In Nyāya, the term used for a category or topic of debate, of which there are sixteen in all. The Vaiśeṣika padārthas (categories of existence) are subsumed under the second Nyāya padārtha (prameya). *See also* NYĀYA.

Padārthadharmasaṃgraha *See* VAIŚEṢIKA.

paddhati The generic term for a (usually *Tantric) ritual manual.

Padmā ('Lotus') An epithet of *Lakṣmī, the goddess of wealth.

padma ('lotus') An *auspicious plant with a wide range of symbolic meanings, including *purity, creation, and wealth.

Padmanābha ('Lotus-Navel') An epithet of *Viṣṇu, derived from the *Purāṇic cosmogonic myth that at the beginning of each *kalpa a *lotus sprouts from the navel of the sleeping god, thus inaugurating a new cycle of creation. The name is particularly associated with the image of Viṣṇu in the *temple at *Trivandrum in Kerala, where, during the 18th century CE, the *king of Travancore abdicated in favour of the deity.

Padmapāda (*c.*8th century CE) One of Śaṅkara's two chief disciples. His commentary (*Pañcapādikā*) on the first four *sūtras of Śaṅkara's **Brahmasūtrabhāṣya* is at the start of a commentarial tradition which leads to the *Vivaraṇa subschool of *Advaita Vedānta.

Padma Purāṇa Classified as one of the eighteen 'great **Purāṇas*' (*mahāpurāṇas*) in the *sāttvika group, i.e. those said to relate to *Viṣṇu, the *Padma* is a voluminous and composite work, which appears to have borrowed widely from other *Purāṇas*. It exists in two recensions, the Bengali and the Western; the former is considered the earlier, but it has proved impossible to establish an absolute date for either version. It takes its name from the lotus (*padma) which springs from Viṣṇu's navel at the beginning of a new world-age (*kalpa), but exhibits a variety of sectarian affiliations.

padmāsana ('lotus position') Sitting with the legs crossed and the heels placed on the thighs—the best known of the postures (*āsanas) assumed in *yogic practice and *meditation.

padmāsana

Paippalāda *See* ATHARVA VEDA.

Paiśāca marriage *See* MARRIAGE.

Paiśācī ('language of *piśācas (demons)') A language apparently spoken in ancient India, but no longer extant. Guṇāḍhya's lost **Bṛhatkathā* is supposed to have been composed in it.

Pāla (8th–12th century CE) The name of an eastern Indian dynasty with its centre at *Magadha. Its *kings were notable patrons of *Buddhism.

Paḻani (Pazhani) The most important of six *temple *pilgrimage centres (*tīrthas) in Tamil Nadu associated with *Murukaṉ. The hilltop temple, which contains an *image of Murukaṉ as Daṇḍapāṇi ('staff-wielder'), is about 60 miles east of *Madurai, and attracts millions of pilgrims every year.

Paḻḻava A South Indian dynasty (*c.*4th–8th centuries CE). From their capital at *Kāñcīpuram they presided over an exceptional flowering of southern Indian cultural and religious life. Spectacular *temples, at sites such as those at *Māmmalapuram and Kāñcīpuram itself, provide their architectural legacy.

Pampā(devī) The name of a local river goddess at Hampī (*Vijayanagara), who was eventually incorporated into the *Śaiva pantheon through her *marriage to *Virūpākṣa (*Śiva), so becoming a form of his consort, *Pārvatī.

Pañcabadrī *See* BADRĪNĀTH.

Pañcakedār *See* KEDĀRNĀTH (A).

pañcalakṣaṇa ('five distinguishing marks') A classical list of five 'distinguishing marks' (*lakṣaṇas) which are supposed to represent the contents of a **Purāṇa*: 'creation' (*sarga), secondary 'creation' (*pratisarga), genealogy (*vaṃśa), the reigns of the *Manus (*manvantaras), and the history of the patriarchs of the *lunar and *solar dynasties (*vaṃśānucarita).

Pāñcālas In the **Mahābhārata* the people of King *Drupada. Allied to the *Pāṇḍāvas by the latter's *marriage to *Draupadī, they are the sworn enemies of *Droṇa and his *son, *Aśvatthāman.

pañcama *See* CASTE.

pañca-mahāyajña *See* MAHĀYAJÑA.

pañca-makāra ('five Ms') Five substances, beginning in *Sanskrit with the letter 'M', which may be used in *Tantric ritual: māṃsa (meat), matsya (fish), madya (wine), *mudrā (parched grain), and *maithuna ([fluids produced in] sexual union). Viewed as *impure by *Brahmanical religion, they are used materially in 'left-handed' (*vāmācāra) worship, or either substituted or visualized in 'right-handed' (*dakṣiṇācāra) worship of the *Goddess.

Pañcānana ('Five-faced') An epithet of *Śiva, variously explained, but intended to represent him in his totality, i.e. from every aspect.

pañcāṅga *See* CALENDAR.

Pāñcarātra ('five nights') A *Vaiṣṇava ritual and theological tradition, beginning approximately in the early centuries CE, which influenced many other Vaiṣṇava schools, including those in *Cambodia, as well as, to some extent, *Kashmiri Śaivism. In particular, it provided part of the textual, and much of the ritual basis for South Indian *Śrī Vaiṣṇavaism.

The term 'pañcarātra' first occurs in the **Śatapatha Brāhmaṇa* (13.6.1), where, as the result of a *puruṣamedha sacrifice which lasts for five nights (pañcarātra), *Nārāyaṇa is identified with the cosmic *puruṣa. Evidence of a distinct Pañcarātra tradition, however, does not occur until the **Nārāyaṇīya* section of the **Mahābhārata*, and the earliest surviving specifically Pāñcarātrin texts (*saṃhitās) are dated to no earlier than the 5th or 6th century CE. The most significant of these are the *Sāttvata-*, *Pauṣkara-*, and **Jayākhya-saṃhitā*, which helped to set the pattern of southern *Śrī Vaiṣṇava *temple ritual and theology, as indeed did the **Ahirbudhnya-saṃhitā* and the **Lakṣmī Tantra*.

Pāñcarātra theology and the ritual which actualizes it are both highly complex. According to the *Saṃhitās*, *Viṣṇu, by revealing himself in three ways, provides three different levels at which he is accessible to his devotees, depending on their qualification (*adhikāra). As (Para-)*Vāsudeva (= *Kṛṣṇa = Nārāyaṇa = *brahman (neut.) = *puruṣa) he has one supreme, transcendent form, worshipped aniconically by *brahmin *yogins, and iconically by brahmin ritualists. His three vyūha forms are 'emanations' or 'partitions' of Vāsudeva for purposes of cosmological creation and worship. Vāsudeva emanates the first of these, *Saṃkarṣaṇa; Saṃkarṣaṇa in turn emanates *Pradyumna; who then emanates *Aniruddha. In each vyūha, two of Vāsudeva's six divine qualities (*guṇas) predominate: *jñāna (knowledge—all-seeing consciousness) and bala (the strength to sustain the universe) in Saṃkarṣaṇa, *aiśvarya (unimpeded will-power) and *vīrya (energy) in Pradyumna, *śakti (power as phenomenal reality) and *tejas (splendour—independence from causality) in Aniruddha. These forms may be worshipped with *mantras by brahmin ritualists, and by the other three *varnas without their use; it is only required that they should be 'suppliant' (prapanna). Thirty-eight further manifestations of Viṣṇu, known as vibhava, emanate from the Aniruddha vyūha; these include the *avatāras of later Vaiṣṇavism, including the most popular among the Pāñcarātrins, *Narasiṃha. As long as they have undertaken *dīkṣa (initiation), members of any varṇa (but not *untouchables) can worship these vibhava forms. Two further forms were later added to this vyūha hierarchy by the Śrī Vaiṣṇavas: the *antaryāmin ('the inner-controller'—the deity within the embodied self), and the *arcāvatāra ('the descent [into an image] to be worshipped') In these ways a single, undifferentiated, all-encompassing deity is accessed through ritual in multiple ways.

Insofar as non-*Vedic *mantras are used at all levels of Pāñcarātra ritual, it is clearly *Tantric in character. However, in an inversion of the *Śaiva Tantric pattern, the higher the form of the deity, the *purer, the more 'Vedic' in form, and the less powerful, in occult terms, the worship associated with him. Similarly, the most accessible form of the deity—Narasiṃha—is the one most closely aligned to occult power through the use of seed syllable mantras (*bījas).

Pāñcarātrins (Pāñcarātrikas) Followers of the *Pāñcarātra tradition.

Pañcatantra ('Five Books', *c.*300 CE) A renowned collection of Indian 'folk' wisdom. Composed in *Sanskrit by (according to the text itself) an ancient *brahmin called Viṣṇuśarman, the *Pañcatantra* consists of five books of (mostly) animal tales and proverbs, each designed to confront a dilemma in order to make a moral and/or political point. It is not only the best-known collection of its kind in India—where, like its off-shoot, the **Hitopadeśa*, it helped to define the genre of *nīti—but it is also the work of Indian literature most widely disseminated throughout the rest of the world. A Pahlavi translation, now lost, initiated the process that ended in the *Pañcatantra* influencing many well-known Middle-Eastern and Western story collections, such as the *Arabian Nights* and La Fontaine's *Fables*; indeed, according to one calculation, there have been more than two hundred versions in over 50 different languages.

***Pañcaviṃśa Brāhmaṇa* (*Taṇḍya Brāhmaṇa, Mahā Brāhmaṇa*)** One of two **Brāhmaṇas* (the other being the **Jaiminīya*) attached to the **Sāma Veda*.

pañcāyat(a) A council of five, or more, members, which arbitrates in *village disputes, particularly those between *castes.

pañcāyatana pūjā A form of domestic *pūjā associated with orthoprax *smārtas, involving the worship of five deities: *Devī, *Gaṇeśa, *Śiva, *Sūrya, and *Viṣṇu. Their images are differently arranged in the domestic shrine, depending on which deity is placed at the centre. Pañcāyatana pūjā is said to have been promoted by *Śaṅkara.

paṇḍā (H.; from Skt.: paṇḍita) **1.** An hereditary *brahmin priest, acting as a superintendent at a *tīrtha, *temple, or *ghāṭ, and/or as a registrar of the genealogies of high-*caste Hindu families in cities such as *Nasik. **2.** A brahmin cook.

Pāṇḍav(a)līlā ('the play of/about the Pāṇḍāvas') A popular performance tradition in the Garhwal region of *Himālayan Uttar Pradesh. Villagers present **Mahābhārata* stories through a mixture of the staged—recitation of texts, song, ritual processions, and drama—and the spontaneous. The most elaborate performances can build to a climax over thirteen days. The Pāṇdavas are thought to be both semi-divine beings and the *ancestors of the participants, and therefore capable of bestowing favours. Essentially the *līlā is both a form of dramatized ritual worship (*pūjā), and a public entertainment in which the barrier between performers and participants is continually removed.

Pāṇḍavas A collective term used in the **Mahābhārata* for the five sons of *Pāṇḍu (i.e. *Yudhiṣṭhira, *Bhīma, *Arjuna, *Nakula, and *Sahadeva), and, by extension, their followers and relatives. In fact, Pāṇḍu is only their father in name; because of a curse he is prevented from fathering children, and the first three Pāṇḍavas are actually the sons of *Dharma (Yudhiṣṭhira), *Vāyu (Bhīma), and *Indra (Arjuna) by Pāṇḍu's first wife, *Kuntī. Similarly, the twins (*Nakula and *Sahadeva) are the sons of the *Aśvins by Pāṇḍu's co-wife, *Mādrī. The Pāṇḍavas, along with their rivals and cousins, the *Kauravas, are the major protagonists in the conflict for the lordship of *Kurukṣetra, which is the central narrative plank of the *Mahābhārata*. *See also* MAHĀBHĀRATA.

Paṇḍharpur The best-known *tīrtha in Maharashtra, near the Karnataka border. Its *Viṭhobā *temple is the focus of quarterly *pilgrimages by the *Vārkarī Panth, whose presumed founder, *Jñāneśvara and other *sants are closely associated with the town. A major *yātrā, undertaken by over half a million pilgrims, occurs each year during Āṣāḍha (June–July). *See also* PUṆḌALĪKA.

paṇḍit(a) ('learned', 'wise') A generic term for a teacher or a scholar, Anglicized as 'pandit'; it is also used as a synonym for '*brahmin'.

Pāṇḍu ('the pale one') In the **Mahābhārata*, the heir to the *Lunar Dynasty, and the brother of *Dhṛtarāṣṭra. Since he had been cursed to die the moment he made love to a woman, he was father in name only to the *Pāṇḍavas (the sons of his co-wives, *Kuntī and *Mādrī). Eventually, his desire got the better of him.

Pāṇḍuraṅga *See* VIṬHOBĀ.

Pāṇḍya dynasty (Tam.: **Pāṇṭiyaṉ**) (*c.*6th–*c.*10th century/13th century CE) A South Indian dynasty with its capital at *Madurai. (It shared its name with the ancient, mythical rulers of the city.) Subsumed into the *Cōḻa state, it briefly reappeared in the 13th century.

Pāṇini (Dākṣeya) (*c.*4th century BCE) The author of the **Aṣṭādhyāyi*, the near-definitive grammar which codified classical *Sanskrit in under 4 000 *sūtras. Nothing is known about him, although he is reputed to have been born at Śalātura near Gandhāra (straddling parts of modern Afghanistan and Pakistan).

pāpa ('wicked', 'evil', 'bad', 'sin', 'demerit', 'ritually impure') A substantive that is often translated as '*evil' and applied to ethical and/or ritual deficiencies. Consequently, it also characterizes the karmic result of such wrong actions (*karma) for the perpetrator. Its conceptual opposite is *puṇya, which helps to eliminate it. *See also* EVIL.

Parakāla(ṉ) ('Death of his Enemies', *c.*8th–9th century CE) *See* TIRUMAṄKAI ĀḺVĀR.

paramaguru ('supreme teacher') The teacher's teacher (*guru's guru). According to **Manusmṛti* (2.205), the pupil should treat him just as he treats his own teacher.

paramahaṃsa ('supreme goose') A title given to the highest category of *ascetics: those who have achieved *liberation, or the supreme degree of spiritual perfection. *See also* HAṂSA.

paramārtha-satya (pāramārthika-satya) ('supreme truth') According to *Advaita Vedānta, the absolute truth: namely, direct knowledge of reality (*brahman (neut.)). *Śaṅkara contrasts it with the relative truth (*vyavahāra-satya)—knowledge of the world of appearances obtained through the senses and the intellect.

Paramātman ('The Supreme Self') **1.** A term used by *Rāmānuja, to distinguish God (= *brahman = *Viṣṇu) from his dependent 'body'—i.e. the individual selves (individually referred to as pratyagātman) and material reality (*pradhāna/*prakṛti). **2.** In *Vedic and *Epic texts, an epithet of *brahman or God, however conceived.

Parameśvara ('The Supreme Lord') **1.** An epithet of *Śiva, particularly as the Absolute (e.g. as the *pati of *Śaiva Siddhānta theology). **2.** For the *Mahānubhāvas, the one, absolute God, who manifests himself in the form of the 'five *Kṛṣṇas'.

paramparā *See* GURU.

Parāśarasmṛti In its extant form, a relatively late **Dharmaśāstra* text, attributed to Parāśara. It deals with agreed behaviour (*ācāra) and reparations (*prāyaścittas). A gloss on the text is attributed to *Mādhava (1).

Parasurām *See* RĀMNĀMĪS.

Paraśurāma (Bhārgava Rāma, Rāma Jāmadagnya (in *Mahābhārata*)**)** ('Rāma with the battle-axe') According to the *Vaiṣṇava *Purāṇic texts and the **Mahābhārata*, Paraśurāma is the sixth *avatāra of *Viṣṇu; he owes his name to his decapitation of twenty generations of *kṣatriyas in revenge for the killing of his *brahmin father, the *Bhārgava *Jamadagni. He therefore re-establishes the proper *varṇa hierarchy, as conceived by the brahmins. Other stories are told of him: in one, on the order of his father, he beheads his mother, *Reṇukā, but, since this proves his obedience, he is allowed to replace her head and bring her back to life.

parāvidyā ('higher knowledge') In the **Upaniṣads*, transcendent knowledge of *ātman/*brahman, which unlike *aparāvidyā ('lower knowledge'), is uncaused and revealed, and therefore not dependent on the senses and the intellect.

pariah An English word derived from paṟaiyār, a South Indian term for a group of outcastes or *untouchables.

paricāra (Tam.: **paricārakar**) ('servant') A South Indian, *brahmin *temple servant.

parikrama *See* PRADAKṢIṆĀ.

Parikṣit In the **Mahābhārata*, the son of *Abhimanyu and Uttarā, and so the grandson of *Arjuna. *Kṛṣṇa revivifies him in his mother's womb after all the other *Pāṇḍava women have been made barren by *Aśvatthāman. He becomes *king after *Yudhiṣṭhira renounces the throne and retires from the world. It is to Parikṣit's son, King *Janamejaya, that, according to its own framing account, the *Mahābhārata* is first recited by *Vaiśaṃpāyana at a great *snake *sacrifice performed to avenge Parikṣit's death by snakebite. In a somewhat different framing story, Parikṣit also appears as the person to whom the **Bhāgavata Purāṇa* is recited.

pariṇāma *See* SATKĀRYAVĀDA.

parivrājaka ('wanderer') A synonym for a *renouncer, indicating that he has left the household and the village (*grāma) in order to pursue a life of homeless wandering. It may have been applied initially to non-*Vedic renouncers as opposed to *saṃnyāsins.

Parsis (Parsees) ('Persians') The Zoroastrian community in India. The name recalls their migration from Iran to Northwest India in the 10th century CE. In the 19th century most Parsis moved from Gujarat to Bombay (Mumbai), where they came to exercise an economic, political, and cultural influence that belied their small numbers. Parsis operate as a *caste within the wider Indian society, which helps to sustain their religious exclusiveness as well as their economic strength. Zoroastrianism is an ethical dualism in which human beings are thought to play the key role in the cosmic struggle between the entirely good God, Ahura Mazda, and his evil opponent Angra Mainyu. God's creation is thought to be inherently good, and it is the responsibility of humans to care for it. Their ritual practice is focused on fire temples, serviced by priests. The fire at Udvada, north of Mumbai, is claimed to have been burning continuously for a thousand years. Parsis are probably most widely known outside their community for their dakmas, or 'towers of silence', where corpses are placed in the open-air to be consumed by carrion-eaters, such as vultures, in conditions which are considered minimally polluting. Their population (less than 100 000) is continuously dwindling, although they now constitute the largest group of Zoroastrians in the world.

Partition The division of the Indian subcontinent at Independence (1947), which engendered mass migrations and a huge loss of life through communal violence. The end result was the division between the newly created, and predominantly *Muslim state of Pakistan, and modern India with its large Hindu majority.

parvan ('joint', 'knot', 'division') A *Sanskrit term used to designate either a part of a text (e.g. a 'book' of the **Mahābhārata*), or of a division in an astronomical or ritual sequence.

Parvata (Himavat) ('mountain') The personification of the *Himālaya, and the father of *Pārvatī ('the daughter of the mountain').

Pārvatī ('the daughter of the mountain') In classical mythology, a common epithet of *Śiva's consort (also known as *Umā, and by a variety of other names), derived from her father's name (*Parvata). A benevolent form of the Goddess (*Devī), Pārvatī is depicted as a good wife and the devoted mother of her sons, *Gaṇeśa and *Skanda. A number of myths tell of her indefatigable pursuit of the god before their *marriage. Iconographically, Pārvatī is most frequently depicted as a beautiful, two-armed woman, in the company of her husband or family; her vehicle (*vāhana) is a lion. She is not usually worshipped independently.

pāśa ('bond', 'tie', 'noose') In *Śaiva Siddhānta theology (where it is also referred to as aṇu—'subtle'), a term for the material universe—i.e. everything which binds individual souls (*paśu), including *mala, *karma, *māyā, and the *śakti of *Śiva (tirobhāvaśakti).

P

paśu ('beast', 'bound [soul]' = aṇu) In *Śaiva Siddhānta theology, a term, used individually and collectively, for the soul or *ātman, expressing the idea that, short of *liberation, it remains in a state of beginningless bondage to an essential impurity (*mala), and to the other ties (*pāśa) which constitute the material universe. Paśu may be liberated through Śiva's *grace, which is accessed through *dīkṣa.

paśubandha ('animal sacrifice') Part of the requirement of a *Vedic *śrauta ritualist, an independent, animal (he-goat) sacrifice performed half-yearly or yearly, requiring six *priests. It originated as part of the *agniṣṭoma rite, where it continues to be performed as a constituent part of *soma sacrifices. *See also* PRAKṚTI (2).

Pāśupata An extinct, *ascetic *renouncer movement, considered to be the earliest *Śaiva tradition for which evidence survives (in the **Śāntiparvan* of the **Mahābhārata*). Its only surviving text, the *Pāśupata Sūtra*, is attributed to *Lākulīśa, although the extant version, with a commentary by Kauṇḍinya, probably dates from the 8th or 9th century CE. At its widest, the term embraces a number of related Śaiva traditions (including the *Lākulas and *Kālamukhas). More narrowly, it refers to one of two subdivisions of the *Śaiva *atimārga tradition (the other being its off-shoot, the Lākula). According to the *Pāśupata Sūtra*, membership was restricted to *brahmin males who were permitted to renounce from any of the four conventional *āśramas by entering into a 'fifth', the siddhāśrama ('stage of the perfected'). Thereafter, the *siddha moved through five levels of increasing detachment from *Vedic society, off-loading onto the latter all his demeritorious *karma en route. This ascension was marked by a progressively intense identification with *Śiva in his wild and terrible form of *Rudra, which culminated in the *cremation ground, where, living off the offerings left for the dead, he hoped to achieve union with the god. At *death, by Rudra's grace, the Pāśupata would expect to be filled with Rudra's qualities (i.e. omniscience and omnipotence), and so achieve union, although not absolute identity with him. The Pāśupatas, in the widest sense, appear to have exercised considerable ritual and political influence from *c.*7th–11th centuries CE, establishing *temples throughout India.

Pāśupata Sūtra *See* PĀŚUPATA.

Paśupati ('lord of beasts') An epithet of *Śiva/*Rudra, evoking his lordship over everything that lives, including human beings. In this form he is the tutelary deity of *Nepal.

Pātāla A generic term for the seven treasure- and wonder-filled subterranean worlds which, according to *Purāṇic *cosmology, are ruled over by *nāgas and other supernatural beings.

Pāṭaliputra (the modern city of Patnā) Built by Ajātaśatru, Pāṭaliputra was subsequently the capital of the *Mauryan dynasty and its successors in the northern Indian kingdom of *Magadha. Still a major city under the *Guptas, it was mostly in ruins by the 7th century, and declined further thereafter.

Patañjali **1.** (2nd century BCE) A *Sanskrit *grammarian who produced a celebrated commentary (*Mahābhāṣya*) on *Pāṇini's **Aṣṭādhyāyi*.

2. (*c.*3rd–4th century CE) The author (or possibly editor) of the **Yoga Sūtra*. Of the two types of *yoga outlined in what may be a composite text, the 'eight-limbed yoga' (*aṣṭāṅga-yoga) is associated by some with Patañjali himself. He is traditionally, but probably mistakenly, identified with the grammarian (1).

3. The name given to a legendary *ṛṣi and devotee of *Śiva at *Cidambaram. He was said to be the human form of *Śeṣa (depicted with the lower body of a *snake). Two ritual manuals, the *Patañjalipūjāsūtra* and the *Citsabheśvarotsavasūtra* are attributed to him.

pāṭha **1.** The public recitation of *Epic or other religious texts. **2.** The collective name for the three traditional means (*kramapāṭha, *padapāṭha, and *saṃhitāpāṭha) of memorizing and repeating the **Veda*.

pāṭhaśālā A *Sanskrit school, based on the principle of recitation (*pāṭha).

pati ('Lord', 'Master') In *Śaiva Siddhānta theology, the name by which *Śiva (*Parameśvara), as pure *consciousness (cit) and the dispenser of *grace, is distinguished from the other two principal categories of beings, *paśu ('souls') and *pāśa ('bonds'). Pati's realm consists of liberated souls, some of which are united with Śiva but distinct from him, others of which are only partially liberated and assume manifestations to do the Lord's bidding.

pativratā ('devoted to her husband') According to the **Dharmaśāstra* literature, the ideal of *Brahmanical womanhood—the wife who is devoted and faithful to her husband.

patnī ('wife') The sacrificer's (*yajamāna's) wife, whose presence and participation is indispensable for the correct performance of *Vedic *śrauta rituals. She is the female equivalent of the master (pati) of the sacrifice (*yajña).

pātra *See* DĀNA.

Paṭṭadakal (early 8th century CE) The site of a number of large, mostly *Śaiva *temples near Aihole in the Deccan, including a *Virūpākṣa temple. Two of them display notable friezes depicting scenes from the *Epics.

paṭṭar (Tam.; = Skt. bhaṭṭa) A *Śaiva *temple *priest.

Paṭṭiṉattār **(Paṭṭiṉattup Piḷḷaiyār, Paṭṭiṇattaṭikaḷ)** (*c.*1400 CE) A *Tamil *Cittar (*siddha) poet. According to the hagiographies, he gave up a life as a wealthy merchant to become a naked mendicant. His work, which may have been composed by two or three poets of the same name, is collected in anthologies under the name *Tiruppāṭaṟṟiraṭṭu*.

Pattuppāṭṭu ('Ten Songs', *c.*5th century CE) An anthology of ten longer *Caṅkam poems, ranging between approximately 100 and 800 lines in length, of which the most celebrated is probably *Nakkīrar's **Tirumurukāṟṟuppaṭai*, 'Guide to Lord Murukaṉ'.

Paulomī *See* INDRĀṆĪ.

paurāṇika One versed in the **Purāṇas*; a professional performer of a Purāṇic text. The term is also used as a synonym for a follower of the *Purāṇic *smārta tradition. *See also* SMĀRTA.

Paurava ('descendant of Puru') In the **Mahābhārata*, a *king, or other character descended from Puru, and so belonging to the *Lunar Dynasty.

Pauṣkara Saṃhitā *See* PĀÑCARĀTRA.

pavitra *See* SACRED THREAD.

penance *See* PRĀYAŚCITTA.

perception *See* PRATYAKṢA.

Periyāḻvār ('The Great Āḻvār', 9th century CE) An *Āḻvār poet-*saint and *brahmin *priest at the *temple of Śrīvilliputtūr in Tamil Nadu, whose compositions, the *Tiruppallāṇṭu* and the *Tirumoḻi* are included in the **Nālāyirappirapantam*. The thirteen stanzas of the *Tiruppallāṇṭu* are probably the most frequently recited *Śrī Vaiṣṇava verses, since they are at the core of the tradition's ritual practice. Many of Periyāḻvār's poems are dedicated to *Kṛṣṇa as a child and a youth. *Āṇṭāḷ is said to have been his adopted daughter.

Periya Purāṇam ('Great *Purāṇa*') *See* CĒKKIḺĀR.

pēy(s) *See* BHŪTA(s).

pilgrimage (tīrthayātrā) From at least the 3rd or 4th century CE onwards, a major Indian and South Asian religious activity, involving the continuous movement of millions of people for diverse and complex reasons. The literal meaning of the term tīrthayātrā is a 'journey' (yātrā) to a 'ford' or 'crossing-place' (tīrtha). It is the tīrtha, therefore, which is the place or object of a pilgrimage. This most commonly takes the form of a deity enshrined in, or synonymous with, a particular place or *temple, including those identified with particular regions and/or topographic features, such as mountains, *forests, bathing places, or *rivers. (The latter may, of course, be deified in and of themselves.) Living *gurus may also be regarded as tīrthas, and so the objects of yātrā.

The wide range of places and objects designated as tīrthas is accounted for by the metaphorical resonance of the term. A tīrtha is a 'crossing-place', or conduit, between the mundane and the supramundane. Sacred power (often expressed through the deity's 'grace' or *prasāda) is thought to be at its most concentrated and accessible here, and therefore most likely to facilitate the attainment of the pilgrim's (tīrthayātrin's) particular goals, whether soteriological (the attainment of *liberation), or more immediate and wordly. The efficacy of attending a particular tīrtha may fluctuate according to the calendrical cycle, so that the combination of place and time becomes the most significant factor, e.g. with the *Kumbha Melā. Other sites may be especially associated with *saṃskāras, e.g. the connection of rivers, particularly the *Gaṅgā (at *Vārāṇasī and elsewhere), with the *antyeṣṭi or *śrāddha rites, and with *purification in general. Others again, such as the *Vaiṣṇava *Braj and its environs, are bound into patterns of sectarian devotionalism (*bhakti). The motivation for pilgrimage is, however, various. For instance, the journey itself, particularly before, or in the absence of, modern transport, may be seen as a purifying form of *tapas or *prāyaścitta. At its least specific, motivation may be derived from the received idea that it is an individual's religious duty to go on a pilgrimage, albeit as part of a family or other communal group, and that religious merit (*puṇya) will be the reward. For many modern pilgrims, yātrā may be, inter alia, a kind of tourism, offering the excitements of much easier travel than in the past, combined with a shared transformative experience.

Tīrthas, or their equivalents, especially sacred rivers, are first identified in the **Veda*, but it is with the *Epics and

*Purāṇas that the textual evidence and patterns for large scale pilgrimage are extensively elaborated. Based on the conception of *Bharatavarṣa as an inherently sacred landscape in its own right, works such as the **Āraṇyakaparvan* of the **Mahābhārata* depict India as covered by regional and national networks of tīrthas. Visiting them with the correct mental attitude, and bodily self-control, will, it is promised, generate copious 'fruit' (tīrthaphala)—as much as, or more than, *Vedic *sacrifice, according to the *Purāṇas*. From such advertisements, one can infer that, from an early date, tīrthas, as a result of their perceived spiritual power, were also highly significant as centres of economic and political power. As a result, the priestly control of such sites, and who exercises patronage over them, were, and continue to be, matters of contention.

Networks of tīrthas may overlap and interlace. One traditional list, the four *dhāmas or 'dwelling places' (*Badrīnāth, *Purī, *Rāmeśvaram, *Dvārakā), demarcates the geographical extent of India. Another lists the 'seven holy cities': *Ayodhyā, Dvārakā, *Hardwār, *Kāñcī(puram), *Mathurā, *Ujjain, and Vārāṇasī. Other major networks, linked by sectarian foundational myths, include the pan-Indian, *Śaiva *jyotirliṅga network, and the *Śākta *pīthas (= tīrthas), known as *śāktipīṭhas. The more significant Vaiṣṇava sites are often locations associated with the earthly appearances of *Viṣṇu's *avatāras, especially *Kṛṣṇa (e.g. *Vṛndāvana) and *Rāma (e.g. *Ayodhyā). Other networks reinforce local or ethnic boundaries and identities, such as the six temple pilgrimage centres in Tamil Nadu traditionally associated with *Murukaṉ (*Paḻani, Tiruccēntūr, Tiruttaṇi, Tiruppaṛaṅkuṉṟam, Cuvāmimalai, and Kunrāṭal). With the spread of Hindus abroad, local tīrthas (usually focused on temple *images) have now been established in North America and elsewhere.

Piḷḷai Lokācārya (trad. 1264–1369) The major theologian of the southern (*Teṉkalai) school of *Viśiṣṭādvaita *Śrī Vaiṣṇavism. Eighteen texts, mostly in *Maṇipravāḷam, and collected as the *Aṣṭādaśarahasya* ('Eighteen Secrets'), are attributed to him, of which the most important is the *Śrīvacaṉapūṣaṇam* (*Śrīvacanabhūṣaṇa*), a digest of Teṉkalai teaching. Also of significance is the *Mumukṣuppatti* ('The Path for Those Seeking Liberation'), an explication of the *rahasya, or the secret *mantras, central to Śrī Vaiṣṇava practice. Piḷḷai lived in *Śrīraṅgam.

piṇḍa ('rice balls', 'flour dumplings', lit. 'round lump') An essential component of both the *antyeṣṭi funerary rites, and ancestor worship (*śrāddha). Piṇḍa are prepared and offered to make an after-death body for the immediately deceased, and to sustain the ancestors or forefathers (*pitṛs) in the afterlife. The antyeṣṭi rites for the *twice-born usually involve the preparation of sets of sixteen piṇḍa. From the first set, six are offered on the day of *death to ease the recently deceased through various dangers; the other ten are offered on the tenth or eleventh day after death in order to make a new body for the dead person. A second, and sometimes third set of sixteen is prepared and offered on the eleventh or twelfth day (and/or after exactly a year in the fully extended version) as the deceased is ritually bound to the forefathers (*pitṛs) in the culminating *sapiṇḍīkaraṇa rite. This involves the joining of three piṇḍa, representing the male deceased's father, grandfather, and great-grandfather, with a fourth (the deceased himself). In this way they are brought together in a commensal group (characterized by some as *sapiṇḍa) which may be fed collectively in further, periodic śrāddha rituals, such as (for the *śrauta ritualist) the monthly *piṇḍapitṛyajña. In fact, the newly deceased has now replaced his great-grandfather in the group, so his living son will offer piṇḍa to *his* father (the deceased), grandfather, and great-grandfather. Piṇḍa may also be employed in other, subsidiary death rituals.

piṇḍapitṛyajña ('sacrifice to the fathers with balls of rice') A monthly offering (*yajña) of *piṇḍa to the 'fathers' (*pitṛs), prepared and offered into the *dakṣiṇāgni by the *śrauta sacrificer. It is regarded by some as a subordinate part of the *darśapūrṇamāsa sacrifice.

piṅgalā One of the three principal channels or *nāḍī of *yogic and *Tantric physiologies, associated with the sun and the river *Yamunā. It runs up the body to the left of the central channel (*suṣumṇā) to the left nostril.

piśāca A class of flesh-eating and shape-shifting demons, first mentioned in the **Veda*, and ubiquitous in later *Epic and *Purāṇic texts. They are liable to possess human beings, and may need propitiation. The related adjective, *paiśācī, is applied to various categories of things thought to be ghoulish or uncouth.

pīṭha ('seat', 'throne') **1.** The pedestal on which an image of a deity is installed. **2.** *See* ŚAKTIPĪṬHA(S).

p

pitṛ(s) ('father(s)', 'ancestor(s)', 'forefather(s)') In the widest sense, the ancestors of the family or race. More narrowly, the deceased male relatives of the living head of the family, especially the father, grandfather, and great-grandfather, who require feeding in the next life through *śrāddha rituals, and the *pitṛyajñā. *See also* PIṆḌA; PIṆḌAPITṚYAJÑA; PITṚLOKA; PITṚYAJÑA; PITṚYĀNA.

pitṛloka ('world of the fathers/ancestors') According to the **Upaniṣads* (see esp. **Bṛhadāraṇyaka* 6.2.16; **Chāndogya* 5.10.3), the intermediate and impermanent after-death world (*loka), adjacent to the *moon, reached by those who have led proper lives as sacrificers and gift-givers, but who will eventually be reborn. It is contrasted with the permanent state achieved in the *brahmaloka (*devaloka). More generally, the pitṛloka designates the celestial or nether world where the dead forefathers (*pitṛs) reside, and where they need to be fed and sustained for as long as possible by their living sons through the *śrāddha funerary rites, and the *pitṛyajñā. *See also* PITṚYĀNA.

pitṛyajña ('sacrifice to the fathers/ancestors') The daily offering of *food and water (the *tarpaṇa) to the ancestors (*pitṛs), which, according to the **Dharmasāstra* literature, is obligatory for an orthodox *brahmin as one of the five 'great sacrifices' (*mahāyajñas).

pitṛyāna ('the way of the fathers') Also referred to as the 'southern path', one of three paths taken by the self, or its *subtle body, after death, according to the **Upaniṣads* and *Vedāntic theology. (The others are the *devayāna ('the way of the gods'), or the 'northern path', and the path to *Yama's world—known as *saṃyamana.) According to the **Bṛhadāraṇyaka Upaniṣad* (6.2.16), those on the pitṛyāna—those who perform sacrificial actions (*karma) properly, but without knowledge of their real meaning (or of *brahman (neut.), according to *Śaṅkara)—follow the route through the funeral smoke into the night, from the night into the fortnight of the waning moon, from there into the six months when the sun moves south, from those into the world of the fathers (*pitṛloka); from there to the moon, where they become *food, and the gods feed on them (or they starve—i.e. the effects of their *karma wear off). They pass from there into the sky, and so, via, wind, rain, earth, and food, they enter the bloodstream and semen of a human being, and are *reborn to begin the potential cycle again.

polluting *See* PURE AND IMPURE.

pollution *See* PURE and IMPURE.

Poṅgal (poṅgal: lit. 'is it boiling/overflowing?') A four-day *Tamil *festival (known as Makara Saṃkrānti in other parts of India), marking the beginning of the new solar year (between the 12th and 15th of January). It derives its name from one of the central components of the celebrations—married women boiling rice and milk in pots until they overflow. Poṅgal is in many respects an agricultural or harvest festival: the third day, for instance, is devoted to giving thanks to cattle by letting them graze at will.

possessed *See* POSSESSION.

possession (āveśa) A very common phenomenon in popular and *village Hinduism, involving the apparent 'possession' of a (usually lower-*caste) individual by another entity, the presence of which is made evident through various, often extreme, alterations in the possessed's behaviour. A distinction is made between invited, or voluntary, possession by a deity, and uninvited, or involuntary, possession by a malevolent spirit (*bhūta). The former kind of possession is usually for a limited period of time, and takes place in strictly delimited cultural circumstances, such as a ritual, a performance, or a *festival. Nevertheless, for the duration of the possession, onlookers regard the possessed as an embodiment of the deity. On the other hand, a malevolent possession, which is often seen as the cause of physical or mental illness in the possessed, or of some other kind of misfortune, requires exorcism by a diviner (often a local *priest) or a deity (i.e. through its *temple *image). Since the exorcism involves the spirit accounting for its possession, according to anthropologists this is often an opportunity for the possessed to express otherwise socially suppressed grievances, or to articulate family divisions.

power *See* ŚAKTI.

powers *See* SIDDHI(s).

Prabandham *See* ĀḺVĀRS; NĀTHAMUNI.

Prabhākara (7th century CE) A *Pūrva *Mīmāṃsaka exegete. His major work is a subcommentary on *Śabara's *Bhāṣya*, itself a commentary on *Jaimini's **Pūrvamīmāṃsā Sūtra*. Other works are the *Bṛhati* and the *Vivaraṇa*. Differences between Prabhākara and *Kumārila Bhaṭṭa in the interpretation of Śabara's text led to the creation of two *Mīmāṃsā subschools, the *Prābhākara and the *Bhāṭṭa.

Prābhākara A Pūrva Mīmāṃsaka subschool named after its founder, *Prabhākara. *See also* MĪMĀṂSĀ.

Prabhupāda *See* BHAKTIVEDĀNTA SWĀMI, A. C.

pradakṣiṇā ('moving to the right', 'turning the right side towards', 'circumambulation') The *auspicious circumambulation of an *image, place, or revered person, conducted in a clockwise direction, with the object of attention to the walker's right. The design of most *temples includes a passageway, around the *garbhagṛha, designed for the pradakṣiṇā of devotees, and it is often listed as one of the sixteen offerings/services (*upacāras) which are component parts of *pūjā. Circumambulation (also called parikrama) can also take place on a large-scale, encompassing cities, or even the entire subcontinent, as a means of acquiring *puṇya, as a form of *tapas, or as a *pilgrimage.

pradhāna ('principal one', 'primary one') According to *Sāṃkhya-Yoga ontology, the unmanifest *prakṛti, which exists in a state of potentiality prior to the evolution of the universe. It is synonymous with the perfect equilibrium of the three *guṇas.

Pradyumna (Sanatkumāra) 1. According to the **Purāṇas* and the **Mahābhārata*, *Kṛṣṇa's son by *Rukmiṇī, and the father of *Aniruddha. He is one of the five heroes of the *Vṛṣṇi clan, and, according to some accounts, the reincarnation of *Kāma.

2. According to *Pāñcarātra *cosmology, Pradyumna is one of the three *vyūha forms ('emanations') of *Viṣṇu (*Vāsudeva). He is emanated by the *Saṃkarṣaṇa form, and, in turn, emanates the Aniruddha form.

prahasana ('farce') A comic form of *Sanskrit theatre, the 'pure' form of which satirizes reprehensible religious figures, such as hypocritical *ascetics and *brahmins.

Prahlāda *See* HIRAṆYAKAŚIPU.

praiṣa *See* SAṂNYĀSA.

Prajāpati ('Lord of Creatures/Offspring') In the **Ṛg Veda*, an epithet applied to various *devas (such as *Indra, *Agni, *Soma, etc.), emphasizing their procreative function, as well as to the original being, who is therefore the father of all other beings, which he emits, or creates, out of desire. In the **Śatapaṭha Brāhmaṇa* and other later *Vedic texts, Prajāpati merges with the *Puruṣa of the **Puruṣa Sūkta* (*Ṛg Veda* 10.90) to become the unifying deity who is everything that is in its entirety, and more—the thirty-fourth of the traditional 33 devas. He is both the prototypical sacrificer (*yajamāna), and the sacrifice (*yajña)—i.e. 'self sacrifice'—through which the universe is differentiated and then ordered. In the *Purāṇic and *Epic periods, his role as demiurge, or secondary creator is assigned to *Brahmā, with whom he therefore becomes synonymous. Brahmā, in turn, is characterized as the'lord of the *Prajāpatis', his mind-born sons, who are also progenitors.

Prajāpatis ('lords of creatures') According to the **Purāṇas* and other texts, the progenitor sons of *Brahmā (= *Prajāpati), born from his mind. **Manusmṛti* (1.35) gives a list of ten: *Marīci, *Atri, *Aṅgiras, Pulastya, Pulaha, Kratu, Pracetas, *Vasiṣṭha, *Bhṛgu, and *Nārada.

prājāpatya marriage According to **Manusmṛti* and other *Sanskrit **Dharmaśāstra* texts, one of the eight possible types of *marriage, in which the bride is given after the couple have been exhorted to practise *dharma together. There is no agreement about the precise meaning of this, or how it differs specifically from some of the other types of marriage.

Prākrit(s) (from prākṛta—'common', 'natural') A group (sing. and pl.), or any one of a group, of Middle *Indo-Āryan languages, distinguished from the grammatically 'polished' or 'correct' *Sanskrit (saṃskṛta). In its widest sense, Prākrit is synonymous with Middle *Indo-Āryan, and includes the Pāli of the Theravāda *Buddhist canon and the *Aśokan inscriptions, as well as the various dialects ('Prākrits') of the *Jain canonical texts. As a group of literary languages, Prākrit is conventionally divided into four regional types: Māhārāṣṭrī, Śaurasenī, Māgadhī, and Lāṭī, the first of these coming to predominate over time. 'Sanskrit' plays allocate different Prākrits to females, young boys, and lower-*caste men, as well as to comic characters; Sanskrit itself being reserved for higher-caste males.

prakṛti ('matter') **1.** According to *Sāṃkhya-Yoga ontology, the female of the two fundamental principles (the other being the male, *puruṣa) which constitute reality. Invisible and unconscious, prakṛti in its unmanifest form (also known as *pradhāna) is the ultimate cause of all material existence. The evolution of the universe occurs when the perfect equilibrium of the three *guṇas, which are synonymous with the unmanifest prakṛti, is disturbed by the proximity of puruṣa. This results in prakṛti manifesting itself in the form of evolutes, which develop to constitute the material universe and all that it contains, including the physical and mental attributes of human beings—the 25 *tattvas of classical Sāṃkhya. At the cosmological level, the process is never-ending: the tattvas will be reabsorbed into unmanifest prakṛti, only to evolve again in a continuous cycle. For the individual, bondage is the delusion that it is the inherently passive puruṣa which is acting and experiencing the results of action (*karma), when in fact, it is prakṛti, through the guṇas, which is the sole cause of action. In a theistic modification of this (in, for example, the *Bhagavadgītā*), prakṛti and its evolutes are said to comprise God's lower nature, while sentient beings (puruṣas) constitute his higher nature. An even more radical redefinition occurs in *Śākta traditions, where *śakti, the *Goddess, and prakṛti are considered to be identical, a single active *consciousness, in which puruṣa is subsumed.

2. In *Vedic *śrauta ritual, a basic paradigm or model (prakṛti) which is modified to produce a series of more complicated *sacrifices. Three types of sacrifice are considered to be prakṛtis in this sense: the *darśapūrṇamāsa, the *paśubandha, and the *agniṣṭoma.

pralaya ('dissolution') According to *Purāṇic *cosmogony, the destruction of the world in a firestorm (*kālāgni) at the end of a *yuga, or a *kalpa ('day of *Brahmā'). After a hundred years of Brahmā (a 'life of Brahmā), there is a 'great dissolution', or mahāpralaya.

pramāṇa ('means of valid knowledge/cognition') The necessity of establishing what counted as a means of valid knowledge (pramāṇa) was considered an essential prerequisite by all *darśanas (2). The usual list consists of i) *pratyakṣa ('perception'), ii) *anumāṇa ('inference'), iii) *śabda ('authoritative verbal testimony'), iv) *upamāna ('analogy'), v) *arthāpatti ('presumption', 'postulation'), and vi) *abhāva ('non-existence', 'absence'). Bhaṭṭa *Mīmāṃsā and *Vedānta recognize all six of these pramāṇas; *Prabhākara *Mīmāṃsā recognizes i–v; *Nyāya recognizes i–iv; Vaiśeṣika: i–ii (with iii and iv subsumed in i and ii); and *Sāṃkhya and *Yoga i–iii.

prameya *See* NYĀYA; PADĀRTHA.

prāṇa ('vital breath', 'life-force') According to esoteric anatomical ideas, first found in *Vedic texts (especially the **Upaniṣads*), and, later, in *yogic and *Tantric systems, and *Āyurveda, the force that animates the human body, as well as the whole of creation. According to the **Praśna Upaniṣad*, for instance, it is the chief faculty, which arises from the *ātman. (Some consider it synonymous with ātman/*brahman.) As well as a generic term for the various kinds of breath in the body, prāṇa is also used in a specific sense to designate inhalation, or the 'in-breath', as opposed (according to some accounts) to the 'out-breath' (apāna), which controls exhalation and excretion, the 'circulatory breath' (vyāna), diffused throughout the body, which it regulates, the 'up- or out-breath' (udāna), which controls speech and other expectorations from the throat, and the 'central breath' (samāna), which controls digestion. Prāṇa can also be used as a metonym for the senses, or for the whole human being.

prāṇāgnihotra ('the sacrifice to and in the life-breaths') The internalization of the *Brahmanical *śrauta ritualist's twice-daily offering into the sacrificial fire (the *agnihotra)—it now takes place in the breathing, or breaths (*prāṇa), of the *renouncer. The sacrifice and its benefits are therefore both continuous, and continuously under the control of the autonomous individual.

Praṇāmī (Śrī Kṛṣṇa Praṇāmī, Nijānand Sampradāya) A movement, founded in 16th century Gujarat by Śrī Devcandrajī (also known as Nijānand Svāmi) (1581–1655), and spread by his disciple,

Mahāmati Prannāth (Mehrāj Thakur) (1618–1694), which combines *Vaiṣṇava *Kṛṣṇa devotionalism with adherence to the *Muslim Qur'an, and teaches the essential unity of all religions. Since his mother belonged to the Praṇāmī sect, its teachings may have exercised some influence over *Gāndhī.

prāṇapratiṣṭhā ('establishing/installing the life-breath') According to the prescriptions of the **Purāṇas* and **Śilpaśāstra*, the final part of the ritual for consecrating the *mūrti of a deity, in which, through the recitation of a *mantra, the image is ritually infused with *prāṇa, and its eyes opened with a golden needle, thus 'activating' the living presence of the god or goddess, and making them accessible for *pūjā.

praṇava *See* OṂ.

prāṇāyāma ('control of the vital breath') An integral component of most *yogic and *meditational practice. The aim is to still or control the body and mind by restraining the vital breaths (*prāṇa, both widely and narrowly defined), using techniques of patterned breathing. According to *Patañjali's **Yoga Sūtra*, prāṇāyāma is the fourth of the 'outer limbs' of his *aṣṭāṅga-yoga ('eight-limbed yoga'), and one of the prerequisites for more advanced practice.

prapañca ('[verbal] proliferation', 'linguistic snare') Concepts, ideas, and verbal formulations which, for *Vedāntins (and some Mahāyāna *Buddhists), ultimately obscure the non-dual nature of reality.

prapatti (śaraṇāgati ('taking refuge')**)** ('surrender') A devotional stance requiring complete surrender to *Viṣṇu. It is sometimes said to be a *Śrī Vaiṣṇava development of **Bhagavadgītā* 18.66, the so-called 'carama śloka' (the 'final' or 'ultimate verse'): 'Abandoning all duties (*dharma), vow yourself to me alone. Don't agonize, I shall release you from all evils'. According to *Rāmānuja, complete self-surrender makes the devotee, or prapanna (the one who has surrendered), worthy of *karma-destroying divine grace (*prasāda), and so God becomes not only the object, but also the means of *liberation. Rāmānuja appears to regard prapatti as the culmination of *bhakti, but the doctrine was variously interpreted by the subsequent *Teṉkalai and *Vaṭakalai schools. The former regarded *liberation as totally dependent on the freely given grace of the deity; the latter saw it as also dependent upon the prior actions (karma) of the prapanna. For the Vaṭakalai theologian *Vedāntadeśika prapatti (as defined in this way) was a legitimate, but slightly inferior lower-*caste alternative to the more exigent *bhakti-yoga, which was only open to *twice-born males.

Prārthanā Samāj ('Prayer Society') A still extant Hindu society with aspirations for social reform—chiefly improvement in the status of women, universal education, and an end to *caste discrimination—similar to those of the *Brāhmo Samāj (Keshub Chandra *Sen had been an early influence). The Prārthanā Samāj was founded in Bombay in 1867 by Dr Atmaram Pandurang (1823–1898), initially drawing its membership from two western Indian secret societies, which had been experimenting with *food preparation and other practices that cut across orthodox notions of *purity and *pollution. It differed from the Brāhmos in grounding its theistic worship in the *bhakti poetry of the Maharastrian *Vārkarī Panth, especially that of *Tukārām, and in generally taking a less uncompromising attitude in its reforms. Its most prominent early leaders were the High Court judge, M.G. *Ranade, and the *paṇḍit and *Indologist, Sir Ramkrishna Gopal *Bhandarkar.

prasād(a) ('grace', 'favour') **1.** Theologically, a term expressing the free choice, or action, of a deity, or power, to favour a devotee with the means to *liberation (e.g. *knowledge), or liberation itself. This idea that the liberation of the individual depends, ultimately, not on their own actions (*karma), but on a power beyond them, characterized as 'grace' (prasāda) appears in the **Kaṭha* (2.20f.) and **Śvetāśvatara Upaniṣads* (3.20; 6.21), and the *Bhagavadgītā* (e.g. 18.56, 58), and is subsequently taken up by various theistic devotional movements. It probably receives its most sophisticated theological treatment in the *Viśiṣṭādvaita of *Rāmānuja and the works of the *Śrī Vaiṣṇava theologians who follow him. Whether surrender (*prapatti) to the deity is sufficient to incur liberation through his or her grace (which can wipe out the effects of karma), or whether works (karma) are required too, remains a point of constant tension—one that perhaps finds a material resolution in the other major use of the concept of prasāda (2).

2. At the end of a *pūjā, the deity's (or the object of worship's) favour, or prasād(a), is materially conveyed to the devotees through the distribution, by the *priest or priests, of *food, and a wide range of other previously made offerings. This is shared among the participants, regardless of their place in the social hierarchy, and either consumed, or, in the case of non-foodstuffs, worn on the body. Because of their proximity to the deity, such left-overs (themselves known as prasāda) are considered to be 'blessed'—that is to say, imbued with the deity's power and grace. It is these qualities which are then physically transferred to the devotees, bringing about their temporary identification or merger with the god. Typically, prasāda takes the form of a piece of fruit, cooked rice, water, or sweets. Flowers may also be returned, as may ornamentation from the *image of the deity, such as sandalwood paste, *kuṃkum (to *Goddess worshippers), and *bhasman (ash) (to *Śaivas), which is then applied to the forehead or smoothed into the hair. The extent to which societal hierarchical relationships, based on commensality, are mirrored, or transcended, in the offering and consumption of prasāda has been much debated by scholars, but remains ambiguous.

Praśastapāda *See* VAIŚEṢIKA.

Praśna Upaniṣad (early centuries CE) A short prose **Upaniṣad* assigned to the **Atharva Veda*. Its six chapters takes the form of the *ṛṣi Pippalāda's answer to six questions (praśnas) asked by six *brahmins. The questions cover such topics as the nature of creatures and persons, the nature of *prāṇa, and *meditation on *oṃ.

prasthāna traya ('the threefold source') For the *Vedānta tradition, the three essential texts requiring commentary by anyone wanting to found a new (i.e. a sub-)school—viz. the principal **Upaniṣads*, the **Brahmasūtras*, and the **Bhagavadgītā*.

pratigraha ('acceptance of gifts') *See* DĀNA.

pratiloma ('against the hair') According to **Dharmaśāstra*, a name for a mixed *marriage between a man of a lower *varṇa, and a woman of a higher one. The term is also applied to any offspring of that marriage. Its name derives from the perception that, unlike an *anuloma union, it is out of line with the natural order.

Prātiśākhya A class of phonetic treatise (classified as **Vedāṅga*), analysing and detailing the pronunciation of the *Sanskrit in the *śākhās of the **Veda* to ensure the correct performance of ritual.

pratisarga A term used in *Purāṇic *cosmology to designate the secondary 'creation' and dissolution of the world at the beginning and end of each 'day of *Brahmā' (or *kalpa). It is one of the classical 'five distinguishing marks' (*pañcalakṣaṇa) of a **Purāṇa*. *See also* SARGA.

pratiṣedha ('prohibition') *See* MĪMĀṂSĀ.

pratiṣṭhā(pana) ('installation') The ritual for consecrating an image (*mūrti), thus 'activating' the presence of the deity, and making it a living presence available for *pūjā. When this coincides with the opening of a new *temple, it is often accompanied by a prolonged *festival (pratiṣṭhā mahotsava) with elaborate rituals. *See also* PRĀṆAPRATIṢṬHĀ.

Pratyabhijñā ('Recognition [School]') The theological school of *Kashmir(i) Śaivism which provides the monistic underpinning for the *Trika ritual system. It argues for the identity of the individual (as *consciousness) with *Śiva (as total consciousness), and the liberating effect of recognizing that. Somewhat paradoxically, it also teaches that the universe is a manifestation of pure consciousness (i.e. the one Śiva), so that any perceived difference between the world and Śiva is essentially an illusion. Among its theologians are *Somānanda, *Utpala, and, most notably, *Abhinavagupta and his pupil, *Kṣemarāja. It was Abhinavagupta who, in a number of sophisticated and influential commentaries, took the apparent dualism of the Kashmiri tradition's root text, the **Mālinīvijayottara Tantra*, and recast it in terms of the Pratyabhijñā's School's supreme non-dualism.

pratyāhāra ('withdrawal of the senses') According to *Patañjali's **Yoga Sūtra*, pratyāhāra—the withdrawal of the senses from the objects of sense—is the fifth of the 'outer limbs' of his *aṣṭāṅga-yoga ('eight-limbed yoga'), and one of the prerequisites for more advanced practice. The *yogin is to detach himself from the distracting activities and experiences of the sense-organs in order to concentrate on the *self.

pratyakṣa ('perception') A means of valid knowledge (*pramāṇa) accepted by all six schools of philosophy (*darśanas). Precisely what kinds of perception are admitted varies from school to school.

pravara (lit. 'a summons') A list of three, or five, remote ancestors recited by a *brahmin in his daily worship. Marriages between members of families which had a common pravara name (or, in some instances, more than one common pravara name) were forbidden, even if they belonged to different *gotra.

pravṛtti ('engagement') *See* NIVṚTTI.

Prayāga ('the place of sacrifice', now called Allahābād) A major place of *pilgrimage (tīrtha) in Uttar Pradesh, standing at the confluence (saṃgama) of three rivers: the *Gaṅgā, the *Yamunā, and the mythical *Sarasvatī. The site is ancient—in the **Mahābhārata* it is said to be the foremost of all tīrthas, the most sacred in the three worlds (*lokas). The most important of the four *Kumbh(a) Melā sites, in 2001 Prayāga hosted the Mahā ('Great') Kumbha Melā, the final *festival in a cycle of twelve (i.e. the conclusion of a 144 year cycle). This resulted in what has been called the largest human gathering in history, with a crowd of over 30 million (according to some, 70 million, over 44 days).

prāyaścitta ('reparation', 'expiation') A term for a specific restorative action, or penance, designed to atone for infringements of *dharma. The systematic application of prāyaścitta is a major topic in the **Dharmasūtras*, and in **Dharmaśāstra* literature in general. The whole of *Manusmṛti* Ch. 11 is given over to it, as is one of the three chapters of **Yajñavalkyasmṛti*. Typical penances (which may be voluntary or imposed) include reciting *mantras, making offerings, gift-giving (*dāna), and, in particular, *fasting, or *tapas. (The last points back to the *Vedic origins of the concept as an adjunct to ritual.) In this way individuals hope to remove the sin incurred by their transgression, and to *purify themselves. Similarly, prāyaścitta rituals of reparation and *purification have to be carried out by *pūjāris if *temple *images are perceived to have been *polluted in any way.

preman (premā) ('love') A term used, chiefly in *Gauḍīya Vaiṣṇavism, to designate an experience (or *rasa) of divine love concomitant with *liberation, either in this body or at *death. This is engendered by a persistent, selfless, and all-encompassing devotion to *Kṛṣṇa, played out in a meditational practice involving the identification of the devotee (*bhakta) with Kṛṣṇa's lover, *Rādhā.

preta(s) ('deceased') A term applied to the spirits of the dead, caught between this world and the next (in what is sometimes termed the pretaloka), waiting to join their forefathers (*pitṛs). This can only be achieved by their living descendants properly performing the *śrāddha rites; if they neglect to do this, then the dead remain in the preta state, and exercise a malign influence on the living. *See also* BHŪTA(S); PUTRA.

priest A generic term for someone whose occupation it is to perform rituals or *pūjā. All the larger *Vedic *śrauta rituals required the collaboration of four groups of hereditary *brahmin priests (one representing each *Veda*): the *adhvaryus (**Yajur Veda*), the *hotṛs (**Ṛg Veda*), the *udgātṛs (**Sāma Veda*), and the *brahmans (masc.) (**Atharva Veda*). In the medieval and modern periods, a *brahmin priest may be attached to a *temple as a *pūjāri, or act as a domestic priest or *purohita (or sometimes both). *Brahmins usually cater for a higher *caste clientele, and serve the great pan-Indian gods, such as *Viṣṇu and *Śiva. They are, however, considered hierarchically inferior to those brahmins who are not professional priests. Non-brahmin priests serve the lower castes, and non-*Sanskritic *village deities. A priest serving a particular temple or area usually belongs to a specific sub-caste, and the job may be hereditary. *See also* BRAHMIN; PŪCĀRI; PŪJĀRI; ṚTVIK.

Pṛthā *See* KUNTĪ.

Pṛthivī ('the broad and extended') The earth personified as a goddess. In the **Ṛg Veda*, she is frequently paired with the sky-god (*Dyaus), as Dyāvāpṛthivī, the parents of the gods, and the totality of the material world. *See also* BHŪ DEVĪ.

pūcāri A term used in South India for a non-*Brahmin priest, serving a *village *temple and its deities, using vernacular *mantras.

pūjā ('worship', 'veneration', 'homage') At its most general, any form of ritualized veneration or devotion (*bhakti) directed towards any being (or object) deemed worthy of such attention. More specifically, 'pūjā' denotes the ritual worship of a deity in the form of an image (*mūrti), typically involving the presentation of *vegetarian and other offerings, and their return to the worshipper in the form of *prasāda. Such worship may be of an *iṣṭa- or *kula-devatā in a domestic shrine, a *grāma-devatā in the form of (e.g.) a rock or a tree in the open, or a great sectarian deity in a *temple. The frequency, scale, and precise detail of a pūjā depend on the nature and location of the mūrti, the prescriptions of sacred texts or ritual manuals (**paddhati*), the nature of the occasion, and the intentions of the participant(s). The spectrum ranges from the recitation of a short invocatory *mantra and the waving of an incense stick in front of an image on a calendar, or dangling in a three-wheeler, through simple offerings of flowers, sweets, and water, accompanied by *darśana and the receipt of prasāda, to elaborate ritual sequences, performed up to four or five times a day by professional temple-*pūjāris. This range is further extended in various *līlās, and the complex temple and processional rites which accompany the numerous *festivals celebrated across the year. Nevertheless, with the exception of the semi-congregational singing of *kīrtanas or bhajans by certain bhakti groups, the precise form and purpose of a particular pūjā, and its expected benefits, remain predominantly a matter between the individual and the deity. What counts most is the concentrated intimacy of their relationship—a connection which, in the bestowal of prasāda, amounts to a temporary identification, or merger, of the devotee and the god.

Temple pūjā, usually performed by pūjāris, and the more elaborate domestic forms of devotion, usually performed by domestic *priests or *purohitas, include, as key components, ritual sequences, such as darśana and *āratī, which may also be discrete acts of worship in themselves. Through the recitation of particular mantras, and the sounding of bells, drums, and other instruments, a typical sequence begins with the making-present of the deity, known as its awaking or 'bidding' (*āvāhana), and ends with its 'dismissal (*visarjana). In-between, the god or goddess, in the form of the mūrti, is treated as an honoured guest: the aim is to please, entertain, and win favour by giving service (*upacāra) through offerings and rites (also collectively and individually known as upacāra). These may include *bathing the image, dressing it, fanning it, anointing it with sandalwood, offering it *food, water, flowers, *tulasī leaves, *kuṃkum, incense, and other substances (including fire through the performance of *āratī), and the circumambulation (*pradakṣiṇā) of the *garbhagṛha, all accompanied by the chanting of mantras (the essential part of each action), or, in some cases, the singing of *bhajans. Some of the offerings made are kept by the temple, and some are returned to the worshippers as prasāda, the tangible form of the deity's blessing—a blessing which, in the context of temple pūjā, may extend beyond the individual to the temple complex itself, and even the surrounding country (or, in the past, the *king and his kingdom).

Pūjāprakāśa *See* MITRAMIŚRA.

pūjāri A *priest employed by a *temple to perform *pūjā. In any given temple complex, the pūjāris may belong to a particular sub-*caste. See also PRIEST.

puṃsavana ('generation of a male') The *saṃskāra, or life-cycle ritual, designed to bring about the birth of a male child. It is supposed to take place during pregnancy, but there is disagreement among the sources on *dharma about precisely when, or the particular form it should take. A number of accounts involve inserting a pounded substance (prepared, for example, from a *nyagrodha tree) into the wife's right nostril.

punar-mṛtyu ('re-death') According to *Brahmanical speculation, the eventual fate of those who had created an afterlife for themselves through ritual, since the effects of the latter would eventually run out. *See also* KARMA; REBIRTH.

Puṇḍalīka (11th/12th century CE?) A near-mythical *saint connected to the instigation of the *Viṭhobā *temple cult at *Paṇḍharpur. According to a foundation myth, given in the *Pāṇḍuraṅgamāhātmya* (part of the *Skanda Purāṇa*), Puṇḍalīka, a reformed character, who had become entirely devoted to his parents, was interrupted one day by Viṭhobā, seeking hospitality. Barely pausing in his ministrations to his father, Puṇḍalīka threw a brick for the god to stand on, clear of the mud, while he waited. This is said to be the same brick upon which Viṭhobā now stands in the temple. Puṇḍalīka himself is worshipped in a separate *samādhi in Paṇḍharpur.

puṇḍra *See* TILAK(A).

puṇya ('merit', 'good', 'right', 'virtuous', 'sacred', 'holy', 'meritorious', 'ritually pure') Religious merit accruing to the individual as the result of correct ritual and/ or ethical actions (*karma), on the assumption that a store of it will lead to good things in this life and the next. It is frequently used as a measure by which to assess the relative worth of particular actions: e.g. *Manusmṛti* (3.87) claims that a *householder obtains as much merit by giving alms food to a *Vedic student, as he would by giving a *cow to a poor man. Used adjectivally, it may be considered synonymous with *dharmic conduct—a 'good' or 'proper' action, however defined. Puṇya's conceptual opposite is *pāpa.

puṟam (Tam.: 'the exterior world') A category of *Tamil literature which deals with the 'exterior world', i.e. life outside the family (from the valour of *kings, to wars, to ethics, to *death and dying), as opposed to *akam literature which deals with love between men and women. The best-known anthology of puṟam poetry is the **Puṟanāṉūṟu*.

Puṟanāṉūṟu ('The Four Hundred [Poems] About the Exterior', 1st–3rd centuries CE) The best-known anthology of *Tamil *puṟam poetry, and one of the earliest surviving works in the language. It represents the work of more than 150 high-*caste poets, including at least ten women, who attached themselves to particular *kings, or moved from court to court. Their sophisticated literary compositions were modelled on the songs of low-caste drummers and bards.

Purāṇa(s) ('ancient', 'old', 'previous') A huge body of narrative texts, originally mostly in *Sanskrit verse, purporting to deal with an ancient past—one predicated on a cyclical and continuous *cosmogony, divided into various ages (*yuga). Along with *itihāsa (the *Epics), the *Purāṇas* embody the tradition (*smṛti) which informs theistic Hinduism from a *Brahmanical perspective. More than any other body of Hindu literature, these exceptionally popular texts have proved impossible to date with any confidence, since the extant versions are often composite, and may have been expanded, or even contracted, from earlier versions. (There is an Indian tradition that there was a single, original *Purāṇa*, composed by *Vyāsa.) Drawing eclectically on orally transmitted material, some of which may indeed be very old, and, possibly a lost '*Purāṇaveda*' or *Purāṇa *Saṃhitā*, some of the apparently earlier *Purāṇas* may have been Brahmanical compilations made during the 4th to 5th centuries CE. Nevertheless, substantial material continued to be added, and some of the texts in the standard lists may be as late as the 16th century. Although the earlier *Purāṇas*' relation with *Vedic texts remains a matter of debate (as does their provenance as oral and/or written texts), the overall strategy of the authors, or compilers, was clearly to legitimate, or *Sanskritize, the monotheistic sectarianism of *bhakti in the light of *Vedic orthodoxy. Traditionally, the texts, which usually take the form of a dialogue, in which questions are answered by an authoritative narrator (*sūta), were performed (effectively constructed) in *temples and elsewhere by interpretative professionals (*paurāṇikas), according to their own conventions and those of the locality.

The Brahmanical tradition makes a distinction between eighteen 'great', or *mahāpurāṇas*, and eighteen *upapurāṇas* (characterized as 'minor' or 'sub'-*Purāṇas*), although there is little consensus about which texts belong to the latter category, or their effective authoritative status. (And there are, in fact, far more than 36 *Purāṇas*.) A standard list of the *mahāpurāṇas*, taken from some of the individual *Purāṇas* themselves, includes the following: 1) **Brahma/ Brāhma*, 2) **Brahmāṇḍa*, 3) **Brahmavaivarta*, 4) **Mārkaṇḍeya*, 5) **Bhaviṣya(t)*, 6) **Vāmana*, 7) **Viṣṇu*, 8) **Bhāgavata*, 9) **Nārada*, 10) **Garuḍa*, 11) **Padma*, 12) **Varāha*, 13) **Vāyu* or **Śiva*, 14) **Liṅga*, 15) **Matsya*, 16) **Kūrma*, 17) **Skanda*, 18) **Agni/Āgneya*. A further traditional, but largely artificial, classification groups the *mahāpurāṇas* according to the three *guṇas, each with its related deity: so 1–6 are regarded as *rājasa and belonging to Brahmā, 7–12 as *sāttvika and belonging to Viṣṇu, and 13–18 as *tāmasa and belonging to *Śiva. In terms of sectarian content, however, many *Purāṇas* show, at best, a mixed affiliation, although *Viṣṇu may be considered the dominant deity in the *mahāpurāṇas*.

According to a tradition established by *Amarasiṃha in the 5th century CE, a *Purāṇa* is supposed to deal with five topics (*pañcalakṣaṇa): 'creation' (*sarga), secondary 'creation' (*pratisarga), genealogy (*vaṃśa) of the gods, the reigns of the *Manus, and the history of the patriarchs of the *lunar and *solar dynasties (*vaṃśānucarita). In fact all *Purāṇas* have relatively little to say on these particular topics, and a great deal to say on many others, especially the mythologies of Viṣṇu and Śiva. The prominent, *bhakti-suffused *Vaiṣṇava strand of the *mahāpurāṇas* deals extensively with Viṣṇu's *avatāras (especially *Rāma and *Kṛṣṇa), and their incidence in terms of cosmogony, *cosmology, and cyclical time. Interlocking material concerning Śiva and his family—*Pārvatī, *Gaṇeśa, and *Skanda—and the origins of *liṅga worship are also prominent, as are myths of *Devī, and, especially in some of the *upapurāṇas*, a concern with *Śākta worship. Other gods, notably *Brahmā, also receive extended glorification. Local deities and traditions are merged with, or subsumed in, wider pan-Indian movements. A further prominent aspect of the *Purāṇas*, which has been taken with increasing seriousness by some historians, is the presence of extensive genealogies, listing various royal dynasties. In short, most of the major concerns of post-Vedic Hinduism, including *pūjā and other rituals, *temples, *festivals, *pilgrimages, and *tīrthas, as well as the popular stories about the great gods, find their locus classicus in these texts. *See also* entries for individual PURĀṆA(S); STHĀLAPURĀṆA.

Purandaradāsa (*c.*1485–1565) A Kannada *bhakti poet and devotee of *Viṭṭhala/*Kṛṣṇa. Born in Pune (Maharashtra), popular stories portray him as having worked as a moneylender, before miraculously being turned to a life of devotion, centred on the *temple at *Paṇḍharpur. A contemporary of *Kanakadāsa, he was a follower of the *Haridāsakūṭa, who were probably responsible for memorizing and preserving the 1 000 and 1 500 songs reliably attributed to him. Although his songs only survive in settings made by later musicians, he is highly esteemed as the initiator of the Karnatic classical music tradition.

Purāṇic ('relating, or related to, the *Purāṇas*') An adjective, often linked with *itihāsa ('Epic'), indicating the time-period, or the typical content, associated with the *Purāṇas*; it is sometimes used almost synonymously with terms such as 'medieval Hinduism', 'theistic Hinduism', or simply just 'Hinduism', in contradistinction to '*Vedic' or '*Brahmaṇical' religion. A clearer distinction, however, is that made between between 'Purāṇic' and '*Tantric', where the former designates *Veda-aligned, Brahmanical forms of practice, and the latter practices based on non-Vedic, Tantric revelation.

pure and impure (śuddha and aśuddha) A key binary opposition, underlying much Hindu thought and practice, and maintained by the prescriptions of *Dharmaśāstra*. It is predicated, in the first instance, on the *Brahmanical idea that the *twice-born *varṇas, and *brahmins in particular, possess an inherent ritual purity (śauca, śuddhi) by virtue of their birth. They can, however, be polluted by contact with i) a wide variety of substances, such as bodily fluids, hair, and nail cilippings, leather products, and various foodstuffs (particularly those improperly prepared, or subject to pollution through the relative impurity of the cook), ii) life events, such as birth, *death, menstruation, and iii) members of the lower *castes, particularly those who are considered *avarṇa or '*untouchable'. Conversely, it is precisely these lower castes which are thought to possess an inherent ritual impurity (aśauca, aśuddhi), and it is to them that are assigned what are thought to be major polluting tasks, such as barbering, laundering, and the disposal of corpses. (In other words, lower castes take on the major pollutions (aśauca) of death, excretion, and other bodily functions for the castes above them.) Change of occupation makes no difference: if a caste is thought of as impure, then its members, regardless of their actual occupations, are thought of as polluting to those above them in the hierarchy. Most such pollutions are temporary, insofar as they dissipate over time, or can be removed through *prāyaścitta, and rituals of 'purification' (śauca)—typically taking a '*bath', since water is seen as a major, ritually purifying agent. This explains the necessity for orthodox brahmins to take a daily bath to maintain their purity: those at the top of the hierarchy being at the same time the most vulnerable to, and the most capable of, absorbing impurity.

The performance of ritual, in particular, requires those involved to purify themselves prior to their involvement. Consequently, those suffering from temporary pollutions, particularly women who are subject to menstruation and childbirth (which in themselves make women inherently less pure than men), are excluded for the duration from activities such as *temple-going, or approaching an *image. (In many cases this embargo is also applied to the lower castes and *mlecchas or foreigners.) An exception to this requirement to maintain ritual purity, which proves and trades on the rule, is the deliberate use of various impure substances (*pañca-makāra) in some types of *Tantric rite, as a means of acquiring powers (*siddhis) through transgression.

Ideas of purity and impurity are extended by analogy to mental or internal processes in (e.g.) *yoga, and to *ethics, although ritual purity or impurity, with its physical co-requisites, may still be seen by some as the index of an equivalent inner state. In the case of ritual purity, it may, indeed, be seen as a prerequisite of, or preparation for its inner analogue. Others may explicitly deny the connection.

Purī The name of a district and a city in Odisha (Orissa). The latter has been a major Hindu *pilgrimage site (replacing an earlier *Buddhist site) since at least the 15th century CE, and is regarded as one of the four *dhāmas (dwelling places of the gods). It houses the *Jagannātha *temple complex, sacred to *Kṛṣṇa, and its associated annual *ratha-yātrā, or 'chariot *festival'. It is also the site of one of the four *Daśanāmi *maṭhas (monasteries) founded, according to tradition, by *Śaṅkara in the 8th century CE.

purification *See* PURE AND IMPURE.

purity *See* PURE AND IMPURE.

purohita In *Vedic times, a *king's chief *priest or court chaplain, a position of immense political influence. The term is now used of a domestic priest who performs rituals for a particular family or group of families.

Puru In the **Mahābhārata*, a progenitor of the *Lunar Dynasty; the son of *Yayāti.

Purūravas The son of *Iḷā, and so the first *king of the *Lunar Dynasty. The story of his love for the celestial nymph, Urvaśī, their separation, and eventual reunion, was first suggested in the **Ṛg Veda* (10.95); it was subsequently expanded in the **Brāhmaṇas*, the **Purāṇas*, and the **Mahābhārata*, and became the subject of *Kālidāsa's play, *Vikramorvaśīya* ('Urvaśī Won by Valour'). In some *Vedic texts the couple's names are given to personifications of the two fire sticks (*araṇi).

puruṣa ('[male] person', man', '(hu)man', 'spirit'/'soul', 'supreme Being') A late *Ṛg Vedic hymn, the **Puruṣasūkta* (**Ṛg Veda* 10.90), envisages creation and the hierarchical ordering of society as a self-creating sacrifice (*yajña) in which the cosmic man (puruṣa), representing the totality of things, is both the subject and the object of the sacrifice made by the gods (*devas). In the **Śatapaṭha Brāhmaṇa*, and elsewhere, this cosmic puruṣa merges with the demiurge, *Prajāpati, to become the unifying deity who is everything in its entirety, and more. Since the puruṣa is the totality of things, he is also the essence of the individual, and a number of **Upaniṣads* (e.g. the **Kaṭha*) use the term with this more specialized or delimited meaning (partly synonymous with *ātman) to differentiate the undying, immaterial soul from the impermanent, material body in which it is housed. *Sāṃkhya develops this further into an absolute dualism between inherently passive, conscious, male 'spirits' (puruṣas), and exclusively active, female 'matter' (*prakṛti). Puruṣas here, and in the **Bhagavadgītā*, where, as sentient beings, they constitute God's higher nature, are referred to in the plural. *Patañjali's **Yoga-Sūtra*, adds a special kind of omniscient puruṣa to this plurality, known as *Īśvara ('Lord', 'God'), an object of *meditation who is untouched by *karma or other defilements. In some *Śākta traditions, puruṣa is subsumed in the single active consciousness which is the *Goddess.

puruṣārtha ('aims or goals of human life') According to *Brahmanical sources, there are four legitimate 'aims or goals of human life': *dharma (conforming to duty—i.e. behaviour defined as virtuous and 'lawful'), *artha (pursuing and acquiring material wealth and worldy success), *kāma (pursuing pleasure in all its forms), and *mokṣa (seeking salvation or liberation). Grouped together, the first three are referred to as trivarga ('the group of three'), the 'three conditions', or 'values', ideally associated with *householder life, and current as an idea from about the 3rd century BCE. The wider fourfold grouping probably reflects a theological and historical process, first evident in later parts of the *Epics, through which mokṣa is added to the list (to make a 'group of four' or caturvarga) in order to accommodate the renunciatory way of life, which has liberation as its goal.

Whatever its origins, the fourfold puruṣārtha reflects a real tension between those leading potentially incompatible ways of life, particularly the majority, the followers of the prescribed social norm (dharma), and individuals who renounce such norms in order to pursue mokṣa. By being inclusive, or synthetic, the concept of puruṣārtha attempts to relieve this theological tension, although, according to some, it is no more successful in that respect than a related but separate ideological construct, the *āśrama system. However, both theories are understood by most contemporary Hindus as recommending the pursuit of mokṣa only in the final part of one's life, after one's dharmic obligations have been fulfilled. Moreover, within the trivarga scheme alone, there is room for a complex debate about the relative importance of the particular goals, and how, precisely, they should be defined or ranked in relation to each other. Inevitably, the **Arthaśāstra* sees artha as the key aim which allows the others to flourish, and the **Kāmasūtra* takes a similarly partisan stance. Other textual sources, such as the **Mahābhārata*, dramatize unresolved and sometimes competing views. While conformity to dharma, unsurprisingly, is the cornerstone of **Dharmaśāstra* texts, some passages also recommend that all three aims should be followed simultaneously. Echoing this, many popular stories demonstrate how social harmony and individual good depend on maintaining a balance between the three aims, which, from a wider perspective, is itself an essentially dharmic view.

puruşamedha *See* HUMAN SACRIFICE.

Puruşasūkta ('hymn of the man') The name given to **Ṛg Veda* 10.90, a late *Vedic hymn which envisages creation and the hierarchical ordering of society as a self-creating sacrifice (*yajña) in which the cosmic man (*puruşa), representing the totality of things, including the **Veda* itself, is both the subject and the object of the sacrifice made by the gods (*devas). In other words, it is the sacrifice itself which establishes the proper order (i.e. *dharma) and interconnectedness of everything. As part of this (and for the first time in a textual source), the ideal ordering of society is represented as a division into four 'classes' (*varṇas) (v. 12), each connected with the part of the puruşa's body which represents its particular social function: the *brahmin is his mouth, the *kşatriya his arms, the *vaiśyas his thighs, and the *śūdras his feet. Several aspects of this model had a paradigmatic influence on subsequent thought, especially i) the depiction of the universe and everything it contains as a monistic whole, and ii) the ordering and maintenance of the universe as a sacrificial activity.

Puruşottama ('supreme person') An epithet of *Vişṇu/*Kṛşṇa. In the **Bhagavadgītā* (11.3), *Arjuna uses the term to address Kṛşṇa. It is also the form the god takes in the *Jagannātha *temple in *Purī. *Rāmānuja regards the term as synonymous with *brahman.

Puruşottamācārya (13th century CE?) Named as an early *ācārya in the *Nimbārka *sampradāya, although the lineage is historically unreliable. The *Vedāntaratnamañjuşa* is attributed to him, as is a 'biography' of Nimbārka, the *Ācāryacarita*; the latter, however, cannot be dated to earlier than the 16th century.

Pūrva Mīmāṃsā *See* MĪMĀṂSĀ.

(Pūrva-) Mīmāṃsā Sūtra *See* JAIMINI; MĪMĀṂSĀ.

pūrvapakşa ('the first side') The technical term for the preliminary position, or prima facie view in a theological or philosophical argument. It usually takes the form of an objection put into the mouth of an opponent (real or imagined).

Pūşan ('nourisher') A *Vedic *deva; one of the *Ādityas, according to the later, extended list of twelve, his name refers to his role as a giver of fertility; he is also seen as the 'pathfinder' or 'guide' to fertile pastures, etc.

Puşkar A lake in Rajasthan, sacred to *Brahmā, and both the starting and finishing point for various long distance *pilgrimages. It is listed among the *tīrthas in the **Mahābhārata's* **Āraṇyakaparvan*.

Puşţimārga ('path of grace/well-being') A *Vaişṇava *bhakti path, established by *Vallabha, and the core element in the religious practice of the *Vallabhasampradāya. Devotion is directed towards the *Kṛşṇa whose early life and 'divine play' (*līlā) among the *gopīs in *Vṛndāvana is evoked in the **Bhāgavata Purāṇa*. For the devotee, an increasing and graded immersion in these events as a participant, up to the contemplation and enactment of the 'divine play', is dependent at every level, on the grace (puṣṭi) of Kṛṣṇa, as is eventual *liberation. In practice this entails the disinterested service (*sevā) of, and complete surrender to, the deity, who is housed in a *temple, known as a *havelī, where he makes himself available for the *darśana of his devotees on eight occasions during the day. These coincide with activities such as waking, eating, dressing, taking his *cows out to graze, napping, bringing his herd back at dusk, and going to bed. As this suggests, he is viewed as being literally and fully embodied in the *image, which therefore requires near continuous attention (i.e. waking, *bathing, dressing, feeding, entertaining, and putting to sleep). Some devotees favour an attitude of parental love towards the child Kṛṣṇa. A characteristic practice is the congregational singing of *kīrtanas before the image, partly formed from the works of a group of eight bhakti poets (aṣṭachāp(a)). Kṛṣṇa is also thought to be embodied in the *guru or *gosvāmī (i.e. Vallabha and his successors). Particularly popular among the commercial *castes of northern and western India, the Puṣṭimārga established its major *tīrtha at *Nāthdvāra in Rajasthan, where the focus of attention is the image of Kṛṣṇa as *Śrī Nāthjī (in the havelī of the same name). *See also* VALLABHASAMPRADĀYA; ŚUDDHĀDVAITA.

Pūtanā ('stinking') A demoness, inimical to children, who takes the form of a beautiful woman in order to kill the infant *Kṛṣṇa by suckling him on her poisoned breast. Instead, the god sucks out both her milk and her vital breath, and Pūtanā goes to *heaven, simply because she offered her breast to the god, regardless of her *evil intention. The story is told in the **Bhāgavata Purāṇa* and elsewhere.

putra ('son') A *Sanskrit term for which the traditional, but probably false, etymology is 'preserving (tra) from the *hell called Put'. It reflects the fact that, according to the *Brahmanical legal texts (**Dharmaśāstra*), only an eldest son can perform his father's funeral rites (*antyeṣṭi/ *śrāddha), and so ensure that a body is created for him in the next world, where he can be united with his ancestors. Failing this, the deceased will wander as a homeless *preta, or be reborn in the hell called Put, to which those without male children are condemned. This belief is frequently used as an explanation for the widespread and continuing obsession with producing a male heir, and the concomitant devaluation of female offspring.

putrikā In **Dharmaśāstra* and the *Epics, the daughter of a *king who has no sons (*putras). The king arranges her *marriage in order for her to produce a male offspring whom he can adopt as his heir (known as the putrikāputra, the 'son of the putrikā').

Q

'qualified nondualism' An older translation of the term *Viśiṣṭādvaita ('non-dualism of the qualified').

R

Rādhā The *gopī singled out from the others as *Kṛṣṇa's particular lover and consort in *Jayadeva's **Gītagovinda*, an erotic pairing which thereafter became the key component of *Gauḍīya Vaiṣṇava theology and practice, in so far as *Caitanya, the *Gosvāmīs, and numerous *bhakti poets saw it as a template for the relationship between God (*Bhagavān) and his devotees (*bhaktas). By identifying with Rādhā in her all-encompassing, secret, and intense, because conventionally adulterous, longing for Kṛṣṇa, on a register that stretches from separation (*viraha) to (re)union, the devotee can aspire to experience a divine love (*preman) concomitant with *liberation. The imitation of the 'divine play' (*līlā) of the couple in *Braj, leads to a permanent 'play' in its heavenly analogue. Rādhā, at one level a cow-herder married to the *gopa, Ayanagoṣa, is also regarded as an incarnation of the goddess *Lakṣmī, i.e. *Viṣṇu/Kṛṣṇa's consort or wife. The Rādhā-Kṛṣṇa relationship has been, and remains, an immensely popular subject for artists.

Rādhā and Kṛṣṇa

Radhakrishnan, Sarvepalli (1888–1975) A *Tamil born academic philosopher, and an influential public figure—he was Vice-President (1952–62) and then President (1962–67) of the Republic of India, Radhakrishnan acted as an exponent of what he saw as the rational core of traditional Indian thought (essentially *Advaita Vedānta) to an anglophone Western audience. At the same time he attempted to introduce elements of Western idealism into contemporary Indian philosophy. His aim was soteriological: the world could be saved by the individual rediscovery of humanity's spiritual nature.

Educated in *Christian-run establishments, he held chairs of philosophy at Mysore and Calcutta universities, and was elected the first *Spalding Professor of Eastern Religions and Ethics at Oxford University (1936–39), where he had previously lectured on Comparative Religion. He was also Vice-Chancellor of *Benares Hindu University (1939–48), and India's ambassador to UNESCO and the Soviet Union. His many publications and lectures include: *Indian Philosophy* (2 vols. 1923, 1927), *The Philosophy of the Upanishads* (1924), *The Hindu View of Life* (1926), *An Idealist View of Life* (1932), *Eastern Religions and Western Thought* (1939), *Religion and Society* (1947), *The Bhagavadgītā* (1948), *The Principal Upanishads* (1953), and *Indian Religions* (1979).

Radhasoami Satsang A *nirguṇa devotional movement originating in northern India in the 19th century. The founding figure was Śiv (Shiv) Dayal Singh

(1818–78), although the Satsang (the association of his faithful followers) was formed in 1861 only at the urging of his disciple, Rai Saligram (1829–1898). In his 'Essential Declarations' (H.: Sār bacan), Śiv Dayal Singh referred to God as 'Rādhāsvāmi' (hence 'Radhasoami'), but there is no detectable connection to the *Vaiṣṇava *Rādhā—this Supreme Being is conceptualized as unambiguously impersonal. Nevertheless, the *gurus of the tradition, starting with Śiv Dayal Singh himself (also called 'Radhasoami' or 'Soamiji'), are worshipped (whether living or dead) as incarnations of Radhasoami, and as the santsatgurus (the 'true teachers'), the only available guides to *liberation. Their teaching maps a *yogic ascent, through a tripartite cosmic hierarchy, which leads from imprisonment in matter to spiritual reunion with Radhasoami. The means to achieving this is through a 'secret' technique known as surat-śabd-yoga, meditation on the inner, eternal sound (*śabda) which is embodied in the guru.

As Śiv Dayal Singh's successor, Rai Saligram systematized the theology of the Satsang, at the same time opening it to all those willing to undertake guru *bhakti and follow a disciplined lifestyle, including *vegetarianism. During the time of Rai Saligram's successor, Brahma Shankar Misra (1861–1907), the Radhasoamis divided into the Beas Satsang, and two divisions of the original Agra Satsang, thereafter known as the Soami Bagh and the Dayal Bagh. The Beas group was led by a Punjabi *Sikh, Jaimal Singh (1838–1903). Under his successor, Savan Singh (1858–1948), it became the most popular Radhasoami Satsang, with a following including Western converts as well as Punjabis. A satellite organization is the Delhi-based Ruhani Satsang. Retrospectively, the Beas Satsang has attempted to a establish a *guruparamparā stretching back to the medieval *Sants and the Sikh gurus.

Rādhavallabhī ('Those who regard Kṛṣṇa as the lover of Rādhā', or 'Rādhā's Lovers') A North Indian *Vaiṣṇaiva *bhakti *sampradāya, founded by *Hitaharivaṃśa when he consecrated an image of *Kṛṣṇa called Rādhavallabha ('Lover of *Rādhā') at *Vṛndāvana in 1535, and continued, after his death, by his son *Kṛṣṇadāsa. The sampradāya was dedicated to the worship of Rādhā through an attitude of sakhya-bhakti, in which the devotee assumed the role of a female attendant or close girl-friend (*sakhī) of Rādhā, the better to contemplate the eternal union of her and her husband Kṛṣṇa; the ultimate aim of this practice was to engender a liberating emotion or aesthetic experience (*rasa) of joy (hita). All other concerns, whether ritual, theological or philosophical, were treated as essentially irrelevant to this devotion. The *Sakhībhāvas may have been an offshoot of the Rādhavallabhīs, although little is known about the history of either tradition.

rāg(a) ('[red] dye', 'passion') **1.** In classical Indian music, one of a series of notes on which melodies are improvised. Textbooks came to number them in their hundreds, classified according to the time of day or night during which they should be performed. Many are associated with particular *rasa, and are thought to evoke, or 'colour', various emotions, especially those associated with *bhakti; they are also connected with specific deities and *Purāṇic myths. Personified, they take the male (rāga) and female (rāginī) forms which, in a synaesthetic transformation, are visualized in the miniature paintings of the Rāgamālā tradition. **2.** ('passion', 'attraction', 'attachment') According to *Patañjali's **Yoga Sūtra*, one of the five *kleśas, or defilements, which perpetuate an individual's *karmic bondage.

rāgānugābhakti A phase of devotion (*bhakti) in a sequence devised by the

r

*Gauḍīya Vaiṣṇava theologian, Rūpa *Gosvāmī in his *Bhaktirasāmṛtasindhu* ('Ocean of the Immortal Nectar of Devotion'). It is known as the 'following (anugā) of passion (rāga)', because it is modelled on the devotion of the *gopīs for *Kṛṣṇa. It is contrasted with vaidhībhakti, devotion according to rules (vidhis), in which Kṛṣṇa is worshipped in a more conservative fashion.

Rāghava *See* RAGHU; RĀMA.

Raghu A *king of the *Solar Dynasty, the great grandfather of *Rāma, hence the latter's epithet, Rāghava ('Descendant of Raghu'). He lends his name to a long poem by *Kālidāsa, 'The Dynasty of Raghu' (*Raghuvaṃśa*).

Raghunātha Bhaṭṭa *See* GOSVĀMĪS.

Raghunātha Dāsa *See* GOSVĀMĪS.

Raghunātha Śiromaṇi (15th–16th century CE) A Bengali Navya-*Nyaya author, who, in his *Padārthatattvanirūpaṇam* ('Examination of the Reality of the Categories'), attempted a radical revision of the categories (*padārthas) of the Nyāya-*Vaiśeṣika tradition.

rahasya ('secret [teaching/doctrine]') At its most general, any *Śrī Vaiṣṇava doctrinal work in *Maṇipravāḷam; more specifically, the term applied to the three secret *mantras which are central to their practice: the Tirumantra, the Dvayam, and the Caramaśloka (*Bhagavadgītā* 18.66). Essentially expressions of homage to *Nārāyaṇa, and the intention to take refuge in him, these three are regarded as a concentration of the entire teaching, delivered by *Viṣṇu himself. Received at *initiation, they are to be recited and meditated upon daily, as well as playing an integral role in *temple ritual. Since they were perceived to contain Śrī Vaiṣṇava doctrine in *nuce*, a large and elaborate commentarial literature developed around them, including works by *Piḷḷai Lokācāriyar and *Vedāntadeśika.

Rahasya Traya ('The Three Secret [Teachings]') A short addendum to the **Devī Mahātmya*, giving an esoteric interpretation of the *Mahātmya's* three main episodes.

Rāhu An *inauspicious demon, associated with eclipses; he is said to consume the *amṛta which fills the *moon. According to traditional astrology (*jyotiṣa), Rahu and Ketu, as, respectively, the ascending (northern) and descending (southern) nodes, make up two of the 'nine planets' (*navagrahas). Rāhu kāla ('Rāhu time') is an inauspicious period, which varies from day to day; it is to be avoided if embarking on some new or doubtful enterprise.

Raidās(a) (Ravidās(a)) (late 15th/early 16th century?) A *bhakti poet in the North Indian *sant tradition, and founder of the Raidāsī tradition, it is claimed that he was a student of *Rāmānanda. Born in *Vārāṇasī, Raidās was an *untouchable, belonging to the *camār *caste of leather-workers, or cobblers, and he has subsequently been regarded as their patron saint. Like *Kabīr, with whom he is sometimes associated in the hagiographies, he regarded conventional worldly or religious behaviour, especially caste differentiation, as irrelevant to salvation, which was entirely dependent upon the *grace of God. Usually said to be a *nirguṇa *bhakta, his poetry also sometimes indicates a more personal devotion to *Rām. Composed in *Hindi, his verses were included, and preserved, in the *Sikh **Ādi Granth*, and the collections of the *Dādūpantha tradition. Raidās has himself become an object of devotion for those belonging to the movement named after him, the Raidāsīs, who emphasize his critical stance towards the behaviour of the higher castes, especially the *brahmins, and celebrate their own, autonomous religious identity. Since the late 19th century, the Raidāsīs of the Punjab, in particular, have been culturally and politically active on behalf of their community.

Raidāsīs *See* RAIDĀS(A).

Rai Saligram (1829–1898) *See* RADHASOAMI SATSANG.

rāja-dharma *See* KINGSHIP.

rājanya ('kingly') An ancient name for the *kṣatriya *varṇa.

Rājarājeśvara temple *See* TAÑJĀVŪR.

Rājarājeśvarī *See* TRIPURASUNDARĪ.

rajas ('activity', 'passion') According to *Sāṃkhya-Yoga ontology, one of the three *guṇas, or strands, of material nature (*prakṛti), rajas is characterized as 'passionate'; concomitantly, it represents the principle of kinesis or energy. Since the tripartite guṇa division is extended to various other categories, rajas is also, for instance, used to characterize a group of (rājasa) **mahāpurāṇas* belonging to *Brahmā, and certain 'hot' (i.e. stimulating) *foods.

rājasa *See* RAJAS.

rājasūya ('royal consecration') By the *Brahmanical period, an elaborate and complex *Vedic *śrauta ritual, extending over a period of two years or more. Only a *kṣatriya could perform it, since it is the means by which the sacrificer (*yajamāna) is anointed and becomes a *king. As the *sacrifice affirms the king's sovereignty over the realm and its inhabitants, at the same time, it is supposed to reinforce the superior ritual status of the *brahmins. There are many sequences—according to the **Śatapatha Brāhmaṇa*, it subsumes all other rituals—including a ritualized dicing match. The *dakṣinā (2) is huge. In the **Sabhāparvan* of the **Mahābhārata*, *Yudhiṣṭhira performs a rājasūya, which is followed by the famous dicing match.

rājayoga ('royal yoga') A synonym for the classical *Yoga system expounded in *Patañjali's **Yoga Sūtra*.

Rajneesh, Bhagwan Shree ('Osho') (1931–1990) Born a *Jain, Mohan Chandra Rajneesh began his adult career as an academic teacher of philosophy, but at the age of 35 became a self-appointed *guru. His *āśram in Pune became a magnet for those wishing to experience the eclectic mix of psychotherapeutic, spiritual, and meditational exercises on offer, as well as the 'free' sex. His close followers were initiated as 'sannyāsins', distinguished by their orange robes (hence the epithet, the 'Orange People'), a new name, and the wearing of a *mālā of wooden beads containing Rajneesh's picture. In 1981 he unexpectedly appeared in the USA, where he settled on a ranch in Oregon. Here, under the direction of his PA, Ma Anand Sheela, and in increasingly repressive circumstances, his followers set about building a city known as Rajneeshpuram. The enterprise ended in scandal, the arrest of Sheela, and the expulsion of Rajneesh from the USA in 1985. Returning to Pune, he changed his name to 'Osho' ('Friend'), and reconstituted the organization, including a change of uniform. Since his death, his followers have continued to run the āśram, now known as the Osho Commune International, and to propagate a mixture of athletic and meditational practices, drawing as much on popularized forms of *Buddhism and New Ageism, as on anything identifiably Hindu. Those wishing to stay are required to pay an entry fee and take an AIDS test.

Rājpūts ('sons of kings', Skt.: rāja-putra—'king's son') A generic term for the approximately twelve million members of a number of clans claiming ancient *kṣatriya status, based in what is now Rajasthan. They may have been descended from the Huns, or other invaders from the north, but, with their rise to political prominence in the 9th and 10th centuries CE, they were provided with royal genealogies which aligned them with either the *Lunar or *Solar dynasties. In particular, a group of four, the Agnikula ('Fire Family'), forged a myth of origin claiming descent from a kṣatriya hero, summoned from a sacrificial fire pit on Mount Ābū in order to deliver the country from invaders. It was they who, after helping them to fight off Arab incursions, gradually replaced the Pratīhāra kings of South Rajasthan. Throughout the 11th and 12th centuries the numerous Rājpūt clans in the region (known as Rājputāna) were largely engaged in fighting each other. Later, they had to contend in various ways with the *Mughals, with a number of principalities—notably *Mewār—holding out until the late 15th and early 16th centuries. Nevertheless, under the emperor *Akbar, and his successors, the Rājpūts were largely incorporated, on favourable terms, into the service of the Mughal state. In spite of intermittent rebellions this remained the case until, following the collapse of the Mughal Empire in the 18th century, and a period at the mercy of the *Marāṭhās, the Rājpūt principalities were assigned the status of subordinate 'princely states' under the British. Since Independence (1947), and the dissolution of the old princely states, the Rājpūts, or those claiming descent from them, have continued to make up the dominant, land-owning *castes in central and northern India.

The Rājpūts are renowned for their fierce martial spirit and heroism, the most spectacular instances being the mass self-immolation of Rājpūt women and children (known as jauhar), preceding the suicidal death of their menfolk in a number of battles with the *Muslims. During the Mughal period, they were major patrons of the arts, particularly of the various traditional schools of painting named after them.

Rākhī Bandhan (Rakṣābandhan) ('bond of protection') A popular *festival held on the full moon day of Śrāvaṇa (July–August) (the same day on which *Śrāvaṇī Pūrṇimā is celebrated), marked by girls and young women tying coloured threads (rākhī) around the wrists of their 'brothers' (a category which may also include other male relatives and friends). The tie (bandhan) symbolizes a request for protection (rākhī/rakṣā), which is answered with a small gift of money. In this way familial love, or some other mutual bond, is confirmed and reinforced. A popular explanation of its origins is given in the myth of *Indra's wife, *Śacī, tying a *mantra-charged thread to his wrist to enable him to defeat the *asuras. Various stories are also told of its historical use in summoning military aid from allies.

rakṣā ('protection') A protective amulet, thread, or *mantra. *See also* Rākhī Bandhan.

Rakṣābandhan *See* Rākhī Bandhan.

rākṣasa marriage *See* marriage.

rākṣasa(s) A collective term for flesh-eating demons and shape-shifting malevolent spirits, believed to haunt the night, especially during the dark lunar fortnight. Small children and women are particularly vulnerable to them, and they are believed to be the cause of all kinds of misfortune. Red-haired, red-eyed, and viciously fanged, they populate the *Epics, and other stories. The *Vedic texts appear to use the term as a derogatory epithet for the *anārya (the non-*Āryans).

Rakteśvarī A family goddess, worshipped by *Nambūdiri Brahmins in Kerala.

Rāma (Rām, Rāma Dāśarathi, Rāmacandra, Rāghava) 1. One of the major Hindu gods, regarded by his devotees as the supreme deity (i.e. God). His oldest surviving appearance is in the narrative which provides the core for the *Epic *Rāmāyaṇa*. Portrayed as a great hero, who destroys the demon *Rāvaṇa, he exhibits all the kingly virtues—he is an ideal son to *Daśaratha, a perfect brother to

*Lakṣmaṇa, and a proper husband to *Sītā. The text not only emphasizes his faultless adherence to the *Vedic *householder's *dharmic norm (not to mention the *sva-dharma of the ideal *king), but it further suggests that, as an *avatāra of *Viṣṇu, he may also be *dharma's ultimate source and support. Although there is scholarly disagreement about whether what are deduced to be the earliest layers of *Vālmīki's *Rāmāyaṇa* really do identify Rāma as God, it is this idea which was taken up in the groundswell of medieval devotional practice (*bhakti). As an object of *temple-based worship from about the 12th century onwards, Rāma came to be widely revered, particularly in northern India, as the one, Supreme God who, through his *grace, can save those devoted to him. His positioning at the heart of *Vaiṣṇava practice was further emphasized by his inclusion, alongside that other 'human' figure, *Kṛṣṇa, in the standard *Purāṇic lists of Viṣṇu's avatāras; but it was in devotional texts, such as the 12th-century *Tamil **Irāmāvatāram*, the 15th-century *Sanskrit **Adhyātma Rāmāyaṇa*, and, especially, *Tulsīdāsa's 16th-century *Hindi retelling of Vālmīki, the **Rāmcaritmānas*, that Rāma's full theological and cultic preeminence came to the fore. Since then, Rāma's story has been inexhaustibly re-enacted in the *Rāmcaritmānas*-derived *Rāmlīlas of northern India, evidence not just of the great popularity of the god himself, but also of those associated with him, particularly his consort, Sītā, and his greatest devotee, *Hanumān, the monkey-hero of the *Rāmāyaṇa*. It is the latter's devotion which has provided many *bhaktas with a role model for their own practice.

Since the time of Tulsīdāsa (*c.*1543–1623), in particular, Rāma has proved a rich inspiration for artists. Iconographically, a typical depiction shows him as a two-, or sometimes four-armed warrior, wielding the bow he broke in order to win Sītā's hand in *marriage. Reflecting his immense, pan-Indian popularity, there are Rāma *temples across the subcontinent (and an important one to Sītā at *Janakpūr in *Nepal); however, the hero-god's supposed capital and birthplace ('Rāmajanmabhūmi'), *Ayodhyā, remains the focal point for Rāma bhakti organizations, such as the *Rāmānandīs. Recently, the city has become a target for the politicized attention of the *BJP and its satellite organizations, with Rāma coopted as the god of a militant Hindu nationalism. *See also* RĀMĀYAṆA. **2.** Many Hindus, drawing on the practice of the North Indian *sants, use the *Hindi word 'Rām' as an unselfconscious synonym for 'God', even when conceived as the undifferentiated and unqualified *nirguṇa absolute.

Rāma

Rāmadāsa (Rāmdās) (1608–1681) A Maharashtrian poet-saint (*sant) and *Vaiṣṇava religious leader. A *brahmin devotee (dāsa means 'servant') of *Rāma (although he was originally a follower of the *Vārkāri Panth), he founded a series of *temples and *maṭhas across the region. His teachings, notably in the encyclopaedic **Daśabodha*, advocate a militant Hindu nationalism, which appears to have been closely aligned to the *Marāṭhā resistance to *Mughal rule led by King *Śivājī. Rāmadāsa is said to have been the king's *guru, and a rival of the *Sanskrit *paṇḍita, *Gāgābhaṭṭa, who performed the monarch's coronation in 1674. The *sampradāya founded by him, whose members are known as the Rāmadāsīs (Rāmdāsīs), went into decline with the end of the Marāṭhā kingdom in 1817, but has revived again with the rise of post-Independence Maharashtrian nationalism. It is based at Sajjangad, near the city of Satara, south of Pune. Now a Vaiṣṇava *tīrtha, the fort of Sajjangad was gifted to Rāmadāsa by Śivājī, and contains the saint's *samādhi.

Rāmadāsīs *See* RĀMADĀSA.

Rāma Jāmadagnya *See* PARAŚURĀMA.

Rāmakaṇṭha (Bhaṭṭa Rāmakaṇṭha) (*c.*950–1000 CE) An important Kashmirian *Śaiva Siddhānta theologian who wrote commentaries on a number of **Tantras*, including the *Kiraṇa*. His father, Nārāyaṇakaṇṭha, was also a commentator in the school.

rāmakathā ('The Story of Rāma') *See* RĀMĀYAṆA.

Rāmakṛṣṇa (Ramakrishna, 'Rāmakṛṣṇa Paramahaṃsa') (1836–1886) A highly influential Bengali *guru and religious exemplar, frequently described as a 'mystic', because of his assertion, derived from numerous, and diversely inspired, ecstatic experiences, that all religions represent aspects of a single truth. Born into a rural family of poor *Vaiṣṇava *brahmins (as Gadadhar Chatterji), after a minimal education, he moved to Calcutta in 1855, and, alongside his elder brother, became a *priest at the new *Kālī *temple at *Dakṣineśvara. It was there that he showed an increasingly emotional devotion to the *Goddess, culminating in a series of visions and trances which effectively incapacited him for worldly purposes. Thereafter, he lived at the temple as a spiritual practitioner and ascetic. In 1859, his family married him to a five-year-old girl, *Śāradā Devī. Once she was 17, she joined him in Calcutta, where, rather than being a wife in any conventional sense, she acted as his disciple, and he worshipped her as an incarnation of the Goddess. Taking their cue from this, his other followers subsequently revered her as the 'Holy' or 'Divine Mother', Rāmakṛṣṇa's name for Kālī. For some years, under the influence of a female brahmin initiate, he followed a form of *Tantric practice. This was succeeded by a time as the pupil of an *Advaita *saṃnyāsin called Totapuri, under whom he achieved nirvikalpa *samādhi (non-differentiation from *brahman). It was this aspect of their master's experience and teaching which was ultimately taken up by *Vivekānanda and *the *Rāmakṛṣṇa Mission, but Rāmakṛṣṇa himself continued to experience ecstatic trances and visions, notably of *Kṛṣṇa-*Gopāla, Mohammed, and Jesus. The perception that his wide variety of methods all led to the same experience, caused him to conclude that all paths converged on the same goal. He was highly celebrated in Calcutta, where large crowds gathered to see and hear him, and also eventually in the Western world as well. Rāmakṛṣṇa wrote down nothing himself, but his followers recorded many of his sayings and conversations. These later became the basis of texts such as *The Gospel of Ramakrishna*, and he was a catalytic influence on the intellectuals and teachers who came to propound *Neo-Vedānta and other forms of *Neo-Hinduism.

Rāmakṛṣṇa Maṭha (Ramakrishna Matha, Belūr Maṭha) A *temple on the right bank of the Hughli river in Kolkata (Calcutta). It became the headquarters of the *Rāmakṛṣṇa Mission (established 1897), when it moved there from Barangore (also in Calcutta) in 1899.

Rāmakṛṣṇa Mission (Ramakrishna Mission) An influential and socially active, male monastic association, founded in 1897 by *Vivekānanda, with the motto: 'For one's own salvation and for the welfare of the world'. It is named after Vivekānanda's teacher and inspiration, *Rāmakṛṣṇa, and developed out of the monastic Order established by Rāmakṛṣṇa's disciples at his death. Its ideology, however, is very much that of its founder: 'Hinduism' (essentially *Advaita Vedānta) is presented as a world religion, based on what are perceived to be universally valid, and scientifically consonant, ethical principles. This has proved attractive to the educated, English-speaking, middle-classes. For the first 23 years of its existence, the Mission's spiritual head was Rāmakṛṣṇa's wife and consort, *Śāradā Devī, and she, Rāmakṛṣṇa, and Vivekānanda are revered as the 'Holy Trio' of the contemporary Mission. Its headquarters were established at the *Rāmakṛṣṇa Maṭha near Kolkata (Calcutta) in 1899; it has over 100 centres throughout India, engaged in educational, medical, and other charitable work. Centres have also been established around the world, notably in the USA and Brazil.

Rām(a)līlā ('the play of/about Rāma') Any one of a number of annual North Indian *festivals celebrating and performing the 'play' (*līlā), i.e. the story, of *Rāma and *Sītā. Based on the 16th-century *Hindi version given in *Tulsīdāsa's **Rāmcaritmānas*, the sequence of performances may last up to a week, or, in the case of the most elaborate example, held at *Rāmnagar, near *Vārāṇasī, up to a month, and culminate in the death of *Rāvaṇa, and the triumphant return of Rāma. Many seem to have been developed initally by local Hindu *kings (who were identified at some level with Rāma) as a reaction to *Muslim rule, but Rāmlīlās also continued to expand throughout the period of British dominance and beyond (the ex-king of *Benares continues to sponsor the Rāmnagar līla). The characters of both sexes are usually played by non-professionals, typically *brahmin boys or youths, who are regarded as *incarnations of the figures represented—the entire performance being a form of worship. In Bengal, and elsewhere, the Rāmlīlā overlaps and coincides with the tenth day (*Dasara) of the *Navarātrī *Durgā-pūjā festival.

Ramaṇa Maharṣi (1879–1950) A South Indian *guru who acquired a substantial reputation in both India and the West. Born into a family of *brahmins as Venkataraman Aiyar, he had a religious experience at the age of 17, in which the sudden awareness of the essential *immortality of the *self dispelled his fear of *death. Shortly afterwards he went to live as a *saṃnyāsin on Aruṇācala hill near *Tiruvaṇṇāmalai, where he remained for the rest of his life. His followers established an *āśram there, and he began to attract a wide range of visitors, including well-known Westerners, such as the celebrated analytical psychologist, Carl Jung (1875–1961). Ramaṇa Maharṣi's teaching was informal and unsystematic, but his vision was essentially *Advaitin in nature. He was well known for advocating *meditation on the question 'Who am I?', as a means to eventual realization of pure, non-dual *consciousness. His disciples continue to propagate his teachings and to run the āśram; his teaching and approach have influenced a number of Indian and Western 'gurus'.

Rāmānanda (15th century CE?) The name given to a North Indian *Vaiṣṇava teacher, and devotee of *Rāma and *Sītā, who, it is claimed, founded the *Rāmānandī *saṃpradāya. Little or nothing is known about him outside the details given in, frequently incompatible, hagiographies, and modern scholarship suggests that he may not have been an historical figure at all. Among the claims made are that, before founding his own order, he belonged to *Rāmānuja's lineage (*paramparā), and that he was the teacher of well-known low-*caste *sants such as *Kabīr and *Raidāsa. Whether an entirely mythical figure or not, Rāmānanda is a significant figurehead and perceived point of origin for an important North Indian, *Hindi-speaking *bhakti movement.

Rāmānandīs **(Bairāgīs, Rāmāvats)** Members of a North Indian *ascetic *sampradāya which claims *Rāmānanda as its founder. Historically, the movement, which worships (i.e. serves) either *Rāma alone, or *Rāma and *Sītā as a married couple, has multiplied into a number of diverse forms. Initially, at least, it recruited from all *castes and both sexes, but recent studies have shown that it is now essentially a celibate, male organization, supported by an initiated lay following. Among the ascetics there is considerable diversity of practice: those known as tyāgīs ('renouncers'), who may or may not be itinerants, and the even stricter mahātyāgīs ('great renouncers'), smear themselves in *ashes, taking on the outward appearance of *Śaiva ascetics; a subgroup regard themselves as *Nāgas. The other major group (or collection of sects), characterized as rasiks (lit. 'connoisseurs'; H.: 'passionate devotionalists'), live in *temples or monasteries under the direction of a senior *brahmin *ascetic (mahant), who is himself the object of devotion. In what is probably a borrowing from *Kṛṣṇa devotionalism, temple ritual is directed towards assisting the newly married Rāma and Sītā in their love-play, and may involve male devotees dressing as women, in imitation of a feminized *Hanumān. Taken as a whole, the Rāmānandīs are probably the largest and wealthiest ascetic organization in Hindi-speaking northern India. Since the 18th century, they have dominated religious life in *Ayodhyā and *Janakpūr (which they effectively founded as a modern city). A number of prominent North Indian *bhaktas are said to have been Rāmānadīs, most notably *Tulsīdāsa, whose **Rāmcaritmānas* provides the theological and ritual framework for the sampradāya.

Rāma navamī ('the ninth of Rāma') The *festival celebrating the birthday of *Rāma, held on the ninth day of the month of Caitra (March–April). In some areas it is a nine-day festival, coinciding with the spring festivities (*Vasantotsava), or *Holī. The **Rāmcaritmānas* is continuously recited in the days leading up to the festival, and there are *ratha yātrās of Rāma, *Sītā, *Lakṣmaṇa, and *Hanumān, the latter being a particular focus of attention. In modern times, *Ayodhyā has attracted huge crowds for this event.

Rāmānuja (d. 1137, trad. 1017–1137) The third *ācārya (after *Nāthamuni and *Yāmuna) in the South Indian *Śrī Vaiṣṇava tradition, and the leading theologian of *Viśiṣṭādvaita ('non-dualism of the qualified'). According to biographies written some considerable time after Rāmānuja's death, he was born into a *smārta *brahmin family near the modern city of Chennai (in Tamil Nadu). He had a *Vedic education and studied under an *Advaitin teacher, *Yādava Prakāśa, with whom he is supposed to have quarrelled; it is claimed that he immediately succeeded Yāmuna as the leader of the Śrī Vaiṣṇavas. Although this precise sequence of events is unlikely, he did, at some point, renounce and take over both the leadership of the community and the management of the *Śrīraṅgam *temple. The intolerant *Śaiva sectarianism of the local *Cōḷa ruler is said to have driven him north to Karnataka, where he is supposed to have converted the *Jain *Hoysaḷa king to *Vaiṣṇavism. He is also said to have travelled as far north as Kashmir, propagating his teachings and ritual devotionalism across the subcontinent, before eventually returning to Śrīraṅgam, where he died.

Nine works are attributed to Rāmānuja, of which the most influential are his discursive commentary on *Bādarāyaṇa's *Brahmasūtra*, the *Śrībhāṣya*, a summary of his main theological position given in the *Vedārthasaṃgraha*, and a devotional *Bhagavadgītā* commentary, the *(Bhagavad)Gītābhāṣya*. He sets out to demonstrate the truth of his, and therefore of the Śrī Vaiṣṇava, understanding of the *Vedānta (i.e. the **Upaniṣads*), in the process rejecting the *Advaitin stance of *Śaṅkara, and the *nāstika views of the *Buddhists and the *Jains. Rāmānuja maintains that the individual self and *brahman (= God) are not completely identical: rather, individual selves and the material world are both real and at the same time 'modes' (prakāras) of brahman. In this way they are analogous to God's 'body': inhabited by the *Paramātman (= God), they are ultimately dependent upon Him. To attain *mokṣa, it is necessary to practise both ritual and *meditation on the **Veda* (i.e. brahman). *Bhakti, in the form of *prapatti (derived from the devotional tradition of the *Āḻvārs), plays a key role in this soteriology, since, given that *karmic bondage is real, not illusory, liberating *knowledge of brahman can be initiated in the mind of the devotee only by the grace (*prasāda) of God (Paramātman = brahman = *Viṣṇu), who is pleased by the *bhakta's performance of daily ritual and worship. (In other words, complete self-surrender makes the devotee worthy of *karma-destroying divine grace.) In this way, Rāmānuja justifies the (*Pāñcarātra) temple ritual of the Śrī Vaiṣṇavas, while connecting it to Vedic orthodoxy, and so demonstrates to his followers that they are really *Vaidikas (essentially, the *only* true Vaidikas). At the same time, he validates the devotionalism of the *Tamil Āḻvār tradition, and legitimates the ritual recitation of their texts as part of temple worship. For these reasons, he is regarded by all subsequent Śrī Vaiṣṇavas as their most important theologian and teacher, and is considered the effective founder of the Viśiṣṭādvaita school of philosophy.

Ramanujan, Attipat Krishnaswami (A. K. Ramanujan) (1919–1993) A brilliant poet, translator, essayist, and a pioneer of academic interdisciplinarity, Ramanujan was one of the first to open a Western door onto non-Sanskritic South Indian languages, literature, and folklore. Born in Mysore, he was fluent in both *Tamil and *Kannada, although he wrote mostly in English. Initially educated in India, he moved to the USA in 1959; after receiving his PhD in linguistics from Indiana University, he taught mostly in the South Asian Studies programme at the University of Chicago, where in due time he was elected to a Chair. The recipient of numerous awards and prizes, a good number of his most important publications have been collected in *The Collected Essays of A. K. Ramanujan* (OUP: Oxford, 1999) and *The Oxford India Ramanujan* (OUP: New Delhi, 2004). Included in the the latter are his celebrated translations of South Indian *bhakti poetry, such as *Speaking of Śiva* (1st published 1973), a collection of *Liṅgāyat poems.

rāmarājya ('reign of Rāma') On the model of *Rāma's reign, which was viewed as the epitome of *dharmic governance, a time when socio-political and religious conditions conform to an ideal standard. The goal of many Hindu nationalists is to institute such a reign in modern India.

Rāma Rājya Pariṣad *See* KARPĀTRĪJĪ MAHĀRĀJ.

Rāma Tīrtha, Svāmi (1873–1906) A maths teacher who became a *saṃnyāsin and a proponent of *Advaita Vedānta. Born in the Punjab as Gossain Tīrtha Rāma, he had started his religious career as a devotee of *Kṛṣṇa; subsequently, he turned to Vedānta, and was inspired to renounce after seeing *Vivekānanda. Rāma Tīrtha travelled to Japan and the USA, where he attracted a substantial following. His collected writings have been published in several volumes as *In the Woods of God-Realization*. A Mission which takes his name is based at an *āśram in Uttaranchal.

Rāmāvats *See* RĀMĀNANDĪS.

Rāmāyaṇa ('The Adventures of Rāma') In the form attributed to the legendary sage *Vālmīki, one of two great *Sanskrit *Epics (the other being the **Mahābhārata*), a narrative poem of approximately 25 000 *ślokas (couplets), divided into seven books (kāṇḍas). The text as we now have it seems to have developed over a long and complex period of oral composition, starting *c.*500 BCE. By the early centuries CE, this telling of 'The Story of *Rāma' (rāmakathā), which is generally thought to have provided the literary template for the profusion of later tellings (whether in Sanskrit, or in one of a huge number of vernaculars), had permeated the subcontinent in a considerable variety of oral and written versions. The extant variations have been grouped into northern and southern recensions, showing considerable differences in detail and expression; however, Vālmīki's basic narrative is clear. A highly condensed summary is as follows:

Book 1: *Bālakāṇḍa* ('The Childhood Book'). Like the final kāṇḍa, this is usually thought to be a later addition to the main text, intended to frame the narrative and shape the way in which it is read. Vālmīki himself is established as the original poet (ādikavi), and the *Rāmāyaṇa* as the first epic poem (ādikāvya). Rāma's pedigree as an exemplary, not to say perfect man, and as an *avatāra of *Viṣṇu is established. Miraculously born into the *Solar Dynasty at *Ayodhyā, as the eldest of King *Daśaratha's four sons, Rāma goes through various initiatory adventures, culminating in his breaking *Śiva's bow, and thus winning the hand of *Sītā.

Book 2: *Ayodhyākāṇḍa* ('The Ayodhyā Book'). The ageing Daśaratha decides to consecrate Rāma as the heir apparent. At the instigation of her servant, the king's second wife, *Kaikeyī intervenes, forcing her husband, in fulfilment of a vow, to exile Rāma to the *forest for fourteen years, and install her own son, Rāma's half-brother, *Bharata (3), in his place. Acceding without protest to his father's wish, Rāma sets out for the wilderness, accompanied, at their own insistence, by Sītā and his brother *Lakṣmaṇa. Daśaratha dies; Bharata, returning to Ayodhyā, wants to give the throne up to Rāma, but the latter refuses, wishing to follow his father's instructions to the letter. Bharata places Rāma's sandals on the throne, and acts as regent during his brother's exile.

Book 3: *Araṇyakāṇḍā* ('The Wilderness/Forest Book'). Rāma and his party move deep into the *Daṇḍaka Forest. He becomes involved in protecting the *ascetics living there from fearsome *rākṣasas, among them *Śūrpaṇakhā, the sister of the ten-headed rākṣasa king, *Rāvaṇa. In revenge for her mutilation by Lakṣmaṇa, Śūrpaṇakhā incites Rāvaṇa to abduct Sītā and carry her off to the island of *Laṅkā. Rāma and Lakṣmaṇa search for her, to no avail.

Book 4: *Kiṣkindhākāṇḍa* ('The Kiṣkindhā Book'). Rāma and Lakṣmaṇa meet *Sugrīva, the *Vānara (monkey-) king, who has been exiled from his capital, Kiṣkindhā, by his brother, *Vālin. They help him to regain his throne; in return he helps them to trace Sītā. Discovering that she is being held somewhere in Laṅkā, Sūgrīva's minister, *Hanumān, who is capable of leaping the ocean, sets out to contact her.

Book 5: *Sundarakāṇḍa* ('The Beautiful Book'). Eventually discovering the disconsolate Sītā, who is still holding out against Rāvaṇa's threatening advances, Hanumān reveals himself by presenting her with Rāma's signet ring. He offers to carry her home, but she prefers to be rescued by her husband alone. She gives Hanumān a jewel to present to Rāma, but, instead of returning with it immediately, he lays waste to Laṅkā. In this he is unwittingly assisted by Rāvaṇa, who, in setting fire to his tail, provides him with a brand to complete the destruction. Leaping the ocean again, and returning to Kiṣkindhā, he reports his success to Rāma and the others.

Book 6: *Yuddhakāṇḍa* ('The War Book') (alternatively, *Laṅkākāṇḍa*—'The Book of Laṅkā'). Rāma and his army of monkeys build a causeway to Laṅkā, where they lay siege to Rāvaṇa's stronghold. A lengthy see-saw battle ensues, described in great detail; by the end of it all the rākṣasas have been killed, including, at the last, Rāvaṇa at the hands of Rāma himself. At this point, Rāma rejects Sītā, suggesting that she may have been sullied by her stay in another man's house. He fought not for her, but for honour. Despairing, Sītā demonstrates her virtue by immolating herself on a pyre. The gods intervene, and Rāma receives her back; he had never doubted her himself, but her fidelity had to be proven in public. They all fly back to Ayodhyā in Rāvaṇa's chariot, and, having fulfilled his duty to his father, Rāma is installed as king.

Book 7: *Uttarakāṇḍa* ('The Last Book'/'The Book of Further Adventures'). A period of married bliss is undermined by rumours in Ayodhyā that Sītā may have been violated by Rāvaṇa during her captivity. To avoid this casting doubt on his honour, or undermining his status as a perfect *king, Rāma orders Lakṣmaṇa to abandon the queen in the forest. There, in Vālmīki's hermitage, she gives birth to Rāma's twin sons, *Lava and *Kuśa. Vālmīki teaches them the text of the *Rāmāyaṇa*, which they recite to Rāma himself during a horse sacrifice (*aśvamedha). Rāma recalls Sītā from the forest. When urged once again to affirm her fidelity in public, Sītā calls on her mother, the Earth (*Bhū Devī) to witness her *purity of thought and action by swallowing her up. This duly happens, and Rāma is left in a frenzy, from which he only recovers when reminded by *Brahmā that he is none other than Viṣṇu himself. After ruling for many years, he divides up his kingdom between his sons, enters the river Sarayū, and ascends to *heaven as the god that he really is.

Vālmīki's poem contains the earliest surviving version of 'The Story of Rāma' (rāmakathā), and it serves as a model for many of the versions which follow, but by no stretch of the imagination is it the only, or, for any given audience, necessarily the most significant telling of the tale. A. K. *Ramanujan asked a now celebrated question—'How many *Rāmāyaṇas*? Three hundred? Three thousand?'—in order to draw attention to the fact that, throughout South, Southeast, and East Asia, there have been multiple tellings and retellings of this particular narrative for two-and-a-half thousand years or more, making it one of the best-known, best-loved, and most widely disseminated stories in the history of the world, although much of the West remains oblivious to it. Every one of these tellings or enactments has, to a greater or lesser extent, shaped the text to its own ends, often providing revisionist versions which run counter to Vālmīki and the norms of *Brahmanical *dharma. Indeed, some tellings, such as those of the *Jains, have been reformulations or reversals from the perspective of an entirely different religious tradition. The most widely disseminated and influential version in India is probably *Tulsīdāsa's 16th-century Hindi retelling of Vālmīki, the **Rāmcaritmānas*, which turned the story into a fully fledged *bhakti text, and provided the basis for the extraordinarily popular *Rāmlīla reenactments. Other important versions include the 12th-century *Tamil **Irāmāvatāram*, and the 15th-century Sanskrit **Adhyātma Rāmāyaṇa*. One of the most recent retellings was a sensationally popular, although, for some scholars, controversial (because it threatened to homogenize and supersede all other versions) Indian television serialization in the late 1980s.

Rāmcaritmānas (***Rāmacaritamānasā, Ramacharitamanasa***) ('The Lake of Rāma's Deeds', 16th century) A poetic retelling by *Tulsīdās(a) of *Vālmīki's **Rāmāyaṇa* (as filtered through the **Adhyātma* and **Bhuśuṇḍi Rāmāyaṇas*) in the eastern dialect of *Hindi known as Avadhī. Tulsīdāsa is said to have begun his poem of over 10 000 lines in *Ayodhyā in 1574, and completed it several years later in *Vārāṇasī. By turning the account of *Rāma's actions into a fully fledged *bhakti text, Tulsīdāsa produced what quickly became the most widely disseminated, popular, and influential version of the story in northern India, in the process determining the whole character of late medieval and modern devotionalism in the area. Throughout the poem, Rāma's identity as the supreme deity, his *dharmic and kingly perfection, and his gracious attitude to his subjects, are continually to the fore; all the other characters, including, in the end, *Rāvaṇa, become his devotees, in an exemplary display of the only feasible reaction to such royal divinity. The ideal devotee in this respect, and the model for all human *bhaktas, is Rāma's humble monkey-servant, *Hanumān. Above all, it is hearing and repeating Rāma's name ('Rām' in Hindi) which saves. For the audience, the poem itself is therefore instrumental in their *liberation (it is widely regarded as the 'Hindi **Veda*'), as are the extraordinarily popular, *Rāmcaritmānas*-derived, *Rāmlīla re-enactments of northern India. Tulsidāsa's emphasis on the maintenance of essentially *Brahmanical *dharma, and conformity to the norms of social *purity (e.g. in his treatment of *Sītā), mark him out from the frequently more antinomian poets of the *Kṛṣṇa bhakti movements, although the inclusivism of the text, and the variety of its source material, allow for various counter readings.

Rāmdās *See* RĀMADĀSA.

Rāmdāsīs *See* RĀMADĀSA.

Ram Dass *See* BHAGAVAN DAS.

Rāmeśvaram ('Lord Rāma') A major *tīrthā situated on an island off the coast of Tamil Nadu, opposite Sri Lanka. Connected to the mainland by a causeway, it is supposed to mark the place where *Rāma, after crossing back from Sri Lanka, did *pūjā before a *Śiva *liṅga in order to purify himself for the killing of *Rāvaṇa. The liṅga is housed in the 17th-century Rāmaliṅgeśvara *temple complex, mostly built during the *Nayaka period. A smaller temple holds Rāma's footprint; there is also a place where he is supposed to have bathed. Rāmeśvaram is counted as one of the four *dhāmas, or 'dwelling places'.

Rāmmohun Roy *See* ROY, RĀMMOHUN.

rāmnām (H.: 'the name of Rāma', 'God's name') The constant repetition of the name of *Rām(a), employed by some *Vaiṣṇava *bhakti sects as a devotional practice and a means to *liberation.

Rāmnāmīs Members of a politically and socially influential *Rāma *bhakti movement (the Rāmnāmi Samāj), composed of *Harijans (*untouchables), living in the central Indian state of Chhattisgarh (before 2000 CE a region of Madhya Pradesh). The Samāj was founded in the 1890s by an illiterate untouchable leather-worker (*camār) called Parasurām, who was devoted to the **Rāmcaritmānas*, and especially to the practice of *rāmnām, the constant repetition of Rāma's name. This, and the recitation of other verses from the *Rāmcaritmānas*, takes place in the Rāmnāmīs' group *bhajans, and at their annual *melā. They inscribe the *mantra on their clothes, the walls of their homes, and tattoo it on their bodies (a practice viewed as sacrilegious by higher *caste devotees of Rāma). A distinctive peacock-feather headdress may also be worn during recitations. Over time, the Rāmnāmīs have developed their own telling of the 'story of Rāma', edited from the *Rāmcaritmānas* to remove the *Brahmanical elements from the narrative. Their existence as a unique group now appears to be under threat from diminishing recruitment.

Rāmopākhyāna ('The Story of Rāma') The name given to the version of the *Rāma narrative told in the **Āraṇyakaparvan* of the **Mahābhārata*. Most current scholarship believes it to have been derived from a memorized version of the story drawn from the northern recension of the **Rāmāyaṇa* prior to the completion of that text as we now have it. It differs in several respects from the *Rāmāyaṇa*, notably in its treatment of Rāma as a human hero, and in the absence of either *Sītā's banishment after the return to *Ayodhyā, or her final disappearance into the earth.

Rāmprasād Sen (*c.*1718–1775) One of the originators of the Bengali tradition of *Śākta poetry, known as *śākta padāvalī, and its best-known exponent. Nothing is known of his life beyond later hagiography (the first biography appeared in 1853), although he seems to have lived just north of Kolkata (Calcutta). Over 300 poems addressed to *Kālī as the terrifying, bloodthirsty, and unpredictable mother goddess, are attributed to him. Recent analysis suggests that his work is essentially *Tantric and monistic in character, although it also contains seeds of the *bhakti religion which provided its appeal for many 19th- and early 20th-century commentators.

Ranade, Mahadev Govind (1842–1901) A historian, social and economic reformer, and High Court Judge in Bombay (Mumbai). The most influential leader of the *Prārthanā Samāj ('Prayer Society'), he campaigned for the abolition of *child marriage, the rights of widows (and of women more generally), and an end to *caste discrimination. His work was continued by G. K. *Gokhale, and others.

Raṅganātha ('Lord of Raṅgam', 'Lord of the Stage', 'Lord of the Island') The name given to the *arcā, or form of *Viṣṇu, in the *temple at *Śrīraṅgam in Tamil Nadu, where he is depicted asleep on the cosmic serpent, *Śeṣa. A smaller, upright *image of the god is used for processions.

rasa ('flavour', 'savour', 'juice', 'aesthetic experience') A term originating in aesthetic theory (an early discussion is in *Bharata's **Nāṭyaśāstra*), where it designates an impersonal and universalized experience, or 'mood', of joy and bliss, which is created in an audience out of the principal emotions (*bhāvas (1)) evoked in a drama. Although rasa in itself is a single, ineffable experience of entrancement or aesthetic rapture, it is subdivided for analytical purposes according to the principal feelings which evoke it. There are said to be eight such emotions—love (rati), laughter (hāsa), sorrow (śoka), energy (utsāha), anger (krodha), fear (bhaya), disgust (jugupsā), and amazement (vismaya)—which engender eight corresponding rasa—the erotic (śṛṅgāra), comic (hāsya), pathetic (karuṇa), heroic (vīra), furious (raudra), fearful (bhayānaka), grotesque (bībhatsa), and wondrous (adbhuta). Through his commentary on *Nāṭyaśāstra*, *Abhinavagupta developed a sophisticated theory of aesthetics which regarded rasa as a distinct mode of experience situated between ordinary awareness and enlightenment, although it differs from the latter only in degree. The concept was also imported into the *bhakti environment of *Gauḍīya, and other *Vaiṣṇava devotional movements, where the *bhāva (2) of erotic love, such as that experienced by the *gopīs and *Rādhā, is thought to be salvific when experienced through the associated rasa of pure bliss.

rās(a) līlā ('dance pastime') **1.** Narrowly, *Kṛṣṇa's dance (rāsa) with the *gopīs, described in the **Bhāgavata Purāṇa* (10.33). The women dance in a circle; Kṛṣṇa inserts himself between each pair, so that each individual supposes that he is attending to her alone. For many *Vaiṣṇava *bhakti traditions, this typifies the individual's relationship to God, an experience intensified through various *meditation and visualization practices focused on the rāsa līlā. More widely, the term rāsa līlā refers to the full extent of Kṛṣṇa's divine play (*līlā) with the gopīs—their love, union, incomprehensible separation, and reunion—described in the *Bhāgavata Purāṇa* (10.29–33). In both the narrower and wider senses of the term, rāsa līlā has been a favourite subject for visual artists.

2. (Rāsalīlā) A North and Eastern Indian, ritualized devotional performance, using words, music, dance, and tableaux to enact Kṛṣṇa's early life in *Braj. In the tradition issuing from Braj itself, the material (which is far more extensive than just the rāsa dance which lies at its centre) is performed by troupes of pre-pubescent boys, who now tour India throughout the year. Another notable tradition is that of the complex and elaborate seasonal Rāsalīlas established in Manipur in 1779 by King Chingthangkhomba (Bhagyacandra) (1763–1798)—a synthesis of local practices and *Gauḍīya Vaiṣṇavism, derived from the five chapters on rāsa in the *Bhāgavata Purāṇa* (10.29–33). *See also* LĪLĀ.

rasāyana *See* ALCHEMY.

Rāṣṭrakūṭa The name of a dynasty which ruled the Western and Central Deccan from *c.*750 to 973 CE.

Rāṣṭrīya Svayamsevak Saṅgh(a) (RSS) ('National Volunteer Association') A militant, right-wing Hindu nationalist organization, founded in 1925 by K. B. *Hedgewar, and developed ideologically by Madhav Sadashiv *Golwalkar. Most influential among upper *caste Maharashtrians, it was modelled on the 17th- and 18th-century warrior *ascetic orders, such as the *Ākhāṛās, and organized on paramilitary lines. *Gāndhī's assassin, Nathuram Godse, was a member. It has occasionally been banned, but currently has a membership of over five million, and is the parent organization for a number of other radical groups. It describes itself as a 'cultural' movement rather than a political party.

rasik *See* RĀMĀNANDĪS.

ratha-yātrā ('chariot procession', a ratha-melā—'chariot festival') The procession of a *Vaiṣṇava *image on a wooden chariot (ratha), usually with solid wooden wheels and an architecturally elaborate superstructure. The most celebrated example of a ratha-yātrā is the annual *festival of *Jagannātha, during which a 16-wheeled, 14-metre high, *temple-shaped vehicle is used to pull the image of *Jagannātha through the streets of *Purī.

Rati *See* KĀMA(DEVA).

Rātrī ('night') A *Vedic goddess personifying night; the complementary opposite of *Uṣas, the goddess of the Dawn.

Raudra A follower of the *Śaiva *atimārga, so-called because he identifies with Śiva in his wild and terrible form of *Rudra, the outsider at the *Vedic sacrifice (*yajña).

Rāvaṇa (Daśakaṇṭha, Daśānana ('ten-necked')**)** In the **Rāmāyaṇa*, and other versions of the *Rāma story, the anti-heroic, ten-headed, twenty-armed, lord of the *rākṣasas, who abducts *Sītā and carries her off to his kingdom of *Laṅkā. At the last, he is killed by Rāma. Various stories are told of his origins and character.

He is said to have been a *brahmin, who acquired his power through great austerities (*tapas), and was granted invulnerability (but not from a god in human form). He ousted his half-brother, *Kubera, from the throne of Laṅkā. Renowned for his lust, he does not, however, violate Sītā. Although the epitome of *adharma, for that very reason (i.e. because he opposes *Brahmanical *dharma) Rāvaṇa has become an heroic figure for some, particularly in South India, and among *outcastes.

Ravidās(a) *See* RAIDĀS(A).

ṛc ('praise') A *Vedic verse recited in praise of a deity. *See also* ṚG VEDA.

ṛddhi(s) *See* SIDDHI(S).

rebirth (punar-janman) As a cyclical process, a corollary of *karma doctrine, although the idea probably had independent origins, based on the observation of natural phenomena. It first appears in textual form in the **Bṛhadāraṇyaka Upaniṣad* (Chs. 4, 6) and **Chāndogya Upaniṣad* (Chs. 4, 5). Under the influence of *renouncer ideologies, rebirth comes to be equated with suffering, and both suffering and rebirth (the cycle of *saṃsāra) will continue unless the individual can intervene in the process. Rebirth thus provides a negative contrast to the renouncer's ultimate goal of liberation (*mokṣa), which brings a permanent end to *death, rebirth, and (in many cases) embodiment (i.e. reincarnation). With the development of elaborate *cosmologies, the refinement of karma doctrine, and the need to accommodate *householder aspirations, some rebirth states are portrayed as relatively better than others. It therefore becomes possible to aspire to a better, or a 'good' rebirth—even a rebirth in one of the *heavens—on the understanding that this state will not last forever, and that only mokṣa can bring permanent release. With the rise of *bhakti movements, this idea is further modified, so that, for some, only rebirth as an inhabitant of the deity's heaven (perhaps through the *grace of the deity itself) will bring a permanent end to the cycle. A common signifier of an individual's *yogic or spiritual power is the ability to remember his or her previous births, an attainment not normally given to ordinary individuals. *See also* KARMA; DEVAYĀNA; PITṚYĀNA.

Recognition School *See* PRATYABHIJÑĀ.

redeath *See* PUNAR-MṚTYU.

reincarnation *See* REBIRTH.

Renou, Louis (1896–1966) A great and influential French *Indologist, Renou held the chair in *Sanskrit at the University of the Sorbonne, Paris, where he worked on a wide variety of topics, particularly in the field of *Vedic studies. His many publications include: *L'Inde classique: manuel des études indiennes* (in 2 vols. with Jean Filliozat, Paris: 1949–53); an edition and translation into French of *Pāṇini's **Aṣṭādhyāyī* (Paris: 1966), and *Études védiques et paninéennes* (2 vols., Paris: 1980, 1986).

renouncer (renunciant) At its most inclusive, an English term used to designate anyone who has given up the householder (*gṛhastha) life, and the values associated with it (encapsulated for the *twice-born in the three '*debts'), in order to pursue personal *liberation. The term may be used synonymously with *saṃnyāsin, i.e. someone who has formally taken renunciation (*saṃnyāsa).

Reṇukā According to the **Purāṇas* and the **Mahābhārata*, the wife of *Jamadagni and the mother of *Paraśurāma; the latter beheads her to prove his obedience to his father, but then brings her back to life.

renunciant *See* RENOUNCER.

renunciation *See* SAṂNYĀSA.

revelation A term variously applied to designate an absolutely authoritative, infallible text, prototypically the 'unauthored' (*apauruṣeya) *Veda (i.e. *śruti), but also any text (e.g. a *Tantra) thought to have been revealed by the supreme deity of that particular tradition.

Ṛg Veda ('The *Veda*/Knowledge Consisting of Praise Verses') The first and earliest of the *Vedic *saṃhitās, comprising 1 028 hymns (= 10 000 verses), made up of praise verses (*ṛc) addressed to the *devas as a component part of the sacrificial ritual. The hymns (*sūktas) are oral works dating from between c.1700 BCE and c.1200–1000 BCE. They were composed, in a style and language (Old *Indo-Āryan or *Vedic) that was probably already deliberately archaic, by members of families, or clans of poets (in the core books, chiefly the *Āṅgirasas and *Kāṇvas), in the Greater Punjab area of northwestern India and Afghanistan. (The most frequently invoked deva is the thunderbolt-wielding, *Āryan warrior-king, *Indra.) The vast majority of these hymns were first put into an orally transmitted *saṃhitā* collection, arranged into ten *maṇḍalas, or 'books', possibly around 1200 BCE. This, the only surviving recension of the *Ṛg Veda Saṃhitā* (transmitted as the *Śākala *śākhā), contains a core of relatively early material (books two to eight, plus parts of book one), the 120 hymns that accompany the *Soma ritual of the somewhat later book nine, and the relatively late book ten (plus the rest of book one). Apart from the ritual material, which predominates (reflected in the frequent invocation of the devas *Agni and Soma), the hymns contain allusive and highly poetical references to the social environment, to a complex, ritually congruent mythology, and, particularly in the later books, to speculations about the nature of the cosmos and the individual's place in it (in, for example, the celebrated *Puruṣasūkta). An important assumption underlying the poetry of the *Ṛg Veda* is that, through the formulae of the hymns (referred to as *brahman) and their associated ritual, it verbalizes, and so actualizes, the power, or truth, known as *ṛta, which actively informs and orders the universe.

As employed in the *Brahmanical tradition, alongside the *Yajur-* and *Sāma-Vedas*, the *Ṛg Veda*'s significance lies entirely in its mantric power as the driving force of the ritual—prototypically in the *mantras recited by the *hotṛ at the *śrauta sacrifice. Indeed, for the *Mīmāṃsaka exegetes, all the apparent descriptive or discursive content of the hymns is merely *arthavāda, designed to shore up the sacrificer's performance. More widely, the tradition regards the entire 'Triple' or 'Fourfold Veda' as *śruti, unauthored (*apauruṣeya) *revelation. The poets of the *Ṛg Veda* are therefore not 'authors' or originators in the modern sense, but, in a reflection of what appears to be their own assessment, inspired transmitters or 'seers' (*ṛṣis) of an eternal, if enigmatic truth. *See also* AGNI; COSMOGONY; DEVA; INDRA; ṚTA; SOMA; VEDA(S).

'right-handed path/practice' *See* DAKṢIṆĀCĀRA.

Rishikesh *See* HṚṢĪKEŚ(A).

rites of passage *See* SAṂSKĀRAS.

rivers All subcontinental rivers are considered to be sacred, but seven are usually listed as being particularly so: the *Gaṅgā, *Godāvarī, *Indus, *Kāverī, *Narmadā, *Sarasvatī, and *Yamunā.

Ṛk Saṃhitā The *Ṛg Veda* (*ṛc being sounded and written ṛk before 's', and ṛg before 'V').

ṛṇa(s) *See* DEBT(S).

Romaharṣaṇa One of the names of the *sūta who is said, in the *Purāṇas* and elsewhere, to have been the immediate pupil of the legendary *Vyāsa.

Roy, Rāmmohun (**Rām Mohan**, etc.) (1772–1833) A Bengali intellectual, Roy was an exceptional social and religious reformer, who founded the first modern Hindu reform movement, the *Brāhmo Samāj. Born into a *Vaiṣṇava *brahmin family, he was educated in Arabic and Persian, the usual preparation for Hindus entering the administrative service of the *Mughal Empire and its successor states. Crucially for his later development, this education brought him into contact with the philosophy of the Mutazila rationalists. His first published work was a treatise written in Persian, 'A Gift to Monotheists' (1803), in which he argues for a monotheism based on reason and morality—one which rejects what he saw as the superstitious 'excrescences' of all religions currently practised.

One of the first Indians to be employed by the *East India Company, Roy worked in the Bengal Civil Service from 1803 to 1815. Thereafter, he settled in Calcutta (Kolkata) and devoted himself to promoting reform through various publications in Bengali, Persian, and English, and through public debate, notably with the Baptist missionary, Joshua Marshman (1768–1837). It was the latter encounter, sparked by Roy's publication of *The Precepts of Jesus* (1820), an anti-Trinitarian anthology of *Christian ethical teachings, which helped Roy to propagate what he considered to be the true, ethical Hinduism, shorn of its superstitious and idolatrous practices (*pūjā and *temple ritual), and returned to its pure, monotheistic origins, as represented in his reading of the *Sanskrit **Upaniṣads* and other *Vedānta aligned texts. In this approach he connected himself to Western scientific Rationalism, notably in the form of the strictly monotheistic, 'Christian' dissenting movement, Utilitarianism. It was the latter's form of worship which provided the model for the *Brahmo Sabhā (subsequently known as the Brāhmo Samāj). This Society, founded by Roy in Calcutta in 1828, became the principal vehicle for spreading his ideas to an educated and influential elite throughout the subcontinent.

Alongside his theological agenda, Roy aimed to reform those social practices he saw as concomitant with 'idol worship' and polytheism. Widow immolation (*satī), polygyny, *child marriage, infanticide, caste discrimination, and restrictions on female education were all subject to his criticism and active campaigning. Many credit him as being largely instrumental in the British outlawing of widow immolation in 1829. This, however, brought him into conflict with Hindu traditionalists, and it was during a visit to Britain in 1833, one object of which was to oppose their petition to have the ban reversed, that Roy died in Bristol.

Because of his articulate and sophisticated argument for the essential ethical and rational parity of India and the West (and often, in practice, for the former's superiority), Roy has been characterized by some as 'the father of modern India'. In his assertions that, in essence, all religions are (or should be) the same in their worship of one Supreme Being, and that a reformed, Vedānticized Hinduism was the epitome of such a universal religion, he provided the model for a particularly influential response to Western religion and culture. Through the work of the Brāhmo Samāj and similar organizations, and the influence of such teachers as *Vivekānanda, *Aurobindo Ghose, *Gāndhī, and *Radhkrishnan, this stance came to be regarded by many,

Rāmmohun Roy

particularly in the West, as the new Hindu orthodoxy.

Royal Asiatic Society A Society, founded in London in 1823 by the British *Sanskrit scholar Henry *Colebrooke, for (in the words of its charter) 'the investigation of subjects connected with and for the encouragement of science, literature and the arts in relation to Asia'. It is affiliated to associate societies in Kolkata, Mumbai, Bangalore, Chennai, Bihar, and elsewhere in Asia. It has published a *Journal* since 1834, holds regular seminars and lectures, and houses an extensive library, including a collection of *Sanskrit manuscripts.

ṛṣi(s) ('seer(s)') Ancient seer-poets, or 'sages', to whom the hymns of the **Ṛg Veda* were said to have been revealed. According to *Brahmanical theology, they constitute the third group, alongside the *pitṛs and the *devas, to whom a *debt (in the ṛṣis' case, *Vedic studentship) is owed by all *twice-born men. They appear in the **Veda*, and especially in the *Epics and **Purāṇas* in various groupings, such as the legendary, but variously identified, 'seven seers' (the saptarṣis, also known as the *maharṣis), and the brahmarṣis or 'brahminical sages'. The word is also used in various other compounds, such as rāja(ṛṣi), 'a sage who is a *king', and deva(ṛṣi), 'a divine seer'. More generally, the term may be applied to any ancient sage. In Epic and Purāṇic sources, such ṛṣis make frequent appearances as powerful and sometimes irascible figures, renowned for the intensity of a *tapas which threatens the gods.

RSS *See* RĀṢṬRĪYA SVAYAMSEVAK SAṄGH(A).

Ṛṣyaśṛṅga ('antelope-horned') A legendary *ṛṣi said to have been born of a deer, hence the horn on his head. He officiated at the *sacrifice, sponsored by *Daśaratha, which gave rise to the birth of *Rāma.

ṛta ('divine/cosmic law', 'force of truth, or order') A term occurring in the **Ṛg Veda*, indicating the inherent active power, or truth, which informs and orders the universe and human society. Ṛta therefore underscores all proper cosmic, moral, and ritual activity. It is activated and maintained by the *devas, especially *Mitra and *Varuṇa, and through the verbal formulae employed in the sacrificial ritual (*yajña). Part of what it expresses is the dynamic, but integrated and interdependent nature of all phenomena. It therefore prefigures aspects of later conceptions such as the **Upaniṣadic* *brahman (neut.) and, in particular, *dharma. The latter term, which in the *Ṛg Veda* refers to those (predominantly ritual) actions and laws which maintain ṛta, later becomes synonymous with the underlying order itself, as well as activities which express and maintain it. *See also* ANṚTA.

ṛtvik (ṛtvij) The collective term for the *priests who perform the *Vedic *śrauta sacrifices. They are usually divided into four groups: *advaryus, *brahmans (masc. (1)), *hotṛs, and *udgātṛs.

Rudi *See* NITYĀNANDA INSTITUTE.

Rudra ('Roarer', 'Howler') A *Vedic storm god and father of the Rudras (*Maruts). Subsequently, Rudra is the name given to the wild and terrible form of *Śiva (sometimes referred to as 'Rudra-Śiva'). In the **Ṛg Veda* (where only three hymns are addressed to him directly), Rudra is associated with *Indra and *Agni in their destructive aspects, and with destruction and *death in general. He is described as brown and long-haired, living beyond the *Āryan pale. His epithet, 'śiva' ('benign'), is, however, ambiguous: on the one hand it appears to be euphemistic, insofar as he is considered *inauspicious and excluded from the sacrificial enclosure, on the other hand it reflects his association with healing and medicinal herbs, and his lordship, as *Paśupati, over everything that lives. In the **Śvetāśvatara Upaniṣad* (3.2ff.), Rudra is identified as the supreme, omnipotent

God, and thereafter Rudra and Śiva are usually assumed to be one and the same deity. The early *Śaiva *Pāśupata tradition establishes the pattern by which Rudra comes to represent Śiva's wilder, fiercer, and more esoteric aspects, those connected with the *impurities of *death and the culture of the *cremation ground. It is with this outsider persona that the *Raudras of the *atimārga identify. *See also* KĀLĀMUKHA; LĀKULA.

Rudra-Āgamas *See* ĀGAMA(S).

rudrākṣa ('Rudra-eyed') A berry (from a shrub of the same name) favoured by *Śaivas in the making of rosaries (*mālās).

Rudrānanda, Swami (Swami Rudi) (1928–1973) *See* NITYĀNANDA INSTITUTE.

Rudras *See* MARUTS.

Rudrasampradāya *See* VIṢṆUSVĀMIN.

Rukmiṇī In the **Mahābhārata* one of *Kṛṣṇa's favourite wives, and the mother of his son, *Pradyumna. Kṛṣṇa abducted her from her *asura brother, Rukmin. She is integrated into wider *Vaiṣṇava mythology as an incarnation of *Lakṣmī.

rūpa ('form') The term given to iconic images to distinguish them from aniconic (arūpa) forms. *See also* NĀMARŪPA.

S

Śabara (Svāmin) (*c.*3rd–6th centuries CE, trad. 1st century CE) Author of the *Śābarabhāṣya* or *Bhāṣya*, the earliest extant commentary on *Jaimini's (*Pūrva-*) *Mīmāṃsā Sūtra*, and one of the most important *Mīmāṃsaka texts. It provides the basis for the two further commentaries, by *Kumārila Bhaṭṭa and *Prabhākara (both 7th century CE), which establish the two main Mīmāṃsaka schools.

Śābarabhāṣya *See* ŚABARA (SVĀMIN).

Sabarimala(i) A *pilgrimage site in the western *ghāṭs of Kerala. The focus of attention is the *temple dedicated to *Aiyappaṉ. Devotees undertake an annual (November–January), 41-day pilgrimage, for the duration of which they should act like *renouncers. Participation is open to males (of all *castes), and to females who are prepubescent or postmenopausal.

śabda 1. ('word', 'sound', 'speech', 'language') A term that may signify both conventional speech or language, and the eternal, primeval sound (synonymous with *oṃ.), which, according to some thinkers, underlies all reality. *See also* ŚABDA-BRAHMAN. **2. (śabda-pramāṇa)** ('authoritative verbal testimony') A means of valid knowledge (*pramāṇa) recognized by the six schools of philosophy (*darśanas).

śabda-brahman ('word-brahman', 'word-essence') A concept which appears in (e.g.) the **Maitrāyaṇī Upaniṣad* (6.22) and in *Mīmāṃsaka thought, but finds its most sophisticated development in the work of the *grammarian *Bhartṛhari (1), according to whom the śabda-brahman (the 'eternal verbum' or 'word-essence') is the single principle and ultimate reality out of which the entire universe has evolved. See also BHARTṚHARI (1).

Sabhāparvan ('The Assembly Hall') Book 2 of the *Sanskrit **Mahābhārata*, during which *Yudhiṣṭhira performs a *rājasūya. He subsequently loses everything, including his brothers and himself in a rigged dicing match, organized by *Duryodhana. *Draupadī is humiliated by the *Kauravas, but obtains the *Pāṇḍavas' freedom. They are exiled to the *forest for twelve years, with a thirteenth year to be spent incognito if they are to regain their kingdom.

saccidānanda ('being, consciousness, and bliss') In *Advaita Vedānta, a term composed of three elements *sat ('being'), cit (*consciousness), and *ānanda ('bliss'), conveying the spiritual and unitary character of the absolute (*brahman (neut.)).

Śacī *See* INDRĀṆĪ.

***Sacred Books of the East* (*SBE*)** An influential 49-volume series of 19th-century translations of religious texts into English (still in print), produced for the Clarendon Press, Oxford, between 1879 and 1904. Begun under the editorship of Max *Müller, nearly half the volumes are taken up with Hindu works, notably: selected **Upaniṣads* (trans. Müller), the **Dharma Sūtras* ('The Sacred Laws of the Āryas', trans. *Bühler), the **Śatapatha Brāhmaṇa* (trans. *Eggeling), **Manusmṛti* ('The Laws of Manu', trans. Bühler), and the **Vedānta Sūtras* with the commentaries of *Śaṅkara and *Rāmānuja (both trans. *Thibaut), as well as some *Vedic hymns (trans. *Oldenberg).

sacred syllable *See* OṂ.

sacred thread (yajñopavīta, pavitra, H.: **janëu)** A 'sacrificial' cord with which males of the first three *varṇa are invested at *upanayana. The thin, knotted cord is passed over the head, and is thereafter normally worn suspended over the left shoulder and looped loosely beneath the right arm (the upavīta mode). When performing *śrāddha rites, however, the cord is slung in the opposite direction, over the right shoulder (the prācīnāvīta mode). And when taking part in *impure actions, or excretion and sexual acts, it should be looped around the neck alone (the nivīta mode). According to **Manusmṛti* (2.44), the cord for a *brahmin should be made with a triple strand of twisted cotton thread, for a *kṣatriya with hemp, and for a *vaiśya with woollen strands; each strand is itself to be made up of nine separate threads. Early references in the **Brāhmaṇas* and **Āraṇyakas* suggest that the ritual function of the upavīta was served by special clothing, such as a strip of antelope skin or cloth worn during the sacrifice (*yajña), and then put aside. Similarly, references to the yajñopavīta in various **Dharmasūtra* passages, are interpreted as prescribing a particular way of wearing an upper garment, rather than a dedicated cord as such. Over time, however, the (often continuous) wearing of a cord, or 'sacred thread', came to be considered a symbol of *twice-born status and, in particular, a prerogative of initiated *brahmins.

sacrifice *See* YAJÑA.

Sadānanda 1. (15th century CE) Author of the *Vedāntasāra* ('Essence of Vedānta'), a popular introduction to *Advaita Vedānta. **2. (Sādananda Svāmi)** (1908–1977) The first non-Indian (a German, born Ernst Schulze) to be initiated into the *Gauḍīya Vaiṣṇava movement. He was a disciple of Bhaktisiddānta Sarasvatī (1874–1937) (the son of *Kedarnath Datta).

Sadāśiva ('Eternal Śiva') A relatively mild form of *Śiva, indicated by the absence of a separate consort or *śakti. As the object of *Śaiva Siddhānta ritual worship, he has five functions: the creation/emission, maintenance, and destruction/reabsorption of the worlds, self-concealment, and the bestowal of *grace (anugraha), i.e. *liberation. Conceived as five-faced, three-eyed, and ten-armed, with each of his limbs representing a different quality or power, he is thought to contain five other Sadāśivas, one inside the other, each more subtle than the last. The devotee 'builds' his body in this form, internally, through the recitation of non-*Vedic *mantras, and then meditates on it, with the ultimate object of identifying with (i.e. becoming equal with) Śiva for the duration of the rite.

ṣaḍ-darśana *See* DARŚAN(A) (2).

sādhaka A *Tantric adept or practitioner seeking to obtain powers (*siddhis)—i.e. a *bubhukṣu.

sādhanā ('means of accomplishing something') A generic term for a spiritual practice, i.e. the practical means to a religious end, but often used more specifically to designate *Tantric practice, consisting of both *pūjā and *yoga.

sādhāraṇa dharma A term applied to ethical principles and forms of self-restraint which are considered to be 'common to all', or 'universal' (sādhāraṇa), as opposed to the particularistic *ethics associated with *varṇāśramadharma. Various lists exist, many of them echoing the restraints (*yama) associated with *renouncer groups and practitioners of *yoga. The principal element is often non-violence or non-harming (*ahiṃsā), accompanied by truthfulness (satya), not stealing (asteya), and various bodily and emotional restraints. More abstract virtues, such as knowledge (*jñāna) and wisdom (*vidyā) may also be included. *See also* DHARMA.

sādhu ('holy man', lit. 'good man'; fem. sādhvī: 'holy woman', 'good woman') A common term for a *renouncer or religious mendicant.

sādhvī According to **Manusmṛti*, a 'virtuous woman', i.e. one who follows *strīdharma. Also a term for a *Jain nun.

Sadyojyoti (8th century CE) A Kashmiri *Śaiva Siddhānta theologian. Works attributed to him include the *Mokṣakārikā*, the *Nareśvaraparīkṣa*, and the *Paramokṣanirāsakārikā*. Against the non-dualism of the *Pratyabhijñā School, he argues forcibly for the separation of the individual *self from *Śiva and the material world.

Sāgar Island (Gaṅgāsāgar) A relatively small island situated where the *Gaṅgā flows into the Bay of Bengal. It is the site of a major annual *pilgrimage and great *melā in mid January, also known as Gaṅgāsāgar, although before modern times, travel to the site was particularly hazardous. Pilgrims bathe in the confluence of the river and the sea, make offerings to the sea, and do *pūjā at the (rebuilt) Kapil(a) Muni *temple. Until the beginning of the 19th century, Sāgar had a reputation for attracting suicides and for those wishing to drown their first-born children, both as a form of *prāyaścitta, and to ensure a blessed life for their future offspring. It is now a favourite *tīrtha for *saṃnyāsins, particularly *Nāgas.

saguṇa ('with qualities') An adjectival compound, indicating that God has qualities (*guṇas), properties, or attributes. It is most frequently applied to the embodied or anthropomorphic deity worshipped in *bhakti traditions (e.g. the *Kṛṣṇa of *Vṛndāvana). For *Śaṅkara, the conventional apprehension (*vyavahāra) of *brahman (neut.) as a personal deity and object of devotion (saguṇa brahman—brahman with qualities) is ultimately an incomplete and limited approach to the absolute, which, in reality, is without qualities (*nirguṇa). *See also* NIRGUṆA.

Sahadeva In the **Mahābhārata*, Sahadeva, the son of *Mādrī and the *Aśvins, is the fifth of the five *Pāṇḍava brothers, and the twin brother of *Nakula.

sahaja ('easy', 'natural', 'innate') According to some *Tantric traditions, the experience of the essentially unified nature of all reality is innate (sahaja) to all beings, and it is only the constraints of formal religion which hinder the individual from the blissful realization of this state. *See also* SAHAJIYĀ.

Sahajānanda, Svāmī (1781–1830) *See* SVĀMĪNĀRĀYAṆA.

Sahajānand Sarasvatī, Svāmī (*c.*1889–1950) A *Daśanāmi *saṃnyāsin who became a well-known social and political activist on behalf of the peasants of Bihar and eastern India.

Sahaja Yoga *See* MĀTĀJĪ NIRMALA DEVĪ.

Sahajiyā A *Tantric *Vaiṣṇava tradition, which flourished in Northeastern India, especially Bengal, between the early 17th and the late 19th centuries. Any connection with the much earlier *Buddhist Sahajiyā tradition is not clear, but the Sahajiyās appear to have been influenced by *Caitanya, whom they regarded as their *guru. Their name is derived from the term *sahaja, since their practice is geared to actualizing the 'innate' state of *consciousness in which all duality or difference is unified. This involves various meditational, *yogic, and devotional practices, culminating in the cooperation of properly initiated men and women in ritual sexual intercourse. The man identifies with *Kṛṣṇa, the woman with *Rādhā, although they are considered merely male and female aspects of the one, supreme deity ('Kṛṣṇa'). Through the manipulation of sexual fluids (including the retention of semen), the physical body is converted to an inner or spiritual body in which the practitioners share a state of blissful equilibrium and divine love (*preman)—one which marks a return to the state of unity underlying all creation. Given their practices, it is not surprising that the Sahajiyās maintained a secret tradition, and that their texts, which include hundreds of short songs, and various **Tantras*, were composed in a highly ambiguous and coded form of Bengali known as sandhyā/sandhā-bhāṣā. Their *guru *paramparā is said to be extinct, although their influence is clear on other traditions, such as the *Bāuls.

sahamaraṇa *See* SATĪ.

sahasrāra padma (cakra) *See* HAṬHA-YOGA.

Sai Baba of Shirdi (*c.*1856–1918) A *guru and miracle-worker whose birth name is not known. While still in his teens, he took up residence in a derelict mosque in the village of Shirdi in Maharashtra, where he practised *asceticism and mendicancy for the rest of his life. Gradually his fame as an ascetic and miracle-worker spread throughout India, and he attracted a huge audience. Deified while still alive, he has continued to be worshipped since his death in a Hindu *temple erected on the site of his *samādhi (now a *pilgrimage site), despite the fact that in his gnomic and often bad-tempered pronouncements he had refused to differentiate between the Hindu and *Muslim traditions. Nevertheless, his Hindu devotees consider him an *avatāra of *Dattātreya. He remains one of the most popular modern Indian *saints. Sathya *Sai Baba claims to be his *reincarnation.

Sai Baba, Sat(h)ya (b. 1926) An immensely popular miracle-working *guru; estimates of his worldwide following (for which there are no reliable figures) vary from six million to fifty million. Born Sathyanarayana Raju at Puttaparthi in Andhra Pradesh, at the age of 13 he briefly entered something similar to a coma. On his recovery, he claimed to be the *reincarnation of *Sai Baba of Shirdi, and the *avatāra of the current age. From that point he began to gather a large following of devotees, who have consistently championed his ability to perform a variety of miracles, both locally and remotely (he claims to be God—omnipotent, omniscient, and omnipresent), including healing the incurably sick. A characteristic activity has been the 'mental' production of sacred, miracle-working ash (*vibhūti), either from his person during the daily *darśanas he gives to his followers, or from his pictures. Other objects, such as gold watches and necklaces have also been regularly materialized. In his teaching, Sai Baba advocates the unity of religions, but from a decidely *Vedāntic perspective. He encourages guru- *bhakti (through the singing of *bhajans), a pure life, and the practice of community service and charity (seva). He has not, however, escaped allegations of sexual misconduct, as well as scepticism about his miracles, and materializations, which to some observers seem merely part of the Indian magician's standard repertoire. An extensive organization has grown up around Sai Baba, focused on the Prasthanthi Nilayam *āśram, and its surrounding complex at Puttaparthi, where he is for the most part resident. Educational institutions, charitable trusts, and social projects (according to some figures, as many as 10 000) have been set up around the world in his name, and his influence shows no signs of diminishing. He has predicted that he will live to the age of 95 and be reincarnated as Prema Sai Baba (ambiguously described as an incarnation of either *Śiva or *Śakti).

Said, Edward (1935–2003) *See* ORIENTALISM.

saint *See* SANT.

Śaiva A devotee of *Śiva (also referred to as a Śaivite); or relating, belonging, or sacred to Śiva. Śaiva *ascetics and devotees (as well as images of Śiva himself), can often be distinguished by their sectarian mark (*tilaka): three horizontal lines of white cremation-ground *ash drawn across the forehead, sometimes accompanied by a dot of red powder placed between the eyebrows to represent his *śakti or, according to some, his '*third eye'. Some ascetics also inscribe a crescent moon above the lines. *See* ŚAIVISM.

Śaivāgamas *See* ĀGAMA(s).

Śaiva Siddhānta A major *Śaiva ritual and theological tradition. Originating in Kashmir as the division of the *mantramārga which regarded the ten *Śiva-* and eighteen *Rudra-Āgamas* as direct *revelation from *Śiva himself, Śaiva Siddhānta disappeared from its homeland in around the 12th century, only to re-emerge in South India. There, under royal patronage, it developed into a still extant, *bhakti-infused, *Tantric ritual tradition, sometimes referred to as 'Tamil Śaiva Siddhānta', or simply 'Tamil Śaivism'. In the process, it created a canon, or canons which, in addition to the *Āgamas* (considered the highest authority), included the **Veda*, the bhakti poetry and hagiographies of the *Nāyaṉmār contained in the **Tirumuṟai* anthology, and various theological treatises written between the late 12th and 14th centuries which combined the devotionalism of the Nāyaṉmār with the doctrine of the *Āgamas*. Similarly, all three—*Āgama, Veda*, and Tamil bhakti poetry—were incorporated into the *temple liturgy at *Cidambaram and other sites.

Śaiva Siddhānta doctrine, the essential underpinning for its complex ritual structure, presents reality as composed of three elements: Śiva (*pati), bound souls (*paśu), and bonds (*pāśa); the first two are spiritual in nature, the last material. Śiva (*Parameśvara), who is pure intelligence (cit), is the efficient, but not material cause of the world. Through his *grace, activated in *dīkṣa ('consecration'), the individual soul (*ātman), which is bound by impurities (*mala), is transformed, and—either instantly (in the Kashmiri version) or gradually (in the *Tamil version)—liberated from its bonds. On liberation, the soul realizes its true nature as pure intelligence, and enters the realm of Śiva where it is united with the Lord in omniscience, but remains distinct from him in terms of power.

Ritual for the Śaiva Siddhāntas is the means by which the soul approaches Śiva through the destruction of its bonds. To qualify himself to perform rituals, the individual has to receive at least the first of three levels of dīkṣa from an *ācārya or *guru; those officiating at public *temple rituals have, in addition, to belong to the *Ādiśaiva class of hereditary *priests. Daily ritual, which is open to males of all four *varṇa, is focused on a complex *pūjā addressed to *Sadāśiva. The devotee internally 'builds' the deity's body through the recitation of non- *Vedic *mantras (usually accompanied by *mudrā), and then meditates on it. That is to say, he 'rehearses' the intended transformation, with the ultimate object of identifying with (i.e. becoming equal with) Śiva for the duration of the rite, prefiguring his eventual liberation.

Śaivism A collective term for those traditions (also known as 'Śaiva traditions') which consider *Śiva to be the Supreme deity or absolute (i.e. God); alongside *Vaiṣṇavism and *Śāktism, it constitutes one of the three great sectarian streams in medieval and later Hinduism. Śaiva traditions generally consider the sacred texts which underpin their ritual practices and theology to be the revealed teachings of Śiva himself (śivaśāsana), transmitted through various divine and legendary intermediaries to a *guru lineage, and thence to devotees and initiates. Putting aside the undeciphered ambiguities of the *Indus valley seals, and the *Rudra of the *Vedic hymns, the earliest textual evidence for a theistic form of Śiva worship comes from the *Śvetāśvatara Upaniṣad* (*c*.2nd–1st century BCE), where *Rudra (Śiva) is identified as the supreme deity. At about the same time, references to specific Śaiva devotees start to occur in a number of sources, but most evidently in the burgeoning *Epic and *Purāṇic literature. The first named *Śaiva tradition or sect for which evidence survives (*c*.2nd century CE?) is that of the *ascetic *Pāśupatas. Along with the *Lākulas and *Kālamukhas they constitute one of the two main branches of *Śaivism described in the Śaiva **Āgamas* and **Tantras* (*c*.3rd–7th centuries CE), known as the 'outer path' or *atimārga. The other branch, the 'path of *mantras' (*mantramārga), represents a *Tantric tradition, open to both *householders and ascetics. One division of the mantramārga, represented by the **Bhairava Tantras*, can be traced through the *Kāpālikas and their *Kaula derivatives into what became *Kashmiri Śaivism, which flourished between the 9th and 11th century CE. The other division is represented by the *Śiva-* and *Rudra-Āgamas*, which are authoritative for the *Śaiva Siddhānta tradition. Another popular North Indian Śaiva tradition was the *Nāth Siddha *sampradāya, which emerged in the late 12th or early 13th century CE.

The works of the 63 Śaiva *bhakti poets known as the *Nāyaṉmār, and the great flowering of *temple architecture and sculpture under the patronage of the *Pallavas, *Pāṇḍyas, and *Cōḻas testify to the dominant position of Śaivism in South Indian religion between the 6th and 10th centuries CE. Around the 12th to 13th centuries CE, the Śaiva Siddhānta tradition disappeared from Kashmir and re-emerged in South India, where it came under the dual influence of *Vedānta and the bhakti poetry of the *Nāyaṉmār, which it incorporated into its temple ritual. Other South Indian Śaiva bhakti movements also emerged; notably the *Kannada-speaking *Liṅgāyat(a)s, founded by the poet *Basava in the 12th century, and possibly drawing on Kālāmukha antecedents.

Beyond particular sectarian affiliations, the worship of Śiva and his wider family (*Pārvatī, *Gaṇeśa, *Murukaṉ/ *Kārtikkeya, *Skanda) has come to permeate Hindu religious life throughout the medieval and modern periods. The situation is further enriched by the interplay between Śiva and the Goddess (*Devī), who is conceptualized, to a greater or lesser extent, as his consort, or *Śakti. The degree, therefore to which any particular local tradition can be labelled *Śākta, rather than Śaiva, will vary, depending on how much emphasis it gives to the female aspect of the supreme—a theological situation which is reflected in the long and close historical connection between Śāktism and various forms of Śaivism across the subcontinent.

Śaka A nomadic group, known to some as Scythians. They exercised some military and political influence over the Northwest of the subcontinent between about the 5th century BCE and the 2nd century CE. Their name has subsequently been given to the 'Śaka *era', a period beginning in (the equivalent of) 77/78 CE and now the basis for the Indian National Calendar. The *Buddha (Śākyamuni) was said to have been descended from them.

Śākala A *Vedic *śākhā which is the only extant recension of the **Ṛg Veda Saṃhitā*. Its reciters are said to be followers of a *ṛṣi called Śākalya.

śākhā ('branch', 'division', 'subdivision') Most frequently used to designate a branch of the **Veda*, i.e. the particular version or recension of a text being followed or recited. Those doing the reciting are properly called caraṇa, but the two terms are often used synonymously, so that śākhā also refers to a particular school or tradition of recitation and interpretation (e.g. the *Śākala śākhā of the **Ṛg Veda Saṃhitā*, the **Jaiminīya* śākhā of the **Sāma Veda*).

sakhī ('female friend') The term used by North Indian *Vaiṣṇaiva *bhakti poets, such as *Haridāsa, *Hitaharivaṃśa, and Harirāma *Vyāsa, to designate a close female attendant or girl-friend of *Rādhā. The poet identifies with this sakhī to the point of assuming her role—a devotional stance also employed by the male members of the *Sakhībhāva sect.

Sakhībhāvas (Haridāsīs) ('Those who follow the way of Rādhā's friends') A North Indian *bhakti sect with both *householder and mendicant members, said to have been founded by *Haridāsa, and possibly an offshoot of the *Rādhavallabhīs. Their male members dressed and conducted themselves as though they were the female attendants, or close girl-friends (*sakhīs), of *Rādhā, apparently believing that only *Kṛṣṇa himself is truly male. They appear to have been most numerous in the 17th century, and have achieved a certain notoriety for their transgressive sexual practices, although little is known about the history of their tradition.

Śākta A worshipper of the Goddess as the supreme creative power (*śakti) and/or theological absolute; i.e. a follower, or practitioner, of *Śāktism. *See* Devī.

śākta padāvalī ('Collected Poems of the Goddess') A literary genre, initiated in 18th-century Bengal by *bhakti poets such as *Rāmprasād Sen, and carried on by others, such as *Kamalākānta Bhaṭṭācārya, consisting of collections of devotional poems directed towards the *Goddess, often in the form of *Kālī.

śāktapīṭhas *See* Śaktipīṭha(s).

śakti ('energy', 'power', 'capability') Divine power or energy, personified as a feminine principle, and therefore either as a male god's consort (his active and immanent power), or as the ultimately independent, female absolute—the Goddess or *Devī (also known as Śakti). The English term, *Śāktism, designating the religious practice of those (the *Śāktas) who worship the Goddess as the supreme deity, is derived from this latter sense of Śakti. *See also* Devī.

śaktipīṭha(s) (śāktapīṭhas, pīṭhas ('seats', 'shrines')**)** ('places of power') A pan-Indian network of *Tantric *Śākta *pilgrimage sites, each marking a spot where, according to the myth of *Śiva's dismemberment of *Satī, parts of the *Goddess's body fell to earth and are manifested in the local topography. According to a variety of traditions and textual sources, the network can include anything from 4 to 108 *pīthas, or, indeed, any or all of the innumerable *temples dedicated to *Devī across the subcontinent. *Kāmarūpa in Assam, where a spring-moistened cleft in the rock represents Satī's *yoni, is considered by many to be the original śaktipīṭha, as well as the most important. It is included in the earliest (7th century *Buddhist) list of four 'great' pīṭhas (mahāpīṭha); the others are named as *Jālandhara (in the Punjab), Oḍiyāṇa/Uḍḍiyāṇa (in the Swat Valley), and Pūrṇagiri (no longer known). Another well-known list of 51 śāktipīṭhas includes *Kālīghāṭ and *Jvālāmukhī. *See also* Devī.

Śāktism An English term designating the religious practices and theologies of the *Śāktas—those who worship the Goddess (*Devī) as the supreme and absolute creative power (*śakti). Alongside

*Vaiṣṇavism and *Śaivism, Śāktism has been identified as one of the three great sectarian streams in medieval and later Hinduism. *See* DEVĪ; *See also* TANTRA.

Śakuntalā As portrayed in the *Ādiparvan* of the *Mahābhārata*, the daughter of the *apsaras Menakā (*Menā) and the sage *Viśvāmitra, who, when living in her fosterfather *Kaṇva's *āśram, is seduced by King *Duṣyanta. She gives birth to *Bharata, whom the *king initially refuses to acknowledge as his *son, but Śakuntalā's rhetoric and a divine intervention change his mind. This is the story that *Kālidasa retells, with significant variations, in his *Abhijñānaśākuntalam* ('Recognition of Śakuntalā').

śālagrāma A smooth, rounded stone containing a fossilized ammonite, considered by *Vaiṣṇavas to be imbued with *Viṣṇu himself. It is named after a *village on the Gaṇḍakī in *Nepal, where large numbers of śālagrāma have been found on the riverbed. They are carefully wrapped in a clean cloth and kept as sacred objects in most Vaiṣṇava households, and the water in which they are ritually bathed is drunk as a means of removing *impurity. Various explanations for the stone's power have been given: a common explanation is that the fossilized spirals resemble *Visṇu's *cakra.

Śalyaparvan ('The Book of Śalya') The ninth book of the *Sanskrit *Mahābhārata*, recounting the period in the war during which Śalya takes command of the *Kaurava forces, only to be killed by *Yudhiṣṭhira. Of the Kauravas, only *Aśvatthāman, Kṛpa, Kṛtavarman, and *Duryodhana survive. At *Kṛṣṇa's instigation, Duryodhana is mortally wounded by *Bhīma in contravention of the laws of battle.

samādhi 1. ('absorbed concentration') A state of higher *conciousness, free of *karmic or material bonds, which is reached as the result of practising *yoga. Referred to in the *Maitrāyaṇī Upaniṣad* (6.18), it is treated in detail in *Patañjali's *Yoga Sūtra*, where, as the most advanced 'inner limb' (antar-aṅga) of 'eight-limbed yoga' (*aṣṭāṅga-yoga), virtually the entire first chapter is given over to its explication. Indeed, in his commentary on *Yoga Sūtra* 1.1, *Vyāsa states that 'Yoga is samādhi' (yogaḥ samādhiḥ). Patañjali distinguishes between samprajñāta samādhi, which requires the support of objects of concentration or consciousness, and the higher state of asamprajñāta or 'seedless' (nirbīja) samādhi, which requires no such support: the self (*ātman) is absorbed in the self, a state synonymous with *kaivalya or *liberation, the final goal of yogic practice. The term comes to be used generically to designate higher states of consciousness, the precise definition depending on the tradition in question. **2.** ('memorial') A memorial marking the tomb or *cremation site of a '*saint' or *saṃnyāsin; it may be incorporated into local or wider *pilgrimage patterns. *See also* JĪVANSAMĀDHI.

sāman ('song', 'chant') Any one of the *Vedic verses or chants collected in the *Sāma Veda*. They are first mentioned in the *Puruṣa Sūkta* (*Ṛg Veda* 10.90, v. 9) alongside the praise verses (*ṛc), the metres (*chandas)—i.e. the correct metres to be used in the chants, and the formulae (*yajus) of the *Yajur Veda*.

samāna *See* PRĀṆA.

samāvartana ('returning') The *saṃskāra performed on the return of the celibate *Vedic student (brahmācarin) to his home after the completion of his period of study with his *guru; it thus marks the formal end of the *brahmacarya *āśrama. Its characteristic feature is the taking of a ritual bath (*snāna—sometimes used synonymously with samāvartana), after which, until such time as he is married and becomes a householder (*gṛhastha), the former student is known as a snātaka ('one who has taken the bath'). Copious rules are prescribed for the snātaka in **Dharmaśāstra*, but essentially they are the same as those laid down for the gṛhastha.

Sāma Veda ('The *Veda*/Knowledge Consisting of Chants') The third of the *Vedic **Saṃhitās*, comprising verses or chants (*sāmans) taken from Books 8 and 9 of the **Ṛg Veda* (plus 75 other verses). The *Saṃhitā* is divided between the *ṛc verses (collected in the *Ārcika*), and four collections of chants (gāna) stipulating the complex melodies to which the verses are to be sung by the *udgātṛ priests, mostly during the *soma sacrifice. There are three extant recensions of the text: the *Kauthama*, *Rāṇāyanīya*, and **Jaiminīya* *śākhas.

Sāmba (Śāmba) A son of *Kṛṣṇa; he appears intermittently and briefly in the **Mahābhārata*. According to some *Purāṇic accounts, he is partly instrumental in the beginnings of *sun worship.

Sambandhar *See* CAMPANTAR, TIRUÑĀṆA.

saṃdhyā ('juncture', 'twilight') The juncture of the three divisions of the day (morning, noon, and evening), but principally the morning and evening twilights, at which initiated male members of the upper three *varṇa (but especially *brahmins) are required, according to **Dharmaśāstra*, to perform a ritual, also called saṃdhyā (or saṃdhyopāsana). This consists of the recitation of *Vedic *mantras (especially the *Gāyatrī), restraint of the breath, sipping and sprinkling water, and pouring libations of water to the *sun (regarded as the worshipper's chosen deity or *iṣṭa-devatā). The morning saṃdhyā should be performed standing, facing East, until the sun appears; the evening, sitting, facing Northwest, until Ursa major is visible. The ritual has been much elaborated in some *Sūtras, and, in many instances, *Purāṇic and *Tantric elements have been added.

Saṃhitā(s) ('collection(s)') **1.** Collections containing the original, continuously recited text—the *mantra portions—of the four **Vedas*, i.e. the **Ṛg-*, **Sāma-*, **Yajur-*, and **Atharva-Saṃhitās*, as opposed to the **Brāhmaṇas*, **Āraṇyakas*, **Upaniṣads*, and **Sūtras* subsequently attached to each of the *Saṃhitā*. *See also* MANTRA(S); SAṂHITĀPĀṬHA. **2.** Any collection of methodically arranged texts, e.g. the *Pañcarātra *Saṃhitās*.

saṃhitāpāṭha ('continuous recitation') A means of memorizing and repeating the **Veda* through continuous recitation, which therefore applies the euphonic changes (sandhi) which occur when *Sanskrit words are recited in an unbroken sequence. Another, complementary method (*padapāṭha), involves memorizing each word individually without the application of sandhi. Traditionally, both these means of recitation are employed (along with *kramapāṭha) to ensure the accurate *oral transmission of the text.

Saṃjaya In the **Mahābhārata*, the blind King **Dhṛtarāṣṭra's* driver (*sūta) and his 'eyes'. In the **Bhīṣmaparvan* (Book 6), he is granted spiritual vision by *Vyāsa, and from there until the middle of the **Sauptikaparvan* (Book 10) becomes the main narrator (sūta) of the story.

saṃkalpa ('intention', 'determination', 'will') A formal declaration of intent, amounting to a vow to accomplish a particular action (e.g. a *pilgrimage), or to perform a particular ritual, in order to satisfy a specific purpose or desire. Such a statement is considered a necessary component of all *Vedic rituals.

Śaṃkara *See* ŚAṄKARA.

saṃkara ('mixture') The intermingling of *varṇa and *castes, through intermarriage, and/or one varṇa assuming the traditional role (*svadharma) of another. According to *Dharmaśāstra* and other sources (e.g. the *Bhagavadgītā*) this will lead to a disastrous breakdown in the social and natural orders (*dharma).

Saṃkarṣaṇa According to the *Pāñcarātra tadition, Saṃkarṣana is the first of *Viṣṇu's (*Vāsudeva's) *vyūha forms. In *Epic and *Purāṇic Hinduism, he is synonymous with *Balarāma.

Sāṃkhya (Sāṅkhya) ('number', 'enumeration', 'discrimination') An ancient and highly influential stream in Indian thought, which eventually gives its name to one of the six 'schools of philosophy' (*darśana). Concepts and patterns of ideas subsequently regarded as central to this tradition (sometimes referred to as 'proto-Sāṃkhya'), especially intimations of a fundamental dualism between male spirit and female matter, are evident from the later books of the *Ṛg Veda* onwards. Some **Upaniṣads*, particularly the **Kaṭha* and the **Śvetāsvatara*, employ *tattva-like hierarchies, and analyse *prakṛti in terms of the *guṇas. Much of the **Bhagavadgītā's* underlying ontology and cosmology—what counts as 'knowledge' (*jñāna)—is specifically linked to the term 'sāṃkhya', although both spirit and matter are eventually subsumed in *Kṛṣṇa (God). Elsewhere in the **Mahābhārata*, the **Mokṣadharma* section of the **Śāntiparvan* is aware of already existing Sāṃkhya treatises, as well as Sāṃkhya's connection with, but difference from, *Yoga.

Despite claims that the legendary seer *Kapila composed a now lost *Sāṃkhya Sūtra* (an existing text of this name belongs to the late medieval period), the foundational text of Sāṃkhya as a philosophical system (darśana) is the **Sāṃkhya Kārikā*, written or compiled by *Īśvarakṛṣṇa, perhaps between the 4th and 5th centuries CE, but referring in part to earlier, now no longer extant treatises. It presents a fundamental ontological dualism between inherently passive, conscious, male 'spirits' (*puruṣas), and exclusively active, female 'matter' (*prakṛti). The latter consists of three inextricably intertwined strands, or constituents (the *sattva, *rajas, and *tamas *guṇas), held in unmanifest equilibrium (a state known as *pradhāna) until disturbed by the proximity of spirit (puruṣa). This causes a dynamic interaction between the guṇas through which prakṛti manifests itself in the form of evolutes; these develop to constitute the material universe and all that it contains, including the physical and mental attributes of human beings—enumerated in a list of *tattvas. Including the non-material, non-evolving puruṣa, there are 25 tattvas: prakṛti evolves into *buddhi, buddhi into *ahaṃkāra, ahaṃkāra into *manas and four sets of five *buddhīndriya ('senses'), *karmendriya ('organs of action'), *tanmātra ('subtle elements'), and *mahābhūta ('great elements'). At the cosmological level, the process of evolution is never-ending: the tattvas will be reabsorbed in sequence into unmanifest prakṛti, only to evolve again in a continuous cycle. For the individual, bondage is the delusion that it is the inherently passive puruṣa which is acting and experiencing the results of action (*karma), when in fact, it is prakṛti, through the guṇas, which is the sole cause of action. *Liberation from karma, and so from *rebirth and suffering, is therefore concomitant with successfully discriminating between the puruṣa's apparent state and its actual state. This results in the realization of the spirit's 'isolation' (*kaivalya) from everything else—i.e. from prakṛti and all other puruṣas. The fact that discrimination relies on analysis of the 25 tattvas reinforces their dual nature: their evolution is at the same time a cosmic and a psychological process. The psychological aspect—the realization of the individual's inherently pure *consciousness—was emphasized in *Patañjali's

*Yoga system, which has an entirely Sāṃkhyan metaphysic, and by about the 11th century CE, in spite of some significant commentaries on the *Sāṃkhya Kārikā,* Sāṃkhya (as opposed to 'Sāṃkhya-Yoga') had started to lose its significance as an independent darśana.

Sāṃkhya Kārikā *See* SĀṂKHYA.

Sāṃkhya-Yoga *See* YOGA.

saṃkīrtana *See* KĪRTAN(A).

saṃnyāsa (sannyāsa) ('laying aside', 'renunciation') The way of life of a *Brahmanical renunciant (*saṃnyāsin); also the name of the ritual by which a man becomes such a saṃnyāsin. More loosely, the renunciation of *caste society in order to pursue personal *liberation.

The historical process by which renunciation was incorporated into, or developed out of the Brahmanical 'mainstream' to become an institution which, in ideological terms, is complementary to the life of the householder (*gṛhastha) ritualist, has been much debated. Some scholars have seen it as an organic and logical development of the role of the sacrificer (*yajamāna)—i.e. as the internalization and perfection of the ritual life; others as the result of the gradual incorporation of extra-Brahmanical beliefs and practices into *Vedic orthopraxy; others again as a complex combination of these two processes. Those looking to outside sources have often argued that the institution of renunciation has its origins in the socio-economic changes which affected North India, in particular, from about the 6th century BCE onwards. Urbanization led to the breakdown in family and kinship networks, and, in the light of new uncertainties about how to live properly, gave rise to a religious individualism based on personal choice. The most immediately obvious result of this was the creation over a period of time of the 'alternative' societies of the *Buddhist and *Jain monastic institutions, although these in themselves clearly had *śramaṇa antecedents. There were, however, no such institutional equivalents in the Brahmanical tradition: individuals who leave home to live lives conducive to liberation in the wilderness or forest (*araṇya) appear in some **Upaniṣads* (*Yajñavalkya in the **Bṛhadāraṇyaka* 2.4.1 is described as becoming a *parivrājaka or 'wandering ascetic'), but there is no suggestion that they are joining a parallel community.

Whatever the underlying process or processes, the mechanism for formally positioning renunciation, or for integrating it into the traditional *Brahmanical way of life was the *āśrama system. It is clear from the **Dharmasūtras* that renunciation, however understood, was initially seen as one of a number of voluntary alternatives, any one of which could be chosen as a lifelong āśrama by an adult male after a temporary period of *Vedic studentship under a *guru. By the time of the **Dharmaśāstras*, however, the āśramas had been arranged, for ideological purposes, into a single path through life marked by four successive stages, which each individual was supposed to pass through in turn. The last of these, according to the developed system, was 'saṃnyāsa', a term which had made its initial appearance at the end of the first millennium BCE referring specifically to the abandonment of the Brahmanical fires in a ritual also called saṃnyāsa. (Although it is worth noting that in the **Muṇḍaka Upaniṣad* (3.2.6) (*c.*3rd–1st century BCE) a single occurrence of the term appears to carry the wider sense of a particular ascetic way of life, albeit one conditioned by knowledge of the *Vedānta.) The influential **Manusmṛti*, however, unlike later *Dharmaśāstra* texts, reserves the term 'saṃnyāsin' (6.86) for a man who has retired from the ritual life but lives at home under the protection of his son. For him the fourth āśrama is that of the homeless ascetic seeking *mokṣa.

Once current, the term 'saṃnyāsa' was explicated in various ways: for instance, the **Bhagavadgītā*, a text opposed to the idea of societal renunciation, redefines it as the rejection of actions motivated by desires (18.2), i.e. it internalizes the idea to an attitude rather than an āśrama. At approximately the same time, however (the early centuries CE), 'minor' Upaniṣadic texts, subsequently called **Sāṃnyasa Upaniṣads*, began to appear whose theological purpose was to to provide *Vedic authority for the institution of saṃnyāsa. In the process—and probably reflecting already well-established traditions—they give detailed and variegated information about the way in which saṃnyāsins should conduct their lives. Thereafter saṃnyāsa, as a specific term, continued to be treated in the context of the āśramas—either as the fourth in sequence, or as an alternative lifestyle embarked upon from one of the other orders of life. (Although according to some sources, renunciation from no āśrama at all was a possibility for those who were sufficiently detached.)

The procedure for taking saṃnyāsa, in the sense of the particular ritual of renunciation, is complex. The saṃnyāsin-to-be should belong to one of the upper three *varṇas, and therefore be qualified to perform the Vedic rituals he is about the renounce. Under the direction of *brahmin *priests, he deposits the *fires he has used for his sacrifices into himself, i.e. into his breath; his life thereby becomes a continuous, internalized sacrifice, fuelled by whatever he eats. This marks a break with the ritual world and the householder's life from which there is supposd to be no return. The idea that he is ritually dead (i.e. no longer alive in the normal social and sacrificial sense) is reinforced by various borrowings from the *śrāddha rites, including the abandonment ('cremation') of his sacrificial implements, *sacred thread, and top-knot. This association with *death, and his status as the performer of his own self-sacrifice, make him *impure as far as the rest of the world is concerned. The essential part of the rite is the renouncer's recitation of the praiṣa formula: saṃnyastam mayā—'I have renounced', which he repeats three times. This is followed by a formal vow that he will never kill or do violence to any living creature (*abhaya). He then removes all his clothes, receives a new name from his *guru (another saṃnyāsin), who also gives him what he needs to lead his new ('re-born') life, viz. a begging bowl, a staff, an old garment (sometimes ochre in colour), a water pot, a waistband, and a loincloth. The first three, in particular, continue to act as outward emblems (*liṅgas) of his altered status, although some advanced saṃnyāsins (such as the *Nāgas) may choose to go naked.

Saṃnyāsa Upaniṣads A group of 'minor' **Upaniṣads* through which the *Brahmanical tradition attempted to provide *Vedic authority for the institution of *saṃnyāsa. Brought together under this name by Western *Indologists, they deal with the rules and practices governing the behaviour of various types of *saṃnyāsins, covering a time span from the early centuries CE to the late medieval period.

saṃnyāsin (sannyāsin, sannyāsī) ('renunciant', 'one who has taken saṃnyāsa') In the technical and historical sense of the term, a saṃnyāsin is a member of one of the three higher *varṇas who, through 'taking' *saṃnyāsa, has formally renounced external *Vedic ritual and the life of the householder (*gṛhastha) in order to dedicate himself to the pursuit of *mokṣa. Since the medieval period, 'saṃnyāsin' has also come to be used generically to refer to any 'holy man' or *renouncer who has abandoned the normal restrictions and demands of *caste society in order to pursue personal *liberation—a way of life characterized by celibacy, homelessness, the abandonment of external ritual, economic inactivity, and mendicancy. The term is also applied to members of monastery- (*maṭha-) based renunciant orders, such as the *Daśanāmis (said to have been founded by *Śaṅkara) and the *Nāgas.

Some renouncers imitate lunatic and animal behaviour (following, for example, the *govrata), or in the case of some *Śaivas, imitate *Śiva's antinomian behaviour by living in *cremation grounds; most practise various forms of *asceticism and *tapas in order to subdue the passions, as well as *yoga and *meditation. Because he has internalized his sacrificial fires, and is considered already dead from a ritual perspective, a saṃnyāsin's body is not cremated, but is subject to *burial, or some other means of disposal when he dies in the physical sense. The number of saṃnyāsins (in the wider sense) currently active in India is difficult to assess, but estimates vary from between five to fifteen million. *See also* ASCETICISM; SAṂNYĀSA.

Saṃnyāsī uprising A peasant rebellion against the British *East India Company, organized by groups of *saṃnyāsins (hence the name) after the 1770 famine in Bengal and Bihar. *See also* ĀNANDAMAṬH.

sampradāya ('order', 'tradition', 'sect') A term for an institutionalized order or tradition (usually *smārta in nature), marked by a *guru-pupil lineage or *paramparā. This may be traced back to an historical or mythical founder, or even to God (however identified). Entry requires a special initiation (*dīkṣā), which, depending on the tradition, may be given to *renouncers only, or to *householders as well.

saṃsāra (lit. 'wandering through') In the context of *karma theory, the potentially endless cycle of suffering and *rebirth to which the embodied individual is subject, unless they can achieve *mokṣa. By extension, it also refers to the world as normally experienced.

saṃskāra (śarīra saṃskara) (lit. 'putting together', 'making perfect', 'preparing', 'cleansing') **1.** According to the *Brahmanical tradition prescribed in the **Gṛhyasūtras* and **Dharmaśāstra*, a series of transformative rituals (also referred to as 'rites of passage', or 'life-cycle rituals') which should structure the entire lives of *twice-born *Vedic students and householders (*gṛhastha). From an internal perspective, they have the dual purpose of removing *impurities (e.g. those attending procreation and birth) and generating new qualities; the overall aim is to perfect the individual undergoing them and make him—in some cases her— fit (essentially in the 'body' or śarīra) for each new stage of life in accordance with *dharma. From an external perspective, the saṃskāras are a way of defining (through inclusion and exclusion), reinforcing, and legitimizing social identity. Texts vary as to the precise number of saṃskāras. **Gautama Dharmasūtra* (8.14–24) names 40, many of them the types of fire *sacrifice involved in performing the saṃskāras; the **Gṛhyasūtras* have various lists—numbering anything from 12 to 25 or more. Standardized lists, established in the medieval period, usually include: *garbhādhāna ('impregnation of the womb'), *puṃsavana ('generation of a male'), simantonnayana ('parting the hair' of the pregnant woman), jātakarma ('birth rite'), nāmakaraṇa ('naming' the child), niṣkramaṇa (child's 'first outing'), *annaprāśana (first 'feeding with solid food'), *cūḍākaraṇa ('tonsure'), karṇavedha ('ear piercing'), *vidyārambha ('beginning of learning'), *upanayana ('initiation'), vedārambha ('beginning to study the **Veda*'), keśānta ('first shave'), *samāvartana ('returning' at the end of Vedic study), vivāha (*marriage), *antyeṣṭi (death ritual and funeral rites). Appearing in all lists, and the most significant of these, are the *birth, initiation, marriage, and funeral rites, although probably only the latter two are still widely performed. According to some sources, these saṃskāras are exclusive to males of the upper three *varṇas, others, including *Manusmṛti*, allow them to women and *śūdras providing that they are performed silently, or with non-Vedic *mantras. It is notable that *Manusmṛti* (2.67) states that marriage is the equivalent of upanayana for females—i.e. the rite by which they become full members of traditional Brahmanical society. (For males too, at least in modern times, upanayana may be added to the marriage ceremony, rather than performed separately.) In various localized or family forms, 'rites of passage' in a more general sense, are practised by both genders across all levels of society.

2. According to *Patañjali's *Yoga Sūtra*, saṃskāras are dispositions created in the individual as a result of the *karmic residue which has been produced from their ignorance- and desire-informed actions. When these saṃskāras are activated in the next life, they engender afflictions (*kleśas), which lead to a further cycle of actions generated from negative internal states, and so motor the process of suffering and *rebirth.

Śāṃtanu *See* BHĪṢMA.

samudramathana/samudramanthana *See* CHURNING OF THE OCEAN.

saṃvat *See* ERAS.

saṃyamana ('the path to Yama's world') One of three paths taken by the self, or its *subtle body, after *death, according to the **Upaniṣads* and *Vedāntic theology. (The others are the *devayāna ('the way of the gods'), or the 'northern path', and the *pitṛyāna, ('the way of the fathers'), or the 'southern path'. It is reserved for those who have neither performed their sacrificial actions (*karma) properly, nor attained knowledge of their real meaning (or of *brahman (neut.), according to *Śaṅkara). In some texts the place of this path is taken by *rebirth as a lower life form.

Sanātana Dāsa *See* GOSVĀMĪS.

sanātana dharma ('eternal dharma') An term first used (in a non-specific sense) by reformers, such as *Dayānand(a) Sarasvatī, in reaction to *Christian criticisms of Hindu practices, to evoke what they regarded as true religion—a 'pure', **Veda*-based form of Hinduism, deemed to be universally and eternally valid, which subsumes all other faiths. It has subsequently proved a popular concept among many middle-class and diaspora Hindus.

Śāṇḍilya *See* AGNICAYANA; ŚATAPATHA BRĀHMAṆA.

Saṅgam literature *See* CAṄKAM LITERATURE.

Śaṅkara (Ādi Śaṅkara, Śaṅkarācārya) (*c.*700 CE, trad. 788–820) A highly influential *Vedāntic thinker and exegete. Now credited with the founding of the *Advaita Vedānta tradition, he has been promoted by many, particularly in the modern era, as the greatest Hindu philosopher. Nothing is known of his life beyond the hagiographies; these portray him as a *brahmin from the small village of Kālati in Kerala who became a *saṃnyāsin at the age of seven. According to the tradition, his *guru was called *Govindapāda and his *paramaguru (his teacher's teacher) was *Gauḍapāda. (Gauḍapāda was the reputed author of the earliest identifiable *Advaita text, the **Gauḍapādīya Kārikā*, the basis of a commentary attributed to Śaṅkara.) The boy Śaṅkara moved to *Vārāṇasī, where he acquired his own pupils, including *Padmapāda and *Sureśvara. Moving again, to *Badrinātha, he composed the earliest surviving commentary on the **Brahmasūtras*, supposedly while still only twelve years old. Thereafter, he led the life of a peripatetic debater and teacher, before dying at the age of 32 in the *Himālayas. During his period of wandering he is supposed to have founded an India-wide network of Advaitin monasteries, each with its associated order of *saṃnyāsins, later identified as the *Daśanāmis. There is some evidence, however, that these *maṭhas may have been established much later in the history of Advaita, and it should be noted that while the Daśanāmis have a markedly Śaiva affiliation, it is likely that Śaṅkara himself was born into a *smārta *Vaiṣṇava family. Nevertheless, by around the 10th century CE, through the advocacy of his pupils, and various subcommentators, and the critical response of rival schools, Śaṅkara had become established as the major proponent of Advaita, and a large number of works, both philosophical and devotional began to be attributed to him. Most scholars now agree that only a small proportion of these texts should be unreservedly accepted as the work of the 8th-century Śaṅkara. Apart from one independent text, the *Upadeśasāhasrī* ('Thousand Teachings'), these are all commentaries (*bhāṣyas), namely: the *Brahmasūtrabhāṣya* (also known as the *Śārīrakabhāṣya*), bhāṣyas on the **Bṛhadāraṅyaka* and **Taittirīya Upaniṣads*, and (probably) the **Bhagavadgītā*, as well as the commentary on the **Gauḍapādīya Kārikā* (itself a commentary on the **Māṇḍūkya Upaniṣad*). Some scholars also regard commentaries on the other major **Upaniṣads* (with the possible exception of the **Śvetāśvatara*) as genuine. For Śaṅkara's teachings, *see* ADVAITA VEDĀNTA.

Śaṅkara

Śaṅkarācāryas The generic term for the lineage of senior *saṃnyāsins of the *Śaiva *Daśanāmi *maṭhas, derived from the tradition that *Śankara himself founded the order.

Śaṅkaradeva (16th century CE, trad. 1449–1569) A *bhakti poet, and the founder of the *Vaiṣṇava tradition (sometimes referred to as 'Neo-Vaiṣṇavism') in Assam. Hagiographies tell of a *pilgrimage during which he is supposed to have met other Vaiṣṇavas, including *Caitanya. He advocated a theologically uncomplicated cross-*caste, cross-gender form of devotion, focused on chanting the name (nāma) of God (*Hari), and drawing its authority directly from the **Bhagavātapurāṇa*. Alongside his other devotional works, in both *Sanskrit and Assamese, he is credited with a number of plays and the establishment of a Vaiṣṇava performance tradition. With the support of local *kings, he, or his followers—his chief disciple was Mādhavadeva (trad. 1489–1596)—established a chain of monasteries (sattras/satras) across Assam, and, at the *village level, institutions (nāmagharas), which, combining religious and social functions, acted as a means of bring the diverse tribal population together. The tradition subsequently divided into a number of branches.

śaṅkha A conch-shell. *See* VIṢṆU.

Śāṅkhāyana Reputed author of the *Śāṅkhāyana* **Śrauta-* and **Gṛhya-Sūtras* (also known as the *Kauṣītaki Gṛhya-Sūtra*), both belonging to the *Ṛg Vedic branch of the **Veda*.

Sanskrit (saṃskṛta—'polished', 'correct', 'highly elaborated', 'put together', 'rendered fit', 'grammatically correct') An *Indo-European language belonging (according to the categorization of philologists) to the Indian, or Indic, branch of the Indo-Iranian language group, known as *Indo-Āryan. To distinguish it from the *Prākrits, and modern languages such as

*Hindi, Sanskrit, at it widest, is further classified as 'Old Indo-Āryan', a term combining *Vedic Sanskrit and the classical language codified by the *grammarians, notably *Pāṇini. The hymns contained in the **Ṛg Veda* represent the oldest form of this language available to us. The **Brāhmaṇas* and **Upaniṣads* show some linguistic development (chiefly morphological simplification), and by the time of Pāṇini it had become necessary, for ritual purposes, to preserve the older language in the face of the further changes evident in the Prākrits spoken by ordinary people, as opposed to the Sanskritic language of educated *brahmins—a process which culminated in Sanskrit (as it came to be known) becoming a second, learned language, rather than a mother-tongue acquired in childhood. In addition, liturgical Sanskrit was increasingly considered by orthodox brahmins (such as those belonging to the *Pūrva Mīmāṃsā school) to be an uncreated (*apauruṣeya) sacred language, synonymous with the **Veda*, and only accessible to those members of the higher *varṇas who had undergone the requisite intitiation (*upanayana), followed by a specialized education. Yet, at the same time, classical Sanskrit was gradually developing into a lingua franca, not just for commentarial and philosophical discourse across both Hindu and heterodox (i.e. *Buddhist and *Jain) religious traditions, but also for administrative, intellectual, and artistic purposes, such as the composition of *kāvya, *mahākāvya, and Sanskrit drama. Indeed, the *Epics and early **Purāṇas*, which were composed in forms of Sanskrit slightly later than Pāṇini's, stand at the beginning of a period, stretching from the early centuries CE for a thousand years or more, in which classical Sanskrit acted as a yardstick, not just of religious authority but also of a level of cultural unity across much of the subcontinent. In the late 18th and 19th centuries, the advent of the printing press and the translation (e.g. by Rāmmohun *Roy) of Sanskrit texts, which had previously been the preserve of families of brahmin *paṇḍits, as well as the 'discovery' of Sanskritic culture by Western Orientalists (such as Sir William *Jones), opened up the subcontinent's past to both Indian and Western scholars. In this way, Sanskrit sources, particularly those associated with *Vedānta, helped to shape the views of 19th-century reformers (and reactionaries) about the nature of Hindu culture. While still regarded as a living literary language with immense cultural cachet—it continues to be taught in some schools and many universities in India—Sanskrit's vitality, and the importance of new works composed in it, has, with regional variations, been in decline since at least the 16th century CE. *See also* PRĀKRIT(S); TAMIL.

Sanskritic Derived from the cultural complex associated with the *Sanskrit language.

Sanskritist A *Sanskrit scholar; a student of *Sanskritic culture.

Sanskritization (Āryanization, Brahmanization, Vedicization) A term originally coined by the social anthropologist M. N. *Srinivas to indicate the process by which individuals, or entire lower *caste groups (*jāti) seek to emulate the practices of higher *varna, particularly *brahmins, in order to make their behaviour seem *purer or more orthodox. This may involve changes in dietary habits (e.g. a switch to *vegetarianism), ritual practices (e.g. a switch to non-animal sacrifices), and social norms (e.g. the rejection of *widow remarriage). All this is done in the hope (seldom fulfilled) that such changes will raise their status in the social hierarchy.

The term has come to be used in a wider sense (sometimes called 'universalization') to indicate an historical and cultural process by which local deities, myths, and ritual practices, originally outside or on the margins of *Brahmanical culture, are assimilated into the latter, and so, from its perspective, both legitimized and controlled. For instance, the *Tamil god *Murukaṉ was identified with the *Sanskritic and *Purāṇic *Kārtikkeya/Skanda, and so incorporated into the *Śaiva pantheon; in a similar fashion, local goddesses were assimilated to *Devī, the Great *Goddess, in the *Sanskrit **Devī Mahātmya*. Sometimes a distinction is made between 'Vedicization'—the process by which sectarian works in their entirety are elevated to the status of the **Veda* (i.e. are regarded as *śruti)—and 'Brahmanization', which involves a modification of the content of particular texts.

sant A generic popular term for a 'saint', holy man/woman, or *bhakta. More specifically, a North Indian poet-saint, generally identified as being *nirguṇa *Vaiṣṇava in orientation, although the movement's origins are eclectic and include forms of *Islamic mysticism. In that their ultimate aim is to attain the unspecified Absolute or Name (*Nāma), sants—often including women and members of lower *castes—have been described as non-sectarian, although various specific traditions, such as *Sikhism, crystallized around the poetry they produced. Notable North Indian sants include *Dādū, *Kabīr, *Nānak, *Mīrā(bāī), and *Raidās(a).

The term is also applied to Kannadiga and Maharashtrian poet-devotees; in the latter case, it is used specifically of members of the *Vārkarī *sampradāya or Panth, founded by *Jñāneśvar(a). Classified as Vaiṣṇavas, pursuing *saguṇa forms of *temple devotion, they incorporated strains of *Śaiva devotionalism into an inclusive and hybrid theology. Other notable Vārkarī Panth sants include *Nāmdev, *Ekanātha, and *Tukārāma.

Śāntiparvan ('The Book of the Peace') The twelfth book of the *Sanskrit **Mahābhārata*. After the war *Yudhiṣṭhira wishes to renounce the kingdom, but is persuaded by *Kṛṣṇa and others to pursue his kingly *dharma. He proceeds to *Hāstinapura to be crowned. At Kṛṣṇa's urging, the dying *Bhīṣma addresses a wide-ranging and extensive discourse on religion, ethics, dharma, and *cosmology to the *king, much of it contained in a sub-*parvan, the *Mokṣadharmaparvan* ('The Book of the Universal Principles leading to Liberation').

Santoṣī Mā(tā) ('The Mother Who Gives Satisfaction') A North Indian goddess, apparently hardly known before the 1960s, who has achieved widespread popularity thanks to the box office success of a *Hindi film, *Jai Santoṣī Mā* ('Hail Santoṣī Mā) (1975; remade 2006), which, in telling the story of a young woman's devotion to her, identified Santoṣī as the daughter of *Gaṇeśa. Regarded as manifesting herself in the film (or on the screen during its projection), she has since become the focus of a *bhakti cult, particularly among middle-class urban women. Numerous *temples have been dedicated to her.

sapiṇḍa (lit. 'round lump') A group of blood relatives, perhaps so-called because they are thought to share particles from the same body, or because they are linked through the offering of *piṇḍa to the ancestors (*pitṛ). Classical **Dharmaśāstra* sources generally regard the sapiṇḍa relationship as extending to six generations either side of the father, and five either side of the mother; but the extent and duration of the relationship remains a matter of controversy, since the tracing of sapiṇḍa relationships and their extension over time have considerable and complex implications for the eligibility of potential *marriage partners. The *Hindu Marriage Act* of 1955 declares that '"sapinda relationship" with reference to any person extends as far as the third generation (inclusive) in the line of ascent through the mother, and the fifth (inclusive) in the line of ascent through the father, the line being traced upwards in each case from the person concerned, who is to be counted as the first generation'. It goes on to record what degrees of relationship on this scale would cause a marriage to be prohibited.

sapiṇḍīkaraṇa That part of the funeral rite (*antyeṣṭi/*śrāddha) in which, using *piṇḍa, an after-death body is constructed for the deceased, and he is ritually bound to those forefathers (*pitṛs)—viz. his father, grandfather, and great-grandfather—who are regarded as *sapiṇḍa. *See also* PIṆḌA.

saptamātṛkās ('seven mothers') *See* MĀTṚKĀ(S).

saptapadī *See* MARRIAGE.

saptarṣis *See* ṚṢI; MAHARṢI(S).

Śāradā Devī (1853–1920) Brought up in a poor *brahmin family in rural Bengal, Śāradā was married to *Rāmakṛṣṇa at the age of five. At 17 she joined him at the *temple where he was resident in Kolkata (Calcutta), and thereafter served him as a disciple. He, in turn, identified her as a manifestation of the *Goddess (Devī), and the embodiment of all wisdom. Taking their cue from this, the association founded in his name, the *Rāmakṛṣṇa Mission, subsequently revered her as the 'Holy' or 'Divine Mother', Rāmākṛṣṇa's name for *Kālī. After his death, she became the spiritual figure head of the association, resident at their headquarters at the *Rāmakṛṣṇa Maṭha near Kolkata, and she, Rāmakṛṣṇa, and *Vivekānanda (1863–1902) are worshipped as the 'Holy Trio' of the contemporary Mission.

śaraṇāgati *See* PRAPATTI.

Sarasvatī 1. According to the **Ṛg Veda*, a great sacred *river in the region of the Punjab, which subsequently dried up, disappearing, it is said, into the sands of the Rajasthani desert. There have been modern attempts to chart its original course through satellite photography, and it is now frequently suggested that, as probably the major waterway of the *Indus Valley civilization, it may have dried up or changed course around 2000 BCE. It has therefore become central to some of the arguments about the dating of the *Ṛg Veda* and the origins of *Āryan culture. Whatever its historical role, as one of the subcontinent's seven sacred rivers, the Sarasvatī has long been believed to flow underground from the *Himālayas to *Prayāga, where it resurfaces (invisibly, except to *yogins) to become confluent with the rivers *Gaṅgā and *Yamunā.

2. Appearing in the *Ṛg Veda* as the personification of the river (1), Sarasvatī is subsequently revered as the goddess of speech (*vāc, or vāgdevī), poetry, music, and learning, and as the consort of *Brahmā (whose *haṃsa *vāhana she shares). She has a particular association with the medium of traditional learning, *Sanskrit, and therefore also with the **Veda*. (She is said to have been the inventor of the language, and of *devanāgarī, one of the scripts in which it is written.) Iconographically, she is usually depicted as a fair young woman with four arms, holding or playing a *vīṇā (lute); other insignia include a water pot, the *Vedas* in manuscript form, and a *mālā. She may also hold, or be seated on, a *lotus. In northern India, her annual *festival is held during the spring festivities; in the South, it may be part of the autumnal *Navarātrī festival. Although popular, and worshipped independently (particularly by students, teachers, and artists), Sarasvatī is ultimately taken to be a form of the great *Goddess. She is also popular amongst the *Buddhists and, in particular, the *Jains.

Sarasvatī, Dayānanda *See* DAYĀNAND(A) SARASVATĪ.

S

sarga ('creation') The first of the five 'distinguishing marks' (*pañcalakṣaṇa) which are supposed to represent the contents of a **Purāṇa*. According to traditional *cosmogony, sarga is the 'creation' that takes place at the beginning of each *mahākalpa (or 'life of *Brahmā'), as opposed to the secondary 'creation' (*pratisarga) which takes place at the beginning of each 'day of Brahmā'.

Śārīrakabhāṣya *See* ŚAṄKARA.

Sarkar, P. R. (1921–1990) *See* ĀNAND MĀRG.

Śarva (from Skt. śaru, 'arrow') 'The god who shoots fatal arrows'; one of the names of *Śiva; associated in the *Vedic period with *Rudra and *Bhava.

Sarvadarśanasaṃgraha ('Compendium of All Philosophical Schools') *See* MĀDHAVA (1).

Sarvodaya *See* BHĀVE, VINOBĀ.

Śāstā *See* AIYAPPAN.

śāstra ('teaching', 'instruction', 'treatise') Usually applied as a suffix to words such as **Dharma-* (e.g. *Dharmaśāstra*), **Nāṭya-*, **Jyotiḥ-*, etc., to indicate an authoritative and inclusive *Sanskrit treatise on the subject.

sat ('being') **1.** A term which first occurs in the **Ṛg Veda*, indicating 'being' or 'the real', as opposed to asat ('non-being', 'the unreal'). In *Advaita *Vedānta, sat is combined with cit ('awareness, sentience, *consciousness'), and *ānanda ('bliss') into *saccidānanda, a single term conveying the spiritual and unitary character of the absolute (*brahman (neut.)). **2.** A Substantive with the sense of 'true', 'good', or 'right'.

Śatapatha Brāhmaṇa ('*Brāhmaṇa* with a Hundred Paths', *c.*10th–7th centuries BCE) The **Brāhmaṇa* attached to the **White Yajurveda* (the *Vājasaneyī* **Saṃhitā*). The largest, most variegated, and most important of the *Brāhmaṇas*, it exists in two recensions preserved by, respectively, the Mādhyaṃdina *śākhā (from the *Vājasaneyī Mādhyaṃdina Saṃhitā*), and the Kāṇva śākhā (from the *Vājasaneyī Kāṇva Saṃhitā*). The first five of the fourteen sections of the Mādhyaṃdina are associated with the *ṛṣi *Yajñavalkya, and appear to have originated in eastern India; the next four sections deal with the *agnicayana under the authority of the *ṛṣi Śāṇḍilya, and are of northwestern origin; the last section is composed of an **Āraṇyaka*, which includes, and culminates in, the **Bṛhadāraṇyaka Upaniṣad*. Like all *Brāhmaṇas*, the *Śatapatha*'s function is to explicate *Vedic ritual (including, inter alia, a lengthy discussion of the *aśvamedha), but it also contains much theological, cosmological, and mythological material, and is a major source of information about the nature of *Brahmanical religion and society during this period.

Śatarudrīya ('Hundred Names of Rudra') A hymn cataloguing the names (and therefore the qualities and attributes) of *Rudra. It first appears in the **Vājasaneyī* **Saṃhitā* (i.e the **White Yajur Veda*), and thereafter becomes popular as a powerful *Śaiva *mantra.

Satī 1. In *Purāṇic mythology, the wife of *Śiva (so a form of the *Goddess) and a daughter of *Dakṣa. She is said to have attracted the god's attention through the strength of her devotion to him, manifested in her *yogic practice. Such is the insult suffered when Dakṣa excludes her husband from the *sacrifice that Satī immolates herself in the fire created by her own *yoga. Distraught, Śiva snatches her body from the flames and whirls it around in a wild *tāṇḍava dance, threatening the world and the power of the other gods. *Viṣṇu alleviates the threat by slicing off parts of Satī's body wherever Śiva's feet touch the earth. This dismemberment provides the foundational myth for the *śāktipīṭhas, a pan-Indian network of *Tantric *Śākta *pilgrimage sites, each marking a spot where parts of the *Goddess's body fell to earth and are manifested in the local topography.

2. (satī ('true' or 'virtuous wife')**)** A woman who expresses her faithful devotion to her husband, and avoids the supposed *inauspiciousness of *widowhood, by (in theory, voluntarily) immolating herself on her husband's *funeral pyre, in a practice known as sahamaraṇa ('dying together'), sahagamana ('going together'), or anumaraṇa ('dying after'). In the process, she ensures him a good *rebirth by wiping out the consequences of his (or his entire family's) bad *karmic actions. Although recorded as an option in the *Epics, becoming a satī in this ritual sense has always been regarded as an exceptional rather than a usual practice for widows, and even according to the later *dharma texts that condone it, it should be entered into freely. The first evidence of its actual practice occurs in northern Indian inscriptions from the 5th and 6th centuries CE. By the 12th century, hundreds of commemorative stones (H.: satīcaurā—'satī plinth') to satīs had been erected in the North. Increases in the occurrence of sahamaraṇa have been correlated by some with periods of foreign rule, particularly in Bengal, Rajasthan, and *Nepal, where it has been most prevalent. Its precise origins are obscure, but it has, or has been given, a logical correlation with the *Brahmanical idea of the ritual unity of husband and wife, which is broken by the former's *death, leaving the *brahmin widow who choses to live on in a ritually dead and socially anomalous state. Reinforced by its assimilation to the myth of Satī (1), self-immolation therefore confers immense prestige, not just on the woman herself, but also on her husband's family. Hindu reformers, such as Rām Mohan *Roy, and the scandalized English (who referred to the practice as 'suttee') combined to see the practice of widow-burning made illegal in Bengal in 1829, although many traditionalists campaigned to have the ruling overturned. (It remained legal in Nepal until the beginning of the 20th century.) In spite of clear cases of family pressure and coercion, a persistent ambivalence towards the practice is exhibited by some women themselves. This was evident in the demonstrations of support shown by a vocal minority in the wake of the recent, well-publicized (but illegal) sahamaraṇa of the young widow, Roop Kanwar, in Rajasthan (1987).

satkāryavāda ('doctrine that the effect (pre-)exists in its cause') A philosophical doctrine concerning origination or causation, according to which the material effect is identical with, or pre-exists in, the material cause (e.g. the table as effect pre-exists in the wood). This position is held by the *Sāṃkhya, the *Yoga and the *Vedānta schools (with the exception of *Madhva's *Dvaita Vedānta). Within the Vedānta school, *Śaṅkara holds that the effect and its cause (the world and *brahman (neut.)) are actually identical, a doctrine sometimes referred to as satkāraṇavāda. The corollary of this is that any change is only apparent (the vivartavāda doctrine). For *Rāmānuja, however, change is a real transformation (pariṇāma) of cause into effect (the pariṇāmavāda doctrine).

Sat Nām ('True Name') A term used to refer to the undifferentiated and unqualified (*nirguṇa) absolute by some North Indian *sants.

Sat Puruṣa ('True Person/Spirit') A term used to refer to the undifferentiated and unqualified (*nirguṇa) absolute by some North Indian *sants.

Śatrughna In the **Rāmāyaṇa*, the son of King *Daśaratha and *Sumitrā, the twin of *Lakṣmaṇa, and the half-brother of *Rāma, whom he supported.

satsaṅg(a) ('association with the good') A gathering of like-minded devotees (such as followers of the North Indian *sants), who have come together to practise forms of communal *bhakti, principally the singing of *bhajans, or to hear religious teachings. The membership of a particular satsaṅg may cut across *caste boundaries, at least for the duration of the meeting.

Sāttāda Śrī Vaiṣṇavas (Sātānis) A South Indian community of *Teṉkalai *Śrī Vaiṣṇavas (dating from at least 15th century CE), variously identified in the past as both *brahmins and/or *śūdras. Emphasizing the practice of non-*Vedic rites, the community has been open to all *castes, although they are now effectively treated as a separate caste themselves.

sattva ('pure thought', 'purity') According to *Sāṃkhya-Yoga ontology, one of the three *gunas, or strands, of material nature (*prakṛti), sattva is characterized as 'pure'; concomitantly, it represents the principle of pure thought. Since the tripartite guṇa division is extended to various other categories, sattva is also, for instance, used to characterize a group of (sāttvika) *mahāpurāṇas* belonging to *Viṣṇu, and certain 'cool' (i.e. pure and thought-clarifying) *foods.

Sāttvata (Sātvata) A *Vaiṣṇava tradition, usually considered synonymous with that of the *Pāñcarātrins, although there is some evidence that it once had an independent existence. It derives its name from the *Vṛṣṇi (Sātvata) tribe, for whom *Vāsudeva (later *Kṛṣṇa) may have been a deified hero or *king.

Sāttvata Saṃhitā *See* PĀÑCARĀTRA.

sāttvika *See* SATTVA.

Sātvata *See* VṚṢṆI(S).

satyāgraha *See* GĀNDHĪ, MOHANDAS KARAMCHAND.

Satyaloka *See* BRAHMALOKA.

Satya Pīr A probably mythical *Muslim saint (pīr) whose immensely popular cult originated in Bengal in the 16th century CE. He was revered by Muslims and Hindus alike for his ability to protect against disease and demonic powers, and to aid in the acquisition of wealth. Devotion to him was expressed through a large number of songs and stories about the miraculous effects of his worship, which sat comfortably alongside more specifically Islamic and Hindu practices. Offerings were made as they would be to any local deity, often simply to a wooden plank representing the pīr. From around the early 18th century, however, Hindus began to identify Satya Pīr as Satya *Nārāyaṇa, an *avatāra of *Viṣṇu, and in the face of this incorporation, or *Sanskritization, and their own increasingly exclusive understanding of Islam, Muslims gradually relinquished their devotion to him.

satyayuga *See* KṚTA.

śauca ('purity', 'purification') *See* PURE AND IMPURE.

Śaunaka A legendary *ṛṣi, traditionally credited with the authorship of the **Bṛhaddevatā*. His is also the name given to one of the recensions of the **Atharva Veda*.

Saundaryalaharī ('The Ocean of Beauty') A popular *Śrī Vidyā hymn praising the goddess *Tripurasundarī. The tradition ascribes it to *Śaṅkara, although it seems to owe more to *Kashmiri Śaivism.

Sauptikaparvan ('The Book of the Massacre at Night') The tenth book of the *Sanskrit **Mahābhārata*, recounting how, possessed by *Śiva, *Aśvatthāman carries out his threat to massacre the victorious *Pāṇḍava army as it sleeps, and then unleashes a weapon of total destruction. Kṛṣṇa, however, intervenes to preserve the *Kuru line in the person of the unborn *Parikṣit.

Saura ('relating to Sūrya') A practice, *temple, or text belonging to the Sun god, *Sūrya; a worshipper of Sūrya.

Saura Purāṇa An **upapurāṇa* which, in spite of its name, is *Śaiva in orientation; *Sūrya (hence *Saura) is merely its mouthpiece. A properly Saura **Purāṇa* of the same name is presumed to have once existed, but is now lost.

Savan Singh (1858–1948) *See* RADHASOAMI SATSANG.

Savarkar, Vinayak Damodar (1883–1966) An influential, and highly controversial, right-wing, Hindu nationalist ideologue. Born into a Maharastrian *brahmin family, he was educated in Pune, where he first became politically active. Imprisoned by the British in 1910 for his attempts to engender revolution, he was later released (1924) and eventually became president (1937–42) of the *Hindū Mahāsabhā, through which he promoted the ideology of Hindutva, a term he had championed in *Hindutva: Who is a Hindu* (1923). He was put on trial in 1948 for his alleged involvement in the assassination of *Gāndhī, but acquitted due to lack of evidence. (However, a Government appointed commission in the 1960s suggested that he was indeed implicated.) He was a prolific author of revisionist historical and political works in his native language of Marathi.

Savitṛ ('vivifier') In the **Ṛg Veda*, a name of the Sun god. He is sometimes treated as identical with *Sūrya, and sometimes differentiated from him, representing the latter's divine, vivifying power. The term may also be used of the sun between setting and rising, as opposed to 'Sūrya', which denotes it in the daytime. *See also* SĀVITRĪ MANTRA.

Sāvitrī A highly popular exemplar of the ideal *pativratā, the devoted wife. Her story occurs in the **Āraṇyakaparvan* of the **Mahābharata*, in a section known as the *Pativratāmāhatmya* ('The Glorification of the Faithful Wife'). Through her devotion and courage, her knowledge of *dharma, and the strength of her *tapas, Savitri acquires the power to overcome *Yama (Death), and restore her husband, Satyavat, to life.

Sāvitrī mantra *See* GĀYATRĪ MANTRA.

Sawan Singh *See* SAVAN SINGH.

Sāyaṇa (d. 1387?) The author of the most celebrated commentary on the **Vedas*, the *Vedārtha Prakāśa* ('Light on the Meaning of the *Veda*'). He is said to have been a general and a minister under the *Vijayanagara kings of the 14th century, and the younger brother of the *Advaitin chief minister, *Mādhava. In addition to his extensive *Veda* commentaries, some of which appear to have been collaborations with his brother and his pupils, or the work of later scholars, Sāyaṇa is also credited with numerous works on other aspects of Indian culture, including ritual, grammar (*vyakāraṇa), *Āyurveda, and literature.

Schopenhauer, Arthur (1788–1860) A celebrated German philosopher who was one of the first Western thinkers to take Indian philosophical thought seriously. He was particularly affected by *Buddhism and by the **Upaniṣads*, coming to know the latter through *Anquetil du Perron's 'translation' (1802).

self *See* ĀTMAN; JĪVA; PURUṢA.

Self-Realization Fellowship A California-based organization, founded by Paramahaṃsa *Yogānanda in 1925 for the dissemination of *kriyā-yoga (2), a technique said to be derived from the *yoga taught by *Kṛṣṇa in the **Bhagavadgītā*. It is claimed that this ancient tradition was revived in the 19th century by a mysterious *guru known as Mahāvatar Babaji, who transmitted it to Lahiri Mahasaya (1828–1895). From him it was passed to Sri Yukteswar Giri (1855–1936), and his pupil, Yogānanda. Under the direction of a monastic order, the Self-Realization Fellowship now has *temples and *meditation centres throughout the world. The Fellowship promotes a 'scientific' and universal yoga, drawing on Yogānanda's oral teachings and writings, notably his popular *Autobiography of a Yogi* (1946). Its followers aim to attain a direct personal experience of God, regarded as the culmination of all religious and scientific traditions. The Fellowship is the Western version of its less prominent Indian sister organization, the Yogoda Satsanga Society of India, founded by Yogānanda in 1917, with its headquarters at Dakshineshwar near Kolkata (Calcutta).

Sen, Keshab Chandra (Keshub Chunder Sen) (1838–1884) Born into a *Vaiṣṇava vaidya ('medical') *caste in Calcutta, Sen had a Westernized education. In 1858 he joined the *Brāhmo Samāj, its then leader, the *brahmin Debendranāth *Tagore initiating him as the organization's first non-brahmin teacher (*ācārya) in 1862. Subsequently, a group of Brāhmos gathered itself around Sen which was much more radical in its rejection of traditional Hindu practices and attitudes (including adherence to caste distinctions) than Tagore's followers, and took an aggressively missionary stance, drawing on Western models while rejecting the *Christianity of the missionaries. The tension between the two groups within the Samāj resulted in the split of 1866, with Sen's followers forming the 'Brāhmo Samāj of India'. Thereafter, Sen himself became ever more idiosyncratic in his religious practice (a personal synthesis of Christian and Hindu elements), and increasingly indifferent to social reform. In 1870 he visited England, lecturing on the Asiatic nature of Jesus. In 1878 he married his 13-year-old daughter to the 15-year-old crown prince of a British princely state in a traditional Hindu *marriage ceremony. This apparent approval of *child marriage, and what they regarded as 'idolatry', led to Sen's abandonment by many of his followers, who formed the Sādhāraṇ Brāhmo Samāj in 1878. Sen himself gathered the remnant into the 'Church of the New Dispensation' in 1881, its practices influenced by Vaiṣṇava devotionalism and Sen's admiration for *Rāmakṛṣṇa.

Servants of India Society *See* GOKHALE, GOPAL KRISHNA.

Śeṣa (Ananta, Ādiśeṣa) ('remainder') The thousand-headed serpent upon which *Viṣṇu, canopied by its hood, is depicted as sleeping, either in the interval between *kalpa, or in his *Vaikuṇṭha heaven. Śeṣa is also thought to support the earth, his coils symbolizing eternity. He is celebrated in the annual *Nāga Pañcamī festival. *See also* ĀDIŚEṢA; ANANTA.

sevā ('service') A corollary and expression of *bhakti, particularly for the *Śrī Vaiṣṇavas, it involves all aspects of the respectful and devoted material care of the *arcāvatāra of the deity. By extension, such sevā is also due to one's *guru. Since the 19th century, the term has also acquired a wider meaning, with *Neo-Hindu reformers and others considering it a social as well as a religious duty to 'serve' the poor and disadvantaged.

'seven mothers' (saptamātṛkās) *See* MĀTṚKĀ(S).

'seven ṛṣis' (saptarṣis) *See* ṚṢI; MAHARṢI(S).

Shāh Jahān (1592–1666, r. 1628–1658) The fifth *Mughal emperor, famously responsible for the construction of the Tāj Mahal at Agra as a mausoleum for his wife, Mumtāz Mahal.

Shiv Sena ('the army of Śiva' (= Śivājī)) A militant Maharashtrian Hindu nationalist organization, founded in Bombay (Mumbai) by Bal Thackeray (Thakare) in 1966. Formed to oppose immigration into

S

Maharashtra from other Indian states, it became virulently anti-*Muslim, and was responsible for the rioting and communal violence in Mumbai in 1992, which occurred in the wake of the demolition of the Bābrī Masjid mosque in *Ayodhyā. Adopting a Hindutva stance, Shive Sena has had considerable political success in Maharashtra in coalition with the *Bhāratīya Janatā Party. The organization, or its paramilitary offshoots, have been persistently implicated in acts of organized violence.

siddha ('perfected', 'realized') A generic term for a practitioner (*sādhaka), such as a *yogi or a *Tantric adept, who has attained the goal of his practice (*sādhana), which may include the attainment of supernatural or spiritual powers (*siddhis), and a perfected (siddha) body.

siddhānta ('established end') The technical term for the demonstrated and definitive conclusion to a theological or philosophical argument. It follows the refutation of the *pūrvapakṣa.

Siddha(s) (Yogi(s)) 1. A term applied to members of a variety of medieval *Tantric traditions, and their precursors, indicating that they held certain beliefs and practices in common. These included the conviction that innumerable semi-divine figures, also known as Siddhas, were resident in a *heaven which practitioners could reach through the Tantric, *yogic, or alchemical perfection of their bodies. The goal was to construct an immutable body, capable of supernatural powers (*siddhis). Success resulted in *jīvanmukti, liberation while still embodied, a divinized state of *immortality and power, either here or in the *heaven of the Siddhas. *See also* ALCHEMY; NĀTH SIDDHAS. **2.** *See* CITTAR.

Siddhasiddhānta Paddhati (*c.*13th century CE) A sophisticated *Nāth Siddha *haṭha-yoga text which, in addition to *yoga, deals with esoteric anatomy, *cosmology, and metaphysics.

Siddha Yoga An organization effectively founded by Swami *Muktānanda, under the direction of his *guru, Swami *Nityānanda. Developed in the mid 1950s at an *āśram at Ganeśpuri, near Mumbai (which, under the name Gurudev Siddha Peeth, remains its headquarters), Siddha Yoga was spread to the West in the 1970s, and is now established in over forty other āśrams across the world, of which the most important is the Shree Muktānanda Ashram in New York State. Siddha Yoga's current leader, and 'living master', is Swami *Cidvilāsānanda. The organization propagates a mixture of *Kashmiri Śaivism and *kuṇḍalinī-based *yoga techniques.

siddhi(s) (ṛddhi(s), vibhūti) (lit. 'accomplishment', 'attainment', 'perfection', 'supernatural/spiritual power') One goal—sometimes the primary one—of *Tantric and *yogic practitioners, such as the *siddhas, is to generate and enjoy supernormal powers (siddhis). A standard list of eight is given in the commentary to the **Yoga Sūtra* (3.45): i) the power to become minute as an atom (*aṇimā); ii) the power to become weightless (i.e. to levitate) (laghimā); iii) the power to expand the body or penetrate any object (mahimā); iv) the power to reach across any space or distance (prāpti); v) the power to exert an irresistible will (prākāmya); vi) the power of unbridled control over the elements (vaśitva); vii) the unimpeded power of creation and destruction (īśitva); viii) the power to obtain anything one desires (kāmāvasāyitva). While for the adherents of *Patañjali's classical *Yoga system (*c.*3rd–4th century CE), such siddhis are epiphenomena of *meditation and yogic practice, indicating the success (siddhi) of their continuing practice, ultimately they are also attachments distracting from the goal of spiritual liberation (*mokṣa). For others, however, they are the manifestations of the body's perfection, the corporeal 'immortality' of *jīvanmukti. Devotees of particular siddhas or *gurus may expect them to demonstrate various siddhis as a public manifestation of their yogic attainments (e.g. the 'miracles' of Sathya *Sai Baba).

Sikh The name given to the disciples of Gurū *Nānak, and so by extension to the followers of the religious tradition now known as *Sikhism.

śikhā (H.: **choṭī**) A tuft of hair on the crown of the head, traditionally left unshaven by *brahmins, since it is thought to cover the *brahmarandhra ('*Brahmā's crevice'), the aperture through which the *soul is thought to escape at *death. It is cut off as part of the ritual for becoming a *saṃnyāsin.

Śikhaṇḍin *See* AMBĀ; BHĪṢMA.

śikhara ('pointed', 'peaked') The characteristic tower (usually a series of ascending peaks or spires) erected as a superstructure above the *garbhagṛha, principally in North Indian Hindu *temples. It is supposed to represent the *Himālayas in general, and Mount *Meru, the axis mundi, in particular.

Sikhism (Sikh Panth) An Indian religious tradition, now treated (and treating itself) separately from both Hinduism and *Islam, although in its origins, practices, and beliefs, it has elements in common with both, sharing, in particular, the *bhakti orientation of the North Indian *sants. Gurū *Nānak (1469–1539), regarded with hindsight as the first *Sikh gurū (teacher), and therefore the founder of the tradition, had been influenced by the poetry of *Kabīr. He taught an essentially monotheistic route to *liberation from *karma, to be achieved through *meditation on the divine Name (nām) of the transcendent, but also personal, deity, characterized as the Sat Gurū ('True Gurū'). His hymns and teachings, along with those of the four Gurūs who immediately succeeded him (as well as the verses of earlier sants), were collected by Arjan, the fifth Gurū, in the **Ādi Granth* (1603–4), which became the foundational text of the tradition. The gurū lineage established by Nānak, was dissolved by the tenth gurū, Gobind Singh (1666–1708), who shortly before his death declared that the leadership of the community (made up entirely of lay people) would now be invested in the *Ādi Granth* (henceforward, *Gurū Granth Sāhib*), and the Sikhs who followed its teaching. It was also the militant Gobind Singh who introduced a new category of Sikh, those formally initiated into the Khalsa ('the Pure'), distinguished by five insignia which, in Punjabi, all begin with the letter 'k': uncut hair, a sword, shorts, an iron or steel wristband, and a comb. Sikh worship is largely congregational, focusing on the reading and recitation of the *Gurū Granth Sāhib*, which is installed in temples called gurdvāras/gurdwaras, of which the most sacred is the Golden Temple (Harimandir) at Amritsar. Historically, the Sikh population, which is Punjabi speaking, has been concentrated in the homeland of its founder. Before *Partition this was the wider Punjab; after Partition (1947) Sikhs chose to live in India, mostly in the Indian state also known as the Punjab. In the run-up to Independence, some Sikhs called for an independent state (Khalistan). This led to an ongoing political tension, which periodically flared into violence, notably the storming of the Golden Temple in 1984, followed by the assassination of the Prime Minister, Indira Gandhi, by her Sikh bodyguards, and the subsequent murder of several thousand Sikhs in Delhi and elsewhere. According to the 2001 census there are 19 000 000 Sikhs in India. Since the 1950s there has also been a considerable migration of Sikhs to the UK and North America. The current UK population is probably in excess of 400 000, more than two-thirds of whom are British-born.

Śikṣā One of the six **Vedāṅgas*, consisting of *Sanskrit texts dealing with phonetic analysis. Their aim is to provide instruction in the proper pronunciation of the **Veda*, an essential prerequisite for the effective performance of *Brahmanical ritual.

Śikṣāṣṭaka *See* CAITANYA.

Śilpaśāstra A category of *Sanskrit texts, or manuals, dealing with such arts/crafts (śilpas) as iconography, and the production of paintings and sculptures, particularly of *temple *mūrtis. More broadly it also covers aesthetics, planning and architecture, although the latter is also dealt with in *Vāstuśāstra*, resulting in no clear boundary between the two types of text. *Śilpaśāstras* have been produced from at least as early as the Gupta period (*c.*320 CE–*c.*6th century CE), reflecting diverse traditions across the subcontinent. Influential works of this kind include the *Aparājitapṛcchā* (western India), the *Mayaśāstra* (southern), the *Tantrasamuccaya* (southwestern), and the pan-Indian *Mayamata*. Produced by *brahmins rather than craftsmen, they appear more concerned with theory and tradition—the symbolic meaning and ritual significance of the buildings and their contents—than with practical considerations and particular blueprints.

Śiśupāla In the **Mahābhārata*, an ally of the *Pāṇḍavas who quarrels with *Kṛṣṇa at *Yudhiṣṭhira's *rājasūya, and is killed for his pains. The father of *Dhṛṣṭaketu.

śiṣya ('pupil') *See* GURU.

Sītā (Jānakī ('daughter of Janaka'), **Ayonijā** ('not born from a womb')**)** ('furrow') In the **Rāmāyaṇa*, the daughter of King *Janaka of *Videha, and the wife of *Rāma. Janaka brings her into existence when she springs from the furrow he is ploughing as part of a spring fertility ritual (suggesting, perhaps, an independent origin as an agricultural deity.) At her *svayaṃvara, Rāma breaks *Śiva's bow and so wins her hand in *marriage. Later, when he is exiled from *Ayodhyā, Sītā insists on accompanying her husband into the *forest. It is there that the *rākṣasa king, *Rāvaṇa, abducts her, and carries her off to the island of *Laṅkā, where she virtuously resists his advances. Eventually, she is discovered in her captivity by *Hanumān. He offers to carry her home, but she prefers to be rescued by her husband alone. Rāma arrives with his monkey army and defeats Rāvaṇa. At this point, Rāma rejects Sītā, suggesting that she may have been sullied by her stay in another man's house. Despairing, Sītā demonstrates her virtue by immolating herself on a pyre. The gods intervene, and Rāma receives her back; he had never doubted her himself, but her fidelity had to be proven in public. A period of married bliss follows Rāma's installation as *king, but this is undermined by rumours that Sītā may have been violated by Rāvaṇa during her captivity. To avoid this casting doubt on his honour, or undermining his status as a perfect king, Rāma orders Lakṣmaṇa to abandon the queen in the forest. There, in *Vālmīki's hermitage, she gives birth to Rāma's twin sons, *Lava and *Kuśa. When their identity is revealed, Rāma recalls Sītā from the forest. When urged once again to affirm her fidelity in public, Sītā calls on her mother, the Earth (*Bhū Devī) to witness her *purity of thought and action by swallowing her up, which duly happens.

Sītā has traditionally been regarded as the perfect woman—the epitome of the ideal high *caste Hindu wife—one who is chaste and modest, faithful and devoted to her husband, and rigorous in the protection of her own virtue, as defined by *strīdharmic norms. As Rāma/*Viṣṇu's consort, Sītā is frequently assimilated to *Lakṣmī; for some *Vaiṣṇava *bhakti sects, such as the *Rāmānandīs, she may assume a significance equal to that of her husband. *See also* JANAKPŪR.

Sītā

Śītalā ('the cool one') A name for both 'smallpox' and its goddess, perhaps derived from the shivering fits of the victims. A pan-Indian village deity (*grāmadevatā) with many localized forms, such as *Māriyammaṉ and *Jyeṣṭhā, Śītalā is thought to control the disease by possessing the afflicted; at the same time she protects those who believe in her and propitiate her from infection. In some instances she is treated as a form of *Devī and worshipped accordingly. Unmarried, powerful, and fierce, she demands blood, or other *impure *sacrifices. Personified, Śītalā is depicted as a scarlet, naked woman sitting on an ass, holding a broom, or winnowing fan, and a pot. Since the eradication of smallpox in the 1970s, she has been worshipped by many as an AIDS goddess.

Śiva ('auspicious', 'benevolent', also known by numerous epithets—e.g. Mahākāla, Maheśvara) One of the three great deities of medieval and subsequent Hinduism; he is the focus of worship in the *Śaiva traditions (collectively referred to as *Śaivism). His historical origins are obscure, although some claim to find evidence of a 'proto-Śiva' cult in the material remains of the *Indus Valley civilization. Textual evidence begins with the application of the partly euphemistic epithet 'śiva' ('benign') to the wild and ambiguous deity *Rudra in the **Ṛg Veda*. Considerably later (*c.*3rd–1st century BCE), Rudra is identified as the supreme God in the **Śvetāśvatara Upaniṣad*, and from about the 2nd century CE onwards, Śiva (now subsuming Rudra) becomes the focus of a wide-ranging, pan-Indian *Purāṇic, *Tantric, and *bhakta literature, accompanied by a complex ritual culture and a rich iconography.

Śiva is portrayed in multiple ways, with numerous regional (e.g. *Khaṇḍobā), sectarian (e.g. *Bhairava), and mythological (e.g. *Gaṅgādhara) variations. His anthropomorphic depiction as the great *ascetic, whose mastery of *yoga (the *tapas he has generated) is signified by his '*third-eye', typically shows him smeared in ashes (*bhasman), clad in the skin of a tiger or an elephant, carrying a trident (*triśūla) or *khaṭvāṅga, his hair in a matted top-knot (*jaṭā), crowned by a crescent moon, wearing a garland (*mālā) of *rudrākṣa berries, or of skulls, entwined with snakes and carrying an alms bowl made from a human skull (*kapāla). This continues to provide the model for the outward appearance of many Śaiva ascetics, such as the *Kāpālikas. In general, his representations in painting, sculpture, and narrative are intended to evoke the ambiguity inherent in his power: he is the sexually continent, celibate, *ascetic mendicant—the solitary, matted-haired 'outsider', patrolling the fringes of *Vedic culture, deliberately, and terrifyingly, courting the *impurities of the *cremation ground. At the same time, he is the sensual, erotic, and fertile God in his familial prime, surrounded, in his *Himālayan stronghold, by his wife (*Pārvatī), and children (*Gaṇeśa, *Murukaṉ/

*Kārtikkeya/*Skanda), accompanied by his *vāhana, *Naṇḍin. This dual (for some paradoxical) aspect of Śiva's character is graphically represented in the form in which he is most commonly worshipped, the aniconic *liṅga, usually set in a *yoni. The liṅga represents his male spirit, the yoni, his *śakti, or female power, conceptualized, to a greater or lesser extent, as his consort, the Goddess (*Devī). Taken together, they symbolize the god's unlimited and dynamic potency, his simultaneously fertile and destructive energy. In a further rendition of these contrasting but complementary attributes, Śiva is visualized as the ecstatic, omnipresent, and omnipotent cosmic deity who, as *Naṭarāja, dances the world to destruction, only to create it again as part of the continuing cosmic cycle. Although his *temples and *tīrthas are ubiquitous, he is particularly associated with the city of *Vārāṇasī. *See also* PAŚUPATI; RUDRA; ŚAIVISM.

Śivādvaita (Śrīkaṇṭha school) A South Indian *Śaiva theological school, associated with Śrīkaṇṭha (*c.*1200 CE?) which, as its name suggests, viewed *Śiva and *brahman (neut.) as being one and the same, subsumed in the title Paramaśiva ('Supreme / Transcendent Śiva'). Similarly, in his commentary on the **Brahma Sūtras*, Śrīkaṇṭha claims that the **Veda* was the work of Śiva, and that it is identical with the *Śiva *Āgamas*. The teachings of the school were expanded by *Appaya Dīkṣita.

***Śivāgamas* (*Śiva-Āgamas*)** *See* ĀGAMA(S).

Śivajī (Shivaji) (1627–1680) The leader of the *Marāṭhā resistance to the *Mughal rule of *Aurangzeb. He successfully established an independent kingdom in Maharashtra, and at his coronation in Pune in 1674 (conducted by the *Sanskrit *paṇḍita, *Gāgābhaṭṭa) he had himself declared a *kṣatriya Hindu *king. His teacher was said to have been the *Vaiṣṇava *sant, *Rāmadāsa. Subsequently deified by his followers, Śivajī has proved a hero to nationalists such as *Tilak, who inaugurated a *festival in his name; and in 1966 Bal Thackeray (Thakare) named his militant Maharashtrian Hindu nationalist organization, *Shiv Sena ('Śivajī's Army'), after him.

Śivajñānabodham See MEYKAṆṬĀR.

Śivakāmasundarī ('Śiva's beautiful beloved') The name of the goddess who is *Śiva *Naṭarāja's consort at *Cidambaram. She is installed in both the god's *temple, and in her own nearby shrine.

Śivānanda, Swami (1887–1963) A *saṃnyāsin who founded the *Divine Life Society. Born into a distinguished *brahmin family, he trained and practised as a medical doctor in India and Malaya before formally renouncing at *Hṛṣīkeśa in 1924. After over a decade of wandering mendicancy, he founded the Divine Life Society in 1936, with its headquarters at the Śivānanda Āśram in Hṛṣīkeśa. The doctrinal basis of his teaching was a form of *Advaita Vedānta universalism (the *Christian, Francis of Assisi (1182–1228) is included in a list of the Society's saints); in practice, this was conveyed through a concern for the poor and the sick—the Society runs hospitals and *Āyurvedic dispensaries—and the advocacy of a synthetic form of *yoga. Śivānanda was succeeded by his pupil, Swami *Cidānanda (b. 1916).

***Śiva Purāṇa* (*Vāyu Purāṇa*)** Classified as one of the eighteen 'great **Purāṇas*' (*mahāpurāṇas*) in the *tāmasa group, i.e. those said to relate to *Śiva, it is highly composite in nature. In addition to the usual contents, it contains early material on *Lākulīśa and the *Pāśupata tradition.

Śivarātri (Mahāśivarātri ('Great Night of Śiva)**)** ('Night of Śiva') An annual pan-Indian *festival in honour of *Śiva, held on the fourteenth day of the dark lunar fortnight during the month of Māgha (January–February), or Phālguna (February–March), depending on the *calendar being used. It involves fasting, and performing four different Śiva *pūjās, with *bilva leaves and water, at intervals during a night time vigil. An explanatory myth tells of how a hunter spends a foodless night sheltering from wild animals in a *bilva tree. Some water and the leaves of the tree fall onto a Śiva *liṅga concealed below. Consequently, the hunter is liberated as result of his inadvertent pūjā.

Śiv Dayal Singh (Shiv Dayal Singh) (1818–1878) *See* RADHADOAMI SATSANG.

Skanda *See* KĀRTTIKEYA; MURUKAṈ.

Skanda Purāṇa Classified as one of the eighteen 'great *Purāṇas*' (*mahāpurāṇas*) in the *tāmasa group, i.e. those said to relate to *Śiva. Named after Śiva's son, *Skanda, it is the longest of the *Purāṇas*, but as it now exists lacks all unity or overall coherence. Effectively an assembly of individual texts, some of which are relatively recent, it deals, inter alia, with such topics as *tīrthas (including a long section on *Kāśī), and the origins of *castes and tribal groups.

śloka A metrical form, consisting of four *pādas, or quarter-verses, of eight syllables each. It developed out of the *Vedic *anuṣṭubh to become the principal *Epic metre.

smallpox *See* ŚĪTALĀ.

smārta ('based on tradition') An adjective applied to orthoprax *brahmins who, through the medieval period, followed *smṛti, in the sense of conforming to the prescriptions of *Dharmaśāstra* (**Manusmṛti*, etc.) in general, and *varṇāśramadharma in particular. Smārtas are also referred to as *paurāṇikas, in so far as their theology and ritual is drawn from the *Purāṇas*, notably in their performance of *pañcāyatana pūjā, the domestic worship of the five deities, *Devī, *Gaṇeśa, *Śiva, *Sūrya, and *Viṣṇu. (In this way they were distinguished both from *śrautas, and from the followers of *Tantric traditions.) Since about the 9th or 10th century CE, many smārtas have aligned themselves with *Śaṅkara's *Advaita Vedānta theology, at the same time showing a tendency to elevate Śiva above the other four deities, in so far as they equate him with the Advaitin's absolute *brahman (neut.). The term 'smārta' is, however, also applied to brahmins in the *Śrī Vaiṣṇava tradition. Today, the South Indian *Aiyar smārta brahmins are notable for the role they play in *Śaiva *temple ritual at *Cidambaram, where they help to conduct the ritual according to *Vedic rather than Tantric rites (i.e they use Vedic *mantras). Smārta practice remains an index of orthopraxy, and its followers exemplars of orthodoxy, even though in both their ideology and their ritual they clearly absorbed (and *Brahmanized) elements from the esoteric Tantric traditions.

śmaśāna *See* CREMATION GROUND.

smṛti *See* ŚRUTI AND SMṚTI.

snakes *See* NĀGA(S).

snāna ('bathing', 'washing') A ritual bath, either of the *image of a deity during *pūjā, or taken by a worshipper or ritualist, as a *purificatory measure, and/or to mark the boundaries of a ritual or *āśrama. It typically involves pouring water over the head. *See also* SAMĀVARTANA.

snātaka *See* SAMĀVARTANA.

Ṣoḍaśī ('consisting of sixteen') One of the *Mahāvidyā transformations of *Devī. She is also identified with *Kāmākhyā and *Tripurasundarī.

Solar dynasty *See* SŪRYAVAṂŚA.

soma 1. ('the pressed out one') The name given by the *Vedic Indians to i) a plant, ii) the plant's juice when ritually extracted and prepared as a libatory drink, and iii) that libation conceptualized as a god (*deva). Soma was central to the ritual practices evoked in the hymns of the *Ṛg Veda* (the 120 hymns of *maṇḍala nine are devoted to it). Prior to the sacrifice, the soma had to be brought from the mountains by an outsider, or a *śūdra, and exchanged for a *cow. (In general, soma is seen as having to be 'won'.) The subsequent ritual required the pressing between stones of the rehydrated stalk of the plant; the resulting tawny juice was filtered and mixed with other fluids, such as milk and water, before being poured into three jars or vats, from which it was offered to the gods by way of the fire (*agni), and imbibed by the officiating *brahmin priests.

According to the mythology of the **Brāhmaṇas*, it is because they drink the soma prepared for them in the sacrifice that the gods are immortal (*amṛta). Thus transformed, soma itself is regarded as being synonymous with amṛta, the 'nectar of immortality' (ambrosia); indeed, as a god, it is said to have descended from heaven to earth in the first place. The priests, who have likewise drunk soma, ascend to the sky or to *heaven, and experience 'immortality' for the duration of the ritual (or for as long as the effect of the soma lasts), in anticipation of permanent immortality in the future. In the words of one hymn: 'We have drunk soma; we have become immortal (amṛta); we have gone to the light; we have found the gods (devas)' (*Ṛg Veda* 8.48.3).

Beyond this, soma's effects are variously suggested in the Vedic hymns. Because 'King Soma' (as he is frequently characterized in the hymns) is powerful, he is dangerous, but he also bestows his power, especially on the god *Indra, to whom he is most frequently offered, and by extension to the human drinker who identifies with Indra. Some evocations suggest ecstatic, consciousness-transforming, and 'out of the body' states, and therefore imply some 'immortal' entity which can be separated from the body. The extent to which these are descriptions of real psycho-physical transformations, as opposed to rhetorical tropes, or metaphorical evocations of a libation also regarded as a deity, is uncertain. Partly as a result of this, the drink's actual properties, and thus the soma plant's botanical identity, have remained sources of controversy. Notable candidates put forward by modern scholars have been the hallucinogenic, fly-agaric mushroom (*amanita muscaria*), and the stimulant, ephedra. The latter is also claimed as the identity of haoma, a major component of *Zoroastrian ritualism and the Iranian equivalent to soma. The prevailing view is that the psychotropic effects were real enough in the early Vedic period, and probably a common feature of Indo-Iranian religious practice for a long time before that.

From at least the time of the **Brāhmaṇas* onwards various soma sacrifices—paradigmatically the *agniṣṭoma—were considered the essential culmination to the annual cycle of hierarchically ordered *śrauta rituals. In addition, the agniṣṭoma provided the framework for such elaborate optional rites as the *agnicayana, and was an indispensable component of other major śrauta rituals, such as the *rājasūya or 'royal consecration'. The original soma plant was, however, increasingly replaced by various substitutes. According to some, it had been deliberately 'forgotten', or lost as the centre of Vedic civilization moved further from the plant's habitat in the mountains (referred to as Mūjavat in the *Ṛg Veda*). Soma's immediate effects—or the lack of them—were, in any case, now considered irrelevant in the context of a sacrificial 'theology' that demanded complete accuracy in the performance of the ritual as a means to achieving its stated ends. In its substituted form, soma was therefore one more, albeit essential, component in an elaborate hierarchy of rites entered on by the *āhitāgni, or śrauta ritualist. And like other elements of the ritual, it was now subordinate to the power of the brahmins ('the gods on earth') who, through their knowledge of the sacrifice—of how to prepare and offer soma in conjunction with the correct *mantras—guaranteed their own immortality as well as the proper functioning of the cosmos. Nevertheless, by establishing a link between the state of the gods ('immortality') and the internal state of the individual, soma continued to provide both a paradigm and a precedent for the transformation of *consciousness in Indian religious traditions well beyond the confines of the śrauta ritual, regardless of whether such transformation was externally stimulated or internally generated through, for instance, meditational or *yogic practice.

2. In late Vedic and *Brahmanical mythology, Soma is identified with the moon, probably on the principle that the moon is a receptacle for the heavenly soma (*amṛta*) which the gods drink causing it to wane. This identification is clearly linked to Soma's wider responsibility as a god for the circulation of the cosmic waters, and so with the cycle of life and death. In classical *Sanskrit 'soma' is simply synonymous with other words for 'moon'.

Somadeva (*c.*1050 CE) *See* KAṬHĀSARITSĀGARA.

S

Somānanda (*c.*900–950 CE) A precursor of *Abhinavagupta in the *Pratyabhijñā School of *Kashmir(i) Śaivism. His major work was the **Śivadṛṣṭi* ('Vision of Śiva').

Somanātha *See* SOMNĀTH.

Somaśambhu (latter half of the 11th century CE) The author of an important *Śaiva Siddhānta ritual manual (*paddhati), which is named after him, the *Somaśambhupaddhati*. He is said to have been the abbot of a South Indian monastery.

Somaskanda ('with [sa-] Umā and Skanda') The name for *Śiva presented in a sculptural grouping (notably in some South Indian bronzes) with his consort *Umā and, between them, the infant *Skanda. He is worshipped in this form in, for example, the *Mīnākṣī-Sundareśvara *temple at *Madurai, and the Tyāgarāja temple at *Tiruvārūr.

Somavaṃśa *See* CANDRAVAṂŚA.

Somnāth (Somanātha) A celebrated *Śaiva *temple town and *tīrtha on the West coast of Gujarat. Sacked by the *Muslim marauder, Maḥmūd of Ghazna (971–1030 CE) in 1025/6, the main temple has been rebuilt several times since, most recently in the 1990s. It is one of the twelve *jyotirliṅga sites.

Somnāthpuram The name of a site in Karnataka containing a complex of *Hoysaḷa temples, among which the Keśava temple (mid 13th century) is the only surviving complete example of the style.

son *See* PUTRA.

soul *See* ĀTMAN; JĪVA; PURUṢA.

south *See* DAKṢINĀ (1).

Spalding Chair of Eastern Religions and Ethics A post endowed by H. N. Spalding (1877–1953) at All Souls College, Oxford University in 1936. A number of distinguished *Indologists have been elected to the Chair, including the first holder, Sarvepalli *Radhakrishnan (1936–9), R. C. *Zaehner (1952–74), and Bimal Krishna *Matilal (1977–91).

Spanda ('Vibration') Claimed by some to be a School of *Kashmir Śaivism founded by *Vasugupta. Its existence is largely predicated on a series of commentaries on the *Spandakārikā* ('Stanzas on Vibration', authorship uncertain). This tradition appears to have been shaped by *Kṣemarāja, and so the Spanda 'School' seems to be effectively a satellite of the *Trika and *Pratyabhijñā Schools.

spanda ('vibration') A term applied by *Bhartṛhari to evoke the way in which linguistic activity works—as a vibration of *consciousness. The idea was developed as a key component in the theology of *Kashmiri Śaivism, where spanda refers to the subtle, creative vibration of the Absolute consciousness.

sphoṭa (lit. 'a boil', 'bursting') According to the theory of speech (*śabda) developed by *Bhartṛhari, sphoṭa is the underlying or inner speech which, having evolved out of the Absolute, or *śabdabrahman, is an integral part of everyone's *consciousness. This manifests itself as articulate sound (*dhvani/*nāda), or a series of sounds, at which point the meaning of the sentence, etc., is disclosed or 'bursts forth'. Sphoṭa is therefore the bearer of the meaning, or 'that from which the meaning bursts forth', and it is nāda which makes it manifest. The theory was further developed by *Maṇḍana Miśra in works such as the *Sphoṭasiddhi* ('The Establishment of the Essence of Meaning'), where he attempted to establish sphoṭa as the underlying metaphysical and epistemological principle of *Advaita Vedānta.

spirit *See* PURUṢA.

śraddhā ('faith', 'confidence') An essential component of *Vedic ritual—the confidence and belief that the rite will produce the intended results, almost equivalent to a contract with the *devas. The term comes to be used in a more general sense (in, for example the **Bhagavadgītā* 18.71) to express confidence in a teaching, and also, therefore, in its promised outcome.

śrāddha (derived from śraddhā, 'faith') **1.** Sometimes used as a synonym for the *antyeṣṭi rites, although, strictly speaking, it only applies to that group of supplementary rituals which, starting with the smashing of the corpse's skull, focus on making an after-death body for the deceased through *sapiṇḍīkaraṇa. **2.** ('ancestor worship') A general term for the ritual feeding of the ancestors (*pitṛs) at regular post-death intervals to ensure that they continue to thrive in the afterlife, the most basic form being the daily offering of water (*tarpaṇa) as part of the *mahāyajña. More extensive rites involve the offering of *piṇḍa.

śramaṇa ('striver') A term for a heterodox *ascetic, often contrasted with the orthodox brāhmaṇa (*brahmin) who accepts the authority of the **Veda*. In the plural, it is usually applied to the disparate groups of *renouncers who were experimenting with various forms of *yoga and *tapas in the period leading up to the historical founding of *Buddhism and *Jainism—traditions which emerged from this background. The term is also used more generally for anyone undertaking an ascetic or renunciatory discipline.

śrauta In *Vedic or *Brahmanical religion, an adjective applied to a person, practice, or text 'related or adhering to the ritual actions enjoined in *śruti' (i.e. the **Veda*). It therefore refers to the expanded and extended public ritualism of those who choose to perform the śrauta *sacrifices (śrauta-*yajñas), as opposed to the limited, single fire (*ekāgni) ritualism of the domestic (*gṛhya) sacrificer. The minimum qualification for a śrauta sacrificer (known as the *yajamāna—'the patron of the sacrifice') is birth into one of the three higher *varṇas, to have received *upanayana, to be married (the yajamāna and his wife act as a ritual unit), and to have set up the *gṛhyāgni ('domestic fire'). From the latter, three (or in some Vedic schools, five) sacred fires are installed: the *gārhapatyāgni, *the āhavanīya, and the *dakṣināgni (the fourth and fifth being the sabhya and the āvasathya). Sacrifices are performed in an enclosure set up for the duration, composed of the three (or five) fires, and a *vedi, or altar. The basic components of the sacrifice are Vedic *mantras enjoining the action, the action itself (an offering to a deity or the *pitṛs, made into a fire), and the fees (*dakṣinā) paid to the officiating *priests. Once the sacred fires have been installed, the yajamāna has an obligation to carry out a particular sequence of rites for the rest of his life (unless he becomes a *saṃnyāsin, or infirm), each rite presupposing that preceding it. The sequence is as follows: the *agnihotra, the *darśapūrṇamāsa, the *caturmāsya, the *paśubandha, the *agniṣṭoma. Notable optional śrauta rites include the *agnicayana, and, for *kings, the *rājasūya and the *aśvamedha. All the larger *śrauta rituals (i.e.those succeeding the agnihotra) require the collaboration of four groups of hereditary *brahmin priests (one representing each *Veda): the *adhvaryu priests (*YajurVeda), the *hotṛs (*Ṛg Veda), the *udgātṛs (*Sāma Veda), and the *brahmans (masc.) (*Atharva Veda), the last being a somewhat later addition.

The practice and theology of śrauta ritual were explicated at length in the *Brāhmaṇas, which provided the core material for *Mīmāṃsaka analysis. (The *Śrautasūtras are simply concerned with the detailed rules for correct performance.) Śrauta ritual's paradigmatic significance is therefore immense, but its actual practice must have always been limited, given the expense and time involved. Even in the *Brāhmaṇas* themselves, condensed or internalized forms of ritual are being advocated, a process carried further still in the *Āraṇyakas* and **Upaniṣads*. Nevertheless, some brahmins, notably the *Nambūdiris of Kerala, appear to have maintained the tradition for 2 000 years or more. *See also* YAJÑA.

Śrautasūtra (*c.*800–300 BCE) A category of late *Vedic texts, classified as belonging to (or synonymous with) the **Kalpasūtra* literature of the **Vedāṅga* (and therefore as *smṛti), which deals with the detailed (and, according to some, idealized) rules for the proper performance of *śrauta ritual (śrauta-yajña). The earliest text of this type (and the earliest **sūtra* text of any kind) is that of *Baudāyana.

śravaṇa ('hearing') According to the *Vedānta tradition, hearing revelation (*śruti) is the prerequisite for thinking (*manana) and then meditating (*nididhyāsana) on it.

Śrāvaṇī Pūrṇimā ('the full moon day of Śrāvaṇa' (July–August)) An annual *festival, held on the day indicated by its name, during which *brahmins (and other initiated *twice-born males) renew their *sacred threads. It is celebrated at the same time as the more popular *Rākhī Bandhan.

Śrī **1.** *See* LAKṢMĪ. **2.** An honorific prefix used, in the sense of 'holy', 'sacred', 'revered', before the names of gods (e.g. Śrī *Rāma), *gurus, (e.g. Śrī *Rāmakṛṣṇa), and texts (e.g. Śrī **Bhāgavata*).

Śrī Aurobindo *See* AUROBINDO GHOSE.

Śrībhāṣya *Rāmānuja's commentary on *Bādarāyaṇa's **Brahmasūtra*.

śrīcakra ('auspicious wheel') *See* ŚRĪYANTRA.

Śrīdevī ('the Auspicious Goddess') Another name for *Tripurasundarī.

Śrīharṣa (12th century CE) A *Śaṅkaran *Advaita Vedāntin who was a trenchant critic of the *Nyāya interpretation of the *pramāṇas.

Śrīkaṇṭha (*c.*1200?) *See* ŚIVĀDVAITA.

Śrīkula ('belonging to the family of the Auspicious Goddess') Within *Śākta *Tantrism, a designation of those schools, originating in the early medieval *Kaula tradition and then flourishing in South India (notably in the *Śrī Vidyā tradition), whose *Tantras are used to worship the Goddess (*Devī) in her benevolent forms, such as Śrīdevī / *Tripurasundarī.

Śrī Nāthjī The name given to the image of *Kṛṣṇa, installed in the *havelī of the same name, at *Nāthdvāra in Rajasthan, where it is worshipped by the *Puṣṭimārga *Vallabhasampradāya. It is thought to portray the youthful god as *Govardhanadhara, i.e. with his left-arm upraised in the act of lifting *Govardhana. According to the *Vallabha hagiographical literature, the arm of the image began to appear out of a crack in Govardhana hill (near *Braj) at the beginning of the 15th century, but only made a complete appearance with the birth of Vallabha (*c.*1479), who subsequently declared it to be a svarūpa ('own form') of Kṛṣṇa (i.e. an actual, embodied form of the deity). During a period of persecution by the *Mughal emperor *Aurangzeb, Vallabha's successor's fled with the image, eventually housing it in Braj in 1671. (According to some accounts, it had been looked after by *Gauḍīya Vaiṣṇavas until this point.) The image itself is carved into a rectangular block of black stone, set into a cavity. In reproductions it is invariably shown wearing one of 25 different costumes, typically with an elaborate turban, and with lotus stalks protruding from under its right armpit.

Srinivas, M. N. (1916–1999) A prominent Indian social anthropologist, well known for his work on the *caste system and the development of the *Sanskritization theory. Educated at the Universities of Bombay and Oxford, he conducted fieldwork in rural South India; he was the recipient of many honours both in India and abroad. Included among his many important publications are *Religion and Society Among the Coorgs of South India* (1952), *The Remembered Village* (1976), and *The Dominant Caste and Other Essays* (1995).

Śrīpati (14th century CE, or earlier) The founder of a *Śaiva *Vedānta *sampradāya. A *Liṅgāyata, in his *Śrīkarabhāṣya* he draws on *Rāmānuja's *Viśiṣṭādvaita, adopting an essentially *bhedābheda stance, characterized as Śaktiviśiṣṭādvaita (Śaktiviśeṣādvaita), 'non-dualism qualified by *Śakti'.

Śrīraṅgam ('sacred stage') A South Indian *temple complex, the largest dedicated area of this kind on the subcontinent, situated on an island (raṅgam) in the *Kāverī river in the Tiruchirāppaḷḷi district of Tamil Nadu. A major *pilgrimage site for all Hindus, it houses the *Śrī Vaiṣṇava *Raṅganātha temple, dedicated to *Viṣṇu, and known to devotees as 'The Temple' (kōyil). In addition, it contains numerous other shrines, not only to *Lakṣmī, and the *avatāras of *Viṣṇu, but also to the *Āḻvārs, and to various Śrī Vaiṣṇava *ācāryas who were based there, including *Rāmānuja, who took over the management of the temple for periods in the 11th/12th century CE. The earliest extant architecture on the site dates from the late *Cōḻa period, although Śrīraṅgam had been celebrated by the Āḻvār poets and others well before that, and its chronicles, the *Kōyil Oḻuku* and the *Śrīraṅga Māhātmya* claim that it was an important *tīrtha from the early centuries CE. Expanded under the patronage of various dynasties between the 13th and 17th centuries (notably under the *Vijayanagara kings), parts of the temple were still being completed at the end of the 20th century. Its basic design is as an enclosure with a perimeter of over 3 km, divided by seven rectangular concentric walls; large and elaborate *gopura are stationed along roads leading in from the four cardinal points.

Śrīśailam An important *tīrthā, thought to be both a *jyotirliṅga and a *śaktipīṭha, on the banks of the river Kṛṣṇā in Andhra Pradesh, which is particularly popular during *Śivarātri. It is the site of the *Mallikārjuna *temple.

Śrī Vaiṣṇava The adjective applied to the tradition of *Śrī Vaiṣṇavism—its followers being referred to as Śrī Vaiṣṇavas.

Śrī Vaiṣṇavism The name commonly applied to the religion practised by members of the major *Tamil *Vaiṣṇava *sampradāya, the ritual practices and theology of which are derived from the teachings and commentaries of the *Viśiṣṭādvaita *ācāryas. Its name is said to be derived from the prominence it ascribes to *Viṣṇu's consort, Śrī (*Lakṣmī) as the vehicle of grace (*prasāda). Śrī Vaiṣṇavism has a complex textual basis, both *Sanskritic and Tamil, drawing on *Purāṇic and *Vedāntic sources, as well as the ritual practices of the *Pāñcarātra, and the *bhakti poetry of the *Āḻvārs. Its alternative name, ubhaya vedānta ('the wisdom of both'), indicates that it regards the *Vedic texts and the poetry of the Tamil saints as complementary and equal sources of authority and revelation. The tradition ascribes its foundation to *Viṣṇu himself; via Śrī, the deity's teaching was eventually mediated to *Nammāḻvār, and from him to the first ācārya of the tradition, *Nāthmuni. It was the *brahmin Nāthmuni who is said to have codified the the Tamil poetry of the Āḻvārs in the *Nālāyirappirapantam and introduced its recitation as part of Śrī Vaiṣṇava daily ritual, thus establishing its claim to be the equivalent of *Vedic *śruti. He was succeeded in the lineage by his grandson, *Yāmuna, whose works claim the *Pāñcarātra *saṃhitās (the basis of Śrī Vaiṣṇava *temple ritual), and texts such as the **Bhagavadgītā*, which *Brahmanical orthodoxy had regarded as *smṛti, as sources of revelation equal to, and alongside the **Vedas*. It was the third ācārya, *Rāmānuja, who drew these ritual and theological strands together into a coherent, doctrinal whole. By connecting the Pāñcarātra temple ritual of the Śrī Vaiṣṇavas to Vedic orthodoxy at a soteriological level, he demonstrated to his followers that they were really *Vaidikas (essentially, the *only* true Vaidikas). At the same time, he validated the devotionalism of the Āḻvār tradition, and legitimated the ritual recitation of their texts as part of temple worship. For these reasons, he is regarded by all subsequent Śrī Vaiṣṇavas as their most important theologian and teacher, and is considered the effective founder of the Viśiṣṭādvaita school of philosophy. Those following him in this tradition eventually divided into northern (*Vaṭakalai) and southern (*Teṉkalai) divisions, a schism based largely on differing interpretations of Rāmānuja's *prapatti ('surrender') doctrine. The two major theologians associated (perhaps retrospectively) with these schools are *Piḷḷai Lokācārya and *Vedāntadeśika.

Although Śrī Vaiṣṇava devotionalism is open to women and members of the lower *castes, the tradition's ācāryas and *priests have been almost exclusively brahmin. This is also true of the heads of the Śrī Vaiṣṇava monastic orders (which first started to appear around the 14th century CE), although they were prepared to initiate ordinary *saṃnyāsins from the lower castes. A partial exception to this general pattern is provided by the *Sāttāda community of Teṉkalai Śrī Vaiṣṇavas (dating from at least 15th century CE), who have emphasized the practice of non-Vedic rites, and so been open to leadership by both brahmins and *śūdras. In general, the Vaṭakalai school has been more insistent on retaining distinctions of caste and *purity at a formal level than has the Teṉkalai. Closely associated with Rāmānuja and the other ācāryas, the geographical focus of the Teṉkalai tradition in particular, and its major *tīrtha, is the great temple complex of *Śrīraṅgam in Tamil Nadu. *Kāñcīpuram is an important centre for the Vaṭakalais.

For a summary of key Śrī Vaiṣṇava doctrines, *see* RĀMĀNUJA.

śrīvatsa ('beloved of Śrī') A distinguishing and *auspicious curl, sometimes shown as a cruciform flower, found on depictions of *Viṣṇu and *Kṛṣṇa, where it is placed on the chest of the deity. It is also part of the iconography of *Jain tīrthaṅkaras (*Jinas).

Śrī Vidyā ('Auspicious Wisdom') A *Tantric *Śākta cult focused on the ritual worship of the all-powerful goddess *Tripurasundarī. The tradition takes its name from the śrīvidyā *mantra which, along with the *śrīyantra, is one of the principal forms in which she is worshipped. The cult claims to have originated as the southern transmission of the *Kaula system of Tantric *Śaivism, developing out of the *Tantras of the *Śrīkula schools. In moving south, it assimilated elements of *brahmin, *Vedānta culture, and has become associated with both the monasticism of the *Daśanāmi *maṭhas, and the *Śaiva/Śākta *temple culture of South India. *See also* TRIPURASUNDARĪ.

śrīyantra A *yantra (śrīcakra and Tripuracakra) used in the *Tantric *Śrī Vidyā worship of the goddess *Tripurasundarī, where it represents both the goddess herself (in her supreme form) and the cosmos. A two- (sometimes three-) dimensional geometric figure, it is composed of five downward- and four upward-pointing intersecting triangles, representing, respectively, *Śakti and *Śiva, who emanate, like the cosmos, from the dot (*bindu (4)) at the centre. The triangles are surrounded by two concentric circles of *lotus petals, and the whole enclosed within a square broken by four apertures. Ritual worship of this figure, accompanied by recitation of the śrīvidyā *mantra (the goddess in her subtle form), is thought to realize the deity and her power in the body of the initiate. The yantra has been installed in many South Indian *Śākta *temples, and now has wide popular currency.

Śṛṅgeri. A town in the hills of Karnataka, once patronized by the *Vijayanagara dynasty. As one of the four *Daśanāmi *maṭhas (monasteries) founded, according to tradition, by *Śaṅkara in the 8th century CE, it is an important centre for both *Śaivism and *Advaita Vedānta. A number of famous *Śaṅkarācāryas have held the seat, including *Sureśvara and *Mādhava.

śruti and smṛti A traditional classificatory dualism which distinguishes between two types of authoritative religious texts, based on their perceived origins and, to a lesser extent, their modes of transmission. Whereas texts classified as smṛti, or 'remembered' (i.e. memorized), are regarded as having been mediated through human authorship, those classified as śruti, or 'heard', are regarded as 'revelation', in the sense of having been revealed to (or 'heard' by) inspired *ṛṣis. Śruti thereby has the status of a direct, uncreated, and eternal transmission from a non-human power—i.e. the Absolute, however defined or evoked. The two classes are linked, however, in so far as smṛti texts constitute a 'tradition', which, although more immediately human in origin, ultimately looks to, and derives its authority from parts of śruti which are now assumed to be obscured.

For *Brahmanical orthodoxy, śruti is composed of the *Veda—i.e. the *Ṛg-, *Sāma-, *Yajur-, and *Atharva-Saṃhitās, with their *Brāhmaṇas, *Āraṇyakas, and *Upaniṣads—while smṛti is composed of a wide range of further literature, including *Sūtra and *Vedāṅga works appended to śruti, the *Epics and Purāṇas, and *Dharmaśāstra (which includes smṛti in a narrower sense, e.g. *Manusmṛti). As well as being revealed, the texts composing the Veda are 'heard' (śruti) in two further senses: first, their primary function is as chanted *mantra, accompanying and actualizing *Vedic ritual; second, they are supposed to be orally transmitted, rather than written down, since their power and sacredness is inherent in their correctly enunciated sound.

For other traditions, however, while there may be little disagreement about the dichotomy per se, what counts as śruti, as opposed to smṛti, varies considerably, with those least tightly aligned to *Brahmanism predictably most at variance with its norm. This ranges from attempts to add a particular text to the Vedic corpus as a 'fifth *Veda*' (a claim often made for the **Mahābhārata*), to subsuming, superseding, or by-passing the *Veda* altogether. The latter strategies are noticeable in the case of **Tantras* and **Āgamas*: the *Śaiva Siddhānta *Āgamas*, for instance, are regarded as direct revelation (śruti) from *Śiva himself. Similarly, for numerous *bhakti texts (e.g. the **Rāmcaritmānas*), the status of their content overrides their apparently human origins, and they are regarded by their devotees as revelation (śruti). Indeed, in an evolutionary trace left by the process of *Vedicization, they may be said to function as both smṛti and śruti.

sthalapurāṇa ('the story of the place') A text, or a section of a text, which provides a foundation myth for a local *temple or *tīrtha, and details the merit (*puṇya) to be gained by visiting that particular site. In style, *sthalapurāṇas* often model themselves on the classical **Purāṇas*, although they employ the local language, rather than *Sanskrit. One of their purposes may be to connect the temple god or goddess with a great, pan-Indian deity. **Māhātmyas* sometimes perform much the same function.

sthānadbhārī A subgroup of *Rāmānandi *Nāgas who take up temporary residence in lodging places (sthāna).

Sthāpatyaveda ('knowledge of architecture') Traditionally regarded as a fourth **Upaveda*; sometimes regarded as synonymous with **Śilpaśāstra*.

stotra A short praise poem or hymn in *Sanskrit verse, usually intended to be sung. They are frequently excerpted or anthologized in *Stotramāla*.

strīdharma ('women's dharma/duty') At its most general, received *Brahmanical views about how a woman should live her life and behave towards the rest of society in accordance with *dharma. More specifically, the compound refers to those (very limited) portions of **Dharmaśāstra* which prescribe the appropriate behaviour for a woman in accordance with her *varṇa, and her current station in life. Within this framework, **Manusmṛti* (5.147ff.), for example, allows her to be a dutiful daughter under the care of her father, a faithful wife under the care of her husband, and a widow under the care of her sons; but at no point at all should she be independent of male control. Being a 'dutiful' or 'faithful' wife in this context entails producing and raising *sons, helping one's husband to perform his enjoined rituals, and retaining one's monogamous *purity. In this way, after *death, one might hope to attain a place in *heaven, alongside one's husband. *See also* MARRIAGE.

Strīdharmapaddhati ('The Manual of Women's Dharma') An 18th-century CE South Indian text by *Trayambakayajvan. The only *Sanskrit work in the *Brahmanical tradition to deal exclusively with *strīdharma, it prescribes in some detail (from the perspective of the orthodox male commentator) the daily life of women.

Strīparvan ('The Book of the Women') The eleventh book of the *Sanskrit **Mahābhārata*, recounting how *Gāndhārī, and the surviving women on both sides of the conflict, grieve for those killed in the battle, as their *funeral rites are performed on the banks of the *Gaṅgā.

*Kuntī discloses *Karṇa's true parentage to her surviving *Pāṇḍava sons.

studenthood/studentship *See* BRAHMACARYA.

Subhadrā *Kṛṣṇa's sister. In the **Mahābhārata* she is married to *Arjuna, and is the mother of their son, *Abhimanyu. *See also* JAGANNĀTH(A).

subhāṣita ('well-spoken') An admired *Sanskrit verse or stanza; thousands were collected in various anthologies.

Subrahmaṇya *See* KĀRTTIKEYA; MURUKAṈ.

subtle body *See* SŪKṢMA ŚARĪRA.

Sudarśana ('beautiful to see') *Viṣṇu's discus or *cakra (2) personified as a god. In South Indian iconography, he is portrayed as a young man, sometimes with many arms.

śuddha ('pure') *See* PURE AND IMPURE.

Śuddhādvaita ('pure non-dualism') The name *Vallabha gave to the theology underlying his *Puṣṭimārga. Denying the *Advaita reading of *māyā, Vallabha maintains the reality of the world, which he sees as identical with *Kṛṣṇa (= *brahman (neut.)). Individuals too are ultimately parts of Kṛṣṇa, but they remain ignorant of their true nature, and so subject to *rebirth, unless freed by his *grace. This is facilitated by the disinterested service (*sevā) of, and complete surrender to, the deity in *temple *bhakti. Śuddhādvaita is claimed to be partially derived from the no longer extant works of the *Vedāntin, *Viṣṇusvāmin.

śuddhi ('purity') *See* PURE AND IMPURE.

śūdra A member of the fourth *varṇa, the 'servant' or 'serf' class. Depicted in the *Vedic **Puruṣasūkta* as being born from the cosmic *puruṣa's feet, it is the śūdras' duty, according to *Brahmanical orthodoxy, to serve the three higher varṇas (i.e. the *brahmins, *kṣatriyas, and *vaiśyas). So according to **Manusmṛti* (1.91), for instance, 'ungrudging service' of the other classes is the only legitimate activity for a śūdra. Correspondingly, they were excluded from the *saṃskāra that gave the *twice-born access to the **Veda*: no śūdra could receive *upanayana and proceed to Vedic studentship. (For their own saṃskāra, Purāṇic rather than Vedic *mantras are used.) Unlike the lowest *jātis in the *caste hierarchy, such as the *caṇḍālas, the śūdras, although socially and, for most of Indian history, legally disadvantaged, are at least considered to lie within the varṇa system. At the *village level, particularly in South India, the dominant, land-holding caste (jāti) often belongs to the śūdra varṇa, and so, in those cases, it is the śūdras who effectively hold power locally, dispensing patronage under the *Jajmānī system.

Sufism The name given to the 'mystical' tradition in *Islam.

Sugrīva In the **Rāmāyaṇa*, the *Vānara (monkey-) king, who, in return for the assistance of *Rāma and *Lakṣmaṇa in restoring him to his throne, helps them, in turn, with his army of monkeys, to locate and rescue the abducted *Sītā.

Śukasaptati ('Seventy Tales of the Parrot', date uncertain) A celebrated anonymous collection of stories about love (*kāma) and adultery. Many of its stories found their way West, via Persian translations.

Śukla Yajur Veda See WHITE YAJUR VEDA.

sūkṣma śarīra (liṅga śarīra) ('subtle body') In *Tantric, *yogic and *Sāṃkhya physiology, the invisible body which provides the vehicle for the transmigrating *soul, as it moves from one 'gross' (i.e. palpable) body (sthūla śarīra) to another. In *haṭha-yoga, and related systems, it is said to be composed of the individual's *prāṇa, the life-force which animates the gross body. In general, it has been used from *Upaniṣadic times onwards as a synonym for the embodied self (*jīva, etc.), as distinct from the physical body.

sūkta ('well-recited') A *Ṛg Vedic hymn (e.g. the *Puruṣasūkta*), consisting of individual verses (*ṛc).

Śulvasūtra (Śulbasūtra) A category of text, supplementing the **Śrautasūtras* (but sometimes classified as a separate type of **Kalpasūtra*), which prescribes the geometric layout of the *śrauta sacrificial area or altar (*vedi).

sumaṅgālī (H.: 'most auspicious') A newly married, and therefore *auspicious wife. Also a wife whose husband is still living.

Sumitrā In the **Rāmāyaṇa*, the junior wife of King *Daśaratha, and the mother of *Lakṣmaṇa and *Śatrughna.

sun *See* SŪRYA.

Sundarakāṇḍa ('The Beautiful Book') The fifth book of *Vālmīki's **Rāmāyaṇa*, in which *Rāma and *Lakṣmaṇa meet *Sugrīva and *Hanumān.

Sundarar *See* CUNTARAR.

Sundareśvara ('The Beautiful Lord') The name given to *Śiva as *Mīṇākṣī's consort at *Madurai. *See also* MĪṆĀKṢĪ.

Śuṅga dynasty The rulers of central India from the fall of the *Mauryan dynasty (*c.*185 BCE) until their own fragmentation in 75 BCE.

Suntarar *See* CUNTARAR.

sura ('god') Synonymous with *deva, probably on the basis that it is the opposite of *asura, an 'anti-god' or demon in the post *Ṛg Vedic understanding of the term.

Surabhi *See* KĀMADHENU.

Sūrdās (Sūradāsa) (late 15th century CE?, trad. 1479–1584) The most popular of the *Hindi poet-saints (*sants) of northern India, belonging to the *saguṇa *bhakti tradition of those devoted to *Kṛṣṇa. Modern scholarship suggests that Sūrdās's biography was almost entirely constructed by the *Vallabhas in order to co-opt an already popular figure into their *sampradāya. According to this account, he was a *brahmin, blind since birth, who, after a meeting with *Vallabha, became his pupil and produced what have since become immensely popular poems on themes consonant with Vallabhan theology. Particularly valued are those poems, addressed to the infant *Kṛṣṇa from the perspective of parental devotion, in which an apprehension of the overwhelming nature of divinity suddenly erupts into everyday family life. These, and some five thousand other songs are collected in the *Sūr Sāgar* ('Sūr's Ocean'), which, despite its blanket attribution to Sūrdās, is clearly an anthology of various North Indian oral traditions from which it is difficult to disentangle specific authors. However, analysis has shown that earliest stratum of this material, which may be by an 'original' Sūrdās, is largely devoted to *viraha poems, voiced through or for the *gopīs in their distraught longing for the absent Kṛṣṇa. In addition to their place in Vallabha *temple liturgy, the poems attributed to Sūrdās, are seemingly ubiquitous amongst North Indian *bhaktas, and his legendary life-story is widely celebrated.

Sureśvara (*c.*8th century CE) An *Advaita Vedāntin commentator, said to have been one of *Śaṅkara's two chief disciples. He is notable for arguing (in contradiction of his teacher's view) that *avidyā is the material cause of the universe, and thus inherent in *brahman (neut.). As well as the independent *Naiṣkarmyasiddhi* ('The Demonstration of the State of Non-Action'), he wrote numerous glosses (*vārttikas*) on *Vedāntic texts, including Śaṅkara's commentaries.

Śūrpaṇakhā ('whose nails are like winnowing fans') In the **Rāmāyaṇa*, the sister of the *rākṣasa king, *Rāvaṇa. Spurned in love by both *Rāma and *Lakṣmaṇa, she attacks *Sītā. Lakṣmaṇa cuts off her nose and ears, and in revenge for this mutilation, she incites Rāvaṇa to abduct Sītā and carry her off to the island of *Laṅkā.

Sūrya Both the astronomical sun, and the Sun deity. In the *Vedic hymns he is either synonymous with, or complements, *Savitṛ, the 'vivifier', who is worshipped in the archetypal *Brahmanical *mantra, the *Gāyatrī. In the post-Vedic period many of his *Ṛg Vedic functions and mythological characteristics appear to have been assimilated to *Viṣṇu. However, towards the end of the first millennium BCE, a separate cult of sun worship, directed towards a fully anthropomorphized Sūrya, with all the attributes of a great soteriological deity, was established in northern and western India, probably under the influence of Iranian *Zoroastrianism. *Epic and *Purāṇic evidence, and lists of no longer extant *Saura **Tantras*, testify to the importance of this cult throughout the medieval period. Most striking are the remains of dedicated sun *temples and their associated *Tantric sculptures, notably, the immense 13th-century ruin at *Konarak in Orissa, built to represent the god's chariot, drawn by seven horses. It has been suggested that the cult of Sūrya was eventually assimilated into *Śaivism, but the echo of its importance remains in the *pañcayatanapūjā, in which the Sun god is one of the five great deities worshipped by *smārta *brahmins. (If the suggestion that Śaṅkara promoted this kind of worship in the 8th century CE is correct, then this further substantiates the importance of Sūrya at this time.) In his sculptural representations, Sūrya is invariably portrayed wearing knee-high boots (according to some, evidence of his foreign origins); he is also shown with *lotuses in his hands to evoke his animating power.

Sūryavaṃśa ('The Solar Dynasty') According to myth, one of the two great dynasties of ancient India, the counterpart to the *Candravaṃśa or 'Lunar Dynasty'. The descendants of *Iḷa's eldest son, *Ikṣvāku, including, notably, *Rāma, belong to the Sūryavaṃśa.

Suśruta *See* ĀYURVEDA.

suṣumṇā The central channel of the spinal cord, one of the three principal *nāḍī of *yogic and *Tantric physiologies. It has a fiery quality, and is associated with the river *Sarasvatī. *See also* KUṆḌALINĪ.

sūta A charioteer (i.e. the driver of a chariot carrying a *king or a *kṣatriya), who, in the *Epics and *Purāṇas, is also a narrator or royal bard (e.g. *Saṃjaya in the **Mahābhārata*). According to **Manusmṛti* (10.11) a sūta (regarded as the member of a *caste) is the offspring of a mixed union, the son of a kṣatriya man by a *brahmin girl. The relationship, historical or theoretical, between these various roles, remains unclear, as does the precise social status of the sūta. It may be noted that *Kṛṣṇa acts as *Arjuna's driver in the **Bhagavadgītā*.

sūtra ('thread', 'line', 'cord') A text made up of a cumulative series, or 'line', of essential rules relating to a specific topic, such as ritual, *grammar, or *yoga. These sūtras are presented in an aphoristic or abbreviated style which usually requires a commentary (oral or written) in order to be understood. (In other words, its meaning is yielded mnemonically to those qualified to understand it.) The earliest examples of texts of this kind are the *Vedic **Śrauta Sūtras*. A benchmark of compression was set by *Pāṇini's **Aṣṭādhyāyi* grammar in which he analysed the whole phonology and morphology of *Sanskrit in fewer than 4000 sūtras. Other notable examples of the genre include *Bādarāyaṇa's *Brahmasūtra* (a cornerstone of the *Vedānta tradition, since anyone wanting to found a new subschool is expected to provide a commentary (*bhāṣya) on it), and *Patañjali's **Yoga Sūtra*.

suttee *See* SATĪ (2).

Svacchandabhairava (Aghora) ('Autonomous Bhairava') A form of *Śiva, popular in *Kashmir since the medieval period. Originally the focus of the *Tantric mantrapīṭha ('seat of mantras') cult of *Kāpālika *Śaivism, formulated in the *Svacchandabhairava Tantra* (a subdivision of the **Bhairava Tantras*), he is visualized as a five-faced, eighteen-armed figure, accompanied by his consort in a circle of *cremation grounds.

svadharma ('inherent duty') According to **Dharmaśāstra*, the duty (*dharma) thought to be enjoined on an individual by virtue of their birth into a particular *varṇa, and modified according to their gender and stage of life (*āśrama). Put simply, it is, for example, a *kṣatriya's svadharma to rule, a *śūdra's to serve. Neglect of one's svadharma is thought to bring dire karmic consequences for the individual, and disorder for society (i.e. it affects dharma at both the micro and macro levels). As *Kṛṣṇa tells the vacillating warrior *Arjuna in the **Bhagavadgītā* (3.35): 'It is better to practise your own inherent duty (svadharma) deficiently than another's duty well. It is better to die conforming to your own duty; the duty of others invites danger'. *See also* DHARMA; VARṆĀŚRAMADHARMA.

svādhyāya The study of the **Veda*, considered to be a daily duty for all orthodox *brahmins. Usually translated as 'study', or 'self-study', it refers to the recitation or repetition of *Vedic *mantras, either sotto voce or aloud. For some it comes to be regarded as equivalent in power and effect to performing sacrificial ritual.

svāhā In the *Vedic *yajña, an exclamation made during the offering of the oblation into the fire.

svāmi (Skt.: svāmin—'lord', 'master', Ang.: 'swami') An honorific, commonly addressed to a *guru or a deity.

Svāminārāyaṇa (Swaminarayan, Swami Narayan, Svāmī Sahajānanda) (1781–1830) The founder and devotional focus of a Gujarati *Vaiṣṇava *bhakti movement, now named after him (the 'Svāminārāyaṇas' or 'Svāminārāyaṇa movement'). Born near *Ayodhyā, he became a wandering mendicant while still a child. In 1800 he joined a group of Gujarati *ascetics under the leadership of a teacher called Rāmānanda (who claimed to be in *Rāmānuja's lineage). When Rāmānanda died in 1802, Sahajānanda (now called Svāminārāyaṇa) succeeded to the leadership of part of the group, which, over the rest of his lifetime, rapidly developed into a full-blown order of around 2000 initiated *ascetics. At the same time, Svāminārāyaṇa instituted a lineage of male *householder devotees (in the first instance, two of his nephews) to administer the organization, which initiated both ascetic and lay followers. Svāminārāyaṇa's message, spread through preaching tours of the area, was recognizably *Vaiṣṇava in its devotionalism, and had much in common, particularly in its recommended pattern of worship, with the teachings of the *Vallabha *Puṣṭimārga. At the same time, it propagated both a conservative (according to some 'puritanical') *Brahmanical orthodoxy in relation to maintaining *caste distinctions and ritual *purity (including the separation of men and women during worship), and a socially reforming stance towards such practices as female infanticide, *satī, and enforced *widowhood. It was also adamantly opposed to *animal sacrifice, and demanded strict *vegetarianism from its members. In 1906 the movement split into two, with a new school, the Akshar Puroshottam Sanstha (Akṣara Puruṣottama Saṃsthā), claiming that the true spiritual descent from Svāminārāyaṇa had been carried, not through the ācāryas, but through a lineage of disciples or 'abodes of God' (Akshars), starting with Guṇātītānanda (Gunatitanand) (1785–1867). Both schools regard Svāminārāyaṇa himself as an unmitigated and full manifestation of *Nārāyaṇa (Viṣṇu), also known as *Puruṣottama. Initiates take refuge in him, and his image is central to *temple worship, with *Kṛṣṇa and *Rādhā given secondary roles. In addition, followers of the Akshar Puroshottam Sanstha hold that Svāminārāyaṇa (i.e. God) is eternally present in 'perfect devotees', i.e. the heads of their order (pre-eminently Guṇātītānanda), so their *images too are the objects of temple *pūjā. Textually, the movement aligns itself with the *Veda*, but pays most attention to the scriptural presence of Svāminārāyaṇa collected in his sayings (*Vacanāmṛta*) and teachings (*Śīkṣāpatrī*). Svāminārāyaṇa temples, and other institutions associated with the movement, are found throughout the towns and *villages of Gujarat, as well as abroad. It has proved particularly successful among the middle-ranking *castes of the commercial and business classes. (The increasingly popular Akshar Puroshottam Sanstha abolished distinctions in the ascetic order between brahmins, other *dvijas, and *śūdras in 1981, but castes below śūdra level have never been admitted to either school.) The movement is currently estimated to have around five million followers, including a large proportion of Gujaratis living overseas. A spectacular new Akshar Puroshottam Sanstha mandir (temple), said to be the largest Hindu temple outside India, was opened in Neasden, North London in 1995.

Svāminārāyaṇa

Svāminārāyaṇa movement/Svāminārāyaṇas *See* SVĀMINĀRĀYAṆA.

svarga ('heaven') In *Ṛg Vedic* mythology, the term 'svarga' is usually associated with *Indra's heaven (*Indraloka) or *svar(loka), the sky. By the time of the **Brāhmaṇas*, it is also being used to indicate a particular 'world' (svarga-*loka) or ontological state, synonymous with 'immortality', which the ritualist creates through the correct performance of the *Vedic sacrifice (*yajña), a sacrificial analogue of the permanent heaven inhabited by the *devas (the deva-loka/svarga-loka). In the *karmic systems that start to appear with the early **Upaniṣads*, the heavens or lokas associated with supernatural beings and gods, which belong to *saṃsāra and from which the occupants will ultimately be reborn, are differentiated from *mokṣa, which (for *Advaita Vedānta, for instance) designates a permanent state of liberation beyond a particular physical or cosmological location. With the rise of *bhakti, and the great sectarian gods, this distinction blurs again, in so far as liberation may be realized through the *grace of a personal God, who, at the death of the faithful *bhakta, transports him or her to permanent and blissful residence in a particular heaven or paradise (such as *Viṣṇu's *Vaikuṇṭha heaven). To some extent consonant with this, *Purāṇic *cosmology posits multiple, hierarchically arranged heavens, topped by the indestructible but ambiguous *Brahmaloka.

Svargārohaṇaparvan ('The Book of the Ascent to Heaven') The eighteenth and final book of the *Sanskrit **Mahābhārata*, recounting how *Yudhiṣṭhira finally enters *heaven only to see his enemies enthroned, while his brothers and wife are moaning in *hell. However, the gods reveal this to be an illusion: both *Kauravas and *Pāṇḍavas now reside in a heavenly region, free of enmity and suffering. The text then closes its narrative framing stories.

svar(loka) ('heaven') **1.** In *Vedic *cosmology, either the sky, or synonymous with *Indra's heaven (*Indraloka). In *Purāṇic cosmology it is said to contain the moon, its 28 mansions (*nakṣatras), the planets and stars. **2.** As svaḥ/svar ('heaven') one of the three exclamations (*vyāhṛtis) to be pronounced twice daily by orthodox *brahmins at the twilight (*saṃdhyā) ritual.

svastika (swastika) A pan-Indian *auspicious sign, variously explained, but probably in origin a solar symbol. Some derive it from the *Sanskrit su + asti, 'well being'/'good fortune'; some also distinguish between svastikas with right-handed (clockwise-pointing) arms, which are auspicious, since they represent the sun ascending towards the summer solstice, and those with left-handed (anti-clockwise-pointing) arms, which are inauspicious since they represent the sun descending towards the winter solstice.

svatantra ('independent', 'having one's own school') An adjective describing self-appointed, or self-initiated *renouncers and *sādhus—i.e. those who have not formally joined a *sampradāya or *ascetic lineage.

Svātmarāma *See* HAṬHAYOGA-PRADĪPIKĀ.

svayambhū ('self-existing', 'uncreated', 'independent') An epithet applied to *brahman (neut.), and to any deity, especially *Viṣṇu and *Śiva, regarded as the Absolute.

svayambhū liṅga ('self-existent liṅga') A *liṅga embodied in, or by, a natural object, such as a stone or block of ice. Because it has manifested itself without human involvement, it is thought to be particularly powerful.

svayaṃvara ('self-choice') For the daughter of a royal or a *kṣatriya family, a way of selecting a husband which takes the form of either of a public contest between her suitors, or an assembly at which the bride-to-be simply chooses between them. Perhaps the best-known instances occur in the **Mahābhārata*, where *Arjuna wins *Draupadī by this method, and *Damayantī prefers *Nala to any of the assembled gods.

Śvetāmbara ('white-clad') The name given to one of the two major *Jaina sects, so-called because their *ascetics wear white robes. *See also* DIGAMBARA.

Śvetaketu *See* CHĀNDOGYA UPANIṢAD.

Śvetāśvatara Upaniṣad ('The *Upaniṣad* of the Man with the White Mule', *c.*2nd–1st century BCE, or later) An important, probably quite late, **Upaniṣad*, traditionally attached to the **Black Yajur Veda*, but apparently addressed to *ascetic *renouncers. It presents a complex picture of a number of theological, philosophical, and *yogic cross-currents, as well as the earliest textual evidence for a theistic form of *Śiva worship. While looking back to the **Veda*, and the monism of the early **Upaniṣads*, the *Śvetāśvatara* draws on *Sāṃkhya ontology, although, in a manner similar to that seen in the **Bhagavadgītā* (with which it shares a number of verses), the dualism of *puruṣa and *prakṛti is ultimately subordinate to a single, all-powerful deity. This one God, referred to as *Rudra (*Śiva), creates the world, exists in it through his creatures, and yet transcends it. The individual attains *liberation through the proper knowledge of God, and through worshipping him. Towards the end of the *Upaniṣad*, concepts such as *grace, and, in the final verse, *guru worship and *bhakti (seemingly its earliest textual occurrence) are also raised. Although these may be later additions to the core text, they explicitly align the *Śvetāśvatara* and its contents with one of the dominant trends of medieval Hinduism.

swami *See* SVĀMI.

Swaminarayan *See* SVĀMĪNĀRĀYAṆA.

T

Tagore, Debendranāth (1817–1905) A Bengali social and religious reformer. His *brahmin father, Dwarkanāth, was an immensely wealthy Calcutta businessman and philanthropist who was a friend and supporter of Rāmmohun *Roy. Educated in one of Roy's schools and at the westernized Hindu College, Debendranāth took over the leadership of the *Brāhmo Samāj after Rāmmohun's death. Like his mentor, he was adamantly opposed to 'idolatry', and in a reorganization of the Samāj in 1843, he instituted a 'Brāhmo Covenant', requiring the now specific membership to worship one God. His attempts to justify this position as consonant with an essentially *Advaitin reading of the authority of the **Veda* proved untenable, although he remained associated with the more traditionally Hindu wing of the Samāj. After Keshub Chandra *Sen's more radical group (the 'Brāhmo Samāj of India') split away in 1866, Tagore remained in charge of the renamed *Ādi Brāhmo Samāj ('Original Brahman Association'), which over time dwindled into little more than an association of family and friends, based around his rural retreat at Śāntiniketan, northwest of Calcutta. Alongside an attempt to formulate a pattern of non-idolatrous ritual, Tagore compiled a selective anthology of what he considered to be true Hindu *dharma, his religious perspective increasingly underwritten by his own experiences of direct revelation. He was the father of Rabindranāth *Tagore. *See also* BRĀHMO SAMĀJ.

Tagore, Rabindranāth (1861–1941) A hugely influential and well-loved Bengali poet, playwright, short-story writer, novelist, essayist, composer, and painter who became the first Indian to be awarded the Nobel prize for literature. The fourteenth of Debendranāth *Tagore's fifteen children, he was brought up in the milieu of his father's *Ādi Brāhmo Samāj, but came to formulate his own religious, political and aesthetic positions, influenced by the **Upaniṣads* and Bengali *Vaiṣṇavism (including the poetry of the *Bāuls). He became well-known in the English-speaking West through his own translation of his book of Bengali poems, *Gitanjali* (B.: *gītāñjali*), which he brought with him on visits to Britain and America in 1912. With the support of poets such as W. B. Yeats (1865–1939) and Ezra Pound (1885–1972), he received the Nobel prize a year later, and a knighthood from the British in 1915 (returned in protest at the Amritsar massacre in 1919). Initially a supporter of nationalism, he subsequently publicly distanced himself from *Gāndhī's strategy of civil disobedience, although they were reconciled at the end of the latter's 1932/3 *fast. At Śāntiniketan ('Abode of Peace'), the Tagore family estate northwest of Calcutta, Rabindranāth created a school, and later an international cultural and artistic centre, the Viśva Bhārati University (1921). Through the 1920s and 30s, Tagore was a tireless traveller and lecturer around the world, promoting his ideals of education, equality for all, anti-materialism, and internationalism. Although his literary reputation in the West rapidly declined as the style of his own translations went out of fashion, he remains a key figure, not just in the modernization of

Bengali literature, but in the revitalization of Indian culture in the 20th century. His works, especially his songs, remain popular throughout Bengal, and he has been a formative influence on many subsequent creative artists, such as the film-maker Satyajit Ray (1921–1992).

Taittirīya *See* TAITTIRĪYA SAṂHITĀ.

Taittirīya Āraṇyaka The **Āraṇyaka* belonging to the **Taittirīya Saṃhitā* of the **Black Yajur Veda*, and a supplement to the **Taittirīya Brāhmaṇa*. Chapters seven to nine constitute the **Taittirīya Upaniṣad*, and ten, the **Mahānārāyaṇa Upaniṣad*.

Taittirīya Brāhmaṇa The **Brāhmaṇa* belonging to the **Taittirīya Saṃhitā* of the **Black Yajur Veda*, and probably the oldest extant *Brāhmaṇa* text. It contains passages that may have originally been part of the lost *Kāṭhaka Brāhmaṇa*.

Taittirīya Saṃhitā The foundational texts of the Taittirīya branch (school) of the **Veda*, and one of the four collections constituting the **Black Yajur Veda*. Its **Brāhmaṇa*, **Āraṇyaka*, and **Upaniṣad*, which are closely linked to each other, all bear the same name, possibly derived from that of a legendary teacher, Tittiri.

Taittirīya Upaniṣad An **Upaniṣad* constituting chapters (vallīs: 'creepers') seven to nine of the **Taittirīya Āraṇyaka*, and therefore belonging to the **Taittirīya Saṃhitā* of the **Black Yajur Veda*. An early prose *Upaniṣad*, it was probably compiled between the 6th and 5th centuries BCE, possibly in the northwestern part of the North Indian *Brahmanical homelands (*Kuru-Pañcāla). It deals, inter alia, with the hidden connections between the ritual and the cosmos, the recitation of the **Veda*, the equivalence of *brahman (neut.) and *oṃ, the nature of *ātman, and, in a dialogue between *Bhṛgu and his father *Varuṇa, the nature of brahman (neut.) and how to attain it. Also notable is the way in which *food is characterized as the foremost of beings, since all creatures are born out of it, live by it, and pass into it; in this way it is equated with brahman.

Taleju *See* NEPAL.

tamas ('darkness', 'inertia') According to *Sāṃkhya-Yoga ontology, one of the three *guṇas, or strands, of material nature (*prakṛti), tamas is characterized as 'dark'; concomitantly, it represents the principle of inertia. Since the tripartite guṇa division is extended to various other categories, tamas is also, for instance, used to characterize a group of (tāmasa) **mahāpurāṇas* belonging to *Śiva, and certain 'dull' (i.e. mind-stupefying) *foods.

tāmasa *See* TAMAS.

Tamil **1.** One of the major *Dravidian languages of South India. There are approximately 60 million Tamil speakers at the beginning of the 21st century, mostly in the state of Tamil Nadu, but including over 3–4 million in Sri Lanka and elsewhere in the Southeast Asian Hindu *diaspora. It has an extremely rich and varied literature, including, for example, the poetry included in the *Caṅkam anthologies, and the influential *bhakti poetry of the *Āḻvārs and *Nāyaṉmār. *See also* DRAVIDIAN. **2.** The term is also applied to those who speak Tamil, and, by extension, to the cultural complex of southern India, sometimes in pointed contradistinction to the *Āryan *Sanskritic culture which originated in the North, but more commonly to the de facto mixture of indigenous Tamil and *Brahmanical (or *Sanskritized) cultures which has characterized Tamil religion (Hindu, *Buddhist, and *Jain) since around the 3rd or 4th centuries CE.

Tamiḻttāy ('Mother Tamil') A goddess personifying the *Tamil language and acting as the guardian deity of its speakers. She first appears towards the end of the 19th century as a Tamil analogue to the *Sanskritic *Bhārat Mātā ('Mother India').

tāṇḍava *See* ĀNANDATĀṆḌAVA

Tañjāvūr (Tanjore/Thanjavur) A major South Indian *temple complex in Tamil Nadu, close to the *Kāverī river. Once the capital of the *Cōḻa kings, it is the site of one of the largest temples in India, the Rājarājeśvara, or Bṛhadīśvara (consecrated 1009/10), built by King Rājrāja, and dedicated to *Śiva.

tank A pool of water, often rectangular and stepped, which is thought to be an essential component of a major *temple complex (unless it is already next to the water of a *river). Worshippers purify themselves by taking a *bath there before entering the temple proper. The tank may be used for annual *festivals, such as the *Kṛṣṇa Jayantī, during which a movable image of the deity is floated in the pool, and perhaps eventually submerged.

tanmātra(s) ('subtle element(s)') According to *Sāṃkhya ontology, the five 'subtle material elements' (sound, touch, form, taste, smell) evolve from *prakṛti.

Tantrāloka ('Light on Tantra') An immense work by *Abhinavagupta (summarized in his *Tantrasāra*) explicating the non-dual system of *Kashimiri Śaivism; it is derived from his analysis of the **Mālinīvijayottara Tantra*.

t

Tantra(s) (lit. 'extension', 'warp', 'loom', 'threads', 'text') A class of text, found in all the major Indian traditions (*Śaiva, *Vaiṣṇava, *Śākta, *Buddhist, *Jaina), specifying—perhaps 'weaving together'—particular non-*Vedic ritual practices and doctrines, and constituting a special, extra-Vedic revelation, only accessible to initiates (i.e. those who have taken *dīkṣā). In the plural, the term is sometimes used as a synonym for Śākta *Tantras*, which are thought to be the prime exemplars of the type, with Śaiva and Vaiṣṇavasa *Tantras* being referred to by the more specific terms, **Āgama* and **Saṃhitā*. By extension, the term 'Tantra' is also used, generically, to describe the spectrum of religious practices and underlying theologies derived from, or associated with these texts, a phenomenon also referred to as 'Tantrism'. (At its most restrictive, the adjective 'Tantric' applies to any ritual using non-Vedic *mantras—i.e. those taken from a *Tantra* rather than the *Veda*.) Similarly, those who follow such practices are called (or call themselves) tāntrikas, or 'Tantrics'. By a further extension, particular practices and techniques (both soteriological and magical), which to some degree resemble those found in the *Tantras*, are more widely and inclusively characterized as 'Tantric'. Since such elements may be thought to inform, to a greater or lesser extent, all Hindu practice (with the exception of the most orthodox—i.e. the most strictly and exclusively Vedic), the term 'Tantra' or 'Tantrism' becomes, at its loosest, almost synonymous with 'medieval and modern Hinduism'.

Many of the phenomena associated with Tantra in its developed form (such as *yogic practices, the transformation of the body, the pursuit of supernormal powers (*siddhis), magic, *alchemy, and sexual ritual) are assumed to have been part of the substratum of the now largely invisible, popular religious practice of ancient India. ('Invisible' because—with the partial exception of the **Atharva Veda*—it was non-Vedic, and so non-textual.) It was only when drawn into the service of, or linked with, the textual revelation and theology of specific *Tantras* that such practice came into historical view. The earliest surviving texts of this type, dating from no earlier than the 5th or 6th century CE, are the *Saṃhitās* of the Vaiṣṇava *Pāñcarātrins, and, somewhat later, a variety of North Indian Buddhist *Tantras*.

Another early medieval Tantric tradition was that of the Śaiva *Kāpālikas which drew on the revelatory authority of the **Bhairava Tantras* to follow *impure practices opposed, and inimical, to *Brahmanical orthodoxy. At the same time, through a complex of *Kāpālika-derived traditions (known as *Kaula or 'Kaulism'), which involved ritual devotion to families of ferocious goddesses (*yoginīs), *Goddess, or Śākta worship was developing. This fed into the *Krama and *Trika systems of *Kashmiri Śaivism (9th–11th century CE), where, through the works of the *Pratyabhijñā school theologians, such as *Abhinavagupta and his pupil, *Kṣemarāja, Tantra developed its most sophisticated and complex soteriological and ritual strategies. Kaulism also generated such later Tantric traditions as the cult of *Śrī Vidyā, focused on the ritual worship of the all-powerful goddess *Tripurasundarī.

In general, Śākta Tantra schools are broadly aligned with either fierce or benevolent forms of the goddess, and categorized, on a similar division of their *Tantras*, as either *Kālīkula, 'belonging to the family of the Black Goddess' (originating in Northeastern and Northern India) or *Śrīkula, 'belonging to the family of the Auspicious Goddess' (originating in Kashmir and the South, notably in the Śrī Vidyā tradition). More widely, because of Tantra's preoccupation with the attainment and manipulation of the female energy or power (*śakti) which informs all existence, nearly all worship of the Goddess (Śakti personified), is imbued to a greater or lesser extent with *Tantric elements.

Another major Śaiva Tantric stream (in the broader sense) is that represented by the lower *caste *Siddhas, and more particularly the *Nāth Siddhas or *Yogis, whose *sampradāya emerged in the late 12th or early 13th century CE. Practitioners of *haṭha yoga and alchemy, and renowned as the possessors of this-worldly supernatural powers (siddhis), their principal aim was to achieve immortality within, and through, a perfected (*siddha) physical body.

The Tantric and Vedic streams of Hinduism, although at one level opposites in a conceptual polarity, have in practice frequently complemented, intertwined, or been layered onto each other in highly complex ways. (Although, from the sectarian tāntrika's point of view, Tantric revelation and the Tantric sādhanā are always more powerful and effective.) This can be seen most obviously in those mainstream Hindu traditions which were shaped into their present forms in the late medieval period, such as the *Śaiva Siddhānta and the *Śrī Vaiṣṇava, whose textual authorities are, inter alia, both Tantric and Vedic, and whose *pūjā is derived directly from Tantric models.

Once secretly initiated by his *guru (who may later initiate him into higher and increasingly esoteric forms of practice), the tāntrika or *sādhaka is expected to perform a daily Tantric *pūjā ritual for the rest of his life. (This is in addition to any non-Tantric rituals he may also practice.) Typically this involves techniques such as *kuṇḍalinī yoga, in which the individual's power or śakti is first visualized at the base of the spine and, through further visualizations, forced to the crown of the head, an ascension which generates ever-increasing spiritual powers (siddhis) in the practitioner. Techniques like this are given specific applications in particular traditions, so, in the Śrī Vidyā cult, for instance, kuṇḍalinī is conceptualized as the Goddess, i.e. as *Śiva's Śakti (a cosmic power), the aim being to unify the male and female principles in the practitioner's body. In other words, the sādhaka's body (the microcosm) is homologized to both the deity and the cosmos (the macrocosm), expressing and literally embodying the fundamental unity of existence. Such unity may also be evoked, and the power which informs it manipulated, through the ritual utilization of what, from the Vedic perspective, are *impure substances, such as the *pañca-makāra. These include sexual intercourse with a ritual partner, and other practices associated with the so-called 'left hand path' or *vāmacāra. The Śrī Vidyā also provides instances of other characteristic Tantric techniques, such as the use of geometric figures or *yantra (or in other contexts *maṇḍala); these are accompanied by the recitation of *mantras, particularly seed (*bīja) mantras (the sonic form of the deity) to realize the Goddess and her power in the body of the initiate. The specific aim of Tantric practice depends upon the particular tradition; in general terms, it may be the cultivation of both supernormal powers (siddhis) and liberation (*mokṣa), since the two are usually conceived as being part of a continuum. Once visualized, however, the deity (for the duration of the rite, the practitioner) may be invoked for any end, and some tāntrikas are concerned solely with the magical manipulation of the material world.

Tantrasadbhāvatantra (*c.*8th century CE) A **Tantra* containing what may be the earliest direct reference to *kuṇḍalinī.

Tantrasamuccaya A 15th-century CE text by Cēnnāsu Nārāyaṇam Nampūtirippāṭu which is one of the main textual sources for the *temple-based, *Tantric ritual tradition of the *Nambūdiri Brahmins of Kerala.

Tantrasāra ('Essence of Tantra') **1.** Abhinavagupta's own summary of his **Tantrāloka*, and an important text in its own right for *Kashimiri Śaivism. **2.** *See* KṚṢṆĀNANDA.

Tantrasārasaṃgraha ('Compendium of the Essence of Tantra') **1.** One of the many works attributed to the *Dvaita Vedāntin, *Madhva. **2.** A 15th/16th-century CE Keralan medical manual attributed to Nārāyaṇa.

tantraśāstra *See* MANTRAŚĀSTRA.

Tantravārttika *See* KUMĀRILA BHAṬṬA.

Tantric *See* TANTRA(S).

tāntrika *See* TANTRA(S).

Tantrism *See* TANTRA(S).

tapas *See* ASCETICISM.

tapasvin An *ascetic. *See* ASCETICISM.

Tārā (Tārakā) ('saviour', 'star') **1.** A *Tantric goddess, numbered among the *Mahāvidyās; probably introduced into Hinduism from *Buddhism, via Tibet. **2.** A name of *Kālī. **3.** In *Vedic and *Purāṇic mythology, the wife of *Bṛhaspati.

Tarkaśāstra ('Science of Reasoning') *See* NYĀYA.

Tārkṣya *See* GARUḌA.

tarpaṇa. The offering of water made to the ancestors (*pitṛs) as part of the *mahāyajña and *śrāddha rituals. It typically involves pouring water through the hands.

tattva (lit. 'thatness', a true or real state, principle, or element) A fundamental category, or real (i.e. ontologically real) constituent, of existence, usually arranged in a hierarchy of other tattvas. The paradigmatic instance is the hierarchy of 25 tattvas enumerated in classical *Sāṃkhya texts. Tattvajñāna—'knowledge of the principles'—is in some respects equivalent to the Western term 'philosophy'.

Tattvacintāmaṇi ('Thought-Jewel of Reality') *See* GAṄGEŚA.

tat tvam asi *See* MAHĀVĀKYA.

Tattvaprakāśa *See* BHOJADEVA.

teacher *See* GURU.

tejas ('brilliance', 'vital power', 'lustre') The semi-material quality of splendour, or vital energy predicated of gods and other great beings.

temple (mandir(a) ('dwelling), Tam.: **kōyil)** There is little extant evidence of the construction of free-standing Hindu temples before the 5th century CE, but it may be supposed that wooden, and possibly also stone structures were in existence in some places from around the 2nd century BCE. The expansion of temple building across the subcontinent from the 4th century CE onwards, engendered and maintained by royal patronage, naturally coincides with the rise of the great sectarian deities, and the associated practices of *bhakti and *pūjā. Although subject to waves of warfare and *Muslim iconoclasm in the north, the enthusiasm for constructing temples has hardly diminished over 1 500 years (although perhaps at its peak in terms of ambition and scope between the 11th and 16th centuries), and even the smallest *villages usually contain one or more mandiras, ideally situated next to a *river, or provided with a *tank. At the other end of the scale, numerous temple cities and complexes, maintained by cadres of *priests or *pūjāris, have become the regional and national focal points of devotion, *festivals, and *pilgrimage. Important temples have their own **sthalapurāṇas*, recounting their histories and foundation myths, as well as linking them to wider pan-Indian patterns of devotion.

Architectural historians distinguish broadly between two styles of temple: the Northern or *Nāgara, and the Southern or *Drāviḍa. Characteristic of the former is the *śikhara or tower, a series of ascending peaks or spires erected above the *mūrti in its *garbhagṛha. In addition to their own towers, the more elaborate examples of the Southern style are notable for their ornately decorated towered gateways, or *gopuras. Conceptually, temples of both types are seen as the actual home, or residence of the deity embodied in the *mūrti. Since God is at the centre of the cosmos, the temple is therefore presented in the **Vāstuśāstra* literature (concerned with architectural theory) as a microcosmos or *maṇḍala, with the deity in the *garbhagṛha at its centre, surrounded by a 'court' of consorts, vehicles, (*vāhanas), and attendant deities (often housed in subsidiary shrines). In a larger or better-endowed temple, the devotee, having bathed in a river or tank at the entrance, will pass many other mūrti as he or she moves ever further into the building, passing from what may be an elaborately carved exterior, depicting scenes from the *Epics and **Purāṇas*, to a plainer, cave-like interior. Such progress usually takes the form of an *auspicious circumambulation (*pradakṣiṇā) of both the rectangular superstructure and the garbhagṛha itself, culminating in *darśan of the main sectarian deity, and receiving the *prasād(a) distributed by the *priests at the end of pūjā. (Although it is always possible for individuals to conduct their own pūjā in public temples.)

Many temples are owned by individual families, groups of families (*kulas) or *caste groups. The great public temples, once under the patronage of *kings, or protected by the colonial authority, are now administered by hereditary families of priests, or by trusts on behalf of the state government. During the medieval period, Hindu temples were also widely constructed across *Java, *Bali, *Cambodia (including the celebrated *Angkor Wat), and Vietnam; and with the modern emigration of substantial Hindu populations to Africa and the West, Hindu temples, usually built to traditional patterns, can now be found across the globe. *See also* PŪJĀ; VĀSTUPURUṢA.

Teṉkalai One of the two major divisions of the *Viśiṣṭādvaita (*Śri Vaiṣṇava) school of philosophy. It was formed in the13th century CE, largely as the result of differing interpretations of Rāmānuja's *prapatti ('surrender') doctrine. Referred to as the 'southern' division, and associated with the theologian *Piḷḷai Lokācāriyar, the Teṉkalai regarded *liberation as totally dependent on the freely given grace (*prasāda) of the deity, a position compared to a cat picking up its kittens, regardless of their will. The geographical focus of the Teṉkalai tradition, and its major *tīrtha, is the great *temple complex of *Śrīraṅgam in Tamil Nadu. A sub-group of Teṉkalais, the *Sāttāda Śrī Vaiṣṇavas, has been active since the 15th century. *See also* VAṬAKALAI.

Tēvāram ('Garland of God', *c.*7th century CE) A collection of *Tamil *Śaiva Siddhānta *bhakti hymns attributed to the three *Nāyaṉmār, *Campantar, *Appar, and *Cuntarar. It constitutes the first seven books, and probably the best known part, of the **Tirumuṟai*, although it did not come to be known as the *Tēvāram* until around the 17th century.

teyyam (M.: 'god') One of a group of northern Keralan deities (teyyams). Usually female, they are worshipped in a network of local shrines with non-*vegetarian offerings, and through the *festival performance of teyyāṭṭam, or 'god dances'. The latter are undertaken by low-*caste male dancers (also called teyyams). Wearing elaborate individual costumes and make-up, the dancer is ritually possessed by, and so embodies, the teyyam.

ṭhag(s) (H.: 'robber', Ang: 'thug') Gangs of 18th- and 19th-century robber-murderers who preyed on travellers. They were said (on little firm evidence) to have offered their victims to the goddess *Bhavānī (*Kālī), and to have belonged to a secret cult. Probably never numbering more than a few hundred at any one time, they had been eliminated by the end of the 19th century, but this has not denied them a lurid afterlife in corners of the Western imagination.

Theosophical Society An organization co-founded in the USA in 1875 by Helena Petrovna ('Madame') Blavatsky (1831–1891)—a self-styled mystic and occultist of Russian origin—and Colonel Henry S. Olcott (1832–1907). In 1878 Blavatsky moved to India, taking the headquarters of the Society with her to Adyar, a suburb of Madras (Chennai), which remains its international headquarters. She was intent on blending Eastern (mostly Hindu) spirituality, including such ideas as *karma, and reincarnation (*rebirth), with what she thought of as Western science. This amalgam of ideas is reflected in her publications, notably *Isis Unveiled* (1877), *The Secret Doctrine* (1888), and the Journal she founded, *The Theosophist.* Perhaps the Society's most notable member has been Annie *Besant, who succeeded Colonel Olcott as president in 1907, and was later responsible for the education and training of Jiddu *Krishnamurti.

Thibaut, Georg F. W. (1848–1914) A German *Indologist who, for a time, worked as Max *Müller's assistant in Oxford. He moved to India in 1875, where he held several academic posts. Apart from his pioneering work on Indian astronomy and mathematics, he is probably best known for his English translations of *Śaṅkara's and *Rāmānuja's commentaries on the *Vedānta Sūtras* (**Brahmasūtras*) (1890, 1896, 1904) for the **Sacred Books of the East.*

third eye An attribute of *Śiva, hence the epithets Trinetra and Trilocana ('Three-Eyed'). In iconography it appears as a closed, vertical third eye in the god's forehead, symbolizing both his spritual perception—his omniscience—and his latent destructive power. Thought to be derived from the strength of his *tapas, and so a channel for heat and light, it is said to be the means by which he incinerates the universe at the end of a world age (*yuga). A number of stories characterize its power. In one, *Pārvatī inadvertently causes the world to go dark by teasingly covering his seeing eyes; his third eye appears to set things right. In another, he opens his third eye to incinerate the god of love, *Kāma, who has disturbed his austerities.

Thoreau, Henry David (1817–1862) A major American writer and thinker who, like *Emerson, was classified as one of the New England Transcendentalists. He was influenced by a number of Hindu sources, including his reading of Charles *Wilkins' 1785 translation of the **Bhagavadgītā*. The intellectual debt was repaid to *Gāndhī, whose satyāgraha strategy was influenced by Thoreau's essay on 'Civil Disobedience'.

thugs *See* ṬHAG(S).

tilak(a) (puṇḍra) A mark applied principally to the forehead, but also on occasion to other parts of the body, with a paste made from a colouring substance, such as sandalwood or *ash. Its significance depends on the context: inter alia, it may signify an individual's current social status (e.g. a red dot indicating that a woman is married), a temporary condition, such as a special consecration (*dīkṣā), the receipt of *prasāda after making a *pūjā, the membership of a particular *ascetic or sectarian order, or it may be merely decorative. In the case of sectarian marks, the lines (usually black, red, yellow, and white) may be extensive, covering the entire forehead. A common feature of *Vaiṣṇava markings is a figure curved upward like the letter U from the meeting point of the eyebrows, with a vertical red line between its arms; the *Śaiva tilaka or tripuṇḍara consists of three horizontal lines of *ash, with or without a central dot or '*third eye'; Śākta tilakas are usually variations on the Śaiva pattern, or a stylized third eye.

Tilak, Bal(a) Gangadhar(a) (1856–1920) A Maharastrian *brahmin who became one of the chief political agitators on behalf of Hindu Nationalism and a swift end to British rule. He propagated his views through the editorship of *Kesarī*, a Marathi newspaper, and was imprisoned three times by the British on charges that included sedition. He published two books in English, attempting to prove the prehistoric origins of the **Vedas*, but probably his most widely read and influential work (written while exiled in Burma) was his Marathi commentary on the **Bhagavadgītā*, the *Gītārahasya* (1915; English trans., 1936). According to this, *Kṛṣṇa's teaching was a call for the restoration of Hindu *dharma through violent political action. Tilak also promoted and expanded the annual Maharastrian *Ganeśa Catūrthi *festival as an opportunity for the large-scale public expression of Hindu nationalist sentiments, and inaugurated a festival in honour of the *Marāṭhā Hindu *king, *Śivajī.

time *See* CALENDAR; COSMOGONY; KĀLA; KALPA; MAHĀKALPA; YUGA.

tīrtha ('ford') See PILGRIMAGE.

tīrthaṅkara ('ford-maker') See JINA.

tīrthaphala *See* PILGRIMAGE.

tīrthayātra *See* PILGRIMAGE.

Tiru A *Tamil word meaning 'holy' or 'sacred' (equivalent to *Sanskrit *Śrī). It appears as a prefix to many Tamil names, place names, and the titles of texts.

Tiruchirāppaḷḷi (Tiruccirāppaḷḷi) A site in Tamil Nadu, on the south bank of the *Kāverī, opposite *Śrīraṅgam. It contains two 7th/8th century CE rock-cut shrines to *Śiva.

Tirukkōṭṭiyūr A *temple site near *Madurai, where *Rāmānuja is said to have publicly declaimed the *mantra, 'Oṃ namo Nārāyaṇāya' (considered the essence of the **Vedas*), from the top of the *temple tower in defiance of the wishes of his initiating *guru. The goddess *Apirāmī is worshipped there.

Tirukkōvaiyār *See* MĀṆIKKAVĀCAKAR.

Tirukkuṟaḷ **(*Kuṟaḷ*)** A popular early *Tamil text, composed sometime in the first millennium CE, and attributed to a legendary figure called Tiruvaḷḷuvar. Nothing, including his religious affiliation, is known about him, other than what can be inferred from the text itself, and there the evidence is scant and ambiguous. 'Kuṟaḷ' refers to couplets in verse, which deal, according the text's own arrangement, with the equivalents of the *Sanskritic *dharma, *artha, and *kāma (the first three *puruṣārthas). The work is essentially a book of popular wisdom or *ethics. It struck a chord with *Christian missionaries, and has since been widely translated into both Indian and Western languages.

Tirumāl (Māl) *See* MĀYŌṈ.

Tirumaṅkai Āḻvār (Tirumaṅgai, Parakāla(ṉ) ('Death of his Enemies')) (*c.*8th–9th century CE) The most prolific of the South Indian *Āḻvār poet-saints. He seems to have been a local ruler in Maṅkai (Tiruvālināṭu). His hagiographies are sensational: one story tells how he raised money to build shrines at *Śrīraṅgam by robbery, including the theft of a golden *Buddha statue. This accounts for his iconographic depiction as an armed dacoit. Tirumaṅkai's voluminous output demonstrates mastery of *Tamil prosody, as well as considerable learning, and takes up the whole 'Second Thousand' (plus some of the 'Third') of the **Nālāyirappirapantam*.

Tirumantiram **(*Tamiḻmūvāyiram*** ('Tamil Three Thousand')**)** ('Sacred Mantra', 6th/7th century CE?) An early *Śaiva theological work, drawing on the **Āgamas*; attributed to Tirumūlar, it was included as the tenth book of the **Tirumuṟai*.

Tirumoḻi *See* PERIYĀḺVĀR.

Tirumūlar (6th or 7th century CE) *See* TIRUMANTIRAM.

Tirumuṟai ('Holy Book') The vast collection of poetry, hagiographies, and theological material which makes up what is sometimes referred to as the *Tamil *Śaiva Siddhānta canon (although it is only actually part of it). Compiled—although probably not in its final form—by *Nampi Āṇṭār Nampi in the 12th century CE, its contents cover a period from about 500 CE to the mid 12th century. It is divided into eleven 'holy books' (tirumuṟais), plus *Cēkkiḻār's 12th-century hagiographical work, the *Periya Purāṇam* ('Great **Purāṇa*'). (The entire collection was probably not known as the *Tirumuṟai* until around the 14th century.) The *Tirumuṟai* contains the poetry of six *Nāyaṉmār and twenty other Śaiva saints. Its first seven books (known since around the 17th century CE as the **Tevāram*—'Garland of God') contain the *bhakti hymns attributed to the three *Nāyaṉmār, *Campantar (Books 1–3), *Appar (Books 4–6), and *Cuntarar (Book 7). Book 8 contains the works of *Māṇikkavācakar; Book 9, various *temple songs, known as *Tiruvicaippā*; Book 10, Tirumūlar's *Tirumantiram* (6th or 7th century CE); Book 11, a disparate anthology, including works by *Kāraikkāl Ammaiyār, *Nakkīrar, and Nampi himself; Book 12 is Cēkkiḻār's *Periya Purāṇam*.

Tirumurukāṟṟuppaṭai ('Guide to Lord Murukaṉ', *c.* 250 CE?) A long *Caṅkam poem attributed to *Nakkīrar, which marks the beginning of the *Tamil *Śaiva *bhakti tradition. Acting as a kind of *pilgrimage guide, it eulogizes *Murukaṉ and the *tīrthas associated with him. Initially included in the **Pattuppāṭṭu* anthology, in the 12th century, along with eight other compositions attributed to Nakkīrar, it was incorporated into the eleventh book of the **Tirumuṟai* collection.

Tiruñāṉa Campantar (Tiruñāṉa Sambandhar) (*c.*7th century CE) *See* CAMPANTAR; TIRUÑĀṈA.

Tirunāvukkaracu ('Lord of Divine Speech') (7th century CE) *See* APPAR.

Tirupati A hugely popular *Vaiṣṇava *pilgrimage centre at the foot of a forested hill (known as Tirumalai/Tirumala—'Holy Hill') in southern Andhra Pradesh. The hill's summit is the home to the richest, and perhaps most charitable, *temple in India (also referred to as the Tirupati temple). The shrine is dedicated to Veṅkaṭeśvara ('Lord of Veṅkaṭa Hill'), identified as *Viṣṇu, although the term '*Īśvara' indicates the original deity may have been *Śiva. According to one story, it was *Rāmānuja who identified the image as being of Viṣṇu and introduced the ritual used at *Śrīraṅgam to the temple, although Veṅkaṭeśvara had been celebrated in *Āḻvār poetry long before that. Veṅkaṭeśvara's most prolific hymnist was the *Śrī Vaiṣṇava poet-saint, *Annamācārya, who is said to have composed more than 32 000 songs in Telugu in praise of the god. Tirupati's fame and fortune were elevated by the patronage of the *Vijayanagara kings in the 14th to 16th centuries. It is now visited by up to ten thousand pilgrims a day, who collectively make lavish donations (as well as offerings of their hair) in the hope that Veṅkaṭeśvara will grant them all their desires. The temple is serviced by *Vaikhānasa *priests, and renowned for its daily 'wake-up prayer' (suprabhātam), delivered in *Sanskrit.

Tiruppallāṇṭu *See* PERIYĀḺVĀR.

Tiruppāvai *See* ĀṆṬĀL.

Tiruttoṇṭapurāṇam *See* CĒKKIḺĀR.

Tiruvācakam ***(Tiruvāsagam)*** ('Sacred Verses) *See* MĀṆIKKAVĀCAKAR.

Tiruvaḷḷuvar *See* TIRUKKUṞAḶ.

Tiruvaṇṇāmalai A *pilgrimage centre in Tamil Nadu, renowned for its *Aruṇācaleśvara ('The Temple of the Lord of the Red Mountain') complex, dedicated to *Śiva as the lord of a nearby hill. During an annual ten day *festival held in November–December, a great bonfire, representing the god's fiery *liṅga, is lit on the hill's summit.

Tiruvārūr Site of the celebrated *Śaiva Tyāgarāja *temple in Tamil Nadu. The temple in its present form was begun in the *Cōla period, and either added to, or rebuilt, over the next four centuries. Śiva is worshipped there as *Somaskanda.

Tiruvāsagam *See* TIRUVĀCAKAM.

Tiruvāymoḻi ('Sacred Speech') The name given to the collection of *Nammāḻvār's songs, 1 102 verses divided into tens in the 'Fourth Thousand' of the **Nālāyirappirapantam* anthology. It became part of *Śrī Vaiṣṇava liturgy in the 11th century, and is extensively recited at particular *festivals, as well as at every kind of ritual, and as an accompaniment to daily *pūjā in homes and *temples. The collection has engendered numerous oral, performative, and written commentaries. *Śrī Vaiṣṇavas refer to the *Tiruvāymoli* as the 'Tamil *Veda*', regarding it as the equal of the *Sanskrit **Veda*, with the added advantage of being accessible to all. For contents, *see* NAMMĀḺVĀR.

Tiruvempāvai **(*Tiruvembavai*)** *See* MĀṆIKKAVĀCAKAR.

Tiruviruttam A collection of 100 verses by *Nammāḻvār contained in the 'Third Thousand' of the **Nālāyirappirapantam* anthology.

tithi (lunar day) *See* CALENDAR.

Tivviyappirapantam *See* ĀḺVĀRS; NĀTHMUNI.

Tivyaprapantam *See* ĀḺVĀRS; NĀTHMUNI.

Todas A tribal community, much studied by anthropologists, living among the Nilgiri hills of Tamil Nadu. Traditionally, their religious life has been focused on 'dairy-temples', and a hierarchy of sacred buffalo. In the 20th century some Hindu elements have been noted on the margins of their practice.

Tolkāppiyam The first descriptive grammar of the *Tamil language. Probably the work of a *Jain monk of the same name, and composed around the beginning of the 2nd century CE, it also gives significant information on the poetics and religion of the time.

Toṇṭaraṭippoṭi (early 9th century CE) One of the *Āḻvārs. A *brahmin *priest at the *Śrīraṅgam temple, his compositions, the *Tiruppaḷḷiyeḻucci* (a song to wake the deity from sleep) and the *Tirumālai* ('Holy Garland') are contained in the 'First Thousand' of the **Nālāyirappirapantam* anthology.

Transcendental Meditation (TM) A largely traditional, *mantra-based form of *meditation, devised by *Maharishi Mahesh Yogi and propagated by his Transcendental Meditation Society on a global scale.

Trayambakayajvan (18th century CE) A South Indian *brahmin who wrote a commentary on *Vālmiki's **Rāmāyaṇa* (the *Dharmākūtam*) and the **Strīdharmapaddhati* ('The Manual of Women's Dharma').

trayī vidyā *See* 'TRIPLE VEDA'.

tretā yuga *See* YUGA.

Trika *See* KASHMIR(I) ŚAIVISM.

Trilocana ('three-eyed') *See* THIRD EYE.

trimūrti ('having three forms') A grouping of *Brahmā, *Viṣṇu, and *Śiva in *Purāṇic *cosmology, emphasizing their complementary functions as, respectively, creator, preserver, and destroyer. There is an early occurrence of the triad (Brahmā, Viṣṇu, *Rudra) in the **Maitrāyaṇī Upaniṣad* (4.5), where it is assimilated to *brahman (neut.); this sets the pattern for all later theology where, as a group, they are treated as subservient to some greater power or deity, and not as a kind of composite God. *See also* 'HINDU TRINTY'.

Trinetra ('Three-Eyed') *See* THIRD EYE.

'Triple *Veda*' Also known as the 'Threefold Knowledge' (trayī vidyā): the **Ṛg*, **Sāma*, and **Yajur Veda* **Saṃhitā*.

Tripura ('three cities', 'triple city') According to *Epic and Purāṇic myth, a three-tiered flying city made of gold, silver, and iron. Inhabited by three belligerent and seemingly invincible *asuras, it was eventually destroyed at the *devas' behest by *Śiva firing a single arrow from an aerial chariot.

Tripurasundarī ('The Beautiful Goddess of the Three Worlds/Cities') The form of the *Goddess whose *Tantric worship is the focus of the *Śākta *Śrī Vidyā cult, also known as Lalitā ('lovely'), Kāmeśvarī ('the Goddess of Erotic Love'), Mahātripurasundarī, Rājarājeśvarī ('Queen of Kings'), and Śrīdevī ('the Auspicious Goddess'), and identified with various other South Indian goddesses, such as *Kāmākṣī and *Ṣodaśī. Essentially benign and erotic, she is, at the same time, both transcendent and immanent, the absolute power (*śakti) that ceaselessly manifests and reabsorbs the cosmos as eternal and primeval sound (*śabda). She has come to be worshipped in three ways: i) iconically, as a beautiful, red, young woman, red-clothed and with a red garland, four-armed, holding a noose, an elephant-goad, *Kāma's five arrows, and a bow (she is sometimes also depicted as sitting on Sadāśiva— *Śiva as a corpse), to whom *pure, vegetal offerings are made; ii) in a subtle form, through recitation of the śrīvidyā *mantra, composed of fifteen (or sixteen) *bīja or 'seed syllables'; iii) in her supreme form, through *meditation on the *śrīyantra diagram. In this way, those initated into the tradition hope to realize their absolute identity with her as unmitigated and liberating power. Consonant with this specific ritual, *haṭha yogic methods of visualization are also employed, in which the goddess is conceptualized as *kuṇḍalinī, with the aim of uniting the male and female principles in the practitioner's body. *See also* LALITĀSAHASRANĀMA; SAUNDARYALAHARĪ.

Tripurā Upaniṣad (16th century CE?) A *Śrī Vidyā text in praise of the goddess *Tripurasundarī, which, through its title, also attempts to align itself with the *Vedic tradition (one of its two recensions claims to belong, to the **Ṛg Veda*, the other to the **Atharva Veda*). It generated a number of commentaries, including one by Bhāskarāya (1728–50).

Tripurī Pūrṇimā (Kārttika Pūrṇimā) ('[the festival of] the full moon day of [the destruction of] the three cites') A major *Śaiva *festival celebrated on the full moon day of Kārttika (October–November), commemorating *Śiva's destruction of the *asuras in *Tripura.

Tristhalīsetu ('The Bridge to the Three Holy Cities') A *tīrthaphala text composed by Nārāyaṇa Bhaṭṭa in the mid 16th century.

triśūla A trident; *Śiva's most important weapon, and one of the insignia carried by his *ascetic devotees. It is given various symbolic interpretations (e.g. its three prongs represent his power to create, preserve, and destroy). In modern politics, it has been used as a symbol of affiliation to various right-wing movements.

Trivandrum (Ang. of Tiruvanantapuram/Thiruvananthapuram) A *temple city in southern Kerala (the present day State Capital), renowned as a major *pilgrimage centre; the 18th-century temple is dedicated to *Viṣṇu as *Padmanābha.

trivarga ('collection/group of three') A collective name for any three entities or concepts which can be grouped together, such as the three '*twice-born' *varṇas. *See also* PURUṢĀRTHA.

Trivikrama ('he who takes three steps') An epithet of *Viṣṇu who, in an *Epic and *Purāṇic myth associated with his *Vāmana *avatāra, encompasses the entire universe in three strides. Earlier versions of the story, in for example, the **Śatapatha Brāhmaṇa* (1.2.5.1–9), have a sacrificial significance, in so far as the *yajamāna imitates the three strides, and so converges with the god, who becomes the embodiment of the *sacrifice. For the content of the myth, *see* BALI (1).

Tukārāma (Tukārām) (*c.*1607–1649) A renowned and popular Maharashtrian poet-saint (*sant). According to the hagiographies, he was born into a low-*caste, but relatively prosperous family at Dehu near Pune. While still in his teens, he suffered a series of family disasters, including the loss of his first wife and eldest son in a famine. Although married to an allegedly shrewish second wife, he thereafter devoted his time to going on *pilgrimages, or singing ecstatic abhaṅgas (*bhajan(a)) to *Viṭhobā in and around *Paṇḍharpur. He was said to have drawn a large following, but also to have antagonized the local *brahmins and landholders, who gave the order for his poems to be thrown into a river, only for them miraculously to resurface. He disappeared in 1649, according to some accounts in an ascension to *Viṣṇu's heaven engineered by *Garuḍa.

Over 4600 abhaṅgas are credited to Tukārāma, although perhaps only a quarter of that number is likely to belong to the 17th century. The accretion is a mark of his importance to the members of the *Vārkarī Panth, who make copious use of the songs in their devotional practices, especially during their regular pilgrimages to Paṇḍharpur. As a result, Tukārāma has strongly influenced the style of some subsequent Marathi literature (a small number of the abhaṅgas are in *Hindi). The poems vary in content, but they are consistently critical of *Brahmanical learning and the putative authority of the **Veda*: all religious practices converge on, and are resolved in, devotion to Viṭhobā.

tulasī (tulsī) (*Ocymum sanctum*) The sweet basil plant, regarded by *Vaiṣṇavas as sacred to *Viṣṇu (especially as *Rāma). Often used in ritual, it is grown in special containers in the precincts of *temples, or in household shrines. Its berries are used to make *mālās.

Tulsīdās(a) (*c.*1543–1623) Author of the celebrated *Hindi *bhakti poem, the **Rāmcaritmānas*. Born into a *brahmin family at either Rājāpur or *Ayodhyā, he is said to have been abandoned as a child and brought up by a *Vaiṣṇava *sādhu. (The name by which he is known means 'Servant of the *Tulasī Plant'.) He begun his most famous poem in *Ayodhyā in 1574, and completed it several years later in *Vārāṇasī, where he seems to have spent most of his remaining life. Both before and after the *Rāmcaritmānas*, he produced a substantial body of devotional work, which has been largely overshadowed by his retelling of *Rāma's story. Around a dozen surviving texts are thought to be genuine, most of them further poems derived from the story of Rāma and *Sītā (*Dohāvalī, Kavitāvalī*), and from places and deities associated with them (*Vinaypatrikā*). There is also a popular collection of songs addressed to *Hanumān (*Hanumān Bāhuk*).

Tvaṣṭṛ In the **Ṛg Veda*, the architect, or carpenter, of the *devas; so according to some passages, the demiurge or fashioner of the world, and, as such, *Indra's father. In *Purāṇic mythology he is replaced by, or subsumed into, *Viśvakarman.

twice-born *See* DVIJA.

tyāga *See* TYĀGIN.

Tyāgarāja (1767–1847) A celebrated classical musician, *Rāma *bhakta, and composer of *kīrtanas. Born in *Tiruvārūr, he spent most of his life in Tiruvaiyāṟu, near *Tañjāvūr in Tamil Nadu; his words and music, including two devotional music dramas, were collected by his disciples.

Tyāgarāja temple *See* TIRUVĀRŪR.

tyāgin One who has undertaken tyāga ('renunciation'); in other words, someone who has either given up something specific for religious purposes—perhaps in the form of a donation (*dāna)—or renounced worldly concerns and possessions altogether, and so become a *renouncer or *saṃnyāsin.

t

U

udāna *See* PRĀṆA.

Udāsīs A group of *ascetics usually classified as Hindu, although they are closely aligned to the *Sikhs. They are said to have been established by Śrī Candra, the eldest son of Gurū *Nānak. Until the early 20th century, when they lost control to less Hindu-oriented Sikhs, their abbots (mahants) controlled many of the most important Sikh centres. As well as worship of the *Gurū Granth Sāhib*, the Udāsīs perform *pañcāyatana pūjā.

Udayagiri A site, not far from modern Bhopāl in Madhya Pradesh, containing twenty Hindu cave *temples with rock cut sculptures dating from the *Gupta period.

Udayana (12th century CE) *See* NYĀYA.

Uddālaka Āruṇi A celebrated *Vedic teacher and debater; a *brahmin from the *Kuru-Pañcāla region of northern India, he appears in the **Śatapatha Brāhmaṇa*, and both the **Bṛhadāraṇyaka* and **Chāndogya* **Upaniṣads*. In the latter text, he is the teacher of *Yājñavalkya and the father of Śvetaketu, to whom he delivers the famous instruction concerning the world being in essence the *ātman, concluding with the refrain: tat tvam asi ('You are that' or 'That's how you are'). In the **Kaṭha Upaniṣad*, *Naciketas and his father are said to be Uddālaka's descendants.

Uddyotakara Bhāradvāja (6th century CE) A *Nyāya teacher; author of the *Nyāyavārttika* ('Elucidation of Nyāya'), and perhaps the first to argue for the reality of *God (*Śiva) from a Nyāya perspective.

udgātṛ (Udgātar) A member of one of the four groups of *priests responsible for performing the *Vedic *śrauta ritual. The udgātṛ is the priest of the **Sāma Veda*, responsible for the complex melodic singing of the *sāmans, mostly during the *soma sacrifice, a kind of chanting referred to as udgītha.

udgītha *See* UDGĀTṚ.

Udyogaparvan ('The Book of the Preparations') The fifth book of the *Sanskrit **Mahābhārata*, recounting the way in which the *Kauravas and *Pāṇḍavas prepare for the coming battle at *Kurukṣetra. It is from this point onwards that *Kṛṣṇa becomes a principal character in the epic in his role as the protector of the Pāṇḍavas and their cause.

Ugraśravas The *sūta who, in the outer framing story of the **Mahābhārata*, first recites the text to the assembled *ṛṣis in the Naimiṣa forest. He had himself heard it recited by *Vyāsa's pupil, *Vaiśampāyana, at *Janamejaya's *snake *sacrifice.

Ujjain (H., Skt.: Ujjayinī) One of India's 'seven holy cities'; situated in modern Madhya Pradesh on the banks of the river Siprā, it is one of the four *pilgrimage sites (tīrthas) at which, every twelve years, a *Kumbh(a) Melā is held. The city has been an important political, economic, and cultural centre since *Mauryan times. *Kālidāsa, who may have lived there, provides a romantic evocation of the city in his *Meghadūta* ('The Cloud Messenger').

Umā (Pārvatī) A name of the goddess who is *Śiva's consort. She is the daughter of *Himavat and *Menā. See PĀRVATĪ.

Umā

Umāpati Śivācārya (Tam.: **Umāpati Civāriyar**) (early 14th century CE) A *Śaiva Siddhāntin, who was a *priest at the *Cidambaram *temple in Tamil Nadu. A number of works are attributed to him, including a wide-ranging poem on *Śiva *Naṭarāja performing his *ānandatāṇḍava ('dance of bliss') at Cidambaram, the *Kuñcitāṅghristava* ('Hymn of Praise to the Curved Foot'), and *Kōyil Purāṇam*, a *Tamil version of the 12th-century **sthalapurāṇa* text, the *Cidambara *Māhātmya*, a *bhāṣya on a Śaiva Siddhānta **Āgama*, the *Pauṣkara*, and an anthology from the *Āgamas*, the *Śataratnasaṃgraha* ('Collection of a Hundred Jewels'). *See also* KOṬIKKAVI.

untouchables An English term designating members of *castes which, from the the point of view of *brahmin ideology (as represented in the *varṇa system), lie outside the system altogether (i.e. they are *avarṇa), hence the synonymous term, 'outcaste'. (In other words, they lie below *śūdras in the hierarchy.) Particularly in the 20th century, they have been referred to by numerous other terms, including 'depressed classes', *dalit ('the oppressed'), 'scheduled castes', and 'scheduled tribes' (tribal peoples also being classified as outside the varṇa system). Untouchability was formally outlawed by the Indian constitution of 1950 in one of a series of continuing attempts to raise the social and economic status of such groups (which constitute more than one fifth of India's population), often in the face of considerable resistance from those above them in the caste hierarchy. The term 'untouchable' derives from the brahmin perception that physical contact with a member of the lower castes is a source of ritual *pollution. (This principle may be extended to more remote 'touching', such as that which takes place through sight or the casting of a shadow.) *See also* CAṆḌĀLA; HARIJANS; PARIAH.

upacāra(s) ('service', 'attendance', 'reverence') A collective name for the offerings, and attendant rites (or, in the singular, for any one of them) made in a particular *pūjā. A standard (although minimally variable) list of sixteen upacāras, sometimes considered the minimum permissible in *temple worship, includes: 1) *āvāhana—the 'bidding', making-present, or awaking of the deity; 2) *āsana—the offering of a seat (i.e. the deity's ritual installation); 3) pādya—washing its feet; 4) *arghya—offering it water, as part of a formal welcome; 5) *ācamanīya—offering it water to rinse the mouth; 6) *snāna (*abhiṣeka)—bathing it; 7) vastra—dressing it; 8) *yajñopavīta—giving it a new sacred thread; 9) gandha—anointing it with (e.g.) sandalwood, and/or a sectarian mark (*tilaka); 10) puṣpa—offering it flowers/garlanding it; 11) dhūpa—burning incense before it; 12) dīpa—waving a light before it (= *āratī); 13) naivedya—feeding it (i.e. offering it foodstuffs, also referred to as *prasāda); 14) namaskāra—paying homage, and/or prostrating to it; 15) *pradakṣinā—the circumambulation of the deity in its *garbhagṛha; 16) *visarjana—the 'dismissal' of the deity, formally closing the pūjā.

Upadeśasāhasrī ('Thousand Teachings') *See* ŚAṄKARA.

Upāgama A class of texts subsidiary, or complementary to the *Śaiva Siddhānta **Āgamas* or **Tantras*.

upamāna ('analogy') Recognized as a means of valid knowledge (*pramāṇa) by the *Nyāya, *Vaiśeṣika, *Mīmāṃsā, and *Vedānta *darśanas.

upanayana (lit. 'leading', 'taking near', 'initiation') According to the tradition prescribed in the **Gṛhyasūtras* and **Dharmaśāstra*, one of the most important *saṃskāras for a male belonging to one of the three higher *varṇas. Most immediately, it marks the beginning of a period of *Vedic studentship (*brahmacarya) under the direction of a teacher (*ācārya), which, once completed, qualifies the individual, at *marriage, to set up the sacred fires and become a *gṛyha or *śrauta ritualist. In the longer term, therefore, upanayana is an essential prerequiste for becoming a householder (*gṛhastha), and so a full member of traditional, high-*caste *Brahmanical society. In this way it constitutes an individual's 'second birth', hence the epithet *dvija, 'twice-born', applied to those who have undergone it.

What in the early Vedic period is a relatively simple ritual becomes, in the *dharma literature, a matter of some complexity, with considerable variations, depending on whether the inititiate belongs to the *brahmin, *kṣatriya, or *vaiśya varṇa. There is no general agreement about the proper age for upanayana, but usually some point between the individual's eighth and twenty-fourth birthdays is prescribed, on the principle the higher the varṇa the lower the age. Among a complex of symbolic actions which purify the individual prior to his being given access to the **Veda*, the initiate has his hair shaved and his nails cut; he is ritually bathed and dons a new garment (traditionally an antelope skin and a girdle of twisted *muñja grass); he may also be taught a basic form of *prāṇāyāma. As a specific initiation into the *Veda*, his teacher then whispers the *Gāyatrī mantra into his ear, and gets him to repeat it. Most of this is accompanied by oblations into the fire and *mantras, and the initate himself is taught some basic ritual gestures. The upanayana is concluded by a meal, marking the boy's transition from a dependent child to adulthood, and, for those undertaking the *āśrama of brahmacarya, a symbolic entry into the actual process of soliciting alms. The investiture with a *sacred thread (yajñopavīta)—subsequently performed as a central part of the ritual, before the revelation of the Gāyatrī mantra—was absent from earlier accounts of upanayana, but over time it has come to be synonymous with it. In the modern period (with the exception of some traditional *brahmin familes) the ritual has generally been compressed or collapsed into the marriage ceremony, mirroring **Manusmṛti*'s view that marriage is the equivalent of upanayana for females.

Upāṅga A name sometimes given to a group of texts considered supplementary to the **Veda*, namely, the **Purāṇas*, the **Nyāya* and **Mīmāṃsā* **Śāstras*, and **Dharmaśāstra*.

Upaniṣadic Belonging to, or related to, the **Upaniṣads*.

Upaniṣad(s) The fourth layer of *Vedic literature according to the traditional division, the *Upaniṣads* are also referred to as the *Vedānta—the conclusion, essence, or culmination of the **Veda*. A distinction is normally made between an effectively closed canon of principal, or major, early *Upaniṣads*, composed or compiled between approximately the 7th century BCE and the early centuries of the Common Era, and a still open-ended category of 'minor' *Upaniṣads*. Collections of the major early *Upaniṣads* usually include the following (listed in a tentative chronological order): **Bṛhadāraṇyaka*, **Chāndogya*, **Taittirīya*, **Aitareya*, **Kauṣītaki*, **Kena*, **Kaṭha*, **Īśā*, **Śvetāśvatara*, **Muṇḍaka*, **Praśna*, **Māṇḍūkya*, and **Maitrāyaṇī*. (Medieval anthologies, however, often contain much longer lists of what are regarded as 'major' *Upaniṣads*.) The minor *Upaniṣads* consist of texts numbered in their hundreds which employ the cachet of the name for their own purposes—e.g. those collected as **Saṃnyāsa Upaniṣads*.

Each extant early *Upaniṣad* is attributed to, and was originally orally transmitted by, a particular *Vedic school or *śākhā. (So, for example, the *Taittirīya Upaniṣad*, belongs to the **Taittirīya Saṃhitā* of the **Black Yajur Veda*.) The division between **Āraṇyaka* and *Upaniṣad* is not always clearly demarcated, either in terms of content or classification: the last book of the **Śatapatha Brāhmaṇa*, for instance, is referred to as an *Āraṇyaka*, but so is the *Upaniṣad* that completes it, the *Bṛhadāraṇyaka*.

The earliest *Upaniṣads*, such as the *Bṛhadāraṇyaka* and the *Chāndogya*, remain closely linked to Vedic ritualism; they continue the speculation on the underlying meaning of ritual found in the texts that chronologically precede them, the **Brāhmaṇas* and *Āraṇyakas*, particularly in relation to the notion of *bandhu, 'homology' or 'equivalence' (which is also one of the early meanings of 'upaniṣad'). One important result of this is the formulation of an equivalence between the essence of the individual, the *ātman, and the power which underlies the universe, *brahman (neut.). Knowledge (*jñāna)—i.e. the active realization of such an equation—liberates the knower from the cycle of *karma and *rebirth—a complex of ideas which itself first comes to textual light in the *Bṛhadāraṇyaka* and *Chāndogya*. There it is presented as a secret knowledge (upaniṣad) of hidden equivalences, privately transmitted from *teacher to pupil, outside the setting of the village (*grāma). The *Upaniṣads* are therefore the texts which contain this secret teaching, much of it put into the mouths of *kṣatriyas (and sometimes of women). (Some recent scholarship has suggested that these new teachings may be associated with the rapid growth of cities in this period, and represent the views of 'city' *brahmins.) Variations on these themes, and other cosmological and soteriological speculations (many of them related to early *yogic and *Sāṃkhya ideas) were added in the later *Upaniṣads*, with a notable theistic strand emerging in texts such as the *Kaṭha* and the *Śvetāśvatara*. The major *Upaniṣads* are thus the repositories of many of the theological and philosophical ideas which come to dominate later *Vedāntic thought. Unsystematic themselves (but like the rest of the *Veda* regarded as revelation), they were systematized, partly through the synthesis made in the **Brahmasūtra* and the work of its commentators, and partly through numerous commentaries on particular *Upaniṣads*, such as those made by *Śaṅkara, which shaped their thought for the theological purposes of particular *Vedāntic schools. Indeed, as two of the *prasthāna traya, the *Brahmasūtra* and the principal *Upaniṣads* required commentaries from anyone wishing to found a new Vedānta subschool. In more recent times, many of those involved in the Hindu reform movements of the 19th century (such as Rāmmohun *Roy) have eulogized the *Upaniṣads* as containing the basis of a pure, essential (not to say universal) Hinduism. Similarly, the early *Upaniṣads*, cut free of their Vedic moorings, were among the first texts to attract the attention of Western philosophers and *Orientalists. *For summaries of specific content, see the entries on individual Upaniṣads.*

upapurāṇa *See* PURĀṆA(S).

upāsana ('worship') A generic term for devotion to a deity or *guru. Precisely how it is expressed depends upon the particular tradition; common forms include *pūjā, *sevā, and internal worship through *meditation. The term is probably most frequently used by the *Śrī Vaiṣṇavas to characterize their practice of *temple devotion to *Viṣṇu's *arcāvatāras.

upavāsa ('fasting') A common expression of religious commitment, undertaken as part of an *ascetic regime, in fulfilment of particular vow (*vrata), or simply in conformity to a specified calendrical fast day. In scope a fast may range from complete abstinence from all *food and water, to avoidance of specified food stuffs, to reduced consumption for a particular period. The term may also be used in an inclusive sense to cover abstinence from all forms of sensual gratification. *Gāndhī's use of fasting to exert moral pressure on his political opponents was an often effective, and certainly widely publicized, tactic.

Upaveda ('supplementary knowledge') A category of knowledge (art or science) regarded as supplementary to the **Veda*, and sometimes artificially aligned with a particular *Vedic school (*śākhā). Four types are usually specified: *Āyurveda (medicine), *Gandharvaveda (music and dancing), *Dhanurveda (martial arts (lit. 'archery')), and *Sthāpatyaveda (architecture) or, alternatively, **Śilpaśāstra*.

upāya ('means') A means, either to a religious goal or, as in **Arthaśāstra*, to overcoming one's enemies through various stratagems, such as bribery.

Urdū A Persianized version of Hindustānī; written in a modified form of the Perso-Arabic script, it became the national language of Pakistan.

Urvaśī *See* PURŪRAVAS.

Uṣas A *Vedic goddess who personifies the Dawn. The daughter of the Sky, she is one of the few goddesses to appear in the **Ṛg Veda*; hymn 1.48 is addressed to her, and she is closely associated with the *Aśvins (in, for example, hymn 1.92).

Utpala (Utpalācārya, Utpaladeva, Utpalavaiṣāva) (*c*.925–975 CE) *Abhinavagupta's *paramaguru in the *Pratyabhijñā School of *Kashmir(i) Śaivism.

utsava *See* FESTIVAL.

utsavamūrti ('festival image') A portable image (*mūrti) of a deity or *saint, often of bronze, which has been ritually empowered to act as though it were the deity which is permanently installed in the *garbhagṛha. It is paraded from the *temple (or in its precincts) as the focus of a regular ritual or particular *festival, thus enabling a large number of devotees to take *darśana of it. Notable examples include *Jagannātha and his siblings at *Purī, and the portable bronzes of South Indian temples.

uttara A common prefix to the names of texts or objects indicating that they are 'higher', 'later', or 'superior'. By extension, it can also indicate that something is 'higher', 'northern', or 'to the right'.

Uttarakāṇḍa ('The Last Book'/'The Book of Further Adventures') The seventh and final book of *Vālmīki's **Rāmāyaṇa*, which is usually thought to be a later addition to the main text. Doubts are cast on *Sītā's fidelity. To maintain his honour, *Rāma exiles her to the *forest where she gives birth to twin sons. Later, in witness to her *purity, her mother the Earth (*Bhū Devī) swallows her up. Rāma abdicates, and (as *Viṣṇu) ascends to *heaven.

Uttara Mīmāṃsā *See* VEDĀNTA.

Uttaramīmāṃsāsūtra *See* BRAHMASŪTRA(S).

Uttararāmacarita ('Rāma's Last Act') *See* BHAVABHŪTI.

U

V

vāc ('speech') Personified as a goddess in the *Ṛg Veda,* where she is naturally seen as the mother of the *Vedas,* 'speech', or the Word, vāc is also regarded as the power which, through *mantra, underlies the *sacrifice, and so the supreme creative force which at the same time informs, manifests, and exceeds the cosmos. In the **Upaniṣads* she is therefore equated with *brahman (neut.). Later, as the goddess of speech (vāgdevī), vāc becomes synonymous with *Sarasvatī. In *Kashmiri *Śaivism, vāc, as sound, is analysed in a complex and sophisticated way as the *śakti, or energy, of *Śiva, through which he manifests and reabsorbs the universe.

vacana An utterance, particularly a grammatical rule or a religious lyric.

Vācaspati Miśra (10th century CE) A philosopher who wrote empathetic and influential commentaries on texts from a number of traditions, notably *Advaita Vedānta, *Nyāya, and *Sāṃkhya-Yoga. Among these were the *Bhāmati* (a subcommentary on *Śaṅkara's *Brahmasūtrabhāṣya*), the *Nyāyavārtikka* ('Gloss on the True Intention of the Elucidation of Nyāya'), the *Sāṃkhyatattvakaumadi* ('Moonlight on the Sāṃkhya *Tattvas'), and the *Tattvavaiśāradi,* a gloss on *Vyāsa's **Yoga Sūtra* commentary. Such was his versatility, he was characterized as 'sarvatantrasvatantra'—'independent master of all systems'.

vāda A scholastic or philosophical debate, conducted according to agreed procedures or rules, laid down in debating manuals (*vāda-śāstra*).

vāghyā A class of male devotees, temporary and permanent, who are attendant upon *Khaṇḍobā in Maharashtra, especially in his *temple at Jejurī. Identifying with the dogs that accompany Khaṇḍobā's hunt, they have a particular repertoire of songs, and may be called upon to perform special domestic rituals.

vāhana ('vehicle') The term for a deity's vehicle, mount, or attendant, usually an animal, such as the bull, *Nandin (*Śiva), or a mythical creature, such as the half-bird half-man, *Garuḍa (*Viṣṇu). A vāhana may have its own shrine in a *temple and be the focus of associated *pūjā. Vāhanas figure prominently in *Purāṇic mythology.

vaidhībhakti *See* RĀGĀNUGĀBHAKTI.

vaidika ('relating to the *Veda*') A substantive designating a *brahmin well-versed in the **Veda,* and/or someone who follows *Vedic as opposed to (e.g.) *Tantric rituals.

Vaikhānasa A *Vaiṣṇava tradition which, since around the 10th century CE, has been preserved in the ritual practices of the South Indian *temple *brahmin *priests of the same name, notably at *Tirupati. It claims unbroken descent from the *Taittirīya ritualists of the **Black Yajur Veda,* and so regards itself as a *vaidika tradition. Its worship of *Viṣṇu is derived from the *Vaikhānasa(smārta) Sūtra* (4th century CE), and from *Saṃhitās* expounding a ritual theology which employs a similar vocabulary to that found in the *Pāñcarātra *Saṃhitās,* although it interprets it in its own way.

The tradition takes its name from its legendary founder, Vikhanas.

Vaikuṇṭha The name of *Viṣṇu's heaven or *loka. (So Viṣṇu himself is sometimes known as Vaikuṇṭhanātha—'Lord of Vaikuṇṭha'.) In *Purāṇic *cosmology, Vaikuṇṭha is located at the top of the cosmic egg (*Brahmāṇḍa), or on Mount *Meru. Through Viṣṇu's *grace, his devotees may join him there in a perfected body and an eternally loving relationship.

Vaikuṇṭha Ekadaśi A major annual *Vaiṣṇava *festival held at the *Śrīraṅgam *temple complex in Tamil Nadu in Pauṣa (December–January). For the ten days preceding the festival, Viṣṇu is ritually dressed as the female *Mohinī. On the eleventh day (ekadaśi), the god is clothed in pearl armour, and, followed by thousands of devotees, paraded through the 'Gate of Vaikuṇṭha' (normally shut for the rest of the year) to take up his place at the head of his royal assembly in the great hall.

Vaikuṇṭha Perumāḷ A renowned 8th-century *Vaiṣṇava *temple at *Kāñcīpuram, its iconography is apparently derived from *Pāñcarātra theology. In addition, it celebrates the achievements of the *Pal̲l̲ava dynasty.

vairāgya Indifference to, or loss of interest in, worldly objects and desires. A synonym for *asceticism, *tyāga, etc.

Vaiśaṃpāyana According to the *Mahābhārata's* own framing account, the pupil of *Vyāsa who, at his teacher's bidding, first recites the text to King *Janamejaya at the great *snake *sacrifice performed to avenge *Parikṣit's death by snakebite.

Vaiśeṣika (from viśeṣa—'specific', 'distinct', 'particular') 'The School of Particularism', listed in modern works as one of the six *darśana or 'schools of philosophy', where it is paired with the *Nyāya school. The foundational Vaiśeṣika text is *Kaṇāda's *Vaiśeṣikasūtra* (probably a composite work, put together around the turn of the Common Era), which attempts to identify the fundamental (i.e. particular) constituents of the material universe. The next earliest surviving Vaiśeṣika text is Praśastapāda's *Padārthadharmasaṃgraha* ('Compendium of Properties of the Categories', early 6th century CE), a discursive commentary on Kaṇāda, which gave rise to a commentarial tradition of its own. This culminated in *Udayana (12th century), whose works effectively mark Vaiśeṣika's convergence with the Nyāya tradition.

A number of scholars have characterized a reconstructed early Vaiśeṣika as an incipient philosophy of nature, an attempt to enumerate and explain the fundamental, irreducible categories (*padārthas) of existence, with only a limited, and incidental interest in soteriology. According to the commentators, the basic categories are substance (*dravya), quality (*guṇa), action/motion (karman), universals (sāmānya), particularity (*viṣeṣa), and inherence (samavāya—which supports the relationship between entities). A seventh padārtha, non-existence, or absence (abhāva), was added in the 11th century CE. In the Nyāya-Vaiśeṣika, these seven were subsumed into *prameya, the second category of Nyāya—the Vaiśeṣika padārthas thereby effectively providing an atomistic, mechanistic ontology for the merged tradition. *See also* NYĀYA.

Vaiśeṣikasūtra *See* VAIŚEṢIKA.

Vaiṣṇava(s) As a noun, a devotee, or devotees of *Viṣṇu (also referred to as Vaiṣṇavites), of whom the two most numerous groups are worshippers of *Kṛṣṇa and *Rāma, classically regarded as *avatāras of *Viṣṇu. Vaiṣṇavas can sometimes be distinguished by their sectarian mark (*tilaka), a figure curved upward like the letter U from the meeting point of the eyebrows, with a vertical red line between its arms. As an adjective, anything relating, belonging, or sacred to Viṣṇu. *See* VAIṢṆAVISM.

Vaiṣṇavism A collective term for those traditions (also known as 'Vaiṣṇava traditions') which consider *Viṣṇu (or one of the *avatāras associated with him, principally *Kṛṣṇa and *Rāma) to be the Supreme deity or absolute (i.e. God); alongside *Śaivism and *Śāktism, it constitutes one of the three great sectarian streams in medieval and later Hinduism.

The history and interplay of Vaiṣṇava traditions is complex, but some broad patterns can be discerned. Viṣṇu has a minor role in the **Veda*, but the earliest evidence of exclusive worship of a proto 'Vaiṣṇava' deity occurs in 5th and 6th century BCE references to devotees of *Vāsudeva. By the time of the **Mahābhārata*, Vāsudeva has merged with Kṛṣṇa, the deified chief of the North Indian *Yādavas, to become Vāsudeva-Kṛṣṇa, who is thought to be synonymous with, or an *avatāra of, the Vedic Viṣṇu. Vāsudeva (= Kṛṣṇa) was worshipped, alongside *Nārāyaṇa, and Saṃkarṣaṇa (= *Balarāma), by the *Bhāgavata cult, which originated in western India around 150 BCE or earlier. Devotion to Nārāyaṇa probably derives from the emerging *Pāñcarātra tradition, which itself comes into full view as a distinctive Vaiṣṇava ritual and theological tradition in the **Nārāyaṇīya* section of the **Mahābhārata*. A *vaidika Vaiṣṇava tradition, that of the *Vaikhānasas, which was subsequently preserved in the ritual of South Indian *temple *priests, also appears at around this time.

As *Bhagavān, the god of the Bhāgavatas and the personal omnipotent deity of the **Bhagavadgītā*, Vāsudeva-Kṛṣṇa was, by the 4th century CE, further fused with the cowherd god, Kṛṣṇa-*Gopāla. This Kṛṣṇa first comes to light in the appendix to the *Mahābhārata*, the **Harivaṃśa*, which provides the model for later accounts of Kṛṣṇa's life and deeds, such as those in the **Viṣṇu Purāṇa* and the **Bhāgavata Purāṇa*. Concentrating on Kṛṣṇa's life with the *gopīs in *Vṛndāvana, and the erotic love between *Rādhā and Kṛṣṇa, these in turn provide the narrative and theological basis for the great medieval and modern *bhakti movements, including the *Rādhavallabhīs and, most importantly, the *Gauḍīya Vaiṣṇavas. Also in northern India, Rāma, the hero of the **Rāmāyaṇa*, had become an increasing focus of bhakti from at least the 12th century onwards, but only came to full theological and cultic preeminence in the wake of *Tulsīdāsa's 16th century **Rāmcaritmānas*, and the *Rāmlīlas derived from it. Notable among influential North Indian Rāma-worshipping *sampradāyas is that of the *ascetic *Rāmānandīs, founded by *Rāmānanda in the 15th century.

Between the 10th and 13th centuries, three major Vaiṣṇava *Vedāntic sampradāyas came to prominence: *Madhva's *Dvaita Vedānta, *Nimbārka's *Dvaitādvaita, and *Viśiṣṭādvaita (effectively founded by *Rāmānuja). A fourth school, based on the no longer extant works of *Viṣṇusvāmin, is claimed to have developed into the largely northern and western Indian *Puṣṭimārga or *Vallabhasampradāya, founded on the teachings of *Vallabha. Other important Vaiṣṇava bhakti traditions originating in western India in the medieval period are the *Mahānubhāva Saṃpradāya (devoted to Kṛṣṇa), and the *Vārkāri Panth (devoted to *Vithobā), said to have been founded by the Marathi poet saint, *Jñāneśvara.

With its ritual practices and theology deriving from the teachings and commentaries of the *Viśiṣṭādvaita *ācāryas, especially Rāmānuja, the foundations of the major *Tamil *Vaiṣṇava *saṃpradāya, commonly referred to as *Śrī Vaiṣṇavism (the *Śrī referring to Viṣṇu's consort), are also laid down in this period. ŚrīVaiṣṇvism draws on complex antecedents, including *Purāṇic and *Vedāntic sources, the ritual practices of the *Pāñcarātra, and the vernacular Tamil *bhakti poetry of the *Āḻvārs. The latter—a disparate but highly influential tradition of South Indian poet-saints—had been active between the 6th to 9th centuries CE, their poetry and 'theology' predicated on an absolute and ecstatic devotion to *Māyōṉ (Viṣṇu/Kṛṣṇa in one or more of his various forms), as present in the *arcāvatāras installed across a network of South Indian *temples. Notable among Vaiṣṇava traditions founded or reformed since the 18th century are the Gujarati *Svāminārāyaṇa movement, and the influential *International Society for Krishna Consciousness, established by *Bhaktivedānta Swāmi.

Vaiṣṇo Devī (Vaiṣṇavī) A form of the *Goddess manifested in a cave rock formation with three heads (piṇḍas) near the town of Katra in the *Himālayan foothills of Jammu and Kashmir. An immensely popular *tīrtha, it is claimed to be the second most visited *pilgrimage site in India (after *Tirupati). The site is also said to be a *śāktipīṭha.

Vaiśvadeva ('relating to all the gods') One of the elements of the *Vedic *śrauta ritual, the *cāturmāsya, involving an offering made to all the gods (*viśvedevas), who are visualized as inhabiting the house; it culminates in an offering of cooked food (*bali) to *Agni.

vaiśya ('commoner') A member of the third *varṇa, traditionally the economically productive classes, e.g. farmers, merchants, bookkeepers, and moneylenders.

Vājasaneyī Saṃhitā The collective name given to the **Saṃhitā* of the **White Yajur Veda*, in reality two collections, each preserved by its own school (*śākhā): the *Vājasaneyī Mādhyaṃdina Saṃhitā* and the *Vājasaneyī Kāṇva Saṃhitā*.

vajra ('thunderbolt', 'lightning') *Indra's favourite weapon, variously depicted as, for instance, a circular discus or a double-headed trident. In later Indian religion vajra also comes to mean 'diamond', the primary sense in which *Tantric *Buddhism uses the term to represent enlightenment.

Vākātaka The name of a dynasty ruling Central India and the Deccan during the 4th and 5th centuries CE.

Vākyapadīya *See* BHARTṚHARI.

Vālakhilya A group of eleven *Vedic hymns, attached to the eighth *maṇḍala of the **Ṛg Veda*, thereby swelling the total number of hymns in the **saṃhitā* from 1017 to 1028.

Vāli(n) (Bālin) In the **Rāmāyaṇa*, the *Vānara (monkey-) king, who has taken the throne from his brother, *Sugrīva. The latter subsequently overthrows and kills him with *Rāma's help.

Vāliyōṉ *See* BALARĀMA.

Vallabha (Vallabhācārya) (1479–1531) The founder of the *Vaiṣṇava *bhakti path, the *Puṣṭimārga, also known as the *Vallabhasampradāya, or *Śuddhādvaita school. According to the hagiographies, he was born into a family of Telugu *brahmins, and spent his childhood receiving a *Vedic education in *Vārāṇasī. Thereafter he became an intinerant teacher and debater, formulating his Śuddhādvaita theology, said to be derived from the no longer extant *Vedāntin tradition of *Viṣṇusvāmin. He was devoted to *Śrī Nāthjī, a form of *Kṛṣṇa which had partially manifested itself out of a crack in Govardhana hill (near *Braj) at the beginning of the 15th century, only to make a complete appearance to coincide with the birth of Vallabha himself. He subsequently declared it to be a svarūpa ('own form'), i.e. an actual, embodied form of the deity. Vallabha is said to have married on Kṛṣṇa's instructions, producing two sons to act as his spiritual successors, Gopīnātha (who died young) and Viṭṭalanātha. Shortly before his death in Vārāṇasī, Vallabha became a *saṃnyāsin. Over eighty *Sanskrit works are attributed to him, including commentaries on the **Bhāgavata Purāṇa* and the **Brahmasūtras*.

Vallabhasampradāya A western Indian Vaiṣṇava *householder *bhakti movement, based on the *Śuddhādvaita theology developed by Vallabha. Its devotional practice is characterized as the *Puṣṭimārga, since soteriological progress and, eventually, *liberation, is dependent at every level, on the grace (puṣṭi) of *Kṛṣṇa—especially of Kṛṣṇa as *Śrī Nāthjī, his svarūpa ('own form') installed at *Nāthdvāra in Rajasthan. The *sampradāya was developed by Vallabha's second son, Viṭṭalanātha, who assigned a further Kṛṣṇa image to each of his seven sons, to be installed in separate North or West Indian *temples. In this way he established, through his male line, a householder *guru lineage for the sampradāya. Viṭṭalanātha is also credited with establishing a liturgy composed of the *kīrtanas of eight bhakti poets (aṣṭachāp(a)) for use during service (*sevā) of the deity. *See also* PUṢṬIMĀRGA; ŚUDDHĀDVAITA.

Vālmīki The legendary sage to whom the *Sanskrit **Rāmāyaṇa* is attributed. The text itself establishes him as the original poet (ādikavi); furthermore, he takes an active part towards the end of the story, sheltering *Sītā in his hermitage, where she gives birth to *Rāma's twin sons, *Lava and *Kuśa, to whom Vālmīki himself teaches the text of the *Rāmāyaṇa*.

V

Valmikis *See* BALMIKIS.

vāmācāra ('left-handed path/practice') A form of *Tantric practice, often characterized as 'extreme' or 'transgressive', marked by the use of the *pañca-makāra ('five Ms'), *impure substances, in contrast to the relative purity of the *dakṣiṇācāra ('right-handed practice/path').

Vāmana ('The Dwarf') According to the *Vaiṣṇava *Purāṇic texts, Vāmana is the fifth *avatāra of *Viṣṇu; he manifests himself to save the three worlds from the threat of the *asura *Bali. Securing land from Bali equivalent to three strides, the Dwarf instantly becomes large enough to cover the universe in two steps, whereupon Bali presents his head to accommodate Vāmana's third stride (hence Viṣṇu's epithet, *Trivikrama). As a dwarf he is usually depicted as a *brahmin carrying his water-pot (*kamaṇḍalu). *See also* BALI.

Vāmana Purāṇa (*c.*9th century CE?) Classified as one of the eighteen 'great **Purāṇas*' (*mahāpurāṇas*) in the *rājasa group, i.e. those said to relate to *Brahmā. An eclectic text, which, in spite of its title, and a prolonged account of the *Vāmana story, contains at least as much *Śaiva as *Vaiṣṇava material.

vaṃśānucarita The genealogies (*vaṃśas) of royal dynasties given in the **Purāṇas*.

vaṃśa(s) (lit. 'bamboo joint(s)') The genealogies of gods, and other personified or supernatural beings, given in the **Purāṇas*.

vānaprastha ('forest dweller/hermit') According to the *āśrama theory, a high *caste male who has undertaken the *forest dwelling stage or order (vānaprasthya). In the **Dharmasūtras*, where it may be chosen as a life-long āśrama, vānaprasthya is undertaken either by a celibate individual, who sets up a single ritual fire and lives alone in the wild on roots and fruits, or a married householder (*gṛhastha) who retires with his wife, his ritual fires, and, according to some, even his children to a dwelling outside the village (*grāma). In *Dharmaśāstra*, where it is regarded as the third element in a sequence of āśramas, vānaprasthya is clearly conceived of as a kind of later life retirement: when he is grey and has grandchildren, the householder, with or without his wife, hands over his family responsibilities to his sons and retires to concentrate on his religious (primarily ritual) life, outside the village. It is possible that, as an āśrama, vānaprasthya was always largely a theoretical category. This is not to say that many older married householders have not undertaken a kind of retirement, but few seem to have literally taken to the forest as hermits, or cut themselves off from *village (or urban) society entirely.

vānaprasthya *See* VĀNAPRASTHA.

Vānara (lit. 'moving in the forest'?) In the **Rāmāyaṇa* (and elsewhere), vānara is the term normally translated as 'monkey', indicating *Sugrīva, *Hanumān, *Vālin, etc.; the vānaras are therefore the members of the monkey army raised to assist *Rāma in his attack on *Laṅkā. According to some, however, the term should be taken as referring to a forest-dwelling tribal people.

Van Buitenen, J. A. B. (1928–1979) A Dutch born American *Indologist, Van Buitenen was the first holder of the Bobrinskoy Chair of *Sanskrit and Indic Studies at the University of Chicago. He is best remembered for his work on *Rāmānuja, and as the translator into English of the first five books of the Critical Edition of the **Mahābhārata.*

Vande Mātaram *See* BANDE MĀTARAM.

varada-mudrā ('wish-giving gesture') A common iconographic *mudrā, displayed as a hand with the palm turned towards the viewer and the fingers pointing down, indicating the deity's ability to give boons or grant the devotee's wishes.

Varadarāja(svāmī) A form of *Viṣṇu displaying the *varada-mudrā, worshipped in a number of *Tamil *temples (for example, at *Kāñcīpuram).

Varāha ('The Boar') According to the *Vaiṣṇava *Purāṇic texts, Varāha is the third *avatāra of *Viṣṇu. Taking the form of a boar, he kills the *daitya *Hiraṇyākṣa and then rescues the earth (personified as *Bhū Devī), whom the daitya has thrown into the ocean, by lifting her on his tusks. Depictions of this cosmogonic myth usually show Varāha with a boar's head and a man's body; in the earlier iconography the goddess clings to a tusk, in the later, a more literal portion of the earth is raised up.

Varāhamihira (mid 6th century CE) An important Indian astronomer and mathematician; the author of the **Bṛhatsaṃhitā* ('The Great Compendium'). His *Pañcasiddhāntikā* provides early instances of zero being used as both a symbol and a number.

Varāha Purāṇa (*c.*10th–12th centuries CE?) Classified as one of the eighteen 'great **Purāṇas*' (*mahāpurāṇas*) in the *sāttvika group, i.e. those said to relate to *Viṣṇu, much of the *Varāha* is taken up with *Vaiṣṇava devotional material. It has been analysed as containing four distinct sections: the first is largely taken up with *Pāñcarātra-like material; the second is *Bhāgavata in orientation, with a *māhātmya glorifying *Mathurā; the third gives an account of *Nāciketas in *Yama's kingdom; the fourth is mostly concerned with *Śaiva sites in *Nepal.

Varāhī A goddess, the *śakti of *Viṣṇu's Boar *avatāra, *Varāha; she is one of the seven *Mātṛkās.

Vārāṇasī (Banāras, Benares, Kāśī) (from Pāli: Bārānasi) The most celebrated and sacred of the seven ancient holy cities of India, situated on the west bank of the *Gaṅgā (Ganges) in modern day Uttar Pradesh. Its name is popularly derived from the city's situation between two rivers, the Varaṇā and the Asi, but it is likely that it was actually named after a single ancient river, the Varāṇasī. An even older name is Kāśī ('shining'), shared with an ancient kingdom of which it was the capital in the early part of the 1st millennium BCE. By the *Epic and *Purāṇic period the city was well established as both the archetype, and the most powerful, of all *tīrthas—indeed, all other tīrthas are thought to be contained within its *temples, *tanks, and lakes. Glorified in numerous **māhātmyas* and Purāṇic passages, it is the focus of a whole series of homologies which at the same time place it at the centre of the world, make it the entire cosmos (the microcosmos), and situate it as the ford or doorway to *heaven or liberation (*mokṣa). This last transition is thought to be guaranteed by dying there—the specific aim of many elderly and infirm *pilgrims. Conceptually, the entire city may therefore be regarded as one great cosmic *cremation ground. The two best-known material cremation grounds, however, are the Hariścandra and Maṇikarṇikā 'burning *ghāṭs'. These are situated on the Gaṅgā, the sacred river whose own powers are regarded as particularly concentrated at Vārāṇasī, where its bathing ghāṭs draw huge crowds of pilgrims.

Although, like the universe itself, the home to every deity, Vārāṇasī has a relationship with *Śiva that amounts to identification (an alternative name is Avimukta—the city that is 'never abandoned' by the god). As Kāśī, the 'shining' city, it is assimilated to his fiery *liṅga (*jyotirliṅga), and is therefore regarded as being at the centre of his cosmic destructive and recreative activities. Iconic liṅgas are ubiquitous, and provide one of the conceptual grids on which the city is laid out; the most important is the jyotirliṅga installed at the much rebuilt *Viśvanātha temple. An ancient centre of traditional *Sanskritic learning, since 1916 Vārāṇasī has been home to what is now the largest residential university in India, *Benares Hindu University.

V

Vardhamāna (*c.*14th century CE) *See* NYĀYA.

Vardhamāna Mahāvīra *See* MAHĀVĪRA.

Vārkarī Panth (Wārkarī Panth) ('Pilgrims' Path') A Marathi *Vaiṣṇava *bhakti movement, whose (mostly *householder) followers are devoted to *Viṣṇu as *Viṭhobā. Their principal religious practice takes the form of quarterly *pilgrimages to Viṭhobā's *temple at *Paṇḍharpur in Maharashtra, culminating each year in a major *yātra undertaken by over half a million pilgrims in Āṣāḍha (June–July). During the pilgrimage, Vākarīs sing the songs (abhaṅgas) of the numerous poet-saints (*sants) associated with the tradition, whom they also worship, making separate pilgrimages to their *samādhis. The presumed founder of the Panth is *Jñāneśvara, whose decorated chariot, or pālkhī, carrying the imprint of his feet, plays a major part in the pilgrimage. Among other important Vārkarī poet-saints (male and female, low and high *caste) are *Janābāī, *Nāmdev, *Muktābāī, *Cokāmeḷā, *Gorā-kumbhār, *Ekanātha, *Bahiṇābāī, *Tukārām, and *Mahīpati, the last of whom produced collections of Marathi stories about the other saints.

varṇa ('class', lit. 'colour') The principle by which, according to *Brahmanical ideology, society is ideally ranked in a complementary hierarchy of four 'classes' or varṇas (*brahmins, *kṣatriyas, *vaiśyas, and *śūdras), differentiated by particular social functions assigned by birth. As a means of classification, the principle was extended into the natural and supernatural worlds, thereby further legitimating the social structure. For a more detailed discussion, *see* CASTE.

varṇadharmī bhakti A term sometimes applied to the kind of devotion (*bhakti) initiated in North India by *brahmin poets, *sants, and teachers who subscribed at some level to the *Brahmanical ideology of class (*varṇa) and *caste (e.g *Caitanya, *Vallabhācarya, *Tulsīdāsa), although their followers came from all levels of society. *See also* AVARṆADHARMĪ BHAKTI.

varṇasaṃkara ('mixing of classes') The result of sexual relations and *marriage between different classes (*varṇas), particularly a high *caste man with a lower caste woman. According to **Dharmaśāstra*, this brings bad results for all concerned, especially any offspring. As the **Bhagavadgītā* (1.41ff.) puts it, intermingling (varṇasaṃkara) leads to obliteration of the family, including the ancestors (*pitṛs).

varṇāśramdharma (caturvarṇāśramadharma ('The Duty of the Four Classes and Stages of Life')**)** ('The Duty of Class and Stage of Life') An inclusive term for the principles which, according to *Brahmanical *dharma texts (**Dharmasūtras* and **Dharmaśātra*) should inform the entire life of each member of society, i.e. conformity to the role incumbent upon them by birth into a specific *varṇa or 'class', in the light of their current *āśrama or 'stage of life'; in other words, compliance with their *svadharma. *See also* ĀŚRAMA; DHARMA; SVADHARMA; VARṆA.

Varuṇa In the **Ṛg Veda*, and later, one of the *Ādityas, a kingly *deva ruling over the cosmic and ethical order (*ṛta). He is inevitably paired with *Mitra, the deva responsible for tribal and social order; so much so that they are most usually invoked as the composite or single deity, *Mitra-Varuṇa. Varuṇa's roots are *Indo-European, and he is sometimes referred to as an '*asura', signalling his likely connection with the Iranian god Ahura (= asura) Mazdā. There is an obvious decline in his significance from the early *Vedic period onwards.

Vasantotsava ('spring festival') The collective name for the ancient tradition of various *festivals (utsavas) held to celebrate the beginning of spring (vasanta) in Phālguna (February–March) or Caitra (March–April). Common elements may include the celebration of fertility and love. Probably the best-known festival of this type is *Holī.

Vasiṣṭha A *Vedic *ṛṣi, said to have composed the seventh 'book' (*maṇḍala) of the **Ṛg Veda* in which he features himself. Thereafter, he appears as a legendary figure in the *Epics and **Purāṇas*. A progenitor son of *Brahmā (a *Prajāpati), and the ideal *brahmin, he is listed as one of the seven great seers (*maharṣis). A number of post-Vedic works are attributed to him. He is portrayed as the arch-rival of *Viśvamitra.

Vasiṣṭha Dharmasūtra (*c.*1st century BCE–1st century CE) One of the four extant **Dharmasūtra* texts, the *Vasiṣṭha* is conventionally ascribed to the *Vedic *ṛṣi, *Vasiṣṭha. Although it has no formal connection with any *Vedic school, it has traditionally been associated with the **Ṛg Veda*. It deals with such topics as the conduct of men and women, *caste laws and purificatory rituals, the *āśramas, the duties of the *king, matters of etiquette, and various penances (*prāyascittas).

vāstupuruṣa (vāstunara)('the person/man in, or of, the foundations'). The figure of a person (*puruṣa) bound diagonally into a square or quadrangle (referred to as a *maṇḍala), representing the ground plan for a building, particularly a *temple. The *Vedic gods, with *Brahmā at the centre, are supposed to be pressing the puruṣa into the ground, the whole presenting a divinely appointed template for the ordered construction of the building. The geometry is worked out in considerable detail in **Vāstuśāstra*.

Vāstuśāstra *See* ŚILPAŚĀSTRA.

Vasudeva (Ānakadundubhi) According to texts such as the **Harivaṃśa*, a *Yādava chieftan who was the father of *Kṛṣṇa and *Balarāma, by his seventh wife, *Devakī.

Vāsudeva ('son of Vasudeva') A patronymic of *Kṛṣṇa. Apart from some ambiguous appearances in the *Vedic literature, the earliest references to *Vāsudeva, a god identified as a precursor of the *Epic and *Purāṇic Kṛṣṇa, occur in *Sanskrit sources of the 5th and 6th centuries BCE, and in the works of Greek historians. This Vāsudeva may have originated as the deified hero or king of the *Vṛṣṇi (Sātvata) tribe. He was subsequently amalgamated with Kṛṣṇa, the similarly deified chief of the *Yādavas of Dvāraka, so that, by the time of the *Sanskrit **Mahābhārata*, Vāsudeva-Kṛṣṇa appears as a single deity, thought to be synonymous with, or an *avatāra of, the Vedic god, *Viṣṇu. The compound 'Vāsudeva-Kṛṣṇa' is therefore most frequently used to distinguish the god of the *Bhāgavatas (2) and the **Bhagavadgītā* from Kṛṣṇa-*Gopāla, the cowherd deity who becomes the focus of so many medieval *bhakti traditions. From the perspective of devotion, however, the two are subsequently considered to be one and the same. 'Vāsudeva' is also the name given to the supreme, transcendent form of Viṣṇu in *Pāñcarātra theology.

Vāsudeva

Vasugupta (*c*.875–925) According to tradition, a *tāntrika and precursor of *Abhinavagupta, who, on the prompting of a dream, discovered the important *Kashmiri Śaiva text, the **Śiva Sūtras* inscribed on a rock in the mountains.

Vāsuki In *Purāṇic myth, a *nāga king, sometimes conflated with *Śeṣa. He is said to have been used as a cord to rotate Mount *Mandara at the *Churning of the Ocean.

Vasu(s) ('good', 'beneficent') In the **Ṛg Veda*, a class of eight gods associated with *Indra, viz. Āpa (water) (sometimes Ahan (day)), Dhruva (pole star), Soma (moon), Dhara/Dhava (earth), Anila (wind), Anala/Pāvaka (fire), Prabhāsa (light), Pratyūṣa (dawn). Vasus are also classified as *Viśvedevas, and linked with atmospheric powers. In the **Mahābhārata*, as the result of a curse, they appear as the sons of the celestial *Gaṅgā, all of whom, bar the eighth, *Bhīṣma, are drowned by their mother at birth in order to return them to the sky.

Vāta ('wind') *See* VĀYU.

Vaṭakalai (Vaḍagalai) One of the two major divisions of the *Viśiṣṭādvaita (*Śrī Vaiṣṇava) school of philosophy. It was formed in a 13th century CE, largely as the result of differing interpretations of Rāmānuja's *prapatti ('surrender') doctrine. Referred to as the 'northern' division, and associated with the theologian *Vedāntadeśika, the Vaṭakalai regarded *liberation as not simply dependent on the freely given grace (*prasāda) of the deity, but also on the prior actions (*karma) of the devotee, a position compared to a young monkey making the effort to cling to its mother's body. *Kāñcīpuram is an important centre for the Vaṭakalais. *See also* TEṈKALAI.

Vātsyāyana 1. (Pakṣilasvāmin) (latter half of 5th century CE) Author of the *Nyāyabhāṣya*. *See* NYĀYA. **2.** (*c*.3rd–4th century CE). *See* KĀMA SŪTRA.

Vāyu (Vāta) ('air', 'wind') The wind, and its personification as a *Vedic god. Close to *Indra, whom he transports across the world in a chariot drawn by a team of horses, he is also an agent of *purification. In the *Puruṣasūkta (Ṛg Veda 10.90.13), he is said to have been born from the vital breath of *puruṣa. Subsequently, his importance declines, although he continues to appear in various lists, both as a force of nature and its personification (as the *aṣṭadikpāla of the northwest, for example), and as an element (the air). In the *Mahābhārata* and *Rāmāyaṇa* he is the father of *Bhīma and *Hanumān.

Vāyu Purāṇa See ŚIVA PURĀṆA.

Vedāṅga ('limb of the *Veda*') Any one of a group of six categories of texts regarded as supplementary to the *Veda*, i.e. designed to ensure the correct performance of *Brahmanical ritual. Partly in *sūtra form, they probably started to appear from around the 5th century BCE. The six categories are composed of texts dealing with *Śikṣā (phonetic analysis), *Vyākaraṇa (grammar), *Chandas (metre and prosody), *Nirukta (etymological analysis), *Jyotiṣa (astronomy, astrology, and mathematics), and *Kalpa (ritual and *dharma).

Vedānta ('the conclusion, essence, or culmination of the *Veda*') **1.** A term for the **Upaniṣads*. **2.** A highly influential theological and philosophical tradition, also known as Uttara Mīmāṃsā—'Later Exegesis'. The Vedānta tradition incorporates a number of different schools, although in modern works it is listed (as a composite) as one of the six 'orthodox' *darśanas or 'schools of philosophy', where it is paired with *Pūrva Mīmāṃsā ('Prior Exegesis'), which it both complements and succeeds. Vedānta derives its name from its basic dependence on the teachings of the principal *Upaniṣads* and their attempted synthesis in *Bādarāyaṇa's **Brahmasūtra(s)*, two of the three essential texts (*prasthāna traya, the third being the **Bhagavadgītā*) which, in the developed tradition, required commentary by anyone wanting to found a new Vedāntin school or *sampradāya. The major concern is to define the nature of *brahman (neut.), and brahman's relationship to everything else, especially the embodied individual or '*self'.

The earliest surviving commentary on the *Brahmasūtras* is the *Brahmasūtrabhāṣya* of *Śaṅkara, who is now credited with founding the *Advaita Vedānta tradition, although he clearly had a number of precursors, including his *paramaguru, *Gauḍapāda. Śaṅkara argues for an ultimately non-dual (advaita) 'relationship' between the absolute (brahman), the individual (*ātman), and the world: brahman alone is real. Nearly all other Vedāntic schools modify this line to a greater or lesser degree, arguing that brahman (often theistically interpreted), the individual, and the world are to some extent different from each other. So the effective founder of the *Viśiṣṭādvaita ('non-dualism of the qualified') school, *Rāmānuja, maintains that the individual self and *brahman (= God) are not completely identical: rather, individual selves and the material world are both real and at the same time 'modes' (prakāras) of brahman, and so ultimately dependent upon Him. *Nimbārka, the founder of *Dvaitādvaita ('dualistic non-dualism'), takes a somewhat similar position, but, unlike (at least, according to his own account) Rāmānuja, he propounds the *bhedābheda ('identity in difference') doctrine, first established by *Bhāskara (1). *Madhva, the founder of the *Dvaita Vedānta ('Dualistic Vedānta') *sampradāya, goes much further, maintaining an absolute and irreducible distinction between the world and brahman, its creator and Lord (equated with *Viṣṇu). Apart from the five teachers already mentioned, standard lists of the founders of

Vedāntin sampradāyas include, inter alia, *Śrīkaṇṭha, *Śrīpati, *Vallabha (*Śuddhādvaita), *Vijñānabhikṣu (avibhāgādvaita—'indistinguishable non-dualism'), and *Baladeva (2) (*acintya-bhedābheda). Many of these teachers are *Vaiṣṇavas, and it is clear that those medieval *bhakti movements wanting to align themselves with *Vedic orthodoxy found a particularly compatible theological partner in dualistic Vedānta.

Vedānta, both in the general sense of the teaching of the *Upaniṣads* about brahman, and in the particular interpretation of the Advaita school, was taken up enthusiastically by 19th century reformers and teachers, such as *Vivekānanda, who presented it as the pure core of Hindu thought. This proved appealing both to the Indian middle classes and to Westerners—so much so that, for many, what is sometimes called *Neo-Vedānta has become synonymous with Hinduism as a world religion.

Vedāntadeśika **(Veṅkaṭanātha, Veṅkaṭeśa,** Tam.: **Vētānta Tēcikar)** (*c.*1269–1307/trad.1369) The main *Vaṭakalai theologian, and probably the most important *Śrī Vaiṣṇava teacher after *Rāmānuja. Beyond hagiography little is known of his life. He is said to have been born at Tūppiḷ, near *Kāñcīpuram, and to have spent his life in the major centres of *Tamil Śrī Vaiṣṇavism, such as *Śrīraṅgam. Vedāntadeśika is close to Rāmānuja in his theology, and wrote a number of subcommentaries on the latter's works. Prolific both as a poet and theologian, he composed a wide variety of works in *Sanskrit, Tamil, and *maṇipravāḷa. These include his defence of Vaiṣṇavism in works such as the *Rahasyatrayasāra, Paramatabhaṅga* (*Paramatapaṅkam*), and *Nyāyasiddhāñjana.* Also notable is the *Varadarājapañcāśat*, a popular eulogy addressed to *Viṣṇu as *Varadarāja, which condenses the principles of Vedāntadeśika's teaching into 50 verses. *See also* PRAPATTI; VAṬAKALAI.

Vedāntasāra ('Essence of Vedānta') *See* SADĀNANDA (1).

Vedānta Society An organization founded by Svāmī *Vivekānanda in New York in 1895, during a two-year visit to the West. It became the parent body for the propagating the teachings of the *Rāmakṛṣṇa Mission in the West.

Vedāntasūtra(s) *See* BRAHMASŪTRA.

Vedāntin A follower of, or teacher in, the *Vedānta tradition.

Vedārthasaṃgraha See RĀMĀNUJA.

Veda(s) ('knowledge') At its narrowest and most material, the term, both singular and plural, refers to a body of *Sanskrit (Old *Indo-Āryan) texts which, in the first instance, was composed, recited, and *orally transmitted (in various *śākhās) by the people who referred to themselves as *Āryans. The earliest layer of this material (dating from between *c.*1700 BCE and *c.*1200–1000 BCE) is constituted by the hymns (*sūktas) of the **Ṛg Veda Saṃhitā.* For ritual and liturgical purposes, these oral compositions were reconstituted in two further collections (**saṃhitās*), the **Sāma* and **Yajur Vedas*, making up a canon referred to as the 'Triple Veda', or 'Threefold Knowledge' (trayī vidyā). With the addition of the **Atharva Veda Saṃhitā* at a later date, this *Veda* became 'fourfold'. Further texts, containing prose explanations (brāhmaṇas) of ritual acts, and other material, were attached to each of the *saṃhitās* or *mantra collections. In roughly chronological order, these were classified as **Brāhmaṇas*, **Āraṇyakas*, and **Upaniṣads*. The whole canonical body, in this expanded sense, is also referred to as the '*Veda*' or '*Vedas*'.

This body of literature was (and is) regarded by its custodians, the *brahmins, and the *Brahmanical tradition in general, as revelation (*śruti)—that is to say, it is a direct, uncreated, and eternal transmission from the Absolute (however conceived), which has simply been 'heard' (śruti) by, or revealed to, inspired *ṛṣis. (In a similar construction, the seen or heard *Veda* is characterized as only a fraction of that eternal, unseen and unheard *Veda*, which both underwrites and transcends all existence.) The *Veda* therefore has an absolute authority, and those refusing to acknowledge it are regarded by 'orthodoxy' (e.g. **Manusmṛti*) as beyond the pale (*nāstikas). Indeed, the brahmins' own claim to authority rests precisely on their knowledge of, and more importantly, their exclusive access to the *Veda*—an ownership which enables them to actualize its power through mantra and ritual.

The later religious texts created by human authors (such as **Dharmaśāstra* and the *Epics and *Purāṇas*), which make up the orthodox Brahmanical tradition and are classified as *smṛti, are ultimately thought to be authoritative only in so far as they are supported by the *Veda*. The demonstration of such support may, however, require considerable commentarial exegesis. Where a text, such as the **Mahābhārata* or the **Nāṭyaśāstra*, is regarded as particularly significant, the claim may be made that it is actually a 'fifth *Veda*'. In a similar fashion, a text may be characterized as the *equivalent* of the *Veda* for a particular group. In this way the *Veda* as an idea, regardless of its actual contents, constitutes the paradigm or prototype of all authoritative texts. Even those claiming supreme authority for their own, non-*Vedic textual tradition, such as the *Śaiva Siddhāntins, may acknowledge the authority of Vedic revelation before claiming that their own revelation is even more powerful, and supersedes it. It is almost as though the cachet and scope of the *Veda* have expanded in inverse ratio to the knowledge of its contents: it has become a commonplace for some that it contains all knowledge, including purportedly modern scientific and technological advances, although few, if any, are in a position to verify the assertion. In the underlying, universalizing sense of the term, as opposed to the narrower application to a particular body of texts, such claims are, in any case, tautological, and, like assertions about any absolute, must remain potently unverifiable. *See also* ŚRUTI AND SMṚTI.

vedi An elevated, or possibly excavated piece of ground, often of roughly rectangular proportions, but with a narrow waist, which is used during the *Vedic *śrauta ritual as an altar—a place where the sacrificial instruments and oblations are placed. It is considered a 'seat' for the *devas attending the sacrifice (*yajña), and is therefore strewn with *darbha grass. The term is also used for the more elaborate firebrick altars constructed for rituals such as the *agnicayana. The term 'mahāvedi' ('great altar')—and sometimes 'vedi' itself—may be used of the entire sacrificial enclosure, including the sacrificial fire or fires. Prescriptions for the construction of the vedi (i.e. the sacrificial area) are given in the **Śulvasūtras*.

Vedic *See* BRAHMANISM.

Vedicization *See* SANSKRITIZATION.

Vedic student *See* BRAHMACĀRIN.

Vedism *See* BRAHMANISM.

vegetarianism *See* FOOD; *See also* AHIṂSĀ.

Vēḷāḷa (Tam.: **Veḷḷāḷa**) The name of an influential South Indian agricultural (*śūdra) *caste, which plays a prominent part in the patronage and administration of some *Śaiva *temples.

Veṅkaṭeśvara ('Lord of Veṅkaṭa Hill') *See* TIRUPATI.

Vēntaṉ (Tam.: 'the King') The equivalent of *Indra in *Tamil literature and devotion.

V

vetāla A demonic spirit, prone to inhabiting and reanimating corpses.

vibhava *See* PĀÑCARĀTRA.

vibhūti **1.** *See* BHASMAN. **2.** A synonym of *siddhi, and the name given to the third *pāda of the **Yoga Sūtra*.

Videha An ancient Indian kingdom in the Northeast, with its capital city at *Mithilā.

vidhi ('injunction', 'rule', 'precept') According to the *Pūrva *Mīmāṃsaka exegetes, vidhi is the division of the **Veda* into which injunctions fall (for example, injunctions such as: 'He should sacrifice', or 'He should perform'). As prescribed ritual action, vidhi is the sole means of knowing *dharma; the rest of the *Veda* is either *arthavāda (eulogy) or pratiṣedha (prohibition).

vidyā ('knowledge', 'science', 'philosophy') A term which, depending on the context, can be used to denote the **Veda*, *śruti and *smṛti combined, *jñāna, any art, science, or body of knowledge (music, astronomy, architecture, etc.), or magical and supernatural practices aligned to *Tantra. Various lists of vidyās appear—**Manusmṛti* (7.43) recommends five types for a *king: the triple *Veda*, the science of government, logic, knowledge of the *ātman, and the practical sciences of commerce, agriculture, etc. In *Advaita Vedānta, vidyā (knowledge) is the ability to distinguish between what is superimposed on the self (through *adhyāsa) and its true nature, which is *brahman (neut.). With this discrimination (*viveka), *avidyā (ignorance) is dispelled and liberating knowledge achieved.

V

vidyādhara ('bearer of magical practices') One of a legendary class of wizards, often living in the mountains, well versed in shape-sifting, the casting of spells, and other magical 'sciences'.

Vidyāpati (14th century CE) A *Vaiṣṇava *bhakti poet and playwright. A *brahmin based in the court of King Śivasiṃha in *Mithilā, he composed lyric devotional sequences (padāvalī) about the longing of *Rādhā and the *gopīs for *Kṛṣṇa, modelled on the **Gītagovinda* of *Jayadeva and following the conventions of court poetry, but using Maithilī, a north Indian vernacular which bridges *Hindi and Bengali. He also wrote in *Sanskrit and *Apabhraṃśa. Literary historians regard him as an important link between Jayadeva and later bhakti poets such as *Caitanya.

vidyārambha ('beginning of learning') One of the standard *saṃskāra, marking the beginning of a basic education (i.e. learning how to read), usually undertaken around the age of five.

Vidyāraṇya *See* MĀDHAVA (1).

Vigneśvara *See* GAṆEŚA.

vijayā *See* BHAṄGĀ.

vijaya-daśamī **(vijayadashami)** *See* DASARA.

Vijayanagara ('city of victory') The name both of a once great city (previously known as Hampī, the modern Vidyānagara) in central Karnataka, and of the renowned South Indian Hindu empire (14th–16th century), encompassing much of the Deccan, which was named after it. Under the patronage of *kings such as Deva Rāya I (r. 1422–46), Kṛṣṇadeva Rāya (r. 1509–29), and Acyuta (r. 1529–42) many large *temples were built, such as the great *Viṭṭhala temple, and the Tiruveṅgalanātha (Acyuta Rāya) *Vaiṣṇava temple complex, both now in a ruined state at Vijayanagara itself. A number of temples were also dedicated to *Śiva as *Virūpākṣa, the guardian deity of the dynasty. The empire was eventually defeated by the *Muslim sultans to the north in 1565, and the city sacked.

vijñāna *See* CONSCIOUSNESS.

Vijñānabhikṣu (latter half of 16th century CE) A philosopher and theologian who attempted to synthesize *Sāṃkhya, *Yoga, and *Vedānta in a system known as avibhāgādvaita ('indistinguishable non-dualism'), but essentially taking a *bhedābheda stance. He wrote commentaries on all three traditions, including the *Vijñānāmṛtabhāṣya* on the **Brahmasūtras*, and the longest sub-commentary on the **Yoga Sūtra*, the *Yogavārttika*.

Vijñāneśvara (11th century CE) *See* MITĀKṢARĀ.

vikrama *See* ERAS; VIKRAMĀDITYA.

Vikramāditya A legendary *king, whose name is given to the *vikrama era, beginning in 57/58 BCE, supposedly the beginning of his reign.

village *See* GRĀMA.

vil pāṭṭu *See* 'BOW SONGS'.

vimāna 1. According to *Purāṇic myth, the name given to a type of 'aerial chariot' which conveys the gods about the world. **2.** The characteristic pyramidal tower erected as a superstructure above the *garbhagṛha, principally in South Indian Hindu *temples.

vīṇā A seven-stringed bamboo lute, with a gourd or gourds attached at each end to enable the instrument to resonate. In some form, the vīṇā is said to have great antiquity; in iconography it is used to symbolize mastery of music and the arts. *Sarasvatī (2) is often depicted playing the vīṇā.

Vinatā According to *Purāṇic legend, one of the two wives of the *ṛṣi *Kaśyapa. Imprisoned by her co-wife, *Kadrū, she is freed by her son, *Garuḍa.

Vināyaka ('remover of obstacles') An epithet of *Gaṇeśa.

Vindhyavāsin (*c.*4th century CE) The founder of a *Sāṃkhya *sampradāya which may have influenced *Patañjali's *Yoga School.

Vindhyavāsinī A celebrated *Śāktā *temple and *pilgrimage site, named after a fierce form of the Goddess (*Devī). Situated on the banks of the *Gaṅgā, near Mirzapur in Uttar Pradesh, it is regarded as a *śaktipīṭha.

Viniyoga An eclectic and individually-tailored style of *haṭha yoga developed by Tirumalai Krishnamacharya, and taught by his son T. K. V. Desikachar. The latter established his headquarters, the Krishnamacharya Yoga Mandiram (KYM), in Chennai (Madras) in 1976. The organization no longer favours the term 'Viniyoga' to describe its therapeutic method, although it has spread around the world under this name.

viniyoga ('application') A technical term for applying *Vedic *mantras during the ritual, as spelt out in the **Śrautasūtras*.

Vinobā Bhāve (1895–1982) *See* BHĀVE, VINOBĀ.

violence *See* HIṂSĀ.

vīra ('hero') An epithet of both martial and spiritual heroes. It may therefore be applied to gods, great *ascetics, and *saints, as well as to military heroes; the latter may, in their turn, also come to be deified as local gods.

Vīrabhadra ('distinguished hero') The ferocious form, generated from his mouth or his sweat, in which *Śiva, in his rage, destroys *Dakṣa's sacrifice. He is often portrayed in this way guarding the entrances to *temples, and is popularly worshipped in this form in the Deccan and South India.

viraha bhakti ('love in separation') The kind of *Kṛṣṇa devotionalism (*bhakti) practised by the *Āḻvārs, *Caitanya, *Sūrdās, and others, in which the poet-devotee identifies with the intense emotions experienced by *Rādhā and the *gopīs when they are separated from the object of their love (Kṛṣṇa), ultimately engendering an ecstatic experience of divine love.

Virāj In the **Veda*, the first offspring of *Brahmā, variously characterized as either male or female. Virāj often has a creative function; in the **Puruṣasūkta*, *puruṣa is born from her, and she is born from puruṣa. S/he is also identified with *Prajāpati, and in *Puraṇic times with *Viṣṇu or *Kṛṣṇa.

Virajānanda, Svāmī *See* DAYĀNAND(A) SARASVATĪ.

vīrakal ('hero stone') A type of stone memorial, particularly popular in the Deccan, commemorating the place where heroic deeds have been performed, or where a hero (*vīra) has died. They usually also depict the hero in heaven (*svarga).

Vīramitrodaya *See* MITRAMIŚRA.

Vīraśaivas *See* LIṄGĀYAT(A)S.

Virāṭaparvan ('King Virāṭa') Book 4 of the *Sanskrit **Mahābhārata*, recounting the *Pāṇḍavas' thirteenth year of exile in disguise (*Arjuna posing as a eunuch) in the service of King Virāṭa of the *Matsyas. Notable episodes include *Bhīma's killing of one of the king's generals, Kīcaka, who had attempted to seduce Draupadī, and the marriage of Virāṭa's daughter, Uttarā to *Abhimanyu, sealing the alliance between the Matsyas and the Pāṇḍavas.

Virūpākṣa (lit. 'having malformed eyes' = 'having three eyes') An epithet of *Śiva. Notable temples dedicated to the deity in this form can be found at *Paṭṭadakal, and Hampī (*Vijayanagara), where, as the guardian deity of the Vijayanagara dynasty, he was married to *Pampā(devī), a local river goddess, and so is also known as Pampāpati ('Pampā's lord').

vīrya ('energy') A quality associated with heroes (*vīra) and deities, especially *Viṣṇu in his *Saṃkarṣaṇa *vyūha form.

Viśākhadatta (early 5th century CE?) Author of one of the best known *Sanskrit dramas, *Mudrārākṣasa* ('[Minister] Rākṣasa's Seal'), which has a seemingly historical, and certainly a political plot. The author is said to have been a prince at the *Gupta court.

visarjana ('dismissal') The formal 'dismissal' of the deity that closes a period of worship—one of the sixteen offerings/ services (*upacāras) which are component parts of *pūjā. With permanently consecrated *images, in which the deity is thought to be ever-present, this is more of a framing device to close the offering ritual, and a reminder of the unrestricted nature of God, than a real dismissal. With images that are not permanently consecrated, it constitutes an actual dismissal of the deity. *See also* ĀVĀHANA.

viśeṣa ('characteristic difference', 'peculiarity', 'individuality', 'particularity') According to the *Vaiśeṣika tradition, which derives its name from the term, 'particularity' is one of the fundamental, irreducible categories (*padārthas) of existence. Discrete particularities (viśeṣas) are usually contrasted with universals (sāmānyas).

Viśiṣṭādvaita ('non-dualism of the qualified') One of the major theological cum philosophical schools of the *Vedānta *darśana. Brought to maturity by *Rāmānuja, its teachings provide the doctrinal basis for *Śrī Vaiṣṇavism. Rāmānuja maintains, against *Śaṅkara's nondualism (*Advaita), that the individual self and *brahman (= God) are not completely identical: rather, individual selves and the material world are both real and at the same time 'modes' (prakāras) of brahman. In this way they are analogous to God's 'body': inhabited by the *Paramātman (= God), they are ultimately dependent upon Him. For Rāmānuja, therefore, the universe of multiplicity and change, rather than being ultimately an 'illusion' (*māyā), and thus a function of ignorance (*avidyā) (as Advaita would have it) is, in fact, a real transformation (pariṇāma) of a pre-existing cause (brahman). Māyā therefore represents the way in which God manifests the reality of material nature (*prakṛti.)

The first *ācārya of the Viśiṣṭādvaita school is said to have been *Nāthamuni; he was succeeded by two of his disciples, Puṇḍarīkākṣa and Rāma Miśra, but no complete works survive from these three early teachers. Rāma Miśra is said to have taught Nāthmuni's grandson, *Yāmuna, regarded as the second ācārya in the lineage; his pupils in turn are claimed to have taught the third ācārya, Rāmānuja. Notable teachers after Rāmānuja include *Vedāntadeśika and *Piḷḷai Lokācārya, the major theologians of, respectively, the *Vaṭakalai and *Teṉkalai subschools. *See also* BHEDĀBHEDA(VĀDA); RĀMĀNUJA; SATKĀRYAVĀDA; ŚRĪ VAIṢṆAVISM.

Viṣṇu ('all-pervader') One of the three great deities of medieval and subsequent Hinduism; he and his *avatāras (especially *Kṛṣṇa and *Rāma) are the focus of worship in the *Vaiṣṇava traditions (collectively referred to as *Vaiṣṇavism). Viṣṇu first appears in the **Ṛg Veda* as a beneficent but less than prominent solar deity, closely allied to *Indra. His sun-aligned, all-pervasive nature, is extended in the **Brāhmaṇas* in a myth in which, as *Trivikrama, he encompasses the entire universe in three strides. This assimilates him to the sacrificer (*yajamāna) at the centre of the universe; by a further homology, he is said 'to be', or to embody, the sacrifice (*yajña).

The process by which this *Vedic deity fuses with other, originally independent gods, such as *Vāsudeva-Kṛṣṇa and *Nārāyaṇa, is both complex and not fully traceable. The 'emanation' (*vyūha) doctrine of *Pāñcarātra theology, and the burgeoning *avatāra doctrine were, however, powerful integrating mechanisms. Through the latter, which first appears in the *Epic literature, Kṛṣṇa and Rāma (who become the chief deities of the Vaiṣṇava *bhakti traditions) are shown to be incarnations, or 'descents' of the supreme God, *Viṣṇu. By way of these avatāras, Viṣṇu, who ultimately transcends all particular forms, undertakes what, by then, is perceived to be his chief cosmic function, the periodic restitution and preservation of *dharma, which includes the sacrificial and social orders. At the same time, a rich mythology dramatizing this function starts to appear in the **Purāṇas*; and it is from these myths that the multiple iconographic representations of the god and his family are derived.

Standard depictions of Viṣṇu (as opposed to his avatāras) show him as an upright, four-armed, kingly figure, wearing royal clothes and jewellery, and an elaborate, often cylindrical crown (kirīṭa). He carries a conch-shell (śaṅkha), a club (*gada), a discus (*cakra (2)) and a lotus (*padma); alternatively, one hand may be raised in either the *abhaya- or the *varada- *mudrās, another may rest on his hip. He wears the *Brahmanical *sacred thread (yajñopavīta), and, on his chest, a curl (sometimes a cruciform flower) called the *śrīvatsa ('beloved of *Śrī), as well as a jewel (kaustubha), obtained at the *Churning of the Ocean. The conch and the discus, in particular, symbolize the presence of the god, as do his footprints. Paintings show him with a dark blue body. Typically, he is accompanied by his consort *Lakṣmī (also known as Śrī); a secondary consort, usually only represented alongside Śrī, is *Bhū Devī, the 'Goddess Earth'. *Garuḍa acts as his vehicle (*vāhana). *See also* ANANTAŚAYANA; AVATĀRA; KṚṢṆA; RĀMA; VAIṢṆAVA; VAIṢṆAVISM.

Viṣṇu Purāṇa (before 1000 CE) Classified as one of the eighteen 'great *Purāṇas*' (*mahāpurāṇas*) in the *sāttvika group, i.e. those said to relate to *Viṣṇu. The six books (aṃśas) of the *Viṣṇu* are, indeed, entirely *Vaiṣṇava (*Pāñcarātra) in content, including a lengthy rendition of *Kṛṣṇa's life. This may have been derived from the **Harivaṃśa* (although some have argued for the *Viṣṇu*'s priority), and may, in its turn, have influenced (or, according to some, been influenced by) the **Bhāgavata Purāṇa*. More than most *Purāṇas*, the *Viṣṇu* also deals with the traditional *pañcalakṣaṇa.

Viṣṇusahasranāma ('thousand names of Viṣṇu') A popular *mantra which takes the form of a litany of Viṣṇu's names and epithets, derived from lists in the **Anuśāsanaparavan* of the **Mahābhārata* and the **Padma Purāṇa*. A commentary on the mantra, the *Viṣṇusahasranāmabhāṣya*, is attributed to *Śaṅkara.

Viṣṇuśarman *See* PĀÑCARĀTRA.

Viṣṇusmṛti **(*Viṣṇudharmasūtra*, *Viṣṇudharmaśāstra*)** A **Dharmaśāstra* text in 100 chapters which, in an early form, may have belonged to the **Kāṭhaka Saṃhitā* of the **Black Yajur Veda*. Much of its material appears to be drawn from other texts, such as **Manusmṛti*. Framing chapters put its teaching into the mouth of *Viṣṇu's *varāha *avatāra. It was the subject of an important 17th-century CE commentary (*Vaijayantī*) by Nandapaṇḍita.

Viṣṇusvāmin (*c.*13th century CE?) A South Indian *Vaiṣṇava *Vedāntin teacher, said to be a precursor of *Vallabha and the *Śuddhādvaita school. His own school has been called the Rudrasampradāya, and seems to have focused on Viṣṇu's *Narasiṃha *avatāra, but since Viṣṇusvāmin's works are no longer extant, the nature of his teaching remains obscure, and can only be glimpsed in the works of others. According to the hagiographies, he was a South Indian *brahmin who moved north, and, by some accounts, he was the *guru of *Jñāneśvara.

Viśva Hindū Pariṣad (Vishva Hindu Parishad, VHP) ('World Hindu Council') A right-wing Hindu nationalist organization, founded in 1964 by Swami *Chinmayānanda. The VHP has become politically active since the 1980s, and has been at the forefront of the often violent struggle to build the Rāmajanmabhūmi *temple in *Ayodhyā.

Viśvakarman ('maker of all') In the **Ṛg Veda*, the creative principle, personified as the *deva who creates the world through *sacrifice; he is therefore often identified with *Prajāpati. He is imagined as having eyes, faces, arms, and feet on all sides. In *Purāṇic mythology Viśvakarman is elided with *Tvaṣṭṛ, and conceptualized as the universal architect (i.e. the architect of the gods). He presides over the **Sthāpatyaveda*.

Viśvāmitra ('friend of all') One of the *Vedic *maharṣis; the third *maṇḍala of the **Ṛg Veda* is attributed to him. Thought to be a rājarṣi or royal sage, i.e. of *kṣatriya birth, he attained *brahmin status through the strength of his *tapas (despite being seduced by *Menā and fathering *Śakuntalā). In the *Epic and *Purāṇic myths, he is portrayed as the arch-rival of *Vasiṣṭha.

Viśvanātha (Viśveśvara) ('Lord of the Universe', 'Universal Lord') An epithet of *Śiva, and the name of a famous *temple in *Vārāṇasī housing his *jyotirliṅga.

viśvarūpa ('universal form', 'all forms') A form of a deity, principally *Viṣṇu, demonstrating the way in which he encompasses the universe. The best-known description occurs in the **Bhagavadgītā* (11.3ff.), after *Arjuna asks to see *Kṛṣṇa's supreme form. Iconographic renditions show Viṣṇu with many heads and arms.

viśvedeva ('relating to all the gods', from viśve devāḥ, the masculine plural form of viśvadeva, 'all divine') A class of minor *Vedic deities. Offerings are made to them in the *Vaiśvadeva ritual.

Viṭhobā (Viṭṭhala, Pāṇḍuraṅga ('The White One')**)** A popular Maharastrian deity, identified with *Viṣṇu/*Kṛṣṇa, whose *temple at *Paṇḍharpur is the focus of quarterly *pilgrimages by the *Vārkarī Panth, culminating each year in a major *yātra undertaken by over half a million pilgrims during Āṣāḍha (June–July). The origins of Vithobā worship are not clear, although it may have originated in Karnataka, where the god is also popular (a great royal temple was dedicated to him at *Vijayanagara in the mid 16th century). Some scholars have suggested that the *Vaiṣṇaiva Viṭhobā at Paṇḍharpur replaced an originally *Śaiva deity (Pāṇḍuraṅga). According to the temple's foundation myth, given in the *Pāṇḍuraṅgamāhātmya* (part of the **Skanda Purāṇa*), *Puṇḍalīka, a reformed character, who had become entirely devoted to his parents, was interrupted one day by Viṭhobā, seeking hospitality. Barely pausing in his ministrations to his father, Puṇḍalīka threw a brick for the god to stand on, clear of the mud. This is said to be the same brick upon which Viṭhobā now stands in the temple.

Viṭhobā has been described as virtually a god without qualities. By the Vārkarīs he is considered to be a svarūpa or natural form of *Viṣṇu, but has no particular iconography apart from the brick on which he stands in the temple at Paṇḍharpur. The family of hereditary *brahmin *priests (baḍvās), which serves him throughout the year, simply treats him as Viṭhobā, sui generis. Statues depict a figure wearing a high crown, with its (two) arms akimbo. Mirroring the temple image, he is usually shown as dark, or black.

Viṭṭhala *See* VIṬHOBĀ.

Viṭṭalanātha (1516–1586) *See* VALLABHA; VALLABHASAMPRADĀYA.

vivāha *See* MARRIAGE.

Vivaraṇa A school of interpretation within the *Advaita Vedānta tradition, following the lead of *Śaṅkara's pupil *Padmapāda in its reading of the master's thought. As well as stressing the importance of *Vedic study, and direct experience of *brahman (neut.), over activities such as *yoga, the Vivaraṇa also regarded ignorance (*māyā) as a cosmic phenomenon relating to brahman, and was thus opposed to the rival *Bhāmatī school.

viveka ('discrimination', 'distinction') A key requirement for making soteriological progress, especially in *Advaita Vedānta, where in texts such as *Śaṅkara's *Vivekacūḍāmaṇi* ('Crest Jewel of Discrimination') it is characterized as the ability to discriminate between the permanent or eternal (*brahman (neut.)), and the impermanent or noneternal—i.e. the ability to distinguish between what is superimposed on the *self, through *adhyāsa, and its true nature.

Vivekānanda, Svāmī (Swami Vivekananda) (1863–1902) A teacher and *saṃnyāsin, he was the best-known and the most influential disciple of *Rāmakṛṣṇa, and the driving force behind the *Rāmakṛṣṇa Mission. Born Narendranath Dutta, he was a member of the *Brahmo Samāj, and training to be a lawyer, when he encountered Rāmakṛṣṇa, and as the result of an intense religious experience became one of his disciples. After his master's death he became a saṃnyāsin, travelling the length and breadth of India on foot, meditating and propagating his interpretation of Rāmakṛṣṇa's teaching. This he regarded as essentially a form of *Advaita Vedānta (subsequently dubbed *Neo-Vedānta), conceptualized as the essence of both Hinduism and every other religion. He promoted this 'Hinduism' as a world religion (in a sense, *the* world religion), based on what he perceived to be universally valid, and scientifically consonant, ethical principles. It was this proposal—that, beneath their apparent diversity, all religions are really one, combined with a plea for universal tolerance, which attracted so much attention at the Chicago World Parliament of Religions in 1893 (where he had been sent, by a local prince, as the 'Hindu' delegate), and gave Vivekānanda a worldwide reputation. Building on a receptivity to his ideas in the West, he established the *Vedānta Society in New York in 1895, before returning to India in 1897, where he transformed the monastic order, which had been established after Rāmakṛṣṇa's death by his disciples, into the *Rāmakṛṣṇa Mission, a charitable and educational organization, based at the *Rāmakṛṣṇa Maṭha in Calcutta, but active throughout the subcontinent and beyond. Vivekānanda, Rāmakṛṣṇa, and *Śāradā Devī, continue to be revered as the 'Holy Trio' of the contemporary Mission. A key figure in the development of what has become known as *Neo-Hinduism, Vivekānanda's teachings had a considerable appeal amongst the English educated middle-classes, and he was among those who prepared the way for the Independence movements of the early 20th century. His shaping of the popular Western view of Hinduism as synonymous with Advaita Vedānta has cast a long and, according to many academics, distorting shadow.

Vivekasindhu *See* MUKUNDARĀJA.

vow *See* VRATA.

Vraj(a) *See* BRAJ.

vrata ('vow') A vow taken by an individual as part of a monastic or *ascetic discipline, as a penance (*prāyaścitta), or as a specific undertaking made in return for the hoped-for favour of a deity (in, for example, healing the sick, or helping with family or financial difficulties). In the latter case, fulfilment of the vow typically involves such activities as fasting (*upavāsa), the recitation of *mantras, or going on a *pilgrimage. Traditionally, vrata are most frequently undertaken by women, either for the benefit of the whole family, or as a means of personal empowerment. *See also* MAHĀVRATA.

Vrātyas (perhaps derived from vrāta—'group') A band of roaming and aggressive warriors who appear in the **Veda* (most notably in the **Atharva Veda*, Book 15), where they are described as turbanned and wearing the skins of rams. Sometimes characterized as being non- *Āryan, or on the fringes of *Vedic society, they are more likely to have been a particular group of young Āryan men, engaged in cattle raiding, and leading a near independent life with its own rituals, some of them sexual as well as proto- *yogic in nature, possibly for a limited period. This was, or could be, brought to an end, and the Vrātyas and their booty reintegrated into society, through a special *purificatory ritual called the vrātyaṣṭoma.

vrātyaṣṭoma *See* VRĀTYAS.

Vṛkodara *See* BHĪMA.

Vṛndāvan(a) (Vrindaban, Brindāvana, Brindaban) ('the forest of Vṛndā') The specific area of *forest, on the banks of the *Yamunā river (now in the western part of the *Mathurā district of Uttar Pradesh), in which *Kṛṣṇa-*Gopāla is said to have grown up. The name is frequently used as a synonym of the surrounding region, *Braj (Vraj). *See also* BRAJ.

Vṛṣṇi(s) The name of a tribe, also known as the Sātvatas or Yādavas, for whom *Vāsudeva (later *Kṛṣṇa) may have been a deified hero or *king. In the **Mahābhārata* they are considered Kṛṣṇa's 'race', and under his protection.

Vṛtra ('coverer', 'enemy') In the **Ṛg Veda*, a drought- and chaos-causing demon (sometimes said to be a serpent), connected with the darkness of unyielding rain clouds, and, according to some, with the pent up disorder that precedes creation. *Indra, his great adversary, kills him and frees the waters, in the process differentiating and ordering the world.

vyāhṛti ('utterance', 'exclamation') In the plural, the sacred sounds evoking the seven levels of the universe. The first three of these— *bhū ('earth'), *bhuvaḥ ('atmosphere'), and *svar ('heaven')—are known as the 'great calls' (mahāvyāhṛti). According to *Manusmṛti* (2.76ff.), the *brahmin who, at the morning and evening *saṃdhyās, recites these 'great calls', preceded by *oṃ, and followed by the *Gāyatrī *mantra, obtains the *merit of reciting the entire **Veda*. (The complete list of seven, in ascending order, is: bhū (bhūr), bhuvaḥ (bhuvar), svar, mahar, janar, tapar, and satya.)

vyākaraṇa ('linguistic analysis', 'grammar') Classified as one of the six **Vedāṅgas*, but also regarded as an independent philosophical system, or *darśana, largely thanks to *Bhartṛhari (1). The analysis of grammar is considered to be the prerequisite of any proper *Sanskritic study, and invariably begins with the **Aṣṭādhyāyi* of *Pāṇini. Other important grammarians and linguistic thinkers include *Patañjali (1) and *Maṇḍana Miśra. For a summary of the underlying theology of vyākaraṇa, *see* BHARTHARI.

vyāna *See* PRĀṆA.

Vyāsa 1. (Kṛṣṇa Dvaipāyana) A legendary *ṛṣi; as the prototypical, author/editor, he is usually thought to be omniscient. Vyāsa is said to have compiled the authorless (*apauruṣeya) **Veda*, dividing it into its four **saṃhitās*. There is also a tradition that he composed a single, original *Purāṇa*, which becomes the source of all the other **Purāṇas*. The *Mahābhārata*, too, attributes its own composition to Vyāsa, who instructs his pupil *Vaiśaṃpāyana to recite it for the first time at *Janamejaya's *snake *sacrifice. (According to one popular legend, he dictated the written text to *Gaṇeśa.) Like a post-modern author, he then proceeds to intervene at various crucial points in his own narrative: for instance, he fathers *Dhṛtarāṣṭra and *Pāṇḍu. In general, otherwise unattributed texts requiring the authority of antiquity tend to be credited to him. **2.** (*c.*4th–7th century CE) Author of the first and most influential commentary (the *Yogabhāṣya*) on *Patañjali's **Yoga Sutra*. The name may be a deliberate attempt to connect the commentator with the legendary sage (1.).

Vyāsa, Harirāma (16th century CE) A prolific North Indian *Vaiṣṇaiva *bhakti poet who was a devotee of *Rādhā and *Kṛṣṇa. In his works, composed in *Braj bhāṣā *Hindi and collected in anthologies called *Vyāsa-vāṇī* ('The Word of Vyāsa'), he identifies himself as a close female attendant or girl-friend (*sakhī) of Rādhā; although, unlike many bhakti poets, he concentrates more on the fulfilment of Rādhā's love for Kṛṣṇa than on their separation (*viraha). Vyāsa is linked with Svāmī *Haridāsa and *Hitaharivaṃśa as one of the 'triad of Hari', also known as the 'triad of connoisseurs' (rasika-trayī) because of their concern to evoke a sense of aesthetic delight or *rasa in their audience.

Vyāsatīrtha (Vyāsarāja) (1447–1539?) A theologian, logician, and *Vaiṣṇava *bhakta in the tradition of *Madhva's *Dvaita Vedānta. Author of the *Nyāyāmṛta* ('The Nectar of Logic').

vyavahāra ('conduct', 'behaviour', 'legal procedure) According to **Dharmaśāstra*, the civil and criminal law through which *kings should administer their justice.

vyavahāra-satya (vyāvahārika-satya) ('relative, practical, or conventional truth') According to *Advaita *Vedānta, knowledge of the world of appearances obtained through the senses and the intellect. *Śaṅkara contrasts it with *paramārtha-satya ('supreme or absolute truth')—direct knowledge of reality, i.e. of *brahman (neut.).

vyūha *See* PĀÑCARĀTRA.

V

W

Wārkarī *See* Vārkarī Panth.

Weber, Max (1864–1920) An eminent and highly influential German sociologist. He wrote quite extensively on both Hinduism and *Buddhism from a theoretical perspective. Among his works is *The Religion of India: The Sociology of Hinduism and Buddhism* (1921) (English trans. by Hans H. Gerth and Don Martindale, 1958).

wedding *See* marriage.

***White Yajur Veda* (*Śukla Yajur Veda*)** One of the two major recensions of the **Yajur Veda*. The adjective 'White' or 'Pure' distinguishes it from the other recension, the **Black Yajur Veda* (*Kṛṣṇa Yajur Veda*), as does the fact that its *mantras or *yajus are not mixed with explanatory prose formulae (**brāhmaṇas*). (These are collected separately in its **Brāhmaṇa*, the **Śatapatha*.) The *White Yajur Veda* is divided between two collections (**saṃhitās*), each preserved by its own school (*śākhā): the *Vājasaneyī Mādhyaṃdina Saṃhitā* and the *Vājasaneyī Kāṇva Saṃhitā*.

Whitney, William Dwight (1827–1894) An eminent American *Indologist, perhaps still best known for his *Sanskrit Grammar* (1st ed. 1879; 2nd rev. ed. 1889) and his linguistic work on the **Veda*.

widow *See* widowhood.

widow-burning *See* Satī (2).

widowhood Traditionally, widowhood is thought to make a woman highly *inauspicious, especially if she belongs to a *brahmin or high-*caste family. She may be expected to shave off her hair, wear plain white clothing, refrain from ritual, and live in seclusion, perhaps in a semi-*ascetic community with other widows. This holds good even for child widows, whose marriage has not been consummated. A childless widow may, in some instances, be cast out, or sent back to her own family by her in-laws. One way to avoid the supposed inauspiciousness of widowhood was for the woman, as a *satī (2), to immolate herself on her husband's *funeral pyre. Remarriage for a high caste widow was considered taboo, although it was legalized for all in the Hindu Widows Remarriage Act of 1856. (The abolition of satī and the permitting of widow remarriage were two of the causes taken up by the Hindu reformers of the 19th century, such as Rāmmohun *Roy.) There are a variety of opinions in **Dharmaśāstra* about whether a widow can inherit her husband's property, although her right to do so (with various provisos), and the equality of women with men in general, has been enshrined in 20th century law (e.g. in the Hindu Marriage Act of 1956).

widow immolation *See* Satī (2).

Wilkins, (Sir) Charles (1749–1846) A pioneering British *Orientalist and *Sanskrit scholar. An employee of the *East India Company, he published *A Grammar of Sanskrit* in 1779, followed, in 1785, by the first complete translation of the **Bhagavadgītā* into a modern European language, and, in 1787, a translation of the **Hitopadeśa* (1787). In 1800, he became the first director of the India House Library in London (subsequently the

India Office Library). He was knighted in 1833.

Wilson, Horace Hayman (1786–1860) An important early *Indologist and *Sanskritist. Wilson lived in India between 1808 and 1832, during which time he was Assay Master of the Calcutta Mint. Under the influence of *Wilkins and **Colebrooke*, he became an accomplished and open-minded Sanskrit scholar. Among his publications was a translation of *Kālidāsa's *Meghadūta* ('The Cloud Messenger') (1813), and the *Sketch of the Religious Sects of the Hindus* (1828; 2nd ed. 1846). In 1832, Wilson was the first person to be elected to the *Boden Professorship of Sanskrit at Oxford University, a post he held until his death.

wind *See* VĀYU.

Winternitz, Moriz (1863–1937) A prolific Austrian *Indologist and *Sanskritist. Educated at the University of Vienna, he was in Oxford from 1888–98, working as Max *Müller's assistant and as librarian of the Indian Institute. He moved to Prague in 1899, where he was appointed to the Chair in Sanskrit in 1902. Among his many publications are an edition of the **Āpastamba* **Gṛhyasūtra* (1887), and his three volume *Geschichte der Indischen Literatur* ('History of Indian Literature') (1904–20).

women's dharma *See* STRĪDHARMA.

Woodroffe, Sir John *See* AVALON, ARTHUR.

word *See* ŚABDA.

world *See* LOKA.

worship *See* PŪJĀ.

Y

Yādava Prakāśa (latter half of 11th century CE) A *Vaiṣṇava *Advaitin, who was said to have been the teacher of *Rāmānuja before they fell out. He was the author of the *Yatidharmasamuccaya* ('Collection of Ascetic Laws'), a book of regulations for *Brahmanical *asceticism.

Yādavas *See* VṚṢṆI(s).

Yadu Founder of the *Yādava dynasty.

yajamāna (lit. 'sacrificing on his own behalf') The patron or sponsor of the *Brahmanical *śrauta sacrifice (*yajña), usually referred to as the 'sacrificer'. The minimum qualification for a yajamāna is birth into one of the three higher *varṇas, to have received *upanayana, to be married (the yajamāna and his wife act as a ritual unit), and to have set up the *gṛhyāgni ('domestic fire'), from which he installs the three (or five) fires necessary for his ritual life as an *āhitāgni. For a fee (*dakṣinā), the *brahmin *priests perform the sacrifice on the yajamāna's behalf; it is the latter, conceptually both the sacrificer and the sacrifice, to whom the results, or 'fruits' of the ritual (good things in this world and the next) accrue. Once the sacred fires have been installed, the yajamāna has an obligation to carry out the sequence of śrauta rites for the rest of his life (unless he becomes a *saṃnyāsin, or infirm), culminating in the sacrifice of himself, i.e. his *cremation. *See also* YAJÑA.

yajña ('sacrifice', 'oblation', 'worship') **1.** Any offering or oblation made to a deity. **2.** The generic term for the complex of *Vedic rituals, including the *śrauta rites, the domestic rites (*gṛhya-yajñas), and various collapsed, internalized, or condensed forms, such as the 'great sacrifices' (*mahā-yajñas). The assumptions which underlie the performance of Vedic yajñā are manifested in the **Brāhmaṇas* (*c.*1000 to 500 BCE), the prose explanations appended to the four **Saṃhitās*. This 'theology' has its basis in the belief that all elements of the universe, human and divine, are interconnected and interdependent. For this reason, everything that happens in the sacrifice is analogous to both individual and cosmic processes; moreover, the sacrifice is the connecting link or conduit between the individual and the universal, and its prototypical performer, the *brahmin śrauta ritualist, is therefore the mediator between the human and the divine. More than this, the sacrificial act (*karma)—giving something up (nominally to a deity)—is the mechanism which creates or activates the connections: if correctly performed, it will automatically achieve the desired and concomitant outcomes. The latter are expressed on two levels: for the individual *yajamāna ('patron of the sacrifice'), the yajña brings good things both here (cattle, sons, a long life) and after death (a place in a permanent *loka or *svarga, i.e. *immortality); for society (and the world) as a whole, sacrifice maintains the natural order. Moreover, sacrifice is thought to be reconstructive or regenerative of the individual as well as the universal. On the model of the *Vedic **Puruṣasūkta*'s cosmic man (*puruṣa), the yajamāna, through his substitutes—the offerings he provides—gives himself up as the material of the sacrifice (something that happens in earnest in the fires of his funerary *cremation.) Sacrifice is therefore thought to be necessary at both the human and cosmic levels: through its perpetual action, both the individual and the world (in the puruṣa, one and the same entity) are constantly recreated and maintained; without its regulative and integrating action everything would fall back into chaos, bringing dire consequences for individuals, society, and the universe as a whole. In other words, it is through the sacrifice that *dharma is realized and maintained. At the centre of this process are the brahmins, the 'gods on earth': only they have access to the **Veda* and so to proper knowledge of the sacrifice, its techniques and inner meaning. Ultimately, only they can maintain human welfare and cosmic order; the gods are merely part of the mechanism. *See also* MĪMĀṂSĀ. For details of ritual procedures, *see* GṚHYA-YAJÑA(S); ŚRAUTA; and entries for individual sacrifices.

Yājñavalkya A legendary *ṛṣi, closely associated with the **White Yajur Veda*, of which he is supposed to have been the first teacher. He appears frequently in its **Brāhmaṇa*, the **Śatapatha*, and its **Upaniṣad*, the **Bṛhadāraṇyaka*. In the latter, he is said to be the teacher of King Janaka of *Videha, and is also described as becoming a *parivrājaka or 'wandering ascetic'. One of his wives is the theologically inquisitive *Maitreyī. A **Dharmaśāstra* text, the **Yājñavalkyasmṛti* is also attributed to him.

Yājñavalkyasmṛti A systematic **Dharmaśāstra* text, attributed to the legendary *ṛṣi *Yājñavalkya, but dating from the 3rd to 4th centuries CE. It is probably the best known work of this type after **Manusmṛti*. It has engendered many commentaries, the most celebrated being the 11th-century CE *Mitākṣarā* ('Comprehensive and Concise') of Vijñāneśvara.

yajñopavīta **1.** *See* SACRED THREAD. **2.** Dressing the deity (*mūrti) in a new *sacred thread—one of the sixteen offerings or services (*upacāras) which are component parts of *pūjā.

Yajur Veda ('The *Veda*/Knowledge Consisting of Mantras/Sacrificial Formulae') The second of the *Vedic **Saṃhitās*, comprising the (mostly) prose formulae (yajus or *mantras), and various instructional additions (*brāhmaṇas), which are muttered by the *adhvaryu *priest to accompany the actions of the *śrauta sacrifice (*yajña). It survives in two major recensions, the **Black Yajur Veda* and the **White Yajur Veda*. *See also* BRĀHMAṆA(S).

yajus The (mostly) prose formulae or *mantras, contained in the **Yajur Veda*, which are muttered by the *adhvaryu *priest to accompany the actions of the *Vedic *śrauta sacrifice (*yajña).

yakṣas (fem.: **yakṣīs, yakṣiṇīs**) A class of semi-divine supernatural beings or 'spirits', closely associated with natural phenomena, especially vegetation and trees, but with the apparent ability to remain invisible, or to take on varied shapes. Probably of non-*Vedic origin, and the object of *village fertility cults, they appear in the **Veda* occasionally, and then routinely in the *Epics and **Purāṇas*, as well as in *Buddhist and *Jain narratives and mythology. Like most supernatural powers, they are regarded as ambivalent towards humans, and require propitiation. Reinforcing their association with wealth, their leader is sometimes identified as *Kubera, who is also connected to the *rākṣasas. They appear amongst the earliest extant Indian iconography, with prosperously rounded bellies (the yakṣas), or as beautiful young women (the yakṣīs). As protective deities, they are subsequently integrated into the wider mythology of Hinduism, Buddhism, and Jainism.

yakṣīs (yakṣiṇīs) *See* YAKṢAS.

Yama (Kāla, Antaka, Dharmarāja) The personification of *death. From the time of the later *Ṛg Vedic hymns onwards, Yama is the name given to the first man to die; he therefore rules over a post-death realm (in the **Purāṇas*, the hellish regions—*narakas) as the *king, god, judge, and punisher (lit. 'restrainer' = yama) of the dead. The theology of the sacrifice (*yajña) views Yama as the creditor par excellence, to whom all mortals are in debt by virtue of their birth. Ritual in part pays, or defers that debt, as may *yogic practices, *knowledge, and *tapas. So, in the **Mahābharata*, for instance, *Sāvitrī, by the strength of her *dharmic knowledge and tapas, is able to rescue her husband from Yama, when the latter appears as a pure black, red-eyed figure, dressed in red, wearing a diadem, and carrying a noose in his hand to bind the *soul of the condemned man. Other depictions of Yama add fangs, a club, a garland of red flowers, and have him riding on his buffalo *vāhana. As the guardian of the South, he is one of the *aṣṭadikpālas.

yama ('[ethical] restraint') The first of the 'outer limbs' (bahir-aṅga) of the *aṣṭāṅga-yoga ('eight-limbed yoga') outlined in *Patañjali's **Yoga Sūtra* (2.28-55; 3.1-8). Yama has five aspects: non-violence (*ahiṃsā), truthfulness (satya), not stealing, or not taking what is not given (asteya), sexual restraint (*brahmacarya), and non-possession/non-possessiveness (aparigraha). The list appears to be part of a general ethical currency common to many *ascetic and *renouncer groups, sometimes referred to as *sādhāraṇa dharma: the headings, if not their interpretation, are identical to the vows taken by the *Jains, and very similar to those taken by the early *Buddhists. Other, sometimes longer, lists of similar restraints are also found in a variety of Hindu sources, including **Manusmṛti* (10.63).

Yamī (Yamunā) *Yama's twin-sister, the first woman to die.

Yamunā (Jumnā, Jamunā) One of India's seven sacred *rivers. Flowing from *Yamunotrī in the *Himālayas to its confluence with the *Gaṅgā (and the mythical *Sarasvatī) at *Prayāga, it passes through *Mathurā, *Vṛndāvana, Delhi, and Agra. Yamunā is personified as a goddess, said to be Yama's twin sister; her vehicle (*vāhana) is a tortoise.

Yāmuna (Yāmunācārya, Āḷavantār) (trad. 918–1038 CE) The second *ācārya of the *Viśiṣṭādvaita school, and so also of the *Śrī Vaiṣṇava tradition. He is said to have been the grandson of the first ācārya, *Nāthamuni, and the predecessor of *Rāmānuja. According to the hagiographies, he was born, like his grandfather, at Vīranārāyaṇapuram, near *Cidambaram; later, under the influence of one of Nāthamuni's disciples, Rāma Miśra, he renounced and moved to *Śrīraṅgam. In works such as the *Āgamapramāṇya* and the *Gītārthasaṃgraha*, Yāmuna claims that the *Pāñcarātra **Saṃhitās* (the basis of Śrī Vaiṣṇava *temple ritual), and the **Bhagavadgītā*, which *Brahmanical orthodoxy had regarded as *smṛti, are sources of revelation equal to, and alongside the **Vedas*. Other works credited to him include the *Siddhi-traya*, the *Mahāpuruṣanirṇaya*, and two devotional poems, the *Stotaratna* and the *Catuḥśloki*. His attempt to explain the relationship between God and individual selves as being analogous to that between the deity and its dependent 'body' was subsequently taken up by Rāmānuja.

Yamunotrī A *tīrtha in the *Himālayas at the source of the *Yamunā river in modern day Uttaranchal (Uttarakhand). Pilgrims worship the divyaśilā ('divine stone'), a pillar of rock, before entering the *temple to the goddess Yamunā which lies below the glacier. The area is also known for its thermal springs. *See also* DHĀMA.

yantra Similar to a *maṇḍala, but the term may in addition be used to describe three-dimensional objects with the same ritual or meditational purposes. In a more restricted sense it refers to a simple maṇḍala—i.e. one having a limited number of lines, arranged in an uncomplicated fashion. *See also* ŚRĪYANTRA.

yantra (*śrīyantra*)

Yāska *See* NIRUKTA (2).

Yaśodā According to *Vaiṣṇava texts such as the **Bhāgavata Purāṇa*, *Kṛṣṇa's cowherd foster-mother, married to *Nanda (1).

yati ('striver') A common term for an *ascetic or *renouncer.

Yatidharmasamuccaya *See* YĀDAVA PRAKĀŚA.

yātrā *See* PILGRIMAGE.

yavanas (fem.: yavanīs) Greeks (Ionians) from Asia Minor who had settled in Bactria. Some scholars think the term had a wider use, and was never restricted to Greeks. In medieval and post-medieval literature, it was also used to refer to *Muslims.

Yayāti In the **Mahābhārata*, a mythical, *Lunar Dynasty *king, the son of *Nahuṣa; as the father of *Puru and *Yadu, he is the progenitor of the *Pauravas and the *Yādavas.

Yellammā A local goddess popular in Maharashtra and Karnataka. A regional manifestation of *Reṇukā, she has an important *temple at Saundatti in northern Karnataka, where it has been the custom for young girls to be presented as co-wives (*devadāsīs) of Yellammā's husband *Jamadagni. Some become prostitutes to the male devotees; the most numerous, however, are the jogammas, many of whom later marry human husbands, and are believed to be *auspicious. There is a small group of male transvestites, known as jogappas, who are also married to the god. *See also* JOGTĪ / JOGTĪṆ.

Yeshwant Rao An '*untouchable' who, according to local legend, gave up his life during the building of the fortress at Jejurī in Maharashtra. As a reward, he was made the gatekeeper of *Khaṇḍobā's *temple, where he has his own shrine, containing his shapeless, rock-based image. Healing powers are attributed to him.

Yoga One of the six 'schools of philosophy' (*darśanas), usually paired with *Sāṃkhya, and sometimes referred to as 'Sāṃkhya-Yoga', or *rājayoga. The school's foundational text is the **Yoga Sūtra* of *Patañjali; scarcely less important is its earliest extant commentary, the *Yogabhāṣya* of *Vyāsa. Yoga's metaphysics is similar to that of Sāṃkhya: it assumes that ontological reality is composed of the 25 *tattvas, to which it adds the 'special *puruṣa', *Īśvara. Its goal is the state of blissful *liberation known as *kaivalya, in which the individual puruṣa is isolated from matter (*prakṛti), and its method is *yoga. Yoga is defined by Patañjali as 'the control of the fluctuations of the mind-field' (cittavṛttinirodha) (*Yoga Sūtra* 1.2). More specifically, this is to be achieved through an 'eight-limbed yoga' (*aṣṭāṅga-yoga), a path of progressive restraint, withdrawal, and inner concentration, culminating in *samādhi (absorbed concentration), a state synonymous with kaivalya. (A somewhat different route to samādhi, designated the 'yoga of action' or *kriyā-yoga, is also outlined in the *Yoga Sūtra*.) *See also* YOGA SŪTRA.

yoga ('act of yoking', 'yoke', 'union', 'method', 'discipline', etc.) A generic term for a wide variety of religious practices. The term is derived from the Sanskrit verbal root 'yuj' ('yoke', 'join', 'unite'), giving rise to a plethora of etymologies concerning what is united with what (body with mind, *self with God, etc.). At its broadest, however, 'yoga' simply refers to a particular method or discipline for transforming the individual (e.g. the three 'yogas' of *karma, *jñāna, and *bhakti in the **Bhagavadgītā*). A narrower reading makes the practice contingent on, or derived from, control of the body and the senses, as in *haṭha-yoga, or control of the breath (*prāṇāyāma) and through it the mind, as in *Patañjali's *rājayoga. At its most neutral, yoga is therefore simply a technique, or set of techniques, including what is usually termed '*meditation', for attaining whatever soteriological or soteriological-cum-physiological transformation a particular tradition specifies. Nevertheless, the theological or metaphysical assumptions of that tradition usually, themselves, shape the specific form—or, at the very least, the analysis of the specific form—that the practice takes: for example, the haṭha-yogic manipulation of *kuṇḍalinī in the *Tantric *Śrī Vidyā tradition, or the divinization and perfection of both human beings and the material world achieved through a *yogic ascent through progressively higher states of *consciousness in the Integral Yoga of *Aurobindo Ghose.

If yoga is taken to be essentially a technique for altering *consciousness, it has a history that reaches back into the *Vedic period, finding an analogue in, for instance, the transformations wrought by the *soma ritual, as well as in the meditational practices adumbrated in the early **Upaniṣads*. As a term, 'yoga' first appears in the last few centuries BCE, in the **Kaṭha* and the **Svetāsvatara Upaniṣads*, in both instances connected to the metaphor of 'reining in' the senses through concentration (i.e. the focusing or minimizing of ordinary mental activity). Similarly, in a text addressed to *householders, the *Bhagavadgītā*, the yogin, whose thought is controlled, is compared to 'an unflickering lamp stationed in a draught-proof place' (6.19). Thereafter, a considerable systematic yoga literature, of which the prototype is the **Yoga Sūtra* of Patañjali, was, and continues to be, produced, much of it highly technical, and requiring the mediation of a *guru, and initiation (*dīkṣā) into a particular *sampradāya. Since the 20th century, yoga (particularly haṭha yoga) has also acquired an enthusiastic following in the West, where it is often seen as a technique for achieving physical and mental fitness, as opposed to attaining more soteriological or metaphysical goals. *See also* SIDDHI(s).

Yogabhāṣya *See* VYĀSA; YOGA SŪTRA.

yogamāyā A term used in the **Bhāgavata Purāṇa* to describe the power (sometimes personified) by which *Kṛṣṇa conceals his true identity as omnipotent God from participants in his *līlā. This prevents them from being overwhelmed and thus allows the 'play' to take place.

Yogānanda, Paramahaṃsa (1893–1952) An influential *guru, particularly in the West, where his *Autobiography of a Yogi* (1st ed. 1946) proved exceptionally popular. Born Mukunda Lal Ghosh in Gorakhpur, Uttar Pradesh, he became the disciple of Sri Yukteswar Giri (1855–1936), whose own guru, Lahiri Mahasaya (1828–1895), had taught Yogānanda's parents. Through this *paramparā, Yogānanda was initiated into *kriyā-yoga, an allegedly ancient tradition revived in the 19th century by Lahiri Mahasaya's teacher, a mysterious *guru called Mahāvatar Babaji. Graduating from Calcutta University in 1915, Yogānanda became a *saṃnyāsin. He founded the Yogoda Satsanga Society of India in Dakshineshwar near Kolkata (Calcutta) in 1917. Travelling to the USA in 1920, he began to teach kriyā yoga in the West, culminating in the establishment in California, in 1925, of the *Self-Realization Fellowship. He continued to travel and give lectures, and, in his final years, to write and revise his *Autobiography of a Yogi*. He died in the USA in 1952; the Fellowship continues to propagate his teachings.

yoganidrā ('meditation sleep') A form of *yogic trance in which the practitioner is in full control of his mind, but oblivious to the external world. The term is also used to characterize *Viṣṇu's cosmic sleep in the interval that comes between two world periods (*kalpas). In the **Devī Mahātmya*, Viṣṇu's yoganidrā is portrayed as synonymous with *Devī.

Yoga Sūtra The foundational text of the *Yoga *darśana, and the first systematic exposition of *yoga, attributed to *Patañjali. The composite text may well be the result of editorial inclusiveness, since it seems to recommend at least two different types of yoga. Its 194 (or 195) *sūtras are divided into four *pādas. The first of these (51 sūtras) deals with *samādhi ('absorbed concentration'), and the general means to attaining it in the context of *Sāṃkhya metaphysics. Pāda two (55 sūtras) deals with *sādhanā ('practice'—i.e. the specific means to attainment), including both *kriyā- and *aṣṭāṅga-yoga. Pāda three (54 or 55 sūtras), entitled *vibhūti, deals with the 'inner limbs' of aṣṭāṅga-yoga, viz. *dhāraṇā (concentration), *dhyāna (meditation), and *samādhi (absorbed concentration), and (in *Vyāsa's commentary, at least) with the supernormal powers (*siddhis) generated as epiphenomena of the practice. Pāda four (34 sūtras) deals with the attainment and nature of *kaivalya (liberation).

The commentary which has done most to shape understanding of the *Yoga Sūtra*, particularly in a *Sāṃkhya context, is the earliest to survive, the *Yogabhāṣya* of *Vyāsa. This gave rise, in turn, to the *Tattvaiśāradī* gloss of *Vācaspati Miśra, and *Bhojadeva's *Bhojavṛtti*. The *Yoga Sūtra* also attracted commentators from the *Vedānta darśana, including the *Yogabhāṣyavivaraṇa* subcommentary on Vyāsa, attributed to *Śaṅkara, and the longest sub-commentary of all, the *Yogavārttika* of *Vijñānabhikṣu. Commentaries of all kinds, now including many in Western and other non-Indian languages, continue to be written on this important text.

***Yogavāsiṣṭha* (*Rāmāyaṇa*)** (*c.*9th–12th centuries CE) An *Advaita Vedānta text which uses the *Epic story to frame a dialogue between *Rāma and *Vasiṣṭha about Advaita and *Yoga.

yogī, yogi(n) **(jogī)** A practitioner of *yoga, or more widely of any religious discipline. Often applied to *renouncers ('full-time practitioners'), it may also be used of *householders for the duration of their practice.

yogī (Śaiva)

yogic An adjective derived from *yoga.

yoginīs Fierce female spirits, or goddesses, which come increasingly to the fore in the ritual practices associated with the **Bhairava Tantras* of the *mantramārga branch of *Śaivism. They belong to variously enumerated (63, 64, 65, etc.) families, but are most closely associated with the eight 'Mothers' (*Mātṛkās). The 11th-century CE Chaunsath Yoginī *temple at Hirapur, near Bhubaneswar in Odisha (Orissa), depicts 64 (Skt.: catuḥṣaṣṭi = chaunsath) yoginīs, as does the 10th-century CE Chaunsath Yoginī temple at Bherāghāt in Madhya Pradesh.

yogī-pratyakṣa The supernormal or direct perception (*pratyakṣa) of the *yogin.

yojana (lit. 'harnessing', yoking') A traditional unit of length, principally employed in *Purāṇic *cosmology to measure the vast dimensions of the universe. Its equivalent in miles has been variously calculated: popular conversions are 1 yojana = 2.5, 4.5, or 9 miles. Less precise calculations based, for example, on the distance a god can fly in a given time are also offered. The term appears to be derived from the distance a team of animals can travel without unyoking.

yoni ('womb', 'uterus', 'vagina', 'vulva') A stylized representation of female genitalia, representing the *Goddess and/or female power (*śakti). The best known iconographic depiction is the near aniconic yoni which provides the pedestal (pīṭha) into which *Śiva *liṅgas are usually set, sometimes shaped as a spout, enabling water, and other substances used in the *abhiṣeka of the liṅga, to drain away. The liṅga and yoni together (representing Śiva and his śakti) are taken to represent the undifferentiated unity of spirit (male) and matter (female),which the god's unlimited, and continuously dynamic potency—his simultaneously creative and destructive energy. The most important, and, according to some, the original *śaktipīṭha is a spring-moistened cleft in the rock at *Kāmarūpa in Assam, which is thought to represent *Satī's dismembered yoni. This provides one of the few instances where the yoni is worshipped separately from the liṅga.

Yuddhakāṇḍa ('The War Book') The sixth book of *Vālmīki's **Rāmāyaṇa*, in which *Rāma and the monkey army cross to *Laṅkā, kill *Rāvaṇa, and rescue *Sītā.

Yudhiṣṭhira ('firm in battle') In the **Mahābhārata*, the son of *Kuntī and the god *Dharma, and the eldest of the five *Pāṇḍava brothers; also known as Ajātaśatru ('he whose conquering enemy has not yet been born') and *Dharmarāja ('King of *Dharma'). As his rival to succeed to the throne, he becomes the focus of his cousin *Duryodhana's persistent malevolence. Fatefully, Yudhiṣṭhira engages in a rigged dicing match, in the course of which he loses everything, including his brothers and himself; this is swiftly succeeded by the Pāṇḍavas' *forest exile. It is not until the end of the war, over thirteen years later, that Yudhiṣṭhira is eventually crowned and performs a great horse sacrifice (*aśvamedha) in atonement for the slaughter. Finally, he renounces the world and sets out for Mount *Meru with his brothers and their wife, *Draupadī. All the others die en route, but after the last of a number of encounters with his father, Dharma, he enters *heaven, where his final illusion is dispelled.

Yudhiṣṭhira represents the perfect *king, for whom conforming to dharma overrides all other considerations. But given that what constitutes dharma in any given instance may be ambiguous (the value of *ahiṃsā measured against the dharma of the *kṣatriya king, for instance), this often leads him into apparently conflicted situations, and protracted dialogues about dharma's true nature. *See also* MAHĀBHĀRATA.

yuga A world age, one of a cycle of four: *kṛta (satya), tretā, dvāpara, and *kali. The terminology is that of dicing: each age is named after the number of spots on separate dice, or perhaps the side of a die (*akṣa), in a descending sequence from 4 (kṛta) to 1 (kali). For humans, this descent—as the values fall, the ages become shorter—represents the cyclical atrophy of *dharma (including a deterioration in the standard of *kingship), and a corresponding increase in *adharma. Each complete cycle (known as a *mahāyuga) culminates in a cosmic dissolution at the end of the kali yuga, followed by a new creation, which starts the cycle again with a new 'golden age' or kṛta yuga. This pattern is tied into the appearance of *avatāras, particularly in *Vaiṣṇava mythology, where the incarnation of *Viṣṇu is always related to a particular yuga, and generally to the rise of adharma. *See also* COSMOGONY.

yūpa ('post', 'pillar') The post or posts to which the victim of the *Vedic *paśubandha (animal) sacrifice was fastened. The cutting and shaping of the yūpa from various trees was itself configured by an elaborate ritual, prescribed in such texts as the **Śatapatha Brāhmaṇa*. Usually octagonal in shape, the yūpa was assimilated to *Indra's *vajra, and by extension to the axis mundi.

Z

Zaehner, Robert Charles (1913–1974) A British *Orientalist and *Sanskritist whose published works spanned *Zoroastrianism, *Islam, comparative religion, mysticism, and Hinduism. From 1952 until his death, he held the *Spalding Chair of Eastern Religions and Ethics in Oxford University, where he had also been educated. His *Hinduism* (1966), and his *Bhagavadgītā* translation and commentary (1969) are still in print.

Zoroastrianism/Zoroastrians *See* PARSIS.

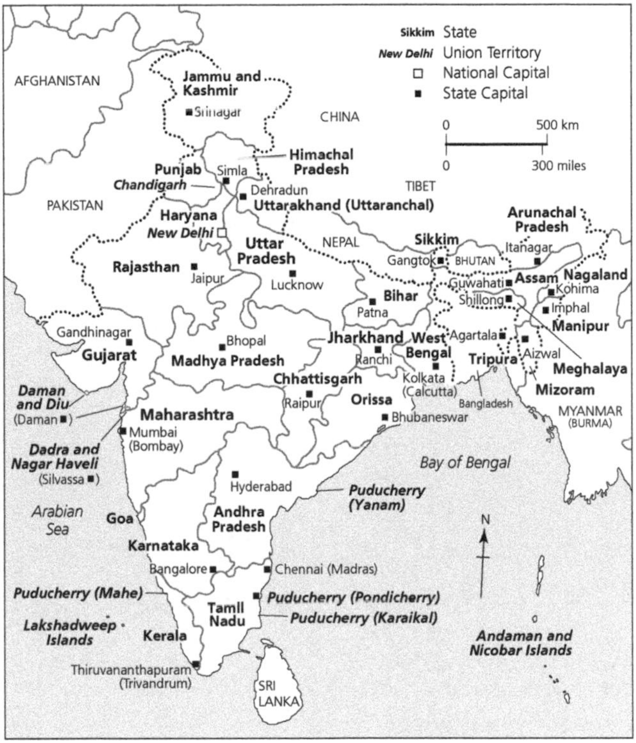

India: States, State Capitals, and Union Territories

Northern and Western India: showing some major Hindu pilgrimage centres and other sites of religious significance

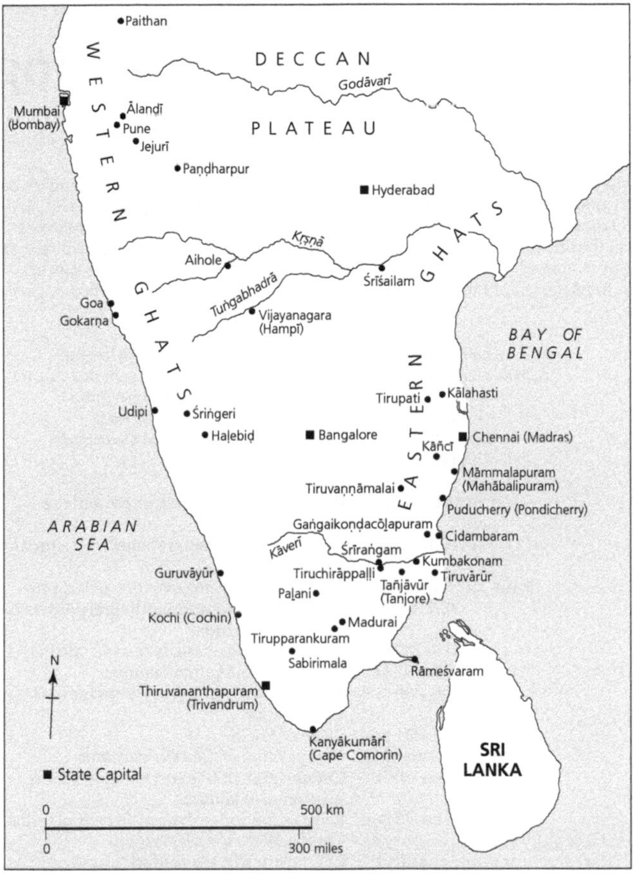

Central and Southern India: showing some major Hindu pilgrimage centres and other sites of religious significance

Chronology

This highly selective chronology uses the Gregorian calendar. (For Indian calendars, see the entry under 'calendar' in the dictionary.) More details concerning the individuals (many of them sants), texts, or dynasties mentioned can be found under the relevant entries in the dictionary. Nearly all dates before the modern period are approximate, and frequently contested; I have, for the most part, reflected the views of the majority of Western Indologists. For further remarks on the difficulty of chronological accuracy, see the Preface.

*c.*2500–*c.*1800 BCE	Indus Valley civilization at its height
*c.*1700–*c.*1200/1000 BCE	Composition of the *Ṛg Veda*; Āryan culture begins to dominate northern India
*c.*1000–500 BCE	Composition of the *Brāhmaṇas*
*c.*700 BCE–100 CE	Composition of the major *Upaniṣads*
*c.*5th century BCE	Life of Mahāvīra
*c.*485–405 BCE	Life of the Buddha
*c.*500 BCE–400 CE	Redaction of the *Mahābhārata* and the *Rāmāyaṇa*
*c.*4th century BCE	Composition of Pāṇini's Sanskrit grammar, the *Aṣṭādhyāyi*
*c.*4th–3rd century BCE	Life of Kauṭilya, author of the *Arthaśāstra*
327–325 BCE	Alexander of Macedonia's military incursion into northern India
*c.*317–185/187 BCE	Reign of the Mauryan dynasty in northern India
*c.*317–297 BCE	Reign of Candragupta Maurya
306–298 BCE	Megasthenes' eight-year stay in India as Ionian ambassador
*c.*272–231 BCE	Reign of Aśoka
*c.*3rd–1st century BCE	Composition of the *Dharmasūtras*
*c.*200 BCE–200 CE	Composition of (*Pūrva-*) *Mīmāṃsā Sūtra* attributed to Jaimini
*c.*185 BCE–75 BCE	Reign of the Śuṅga dynasty in central India
*c.*1st century BCE–2nd century CE	Composition of *Vaiśeṣikasūtra*
*c.*1st century BCE–2nd century CE	Composition of *Manusmṛti*
57/58 BCE	Beginning of the vikrama era
*c.*1st century CE	Composition of the *Bhagavadgītā*
77/78 CE	Beginning of the Śaka era
1st–3rd century CE	Collection of the Tamil *Puṟanāṉūṟu* anthology
mid 1st–3rd century CE	Reign of Kuṣāṇa dynasty in northern India
2nd century CE	Composition of the first Tamil grammar, the *Tolkāppiyam*
early centuries CE	Redaction of the *Brahmasūtra(s)*
*c.*3rd–4th century CE	Composition of Patañjali's *Yoga Sūtra*
*c.*3rd–4th century CE	Composition of Vātsyāyana's *Kāma Sūtra*
*c.*3rd–6th century CE	Life of Śabara
*c.*300 CE	Collection of the *Pañcatantra*
*c.*320 CE–*c.*6th century CE	Reign of Gupta dynasty in northern and central India
*c.*4th century CE	Composition of *Mārkaṇḍeya Purāṇa*
*c.*4th century CE onwards	Expansion of temple building across the subcontinent

*c.*4th–5th century CE	Life of Kālidāsa
4th–5th century CE	Composition of Īśvarakṛṣṇa's *Sāṃkhya Kārikā*
*c.*4th–8th centuries CE	Reign of the South Indian Pal̲l̲ava dynasty
*c.*5th century CE	Life of Bhartṛhari
*c.*6th century CE	Composition of the *Devī Mahātmya*
*c.*6th to 9th century CE	Lives of the South Indian Āl̲vār (Vaiṣṇava) and Nāyan̲mār (Śaiva) bhakti poets
*c.*6th–*c.*10th century CE; 13th century CE	Reign of the South Indian Pāṇḍya dynasty
*c.*700 CE; trad. 788–820 CE	Life of Śaṅkara
*c.*7th century CE	Composition of the Śrī Vidyā *Tantra*, the *Lalitāsahasranāma*
7th–8th century CE	Life of Maṇḍana Miśra
7/8th century CE	Introduction of Islam to the Indian subcontinent
*c.*750–973 CE	Reign of the Rāṣṭrakūṭa dynasty in the western and central Deccan
*c.*8th–9th century CE	Life of the Tamil Śaiva saint and bhakti poet Māṇikkavācakar
8th–12th century CE	Reign of the eastern Indian Pāla dynasty
*c.*9th/early 10th century CE	Composition of the *Bhāgavata Purāṇa*
9th–10th century CE	Composition of the *Mālinīvijayottara Tantra*, the root text of the Kashmiri Śaiva tradition
9th–12th centuries CE	Reign of the central Indian Candella dynasty, builders of Khajurāho
9th–13th centuries CE	Reign of South Indian Cōl̲a dynasty
10th century CE	Migration of the Parsis from Iran to Northwest India
10th century CE	Life of Vācaspati Miśra
*c.*10th century CE	Life of Nāthamuni
trad. 918–1038 CE	Life of Yāmuna
*c.*975–1025 CE	Life of Abhinavagupta
earlier half of 11th century CE	al-Bīrūnī accompanies Maḥmūd of Ghaznī on his raids into northern India
*c.*1050–1350 CE	Reign of the Hoysaḷa Dynasty in South India
*c.*1106–1167 CE	Life of Basava
d. 1137 CE; trad. 1017–1137 CE	Life of Rāmānuja
12th century CE	Compilation of Tamil *Tirumur̲ai* by Nampi Āṇṭār Nampi
12th century CE	Life of Jayadeva, author of the *Gītagovinda*
12th century CE	Composition of the *Hitopadeśa*
*c.*12th century CE	Life of Allama-Prabhu
*c.*12th century CE	Life of Cēkkil̲ār, compiler of the *Periya Purāṇam*
12th–13th century CE	Life of Meykaṇṭār, the first systematic Śaiva Siddhānta theologian
*c.*12th–13th century CE	Disappearance of Buddhism from India
*c.*12th–13th century CE	Life of Nimbārka, founder of the Dvaitādvaita school of Vedānta
1211 CE	Delhi Sultanate (1211–1526) established, marking the beginning of Muslim rule in northern India
13th century CE	Life of Cakradhara, founder of the Mahānubhāva Sampradāya
*c.*13th century CE	Life of Madhva
trad. 1264–1369 CE	Life of Piḷḷai Lokācārya
1269–1307 CE	Life of Vedāntadeśika
trad. 1270–1350 CE	Life of Nāmdev
1275–1296 CE	Life of Jñāneśvara
1293–1338 CE	Life of Cokāmeḷā

14th–16th century CE	Reign of the Hindu Vijayanagara empire in South India and the Deccan
*c.*1398–*c.*1448 CE	Life of Kabīr
*c.*1414–*c.*1480 CE	Life of Narsī Mehtā
*c.*15th century CE	Life of Rāmānanda
1469–1539 CE	Life of Gurū Nānak, founder of Sikhism
1479–1531 CE	Life of Vallabha
*c.*late 15th century CE; trad. 1479–1584 CE	Life of Sūrdās
*c.*1485–1565 CE	Life of Purandaradāsa
*c.*1486–1533 CE	Life of Caitanya
*c.*late 15th/early 16th century CE	Life of Raidāsa
1502–1553 CE	Life of Hitaharivaṃśa
1510 CE	Portuguese establish a colony in Goa
*c.*16th century CE	Life of Mīrābāī
16th century CE; trad. 1449–1569 CE	Life of Śaṅkaradeva
16th–18th century	Mughal rule in India at its peak (dynasty est. 1526)
*c.*1543–1623 CE	Life of Tulsīdāsa, author of *Rāmcaritmānas*
1544–1604 CE	Life of Dādū
1556–1605 CE	Reign of Mughal emperor Akbar
*c.*1607–1649 CE	Life of Tukārāma
1608–1681 CE	Life of Rāmadāsa
1613 CE	British trading post established at Surat
1627–1680 CE	Life of Śivajī
1628–1658	Reign of Mughal emperor Shāh Jahān
1650 CE	(British) East India Company establishes its first factory on the Hughli (Bhāgīrathī) river in West Bengal
1659–1707 CE	Reign of Mughal emperor Aurangzeb
1662 CE	Bombay becomes a British possession
1690 CE	(British) East India Company establishes a trading post at Calcutta
*c.*1718–1775 CE	Life of Rāmprasād Sen
1746–1794 CE	Life of Sir William Jones
1757 CE	Battle of Plassey; British rule in India begins
1785 CE	First complete translation of the *Bhagavadgītā* into English by Sir Charles Wilkins (1749–1846 CE)
1770 CE	Saṃnyāsi uprising against the British East India Company
1772–1833 CE	Life of Rāmmohun Roy
1773–1785 CE	Warren Hastings the first British Governor-General of Bengal
1781–1830 CE	Life of Svāminārāyaṇa
1784 CE	Sir William Jones founds the Asiatic Society of Bengal in Calcutta
1817–1905 CE	Life of Debendranāth Tagore
1823 CE	Foundation of the Royal Asiatic Society in London
1824–1883 CE	Life of Dayānanda Sarasvatī
1828 CE	Foundation of the Brāhmo Samāj by Rāmmohun Roy
1829–1835 CE	Lord William Bentinck Governor-General of India
1829 CE	Satī made illegal in Bengal
1834–1886 CE	Life of Rāmakṛṣṇa
1838–1884 CE	Life of Keshab Chandra Sen
1838–1914 CE	Life of Kedarnath Datta (Bhaktivinoda Ṭhākura)
*c.*1856–1918 CE	Life of Sai Baba of Shirdi

1856–1920 CE	Life of B. G. Tilak
1857 CE	The Great Rebellion ('Indian Mutiny'/'National Uprising')
1858 CE	Direct rule of India by the British Crown
1861–1941 CE	Life of Rabindranāth Tagore
1863–1902 CE	Life of Swami Vivekānanda
1869–1948 CE	Life of M. K. Gāndhī
1875 CE	Foundation of the Ārya Samāj
1877 CE	Queen Victoria declared Empress of India
1883–1966 CE	Life of Vinayak Damodar Savarkar
1885 CE	Foundation of the Indian National Congress (later the Congress Party)
1891–1956 CE	Life of Dr Ambedkar
1895 CE	Foundation of the Vedānta Society in New York by Vivekānanda
1896–1982 CE	Life of Ānandamāyī Mā
1897 CE	Foundation of Rāmakṛṣṇa Mission
1911 CE	Indian capital changed from Calcutta to Delhi
1926 CE	Sathya Sai Baba born
1930 CE	Gāndhī's march against the salt tax
1947 CE	Indian Independence from Britain; Partition of the Indian subcontinent; creation of the Indian Union, and the state of Pakistan; Congress Party elected
1948 CE	M. K. Gāndhī assassinated
1947–1964 CE	Jawaharlal Nehru Prime Minister of India
1950 CE	Indian constitution accepted; India declared a Republic
1964 CE	Foundation of the Viśva Hindū Pariṣad
1966 CE	Foundation of ISKCON in New York by Bhaktivedānta Swāmi (1896–1977)
1980 CE	Formation of the Bhāratīya Janatā Party (BJP)
1984 CE	Prime Minister Indira Gandhi assassinated
1989 CE	Prime Minister Rajiv Gandhi assassinated
1992 CE	Destruction of Bābrī Masjid mosque, Ayodhyā
1996–2004 CE	Coalition governments formed by BJP
2001 CE	Celebration of the Mahā ('Great') Kumbha Melā at Allahābād
2004 CE	Congress Party elected
2008 CE	End of Hindu Kingdom in Nepal

Pronunciation Guide

Many of the headwords and most of the technical terminology in this dictionary are in Sanskrit or one of its derivatives. A minority of headwords (mostly the names of texts, people, or places) are in the Dravidian language of Tamil. Words in related languages, usually following similar principles of pronunciation, are also sometimes used, but this guide confines itself to Sanskrit and Tamil. The use of diacritical marks is a convention designed to represent in Roman script (i.e. in transliteration) the full range of sounds conveyed by Indic scripts such as devanāgarī ('divine city writing'—used to write or print Sanskrit, Hindi, Marathi, etc.), and vaṭṭeḻutu ('rounded writing'—used to write Tamil).

Sanskrit

Sanskrit	as in *English*
a	c*u*t
ā	f*a*r
i	s*i*t
ī	m*e*
u	p*u*t
ū	t*oo*
ṛ	*ri*sk
ḷ	reve*lry*, with the tongue curved back in the mouth and flapped forward
e	pr*ay*
ai	s*i*gh
o	h*o*pe
au	s*ou*nd
c	*ch*urch
v	close to *w*ile
ś	*sh*ame
ṣ	di*sh*
ḥ	as in English, but with a faint echo of the preceding vowel
ṭ, ḍ	as in English, but with the tongue curved back in the mouth
ṅ, ṇ	have a nasal quality
ñ	ca*ny*on
t	as in French *t*out
kh, gh, ch, jh, ṭh, ḍh, th, dh, ph, bh	aspirated—as it ho*th*ouse, she*ph*erd, clu*bh*ouse, etc.; (not as in 'wi*th*', etc.)
ṃ	nasalizes the preceding vowel sound, as in French *bon*

Pronounce other sounds as in standard English.

For more detailed information on the pronunciation of Sanskrit the reader should consult a work such as Michael Coulson's *Sanskrit: An Introduction to the Classical Language* (New York: Teach Yourself Books, Hodder & Stoughton, 1st pub. 1976; numerous reprints).

Tamil

Although the convention for transliterating Sanskrit has been standardized, the transcription of Tamil orthography presents more of a challenge. In this dictionary I have, for the most part, followed the conventions employed by the Madras University *Tamil Lexicon*, and used in works such as K. V. Zvelebil's *Tamil Literature* (Leiden: E. J. Brill, 1975), the main features of which are represented below in a simplified version. Some place names, however, are spelt in the way in which they most usually appear in English sources: e.g. Madurai (instead of Maturai), Cidambaram (instead of Citamparam), a convention designed to represent their approximate pronunciation in English (see below).

As in Sanskrit, with the following distinctions:

ē and ō	long vowels, as in English pr*ay* and h*o*pe (= Sanskrit e and o); in the initial position pronounced, respectively, as *yē* and *wō*
e and o	short vowels, as in English *e*cho and b*o*at; in the initial position pronounced, respectively, as *ye* and *wo*
ai	when final, pronounced as in English th*ey*
ṉ, ṟ	as in English
ṉṟ	*ndr* as in English lau*ndr*y
ṟṟ	*tr* as in English *tr*ee
ḻ	*r* as in American gi*rl* or si*r* (i.e. l with the tongue curved as far back as possible)
c	in the initial position, and between vowels, pronounced as *s* or *sh* after nasals (m, n, etc.) pronounced as *j*
cc	as in English *ch*urch
k	after nasals (m, n, etc.) pronounced as *g* (e.g. ṅk = *ṅg*) between vowels pronounced as *h* or *g* (e.g. akam = a*h*am; Murukaṉ = Murugan)
ṭ, t, p	after nasals, and between vowels, pronounced, respectively, as *ḍ*, *d*, *b*

Principal Sources and Further Reading

This reading list is, of course, indicative rather than exhaustive. It serves two purposes: to acknowledge my principal sources, and to direct those readers in search of more detailed information towards some relevant publications. These are weighted towards the next level of discussion, i.e. introductory and survey articles. The headings under which the list is arranged are supposed to be suggestive, rather than definitive. As a trawl through some of the longer dictionary entries will reveal, many topics run into, or across each other, and the appearance of particular works under one heading rather than another is to an extent arbitrary. Some accessible translations of selected texts, both theological and literary, are also listed for those non-specialists wishing to engage with the primary sources. Where a work has been translated, the date given is that of the translation.

Introductory Works, Surveys, Dictionaries and Essay Collections

Basham, A. L. *The Wonder That Was India: A Survey of the Culture of the Indian Sub-Continent Before the Coming of the Muslims* (London: Sidgwick and Jackson, 1954).

Basham, A. L. (ed.) *A Cultural History of India* (Oxford: Oxford University Press, 1975).

Biardeau, Madeleine *Hinduism: The Anthropology of a Civilization*, trans. Richard Nice (Oxford: Oxford University Press, 1989).

Bonnefoy, Yves (ed.) *Asian Mythologies*, trans. under the direction of Wendy Doniger (Chicago: University of Chicago Press, 1993).

Brockington, J. L. *The Sacred Thread: Hinduism in its Continuity and Diversity* (Edinburgh: Edinburgh University Press, 1981).

Coulson, Michael *Sanskrit: An Introduction to the Classical Language* (New York: Teach Yourself Books, Hodder & Stoughton, 1st pub. 1976; numerous reprints).

Dallapiccola, Anna L. *Dictionary of Hindu Lore and Legend* (London: Thames and Hudson, 2002).

Dasgupta, Surendranath *A History of Indian Philosophy* (Cambridge: Cambridge University Press, 1922–55).

Eliade, Mircea (ed. in chief) *The Encyclopedia of Religions* (New York: Macmillan, 1987).

Flood, Gavin (ed.) *The Blackwell Companion to Hinduism* (Oxford: Blackwell Publishing, 2003).

Flood, Gavin *An Introduction to Hinduism* (Cambridge: Cambridge University Press, 1996).

Frauwallner, Erich *History of Indian Philosophy* Vol. I and II (Delhi: Motilal Banarsidass, 1973).

Fuller, C. J. *The Camphor Flame: Popular Hinduism and Society in India* (Princeton: Princeton University Press, 1992).

Gombrich, Richard *Theravāda Buddhism: A Social History from Ancient Benares to Modern Colombo* (London: Routledge & Kegan Paul, 1988; 2nd edn. 2006).

Halbfass, Wilhelm *India and Europe: An Essay in Understanding* (New York: State University of New York Press, 1988).

Halbfass, Wilhelm *Tradition and Reflection: Explorations in Indian Thought* (Albany: State University of New York Press, 1991).

Hamilton, Sue *Indian Philosophy: A Very Short Introduction* (Oxford: Oxford University Press, 2001).

Hardy, Friedhelm (ed.) *The Religions of Asia* (London: Routledge, 1990).

Hardy, Friedhelm *The Religious Culture of India: Power, Love, and Wisdom* (Cambridge: Cambridge University Press, 1994).

Harris, Ian et al. (ed.) *Longman Guide to Living Religions* (Harlow: Longman Group Limited, 1994).
Hinnells, John R. (ed.) *A New Handbook of Living Religions* (London: Penguin Books, 1997).
Hinnells, John R. (ed.) *Who's Who of Religions* (London: Penguin Books, 1996).
Hopkins, Thomas J. *The Hindu Religious Tradition* (Wadsworth Publishing, 1971).
Kane, Pandurang Vaman *History of Dharmaśāstra (Ancient and Mediaeval Religious and Civil Law)* 5 vols. (Poona: Bhandarkar Oriental Research Institute, 1930–62; 2nd edn. 1968–75).
Keay, John *India: A History* (London: Harper Collins, 2000).
King, Richard *Indian Philosophy: An Introduction to Hindu and Buddhist Thought* (Edinburgh: Edinburgh University Press, 1999)
Klostermaier, Klaus K. *A Survey of Hinduism* (Albany: State University of New York Press, 1994).
Lipner, Julius *Hindus: Their Religious Beliefs and Practices* (London and New York: Routledge, 1994).
Llewellyn, J. E. (ed.) *Defining Hinduism: A Reader* (London: Equinox Publishing Ltd., 2005).
Madan, T. N. (ed.) *Religion In India* (Delhi: Oxford University Press, 1991).
Matilal, Bimal Krishna *The Word and the World: India's Contribution to the Study of Language* (Delhi: Oxford University Press, 1990).
McGregor, R. S. (ed.) *The Oxford Hindi-English Dictionary* (Oxford: Oxford University Press, 1993).
Michaels, Axel *Hinduism: Past and Present*, trans. Barbara Harshav (Princeton and Oxford: Princeton University Press, 2004).
Mittal, Sushil and Gene Thursby (eds.) *The Hindu World* (London: Routledge, 2004).
Mittal, Sushil and Gene Thursby (eds.) *Religions of South Asia: An Introduction* (London: Routledge, 2006).
Monier-Williams, Monier *A Sanskrit-English Dictionary* (Oxford: Oxford University Press, 1st pub. in this edn. 1899; numerous reprints).
O'Flaherty, Wendy Doniger (ed.) *Karma and Rebirth in Classical Indian Traditions* (Berkeley and Los Angeles: University of California Press, 1980).
Pollock, Sheldon (ed.) *Literary Cultures in History: Reconstructions from South Asia* (Berkeley: University of California Press, 2003).
Potter, Karl H. (ed.) *Encyclopaedia of Indian Philosophies*, 11 vols. to date (Delhi: Motilal Banarsidass, 1987–) (see also: http://faculty.washington.edu/kpotter/).
Radhakrishnan, S. and C. A. Moore (eds.) *A Sourcebook in Indian Philosophy* (Princeton: Princeton University Press, 1957).
Ramanujan, A. K. *The Collected Essays of A. K. Ramanujan*, ed. Vinay Dharwadker (Delhi: Oxford University Press, 1999).
Renou, Louis, and Jean Filliozat *L'Inde Classique* 2 tomes (Paris: Librarie d'Amerique et d'Orient, 1985).
Robinson, Francis (ed.) *The Cambridge Encyclopedia of India, Pakistan, Bangladesh, Sri Lanka*, etc. (Cambridge: Cambridge University Press, 1989).
Rodrigues, Hillary P. *Introducing Hinduism* (London and New York: Routledge, 2006).
Stutley, Margaret and James *A Dictionary of Hinduism* (London: Routledge & Kegan Paul, 1977).
Thapar, Romila *A History of India*, Volume One (London: Penguin Books, 1st pub. 1966; repr. 1990).
Weber, Max *The Religion of India*, trans. Hans. H. Gerth and Don Martindale (Glencoe: Free Press, 1958).
Zaehner, R. C. *Hinduism* (Oxford: Oxford University Press, 1966).

Vedic, Vedāntic, and Brahmanical Hinduism (including Renouncer Traditions)

Alston, A. J. *Śaṅkara on the Absolute* (London: Sheti Sadan, 1980).
Basham, A. L. *History and Doctrine of the Ājivikas: A Vanished Indian Religion* (London: Luzac, 1951).
Bronkhorst, J. *The Two Sources of Indian Asceticism* (Bern: European Academic Publishers, 1993)
Bronkhorst, J. *The Two Traditions of Meditation in Ancient India* (Delhi: Motilal Banarsidass, 1993).
Bryant, Edwin *The Quest for the Origins of Vedic Culture: The Indo-Aryan Migration Debate* (New York: Oxford University Press, 2001).

Carman, J. B. *The Theology of Rāmānuja: An Essay in Interreligious Understanding* (London and New Haven: Yale University Press, 1976).
Dumont, Louis *Homo Hierarchicus: The Caste System and its Implications* (Chicago: University of Chicago Press, 1980).
Dundas, Paul *The Jains* (London: Routledge, 2nd ed. 2002).
Gupta, Sanjukta *Advaita Vedānta and Vaiṣṇavism: The Philosophy of Madhusūdana Sarasvatī* (Oxford and New York: Routledge, 2006).
Halbfass, W. *Studies in Kumārila and Śaṅkara* (Reinbeck: Verlag für Orientalistische Fach-Publikationen, 1983).
Heesterman, J. C. *The Broken World of Sacrifice: An Essay in Ancient Indian Ritual* (Chicago: University of Chicago Press, 1993).
Heesterman, J. C. *The Inner Conflict of Tradition: An Essay in Indian Ritual, Kingship, and Society* (Chicago: University of Chicago Press, 1985).
Hirst, J. G. Suthren *Saṃkara's Advaita Vedānta: A Way of Teaching* (London: Routledge Curzon, 2005).
Holdrege, Barbara A. 'Dharma', in Sushil Mittal and Gene Thursby (eds.), *The Hindu World* (London: Routledge, 2004).
Ingalls, Daniel H. H. 'Śaṃkara on the question: Whose is avidyā?', in *Philosophy East and West*, 3 (1953), 69–72.
Jamison, Stephanie W. *Sacrificed Wife/ Sacrificer's Wife: Women, Ritual, and Hospitality in Ancient India* (New York: Oxford University Press, 1996).
Kaelber, Walter O. 'Āśrama', in Sushil Mittal and Gene Thursby (eds.), *The Hindu World* (London: Routledge, 2004).
Kaelber, Walter O. *Tapta Mārga: Asceticism and Initiation in Vedic India* (Albany: State University of New York Press, 1989).
Keith, Arthur Berriedale *The Religion and Philosophy of the Veda and Upanishads*, 2 vols. (Cambridge: Harvard University Press, 1925).
Lipner, Julius *The Face of Truth: A Study of Meaning and Metaphysics in the Vedāntic Theology of Rāmānuja* (Albany: State University of New York Press, 1986).
Lott, E. J. *God and the Universe in the Vedāntic Theology of Rāmānuja: A Study in His Use of the Self-Body Analogy* (Madras: Ramanuja Research Society, 1976).
Malamoud, Charles *Cooking the World: Ritual and Thought in Ancient India*, trans. David White (Delhi: Oxford University Press, 1996).
Marriott, McKim 'Varṇa and Jāti', in Sushil Mittal and Gene Thursby (eds.), *The Hindu World* (London: Routledge, 2004).
McGee, Mary 'Saṃskāra', in Sushil Mittal and Gene Thursby (eds.), *The Hindu World* (London: Routledge, 2004).
Olivelle, Patrick *The Āśrama System: The History and Hermeneutics of a Religious Tradition* (Oxford: Oxford University Press, 1993).
Olivelle, Patrick 'The Renouncer Tradition', in Gavin Flood (ed.), *The Blackwell Companion to Hinduism* (Oxford: Blackwell Publishing, 2003).
Patton, Laurie L. 'Veda and Upaniṣad', in Sushil Mittal and Gene Thursby (eds.), *The Hindu World* (London: Routledge, 2004).
Rocher, Ludo 'The Dharmaśāstras', in Gavin Flood (ed.), *The Blackwell Companion to Hinduism* (Oxford: Blackwell Publishing, 2003).
Smith, Brian K. *Classifying the Universe: The Ancient Indian Varṇa System and the Origins of Caste* (New York: Oxford University Press, 1994).
Smith, Brian K. *Reflections on Resemblance, Ritual, and Religion* (New York: Oxford University Press, 1989).
Tull, Herman W. 'Karma', in Sushil Mittal and Gene Thursby (eds.), *The Hindu World* (London: Routledge, 2004).
Wasson, R. Gordon *Soma: Divine Mushroom of Immortality* (New York: Harcourt Brace Jovanovich, 1968).
Witzel, Michael 'Vedas and Upaniṣads', in Gavin Flood (ed.), *The Blackwell Companion to Hinduism* (Oxford: Blackwell Publishing, 2003).

Texts in Translation

Deutsch, Eliot, and Rohit Dalvi (eds.) *The Essential Vedānta: A New Source Book of Advaita Vedānta* (Bloomington: World Wisdom, 2004).
Doniger, W., with Brian K. Smith (trans.) *The Laws of Manu* (Harmondsworth: Penguin Books, 1991).

O'Flaherty, Wendy Doniger (trans.) *The Rig Veda: An Anthology* (Harmondsworth: Penguin Books, 1981).

Olivelle, Patrick (trans.) *Dharmasūtras: The Law Codes of Āpastamba, Gautama, Baudhāyana, and Vasiṣṭha* (Oxford: Oxford University Press, Oxford World's Classics, 1999).

Olivelle, Patrick (trans.) *Saṃnyāsa Upaniṣads: Hindu Scriptures on Asceticism and Renunciation* (New York: Oxford University Press, 1992).

Olivelle, Patrick (trans.) *The Law Code of Manu* (Oxford: Oxford University Press, Oxford World's Classics, 2004).

Olivelle, Patrick (trans.) *Upaniṣads* (Oxford: Oxford University Press, Oxford World's Classics, 1996).

Roebuck, Valerie J. (trans.) *The Upaniṣads* (London: Penguin Books, 2003).

Epic and Purāṇic Hinduism

Brockington, John L. *Righteous Rāma: The Evolution of an Epic* (Delhi: Oxford University Press, 1984).

Brockington, John L. *The Sanskrit Epics* (Leiden: Brill, 1998).

Courtright, P. B. *Gaṇeśa: Lord of Obstacles, Lord of Beginnings* (New York: Oxford University Press, 1985).

Doniger, Wendy (ed.) *Purāṇa Perennis: Reciprocity and Transformation in Hindu and Jaina Texts* (New York: State University of New York Press, 1993).

Fitzgerald, James L. 'Mahābhārata', in Sushil Mittal and Gene Thursby (eds.), *The Hindu World* (London: Routledge, 2004).

Goldman, Robert P. and Sally J. Sutherland Goldman 'Rāmāyaṇa', in Sushil Mittal and Gene Thursby (eds.), *The Hindu World* (London: Routledge, 2004).

Gombrich, Richard F. 'Ancient Indian Cosmology', in C. Blacker and M. Loewe (eds.), *Ancient Cosmologies* (London: George Allen & Unwin, 1975), 100–42.

Hiltebeitel, Alf *Rethinking the Mahābhārata: A Reader's Guide to the Education of the Dharma King* (Chicago: University of Chicago Press, 2001).

Hiltebeitel, Alf *The Cult of Draupadī*, 2 vols. (Chicago: University of Chicago Press, 1998, 1991).

Hiltebeitel, Alf *The Ritual of Battle: Krishna in the Mahābhārata* (Ithaca NY: Cornell University Press, 1976).

Kloetzli, Randy and Alf Hiltebeitel 'Kāla', in Sushil Mittal and Gene Thursby (eds), *The Hindu World* (London: Routledge, 2004).

Kramrisch, Stella *The Presence of Śiva* (Princeton: Princeton University Press, 1981).

Lipner, Julius (ed.) *The Fruits of Our Desiring: An Enquiry into the Ethics of the Bhagavadgīta for Our Times* (Calgary: Bayeux Arts, 1997).

Matchett, Freda 'The Purāṇas', in Gavin Flood (ed.), *The Blackwell Companion to Hinduism* (Oxford: Blackwell Publishing, 2003).

Rao, Velcheru Narayana 'Purāṇa', in Sushil Mittal and Gene Thursby (eds.), *The Hindu World* (London: Routledge, 2004).

Richman, Paula (ed.) *Many Rāmāyaṇas: The Diversity of a Narrative Tradition in South Asia* (Berkeley and Los Angeles: University of California Press, 1991).

Richman, Paula (ed.) *Questioning Ramyanas: A South Asian Tradition* (Berkeley and Los Angeles: University of California Press, 2001).

Rocher, Ludo *The Purāṇas* (Wiesbaden: Otto Harrassowitz, 1986).

Sörensen, S. *An Index to the Names in the Mahābhārata, with Short Explanations and a Concordance to the Bombay and Calcutta Editions and P. C. Roy's Translation* (1st pub. 1904; repr. Delhi: Motilal Banarsidass, 2006).

Yano, Michio 'Calendar, Astrology, and Astronomy', in Gavin Flood (ed.), *The Blackwell Companion to Hinduism* (Oxford: Blackwell Publishing, 2003).

Texts in Translation

Bryant, Edwin F. (trans.) *Krishna: The Beautiful Legend of God (Śrīmad Bhāgavata Purāṇa, Book X, with Chapters 1, 6 and 29–31 from Book XI* (London: Penguin Books, 2003).

Dimmitt, Cornelia, and J. A. B. van Buitenen (eds.) *Classical Hindu Mythology: A Reader in the Sanskrit Purāṇas* (Philadelphia: Temple University Press, 1978).
Fitzgerald, James L. (trans. and ed.) *The Mahābhārata, Books 11 and 12* (Chicago: University of Chicago Press, 2004).
Ganguli, Kisari Mohan (trans.) *The Mahabharata of Krishna-Dwaipayana Vyasa*, 12 vols. (1884–99; repr. New Delhi: Munshiram Manoharlal, 1970).
Goldman, Robert P. (trans. and ed.; et al.) *The Rāmāyaṇa of Vālmīki: An Epic of Ancient India*, 5 vols. to date (Princeton: Princeton University Press, 1984–).
Johnson, W. J. (trans.) *The Bhagavad Gita* (Oxford: Oxford University Press, Oxford World's Classics, 1994).
Johnson, W. J. (trans.) *The Sauptikaparvan of the Mahābhārata: The Massacre at Night* (Oxford: Oxford University Press, Oxford World's Classics, 1998).
Mallinson, James (trans.) *The Gheranda Samhita* (Woodstock, New York: YogaVidya.com, 2004).
O'Flaherty, Wendy Doniger (trans.) *Hindu Myths: A Sourcebook Translated from the Sanskrit* (Harmondsworth: Penguin Books, 1975).
van Buitenen, J. A. B. (trans. and ed.) *The Bhagavadgītā in the Mahābhārata: Text and Translation* (Chicago: University of Chicago Press, 1981).
van Buitenen, J. A. B. (trans. and ed.) *Rāmānuja on the Bhagavadgītā: A Condensed Rendering of his Gītābhāṣya with Copious Notes and an Introduction* (Delhi: Motilal Banarsidass, 1968).
van Buitenen, J. A. B. (trans. and ed.) *The Mahābhārata*, 3 vols. (Chicago: University of Chicago Press, 1973–8).

For reprints, with transliterated Sanskrit, of the Goldman (ed.), Princeton University Press translations of the *Rāmāyaṇa*, a new translation of the *Mahābhārata* (not yet complete at the time of writing (2008)), and numerous works of classical Sanskrit literature, see The Clay Sanskrit Library, Sheldon I. Pollock (general ed.) (http://www.claysanskritlibrary.com).

Bhakti, Tantra, Yoga, and the Darśanas

Bhardwaj, Surinder M. and James G. Lochtefeld 'Tīrtha', in Sushil Mittal and Gene Thursby (eds.), *The Hindu World* (London: Routledge, 2004).
Cutler, Norman 'Tamil Hindu Literature', in Gavin Flood (ed.), *The Blackwell Companion to Hinduism* (Oxford: Blackwell Publishing, 2003).
Eck, Diana L. *Darśan: Seeing the Divine Image in India* (Chambersburg: Anima, 1981).
Flood, Gavin *The Tantric Body: The Secret Tradition of Hindu Religion* (London and New York: I. B. Tauris, 2006).
Franco, Eli, and Karin Preisendanz 'Nyāya-Vaiśeṣika', in Edward Craig (ed.) *Routledge Encyclopedia of Philosophy* (London: Routledge, 1998).
Freeman, Rich 'The Literature of Hinduism in Malayalam', in Gavin Flood (ed.), *The Blackwell Companion to Hinduism* (Oxford: Blackwell Publishing, 2003).
Freeman, Rich 'The Teyyam Tradition of Kerala', in Gavin Flood (ed.), *The Blackwell Companion to Hinduism* (Oxford: Blackwell Publishing, 2003).
Gonda, Jan *Medieval Religious Literature In Sanskrit* (Wiesbaden: Otto Harrassowitz, 1977).
Gottschalk, Peter 'Indian Muslim Tradition', in Sushil Mittal and Gene Thursby (eds.), *Religions of South Asia: An Introduction* (London: Routledge, 2006).
Gupta, Sanjukta, Dirk Jan Hoens, and Teun Goudriaan *Hindu Tantrism* (Leiden: Brill, 1979).
Lorenzen, David N. (ed.) *Religious Movements in South Asia 600–1800* (Delhi: Oxford University Press, 2004).
Lorenzen, David N. 'Bhakti', in Sushil Mittal and Gene Thursby (eds.), *The Hindu World* (London: Routledge, 2004).
Martin, Nancy M. 'North Indian Hindi Devotional Literature', in Gavin Flood (ed.), *The Blackwell Companion to Hinduism* (Oxford: Blackwell Publishing, 2003).
Padoux, André 'Mantra', in Gavin Flood (ed.), *The Blackwell Companion to Hinduism* (Oxford: Blackwell Publishing, 2003).
Samuel, Geoffrey *The Origins of Yoga and Tantra: Indic Religions to the Thirteenth Century* (Cambridge: Cambridge University Press, 2008).
Sax, William S. (ed.) *The Gods at Play: Līlā in South Asia* (New York: Oxford University Press, 1995).

Vaudeville, Charlotte *Myths, Saints and Legends in Medieval India* (Delhi: Oxford University Press, 1996).

Whicher, Ian *The Integrity of the Yoga Darśana: A Reconsideration of Classical Yoga* (New York: State University of New York Press, 1998).

White, David Gordon *The Alchemical Body: Siddha Traditions in Medieval India* (Chicago: University of Chicago Press, 1996).

Zvelebil, K. V. *Tamil Literature* (Leiden: Brill, 1975).

Śaiva and Śākta Traditions

Brooks, Douglas Renfrew *Auspicious Wisdom: The Texts and Traditions of Śrīvidyā Śākta Tantrism in South India* (Albany: State University of New York Press, 1992).

Brunner-Lachaux, H. *Somaśambhupaddhati*, 3 vols. (Pondicherry: Institut Français D' Indologie, 1963, 1968, 1977).

Coburn, Thomas B. *Devī-Māhātmya: The Crystallization of the Goddess Tradition* (Delhi: Motilal Banarsidass, 1985).

Dhavamony, Mariasusai *Love of God According to Śaiva Siddhānta* (Oxford: Oxford University Press, 1971).

Erndl, Kathleen M. 'Śākta', in Sushil Mittal and Gene Thursby (eds.), *The Hindu World* (London: Routledge, 2004).

Flood, Gavin 'The Saiva Traditions', in Gavin Flood (ed.), *The Blackwell Companion to Hinduism* (Oxford: Blackwell Publishing, 2003).

Hawley, John Stratton, and Donna Marie Wulff (eds.) *Devī: Goddesses of India* (Berkeley: University of California Press, 1996).

Kinsley, David *Hindu Goddesses: Visions of the Divine Feminine in the Hindu Religious Tradition* (Berkeley: University of California Press, 1986).

McDermott, Rachel Fell *Mother of My Heart, Daughter of My Dreams: Kālī and Umā in the Devotional Poetry of Bengal* (New York: Oxford University Press, 2001).

Padoux, André *Vāc: The Concept of the Word in Selected Hindu Tantras* (trans. Jacques Gontier). (Albany: State University of New York Press, 1990).

Sanderson, Alexis 'Purity and power among the Brahmans of Kashmir', in Michael Carrithers, Steven Collins, Steven Lukes (eds.), *The Category of the Person* (Cambridge: Cambridge University Press, 1985).

Sanderson, Alexis 'Śaivism and the Tantric Traditions', in Friedhelm Hardy (ed.), *The Religions of Asia* (London: Routledge, 1990).

Sanderson, Alexis 'Trika Śaivism' in Mircea Eliade (ed. in chief), *The Encyclopedia of Religions*, vol. 13 (New York: Macmillan, 1987).

Shulman, David Dean *Tamil Temple Myths: Sacrifice and Divine Marriage in the South Indian Śaiva Tradition* (Princeton: Princeton University Press, 1980).

Smith, David *The Dance of Śiva: Religion, Art and Poetry in South India* (Cambridge: Cambridge University Press, 1996).

Vaiṣṇava Traditions

Clémentin-Ojha, Catherine 'La renaissance du Nimbarka Sampradaya au XVIe siècle. Contribution à l'étude d'une secte kṛṣṇaïte', *Journal Asiatique*, 278 (1990), 327–76.

Clooney, Francis X. and Tony K. Stewart 'Vaiṣṇava', in Sushil Mittal and Gene Thursby (eds.), *The Hindu World* (London: Routledge, 2004).

Colas, Gérard 'History of Vaiṣṇava Traditions: An Esquisse', in Gavin Flood (ed.), *The Blackwell Companion to Hinduism* (Oxford: Blackwell Publishing, 2003).

Dimock, Edward C. Jr. *The Place of the Hidden Moon: Erotic Mysticism in the Vaiṣṇava-Sahajiyā Cult of Bengal* (Chicago: University of Chicago Press, 1966).

Feldhaus, A. (trans. and ed.) *The Religious System of the Mahānubhāva Sect: The Mahānubhāva Sūtrapāṭha* (Delhi: Manohar, 1983).

Hardy, Friedhelm *Viraha-Bhakti: The Early History of Kṛṣṇa Devotion in South India* (Delhi: Oxford University Press, 1983).

Hopkins, Steven Paul *Singing the Body of God: The Hymns of Vedāntadeśika in Their*

South Indian Tradition (New York: Oxford University Press, 2002).
Lutgendorf, Philip *The Life of a Text: Performing the Rāmcaritmānas of Tulsidas* (Berkeley: University of California Press, 1991).
Singer, Milton (ed.) *Krishna: Myths, Rites, and Attitudes* (Chicago: University of Chicago Press, 1968).
Snell, Rupert *Hita Harivaṃśa: An Edition of the Caurāsī Pada* (London: School of Oriental & African Studies, 1991).

Texts in Translation

Grierson, Sir George, and Lionel D. Barnett (trans.) *Lallā-Vākyāni or The Wise Sayings of Lal Dĕd, A Mystic Poetess of Ancient Kashmir* (London: Royal Asiatic Society, 1920).
Gupta, Sanjukta *Lakṣmī Tantra, A Pāñcarātra Text, Translation and Notes* (Leiden: Brill, 1972).
Hawley, John Stratton, and Mark Juergensmeyer (trans.) *Songs of the Saints of India* (Delhi: Oxford University Press, 2004).
Jackson, William J. (trans.) *Songs of Three Great South Indian Saints* (Delhi: Oxford University Press, 1998).
McDermott, Rachel Fell (trans.) *Singing to the Goddess: Poems to Kālī and Umā from Bengal* (New York: Oxford University Press, 2001).
Miller, Barbara Stoler (trans. and ed.) *Love Song of the Dark Lord: Jayadeva's Gītagovinda* (New York: Columbia University Press, 1977).
Miller, Barbara Stoler (trans. and ed.) *Yoga: Discipline of Freedom: The Yoga Sutra Attributed to Patanjali* (Berkeley: University of California Press, 1996).
Mumme, Patricia Y. (trans.) *The Mumukṣuppaṭi of Piḷḷai Lokācārya with Maṇavāḷamāmuni's Commentary* (Bombay: Ananthacharya Indological Research Institute (1987).
Peterson, Indira Viswanathan (trans.) *The Hymns of the Tamil Saints* (Princeton: Princeton University Press, 1989).
Ramanujan, A. K. (trans.) *Speaking of Śiva* (London: Penguin Books, 1973).
Smith, John D. *The Epic of Pābūjī: A Study, Transcription and Translation* (Cambridge: Cambridge University Press, 1991).
Vaudeville, Charlotte *A Weaver Named Kabir* (Delhi: Oxford University Press, 1993).

Modern and Contemporary Hinduism

Babb, Lawrence *The Divine Hierarchy* (New York: Columbia University Press, 1975).
Ferrari, Fabrizio F. '"Love Me Two Times" From Smallpox to Aids: Contagion and Possession in the Cult of Śītalā', *Religions of South Asia* Vol. 1, No. 1 (2007), 81–106.
Fuller, C. J. *Servants of the Goddess: The Priests of a South Indian Temple* (Delhi: Oxford University Press, 1991).
Hiltebeitel, Alf, and Kathleen M. Erndl (eds.) *Is the Goddess a Feminist?: The Politics of South Asian Goddesses* (New York: State University of New York Press, 2000).
Killingley, Dermot 'Modernity, Reform, and Revival', in Gavin Flood (ed.), *The Blackwell Companion to Hinduism* (Oxford: Blackwell Publishing, 2003).
Kopf, D. *The Brahmo Samāj and the Shaping of the Modern Indian Mind* (Princeton: Princeton University Press, 1979).
Leslie, Julia (ed.) *Roles and Rituals for Hindu Women* (London: Pinter, 1991).
Parekh, Bhikhu *Gandhi* (Oxford: Oxford University Press, 1997).
Pocock, David *Mind, Body and Wealth: A Study of Belief and Practice in an Indian Village* (Oxford: Blackwell Publishing, 1973).
Radice, William (ed.) *Swami Vivekānanda and the Modernization of Hinduism* (Delhi: Oxford University Press, 1998).
Ramaswamy, Sumathi 'The Goddess and the Nation: Subterfuges of Antiquity, the Cunning of Modernity', in Gavin Flood (ed.), *The Blackwell Companion to Hinduism* (Oxford: Blackwell Publishing, 2003).
Ram-Prasad, C. 'Contemporary Political Hinduism', in Gavin Flood (ed.), *The Blackwell Companion to Hinduism* (Oxford: Blackwell Publishing, 2003).
Smith, David *Hinduism and Modernity* (Oxford: Blackwell Publishing, 2003).
Wadley, Susan S. 'Grāma', in Sushil Mittal and Gene Thursby (eds.), *The Hindu World* (London: Routledge, 2004).

Williams, Raymond B. *A New Face of Hinduism: The Swaminarayan Religion* (Cambridge: Cambridge University Press, 1984).

Texts in Translation

Chatterjee, Bankimcandra *Ānandmaṭh or The Sacred Brotherhood*, translated with an introduction and critical apparatus by Julius J. Lipner (New York: Oxford University Press, 2005).
Leslie, Julia (trans. and ed.) *The Perfect Wife: The Orthodox Hindu Woman According to the Strīdharmapaddhati of Trayambakayajvan* (Delhi: Oxford University Press, 1989).
Lopez, Donald S. Jr (ed.) *Religions of India in Practice* (Princeton: Princeton University Press, 1995).
Richards, Glyn (ed.) *A Source-Book of Modern Hinduism* (Richmond: Curzon Press, 1985).

Art, Science, Literature, Politics, Social Life, and miscellaneous topics

Blurton, T. Richard *Hindu Art* (London: British Museum Press, 1992).
Coomaraswamy, Ananda K. *The Dance of Shiva* (New York: The Noonday Press, rev. ed., 1957).
Dehejia, Vidya, John Eskenazi, and John Guy *Chola: Sacred Bronzes of Southern India* (London: Royal Academy of Arts, 2007).
Deshpande, Madhav M. 'Bhāṣā', in Sushil Mittal and Gene Thursby (eds.), *The Hindu World* (London: Routledge, 2004).
Eck, Diana L. *Banaras: City of Light* (New York: Alfred A. Knopf, 1982).
Gellner, David 'Buddhism and Hinduism in the Nepal Valley', in Friedhelm Hardy (ed.), *The Religions of Asia* (London: Routledge, 1990).
Grimes, John A. 'Darśana', in Sushil Mittal and Gene Thursby (eds.), *The Hindu World* (London: Routledge, 2004).
Harle, J. C. *The Art and Architecture of the Indian Subcontinent* (New Haven and London: Yale University Press, 1994).
Howe, Leo *Hinduism and Hierarchy in Bali* (Oxford: James Currey, 2001).
Khare, R. S. 'Anna', in Sushil Mittal and Gene Thursby (eds.), *The Hindu World* (London: Routledge, 2004).
Killingley, Dermot 'Kāma', in Sushil Mittal and Gene Thursby (eds.), *The Hindu World* (London: Routledge, 2004).
Killingley, Dermot '*Mlecchas*, Yavanas and Heathens: Interacting Xenologies in Early Nineteenth-century Calcutta', in Eli Franco and Karin Preisendanz (eds.), *Beyond Orientalism: The Work of Wilhelm Halbfass and its Impact on Indian and Cross-Cultural Studies* (Amsterdam: Poznanī Studies in the Philosophy of the Sciences and Humanities 59, 1997).
Kloetzli, Randy and Alf Hiltebeitel 'Kāla', in Sushil Mittal and Gene Thursby (eds.), *The Hindu World* (London: Routledge, 2004).
Kolatkar, Arun (in English) *Jejuri* (New York: New York Review of Books, 2005).
Lal, Ananda (ed.) *The Oxford Companion To Indian Theatre* (Delhi: Oxford University Press, 2004).
Michell, George *The Hindu Temple: An Introduction to Its Meaning and Forms* (Chicago: University of Chicago Press, 1988).
Michell, George *The Penguin Guide to the Monuments of India, Vol. 1: Buddhist, Jain Hindu* (London: Penguin Books, 1990).
Mitter, Partha *Indian Art* (Oxford: Oxford University Press, 2001).
Narayana, Vasudha 'Ālaya', in Sushil Mittal and Gene Thursby (eds.), *The Hindu World* (London: Routledge, 2004).
Ramanujan, A. K. *The Oxford India Ramanujan*, Molly Daniels-Ramanujan (ed.) (Delhi: Oxford University Press, 2004).
Said, Edward W. *Orientalism* (London: Routledge & Kegan Paul, 1978).
Scharfe, Hartmut 'Artha', in Sushil Mittal and Gene Thursby (eds.), *The Hindu World* (London: Routledge, 2004).
Shulman, David *The King and the Clown in South Indian Myth and Poetry* (Princeton: Princeton University Press, 1995).
Shulman, David *The Wisdom of Poets: Studies in Tamil, Telugu, and Sanskrit* (Delhi: Oxford University Press, 2001).
Wujastyk, Dominik 'The Science of Medicine' in Gavin Flood (ed.), *The Blackwell Companion to Hinduism* (Oxford: Blackwell Publishing, 2003).

Texts in Translation

Anand, Mulk Raj (in English) *Untouchable* (Harmondsworth: Penguin Books, 1940; 1st pub. 1935).

Bhavabhūti *Rāma's Last Act*, trans. Sheldon Pollock (New York University Press, JJC Foundation: 2007).

Hart, George L., and Hank Heifetz (trans.) *The Four Hundred Songs of War and Wisdom: An Anthology of Poems from Classical Tamil. The Puṟanāṉūru.* (New York: Columbia University Press, 1999).

Ingalls, Daniel H. H. *Sanskrit Poetry from Vidyākara's 'Treasury'* (Cambridge: Harvard University Press, 1968).

Kālidāsa *The Recognition of Śakuntalā*, trans. W. J. Johnson (Oxford: Oxford University Press, Oxford World's Classics, 2001).

Miller, Barbara Stoler (ed.) *Theater of Memory: The Plays of Kālidāsa* (New York: Columbia University Press, 1984).

Mokashi, D. B. *Palkhi: An Indian Pilgrimage*, trans. Philip C. Engblom, with Introductory Essays by Philip C. Engblom and Eleanor Zelliot (Albany: State University of New York Press, 1987).

Murthy, U. R. Anantha *Samskara: A Rite for a Dead Man*, trans. A. K. Ramanujan (Delhi: Oxford University Press, 1978; 1st pub. 1976).

Olivelle, Patrick (trans.) *The Pañcatantra* (Oxford: Oxford University Press, Oxford World's Classics, 1997).

Selby, Martha Ann (trans.) *Grow Long, Blessed Night: Love Poems from Classical India* (New York: Oxford University Press, 2000).

Tagore, Rabindranath *Selected Poems*, trans. and ed. William Radice (London: Penguin Books, 2005).

Vatsyayana Mallanaga *Kamasutra*, trans. Wendy Doniger and Sudhir Kakar (Oxford: Oxford University Press, 2002).

Websites

There are hundreds if not thousands of Hindu devotional and sectarian websites. However, many of the sites which students of Hinduism may find useful for academic purposes can be accessed through the links found on the Indology website (http://indology.info/). These include online Sanskrit and Tamil dictionaries, bibliographies, E-texts, maps, fonts, electronic journals, library catalogues, publishers, bookshops, and art. Of particular interest are: the Digital South Asia Library at the University of Chicago (http://dsal.uchicago.edu/index.html/), Karl Potter's 'Bibliography of Indian Philosophies' (http://faculty.washington.edu/kpotter/), and the Clay Sanskrit Library (http://www.claysanskritlibrary.com).

Oxford Quick Reference

The Concise Oxford Dictionary of Quotations
SIXTH EDITION
Edited by Susan Ratcliffe

Based on the highly acclaimed seventh edition of *The Oxford Dictionary of Quotations*, this dictionary provides extensive coverage of literary and historical quotations, and contains completely up-to-date material. A fascinating read and an essential reference tool.

Oxford Dictionary of Quotations by Subject
Edited by Susan Ratcliffe

The ideal place to discover what's been said about what, the dictionary presents quotations on nearly 600 areas of special interest and concern in today's world.

The Oxford Dictionary of Humorous Quotations
Edited by Ned Sherrin

From the sharply witty to the downright hilarious, this sparkling collection will appeal to all senses of humour.

The Oxford Dictionary of Political Quotations
Edited by Antony Jay

This lively and illuminating dictionary from the writer of 'Yes Minister' presents a vintage crop of over 4,000 political quotations. Ranging from the pivotal and momentous to the rhetorical, the sincere, the bemused, the tongue-in-cheek, and the downright rude, examples include memorable words from the old hands as well as from contemporary politicians.

'funny, striking, thought-provoking and incisive ... will appeal to those browsing through it at least as much as to those who wish to use it as a work of reference'
Observer

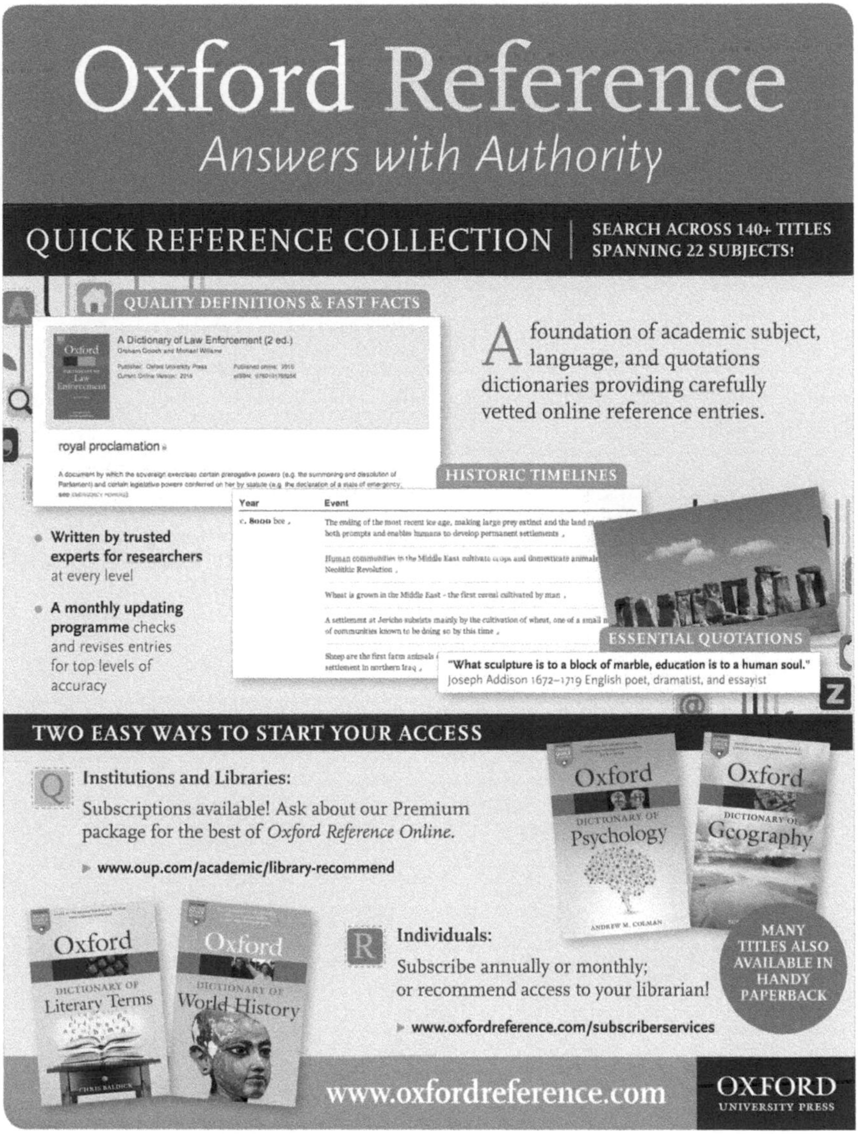
Oxford Reference
Answers with Authority
QUICK REFERENCE COLLECTION
SEARCH ACROSS 140+ TITLES SPANNING 22 SUBJECTS!
QUALITY DEFINITIONS & FAST FACTS
A Dictionary of Law Enforcement (2 ed.)
royal proclamation
A foundation of academic subject, language, and quotations dictionaries providing carefully vetted online reference entries.
HISTORIC TIMELINES
Year
Event
Written by trusted experts for researchers at every level
A monthly updating programme checks and revises entries for top levels of accuracy
ESSENTIAL QUOTATIONS
"What sculpture is to a block of marble, education is to a human soul."
Joseph Addison 1672–1719 English poet, dramatist, and essayist
TWO EASY WAYS TO START YOUR ACCESS
Institutions and Libraries:
Subscriptions available! Ask about our Premium package for the best of Oxford Reference Online.
www.oup.com/academic/library-recommend
Oxford Dictionary of Psychology
Oxford Dictionary of Geography
Oxford Dictionary of Literary Terms
Oxford Dictionary of World History
Individuals:
Subscribe annually or monthly; or recommend access to your librarian!
www.oxfordreference.com/subscriberservices
MANY TITLES ALSO AVAILABLE IN HANDY PAPERBACK
www.oxfordreference.com
OXFORD UNIVERSITY PRESS

Lightning Source UK Ltd.
Milton Keynes UK
UKHW02f0343070818
326869UK00003B/4/P

9 780198 610267